CME PROJECT

Precalculus

PEARSON

Boston, Massachusetts
Chandler, Arizona
...iew, Illinois
...nesota
...rsey

Education Development Center, Inc.
Center for Mathematics Education
Newton, Massachusetts

The Center for Mathematics Education Project was developed at Education Development Center, Inc. (EDC) within the Center for Mathematics Education (CME), with partial support from the National Science Foundation.

Education Development Center, Inc.
Center for Mathematics Education
Newton, Massachusetts

This material is based upon work supported by the National Science Foundation under Grant No. ESI-0242476, Grant No. MDR-9252952, and Grant No. ESI-9617369. Any opinions, findings, and conclusions or recommendations expressed in this material are those of the author(s) and do not necessarily reflect the views of the National Science Foundation.

CME Project Development Team

Lead Developer: Al Cuoco

Core Development Team: Anna Baccaglini-Frank, Jean Benson, Nancy Antonellis D'Amato, Daniel Erman, Brian Harvey, Wayne Harvey, Bowen Kerins, Doreen Kilday, Ryota Matsuura, Stephen Maurer, Sarah Sword, Audrey Ting, and Kevin Waterman

Others who contributed include Steve Benson, Paul D'Amato, Robert Devaney, Andrew Golay, Paul Goldenberg, Jane Gorman, C. Jud Hill, Eric Karnowski, Helen Lebowitz, Joseph Leverich, Melanie Palma, Mark Saul, Nina Shteingold, and Brett Thomas.

PEARSON

13-digit ISBN 978-0-13-350020-2
10-digit ISBN 0-13-350

1 2 3 4 5 6 7 8 9 1

Contents in Brief

Introduction to the CME Project

The CME Project, developed by EDC's Center for Mathematics Education, is a new NSF-funded high school program, organized around the familiar courses of algebra 1, geometry, algebra 2, and precalculus. The CME Project provides teachers and schools with a third alternative to the choice between traditional texts driven by basic skill development and more progressive texts that have unfamiliar organizations. This program gives teachers the option of a problem-based, student-centered program, organized around the mathematical themes with which teachers and parents are familiar. Furthermore, the tremendous success of NSF-funded middle school programs has left a need for a high school program with similar rigor and pedagogy. The CME Project fills this need.

The goal of the CME Project is to help students acquire a deep understanding of mathematics. Therefore, the mathematics here is rigorous. We took great care to create lesson plans that, while challenging, will capture and engage students of all abilities and improve their mathematical achievement.

The Program's Approach

The organization of the CME Project provides students the time and focus they need to develop fundamental mathematical ways of thinking. Its primary goal is to develop in students robust mathematical proficiency.

- The program employs innovative instructional methods, developed over decades of classroom experience and informed by research, that help students master mathematical topics.

- One of the core tenets of the CME Project is to focus on developing students' Habits of Mind, or ways in which students approach and solve mathematical challenges.

- The program builds on lessons learned from high-performing countries: develop an idea thoroughly and then revisit it only to deepen it; organize ideas in a way that is faithful to how they are organized in mathematics; and reduce clutter and extraneous topics.

- It also employs the best American models that call for grappling with ideas and problems as preparation for instruction, moving from concrete problems to abstractions and general theories, and situating mathematics in engaging contexts.

- The CME Project is a comprehensive curriculum that meets the dual goals of mathematical rigor and accessibility for a broad range of students.

About CME

EDC's Center for Mathematics Education, led by mathematician and teacher **Al Cuoco**, brings together an eclectic staff of mathematicians, teachers, cognitive scientists, education researchers, curriculum developers, specialists in educational technology, and teacher educators, internationally known for leadership across the entire range of K–16 mathematics education. We aim to help students and teachers in this country experience the thrill of solving problems and building theories, understand the history of ideas behind the evolution of mathematical disciplines, and appreciate the standards of rigor that are central to mathematical culture.

Contributors to the CME Project

National Advisory Board The National Advisory Board met early in the project, providing critical feedback on the instructional design and the overall organization. Members include

Richard Askey, University of Wisconsin
Edward Barbeau, University of Toronto
Hyman Bass, University of Michigan
Carol Findell, Boston University
Arthur Heinricher, Worcester Polytechnic Institute
Roger Howe, Yale University
Barbara Janson, Janson Associates
Kenneth Levasseur, University of Massachusetts, Lowell
James Madden, Louisiana State University, Baton Rouge
Jacqueline Miller, Education Development Center
James Newton, University of Maryland
Robert Segall, Greater Hartford Academy of Mathematics and Science
Glenn Stevens, Boston University
Herbert Wilf, University of Pennsylvania
Hung-Hsi Wu, University of California, Berkeley

Core Mathematical Consultants **Dick Askey,** **Ed Barbeau,** and **Roger Howe** have been involved in an even more substantial way, reviewing chapters and providing detailed and critical advice on every aspect of the program. Dick and Roger spent many hours reading and criticizing drafts, brainstorming with the writing team, and offering advice on everything from the logical organization to the actual numbers used in problems. We can't thank them enough.

Teacher Advisory Board The Teacher Advisory Board for the CME Project was essential in helping us create an effective format for our lessons that embodies the philosophy and goals of the program. Their debates about pedagogical issues and how to develop mathematical topics helped to shape the distinguishing features of the curriculum so that our lessons work effectively in the classroom. The advisory board includes

Jayne Abbas, Richard Coffey,
Charles Garabedian, Dennis Geller,
Eileen Herlihy, Doreen Kilday,
Gayle Masse, Hugh McLaughlin,
Nancy McLaughlin, Allen Olsen,
Kimberly Osborne, Brian Shoemaker,
and **Benjamin Sinwell**

Field-Test Teachers Our field-test teachers gave us the benefit of their classroom experience by teaching from our draft lessons and giving us extensive, critical feedback that shaped the drafts into realistic, teachable lessons. They shared their concerns, questions, challenges, and successes and kept us focused on the real world. Some of them even welcomed us into their classrooms as co-teachers to give us the direct experience with students that we needed to hone our lessons. Working with these expert professionals has been one of the most gratifying parts of the development—they are "highly qualified" in the most profound sense.

California **Barney Martinez,** Jefferson High School, Daly City; **Calvin Baylon** and **Jaime Lao,** Bell Junior High School, San Diego; **Colorado Rocky Cundiff,** Ignacio High School, Ignacio; **Illinois Jeremy Kahan,** **Tammy Nguyen,** and **Stephanie Pederson,** Ida Crown Jewish Academy, Chicago; **Massachusetts Carol Martignette, Chris Martino,** and **Kent Werst,** Arlington High School, Arlington; **Larry Davidson,** Boston University Academy, Boston; **Joe Bishop** and **Carol Rosen,** Lawrence High School, Lawrence; **Maureen Mulryan,** Lowell High School, Lowell; **Felisa Honeyman,** Newton South High School, Newton Centre; **Jim Barnes** and **Carol Haney,** Revere High School, Revere; **New Hampshire Jayne Abbas** and **Terin Voisine,** Cawley Middle School, Hooksett; **New Mexico Mary Andrews,** Las Cruces High School, Las Cruces; **Ohio James Stallworth,** Hughes Center, Cincinnati; **Texas Arnell Crayton,** Bellaire High School, Bellaire; **Utah Troy Jones,** Waterford School, Sandy; **Washington Dale Erz, Kathy Greer, Karena Hanscom,** and **John Henry,** Port Angeles High School, Port Angeles; **Wisconsin Annette Roskam,** Rice Lake High School, Rice Lake.

Special thanks go to our colleagues at Pearson, most notably Elizabeth Lehnertz, Joe Will, and Stewart Wood. The program benefits from their expertise in every way, from the actual mathematics to the design of the printed page.

Analyzing Trigonometric Functions

2 Complex Numbers and Trigonometry

Contents

3 Analysis of Functions

4 Combinatorics

5 Functions and Tables

6 Analytic Geometry

Contents

7 Probability and Statistics

8 Ideas of Calculus

CME Project
Student Handbook

What Makes CME Different

Welcome to the CME Project! The goal of this program is to help you develop a deep understanding of mathematics. Throughout this book, you will engage in many different activities to help you develop that deep understanding. Some of these instructional activities may be different from ones you are used to. Below is an overview of some of these elements and why they are an important part of the CME Project.

The Habits of Mind Experience

Mathematical Habits of Mind are the foundation for serious questioning, solid thinking, good problem solving, and critical analysis. These Habits of Mind are what will help you become a mathematical thinker. Throughout the CME Project, you will focus on developing and refining these Habits of Mind.

Developing Habits of Mind

Develop thinking skills. This feature provides you with various methods and approaches to solving problems.

You will develop, use, and revisit specific Habits of Mind throughout the course. These include

- **Process** (how you work through problems)
- **Visualization** (how you "picture" problems)
- **Representation** (what you write down)
- **Patterns** (what you find)
- **Relationships** (what you find or use)

Developing good habits will help you as problems become more complicated.

Habits of Mind

Think. These special margin notes highlight key thinking skills and prompt you to apply your developing Habits of Mind.

You can find Developing Habits of Mind on pages 19, 20, 21, 46, 70, 94, 101, 110, 112, 134, 145, 148, 175, 222, 250, 279, 286, 297, 298, 300, 346, 348, 382, 389, 428, 446, 452, 454, 460, 469, 478, 480, 486, 487, 492, 494, 504, 544, 545, 548, 551, 557, 565, 577, 593, 610, 619, 647, 659, 687, 692

Minds in Action

Discussion of mathematical ideas is an effective method of learning. The Minds in Action feature exposes you to ways of communicating about mathematics.

Join Sasha, Tony, Derman, and others as they think, calculate, predict, and discuss their way towards understanding.

Minds in Action prologue

Sasha, Tony, and Derman have just skimmed through their CME Project Precalculus book.

Sasha Did you notice the student dialogs throughout the book?

Derman Sure did!

Tony They talk and think just the way we do.

Sasha I know! And they even make mistakes sometimes, the way we do.

Tony But I like how they help each other to learn from those mistakes. I bet they use the Habits of Mind I saw all over the book, too.

Sasha That's great! They should help a lot.

You can find Minds in Action on pages 18, 44, 63, 113, 117, 172, 211, 219, 221, 279, 285, 308, 328, 357, 398, 421, 427, 451, 486, 509, 543, 555, 558, 583, 608, 643, 645, 648, 666, 683, 684, 685

Exploring Mathematics

Throughout the CME Project, you will engage in activities that extend your learning and allow you to explore the concepts you learn in greater depth. Two of these activities are In-Class Experiments and Chapter Projects.

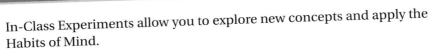

In-Class Experiment

In-Class Experiments allow you to explore new concepts and apply the Habits of Mind.

You will explore math as mathematicians do. You start with a question and develop answers through experimentation.

You can find In-Class Experiments on pages 8, 24, 34, 50, 132, 170, 180, 197, 254, 352, 364, 376, 414, 468, 493, 504, 541, 554, 575, 582, 591, 638

Chapter Projects

Chapter Projects allow you to apply your Habits of Mind to the content of the chapter. These projects cover many different topics and allow you to explore and engage in greater depth.

Chapter Projects
Using Mathematical Habits

Here is a list of the Chapter Projects and page numbers.

Using Your CME Book

To help you make the most of your CME experience, we are providing the following overview of the organization of your book.

Focusing Your Learning

In *Precalculus*, there are 8 chapters, with each chapter devoted to a mathematical concept. With only 8 chapters, your class will be able to focus on these core concepts and develop a deep understanding of them.

Within each chapter, you will explore a series of Investigations. Each Investigation focuses on an important aspect of the mathematical concept for that chapter.

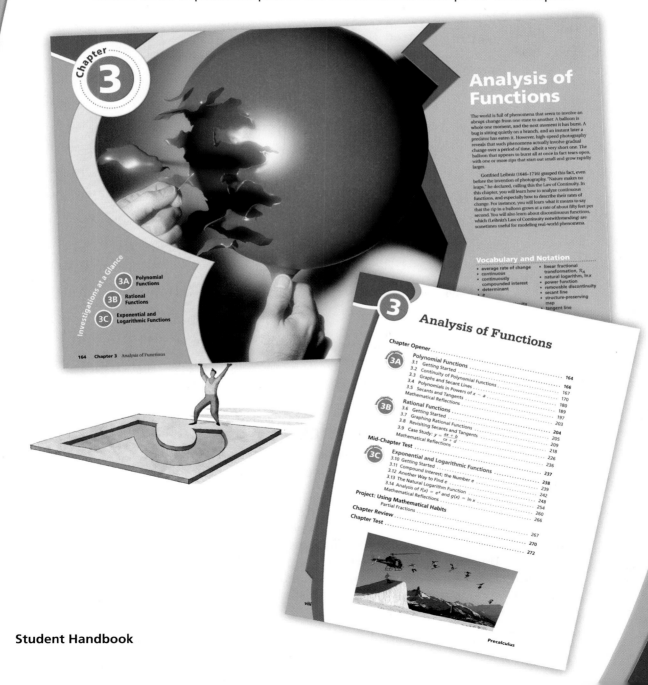

The CME Investigation

The goal of each mathematical Investigation is for you to formalize your understanding of the mathematics being taught. There are some common instructional features in each Investigation.

Getting Started

You will launch into each Investigation with a Getting Started lesson that activates prior knowledge and explores new ideas. This lesson provides you the opportunity to grapple with ideas and problems. The goal of these lessons is for you to explore—not all your questions will be answered in these lessons.

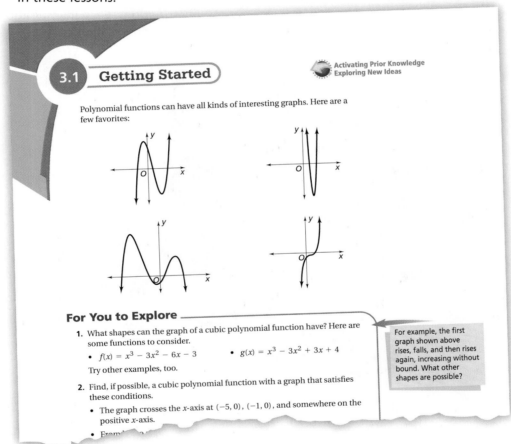

3.1 **Getting Started**

Activating Prior Knowledge
Exploring New Ideas

Polynomial functions can have all kinds of interesting graphs. Here are a few favorites:

For You to Explore

1. What shapes can the graph of a cubic polynomial function have? Here are some functions to consider.
   - $f(x) = x^3 - 3x^2 - 6x - 3$
   - $g(x) = x^3 - 3x^2 + 3x + 4$

   Try other examples, too.

2. Find, if possible, a cubic polynomial function with a graph that satisfies these conditions.
   - The graph crosses the x-axis at $(-5, 0)$, $(-1, 0)$, and somewhere on the positive x-axis.
   - From

   For example, the first graph shown above rises, falls, and then rises again, increasing without bound. What other shapes are possible?

Learning the Mathematics

You will engage in, learn, and practice the mathematics in a variety of ways. The types of learning elements you will find throughout this course include

- **Worked-Out Examples** that model how to solve problems
- **Definitions and Theorems** to summarize key concepts
- **In-Class Experiments** to explore the concepts
- **For You to Do** assignments to check your understanding
- **For Discussion** questions to encourage communication
- **Minds in Action** to model mathematical discussion

Communicating the Mathematics

Minds in Action

Student dialogs

By featuring dialogs between characters, the CME Project exposes you to a way of communicating about mathematics. These dialogs will then become a real part of your classroom!

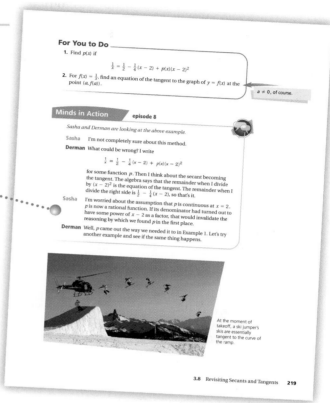

For You to Do

1. Find $p(x)$ if

$$\frac{1}{x} = \frac{1}{2} - \frac{1}{4}(x-2) + p(x)(x-2)^2$$

2. For $f(x) = \frac{1}{x}$, find an equation of the tangent to the graph of $y = f(x)$ at the point $(a, f(a))$.

> $a \neq 0$, of course.

Minds in Action   episode 8

Sasha and Derman are looking at the above example.

Sasha   I'm not completely sure about this method.

Derman   What could be wrong? I write

$$\frac{1}{x} = \frac{1}{2} - \frac{1}{4}(x-2) + p(x)(x-2)^2$$

for some function p. Then I think about the secant becoming the tangent. The algebra says that the remainder when I divide by $(x-2)^2$ is the equation of the tangent. The remainder when I divide the right side is $\frac{1}{2} - \frac{1}{4}(x-2)$, so that's it.

Sasha   I'm worried about the assumption that p is continuous at $x = 2$. p is now a rational function. If its denominator had turned out to have some power of $x - 2$ as a factor, that would invalidate the reasoning by which we found p in the first place.

Derman   Well, p came out the way we needed it to in Example 1. Let's try another example and see if the same thing happens.

At the moment of takeoff, a ski jumper's skis are essentially tangent to the curve of the ramp.

3.8   Revisiting Secants and Tangents   **219**

Reflecting on the Mathematics

At the end of each Investigation, Mathematical Reflections give you an opportunity to put ideas together. This feature allows you to demonstrate your understanding of the Investigation and reflect on what you learn.

Practice

The CME Project views extensive practice as a critical component of a mathematics curriculum. You will have daily opportunities to practice what you learn.

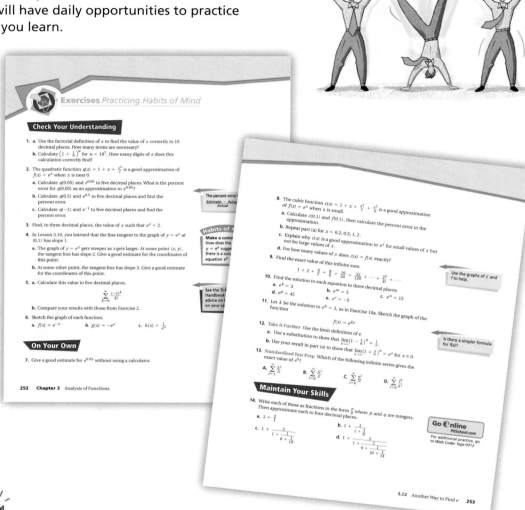

Check Your Understanding

Assess your readiness for independent practice by working through these problems in class.

On Your Own

Practice and continue developing the mathematical understanding you learn in each lesson.

Maintain Your Skills

Review and reinforce skills from previous lessons.

Also Available

An additional Practice Workbook is available separately.

Go Online

Throughout this book you will find links to the Prentice Hall Web site. Use the Web Codes provided with each link to gain direct access to online material. Here's how to Go Online.

1 Go to PHSchool.com.

2 Enter the Web Code.

3 Click Go!

Check out the TI-Nspire™ Technology Handbook on p. 704 for examples of how you can use handheld technology with your math learning!

Go Online Lesson Web Codes

Additional Practice Web Codes: For every lesson, (except Getting Started lessons) there is additional practice online. Access this additional practice using the Web Code format at the right.

Additional Practice

Web Code format: bga-0203
02 = Chapter 2 03 = Lesson 3

Go Online Chapter Web Codes

Chapter	Vocabulary Review	Mid-Chapter Test	Chapter Test
1	bgj-0151	bga-0152	bga-0153
2	bgj-0251	bga-0252	bga-0253
3	bgj-0351	bga-0352	bga-0353
4	bgj-0451	bga-0452	bga-0453
5	bgj-0551	bga-0552	bga-0553
6	bgj-0651	bga-0652	bga-0653
7	bgj-0751	bga-0752	bga-0753
8	bgj-0851	bga-0852	bga-0853

Go Online Additional Web Codes

Math Background

Use **Web Code:** bge-8031 to find additional historical background information. See page 414.
Use **Web Code:** bge-9031 to find additional background information related to the mathematics at hand. See page 10.

Analyzing Trigonometric Functions

As you know, trigonometry describes the relationships between the angles and sides of triangles. When some of the angles and distances between three locations are known, you use trigonometry to calculate the unknown angles and distances.

But its usefulness is even more wide-ranging. It also describes cyclical behavior such as the height of a seat on a Ferris wheel, the heights of the tides, or the monthly sales of sunscreen over a year. To begin, you look at radians, a more natural way to express the domain of the trigonometric functions. You discover special properties of the sine, cosine, and tangent functions. Then you use trigonometric functions to model periodic behavior.

In this chapter, you will develop useful tools. These will prepare you for the study of complex numbers, continuity, limits, and vectors.

Vocabulary

- amplitude
- arc
- asymptote
- central angle
- decreasing
- increasing
- inverse function
- maximum

- minimum
- period
- periodic
- phase shift
- radian
- sinusoidal function
- turning point
- vertical displacement

Investigation 1A

The Cosine and Sine Functions

In *The Cosine and Sine Functions,* you will learn how to measure in radians. You will learn how to think of cosine and sine as functions of radian measure. You will solve equations involving these trigonometric functions.

By the end of this investigation, you will be able to answer questions like these.

1. Where are the turning points of the cosine and sine functions?

2. What is a radian?

3. How can you use a graph of $y = \sin x$ to estimate solutions to the equation $\sin x = -0.6$?

You will learn how to

- understand the relationship between degree and radian measure as the length of an arc on the unit circle subtended by a central angle

- relate the motion of an object around a circle to the graphs of the cosine and sine functions

- solve equations that involve cosine and sine (such as $3 \cos x + 2 = 1$)

You will develop these habits and skills:

- Calculate cosine and sine using radians directly without converting to degrees.

- Visualize periodic functions, and identify their period.

- Understand how to "undo" cosine or sine to solve equations.

- Compare the cosine and sine functions through their relation to the unit circle and through their graphs.

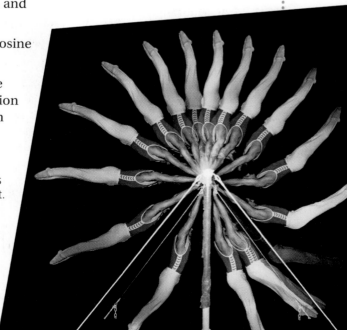

The gymnast traces a circle as he rotates about a fixed point.

1.1 Getting Started

Olivia watches Paul walk around a circle. The circle's radius is 1 meter. Olivia stands at the center, and Paul begins walking counterclockwise. Consider a coordinate grid, with Olivia standing at the origin and Paul starting at the point $(1, 0)$.

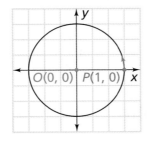

> **Remember...**
> The equation of the unit circle is $x^2 + y^2 = 1$.

As Paul walks an increasing distance around the circle, he passes through many points. The questions in this Getting Started ask about Paul's location after he has walked a specific distance.

For You to Explore

1. How far will Paul walk before returning to the point $(1, 0)$?

2. Draw the unit circle and plot the point where Paul will be after walking each distance.

   a. exactly π meters

   b. exactly $\frac{\pi}{2}$ meters

   c. exactly 3π meters

   d. exactly 3 meters

3. At some point, Paul has walked exactly $\frac{9\pi}{4}$ meters.

   a. What quadrant is Paul in after this much walking?

   b. Draw a unit circle and plot the point where Paul is after walking $\frac{9\pi}{4}$ meters.

   c. Find two other distances Paul could have walked around the circle to end up at this same point.

4. At some point, Paul has walked exactly $\frac{\pi}{3}$ meters. Find the exact coordinates of Paul's location.

5. **Write About It** At some point, Paul has walked exactly $\frac{\pi}{4}$ meters. Explain why his x- and y-coordinates must be equal at this point.

6. **a.** Find the exact coordinates of Paul's location after he walks $\frac{\pi}{4}$ meters.

   b. Find the exact coordinates of Paul's location after he walks $\frac{5\pi}{4}$ meters.

7. **Take It Further** Paul runs 100 meters along the circle. What quadrant is he in at the end of this 100-meter run?

> **Habits of Mind**
> **Recognize symmetry.**
> Is there any symmetry to Paul's location?

> **Remember...**
> *Exact* here means no decimals, just exact fractions or radicals.

Exercises Practicing Habits of Mind

On Your Own

8. How far will Paul walk when he first reaches the point $(0, -1)$?

9. **Write About It** What is the importance of π in measuring the distance Paul has walked? In other words, why are so many of the questions about multiples of π and not integers?

10. **Write About It** Olivia, standing at $O(0, 0)$, says that Paul's $\frac{\pi}{2}$ behaves like $90°$. Explain Olivia's observation.

11. As Paul continues to walk, he will reach $(0, -1)$ again.

    a. Give another distance Paul could walk to reach $(0, -1)$.

    b. Describe a method you could use to generate a large number of these distances.

12. **a.** Draw the unit circle and plot the point where Paul will be after walking exactly $\frac{7\pi}{6}$ meters.

    b. Find the exact coordinates of Paul's location after he walks $\frac{7\pi}{6}$ meters.

13. As Paul walks around the circle, is there ever a time when his y-coordinate is *exactly* $\frac{2}{3}$? If so, how many times will this happen each time Paul goes around the circle? If not, how do you know it can never happen?

14. As Paul walks around the circle, his x- and y-coordinates reach maximum and minimum values. What are these maximum and minimum values, and at what walking distances do they occur?

Maintain Your Skills

15. Copy and complete this table, giving the coordinates of Paul's location after walking each distance. Look for patterns to help make your work easier.

Distance	Coordinates
0	$(1, 0)$
$\frac{\pi}{4}$	$\left(\frac{\sqrt{2}}{2}, \frac{\sqrt{2}}{2}\right)$
$\frac{\pi}{2}$	▨
$\frac{3\pi}{4}$	▨
π	$(-1, 0)$
$\frac{5\pi}{4}$	▨
$\frac{3\pi}{2}$	▨
$\frac{7\pi}{4}$	▨
2π	▨
$\frac{9\pi}{4}$	▨
$\frac{5\pi}{2}$	▨

1.2 Trigonometry With Radians

In Lesson 1.1, Paul walked around a unit circle, and you found the coordinates of his stopping point. You may remember that the coordinates of any point on the unit circle are $(\cos\theta, \sin\theta)$, where θ is the measure of the angle between the positive x-axis and a ray drawn from the origin through the point.

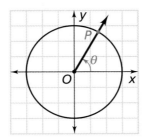

Since the origin is the center of the circle, the angle whose measure is θ is a **central angle.** The part of the circle that is between the two sides of the angle is an **arc.**

There is a direct correspondence between the length of an arc on the unit circle and the measure of the central angle that defines the arc.

> **Remember...**
>
> A central angle for a circle is an angle that has its vertex at the center of the circle.
>
> An arc is a set of points of a circle that lie in the interior of a particular central angle.

Example 1

Problem For an arc length of $\frac{\pi}{3}$, what is the measure of the corresponding central angle?

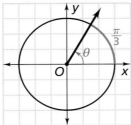

Solution The circumference of the unit circle is 2π. So the arc with length $\frac{\pi}{3}$ would be $\frac{1}{6}$ of the entire circle (since $\frac{\pi}{3} \cdot 6 = 2\pi$). The central angle is $\frac{\theta}{360°}$ of the full circle. Thus,

$$\frac{1}{6} = \frac{\theta}{360°}$$

so $\theta = 60°$.

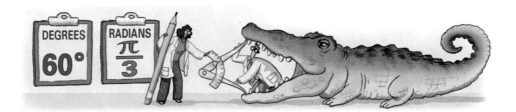

DEGREES
60°

RADIANS
$\frac{\pi}{3}$

For You to Do

1. How long is the arc that corresponds to a 135° central angle?

See the TI-Nspire™ Handbook on p. 704 on how to make this sketch. Some geometry software will calculate actual length in inches or centimeters, not in relative units.

In-Class Experiment

In this experiment, you will build a model using your graphing calculator or geometry software. You will compare distance traveled around a circle, the corresponding central angle, and the coordinates of the stopping point.

Follow these steps to build your sketch:

Step 1 Construct a circle of radius of 1 unit on a coordinate grid.

Step 2 Add a point at $(1, 0)$. Label it A.

Step 3 Construct another point on the circle. Label it B.

Step 4 Have the software display the coordinates of point B.

Step 5 Have the software display the length of $\overset{\frown}{AB}$ (counterclockwise).

Step 6 Have the software display the degree measure of $\angle AOB$.

Drag point B around the circle, and compare the angle measure to the arc length.

For You to Do

2. What is the maximum y-coordinate? For what arc length does it occur?

3. What arc length corresponds to 90°?

4. What angle corresponds to an arc length of $\frac{7\pi}{4}$?

In general, if R is the arc length, and D is the degree measure of the corresponding angle, then

$$\frac{R}{2\pi} = \frac{D}{360°}$$

For You to Do

Find the measure of the angle (in degrees) for each of the following arc lengths.

5. $\frac{\pi}{4}$ **6.** $\frac{4\pi}{3}$ **7.** 4

At this point, you have defined the functions cosine and sine in terms of degrees. The input is the angle measure in degrees and the output is a real number. When you set the calculator in **radian** mode, it gives you the cosine and sine as a function of the length of an arc along the circle, rather than of the central angle.

Why think of a different way to define the trig functions? With this new definition, you can think of both input and output as lengths or distances—the same type of measurement. You input the arc distance from $(1, 0)$ of a point on a unit circle. The cosine function outputs the distance of that point from the y-axis. The sine function outputs the distance from the x-axis.

Think of a radian as an arc of length 1 unit. So π radians would correspond to a central angle of $180°$.

See the TI-Nspire Handbook on p. 704 for details on how to put your calculator in radian mode.

Example 2

Problem Find $\cos \frac{\pi}{3}$ and $\sin \frac{\pi}{3}$.

Solution In the previous example, you saw that an arc of $\frac{\pi}{3}$ on the unit circle corresponds to a $60°$ angle. You might remember $\cos 60°$ and $\sin 60°$, since $60°$ is one of the angles from a 30–60–90 right triangle. So

$$\cos \frac{\pi}{3} = \cos 60° = \frac{1}{2}, \text{ and}$$

$$\sin \frac{\pi}{3} = \sin 60° = \frac{\sqrt{3}}{2}$$

Since your experience now is mostly with degree measure, you may naturally try to convert any radian measure to degrees to find the sine and cosine. With practice, taking this extra step will be unnecessary. Your ultimate goal is to calculate cosine and sine directly from the arc length.

The cosine and sine functions look the same whether you are in degree or radian mode. The only way to be certain which mode is intended is to look at the argument: $\sin 30°$ is different from $\sin 30$. When you see $\sin x$, you can assume x is radians unless you are told otherwise.

As Paul walked around the circle, you may have noticed a correspondence between the distance he walked (the length of an arc if he walked less than once around the circle) and the coordinates of his stopping point. Using radian mode on your calculator, you can calculate the coordinates of his stopping point directly from the distance he actually traveled, without converting to degrees.

For You to Do

Find the exact coordinates of Paul's stopping point after walking each distance.

8. exactly π meters

9. exactly $\frac{\pi}{2}$ meters

10. exactly 3π meters

11. exactly $\frac{9\pi}{4}$ meters

Exercises Practicing Habits of Mind

Check Your Understanding

1. Example 2 showed that $\cos\frac{\pi}{3} = \frac{1}{2}$ and $\sin\frac{\pi}{3} = \frac{\sqrt{3}}{2}$.

   a. The value of $\cos\frac{2\pi}{3}$ is negative, while $\sin\frac{2\pi}{3}$ is positive. What are these values?

   b. Find the values of $\cos\frac{4\pi}{3}$ and $\sin\frac{4\pi}{3}$.

   c. Find the values of $\cos\frac{5\pi}{3}$ and $\sin\frac{5\pi}{3}$.

   d. Find the values of $\cos\frac{6\pi}{3}$ and $\sin\frac{6\pi}{3}$.

2. Find the exact values of $\cos\frac{\pi}{4}$ and $\sin\frac{\pi}{4}$.

3. Copy and complete this table with exact values of cosine and sine. It may help to plot the point $(\cos x, \sin x)$ for each value of x.

x	cos x	sin x
0	■	■
$\frac{\pi}{6}$	$\frac{\sqrt{3}}{2}$	$\frac{1}{2}$
$\frac{\pi}{4}$	■	■
$\frac{\pi}{3}$	$\frac{1}{2}$	$\frac{\sqrt{3}}{2}$
$\frac{\pi}{2}$	■	■
$\frac{2\pi}{3}$	■	■
$\frac{3\pi}{4}$	$-\frac{\sqrt{2}}{2}$	$\frac{\sqrt{2}}{2}$
$\frac{5\pi}{6}$	■	■
π	■	■
$\frac{7\pi}{6}$	■	■
$\frac{5\pi}{4}$	■	$-\frac{\sqrt{2}}{2}$
$\frac{4\pi}{3}$	■	■
$\frac{3\pi}{2}$	0	−1
$\frac{5\pi}{3}$	■	■
$\frac{7\pi}{4}$	■	■
$\frac{11\pi}{6}$	$\frac{\sqrt{3}}{2}$	■
2π	■	■
$\frac{13\pi}{6}$	■	■
$\frac{9\pi}{4}$	■	■
$\frac{7\pi}{3}$	■	■

Go Online
PHSchool.com

For an overview of trigonometry, go to Web Code: bge-9031

4. For several different values of x, calculate the squares of $\cos x$ and of $\sin x$. How do the two values, $\cos^2 x$ and $\sin^2 x$, relate to each other?

Remember...

The square of $\cos x$ is usually written as $\cos^2 x$.

5. a. Is there some number x that makes $\cos x = \frac{4}{5}$? Explain.

   b. If $\cos x = \frac{4}{5}$, what could $\sin x$ equal?

6. Which of the following values is greatest?

   A. $\sin 1$ **B.** $\sin 2$ **C.** $\sin 3$ **D.** $\sin 4$

Don't let your calculator have all the fun!

7. Take It Further

   a. Is there an integer n such that $\sin n > 0.999$? Explain.

   b. Is there an integer n such that $\sin n = -1$? Explain.

On Your Own

8. Locate the point on the unit circle with coordinates $\left(\cos \frac{\pi}{6}, \sin \frac{\pi}{6}\right)$.

9. Explain why $\sin \frac{\pi}{2} = 1$.

10. Simplify the sum $\cos \frac{\pi}{4} + \cos \frac{3\pi}{4} + \cos \frac{5\pi}{4} + \cos \frac{7\pi}{4}$.

11. Suppose $\frac{\pi}{2} < x < \pi$. State whether each of the following is positive or negative.

   a. $\sin x$ **b.** $\cos x$ **c.** $\frac{\sin x}{\cos x}$ **d.** $\cos^2 x + \sin^2 x$

If the length of the arc is between $\frac{\pi}{2}$ and π, the endpoint will be somewhere in Quadrant II.

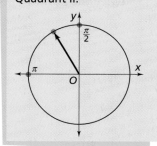

12. What's Wrong Here? Walt can't decide whether $\sin 5$ should be positive or negative.

Walt says, "I drew a unit circle. Five radians is more than π, since π is just over 3. But 5 is less than 2π. Then 5 radians is somewhere around here:

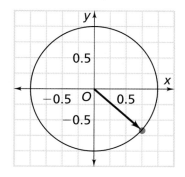

It looks like $\sin 5$ should be negative, but the calculator says that the answer is about 0.087, positive."

Explain what happened. Is Walt right, or is the calculator right?

Go Online
PHSchool.com

For additional practice, go to **Web Code:** bga-0102

13. Find the exact value of $\log_{10}\left(20 \sin \frac{5\pi}{6}\right)$.

14. **Take It Further** Simplify the sum $\cos\frac{2\pi}{5} + \cos\frac{4\pi}{5} + \cos\frac{6\pi}{5} + \cos\frac{8\pi}{5}$.

15. **Standardized Test Prep** Of the following four cosine values, which is the greatest?

A. cos 5.28   **B.** cos 6.28   **C.** cos 7.28   **D.** cos 8.28

Maintain Your Skills

16. In the figure below, the angle of the intercepted arc has length equal to the radius.

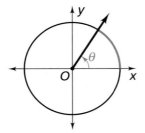

Find the angle to the nearest tenth of a degree.

17. In the figure below, the angle of the intercepted arc has length equal to twice the radius.

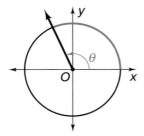

Find the measure of the angle to the nearest tenth of a degree.

1.3 Graphing Cosine and Sine Functions

After Paul has moved α meters around his circle of radius 1 meter, he reaches a certain point, (a, b). You can track how a and b change individually as Paul moves around the circle by making a graph.

The following diagram shows a series of arcs of the same unit circle. Each arc starts from the point $(1, 0)$, and ends at some stopping point (a, b). The arc is highlighted, along with the height of the stopping point. That height is, in fact, the same value as the y-coordinate of the stopping point, b. And b is equal to $\sin \alpha$.

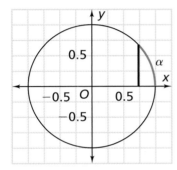 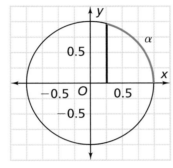 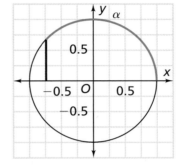

As the value of α, the arc length, increases from 0 to $\frac{\pi}{2}$, the y-coordinate, or $\sin \alpha$, increases from 0 to 1. Then, as the arc length increases from $\frac{\pi}{2}$ to π, the sine decreases from 1 to 0. The graph below shows the results for $0 \le \alpha \le \pi$.

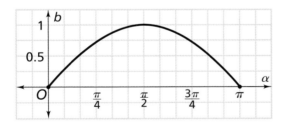

Temporal changes in the height of the sun follow a sine pattern as seen in this time-lapse photograph of the sun's daily cycle from the island of Loppa in Norway, north of the Arctic Circle.

To continue this graph, look at more arcs. As the arc length grows larger than π, the y-coordinate of the stopping point becomes negative.

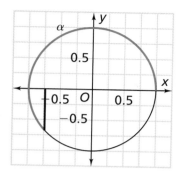 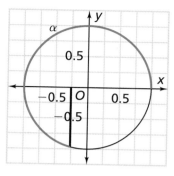 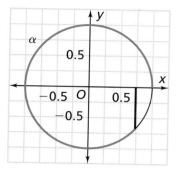

So the sine of arcs that are between π and 2π are all negative. The following graph shows a full rotation around the unit circle.

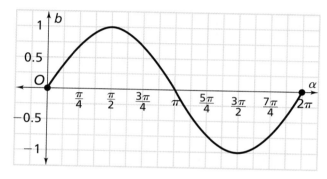

For You to Do

1. Find all numbers x such that $0 \leq x \leq 2\pi$ and $\sin x = 1$.

After Paul has walked 2π meters, he has returned to his starting point. If he continues walking, he ends up retracing his earlier steps. For instance, his stopping point is the same when he walks $\frac{\pi}{4}$ meters and when he walks $\frac{9\pi}{4}$ meters.

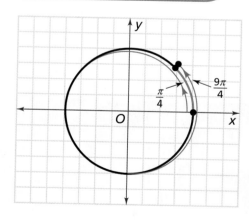

For You to Do

The values of n may or may not be integers.

2. Find 4 values for x such that $\sin x = 1$. Write a general statement in terms of n, such that $\sin n\pi = 1$.

You can generate the graph $a = \cos \alpha$ in a similar manner. As Paul walks from the point $(1, 0)$ to the point (a, b) on his circle, graph the distance he travels α on the horizontal axis and the value of a on the vertical axis. Below is the graph of $a = \cos \alpha$, for domain $0 \leq \alpha \leq 2\pi$.

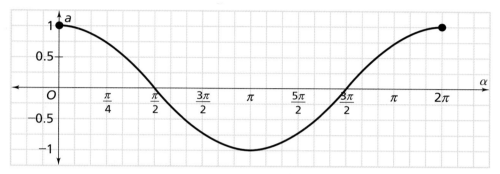

For Discussion

3. Apply the transformation $x \mapsto x + \frac{\pi}{2}$ to the graph of $y = \cos x$. How does this graph compare to the graph of $y = \sin x$?

You built the graphs for both the cosine and sine functions by observing Paul walking around a circle. Since he only walks around in circles, he will continue to move through the exact same set of points each lap around the circle.

When the outputs of a function, like cosine and sine, repeat in a regular pattern, the function is called periodic.

Definitions

A nonconstant function f is **periodic** if there exists a real number $p > 0$ such that, for all x, $f(x + p) = f(x)$.

The **period** of a periodic function is the smallest value p such that, for all x, $f(x + p) = f(x)$.

 **Exercises** *Practicing Habits of Mind*

Check Your Understanding

1. Starting from standard position, an angle that intercepts an arc of length $\frac{4\pi}{3}$ ends in what quadrant?

   A. Quadrant I   **B.** Quadrant II

   C. Quadrant III   **D.** Quadrant IV

2. **a.** If $\cos x = 0.6$, what is $\cos^2 x$? What is $\sin^2 x$?

   b. Find both possible values of $\sin x$.

   c. On the unit circle, show the two possible locations where $\cos x = 0.6$.

3. On the same axes, sketch the graphs of these two equations.

   $$y = \cos x$$
   $$y = 0.6$$

   Use the graphs to estimate the two solutions to $\cos x = 0.6$ in the interval $0 \le x < 2\pi$.

4. You can extend the domain of the cosine and sine functions to include negative values.

   a. What should $\cos\left(-\frac{\pi}{2}\right)$ and $\sin\left(-\frac{\pi}{2}\right)$ equal?

   b. What should $\cos\left(-\frac{\pi}{3}\right)$ and $\sin\left(-\frac{\pi}{3}\right)$ equal?

   > For negative values in the domain, think of Paul walking backward, or clockwise, around his circle.

5. Paul and his twin brother Saul follow the instructions from the Getting Started, except Paul moves counterclockwise and Saul moves clockwise. (Assume they walk at the same speed.)

   a. As Paul and Saul continue, what is the relationship between their x-coordinates?

   b. What is the relationship between Paul and Saul's y-coordinates?

6. Decide whether each statement is always true. Use what you have learned from Paul and Saul in Exercise 5.

   a. $\cos(-x) = -\cos x$ **b.** $\cos(-x) = \cos x$

   c. $\sin(-x) = -\sin x$ **d.** $\sin(-x) = \sin x$

On Your Own

7. Sketch accurate graphs of $y = \cos x$ and $y = \sin x$, where the domain of each is $-2\pi \le x \le 4\pi$.

> **Habits of Mind**
>
> **Visualize.** Think about Paul's walk. How many times around the circle would it be from -2π to 4π?

8. Paul starts at $(1, 0)$ and walks counterclockwise 24 radians along the unit circle. What quadrant is Paul in?

9. On the unit circle, show the two possible locations where $\sin x = 0.8$.

10. On the same axes, sketch these two graphs.

$$y = \sin x$$
$$y = 0.8$$

Use the graphs to estimate the two solutions to $\sin x = 0.8$ in the interval $0 \le x < 2\pi$.

11. Sketch the graph of the equation.

$$y = \sin\left(x + \tfrac{\pi}{2}\right)$$

12. Instead of graphing the arc length against the height, Olivia decides to make graphs of Paul's x- and y-coordinates against time (in seconds).

a. Suppose Paul walks 1 meter per second. How would Olivia's graph compare to her graph of arc length against the height?

b. Suppose Paul walks 2 meters per second. How would Olivia's graph compare to the graph from part (a)?

13. Take It Further Simplify the sum
$\sin \tfrac{2\pi}{9} + \sin \tfrac{4\pi}{9} + \sin \tfrac{\pi}{3} + \cos \tfrac{\pi}{6} + \cos \tfrac{13\pi}{18} + \cos \tfrac{17\pi}{8}$

14. Standardized Test Prep Let x be the length of an arc on the unit circle in standard position. In which quadrants can the arc terminate if the product $(\cos x)(\sin x)$ is positive?

A. I and II **B.** I and III **C.** I and IV **D.** II and IV

For additional practice, go to **Web Code:** bga-0103

Maintain Your Skills

15. Find the corresponding radian measure for each of the following degree values.

a. 30° **b.** 150° **c.** 210° **d.** 330° **e.** 390°

16. Find the corresponding measure in degrees for each of the following radian values.

a. $\tfrac{\pi}{3}$ radians **b.** $\tfrac{2\pi}{3}$ radians **c.** $\tfrac{4\pi}{3}$ radians

d. $\tfrac{5\pi}{3}$ radians **e.** $\tfrac{7\pi}{3}$ radians

> **Remember...**
> The radian measure is the length of the arc on a unit circle cut by a central angle.

1.4 Solving Cosine and Sine Equations

To solve an equation involving a trigonometric function, you begin the same way you begin with an ordinary equation.

Minds in Action   episode 1

Tony and Sasha are trying to solve the equation $4 \sin x + 5 = 7$, *with x in radians.*

Tony   I know we want to solve for x, but what do we do with $\sin x$?

Sasha   Let's use the lumping-together technique from algebra.

Sasha goes to the board and covers up the $\sin x$ *with her hand.*

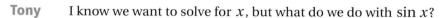

$$4 \, \text{\includegraphics{hand}} \, x + 5 = 7$$

Sasha   See? It now looks like it's saying "4 times something plus 5 is 7." That sounds like a simple equation. So, if we let H stand for $\sin x$, we can write the equation as

$$4H + 5 = 7$$

Tony   I know how to solve that … $H = \frac{1}{2}$.

Sasha   Right. And remember, H was just an alias for $\sin x$. So just replace H with $\sin x$ to get the new equation $\sin x = \frac{1}{2}$.

Tony   And I know how to solve that, too. You just use the $\sin^{-1}$ function and get about 0.52.

> Tony typed $\sin^{-1}(0.5)$ into his calculator. His calculator was in radian mode.

Sasha   We can find the exact answer. Remember, $\frac{1}{2}$ is one of the ratios from a 30–60–90 triangle: $\sin 30° = \frac{1}{2}$.

Tony   And 30° corresponds to $\frac{\pi}{6}$ radians, and $\frac{\pi}{6}$ is about 0.52, the number I got before. So that's it, we're done!

Sasha   Well, um, no. Look at this:

Sasha draws on the board.

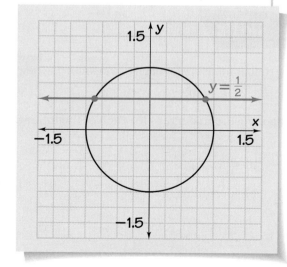

Sasha   See? Sine is the y-coordinate, and there are *two* points on the unit circle whose y-coordinate is $\frac{1}{2}$.

Tony   The point in the first quadrant is the solution we already got, $\frac{\pi}{6}$.

Sasha   And the other solution is in the second quadrant. It's $\pi - \frac{\pi}{6} = \frac{5\pi}{6}$, which is about 2.62.

Tony   Okay, so there are two answers. I wonder why the calculator only gave me one. Anyway, is that all?

Sasha   That's all we'd find on the unit circle. So we can say at least that that's all between 0 and 2π.

> By the end of this chapter, you will see why the calculator only gave Tony one answer.

For You to Do

1. Solve $-8\cos x + 5 = 11$ for x between 0 and 2π radians.

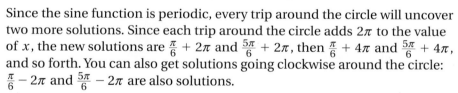

Developing Habits of Mind

Extend the process. The unit circle makes it clear how many solutions there are between 0 and 2π. But if you lift that restriction, you will find infinitely many solutions to Tony and Sasha's equation.

Since the sine function is periodic, every trip around the circle will uncover two more solutions. Since each trip around the circle adds 2π to the value of x, the new solutions are $\frac{\pi}{6} + 2\pi$ and $\frac{5\pi}{6} + 2\pi$, then $\frac{\pi}{6} + 4\pi$ and $\frac{5\pi}{6} + 4\pi$, and so forth. You can also get solutions going clockwise around the circle: $\frac{\pi}{6} - 2\pi$ and $\frac{5\pi}{6} - 2\pi$ are also solutions.

In the end, there are infinitely many solutions. They are of the form $\frac{\pi}{6} + 2\pi n$ and $\frac{5\pi}{6} + 2\pi n$ for all integer values of n.

For Discussion

2. Plot the equations $y = \sin x$ and $y = \frac{1}{2}$ on the same axes. How can you use your graphs to show all the solutions to $\sin x = \frac{1}{2}$?

> Your may not actually *see* every solution, but your graph definitely suggests all the solutions.

Simplify complicated problems. Use the lumping idea that Sasha used to solve trigonometric equations that look like ordinary algebraic equations. For example, the equation

$$10 \sin^2 x - 3 \sin x = 4$$

is a quadratic equation in $\sin x$. That is, if you let $H = \sin x$, the equation becomes

$$10H^2 - 3H = 4$$

You can solve this equation like any other quadratic. When you find two values for H, replace H by $\sin x$ and then solve for x.

For You to Do

3. Solve the equation for all x, where $0 \leq x < 2\pi$.

$$10 \sin^2 x - 3 \sin x = 4$$

Some trigonometry problems are not explicit equations, but ask you to relate cosine and sine for the same angle.

Example

Problem If $\sin \alpha = 0.4$, find all possible values of $\cos \alpha$.

Solution It might help to start with a picture. The figure below shows the two possible points where $\sin \alpha = 0.4$. So the possible values for $\cos \alpha$ will be the x-coordinates of those two points, which seem to be about ± 0.9.

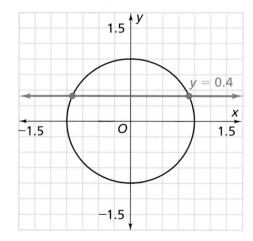

But how do you find the exact answers? You may recall the Pythagorean identity

$$\cos^2 \alpha + \sin^2 \alpha = 1$$

You can use this identity to find the exact answers. Since $\sin x = 0.4$, you have

$$\cos^2 x + (0.4)^2 = 1$$

$$\cos^2 x + 0.16 = 1$$

$$\cos^2 x = 0.84$$

$$\cos x = \pm\sqrt{0.84} = \pm\frac{\sqrt{21}}{5}$$

And $\frac{\sqrt{21}}{5} \approx 0.917$, which is close to the estimate from the graph.

For You to Do

4. If $3\cos x + 4 = 2$, find all possible values of $\sin x$.

Developing Habits of Mind

Look for relationships. When you first saw the identity $\cos^2\theta + \sin^2\theta = 1$, you probably related it to a right triangle.

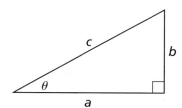

By the Pythagorean Theorem, you know that $a^2 + b^2 = c^2$. You can divide through by c^2 to get

$$\left(\frac{a}{c}\right)^2 + \left(\frac{b}{c}\right)^2 = 1$$

If θ is the angle opposite the side a, then $\cos\theta = \frac{a}{c}$ and $\sin\theta = \frac{b}{c}$. Substitution gives you the identity.

Another way to see the identity is to think about the unit circle. An equation for the unit circle is $x^2 + y^2 = 1$. But remember that any point on the circle is $(\cos\theta, \sin\theta)$. Substitute $\cos\theta$ for x and $\sin\theta$ for y and, you get the identity again.

Exercises *Practicing Habits of Mind*

Check Your Understanding

1. If $0 \leq x < 2\pi$, find the two possible values of x such that $\sin x = -\frac{1}{2}$.

2. Find all possible values of x so that $\sin x = -\frac{1}{2}$.

3. Suppose x is the length of an arc intercepted by an angle in Quadrant III and $\cos x = -0.65$. Find $\sin x$ to four decimal places.

4. If θ is degree measure, and $\sin \theta = \sin 50°$, what are all possible values of θ?

5. If x is the length of an arc intercepted by an angle in Quadrant I, and $\sin x = 0.62$, find $\frac{\sin x}{\cos x}$ to two decimal places.

6. Let $0 \leq x < 2\pi$. Find a trigonometric equation in x with the given number of solutions.

    a. one solution   **b.** two solutions   **c.** 0 solutions

    d. four solutions   **e.** six solutions

7. **Take It Further** Find all solutions to this system of equations, if $0 \leq \theta \leq \pi$ and $0 \leq \alpha \leq \pi$.

$$4 \sin \theta + \cos \alpha = 3$$
$$2 \sin \theta + 4 \cos \alpha = 5$$

8. **Take It Further** Suppose $\sin x = 2 \cos x - 1$.

    Find the two possible values of $\sin x$ if $0 \leq x \leq 2\pi$.

On Your Own

9. Find all solutions to the equation.

$$3 \sin x + 4 = 0$$

10. **a.** Show, using a unit circle, that $\sin 20° = \sin 160°$.

    b. What is the relationship between $\cos 20°$ and $\cos 160°$?

11. If θ is a degree measure, and $\cos \theta = \cos 50°$, what are all possible values of θ?

12. If $\cos x = \frac{1}{3}$, find both possible values of $\sin x$.

13. If $\cos x = \frac{1}{3}$, find the two possible values of x between 0 and 2π.

14. The value of $\sin 56.3° = 0.832$ to three decimal places.

   a. Find all possible angle measures θ, in degrees, for which $\sin \theta = 0.832$.

   b. Take It Further Find all possible angle measures θ, in degrees, for which $\cos \theta = 0.832$.

15. Find all solutions if $0 \le x < 2\pi$.

$$2 \cos^2 x = \cos x$$

16. Take It Further Find all solutions.

$$\cos^2 x + \sin x = 1.$$

17. Standardized Test Prep If $\cos x = \frac{5}{13}$, which of the following could be the value of $\sin x$?

   A. $\frac{5}{12}$ **B.** $\frac{5}{13}$ **C.** $\frac{12}{13}$ **D.** $\frac{13}{5}$

Maintain Your Skills

18. Solve each equation if $0 \le x < 2\pi$.

   a. $\sin x = \frac{1}{2}$

   b. $\sin x = \frac{2}{3}$

   c. $\sin x = \frac{5}{3}$

   d. $5 \sin x = 4$

   e. $3 \sin x + 2 = 0$

   f. $3 \sin x - 5 = 0$

   g. $(3 \sin x + 2)(3 \sin x - 5) = 0$

19. Solve each equation if $0 \le x < 2\pi$.

   a. $\cos x = \frac{1}{2}$

   b. $\cos x = \frac{2}{3}$

   c. $\cos x = \frac{5}{3}$

   d. $5 \cos x = 4$

   e. $3 \cos x + 2 = 0$

   f. $3 \cos x - 5 = 0$

   g. $(3 \cos x + 2)(3 \cos x - 5) = 0$

The surface of the water intersects the circular paddlewheel in two places. A cross-section view would look similar to the graph of the Example on page 20.

Go Online

PHSchool.com

For additional practice, go to **Web Code:** bga-0104

1.5 Analyzing Graphs

When you draw the graphs of linear functions, an important property of the graph is the slope of the line. And the most important property of a line is that it has constant slope: pick any two points on the line and calculate the slope between them, and you will always get the same value.

Only lines have constant slope. But you can think about slope for non-linear functions: you can pick any two points on the graph of any function and calculate the slope between them. But those two points can be anywhere on the graph, so the only information you will get is that comparing several calculations of these slopes can tell you that a function is not linear.

To analyze a graph, it is most useful to think of the slope of a curve at a single point. But how do you calculate slope if you are only considering one point?

In-Class Experiment

In this experiment, you will use your graphing calculator or geometry software to analyze the graph of $y = \sin x$.

Make a figure following these steps.

Step 1 Draw the graph of $y = \sin x$.

Step 2 Put two points on the graph. Label them A and B. Test to make sure the points are on your graph by dragging them around. You should not be able to move them off of your graph.

Step 3 Construct the line through points A and B.

Step 4 Measure the slope of $\overleftrightarrow{AB}$.

> See the TI–Nspire Handbook on p. 704 for details on how to make this construction.

> A line that contains two points of a graph is called a secant line.

Keep point A constant—that will be the point you are analyzing. Move point B slowly toward A, observing the slope. Your goal is to estimate the slope of the line when the two points are as close as the software allows you to make them. In some cases, you may get the two points to coincide, making the line and slope disappear. If that happens, move point B off until the line reappears, and record that slope value as your estimate.

For You to Do

1. Copy and complete the following table by estimating the slope at each value of x to three decimal places. You can use the symmetry of the graph of $f(x) = \sin x$ to help make this task less daunting.

When analyzing the graph of $f(x) = \sin x$ or $g(x) = \cos x$, start with inputs like $x = \frac{\pi}{4}$ or $x = \frac{2\pi}{3}$.

x	$\sin x$	Slope
0	0	
$\frac{\pi}{6}$	$\frac{1}{2}$	
$\frac{\pi}{4}$		
$\frac{\pi}{3}$	$\frac{\sqrt{3}}{2}$	
$\frac{\pi}{2}$	1	
$\frac{2\pi}{3}$		
$\frac{3\pi}{4}$	$\frac{\sqrt{2}}{2}$	
$\frac{5\pi}{6}$		
π		
$\frac{7\pi}{6}$		
$\frac{5\pi}{4}$	$-\frac{\sqrt{2}}{2}$	
$\frac{4\pi}{3}$		
$\frac{3\pi}{2}$	-1	
$\frac{5\pi}{3}$		
$\frac{7\pi}{4}$		
$\frac{11\pi}{6}$	$-\frac{1}{2}$	
2π	0	

As the experiment suggests, you can find the slope of a curve at a particular point A by finding the limit of the slope of a secant $\overleftrightarrow{AB}$, where B is also on the curve, as B gets close to A.

A formal definition requires some ideas of calculus that you will see in Chapter 3.

Exercises *Practicing Habits of Mind*

Check Your Understanding

1. When the graph of the sine function reaches a maximum or minimum value, what happens to the slope of its graph there?

2. What are the maximum and minimum values of the slope of the graph of $y = \sin x$, and where does each occur? Could you answer this question by looking at a graph of the sine function?

3. **a.** Zoom in on the graph of $y = \sin x$ near $x = 0$. What specific line does the graph begin to look like?

   b. What is the slope of the graph of $\sin x$ at $x = 0$?

4. **a.** By plotting points, sketch the graph of function s, where $s(x)$ is the slope of $y = \sin x$ at input x.

   b. What function most closely matches the values of s?

5. **a.** Sketch the graphs of the following two functions on the same axes.

   $$d(x) = \cos^2 x - \sin^2 x$$
   $$e(x) = \cos^4 x - \sin^4 x$$

   b. Take It Further Explain how the functions d and e relate.

On Your Own

6. **a.** For what value of x, where $0 \le x < 2\pi$, is the function $f(x) = \cos x$ a maximum?

   b. For what value of x, where $0 \le x < 2\pi$, is the function $f(x) = \cos x$ a minimum?

   c. How do these values compare to the maximums and minimums of the sine function?

7. **a.** For what inputs is the sine function increasing?

   b. For what inputs is the sine function decreasing?

   c. For what inputs is the cosine function increasing?

A function f is **increasing** on an interval if, for any two values in the interval a and b, $a < b$ implies $f(a) < f(b)$.

A function f is **decreasing** on an interval if, for any two values in the interval a and b, $a < b$ implies $f(a) > f(b)$.

8. A **turning point** for a function is an input x where the function changes from increasing to decreasing, or from decreasing to increasing.

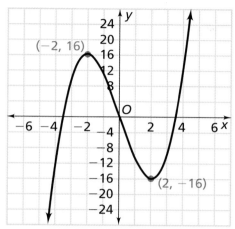

The turning points of $f(x) = x^3 - 12x$ are 2 and -2.

Sometimes the phrase turning point refers instead to the actual coordinates $(x, f(x))$ of the point where this change occurs.

   a. What inputs are turning points for the sine function?

   b. What inputs are turning points for the cosine function?

9. Repeat the In-Class Experiment on page 24 and Problem 1 on page 25 for the function $g(x) = \cos x$. Then sketch the graph of the function r, where $r(x)$ is the slope of g at input x. What function matches the table for r?

10. Sketch the graphs of the two functions $a(x) = \cos^2 x$ and $b(x) = \sin^2 x$ on the same axes.

11. Without graphing, describe the shape of the graph of $c(x) = a(x) + b(x)$, where $a(x)$ and $b(x)$ are the functions in Exercise 10.

12. **Take it Further** Sketch a reasonably accurate graph of $k(x) = 2^{\sin x}$.

13. **Standardized Test Prep** Given $0 < a < b < 17$, which of the following is the maximum value of $a \sin x + b$?

   A. $a + b$ **B.** $b - a$ **C.** $-(a + b)$ **D.** 17

Go Online
PHSchool.com

For additional practice, go to **Web Code:** bga-0105

Maintain Your Skills

14. Sketch the graph of each equation on the interval $0 \le x \le 2\pi$ and find the maximum and minimum.

   a. $y = 5 \sin x$

   b. $y = 5 \sin x + 7$

   c. $y = 5 \sin x - 7$

   d. $y = 10 \sin x + 5$

   e. $y = A \sin x + B$

The **maximum** of a graph is the highest value achieved on the vertical axis. The **minimum** of a graph is the lowest.

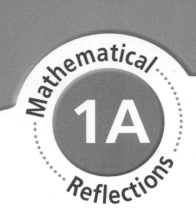

Mathematical 1A Reflections

In this investigation, you learned what radians are and how they relate to degrees. You graphed the cosine and sine functions. You solved equations involving these trigonometric functions. The following questions will help you summarize what you have learned.

1. **a.** What angle measure corresponds to $\frac{9\pi}{2}$ radians?

   b. For what value of x, where $0 \le x < 2\pi$, will both $\cos x = \cos \frac{9\pi}{2}$ and $\sin x = \sin \frac{9\pi}{2}$?

2. **a.** On a unit circle, locate approximately the point with coordinates $(\cos 3, \sin 3)$.

   b. Estimate the values of $\cos 3$ and $\sin 3$.

   c. Use a calculator to find the values of $\cos 3$ and $\sin 3$ to four decimal places.

3. **a.** Using a unit circle, identify the places where cosine and sine are equal.

   b. Find all angle measures θ, where $0 \le \theta < 2\pi$, such that $\cos \theta = \sin \theta$.

4. Using the graphs of cosine and sine on the interval $0 \le x < 2\pi$, find all values of x such that $\cos x = \sin x$.

5. Find all solutions if $0 \le x < 2\pi$.

$$\sin x \cos x - 2 \sin x = \sin x$$

6. Where are the turning points of the cosine and sine functions?

7. What is a radian?

8. How can you use a graph of $y = \sin x$ to estimate solutions to the equation $\sin x = -0.6$?

Vocabulary

In this investigation, you learned these terms. Make sure you understand what each one means and how to use it.

- arc
- central angle
- decreasing
- increasing
- period

- periodic function
- Pythagorean identity
- radian
- secant line
- turning point

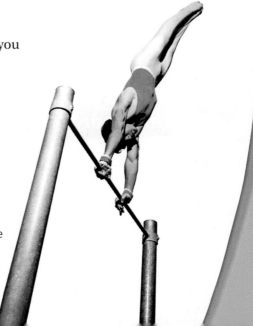

Many athletic activities involve circular motion.

Go Online PHSchool.com

For a mid-chapter test, go to Web Code: bga-0152

Multiple Choice

1. Simplify $\sin \frac{7\pi}{6} \cdot \sin \frac{5\pi}{6} - \cos \frac{7\pi}{6} \cdot \cos \frac{5\pi}{6}$.

   A. 1   **B.** $-\cos 2\pi$ **C.** $\sin \pi$ **D.** 2π

2. The graph below represents which of the following functions?

   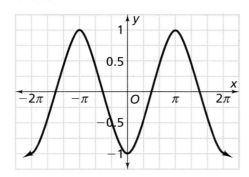

   A. $y = \sin x$ **B.** $y = \sin\left(x + \frac{\pi}{2}\right)$

   C. $y = \cos x$ **D.** $y = \sin\left(x - \frac{\pi}{2}\right)$

3. Which system of equations does the graph represent?

   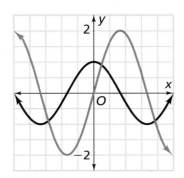

   A. $y = \sin x$ **B.** $y = 2 \sin x$
   $\quad\;\; y = \cos x$ $\quad\;\; y = x$

   C. $y = 2 \sin x$ **D.** $y = -\sin x$
   $\quad\;\; y = \cos x$ $\quad\;\; y = 2 \sin x$

4. Simplify $\sin\left(-\frac{\pi}{6}\right)$.

   A. $\sin \frac{\pi}{6}$ **B.** $-\cos \frac{\pi}{3}$ **C.** $\frac{1}{2}$ **D.** $\frac{\sqrt{3}}{2}$

5. Simplify $\cos 360° + \frac{3}{2} \cos 0° + \sqrt{2} \cos 45°$.

   A. 0   **B.** $\frac{1}{2}$ **C.** $\frac{7}{2}$ **D.** -3

6. Which expression gives all possible solutions to the equation

   $$\cos x = -\frac{1}{2}$$

   if k can represent any integer?

   A. $120° + k360°$ **B.** $\frac{2\pi}{3} + 2k\pi$

   C. $120° + k360°$ and   **D.** $\frac{2\pi}{3}$ and $\frac{4\pi}{3}$
   $\quad\;\; 240° + k360°$

Open Response

7. For each radian value, find the corresponding degree measure.

   a. $\frac{\pi}{6}$ **b.** $\frac{5\pi}{3}$ **c.** 2π **d.** $\frac{7\pi}{6}$

8. Find the maximum and minimum values of the slope of the graph of $f(x) = \cos x$. Where does each occur?

9. Sketch the graph of $y = 6 \sin x + 2$ on the interval $0 \leq x \leq 2\pi$ and find the maximum and minimum.

10. Solve the equation $-\sin x = \frac{1}{2}$ on $-\frac{\pi}{2} \leq x \leq \frac{3\pi}{2}$.

11. If $0 < x < \pi$, is $\sin x$ always positive or always negative? What about $\cos x$? Explain your reasoning.

12. What inputs are turning points for the function $f(x) = 2 \sin x$ on $-\pi \leq x \leq \pi$?

Challenge Problem

13. Find all solutions to $2 \cos^2 x - 5 \cos x + 2 = 0$.

Other Trigonometric Functions

In *Other Trigonometric Functions*, you will study the tangent function and draw its graph. You will define the inverse cosine, sine, and tangent functions. You will also learn about the three other trigonometric functions: secant, cosecant, and cotangent.

By the end of this investigation, you will be able to answer questions like these.

1. How are the six trigonometric functions defined?

2. Why does the $\sin^{-1}$ function on a calculator only return results between $-\frac{\pi}{2}$ and $\frac{\pi}{2}$?

3. How many solutions are there to the equation $\cos x = 0.8$?

You will learn how to

• understand several relationships between the tangent function and the unit circle

• sketch and describe the graph of the tangent function

• define an inverse of cosine, sine, and tangent

• recognize three other trigonometric functions: secant, cosecant, and cotangent

You will develop these habits and skills:

• Use the unit circle to generate the graph of $y = \tan x$.

• Visualize geometrically the tangent and secant functions.

• Restrict the domain of a function to make it one-to-one.

• Solve equations and prove identities using trigonometric functions.

Since the column and its shadow form a right angle, you can use elementary trigonometry to calculate its height.

Activating Prior Knowledge
Exploring New Ideas

To start this investigation, you will have to work with definitions. You will have to recall how to relate the inverse of a function to the function. You will also have to work with definitions of some new functions.

For You to Explore

1. Two of these four functions are inverses of each other. Which two?

 I. $f(x) = 3x + 5$ **II.** $g(x) = 3x - 5$

 III. $h(x) = \frac{1}{3}x + 5$ **IV.** $k(x) = \frac{1}{3}(x + 5)$

 A. I and III

 B. I and IV

 C. II and III

 D. II and IV

2. On the same axes, sketch the graphs of the two functions f and g over the domain $-\pi \le x \le 2\pi$.

$$f(x) = \sin x$$
$$g(x) = \frac{1}{\sin x}$$

3. **Write About It** Consider the two functions in Problem 2. Is g the inverse of f? Justify your answer.

4. **a.** Sketch the graph of $h(x) = \cos x$ on the domain $-\pi \le x \le 2\pi$.

 b. Explain why $h(x)$ does not have an inverse function on this domain.

 c. Can $h(x)$ have an inverse function on some other domain? If so, give an example. If not, explain why not.

5. **Take It Further** Sketch and describe the graph of the equation

$$j(x) = \sin \frac{1}{x}$$

> Make sure you leave enough room for the graph of g. You might want your y-axis to range from -10 to 10.

Habits of Mind

Think it through.
Can you explain why $j(x)$ is not the same as $g(x) = \frac{1}{\sin x}$?

Exercises *Practicing Habits of Mind*

On Your Own

In this investigation, you will be using the cosine and sine functions frequently, as well as these four other functions related to them:

$$\tan x = \frac{\sin x}{\cos x}$$ **tangent** of x

$$\sec x = \frac{1}{\cos x}$$ **secant** of x

$$\csc x = \frac{1}{\sin x}$$ **cosecant** of x

$$\cot x = \frac{\cos x}{\sin x}$$ **cotangent** of x

> The names tangent and secant have geometric meanings, and you will see how those meanings apply to the unit circle later in this investigation.

6. Find the domain and range for the function.

$$g(x) = \csc x$$

> Have you sketched the graph of g earlier?

7. Find each value.

a. $\sec \frac{\pi}{3}$ **b.** $\tan \frac{3\pi}{4}$

c. $\cot \frac{3\pi}{4}$ **d.** $\sec \frac{\pi}{4} \cdot \cos \frac{\pi}{4}$

8. a. Let $x = 1.22$. Which is greater, $\tan x$ or $\sec x$?

b. Let x be the length of an arc intercepted by any angle in Quadrant I. Which is greater, $\tan x$ or $\sec x$? Explain.

9. a. For any value of x where both functions are defined, which is larger: $\tan^2 x$ or $\sec^2 x$?

b. Take It Further Justify, with proof, your answer.

> **Habits of Mind**
>
> **Make a connection.** Think about how to calculate $\tan x$ and $\sec x$. How are they similar? How are they different?

Maintain Your Skills

10. Let $PROD(x)$ be the product of the six trigonometric functions.

$$PROD(x) = \cos x \cdot \sin x \cdot \tan x \cdot \sec x \cdot \csc x \cdot \cot x$$

For each x, calculate $PROD(x)$.

a. $x = \frac{\pi}{4}$ **b.** $x = \frac{\pi}{3}$ **c.** $x = 30°$

d. $x = 0$ **e.** $x = 150°$

11. Find the domain and range of the $PROD$ function given in Exercise 10.

The Tangent Function

You first learned the tangent function in geometry using a right triangle.

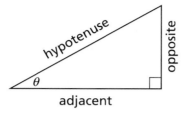

Using that, you defined $\tan \theta$ as

$$\tan \theta = \frac{\text{opposite}}{\text{adjacent}}$$

In Lesson 1.6, you defined tangent as

$$\tan \theta = \frac{\sin \theta}{\cos \theta}$$

For You to Do

1. Show how the two definitions will give the same results for $0° < \theta < 90°$.

By using the words *opposite* and *adjacent,* you are referring to sides of a right triangle. Therefore, the definition of tangent in a right triangle is limited to angle inputs from 0° to 90°.

Since $\cos x$ and $\sin x$ are just numbers, and you have definitions of them for any real value of x (with x in either degrees or radians), you can use the relationship $\tan x = \frac{\sin x}{\cos x}$ to extend the definition of tangent as well.

For Discussion

2. The cosine and sine functions have the same domain: all real numbers. What is the domain of the tangent function?

Remember...

The *natural domain* of a function f is the set of values x for which $f(x)$ is defined. When you are asked "What is the domain of f?" the real question is "What is the natural domain of f?"

You can also relate the tangent function to the unit circle.

In this experiment, you will use your graphing calculator or geometry software to model the tangent function.

Follow these steps to build your sketch:

Step 1 Construct a circle of radius of 1 unit with center at the origin on a coordinate grid.

Step 2 Add a point at $(1, 0)$, and label it A.

Step 3 Construct the graph of the equation $x = 1$.

Step 4 Place another point on the circle. Label it B.

Step 5 Construct a line containing the origin $(0, 0)$ and point B.

Step 6 Construct the intersection between this line and the graph of the equation $x = 1$. Label that point T.

Step 7 Have the software display the y-coordinate of point T.

Step 8 Have the software display the length of $\overarc{AB}$.

Step 9 Have the software calculate the tangent of that arc length.

As you drag your point around the circle, compare the y-coordinate of point T to the value $\tan m\overarc{AB}$.

> See the TI-Nspire Handbook on p. 704 for details on how to make this sketch on your calculator.

> Your geometry software may not be able to graph equations like $x = 1$. In that case, you need to construct a line perpendicular to the x-axis through the point $(1, 0)$.

For You to Do

3. In the experiment, how did the y-coordinate of T compare to the tangent calculation?

4. What happens when you drag B across $(0, 1)$? Explain.

5. What are the coordinates of B if the y-coordinate of T is equal to 2? Is there more than one answer? If so, how are the answers related?

As the experiment suggests, the y-coordinate of the point T is equal to the tangent of the arc measure $m\overarc{AB}$.

 **Exercises** *Practicing Habits of Mind*

Check Your Understanding

1. With a unit circle, draw one line that indicates the two possible solutions to each equation in the interval $0 \le x < 2\pi$.

   a. $\sin x = 0.5$ **b.** $\sin x = -0.7$ **c.** $\cos x = 0.3$

   d. $\tan x = 2.5$ **e.** $\tan x = -0.4$

2. Suppose your calculator could compute only the sine function. Describe how you might calculate $\tan 0.38$.

3. Describe how $\tan x$ relates to $\tan\left(\frac{\pi}{2} + x\right)$.

4. **Write About It** Suppose $\overset{\frown}{AB}$ is on the unit circle with A at $(1, 0)$. In which two quadrants can B be in if the tangent of $m\overset{\frown}{AB}$ negative? Justify your answer in at least two different ways.

5. Is it possible for $\tan x$ to be larger than 200? If so, find a number x such that $\tan x > 200$. If not, explain why not.

6. Answer the following to prove that $x < \tan x$ for $0 \le x < \frac{\pi}{2}$.

   a. Find $\tan \frac{\pi}{6}$, $\tan \frac{\pi}{4}$, and $\tan 1$. For these values, is it true that $x < \tan x$? Calculate $\tan x$ for three other values of x between 0 and $\frac{\pi}{2}$ to show that $x < \tan x$ for each value.

   b. The figure below shows a unit circle and the graph of the equation $x = 1$. α is the length of $\overset{\frown}{AB}$. Find the area of $\triangle OAT$ and sector OAB.

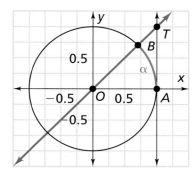

   c. Use the information from part (b) to prove that $x < \tan x$ for $0 \le x < \frac{\pi}{2}$.

> **Habits of Mind**
>
> **Represent a function.**
> Which representation of the tangent function is most helpful here?

7. Use what you know about cosine and sine to copy and complete this table for $f(x) = \tan x$. Look for shortcuts to simplify your work.

x	tan x
0	■
$\frac{\pi}{6}$	$\frac{\sqrt{3}}{3}$
$\frac{\pi}{4}$	■
$\frac{\pi}{3}$	■
$\frac{\pi}{2}$	■
$\frac{2\pi}{3}$	■
$\frac{3\pi}{4}$	-1
$\frac{5\pi}{6}$	■
π	■
$\frac{7\pi}{6}$	■
$\frac{5\pi}{4}$	■
$\frac{4\pi}{3}$	$\sqrt{3}$
$\frac{3\pi}{2}$	undefined
$\frac{5\pi}{3}$	■
$\frac{7\pi}{4}$	■
$\frac{11\pi}{6}$	■
2π	0
$\frac{13\pi}{6}$	■
$\frac{9\pi}{4}$	■

8. **Write About It** Explain why $\tan \alpha$ is equal to the slope from the origin $(0, 0)$ to a point on the unit circle at distance α.

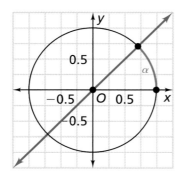

9. For each angle θ in degrees, calculate $\sin \theta$ and $\cos (90° - \theta)$.

    a. $\theta = 30°$ **b.** $\theta = 83°$ **c.** $\theta = 90°$ **d.** $\theta = 160°$ **e.** $\theta = -90°$

10. Here are two relationships for cosine and sine.

$$\sin \left(\tfrac{\pi}{2} - x \right) = \cos x$$

$$\cos \left(\tfrac{\pi}{2} - x \right) = \sin x$$

What can you say about $\tan \left(\tfrac{\pi}{2} - x \right)$? How do $\tan \left(\tfrac{\pi}{2} - x \right)$ and $\tan x$ compare?

11. What is the relationship between $\tan (\pi - x)$ and $\tan x$?

12. What is the relationship between $\tan (\pi + x)$ and $\tan x$?

13. **Standardized Test Prep** Suppose that the walk on the unit circle from the point $(1, 0)$ to point B has length α. Which of the following gives the slope of OB?

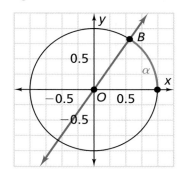

    A. $\sin \alpha$ **B.** $\cos \alpha$ **C.** $\tan \alpha$ **D.** $\cot \alpha$

Maintain Your Skills

14. Let $f(x) = 5 \sin x + 7$.

    a. What is the maximum possible value of $f(x)$? Find two values of x that produce this maximum.

    b. What is the minimum possible value of $f(x)$? Find two values of x that produce this minimum.

    c. How many solutions are there to the equation $5 \sin x + 7 = 0$?

15. For each function, find the maximum and minimum value.

    a. $g(x) = 10 \sin x + 7$ **b.** $h(x) = 20 \sin x + 7$

    c. $j(x) = 20 \sin x + 34$ **d.** $k(x) = A \sin x + B$

Go Online
PHSchool.com

For additional practice, go to **Web Code: bga-0107**

1.8 Graphing Periodic Functions

In the last lesson, you built a model for seeing the tangent function in relation to the unit circle. As you move your point a distance α around the unit circle, the line connecting the origin and your point intersects the graph of the equation $x = 1$ at the point $(1, b)$. You can track how b changes as the point moves around the circle by making a graph.

The following diagram shows a series of arcs of the same unit circle. Each arc starts from the point $A(1, 0)$, and ends at some stopping point B. Draw the line containing the origin O and the point B which intersects the graph of the equation $x = 1$ at point T. You can calculate the y-coordinate of the point T as $\tan \alpha$.

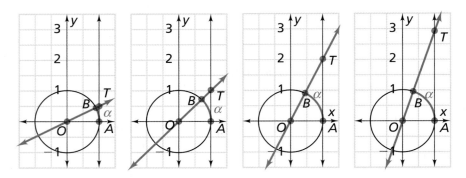

As the value of the arc length α increases from 0 to $\frac{\pi}{2}$, the y-coordinate of T, or $\tan \alpha$, also increases. As B approaches $(0, 1)$ and α approaches $\frac{\pi}{2}$, the y-coordinate of T grows greater and greater.

When B is at $(0, 1)$, $\overleftrightarrow{OB}$ is parallel to the graph of the equation $x = 1$, so there is no intersection point T. The graph shows that the values of the tangent function increase without bound as α approaches $\frac{\pi}{2}$.

An **asymptote** is a line that the graph of a function approaches, but does not intersect. The dotted vertical line in this graph is an asymptote.

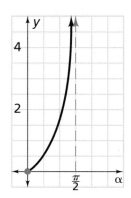

To continue this graph, look at more arcs. When B is in Quadrant II, $\overleftrightarrow{OB}$ intersects the graph of the equation $x = 1$ in Quadrant IV, so the y-coordinate of T is negative.

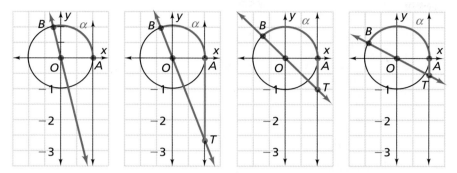

If α is a little less than $\frac{\pi}{2}$, the outputs of the tangent function are large positive numbers. If α is a little more than $\frac{\pi}{2}$, then the outputs of the tangent function are large negative numbers. As α increases from $\frac{\pi}{2}$ to π, the outputs of the tangent function are negative, but increase toward 0.

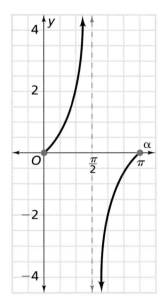

What happens next? As point B moves into Quadrant III, notice what happens to T. It follows the same path as it did when B was in Quadrant I.

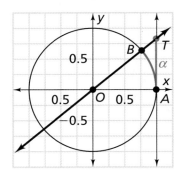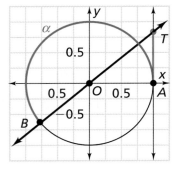

Notice that T is in the same position in both pictures, but B is at opposite ends of a diameter. So $\tan \alpha$ is equal for two different values on the unit circle.

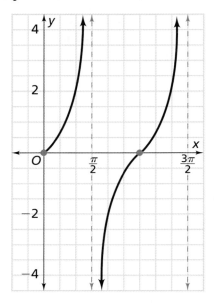

For You to Do

1. Find all numbers x such that $0 \leq x \leq 2\pi$ and $\tan x = 1$.

2. What is the period of the tangent function?

3. Find all real numbers x such that $\tan x = 1$.

Remember...

The period of a periodic function is the least value p such that, for all x, $f(x + p) = f(x)$.

Exercises Practicing Habits of Mind

Check Your Understanding

1. The period of the tangent function is π.

   a. What is the period of $g(x) = \tan 2x$?

   b. What is the period of $h(x) = \tan \frac{x}{2}$?

2. **a.** Use the graph of $y = \tan x$ to find the least value of x such that $x > 0$ and $\tan x = 3$.

   b. How many solutions are there to the equation $\tan x = 3$? What are they?

3. **a.** Sketch the graph of $r(x) = \sin^2 x$.

   b. Find the period of r.

   c. Take It Further Prove, using properties of the sine function, that this is the correct period for r.

4. Consider the function $t(x) = \sin x + x$.

   a. Sketch a graph of this function on the interval $-2\pi \leq x \leq 2\pi$.

   b. Is t a periodic function? Justify your answer.

5. **a.** Find the period of $n(x) = \sin \frac{x}{2}$.

   b. Write About It For a real number $B > 0$, describe how the period of $p(x) = \sin Bx$ relates to the value of B. Include examples when $B > 1$ and when $B < 1$.

On Your Own

6. This lesson showed that this statement is true for every value of x.

   $$\tan (x + \pi) = \tan x$$

   How does $\tan (x + 2\pi)$ relate to $\tan x$?

7. Suppose f is a periodic function with period 10, and $f(3) = 13$. Which of the following must also be true?

   A. $f(10) = 13$ **B.** $f(13) = 3$

   C. $f(-13) = 13$ **D.** $f(83) = 13$

8. Sketch the graphs of $g(x) = \cos 2x$ and $s(x) = \cos^2 x - \sin^2 x$ on the same axes. How do the graphs of g and s compare?

9. Problem 2 on page 31 asked you to graph

$$g(x) = \frac{1}{\sin x} = \csc x$$

Is g a periodic function? If so, what is its period? If not, explain why.

The notation "csc" is short for "cosecant."

10. In Lesson 1.10, you will learn more about three additional trigonometric functions: secant (sec), cosecant (csc), and cotangent (cot). The definitions are as follows.

$$\sec x = \frac{1}{\cos x}, \csc x = \frac{1}{\sin x}, \text{ and } \cot x = \frac{\cos x}{\sin x}$$

For this exercise, consider the function given by the following rule.

$$h(x) = \sin x \cdot \csc x + \cos x \cdot \sec x + \tan x \cdot \cot x$$

a. Use a calculator. Find the value of $h(0.5)$ to three decimal places.

b. Find $h(1)$ to three decimal places.

c. Describe the overall behavior of h.

11. **Take It Further** Let n be a positive integer. For what values of n does the function $z(x) = \sin nx$ have a maximum at the point $\left(\frac{\pi}{2}, 1\right)$?

12. **Standardized Test Prep** Which of the following is the period of $f(x) = \tan ax$?

A. a **B.** $\frac{2\pi}{a}$ **C.** $2a\pi$ **D.** $\frac{\pi}{a}$

Maintain Your Skills

13. Find the period of each function.

a. $f(x) = 5 \sin x + 7$

b. $g(x) = 3 \cos x - 10$

c. $h(x) = 2 \tan x + 1$

d. $j(x) = 4 \sin 2x - 3$

e. $k(x) = 6 \cos 5x + 14$

f. $m(x) = A \sin ax + B$

Go Online
PHSchool.com

For additional practice, go to **Web Code:** bga-0108

1.9 Inverse Trigonometric Functions

In Lesson 1.4, you learned how to solve equations that involve trigonometric functions. Tony found the solution by using the $\sin^{-1}$ function on his calculator, the inverse sine.

In algebra, you learned about inverse functions.

Definition

Suppose f is a one-to-one function with domain A and range B. The **inverse function** f^{-1} is a function with these properties.

- f^{-1} has domain B and range A
- $f(f^{-1}(x)) = x$

You later proved that $f^{-1}(f(x)) = f(f^{-1}(x)) = x$. An important part of this definition and the subsequent theorem is that a function f must be one-to-one in order for the inverse function f^{-1} to exist.

For Discussion

Recall that a function f is one-to-one if $f(a) = f(b)$ only when $a = b$.

1. Explain why a periodic function cannot be one-to-one.

2. Explain why a function that is not one-to-one cannot have an inverse function.

For instance, $f(x) = x^2$ is not one-to-one, because $f(2) = f(-2) = 4$, but $2 \neq -2$.

Since the cosine, sine, and tangent functions are periodic, they cannot be one-to-one. So how can you define inverse trigonometric functions?

Public transportation schedules are periodic. The period may be an hour, a day, or a week but the plane, train, bus, or ferry will eventually retrace its route.

Tony and Sasha are trying to decide what $\tan^{-1}$ *means.*

Tony I'm lost. If the tangent function is periodic, then it can't be one-to-one, so it can't have an inverse. Then what does the $\tan^{-1}$ mean?

Sasha jabs at the keys on her calculator.

Sasha Look. I've calculated the inverse tangent of a bunch of numbers. The answers the calculator gives all fall in the range between about -1.57 and -1.57.

Tony That's a weird number. I wonder where it comes from. Wait a second. Let me check.

Tony hits a few keys on his calculator.

Yes. It looks like your numbers are all between $-\frac{\pi}{2}$ and $\frac{\pi}{2}$.

Sasha Of course, that makes sense. Look. If I draw only one cycle of the graph of $y = \tan x$, between $-\frac{\pi}{2}$ and $\frac{\pi}{2}$, it looks like this.

> One *cycle* of the graph of a periodic function $f(x)$ results as x ranges over one fundamental period.

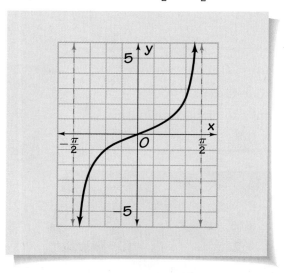

Now it looks one-to-one. Any horizontal line I draw will hit the graph in only one spot.

Tony So if we restrict the domain of tangent to include just the interval $-\frac{\pi}{2}$ to $\frac{\pi}{2}$, it's one-to-one, and the range is all real numbers.

Sasha And then the domain of the inverse tangent function would be all real numbers, and the range would be $-\frac{\pi}{2}$ to $\frac{\pi}{2}$.

For You to Do

3. Sketch a graph of the equation $y = \tan^{-1} x$. How does it compare to the graph of $y = \tan x$ with domain $-\frac{\pi}{2} < x < \frac{\pi}{2}$?

Just as Tony and Sasha did for the tangent function, you can restrict the domains of the cosine and sine functions to make them one-to-one. The figure below shows the graph of one cycle of $y = \sin x$, for $-\pi \leq x \leq \pi$.

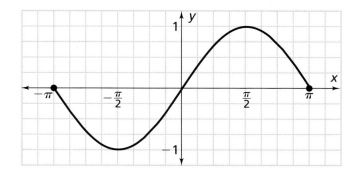

Notice that in most cases, if you draw a horizontal line, it will still hit the graph of $y = \sin x$ in two spots. If you restrict the domain to $-\frac{\pi}{2} \leq x \leq \frac{\pi}{2}$, any horizontal line will intersect the graph in at most one point.

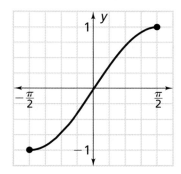

The domain for the inverse sine function is $-1 \leq x \leq 1$, and the range is $-\frac{\pi}{2} \leq x \leq \frac{\pi}{2}$. Its notation is $f(x) = \sin^{-1} x$.

For You to Do

4. Sketch a graph of the equation $y = \sin^{-1} x$.

Restricting the cosine function to a domain between $-\frac{\pi}{2}$ and $\frac{\pi}{2}$ will not work as it did for the tangent and sine functions.

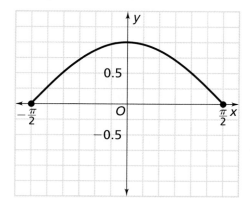

This portion of the cosine graph is not one-to-one, so you must use a different interval. One interval that makes the function one-to-one is $0 \le x \le \pi$.

The domain for the inverse cosine function is $-1 \le x \le 1$, and the range is $0 \le y \le \pi$. Its notation is $f(x) = \cos^{-1} x$.

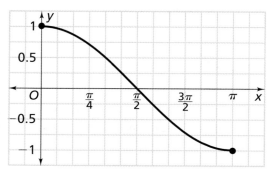

For You to Do

5. Sketch a graph of the equation $y = \cos^{-1} x$.

Developing Habits of Mind

Make strategic choices. Since the cosine, sine, and tangent functions are periodic, you could have chosen to restrict your domain in infinitely many ways. For example, the cosine function is also one-to-one on the interval $-\pi \le x \le 0$. So why are these particular intervals important?

The reason goes back to the unit circle, and even the right triangle. Each interval includes lengths of arcs intersected by angles that terminate in Quadrant I, the angles over which you first defined the functions. So it makes sense to include these angles in the restricted domains. The shape of its graph determines the rest of the interval for each function.

Exercises Practicing Habits of Mind

Check Your Understanding

1. Solve each equation, if possible.

   a. $3 \sin x + 7 = 5$

   b. $5 \cos x - 12 = 14$

   c. $2 \tan x + 3 = -10$

   d. $10 \cos(x + 3) - 7 = 13$

2. Consider the equation $\tan x = 0.75$.

   a. Use a calculator. Find one solution for x to three decimal places.

   b. Use the graph of the tangent function to show where more solutions lie.

   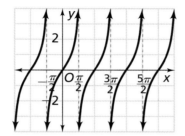

   c. For $\tan x = 0.75$, find the least solution that is greater than your solution in part (a).

3. Consider the equation $\cos x = 0.8$.

   a. Use a calculator. Find one solution for x to three decimal places.

   b. Use the graph of the cosine function to show where more solutions lie.

   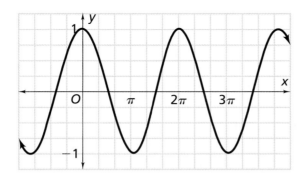

   c. For $\cos x = 0.8$, find the least solution greater than your solution in part (a).

4. Consider the equation $\sin x = 0.6$.

   a. Use a calculator. Find one solution for x to three decimal places.

   b. Use the graph of the sine function to show where more solutions lie.

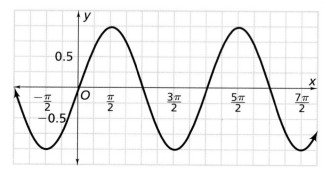

   c. For $\sin x = 0.6$, find the least solution greater than the solution you found in part (a).

5. Determine each value.

   a. $\sin^{-1}\frac{1}{2}$

   b. $\cos^{-1} 0$

   c. $\tan^{-1} 1$

   d. $\cos^{-1} (\cos 120°)$

   e. $\tan (\tan^{-1} 2.14)$

   f. $\cos^{-1}\left(\cos \frac{11\pi}{6}\right)$

6. a. If x is the length of an arc intersected by an angle in Quadrant I and $\sin x = \frac{7}{25}$, find $\cos x$.

   b. Determine the value of $\cos\left(\sin^{-1}\frac{7}{25}\right)$.

> Don't let your calculator have all the fun!

On Your Own

7. Solve each equation, if possible.

   a. $6 \sin 2x + 1 = -2$

   b. $12 \sin 2(x - 3) + 8 = 22$

   c. $3 \sin \pi(x - 5) + 4 = 7$

   d. $36 \cos \left(\frac{2\pi}{30}(x - 3)\right) + 39 = 50$

8. Look back at Exercises 2–4. You should have gotten the same answer for part (a) of each exercise.

   a. Draw a triangle that has one angle of measure corresponding to an arc of length $\tan^{-1} 0.75$. Find integer lengths for each of the sides of the triangle that satisfy the three statements for $\tan^{-1} 0.75$, $\sin^{-1} 0.6$, and $\cos^{-1} 0.8$. What special triangle is it?

   b. Write About It Explain why the answer you got in part (a) from each exercise was the same, but the answer you got in part (c) was not.

9. a. Find the value of $\sin^{-1}\frac{1}{2} + \cos^{-1}\frac{1}{2}$.

b. Find the value of $\sin^{-1}\frac{\sqrt{3}}{2} + \cos^{-1}\frac{\sqrt{3}}{2}$.

c. Find the value of $\sin^{-1}(-1) + \cos^{-1}(-1)$.

d. Take It Further Explain why the pattern in these three results occurs.

10. Is this statement true for every x?

$$\sin^{-1}(\sin x) = x$$

If so, explain why. If not, when is it true and when is it false?

11. Find the maximum and minimum values for each function.

a. $a(x) = 5\sin x + 8$

b. $b(x) = 10\sin x + 17$

c. $c(x) = 10\sin x + 3$

d. $d(x) = 4\sin x - 2$

12. a. Find a function using cosine or sine that has a maximum of 27, and a minimum of 11.

b. Find a function using cosine or sine that has a maximum of 75, and a minimum of 3.

c. Find a function using cosine or sine that has a maximum of 23, and a minimum of -15.

13. Standardized Test Prep Which of the following is true?

A. $\cos^{-1}x = \frac{1}{\cos x}$ **B.** $\cos^{-1}x = \sin x$

C. $\cos^{-1}x = \frac{1}{\sin x}$ **D.** $\cos(\cos^{-1}x) = x$

Maintain Your Skills

14. Find one solution to each equation.

a. $4\cos x + 5 = 7$

b. $4\cos 2x + 5 = 7$

c. $4\cos\frac{x}{2} + 5 = 7$

d. $4\cos \pi x + 5 = 7$

e. $4\cos(\pi(x + 3)) + 5 = 7$

f. $4\cos\left(\frac{2\pi}{10}(x - 3)\right) + 5 = 7$

ON

OFF

Go Online
PHSchool.com

For additional practice, go to Web Code: bga-0109

Taking the output of f as the input for f^{-1} is like flipping a toggle switch twice. In the end, you are back where you started.

Reciprocal Trigonometric Functions

Go Online
PHSchool.com

For more information on trigonometric functions, go to **Web Code:** bge-9031

There are six possible ratios of side lengths of a right triangle. The three more common trig functions, cosine, sine, and tangent.

$$\cos \theta = \frac{\text{adjacent}}{\text{hypotenuse}} \quad \sin \theta = \frac{\text{opposite}}{\text{hypotenuse}} \quad \tan \theta = \frac{\text{opposite}}{\text{adjacent}}$$

The reciprocal of each of these ratios account for the other three.

$$\sec \theta = \frac{\text{hypotenuse}}{\text{adjacent}} \quad \csc \theta = \frac{\text{hypotenuse}}{\text{opposite}} \quad \cot \theta = \frac{\text{adjacent}}{\text{opposite}}$$

You can represent each of these functions on the unit circle as well. Recall in Lesson 1.7 you built a model for tan α. You can use that same model to find sec α.

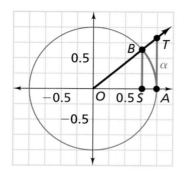

The measure of $\overset{\frown}{AB}$ is α. $\overline{OA}$ and $\overline{OB}$ are both radii. So they each have length 1. As you saw in Investigation 1A, $\cos \alpha = OS$ and $\sin \alpha = SB$. Earlier in this investigation, you saw that $\tan \alpha = AT$, and $\overline{AT}$ is on a line tangent to the unit circle at A.

Recall that a secant line is a line that intersects a curve in at least two points. Notice that $\overline{OT}$ is on a secant line through the center of the unit circle.

In-Class Experiment

Start with the sketch you made in the In-Class Experiment of Lesson 1.7. Follow these steps to add to your sketch.

Step 1 Label the origin as point O.

Step 2 Construct the line segment $\overline{OT}$.

Step 3 Have the software display the length of $\overline{OT}$.

Step 4 Have the software calculate the secant of the radian measure of $\overset{\frown}{AB}$.

As you drag point B around the circle, compare the length of segment $\overline{OT}$ to the value of the secant of the radian measure of $\overset{\frown}{AB}$.

If your software does not calculate sec x directly, have it calculate $\frac{1}{\cos x}$.

For You to Do

1. In the experiment, how did the length of $\overline{OT}$ compare to the secant calculation?

2. What happens to the two values when you drag B across $(0, 1)$? Explain.

For Discussion

3. Your sketch will display the length of $\overline{OT}$ as positive, since length is a measure of distance, which is always positive. The value of the secant function, however, can be negative. For arcs terminating in which quadrants will the secant of the arc be negative? Explain how your sketch shows where the secant is negative.

You can also define the secant, cosecant, and cotangent functions by their relationships to the cosine and sine functions.

$$\sec x = \frac{1}{\cos x} \qquad \csc x = \frac{1}{\sin x} \qquad \cot x = \frac{\cos x}{\sin x}$$

The following figures show the graphs of $y = \sec x$, $y = \csc x$ and $y = \cot x$.

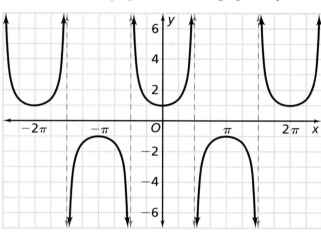

$y = \sec x$

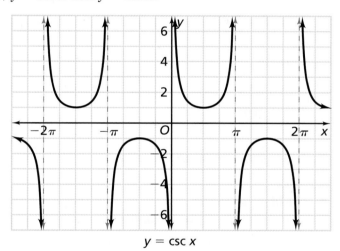

$y = \csc x$

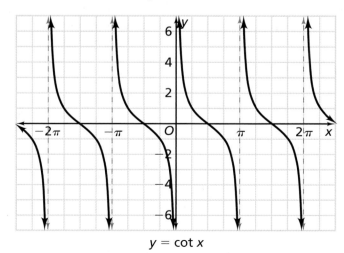

$y = \cot x$

Exercises *Practicing Habits of Mind*

Check Your Understanding

1. Find all solutions to each equation if $0 \leq x \leq 2\pi$.

   a. $\csc x = 2$

   b. $\cot x = \sqrt{3}$

   c. $\sec x = 0$

   d. $\sec^2 x = 1$

Remember...

Use radians unless the degree symbol is present.

2. Consider the functions f and g.

$$f(x) = \sec^2 x + \csc^2 x$$

$$g(x) = \sec^2 x \cdot \csc^2 x$$

   For each value below, calculate $f(x)$ and $g(x)$.

   a. $x = 30°$

   b. $x = \dfrac{\pi}{4}$

   c. $x = 60°$

   d. $x = 120°$

   e. $x = 2$

3. **Take It Further** Show that $f(x)$ and $g(x)$ from Exercise 2 are equal wherever they are defined.

4. The identity $\cos \theta = \sin (90° - \theta)$ is the *co-function identity*. Similar identities exist for the tangent and secant functions.

   a. Give an example to show that $\cot \theta = \tan (90° - \theta)$ for a particular angle measure θ.

   b. Give an example to show that $\csc \theta = \sec (90° - \theta)$ for a particular angle measure θ.

   c. Show that $\cot \theta = \tan (90° - \theta)$ for any angle measure θ in the domain of the cotangent function.

   d. Show that $\csc \theta = \sec (90° - \theta)$ for any angle measure θ in the domain of the cosecant function.

In fact, the *co* part of *cosine* is short for *complement*. Two angles are complementary if the measures add up to 90°.

5. Consider the following graph of the unit circle and the tangent at $(1, 0)$.

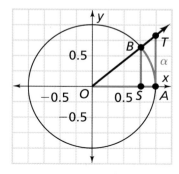

a. Explain why $\triangle OSB \sim \triangle OAT$.

b. Use similar triangles to show that the length of $\overline{OT}$ is $\sec \alpha$.

6. Consider the following geometric series.

$$1 + \sin^2 x + \sin^4 x + \sin^6 x + \cdots$$

As long as $|\sin x| < 1$, this series converges to a specific sum. Which is it?

A. $\cos^2 x$ **B.** $\tan^2 x$

C. $\cot^2 x$ **D.** $\sec^2 x$

> Recall from algebra, if the first term of an infinite geometric series is a and the common ratio is r with $|r| < 1$, the sum is $\frac{a}{1 - r}$.

7. Consider the following geometric series.

$$\sin^2 x + \sin^4 x + \sin^6 x + \sin^8 x + \cdots$$

Assuming $|\sin x| < 1$, which of these is the sum of this series?

A. $\cos^2 x$ **B.** $\tan^2 x$

C. $\cot^2 x$ **D.** $\sec^2 x$

On Your Own

8. Here is the graph of $f(x) = \sec x$ on the interval $-\pi \le x \le 2\pi$.

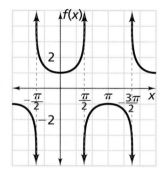

a. Find the domain and range of f.

b. Explain why there is a horizontal gap in the graph between the graphs of the equations $y = -1$ and $y = 1$.

9. Show graphically that there are two solutions to the equation

$$\sec x = -2$$

in the interval $0 \le x \le 2\pi$.

10. Use the results from Exercises 6 and 7 to show the following.

$$1 + \tan^2 x = \sec^2 x$$

11. The Pythagorean identity $\cos^2 x + \sin^2 x = 1$ leads to two other major identities.

a. If you divide through each term of $\cos^2 x + \sin^2 x = 1$ by $\cos^2 x$, you will get the following equation.

$$\frac{\cos^2 x}{\cos^2 x} + \frac{\sin^2 x}{\cos^2 x} = \frac{1}{\cos^2 x}$$

You can simplify each of these terms. What do you get after simplifying?

b. Construct a second identity by dividing through by $\sin^2 x$.

12. Use the picture from Exercise 5 to show the following identity.

$$1 + \tan^2 \alpha = \sec^2 \alpha$$

13. **Take It Further** In Investigation 1A, you looked at the slope of lines tangent to the graph of $y = \sin x$. Those slopes approximated the outputs of the function $f(x) = \cos x$. You can apply the same process to $f(x) = \tan x$. Find a function that matches the slopes you find.

14. **Standardized Test Prep** Which of the following is false?

A. $\sin x \cdot \csc x = 1$ for all x in the domain of the cosecant function.

B. $\cos x \cdot \sec x = 1$ for all x in the domain of the secant function.

C. $\tan x \cdot \cot x = 1$ for all x in the domain of both the tangent and cotangent functions.

D. $\cot x = \frac{\sin x}{\cos x}$ for all x in the domain of the cosine function.

Maintain Your Skills

15. Each of these equations has $x = 30°$ as a solution. Find the other solution in the interval $0 \le x \le 360°$.

a. $2 \sin x = 1$ **b.** $2 \cos x = \sqrt{3}$ **c.** $3 \tan x = \sqrt{3}$

d. $\csc x = 2$ **e.** $\sqrt{3} \sec x = 2$ **f.** $\sqrt{3} \cot x = 3$

16. Calculate each of these to three decimal places.

a. $\sin 40°$ **b.** $\sin(180° - 40°)$ **c.** $\cos 40°$

d. $\cos(360° - 40°)$ **e.** $\tan 40°$ **f.** $\tan(180° + 40°)$

Go **O**nline

PHSchool.com

For additional practice, go to **Web Code:** bga-0110

In this investigation, you learned the relationship between the tangent function and lines tangent to the unit circle. You defined inverse cosine, sine, and tangent functions by restricting domains. You graphed all six trigonometric functions, including secant, cosecant, and cotangent. The following questions will help you summarize what you have learned.

1. Suppose $\tan x = 2.4$. Find the two possible exact values of $\sec x$.

2. Let $A = (1, 0)$, and let $\overset{\frown}{AB}$ be an arc on the unit circle with length α. What is the slope of the line $\overleftrightarrow{OB}$, where O is the origin, in terms of α?

3. Solve the equation $7 \csc 5x - 8 = 6$.

4. Each of these equations has $x = \frac{\pi}{3}$ as a solution. Find the other solution in the interval $0 \leq x \leq 2\pi$.

   a. $2 \cos x = 1$ **b.** $\tan x = \sqrt{3}$ **c.** $\sqrt{3} \csc x = 2$ **d.** $3 \cot x = \sqrt{3}$

5. The figure at the right shows the unit circle with three triangles, $\triangle OSB$, $\triangle OAT$, and $\triangle OPQ$. Point A is at $(1, 0)$ and $\overleftrightarrow{AT}$ is perpendicular to the x-axis. Point P is at $(0, 1)$ and $\overleftrightarrow{PQ}$ is perpendicular to the y-axis. B and T are both on $\overleftrightarrow{OQ}$. You have already seen how $\triangle OSB$ lets you find cosine and sine of α, and how $\triangle OAT$ lets you find tangent and secant of α.

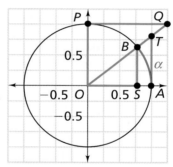

   a. Show that $\triangle OPQ \sim \triangle TAO$.

   b. Use similar triangles to show that the length of $\overline{OQ}$ is equal to $\csc \alpha$ and that the length of $\overline{PQ}$ is equal to $\cot \alpha$.

6. How are the six trigonometric functions defined?

7. Why does the $\sin^{-1}$ function on a calculator in degree mode return only results between -90 and 90 degrees?

8. Solve the equation $\cos x = 0.8$ for x. How many solutions are there?

Vocabulary

In this investigation, you learned these terms. Make sure you understand what each one means and how to use it.

- **asymptote**
- **inverse function**

Sinusoidal Functions and Their Graphs

In *Sinusoidal Functions and Their Graphs*, you will graph translations and dilations of the cosine and sine functions. You will learn how to relate the graphs to the parameters in the sinusoidal forms $A\cos(ax + b) + B$ and $A\sin(ax + b) + B$. You will relate these functions to everyday periodic behavior.

By the end of this investigation, you will be able to answer questions like these.

1. Given the maximum and minimum values of a cosine or sine function, how do you find the amplitude and vertical displacement?

2. How can you make a sinusoidal function that has a specific period?

3. How can you use sinusoidal functions to model periodic phenomena?

You will learn how to
- make sense of sinusoidal functions in the context of previous experience
- understand the geometry of sinusoidal functions
- model with sinusoidal functions

You will develop these habits and skills:
- See the graph of $y = A\sin(ax + b) + B$ is simply a transformation of the basic graph of $y = \sin x$.

The minimum value of a sinusoidal curve that models the height of the tide represents the height of low tide.

1.11 Getting Started

As you work though these problems, make sure to write down any conjectures you have about trigonometric functions and their graphs.

For You to Explore

1. Suppose $f(x) = \sin x$. For each function below, sketch its graph and the graph of $y = f(x)$ on the interval $-\pi \le x \le 2\pi$. Describe how the two graphs relate to each other.

   a. $f(2x) = \sin 2x$ **b.** $f(3x) = \sin 3x$

   c. $f(4x) = \sin 4x$ **d.** $f(10x) = \sin 10x$

> See the TI-Nspire Handbook on p. 704 for ideas about how to graph each function.

2. Let $f(x) = \sin x$ as in Problem 1. For each function below, sketch its graph and the graph of $y = f(x)$ on the interval $-\pi \le x \le 2\pi$. Describe how the two graphs relate to each other.

   a. $2f(x) = 2 \sin x$ **b.** $5f(x) = 5 \sin x$

   c. $\frac{1}{3} f(x) = \frac{1}{3} \sin x$ **d.** $-3f(x) = -3 \sin x$

3. Let $g(x) = \cos x$. Sketch the graph of $g(x)$ on the interval $-\pi \le x \le 2\pi$ along with the graph of each of these functions. Describe how the two graphs relate to each other.

   a. $g(x) + 1 = \cos x + 1$ **b.** $g(x) - 2 = \cos x - 2$

   c. $g(x + 1) = \cos(x + 1)$ **d.** $g(x - 2) = \cos(x - 2)$

4. Sketch the graph of each function.

   a. $A(x) = 3\cos x$ **b.** $B(x) = 3\cos x - 2$

   c. $C(x) = 3\cos(x - 2)$ **d.** $D(x) = 2\sin(x + 1) + 2$

> Note the change in order of operations. Add 1, then take the cosine of the result. As usual, use radians unless the degree symbol is present.

5. Find two functions that have graphs that pass through the point $\left(\frac{\pi}{2}, 4\right)$.

6. The function $f(x) = \sin x$ has period 2π. Find a function in the form $h(x) = \sin ax$ with the following period.

   a. period π **b.** period $\frac{\pi}{2}$

   c. period 4π **d.** period 2

   e. period 1 **f.** period 17

> **Remember...**
> The *period* of a periodic function is the least positive number p so that $f(x + p) = f(x)$ always. On a graph, it is where the function begins to repeat itself.

7. **Take It Further** Determine the number of intersections of the graphs of the following two equations.

$$y = \sin x$$

$$y = \frac{x}{10}$$

On Your Own

8. Find a solution to this equation.

$$6 \cos(\pi(x - 1)) + 2 = 5$$

Exercises 9 through 12 refer to the graph and function below.

$$H(t) = 36 \cos\left(\frac{2\pi}{60} t\right) + 39$$

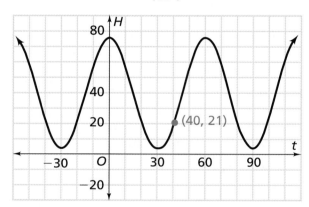

9. Use the graph of *H* to answer these questions.

   a. What is the maximum possible output of *H*?

   b. What is the minimum possible output of *H*?

   c. What is the period of *H*?

10. **a.** What appears to be the average value of *H*?

    b. How far is it from the average value of *H* to the maximum?

    c. How far is it from the average value of *H* to the minimum?

11. According to the graph, $H(40) = 21$.

    a. Using the symmetry of the graph, find the one positive value of $t < 40$ with $H(t) = 21$.

    b. Use the period of this function to find the next two values of *t* with $H(t) = 21$.

12. **a.** Find a value of t, that makes $H(t) = 55$. In other words, find a solution to the equation

$$55 = 36 \cos\left(\tfrac{2\pi}{60} t\right) + 39$$

Round your answer to two decimal places.

b. Find the next two larger values of t with $H(t) = 55$.

13. Determine the number of intersections of the graphs of these two equations.

$$y = \tan x$$

$$y = \tfrac{x}{10}$$

Draw a picture. Try sketching the graphs.

Maintain Your Skills

14. Copy and complete this table. Each column is a new instance of the variables D and A.

D + A			23	46	100	75	−10	x
D	7	−5	10	20				
A	3	7						
D − A					40	3	−32	y

Sinusoidal patterns are common in the natural world.

1.12 Sinusoidal Functions

Habits of Mind

Recognize periodicity. This is a direct consequence of the definition of cosine and sine and the way you extended the definition from acute angles to any angle and then from angles to radians. Look back at the definitions in Investigation 1A.

Unlike polynomials, trigonometric functions are periodic. For example, cosine and sine are periodic with period 2π. For any real number x

$$\cos(x + 2\pi) = \cos x \quad \text{and} \quad \sin(x + 2\pi) = \sin x$$

Because they are periodic, you can use them to model many periodic phenomena like the height of a rider as a Ferris wheel turns or the heights of the tides in the ocean as the day progresses. Actually, you can not model physical situations well directly simply by using cosine and sine. You need a wider class of functions that you could call *sinusoidal*.

Definition

A **sinusoidal function** is a function that is defined by a formula of the form

$$f(x) = A\cos(ax + b) + B \text{ or } f(x) = A\sin(ax + b) + B$$

where A, B, a, and b are real numbers.

As you will see in this investigation, if you model a function with one of these formulas, you can also model the function with the other formula.

Look at an example.

Example

Problem Let

$$H(x) = 36\cos\left(2x - \frac{\pi}{3}\right) + 39$$

a. Sketch the graph of the equation $y = H(x)$.

b. What appears to be the average value of H?

c. How far is it from the average value of H to the maximum?

d. How far is it from the average value of H to the minimum?

e. What is the period of H?

Solution

a. Use Derman's replacing-the-axis method from CME Project *Algebra 2*. First, rewrite the equation

$$y = 36\cos\left(2x - \frac{\pi}{3}\right) + 39$$

as

$$\frac{y - 39}{36} = \cos\left(2x - \frac{\pi}{3}\right)$$

Then let

$$M = 2x - \frac{\pi}{3} \text{ and } N = \frac{y - 39}{36}$$

Upon making these substitutions, you have
$$N = \cos M$$
Its graph appears below.

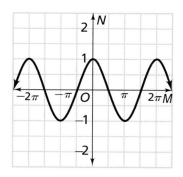

Since
$$M = 2x - \frac{\pi}{3}$$
$$= 2\left(x - \frac{\pi}{6}\right)$$
you have
$$x = \frac{M}{2} + \frac{\pi}{6}$$
And below is a pair of number lines depicting the relationship between M and x.

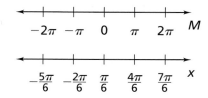

Likewise, $N = \frac{y - 39}{36}$ implies
$$y = 36N + 39$$
which gives the following pair of number lines relating N and y.

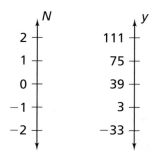

Finally, take the graph of $N = \cos M$ and

• replace the M-axis with the x-axis.
• replace the N-axis with the y-axis.

The resulting graph appears below.

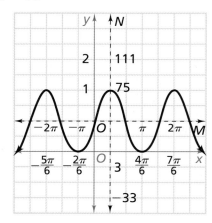

b. The horizontal dotted line, which is the graph of the equation $y = 39$, tells you that the average value of H is 39.

c. The maximum value of H occurs when $\cos M = 1$. The maximum is

$$36 \cdot 1 + 39 = 75$$

Thus, the distance from the average value to the maximum is

$$75 - 39 = 36$$

d. The minimum value of H occurs where $\cos M = -1$. The minimum is 3. Thus, the distance from the average value to the minimum is

$$39 - 3 = 36$$

Note that the average value is equidistant to the maximum and the minimum.

You could also use the graph of H to see the values of the maximum and minimum.

e. Pick the point $\left(\frac{\pi}{6}, 75\right)$ as a reference point. The graph of $y = H(x)$ starts to repeat itself at $\left(\frac{7\pi}{6}, 75\right)$. Thus, the period of H is

$$\frac{7\pi}{6} - \frac{\pi}{6} = \pi$$

Remember...
You can find the period by looking for where the graph begins to repeat itself.

The following definitions introduce some new terms that describe the characteristics of the graph of a sinusoidal function.

Definitions

Let f be a sinusoidal function.

The **vertical displacement** of f is its average value. More precisely, it is the average of the maximum and the minimum values of f.

The **amplitude** of f is the distance from its average value to the maximum or the minimum value.

Note that the amplitude is always positive.

For You to Do

1. Find the amplitude and the vertical displacement of
$$H(x) = 36 \cos\left(2x - \frac{\pi}{3}\right) + 39$$

2. Find the amplitude and the vertical displacement of
$$g(x) = 5 \sin 2x - 7$$

3. Find the amplitude and the vertical displacement of
$$f(x) = A \cos(ax + b) + B$$

The amplitude and the vertical displacement of

$$f(x) = A \cos(ax + b) + B \text{ or } f(x) = A \sin(ax + b) + B$$

describe how the graph of f relates to the graph of $N = \sin M$. More specifically, they describe how you transform the graph of $N = \sin M$ vertically to obtain the graph of $y = f(x)$. The next two concepts deal with how you transform the graph of $N = \sin M$ horizontally to obtain the graph of a sinusoidal function.

Minds in Action   episode 3

Derman and Tony are working on Exercise 6 on page 57.

Derman Okay, we need a function $h(x) = \sin ax$ with period π.

Tony Well, $f(x) = \sin x$ has period 2π and the graph of $y = f(2x)$ is the same as the graph of $y = f(x)$, except it's shrunk horizontally by the factor $\frac{1}{2}$.

Derman So the period of $f(2x) = \sin 2x$ is half of 2π, which is π.

Tony Right. How about a function $h(x) = \sin ax$ with period 2?

Derman We'd want it to shrink by the factor of , I think, 1 over π?

Tony That looks good. I guess it would be $f(\pi x) = \sin \pi x$.

Derman Fine, but what about this period 17? That seems tougher.

Tony It is. But I think you can use the one with period 2. So we could scale it by $\frac{1}{\pi}$ then adjust the coefficient to become 17.

Derman What?

Tony Instead of scaling by $\frac{1}{\pi}$, we could scale by $\frac{17}{2\pi}$.

$$f\left(\frac{2\pi}{17} x\right) = \sin \frac{2\pi}{17} x$$

Derman I put that in the calculator and it worked great! I bet we could do this for any period P by replacing the 17.

Tony Yes. I think that works. We want to scale the graph of $y = f(x)$ horizontally by a factor of $\frac{P}{2\pi}$. So the function would be

$$f\left(\frac{2\pi}{P}\,x\right) = \sin\frac{2\pi}{P}\,x$$

Derman And that has period P.

For Discussion

4. In terms of a, find the period of the sinusoidal function
$$f(x) = \sin ax$$

5. Find the period of the sinusoidal function
$$f(x) = A\sin(ax + b) + B$$

6. Find a sinusoidal function with period 3.

Finally, compare the graphs of

$$y = \cos x \text{ and } y = \cos\left(x - \frac{\pi}{6}\right)$$

which appears below.

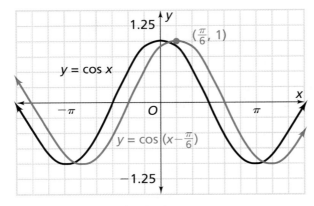

To obtain the graph of $y = \cos\left(x - \frac{\pi}{6}\right)$, shift the graph of $y = \cos x$ to the right by $\frac{\pi}{6}$ units. Thus, the function $y = \cos\left(x - \frac{\pi}{6}\right)$ has a phase shift of $\frac{\pi}{6}$. Here is the precise definition.

Phase shift is positive because you shifted the graph of $y = \cos x$ to the right.

Definition

Let

$$f(x) = A\cos(ax + b) + B \text{ or } f(x) = A\sin(ax + b) + B$$

be a sinusoidal function. The **phase shift** of f is the amount of horizontal translation required to obtain the graph of $y = f(x)$ from the graph of

$$y = A\cos ax \text{ or } y = A\sin ax$$

For You to Do

7. Consider again the function

$$H(x) = 36 \cos\left(2x - \frac{\pi}{3}\right) + 39$$

What is its phase shift? Explain your reasoning.

Exercises Practicing Habits of Mind

Check Your Understanding

1. Here is the graph of a sinusoidal function f.

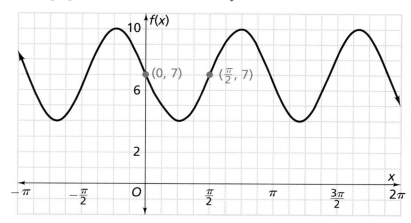

a. Find the amplitude and vertical displacement of f.

b. Find the period of f.

c. If you write f as a cosine, find a value for the phase shift. (There is more than one possible answer.)

d. Write f in the form

$$f(x) = A \cos(ax + b) + B$$

that could generate this graph.

> Some of the values of A, B, a, and b might be negative.

2. Find a function in the form

$$f(x) = A \sin(ax + b) + B$$

that generates the graph in Exercise 1.

3. **Take It Further** It is possible to write a function that generates the graph in Exercise 1 with no phase shift. How?

4. **a.** Find one solution to the equation $4 \cos 2x + 3 = 5$.

   b. Sketch the graph of $y = 4 \cos 2x + 3$. Show how you could use this graph to locate solutions to the equation $4 \cos 2x + 3 = 5$.

   c. Find all solutions to the equation $4 \cos 2x + 3 = 5$.

5. Consider the function

$$g(x) = 13 \sin (4x - \pi) + 10$$

See TI-Nspire Handbook on p. 704 for ideas about how to use a CAS to solve equations like this.

   a. Show that $\left(\frac{\pi}{4}, 10 \right)$ must be on the graph of g.

   b. Find the amplitude and vertical displacement of g.

   c. Find the maximum and minimum of g.

   d. Find the period of g.

   e. Sketch the graph of $y = g(x)$.

6. **a.** Sketch the graph of $h(x) = \cos^2 x$.

   b. Assume this function is sinusoidal. Find its amplitude, vertical displacement, and period.

You will probably have to enter this as $(\cos x)^2$ on the calculator.

7. The graph of $h(x) = \cos^2 x$ appears sinusoidal. Use your results from Exercise 6 to write another expression for $\cos^2 x$ in the form $A \cos ax + B$.

On Your Own

8. Here is the graph of a sinusoidal function.

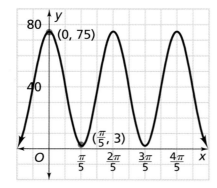

   a. Find the amplitude and vertical displacement of this function.

   b. Find the period of this function.

   c. Explain why you can write this function as a cosine with no phase shift.

   d. Write a function in the form $f(x) = A \cos ax + B$ that could generate this graph.

9. **a.** Show that for all numbers x, $\sin\left(x + \frac{\pi}{2}\right) = \cos x$

   b. Graph the equations $y = \sin\left(x + \frac{\pi}{2}\right)$ and $y = \cos x$ on the same axes.

10. Here is the graph of $g(x) = \cos x \sin x$, the product of the cosine and sine functions.

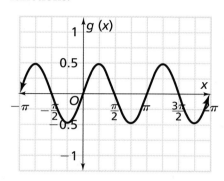

Assume that g is sinusoidal. Find its amplitude, vertical displacement, and period.

11. The graph of $g(x) = \cos x \sin x$ appears sinusoidal. Use your results from Exercise 10 to write another expression for $\cos x \sin x$ in the form

$$\cos x \sin x = A \sin ax + B$$

12. What is the period of the sinusoidal function $f(x) = A \sin(ax + b) + B$?

13. Consider the function

$$h(x) = 20 \cos\left(\frac{2\pi}{7}(x - 4)\right) + 26$$

   Evaluate each of these.

   a. $h(4)$ **b.** $h(11)$ **c.** $h(18)$ **d.** $h(-3)$

   e. Function h is periodic. What is its period?

14. Write an equation for a sinusoidal function with period 5.

15. **Standardized Test Prep** Which of the following represents the average value of the function $f(x) = A \cos(B(x - C)) + D$?

   A. A **B.** B **C.** C **D.** D

Go Online
PHSchool.com

For additional practice, go to **Web Code:** bga-0112

Maintain Your Skills

16. Write an equation for a sinusoidal function with each given period.

   a. π **b.** 4π

   c. 10π **d.** $n\pi, n \neq 0$

1.13 Applying Trigonometric Functions

In this lesson, you will study some applications of sinusoidal functions. Sinusoidal functions model many phenomena in the world, such as the Ferris wheel, the heights of tides, and lengths of days over the course of a year.

For Discussion

1. Suppose $f(t)$ describes the height of a person on a Ferris wheel after some time t. Based on what you know about how cosine and sine functions are defined using the unit circle, explain why $f(t)$ must be a sinusoidal function.

Remember Paul and Saul from Investigation 1A? Well, their younger brother Gaul also walks around a circle, but a much larger one with a radius of 36 feet. Gaul starts at the point (36, 0) and walks counterclockwise. He takes only 60 seconds to travel one lap around the circle.

> The center of the circle is at the origin.

Example 1

Problem

a. Find an equation for the function $h(t)$ that describes Gaul's x-coordinate after t seconds.

b. Suppose instead that the center of the circle is at the point (39, 0). Find an equation for $h(t)$ and sketch its graph.

Solution

a. Since Gaul's circle is the unit circle scaled by a factor of 36, the definition of the cosine function implies

$$h(t) = 36 \cos(at)$$

for some parameter a. You saw in the last lesson that

$$a = \frac{2\pi}{P}$$

where P is the period of h. Since it takes Gaul 60 seconds to make one revolution, you have $P = 60$. Therefore, $a = \frac{2\pi}{60}$ and you have

$$h(t) = 36 \cos\left(\frac{2\pi}{60} t\right)$$

> Given a real number t, locate the point on the unit circle that is at an angle t radians (measured counter-clockwise from the positive x-axis). By definition, this point has coordinates $(\cos t, \sin t)$.

b. If you were to locate the center of the circle at (39, 0). Gaul's *x*-coordinate simply increases by 39 units at every point on his path. Therefore, you have

$$h(t) = 36 \cos\left(\tfrac{2\pi}{60} t\right) + 39$$

Its graph appears below.

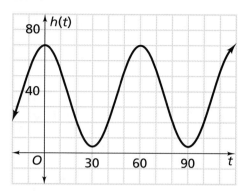

What happens to his *y*-coordinates?

Now consider a Ferris wheel with the following specifications.

- It makes a full revolution every 60 seconds.
- Its maximum height is 75 feet.
- Its minimum height is 3 feet.

Then the center of the Ferris wheel must be at the average of the maximum and the minimum heights.

$$\tfrac{1}{2}(75 + 3) = 39$$

or 39 feet. The radius of the wheel must be the difference of the maximum height and the average value.

$$75 - 39 = 36$$

Or 39 − 3 = 36 feet.

or 36 feet. Let $H(t)$ denote the height of a person on this Ferris wheel t seconds after he or she is at the highest point of the wheel.

For Discussion

2. Explain why

$$H(t) = 36 \cos\left(\tfrac{2\pi}{60} t\right) + 39$$

In other words, explain why $H(t)$ equals the function describing Gaul's *x*-coordinate when his circle has center at (39, 0).

Developing Habits of Mind

Think about it another way. You took a rather rigorous approach to finding an equation for $H(t)$, starting from the unit circle definition of the cosine function. In practice, you often skip these steps and conclude that the height of a person on a Ferris wheel must be sinusoidal because moving around the wheel is like moving around the unit circle.

So, you could write

$$H(t) = A\cos(at + b) + B$$

and proceed to find the parameters A, B, a, and b. From the analysis of the Ferris wheel, you can deduce the following

- The amplitude of $H(t)$ equals the radius of the wheel, and thus $A = 36$.

- The vertical displacement of $H(t)$ is the height of the center of the wheel. Therefore $B = 39$.

- The period of $H(t)$ is 60 and so $a = \frac{2\pi}{60}$.

- $H(t)$ assumes its maximum value when $t = 0$. And since you are modeling $H(t)$ using a cosine function, which also assumes its maximum value at $t = 0$, there is no need for horizontal translation. Thus, the phase shift is zero and so $b = 0$.

Therefore, conclude that

$$H(t) = 36\cos\left(\frac{2\pi}{60}\,t\right) + 39$$

Note that although you could have chosen a sine wave instead, there would be a phase shift involved. Knowing the behavior of the function can help you decide whether to choose a cosine or sine form.

The model comes directly from the geometry of the situation. Here, the person riding the Ferris wheel is moving around a circle, so the definition of cosine and sine dictate that their height over time should be modeled by a sinusoidal function.

> **Remember...**
>
> Circular behavior is often the underlying cause of a sinusoidal function.

> You could have also written $H(t) = A\sin(at + b) + B$.

> Recall that $t = 0$ when the person is at the peak of the wheel.

For You to Do

3. Consider again the Ferris wheel from the discussion above, but this time, suppose you model it with a sine function—in other words, write

$$H(t) = A\sin(at + b) + B.$$

Find the values of the parameters A, B, a, and b.

You can model many phenomena occurring in nature with sinusoidal functions. For example, consider the example of the tide, the periodic rise and fall of the sea level caused by the gravitational pull of the moon. Observations show that when you graph the height of the tide as a function of time, the resulting graph is approximately a sinusoidal curve.

Example 2

Problem Suppose you have the following information about the height of the tide in a particular region.

- The maximum height (i.e., a high tide) of 10 feet occurred at 8 A.M.

- The minimum height (i.e., a low tide) measured 6 feet.

- On average, high tides occur about every 12.4 hours (i.e., 12 hours and 24 minutes).

Assuming that the height of the tide is a sinusoidal function, find the equation for $H(t)$, the height of the tide t hours after midnight.

Solution Since you are assuming that H is a sinusoidal function, write

$$H(t) = A \cos (at + b) + B$$

and proceed to find the parameters A, B, a, and b.

The average height of the tide is

$$\frac{1}{2}(10 + 6) = 8$$

or 8 feet, and thus the vertical displacement of H is $B = 8$. Moreover, the amplitude of H is

$$10 - 8 = 2$$

That is, $A = 2$. Since H has period $P = 12.4$, you have

$$a = \frac{2\pi}{12.4}$$

Now consider the function

$$f(t) = 2 \cos\left(\frac{2\pi}{12.4}t\right) + 8$$

> The period of the tide depends mostly on the earth's rotation and the moon's orbit around the earth. If the moon never moved, the period of the tide would be 12 hours, but the moon moves in its orbit a little over that time. Note that it is an underlying circular motion that is responsible for the sinusoidal tide.

> Or $8 - 6 = 2$.

whose graph appears below.

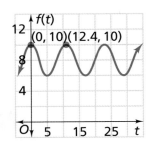

To obtain the graph of H, you need to shift the graph of f to the right by 8 units, reflecting the fact that the high tide occurs at 8 A.M. In other words, H has a phase shift of 8 and thus

$$H(t) = 2 \cos\left(\frac{2\pi}{12.4}(t - 8)\right) + 8.$$

Here is the graph of $y = H(t)$.

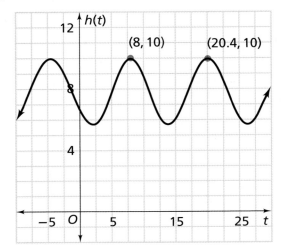

So, $b = -\frac{16\pi}{12.4}$.

For Discussion

4. Explain why, in the above example, you can also obtain the graph of H by translating the graph of f to the left by 4.4 units. What would be the corresponding phase shift and equation for H? And how does this equation relate to the equation

$$H(t) = 2 \cos\left(\frac{2\pi}{12.4}(t - 8)\right) + 8$$

that you obtained in the above example?

Exercises Practicing Habits of Mind

Check Your Understanding

1. The first ever Ferris wheel had a radius of 125 feet, and a maximum height of 264 feet.

   This Ferris wheel made a full revolution every 9 minutes. Write a rule for $H(t)$, the height of a person on this wheel t minutes after they are at the peak of the wheel.

2. Sketch an accurate graph of H from Exercise 1 on the domain $-9 \leq t \leq 9$.

3. **a.** Find, to the nearest second, the elapsed time for a person on the Ferris wheel in Exercise 1 to go from the top of the wheel to a height of exactly 200 feet.

   b. Use the graph of H from Exercise 2 to locate, approximately, the second time that person will be at a height of exactly 200 feet.

   c. Use the symmetry of the graph of H to give an answer to part(b) that is accurate to the nearest second.

> Remember, you will need the amplitude, period, phase shift, and vertical displacement. One of them is zero, probably not the period!

> What equation do you need to solve here? How can backtracking help?

4. On average, high tides occur about every 12 hours and 24 minutes. Suppose a high tide occurred at 8 A.M. this morning.

   a. What time would you predict for the next high tide, and the one after that?

   b. What time would you predict for the next low tide? the next low tide after that?

   c. Sketch, approximately, the graph of the tide's height for 30 hours, starting at 8 A.M. today.

5. A reporting station records a high tide of 9 feet at 8 A.M., then a low tide of 2 feet at about 2:12 P.M. Assuming the height of the tide is a sinusoidal function with period 12.4 hours, find an equation for $H(t)$, the height of the tide t hours after midnight.

6. Sketch the graph of the function you found in Exercise 5.

7. Use the equation you found in Exercise 5 to answer these questions.

   a. What is the predicted tide height at noon? at midnight?

   b. What is the height of the tide at 11:06 A.M.?

   c. Find another time when the tide is the same as it is at 11:06 A.M.

   d. Find a time, to the nearest minute, when the tide is 6 feet high.

8. Consider the Ferris wheel on page 69. The wheel has a radius of 36 feet. You travel around it once per 60 seconds.

   a. Find your speed as you move around the Ferris wheel, in feet per second. Drawing a picture of the situation may help.

   b. How fast are you traveling in miles per hour?

   c. **Take It Further** Consider the graph of H, vertical height on this Ferris wheel. At what times t is $H(t)$ changing the fastest? Use a graphing calculator to determine the maximum change in H as a slope, in feet per second.

On Your Own

9. Sketch the graph of this function over two periods.

$$f(x) = 20 \cos\left(\tfrac{2\pi}{7}(x - 4)\right) + 26$$

10. Which of these is the period of $g(t) = 5 \sin 100\pi t + 3$?

   A. $\tfrac{1}{100}$ **B.** $\tfrac{1}{50}$ **C.** 50   **D.** 100

11. **Write About It** The equation for the Ferris wheel on page 69 is

$$H(t) = 36 \cos\left(\tfrac{2\pi}{60}t\right) + 39$$

   You can simplify the fraction $\tfrac{2\pi}{60}$ to $\tfrac{\pi}{30}$. Why does it make sense not to simplify this fraction?

12. Suppose you get on at the bottom of the Ferris wheel described on page 69. Then you start keeping track of time immediately as it moves.

a. Copy and complete this table for your height on the wheel after t seconds.

Assume the Ferris wheel moves at its full speed immediately. Its period is still 60 seconds.

Time t (seconds)	Height H (t) (feet)
0	3
15	■
30	■
45	■
60	■
75	■
90	■

b. Sketch the graph of height against time for this situation.

c. Write an equation for $H(t)$, the height after t seconds, for this situation.

13. Would you move faster if you sat on the Ferris wheel from page 69 or the Ferris wheel from Exercise 1? One completes its rotation more quickly but is smaller in radius.

There is more than one possible answer here.

14. Tide tables report the times and depths of high tides, and the times and depths of low tides. For example, here is part of a tide from Salem, Massachusetts, dated September 19, 2006.

10:14 A.M.	8.14 feet	High Tide
4:05 P.M.	1.27 feet	Low Tide
10:24 P.M.	8.97 feet	High Tide

These tables do not report the tide heights in between. However, there is a guideline called the Rule of Twelfths that you can use to predict the tide each hour (for six hours) between a high and low tide:

Divide the amount the tide changes from high to low (or from low to high) into 12 equal parts. The first hour's gain (or loss) is 1 part (or, $\frac{1}{12}$ of the total change), the second hour is 2 parts, then 3, 3, 2, and 1.

a. Show that the predicted tide at 11:14 A.M. should be about 7.57 feet.

b. Find the predicted tide for 2:14 P.M. using the Rule of Twelfths.

c. Find the predicted tide for 6:05 P.M.

d. Draw a plot that includes the predicted tides from 10:14 A.M. to 10:24 P.M.

15. Write About It Describe how the Rule of Twelfths is related to sinusoidal behavior. Why does the rule group the equal parts the way it does?

16. Take It Further The function $f(x) = \cos x + \sin x$ is sinusoidal.

a. Using the unit circle, show that the maximum possible value of f is $\sqrt{2}$. For what x does the maximum occur?

b. Show that the minimum possible value of f is $-\sqrt{2}$. Find where it occurs.

c. Write an equation for f based on amplitude and phase shift.

17. Standardized Test Prep A Ferris wheel has a radius of 20 feet. The center is 35 feet above the ground and the wheel is rotating counterclockwise at a rate of 1 revolution every π minutes. Which of the following is a function giving the height of a rider in feet at time t minutes if the rider passes location S (35 feet above the ground) at time $t = 0$?

A. $35 \sin \left(2 \left(t - \frac{\pi}{2} \right) \right) + 20$

B. $20 \sin 2t + 35$

C. $2 \sin 20t + 35$

D. $20 \sin (t - 35) + 2$

Go Online
PHSchool.com

For additional practice, go to **Web Code:** bga-0113

Maintain Your Skills

18. Consider the function

$$H(t) = 36 \cos \left(\frac{2\pi}{60} (t - 15) \right) + 39$$

a. Sketch a graph of H on the interval $0 \le t \le 120$.

b. Find a value of t for which $H(t) = 21$.

c. Use the graph of H to find the three other values of t between 0 and 120 that make $H(t) = 21$.

How might it help to draw a line on top of the graph of H?

19. Find all the values of t between 0 and 120 that are solutions to the equation

$$36 \cos \left(\frac{2\pi}{60} (t - 5) \right) + 39 = 12$$

to two decimal places.

Mathematical 1C Reflections

In this investigation, you studied graphs, properties, and applications of sinusoidal functions. The following questions will help you summarize what you have learned.

1. Suppose a Ferris wheel has a radius of 78 feet and a minimum height of 10 feet. It makes a full revolution every 6 minutes. Let $H(t)$ denote the height of a person on this wheel t minutes after they are at the highest point of the wheel.
   a. Sketch the graph of H on the domain $-6 \le t \le 6$.
   b. Find an equation for $H(t)$.

2. Find the amplitude, vertical displacement, period, and phase shift of the sinusoidal function $f(x) = 21 \cos\left(\frac{2\pi}{3}(x - 5)\right) - 14$.

3. Sketch the graph of the function $f(x) = 10 \sin\left(\frac{4\pi}{5}(x + 2)\right) + 3$ over two periods.

4. Find, to two decimal places, a solution to the equation
   $8 = 10 \sin\left(\frac{4\pi}{5}(x + 2)\right) + 3$.

5. Suppose $f(x) = \sin x$. For each function below, sketch the graph and the graph of $y = f(x)$ on the interval $-\pi \le x \le 2\pi$. Describe how the two graphs relate.
   a. $f(2x) = \sin 2x$ b. $2f(x) = 2 \sin x$ c. $f(x) + 1 = \sin x + 1$

6. Given the maximum and minimum values of a cosine or sine function, how do you find the amplitude and vertical displacement?

7. How can you make a sinusoidal function that has a specific period?

8. How can you use sinusoidal functions to model periodic phenomena?

Vocabulary

In this investigation, you learned these terms. Make sure you understand what each one means and how to use it.
- amplitude
- phase shift
- sinusoidal function
- vertical displacement

The differences in high and low tidal levels can often be dramatic.

Project: Using Mathematical Habits

"Trigonometry" of the Unit Square

The unit circle was the basis for the work in this chapter. You can measure cosine and sine by looking at the coordinates of someone walking α units counterclockwise around the unit circle.

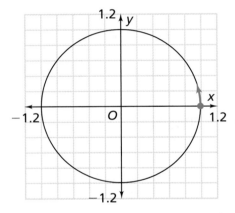

What would happen if everything stayed the same, but you replaced the circle by a square with side length 2?

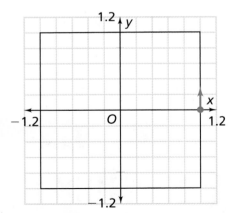

1. Paul walks 2π units around the unit circle. How far does he walk when he goes completely around the square once?

2. Copy and complete this table. Give the coordinates of Paul's location after walking each distance around a square with side length 2.

Distance	Coordinates
0	(1, 0)
$\frac{1}{2}$	$\left(1, \frac{1}{2}\right)$
1	■
$1\frac{1}{2}$	■
2	(0, 1)
3	■
4	■
5	■
6	■
7	■
8	■
9	■
10	■

3. After walking around the square for 3 units, Paul is at the point $(-1, 1)$. If he continues walking, how far has he walked once he reaches these coordinates again? Find a rule that generates all the answers to this question.

4. Determine where an exhausted Paul would be after walking 739 units on the square.

On the unit circle, define the sine function by using the distance walked as the input, and the y-coordinate as the output.

For the unit square, let $SSIN(t)$ be the y-coordinate on the square after walking distance t. Let $SCOS(t)$ be the x-coordinate on the square after walking distance t.

5. Find each value.

a. $SSIN(5)$ **b.** $SSIN(21)$

c. $SSIN(3.6)$ **d.** $SCOS(3.6)$

e. $SCOS(0)$ **f.** $SCOS(2) + SCOS(6)$

g. $SCOS(3) + SCOS(7)$

6. Two examples above suggest that $SCOS(t) + SCOS(t + 4) = 0$. Is this true for all values of t? What is the corresponding identity for the unit circle?

7. Sketch a graph of the $SSIN$ function on the domain $0 \le t \le 16$. Consider the proper range before laying out the axes of your sketch.

8. On the same axes used for the $SSIN$ function, sketch the $SCOS$ function on the domain $0 \le t \le 16$.

9. Here are some questions for further study.

- On the unit circle, $\cos^2 t + \sin^2 t = 1$ for all values of t. Is there any relationship like this on the unit square? What does the graph of $f(t) = SCOS^2(t) + SSIN^2(t)$ look like?

- What would cosine and sine look like for someone walking around a different polygon with center $(0, 0)$ and one vertex at $(1, 0)$? Consider an equilateral triangle, a regular hexagon, a rectangle, and other shapes.

- What does the graph of the tangent function $STAN$ look like for the unit square? Here, define the tangent in any of the ways used for the circle. Will each option for the definition of tangent give the same result?

- What do the graphs of the reciprocal trigonometric functions look like for the unit square?

- Is it possible to model the $SSIN$ and $SCOS$ functions on a graphing calculator?

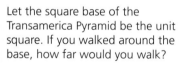

Let the square base of the Transamerica Pyramid be the unit square. If you walked around the base, how far would you walk?

For vocabulary review, go to Web Code: bgj-0151

In **Investigation 1A,** you learned how to …

- understand the relationship between degree and radian measure as the length of an arc on the unit circle subtended by a central angle.

- relate the motion of an object around a circle to the graphs of the cosine, sine, and tangent functions.

- solve equations that involve cosine and sine (such as $3 \cos x + 2 = 1$).

The following questions will help you check your understanding.

1. Draw the unit circle. A toy car is driving along this circle in the clockwise direction, starting from the point $(0, -1)$. After exactly $\frac{\pi}{2}$ meters, the car will be at which point?

   A. $(1, 0)$ **B.** $(-1, 0)$

   C. $(0, 1)$ **D.** $(0, -1)$

2. Evaluate the expression below.
$$\sin 30° + \cos \pi - 3 \cos 60°$$

3. How many radians corresponds to an angle with degree measure $160°$?

   A. $\frac{8\pi}{9}$ **B.** $\frac{3\pi}{4}$

   C. 3π **D.** $\frac{5\pi}{6}$

4. Solve the following system of equations if $0 \le x \le \frac{\pi}{2}$.
$$y = 4 \sin x + 1$$
$$y = 3$$

In **Investigation 1B,** you learned how to …

- understand several relationships between the tangent function and the unit circle.

- sketch and describe the graph of the tangent function.

- define an inverse of cosine, sine, and tangent.

- recognize three other trigonometric functions: secant, cosecant, and cotangent.

The following questions will help you check your understanding.

5. Solve the following equation.
$$\sin x - \sqrt{3} \cos x = 0$$

6. Solve the following equation.
$$2 \cot x = \frac{\cos x}{1 - \cos^2 x}$$

7. What is the period of $f(x) = \tan \frac{x}{2}$?

   A. π **B.** 2π **C.** $\frac{\pi}{2}$ **D.** $\frac{1}{2}$

In **Investigation 1C,** you learned how to …

- make sense of sinusoidal functions in the context of real-world applications.

- understand the geometry of sinusoidal functions.

- model with sinusoidal functions.

The following questions will help you check your understanding.

8. Give two examples of sinusoidal functions that have period $\frac{\pi}{4}$.

9. Sketch the graph of the function.
$$S(x) = 3 \cos (x + 2) + 1$$

Test

Go Online
PHSchool.com

For a chapter test, go
to Web Code: bga-0153

Multiple Choice

1. What is the value of the following expression?

$$\sin \frac{\pi}{2} + 2 \sin \pi - 3 \sin \frac{3\pi}{2}$$

A. 4   **B.** -2 **C.** -3 **D.** 3

2. Which of the following radian measures corresponds to 90°?

A. π **B.** $\frac{\pi}{4}$ **C.** $\frac{\pi}{2}$ **D.** $\frac{3\pi}{2}$

3. Which function has the graph below?

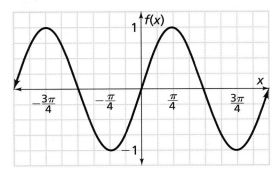

A. $f(x) = \sin x$ **B.** $f(x) = 2 \sin x$

C. $f(x) = 2 \cos x$ **D.** $f(x) = \sin 2x$

4. Which is equal to $\sin\left(\cos^{-1} \frac{1}{2}\right)$?

A. $\frac{\sqrt{3}}{2}$ **B.** $\frac{1}{2}$

C. $\frac{\sqrt{3}}{2}$ or $-\frac{\sqrt{3}}{2}$ **D.** $-\frac{1}{2}$

5. What is the period of the function below?

$$h(t) = \cos 3t$$

A. π **B.** 3π **C.** $\frac{1}{3}$ **D.** $\frac{2\pi}{3}$

6. What is the value of the following expression, where α is some real number?

$$\sin(\alpha + \pi) \cdot \sin\left(\frac{\pi}{2} - \alpha\right) + \cos\left(\frac{\pi}{2} - \alpha\right) \cdot \cos\alpha$$

A. 0   **B.** 2

C. $2 \sin\alpha \cdot \cos\alpha$ **D.** $2(\sin\alpha + \cos\alpha)$

Open Response

7. Answer the following questions. Explaining your reasoning.

  a. For what values of α is $\sin\alpha > 1$?

  b. For what values of α is $\cos\alpha < -1$?

8. Evaluate the expression below, where a and b are real numbers.

$$a^2 \cos 2\pi - 2ab \cos \pi + b^2 \sin \frac{\pi}{2}$$

9. Solve the following equation.

$$4 \cos^2 x - 1 = 0$$

10. Solve the equation below on $0 \le x \le \pi$.

$$3 \tan\left(\frac{x}{2} - \frac{\pi}{3}\right) + \sqrt{3} = 0$$

11. The sea level at a given point on the coast changes sinusoidally as a function of the time t. The following function gives the height x (in meters) of the water.

$$x = 6 + 5 \sin \frac{1}{6}\pi(t - 2)$$

  a. What is the maximum height of the water. What is its minimum height?

  b. If you start measuring the height at 10 A.M., at what time does the high tide occur?

  c. How many hours are there between successive high tides?

12. Solve the following equation.

$$\cot x = \tan x$$

Challenge Problem

13. Find all the solutions of the following equation.

$$\sqrt{3} \sin x - \cos x = 1$$

Chapter 2

Complex Numbers and Trigonometry

What do complex numbers have to do with trigonometry? As it turns out, a whole lot!

In your earlier courses, you may have thought about how trigonometry could be used to rewrite complex numbers. In this chapter, you will first learn how to plot complex numbers on the complex plane. Next, you will discover how to transform any complex number $a + bi$ to a new polar form. Then, using the powerful techniques of complex number calculation, you will generate and prove complicated trigonometric identities.

Scientists and engineers use complex numbers to model electrical circuits and water flow, to process digital signals, and to study nuclear phenomena. But artists use these same numbers to animate fractal domains in virtual reality scenarios, to visualize stunning works of art, and to compose audacious new soundscapes.

Vocabulary and Notation

- argument, arg(z)
- polar coordinates
- complex numbers
- conjugate, $\bar{z}$
- cyclotomy
- discriminant
- identically equal
- identity
- magnitude, |z|

- modulus
- norm, $N(z)$
- polar coordinates
- polar form for complex numbers
- rectangular coordinates
- rectangular form for complex numbers
- roots of unity

Investigation 2A

Graphing Complex Numbers

In *Graphing Complex Numbers*, you will view complex numbers as points in a plane. You will learn two coordinate representations for each complex number.

By the end of this investigation, you will be able to answer questions like these.

1. How can you write a complex number using trigonometry?

2. What are the magnitude and argument of a complex number, and how do you find them?

3. How do you use geometry to calculate $(1 - i\sqrt{3}) \cdot (-3\sqrt{3} + 3i)$?

You will learn how to

- represent complex numbers using both rectangular coordinates and polar coordinates

- determine the magnitude and argument of any complex number

- decide when it is best to use either rectangular or polar coordinates to represent complex numbers

You will develop these habits and skills:

- Graph complex numbers in the complex plane.

- Use geometry to explain arithmetic facts of complex numbers.

- Multiply two complex numbers of the form $r(\cos\theta + i\sin\theta)$.

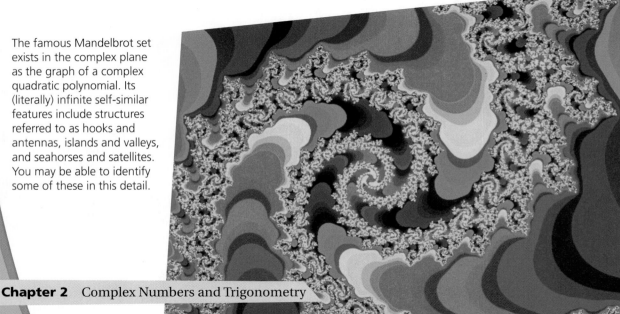

The famous Mandelbrot set exists in the complex plane as the graph of a complex quadratic polynomial. Its (literally) infinite self-similar features include structures referred to as hooks and antennas, islands and valleys, and seahorses and satellites. You may be able to identify some of these in this detail.

2.1 Getting Started

Activating Prior Knowledge
Exploring New Ideas

In an earlier algebra course, you learned about the complex numbers. A complex number is a number that is written in the form $x + yi$, where x and y are real numbers, and i is the imaginary unit, a number that has a square of -1. These Getting Started problems will give you an opportunity to refresh your memory about the arithmetic of complex numbers ($\mathbb{C}$).

For You to Explore

For Problems 1 and 2, calculate each expression. Write each result in the form $x + yi$ with real numbers x and y.

1. a. $(3 + i) + (2 + i)$ **b.** $(3 + i) - (2 + i)$

   c. $(3 + i)(2 + i)$ **d.** $(3 + i)^2$

   e. $(3 + i)^2 \cdot (2 + i)^2$ **f.** $(3 + i)^4 \cdot (2 + i)^4$

> The results from part (c) can help you answer parts (e) and (f).

2. a. $(3 + 5i) + (3 - 5i)$ **b.** $(3 + 5i)(3 - 5i)$

   c. $(-7 + 2i) + (-7 - 2i)$ **d.** $(-7 + 2i)(-7 - 2i)$

   e. $(12 + 5i) + (12 - 5i)$ **f.** $(12 + 5i)(12 - 5i)$

3. Let $z = x + yi$. The complex number $\bar{z} = x - yi$ is the **conjugate** of z.

   a. What is the conjugate of $12 + 5i$?

   b. What is the conjugate of $12 - 5i$?

   c. If $z = x + yi$, show that $z + \bar{z} = 2x$.

   d. If $z = x + yi$, show that the product $z\bar{z} = x^2 + y^2$.

> The real part stays the same. The imaginary part switches its sign. The conjugate of $z = 3 + 5i$ is $\bar{z} = 3 - 5i$.

4. For each point A, find the coordinates of the point A' by rotating A 90° counterclockwise about the origin.

   a. $A = (1, 0)$ **b.** $A = (0, -1)$

   c. $A = (3, 5)$ **d.** $A = (6, -1)$

5. Multiply each complex number z by i.

   a. $z = 1$ **b.** $z = -i$ **c.** $z = 3 + 5i$ **d.** $z = 6 - i$

6. Let $z = x + yi$.

   a. Calculate z^2.

   b. What is the real part of z^2?

   c. What is the imaginary part of z^2?

7. Show that the following equation is true for all x and y.

$$(x^2 - y^2)^2 + (2xy)^2 = (x^2 + y^2)^2$$

Exercises Practicing Habits of Mind

On Your Own

8. Define $f(x) = x^2 - 2x + 2$.

   a. Show that $f(x) = (x - 1)^2 + 1$.

   b. Explain why the graph of f does not have any x intercepts.

   c. Show that $f(1 + i) = 0$.

   d. Find one other nonreal number for which $f(x) = 0$.

9. Find the exact length of each line segment with the given endpoints.

   a. $(0, 0)$ and $(4, 1)$ **b.** $(0, 0)$ and $(2, 1)$ **c.** $(0, 0)$ and $(7, 6)$ **d.** $(0, 0)$ and $(3, 4)$

   e. $(0, 0)$ and $(6, 8)$ **f.** $(0, 0)$ and $(1, \sqrt{3})$ **g.** $(0, 0)$ and (x, y)

10. Compute each of these products.

    a. $(4 + i)(4 - i)$ **b.** $(2 + i)(2 - i)$ **c.** $(7 + 6i)(7 - 6i)$

    d. $(3 + 4i)(3 - 4i)$ **e.** $(6 + 8i)(6 - 8i)$ **f.** $(1 + i\sqrt{3})(1 - i\sqrt{3})$

11. **a.** Let $x = 3$ and $y = 2$ in the equation from Problem 7. Calculate the values of $x^2 - y^2$, $2xy$, and $x^2 + y^2$.

    b. Copy and complete the table at the right.

x	y	$x^2 - y^2$	$2xy$	$x^2 + y^2$
3	2	▨	▨	▨
2	1	▨	▨	▨
3	1	▨	▨	▨
4	3	▨	▨	▨
4	1	▨	▨	▨
5	2	▨	▨	▨

12. **a.** Sketch the graph of $f(x) = \cos^2 x - \sin^2 x$.

    b. Find the amplitude and period of f.

    c. Sketch the graph of $g(x) = \cos 2x$ on the same axes.

    d. Compare the graphs of f and g.

13. **a.** If $z = x + yi$, find the real part of z^3.

    b. Sketch the graph of $h(x) = \cos^3 x - 3 \cos x \sin^2 x$.

    c. Sketch the graph of $j(x) = \cos 3x$ on the same axes.

    d. Compare the graphs of h and j.

Maintain Your Skills

14. Expand each of these expressions.

    a. $(a + b)(a - b)$ **b.** $(a + b\sqrt{2})(a - b\sqrt{2})$ **c.** $(a + b\sqrt{3})(a - b\sqrt{3})$

    d. $(a + b\sqrt{c})(a - b\sqrt{c})$ **e.** $(x + yi)(x - yi)$

2.2 The Complex Plane

Any complex number is made up of two parts, the real part, and the imaginary part. Two complex numbers are equal if and only if their real and imaginary parts are equal. In 1806, Jean-Robert Argand, a Parisian, published his ideas about a geometric representation of complex numbers. He used the *x*-axis to represent the real part, and the *y*-axis to represent the imaginary part.

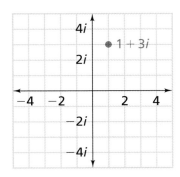

> Another name for the complex plane is the *Argand plane.* Gauss and Caspar Wessel described the complex plane in much the same way around the same time.

In the complex plane, the horizontal axis is the real axis, and the vertical axis is the imaginary axis.

Go Online
PHSchool.com

For a review of complex numbers, go to **Web Code:** bge-9031

For You to Do

1. Identify the complex number represented by each point.

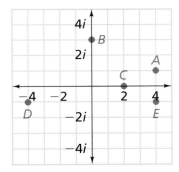

2. Which two of the five points are conjugates of one another?

In an earlier algebra course, you saw that the absolute value of a number *x* is its distance from 0 on the number line. In the same way, the absolute value $|z|$ of a complex number is also the distance from 0 on the complex plane.

Definition

The **magnitude** of a complex number *z*, denoted by $|z|$, is the distance between the complex number and 0 in the complex plane.

> Some older texts call the magnitude of a complex number the *modulus*.

If $z = x + yi$, $|z|$ is the length of the line segment connecting 0 and $x + yi$ in the complex plane, or $(0, 0)$ and (x, y) in the coordinate plane.

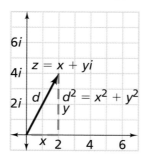

If $d^2 = x^2 + y^2$, then $d = \sqrt{x^2 + y^2}$, so $|x + yi| = \sqrt{x^2 + y^2}$.

For You to Do

3. Find $|-2 + 7i|$.

4. Find a complex number in Quadrant IV with magnitude 13.

See TI-Nspire™ Handbook on p. 704 for advice on calculating magnitude.

You may recall another attribute of a complex number, the *norm*.

Definition

The **norm** of a complex number z, written $N(z)$, is the product of the complex number and its conjugate, $z\bar{z}$.

The norm and absolute value of a complex number are similar, as the following theorem suggests.

Theorem 2.1

The absolute value of a complex number is equal to the square root of its norm.

$$|z| = \sqrt{N(z)}$$

For You to Do

5. Prove Theorem 2.1.

You can think of a real number x as having a size $|x|$, and a positive or negative sign. The absolute value denotes the magnitude of x, and the sign is the direction from 0. So the number 3 is 3 units in the positive direction from 0, and -3 is 3 units in the negative direction from 0.

The complex plane gives a convenient way to think of the direction of a complex number.

Definition

The **argument** of a complex number z, written arg(z), is the measure of the angle in standard position with z on the terminal side.

The argument arg (z) of a complex number is also its direction.

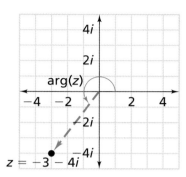

The value arg(z) is expressed in either degrees or radians. To find the argument, you need to use trigonometry.

A good way to think of a complex number and its attributes is to think of it as a vector. Instead of a ray as described in this definition, you could think of the vector **z**.

Example

Problem Find the magnitude and argument of $-2 + 3i$.

Solution The figure below shows $-2 + 3i$ graphed in the complex plane.

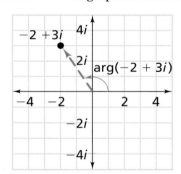

Use the formula $|x + yi| = \sqrt{x^2 + y^2}$ to find the magnitude.

$$|-2 + 3i| = \sqrt{(-2)^2 + (3)^2} = \sqrt{4 + 9} = \sqrt{13}$$

In Chapter 1, you saw that the slope of a line through the origin was equal to the tangent of the angle from the positive x-axis to the line. The slope of the line through the origin and the complex number z is $\frac{3 - 0}{(-2) - 0} = -\frac{3}{2}$. You can find the argument by using inverse trigonometric functions. However, you might need to adjust the result from a calculator to find an angle in the correct quadrant.

Your calculator will say that $\tan^{-1}\left(-\frac{3}{2}\right) \approx -0.9828$, which corresponds to an angle in the fourth quadrant. $-2 + 3i$ is in the second quadrant, so

$$\arg(z) \approx \pi - 0.9828 \approx 2.1588$$

For You to Do

6. Graph and label each of these complex numbers in the same complex plane. For each number, find its magnitude and argument (in degrees between 0° and 360°).

   a. $4 + 3i$ **b.** $4 - 3i$ **c.** $-4 + 3i$ **d.** $-4 - 3i$

Exercises *Practicing Habits of Mind*

Check Your Understanding

Unless otherwise specified, write the argument using radians.

1. For each complex number, find its exact magnitude.

   a. $4 + i$ **b.** $2 + i$ **c.** $3 - 2i$ **d.** $6 + 5i$

2. Compute each product. Compare the result to the magnitudes found in Exercise 1.

   a. $(4 + i)(4 - i)$ **b.** $(2 + i)(2 - i)$
   c. $(3 - 2i)(3 + 2i)$ **d.** $(6 + 5i)(6 - 5i)$

3. For each complex number z, graph z and $i \cdot z$ as vectors in the same complex plane. Estimate arg(z) and arg(iz).

   a. $z = 3 + 2i$ **b.** $z = -1 + 4i$
   c. $z = -1 - 3i$ **d.** $z = 2 - 3i$

4. Find the exact magnitude and argument of each complex number.

   a. $2 + 2i$ **b.** $2 - 2i$ **c.** $-2 + 2i$ **d.** $-2 - 2i$

5. Let z be a complex number. For each of the expressions below, describe how its magnitude and argument compare to $|z|$ and arg(z).

   a. iz **b.** $i^2 z$ **c.** $(-i)z$ **d.** $2z$ **e.** $\frac{1}{z}$

Go Online
PHSchool.com

For additional practice, go to **Web Code:** bga-0202

On Your Own

6. Suppose you triple a complex number z. How do $|3z|$ and arg($3z$) compare to $|z|$ and arg(z)?

7. Write About It Suppose you multiply a complex number z by a real number c. How do $|cz|$ and $\arg(cz)$ compare to $|z|$ and $\arg(z)$?

There may be several cases to consider, since c can be any real number.

8. Let $z = x + yi$, where x and y are positive real numbers.

   a. Graph what z and $\bar{z}$ might look like in the same complex plane.

   b. Graph $z + \bar{z}$.

   c. Show that the four complex numbers 0, z, $\bar{z}$, and $z + \bar{z}$ are the vertices of a parallelogram when plotted in the complex plane.

9. Let $z = \cos t + i \sin t$.

   a. Calculate z^2.   **b.** What is the imaginary part of z^2?

10. Find the vertices of a square in the complex plane.

11. Find the four solutions to the equation $x^4 - 16 = 0$. Plot them in the complex plane.

Two of the solutions are real numbers, and two are not.

12. For each complex number, find the exact magnitude. Also, approximate to two decimal places the argument in degrees.

   a. $(3 + 2i)^0$ **b.** $(3 + 2i)^1$ **c.** $(3 + 2i)^2$

   d. $(3 + 2i)^3$ **e.** $(3 + 2i)^4$

13. For each complex number, find the exact magnitude.

   a. $(1 + i)^2$ **b.** $(2 + i)^2$ **c.** $(3 + i)^2$

   d. $(7 + i)^2$ **e.** $(2 + 3i)^2$

   f. Find a complex number $x + yi$ with a magnitude of 29, where $x \neq 0$ and $y \neq 0$.

14. Find the magnitude and argument of each solution to each equation.

   a. $x^2 - 1 = 0$ **b.** $x^3 - 1 = 0$ **c.** $x^4 - 1 = 0$

15. Establish the identity $(ac - bd)^2 + (bc + ad)^2 = (a^2 + b^2)(c^2 + d^2)$.

16. Standardized Test Prep Which of the following is the product of $-1 + i$ and its complex conjugate?

   A. 0   **B.** -1.1 **C.** -0.9 **D.** 2

Maintain Your Skills

17. Let $\omega = \dfrac{1 + i\sqrt{3}}{2}$. Plot each of the following in the same complex plane.

ω is the Greek letter omega.

   a. ω **b.** ω^2 **c.** ω^3 **d.** ω^4

   e. ω^5 **f.** ω^6 **g.** ω^7 **h.** ω^{12}

Another Form for Complex Numbers

Coordinates are a perfectly good way to describe a point in the plane. The two numbers x and y identify a unique location. You start at the origin. You count $|x|$ units left or right (depending on the sign of x). Then you count $|y|$ units up or down (depending on the sign of y).

Suppose you are walking from the origin to the point (x, y). Regardless of how you define your axes, you could move x units in some direction, then turn 90° clockwise or counterclockwise before moving y units. The key idea is that your second movement would be perpendicular to the first.

But think, for instance, how you would actually move from one point to another. Suppose you were in an open field. You would likely walk in a straight line directly from one point to the other. You would first turn in the proper direction, then walk the proper distance.

This idea, and your work in the previous lesson, suggest another way to identify points in the plane. To get from the origin to the point (x, y), instead of walking two separate distances, you can move just one distance, providing you are heading in the right direction. So if you have two numbers, a direction (given by an angle measurement) and a distance, you can find your point.

Is it easier for you to desribe this fan in terms of polar coordinates or rectangular coordinates?

Facts and Notation

You can locate a point P in the plane in two ways.

Rectangular coordinates: (x, y) denotes distances along two axes that are perpendicular.

Polar coordinates: (r, θ) denotes a direction (an angle θ counterclockwise from the positive real axis) and distance r.

For Discussion

Let P_1 and P_2 be two points in the plane. If $P_1 = (x_1, y_2)$ and $P_2 = (x_2, y_2)$, it is a true statement that

$$P_1 = P_2 \Leftrightarrow x_1 = x_2 \text{ and } y_1 = y_2$$

Can you make the same statement about polar coordinates? Decide if the following statement is true: if $P_1 = (r_1, \theta_1)$ and $P_2 = (r_2, \theta_2)$

$$P_1 = P_2 \Leftrightarrow r_1 = r_2 \text{ and } \theta_1 = \theta_2$$

Consider these questions.

1. Is the statement true for either direction $\Leftrightarrow$?

2. If either implication is not always true, modify the statement to make both implications always true.

Complex numbers of the form $x + yi$ correspond directly to rectangular coordinates of the point (x, y). You can find a complex number if you are given polar coordinates (r, θ).

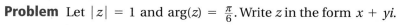

Example

Problem Let $|z| = 1$ and $\arg(z) = \frac{\pi}{6}$. Write z in the form $x + yi$.

Solution From the argument, z is in the first quadrant.

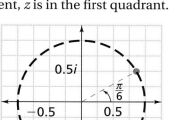

Since $|z| = 1$, z is on the unit circle. So $x \cos \frac{\pi}{6} = \frac{\sqrt{3}}{2}$ and y is $\sin \frac{\pi}{6} = \frac{1}{2}$. Thus, you can write $z = \cos \frac{\pi}{6} + i \sin \frac{\pi}{6} = \frac{\sqrt{3}}{2} + \frac{1}{2}i$.

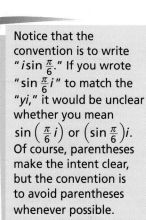

Notice that the convention is to write "$i \sin \frac{\pi}{6}$." If you wrote "$\sin \frac{\pi}{6} i$" to match the "yi," it would be unclear whether you mean $\sin \left(\frac{\pi}{6} i \right)$ or $\left(\sin \frac{\pi}{6} \right)i$. Of course, parentheses make the intent clear, but the convention is to avoid parentheses whenever possible.

For You to Do

For each absolute value and argument, write z in the form $x + yi$.

3. $|z| = 2$ and $\arg(z) = \frac{\pi}{6}$.

4. $|z| = 4$ and $\arg(z) = 135°$.

Just as you can express a point in the coordinate plane in two ways, you can express a complex number in two ways.

Rectangular Form: $x + yi$, where x and y are real numbers.

Polar Form: $r(\cos \theta + i \sin \theta)$, where r is a nonnegative real number and θ is a measurement in either degrees or radians.

By convention, r is not negative. You could express a complex number using $r < 0$, but if r is nonnegative, it will be equal to the magnitude of the complex number.

Facts and Notation

To identify the complex number $\cos \theta + i \sin \theta$, you can use the abbreviation cis θ.

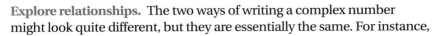

Explore relationships. The two ways of writing a complex number might look quite different, but they are essentially the same. For instance,

$$1 + i\sqrt{3} = 2\operatorname{cis}\frac{\pi}{3}$$

is a true statement. To see why, look at the right side.

$$2\operatorname{cis}\frac{\pi}{3} = 2\left(\cos\frac{\pi}{3} + i\sin\frac{\pi}{3}\right)$$

$$= 2\left(\frac{1}{2} + i\frac{\sqrt{3}}{2}\right)$$

$$= 1 + i\sqrt{3}$$

Either way you write it, you can see that the complex number has a real part and an imaginary part.

In general, you can write a complex number of the form $r\operatorname{cis}\theta$ as $x + yi$ by realizing that

$$x = r\cos\theta, \text{ and}$$

$$y = r\sin\theta$$

Also, if $z = r\operatorname{cis}\theta$, then you know that

$$|z| = r, \text{ and}$$

$$\arg(z) = \theta$$

> So, for any complex number z, you can say
>
> $$z = |z|\operatorname{cis}(\arg(z)).$$

Exercises Practicing Habits of Mind

Check Your Understanding

1. Find the magnitude and argument of each complex number.

    a. $z = 5\operatorname{cis}60°$ **b.** $w = \frac{1}{5}\operatorname{cis}300°$

2. Consider the complex numbers z and w from Exercise 1.

    a. Find the magnitude and argument of z^2.

    b. Find the magnitude and argument of z^3.

    c. Find the magnitude and argument of zw.

3. **a.** In the complex plane, plot (as points) four different numbers with argument $210°$.

   b. Plot the set of all points with argument $210°$.

   c. What complex number has magnitude 10 and argument $210°$?

4. Suppose q is a complex number with $|q| = 4$ and $\arg(q) = \frac{2\pi}{3}$.

   a. Write q using trigonometric functions.

   b. Write q without using trigonometric functions.

5. Let a and b be complex numbers, with $|a| = 5$, $\arg(a) = 60°$, $|b| = 3$, and $\arg(b) = 30°$.

   a. Write a and b in any form.

   b. Calculate the product ab. Find its magnitude and argument.

6. Suppose $z = 3 \operatorname{cis} \theta$ for some value of θ.

   a. Pick seven different values of θ. For each, plot z as a point in the complex plane.

   b. **Write About It** What does the graph of all possible such points look like? Explain.

7. **a.** Show that, for any value of θ, $|\operatorname{cis} \theta| = 1$.

   b. Show that, for any value of r and θ, $|r \operatorname{cis} \theta| = |r|$.

On Your Own

8. Find the magnitude and argument of each complex number.

   a. $5\sqrt{3} - 5i$ **b.** $10 \operatorname{cis} 330°$

   c. $4\sqrt{2} \operatorname{cis} \frac{5\pi}{4}$ **d.** $-4 - 4i$

9. Consider the complex number $z = \operatorname{cis} \frac{\pi}{2}$.

   a. Calculate z^2.

   b. Describe the effect in the complex plane of multiplying a complex number by z.

10. Suppose $z = 5 \operatorname{cis} 160°$ and $w = 2 \operatorname{cis} 110°$. Find $|zw|$ and $\arg(zw)$.

11. Complex number w has magnitude 1 and argument α. Complex number z has magnitude 1 and argument β.

   a. Write expressions for z and w.

   b. Write an expression for the product zw in the form $x + yi$, where x and y are in the set $\mathbb{R}$.

12. For each pair of complex numbers, find the magnitude and direction of z and w. Then find the magnitude and direction of the product zw.

   a. $z = 2 + i$ and $w = 3 + i$

   b. $z = 2 + i$ and $w = 3 + 2i$

   c. $z = 5i$ and $w = 3i$

   d. $z = 2 + i$ and $w = \dfrac{2 - i}{5}$

13. **a.** Based on the results in Exercise 12, describe a relationship between $|z|$, $|w|$, and $|zw|$.

   b. Describe a relationship between $\arg(z)$, $\arg(w)$, and $\arg(zw)$.

   c. Let $z = x + yi$ and $w = c + di$. Show that the relationship you found between $|z|$, $|w|$, and $|zw|$ holds for any choice of z and w.

14. **Standardized Test Prep** In polar coordinates, which of the following is the same as $\left(1, \frac{\pi}{3}\right)$?

   A. $\left(-1, \frac{4\pi}{3}\right)$ **B.** $\left(1, \frac{4\pi}{3}\right)$ **C.** $\left(-1, \frac{\pi}{3}\right)$ **D.** $\left(\frac{\pi}{3}, 1\right)$

> **Remember...**
>
> $|z|$ is the magnitude of the complex number z.

Maintain Your Skills

For additional practice, go to **Web Code:** bga-0203

15. The complex number $z = \sqrt{3} + i$ has magnitude 2 and direction $\frac{\pi}{6}$ (or 30°). For each complex number w listed below, find its magnitude and argument. Then find the magnitude and argument of zw.

   a. $w = 1 + i\sqrt{3}$

   b. $w = 5i$

   c. $w = 10$

   d. $w = 1 + i$

   e. $w = -2 + i$

The Multiplication Law

There are two ways to represent a complex number graphically, as a point and as a vector (a directed distance). Both methods are useful, just as it is useful on the number line to present numbers as both points and arrows.

- Thinking of complex numbers as points allows you to apply all the machinery of geometry to questions about complex numbers. This representation helps you do some very algebraic jobs, including equation solving.

- Thinking of complex numbers as vectors allows you to picture operations like adding two vectors or multiplying by i. Using vectors also allows you to think about the relative size of complex numbers, since a vector has a length.

Throughout this investigation, you have worked on arithmetic of complex numbers. You may have found the following ways of representing complex arithmetic geometrically.

> Throughout this lesson, the representation of complex numbers will alternate between points and vectors. What is most important is that you become comfortable with both representations and that you develop a knack for when to "think point" and when to "think vector."

- You can add two complex numbers by completing a parallelogram. The first two sides are vectors that represent the two numbers.

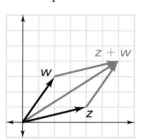

- You can multiply a complex number and a real number k by stretching the vector for the complex number by a factor of k.

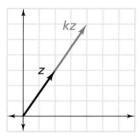

> If $k > 0$, the head of the vector is k times as far from the origin in the same direction. If $k < 0$, the head of the vector is $|k|$ times as far from the origin in the opposite direction.

- You can multiply a complex number by i by rotating the vector for the complex number 90 degrees counterclockwise.

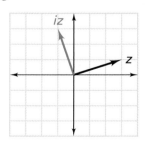

You can also represent the multiplication of two complex numbers geometrically.

Example

Problem Let $z = 3 + 2i$ and $w = 4 + i$. Describe how to find the product zw geometrically.

Solution You already know how to multiply two complex numbers.

$$(3 + 2i)(4 + i) = 3(4 + i) + 2i(4 + i)$$
$$= (12 + 3i) + (-2 + 8i)$$
$$= (12 - 2) + (3 + 8)i$$
$$= 10 + 11i$$

Just graphing the three vectors does not help much.

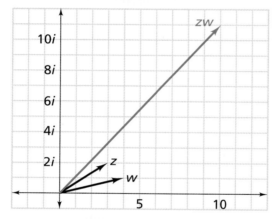

To see the geometry of the multiplication, you need to add a few more lines. Take a look at the first step in the calculation above.

$$(3 + 2i)(4 + i) = 3(4 + i) + 2i(4 + i)$$

On the right side, you have two arithmetic expressions that you know how to represent geometrically.

- $3(4 + i)$ is the product of a real number and a complex number. To show the product geometrically, you stretch the vector $4 + i$ by a factor of 3.

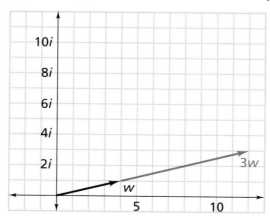

- $2i(4 + i)$ involves two steps. First, you can show the product $i(4 + i)$ by rotating $4 + i$ by 90 degrees counterclockwise.

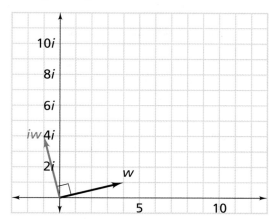

You can show the product of that resulting vector, $-1 + 4i$, and 2 by stretching the vector by a factor of 2.

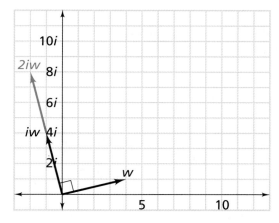

- Finally, add the two vectors by completing the parallelogram.

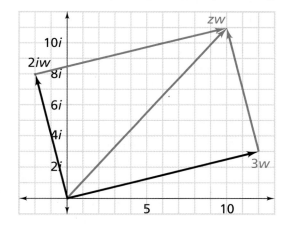

The parallelogram is actually a rectangle, because of the right angle.

The Example shows how to construct the product. But you may find it more difficult to follow the construction steps when finding the product of complex numbers written in cis notation, like $5 \operatorname{cis} \frac{\pi}{6}$ and $2 \operatorname{cis} \frac{\pi}{2}$.

To multiply complex numbers written this way, you can use certain properties of absolute value and argument, some of which you may have picked up in the exercises throughout this investigation. Your results from those exercises suggest the following theorem about the magnitude and argument of products.

Theorem 2.2   The Multiplication Law

Given complex numbers $z = a \operatorname{cis} \alpha$ and $w = b \operatorname{cis} \beta$,

$$zw = (a \operatorname{cis} \alpha)(b \operatorname{cis} \beta) = ab \operatorname{cis}(\alpha + \beta)$$

In other words,

- $|zw| = |z| \cdot |w|$
- $\arg(zw) = \arg(z) + \arg(w).$

You can use $z = 3 + 2i$ and $w = 4 + i$ from the Example to demonstrate both parts of the theorem. Consider this figure.

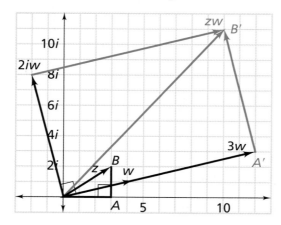

The smaller triangle is made from dropping a perpendicular from B to the real axis. The larger triangle is made from the construction from the examples. The two triangles are similar.

- Both are right triangles: the smaller because you made it by dropping a perpendicular, the larger because the angle at A' is part of a rectangle.

- Two pairs of sides are proportional: since $z = 3 + 2i$, you know that $OA = 3$ and $AB = 2$, so $\frac{OA}{AB} = \frac{3}{2}$. For the corresponding sides on the larger triangle, you have

$$OA' = |3(4 + i)| = |12 + 3i| = \sqrt{12^2 + 3^2} = \sqrt{144 + 9}$$
$$= \sqrt{153} = 3\sqrt{17}$$

and

$$A'B' = \sqrt{(10 - 12)^2 + (11 - 3)^2} = \sqrt{(-2)^2 + 8^2} = \sqrt{4 + 64}$$
$$= \sqrt{68} = 2\sqrt{17}$$

Thus

$$\frac{OA'}{A'B'} = \frac{3\sqrt{17}}{2\sqrt{17}} = \frac{3}{2}$$

Since the ratios are the same, the two pairs of sides are proportional.

Thus, by the SAS Theorem for similar triangles, the two triangles are similar. Now that you know the two triangles are similar, you can show both parts of the theorem.

- Corresponding sides in similar triangles are proportional. Every side in the larger triangle is $\sqrt{17}$ times as long as every side in the smaller triangle, and $\sqrt{17} = |w|$.

  The length of the hypotenuse of the smaller triangle is $|z| = \sqrt{3^2 + 2^2} = \sqrt{13}$. Thus, the length of the hypotenuse of the larger triangle is $\sqrt{13} \cdot \sqrt{17} = |zw|$. Thus, $|z| \cdot |w| = |zw|$.

- Corresponding angles in similar triangles are congruent. Thus, $\angle AOB \cong \angle A'OB'$. By definition, $\arg(z) = m\angle AOB$, $\arg(w) = m\angle AOA'$, and $\arg(zw) = m\angle AOB'$. Notice, though, that

$$\begin{aligned}
\arg(zw) &= m\angle AOB' \\
&= m\angle AOA' + m\angle A'OB' \\
&= m\angle AOA' + m\angle AOB \\
&= \arg(z) + \arg(w)
\end{aligned}$$

You can double check:
$$\begin{aligned}
|zw| &= \sqrt{10^2 + 11^2} \\
&= \sqrt{100 + 121} \\
&= \sqrt{221} \\
&= \sqrt{13} \cdot \sqrt{17}
\end{aligned}$$

For Discussion

1. Using algebra, prove for any two complex numbers $z = a + bi$ and $w = c + di$ that

$$|z| \cdot |w| = |zw|$$

Developing Habits of Mind

Visualize. Another way to envision what is happening with the geometry of complex multiplication is to look at what happens to z. You rotate it by $\arg(w)$, and then dilate it by $|w|$.

So, to multiply any complex number by $1 + i$, rotate it 45°, (since $45° = \arg(1 + i)$). Then scale by $\sqrt{2}$ (since $\sqrt{2} = |1 + i|$). To multiply by i, rotate it 90° and scale by 1.

It might help to think of the transformation of z by seeing how it transforms as part of the triangle *AOB*.

For You to Do

2. Describe multiplication of z by each of these numbers in terms of the rotation and scaling of z.

   a. $\sqrt{3} + i$ **b.** $-i$ **c.** -1

 **Exercises** *Practicing Habits of Mind*

1. Suppose $z = 3 \text{ cis } 120°$.

   a. Find the magnitude and argument of z^2.

   b. Explain why $z^3 = 27$.

2. Write About It If you know the magnitude and argument of z, describe (in words) how to find the magnitude and argument of z^2, z^3, and in general, z^n.

3. Suppose the complex number z^3 has magnnitude 27 and argument 120°. Decide whether each statement about z could be true. Explain.

   a. z has magnitude 9 and argument 40°.

   b. z has magnitude 3 and argument 40°.

   c. z has magnitude 3 and argument 120°.

   d. z has magnitude 3 and argument 160°.

4. Here are two complex numbers z and w drawn in the complex plane. Estimate the magnitude and argument of zw.

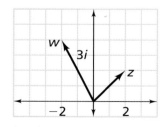

5. Write About It Two complex numbers have arguments that add up to more than 360°. Describe how to find the magnitude and argument of their product.

6. For each z, plot the first few powers of z (that is, $z^0, z^1, z^2, \ldots$). If you take higher powers of z, describe and explain the pattern you see.

   a. $z = i$ **b.** $z = -i$

   c. $z = 1 + i$ **d.** $z = 1 - i$

   e. $z = 2 + i$ **f.** $z = 2 - i$

7. Suppose z and w are complex numbers with magnitude 1. For each complex number, decide whether it must also have magnitude 1.

a. zw **b.** $z + w$ **c.** $\overline{w}$

d. $\frac{1}{z}$ **e.** z^2 **f.** $2z$

8. a. In the complex plane, plot the triangle with vertices $2 + 3i$, $4 + 6i$, and $7 - i$.

    b. Plot the triangle that results if you multiply each vertex by i.

    c. Plot the triangle that results if you multiply each vertex by $1 + i$.

9. The product of two complex numbers is $10i$. Neither is a real number.

    a. Find one possible pair of numbers that works.

    b. Take It Further Given any nonzero complex number z, explain how to find w so that $zw = 10i$.

10. Here are two complex numbers z and w drawn in the complex plane. Estimate the magnitude and argument of zw.

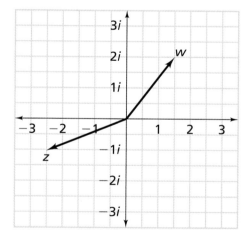

11. Consider the complex numbers $z = 3 - 2i$ and $w = 1 + 3i$.

    a. Plot z and w as vectors. Determine the magnitude and argument of each.

    b. In what quadrant is zw? Explain how you know.

    c. Find the magnitude and argument of zw.

12. This lesson explains how to find the magnitude and argument of the product of two complex numbers, but what about the quotient? Consider the complex numbers $z = 4 + 2i$ and $w = 3 + i$.

   a. Write $\frac{z}{w}$ as $a + bi$ where a and b are real numbers.

   b. Find the magnitude and argument of $\frac{z}{w}$.

   c. Find a relationship between the magnitudes of z, w, and $\frac{z}{w}$. Also find a relationship between their arguments.

13. **Take It Further** Plot the set of all complex numbers that satisfy each equation. Make a new graph for each part.

   a. $|z| = 3$ **b.** $|z| = 1$ **c.** $|z| < 1$ **d.** $|z| > 1$

   e. $|z| = \left|\frac{1}{z}\right|$ **f.** $z^2 = z$ **g.** $|z|^2 = |z|$

14. **Standardized Test Prep** Which of the following is equivalent to multiplying a complex number z by the number i?

   A. reflection of z over the x-axis   **B.** reflection of z over the y-axis

   C. rotation 90° counterclockwise   **D.** rotation 90° clockwise

Maintain Your Skills

For additional practice, go to **Web Code:** bga-0204

15. Simplify each expression. Write the result in the form $x + yi$ where x and y are real numbers.

   a. $1 + i + i^2$

   b. $1 + i + i^2 + i^3$

   c. $1 + i + i^2 + i^3 + i^4$

   d. $1 + i + i^2 + i^3 + i^4 + i^5$

   e. $1 + i + i^2 + i^3 + i^4 + i^5 + i^6$

   f. $1 + i + i^2 + i^3 + i^4 + i^5 + i^6 + i^7 + \cdots + i^{67}$

16. **Take It Further** Let $\omega = \dfrac{-1 + i\sqrt{3}}{2}$.

   Simplify each expression. Write the result in the form $x + yi$ where x and y are real numbers.

   a. $1 + \omega + \omega^2$

   b. $1 + \omega + \omega^2 + \omega^3$

   c. $1 + \omega + \omega^2 + \omega^3 + \omega^4$

   d. $1 + \omega + \omega^2 + \omega^3 + \omega^4 + \omega^5$

   e. $1 + \omega + \omega^2 + \omega^3 + \omega^4 + \omega^5 + \omega^6$

   f. $1 + \omega + \omega^2 + \omega^3 + \omega^4 + \omega^5 + \omega^6 + \omega^7 + \cdots + \omega^{67}$

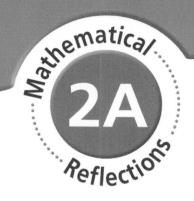

In this investigation, you described complex numbers as points in a plane using both rectangular and polar coordinates. You learned geometric interpretations of addition and multiplication of complex numbers. The following questions will help you summarize what you have learned.

1. Describe the effect of multiplying a complex number by $2i$ in terms of scaling and rotation.

2. Graph all complex numbers having magnitude 2.

3. Name three complex numbers that have argument $120°$.

4. If z is any complex number, show that $z\bar{z} = |z|^2$.

5. Use the result from Exercise 4 to show that $\dfrac{1}{z} = \dfrac{\bar{z}}{|z^2|}$ for any nonzero complex number z.

6. How can you write a complex number using trigonometry?

7. What are the magnitude and argument of a complex number, and how do you find them?

8. How do you use geometry to calculate $(1 - i\sqrt{3}) \cdot (-3\sqrt{3} + 3i)$?

Vocabulary and Notation

In this investigation, you learned these terms. Make sure you understand what each one means and how to use it.

- argument, arg(z)
- cis(θ)
- conjugate, $\bar{z}$
- magnitude, $|z|$
- norm, N(z)

- polar coordinates
- polar form for complex numbers
- rectangular coordinates
- rectangular form for complex numbers

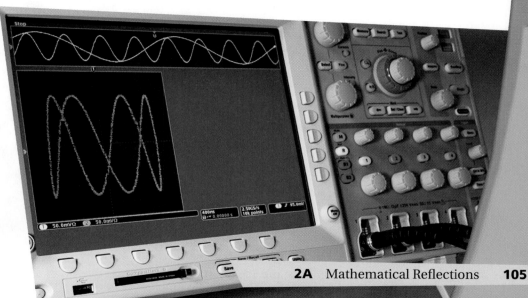

Lissajous figures are the graphs of equations containing cosine and sine functions. You can best observe their lively display on an oscilloscope.

Investigation 2B

Trigonometric Identities

In *Trigonometric Identities*, you will use complex arithmetic to prove basic trigonometric identities. You will learn techniques to validate other identities.

By the end of this investigation, you will be able to answer questions like these.

1. How can you test to see if an equation might be an identity?

2. How can you use complex numbers to find formulas for $\cos 2x$ and $\sin 2x$?

3. How can you use identities to prove other identities?

You will learn how to

- test trigonometric equations to predict whether they are identities

- show the basic addition rules for cosine and sine using the Multiplication Law for complex numbers

- use Pythagorean identities and algebra to prove that a trigonometric equation is an identity

You will develop these habits and skills:

- Manipulate trigonometric expressions.

- Determine useful test cases and techniques to identify identities.

- Use basic rules to generate more complicated rules.

Much like these multicolored plastic toy bricks, you assemble theorems using mathematical objects. If you don't put the pieces together correctly, the resulting structure may fall apart.

2.5 Getting Started

Two expressions are **identically equal** if you can transform one to the other using the basic rules of algebra, and any other proven identities or theorems. An **identity** is any equation that equates two identically equal expressions.

To prove an identity, you have to show that the equation is true for all values of the variable for which both expressions are defined. Even before you prove an identity, however, you should convince yourself that the equation is indeed likely an identity.

> The basic rules of algebra include the commutative, associative, and distributive properties, along with the additive and multiplicative inverses and identities.

Here are two ways to gather evidence that an equation is an identity.

Try some numbers: The fastest way to prove an equation is not an identity is to provide a counterexample. Treat each side of the equation as a separate function. Choose several numbers to plug into each of the functions.

- If the outputs are different, you know the equation is not an identity.
- If the outputs are the same, you have some evidence that the expressions are identically equal.

Compare graphs: Graph each side of the equation as a separate function. If the two graphs look identical, you have good evidence that the equation may be an identity.

For You to Explore

1. For which values of x is the following equation true?
$$\sec^2 x + \csc^2 x = \sec^2 x \cdot \csc^2 x$$
   A. $x = \frac{3\pi}{4}$ **B.** $x = 115°$

   C. $x = \frac{2\pi}{7}$ **D.** all of the above

2. Find the pairs of expressions that are identically equal.

$\cos^4 x - \sin^4 x$	$\cot^2 x$	$\sin^3 x + \sin x \cos^2 x$
$\sin(-x)$	$\cot x$	$\sec^2 x$
$1 + \tan^2 x$	$-\sin x$	$(\csc x + 1)(\csc x - 1)$
$\cos^2 x - \sin^2 x$	$\frac{\csc x}{\sec x}$	$\sin x$

3. Is this statement true? If so, explain why. If not, what changes to the statement will make it an identity? (Your answer should not be of the trivial form $A = A$.)
$$\frac{\cos x + 1}{\sin x} = \frac{\sin x}{\cos x - 1}$$

4. Sketch and describe the graph of $f(x) = \cos^3 x + \cos x \sin^2 x$.

5. Define the function $g(n) = n^2 + n + 41$ for whole-number values of n.

   a. Calculate $g(0)$ through $g(5)$, $g(10)$, and $g(20)$.

   b. The values of $g(0)$ through $g(5)$ are prime. Do you think $g(n)$ will be prime for all values of n? Explain your answer.

6. a. Sketch the graphs of $f(x) = \sin x \cos x$ and $g(x) = \sin 2x$ on the same axes.

   b. Is the equation $\sin x \cos x = \sin 2x$ an identity? Explain your answer.

7. One of these two equations is an identity, and the other is not.
$$(\tan x \sin x)^2 = (\tan x + \sin x)(\tan x - \sin x)$$
$$\sin^2 x + \cos^2 x \csc x = \csc x$$

   a. Pick a value for x and test it in each equation.

   b. Which equation is the identity?

8. What's Wrong Here? Candace thinks the equation $\cos 13x = \cos x$ is an identity.

Candace says, "I decided to test some values. I tried 0 and it worked, I tried $\frac{\pi}{6}$ and it worked, I tried $\frac{\pi}{2}$ and it worked. I even tried $\frac{7\pi}{6}$, and *that* worked! So, I'm convinced, it's an identity."

Help Candace see why this equation is not an identity.

9. a. On the same axes, sketch the graphs of $f(x) = \sin\left(x + \frac{\pi}{3}\right)$ and $g(x) = \cos\left(x - \frac{\pi}{6}\right)$. How do the two graphs compare?

   b. Must the equation
$$\sin\left(x + \frac{\pi}{3}\right) = \cos\left(x - \frac{\pi}{6}\right)$$
   be an identity, according to these graphs?

10. Take It Further Candace found several values of x that make $\cos 13x = \cos x$. Find the total number of values of x with $0 \le x < 2\pi$ that make $\cos 13x = \cos x$.

Exercises *Practicing Habits of Mind*

On Your Own

11. Simplify the following product.
$$(\csc^2 x - 1)(\sec^2 x - 1)$$

   A. $\sin x$ **B.** $\tan^2 x$ **C.** $\sec^4 x$ **D.** 1

12. a. Sketch graphs of $f(x) = \sin x$ and $g(x) = \cos x$ on $-2\pi \le x \le 2\pi$.

   b. Use the graph of f to demonstrate that $\sin(-x) = -\sin x$.

   c. Use the graph of g to demonstrate an identity involving $\cos(-x)$.

> **Remember...**
> Sine is an odd function. Cosine is an even function.

13. Find the pairs of expressions that are identically equal.

$$\sin^4 x - \cos^4 x \qquad \tan^2 x \qquad -\cos^3 x - \cos x \sin^2 x$$
$$\cos(-x) \qquad \tan x \qquad \csc^2 x$$
$$1 + \cot^2 x \qquad \cos x \qquad (\sec x + 1)(\sec x - 1)$$
$$\sin^2 x - \cos^2 x \qquad \frac{\sec x}{\csc x} \qquad -\cos x$$

14. Calculate the product $(\operatorname{cis} x)\left(\operatorname{cis} \frac{\pi}{4}\right)$ to show that

$$\sin\left(x + \frac{\pi}{4}\right) = \frac{\sqrt{2}}{2}(\sin x + \cos x)$$

15. Write this expression as a single trigonometric function of x.

$$\frac{\tan x}{(\sec x + 1)(\sec x - 1)}$$

16. One of these equations is an identity, and the other is not. Determine which equation is the identity by testing values for the variables.

$$\sin(x + y) + \sin(x - y) = 2\sin x \sin y$$
$$\cos(x + y) + \cos(x - y) = 2\cos x \cos y$$

17. Show that these three expressions are all equivalent.

$$\cos^2 x - \sin^2 x$$
$$2\cos^2 x - 1$$
$$1 - 2\sin^2 x$$

18. Find all values of x on the interval $0 \le x < 2\pi$ with $\cos^2 x - \sin^2 x = \frac{1}{2}$.

19. Find all values of x on the interval $0 \le x < 2\pi$ with $\cos^2 x - \sin^2 x = \sin x$.

20. Determine whether or not the equation, $\cos 5x = 2\cos x \cos 4x - \cos 3x$, is an identity. Explain your answer.

> **Remember...**
>
> Two expressions are *equivalent* if you can get from one expression to the other using the basic rules of algebra.

> Do not try to prove it, just decide whether or not you think it is an identity.

Maintain Your Skills

21. In Exercise 1, you may have found that $\sec^2 x + \csc^2 x = \sec^2 x \cdot \csc^2 x$. It is quite rare for two numbers to have the same sum and product.

   a. If $\sec^2 x = 3$, what is $\csc^2 x$?   **b.** If $\sec^2 x = 4$, what is $\csc^2 x$?

   c. If $\sec^2 x = 11$, what is $\csc^2 x$?

   d. If $\sec^2 x = A$, find a formula for $\csc^2 x$ in terms of A.

   e. **Take It Further** What is the smallest possible value of $\sec^2 x + \csc^2 x$? Explain your answer.

22. Simplify $\sin \frac{\pi}{7} + \sin \frac{2\pi}{7} + \sin \frac{3\pi}{7} + \sin \frac{-\pi}{7} + \sin \frac{-2\pi}{7} + \sin \frac{-3\pi}{7}$.

23. Simplify $\cos \frac{\pi}{2} + \cos \frac{\pi}{3} + \cos \frac{\pi}{4} + \cos \frac{-\pi}{4} + \cos \frac{-\pi}{3} + \cos \frac{-\pi}{2}$.

Recall Theorem 2.2, the Multiplication Law for complex numbers. If $z = r_1 \text{ cis } \alpha$ and $w = r_2 \text{ cis } \beta$, then

$$zw = (r_1 \text{ cis } \alpha)(r_2 \text{ cis } \beta) = r_1 r_2 \text{ cis } (\alpha + \beta)$$

If both z and w are on the unit circle, then $r_1 = r_2 = 1$ and you get a simpler expression.

$$zw = (\text{cis } \alpha)(\text{cis } \beta) = \text{cis } (\alpha + \beta)$$

In fact, the product of any two complex numbers on the unit circle will also be on the unit circle.

These facts about complex numbers will help you find many important trigonometric relationships, which involve real numbers only.

> Jacques Hadamard (1865–1963) said, "The shortest path between two truths in the real domain passes through the complex domain."

Developing Habits of Mind

Simplify complicated problems. There are two ways to go about building and proving identities for trigonometric functions.

- Cosine and sine are real-valued functions. They take a real input (like π) and they give you a real output (like $\sin \pi = 0$). You can study their relationships entirely in the real numbers without ever thinking about complex numbers at all. But when you try to prove many of these relationships with real numbers, you end up with long, tedious calculations—not exactly elegant mathematics.

- As you have seen in this chapter, you can use cosine and sine to describe coordinates of complex numbers on the unit circle. This relationship lets you use the properties of complex numbers to prove relationships involving cosine and sine. You can write a proof that could be 15 lines long using real numbers alone in only 1 or 2 lines using complex numbers.

> Cosine and sine are still real-valued functions. They take a real input (the argument of the complex number) and give real outputs (the x- and y-coordinates of the complex number).

You can build many identities involving cosines and sines with mathematical elegance by using complex numbers. You may want to try proving some of these identities with real numbers just to appreciate how nice it is to work with the complex numbers.

Example

Problem Write a formula for $\cos\left(x + \frac{\pi}{3}\right)$.

Solution From the Multiplication Law, you know that

$$\mathrm{cis}\left(x + \tfrac{\pi}{3}\right) = (\mathrm{cis}\,x)\left(\mathrm{cis}\,\tfrac{\pi}{3}\right)$$

From there, expand the cis notation.

$$(\mathrm{cis}\,x)\left(\mathrm{cis}\,\tfrac{\pi}{3}\right) = (\cos x + i\sin x)\left(\cos\tfrac{\pi}{3} + i\sin\tfrac{\pi}{3}\right)$$

$$= (\cos x + i\sin x)\left(\tfrac{1}{2} + \tfrac{\sqrt{3}}{2}i\right)$$

$$= \left(\tfrac{1}{2}\cos x - \tfrac{\sqrt{3}}{2}\sin x\right) + i\left(\tfrac{1}{2}\sin x + \tfrac{\sqrt{3}}{2}\cos x\right)$$

Since

$$\cos\left(x + \tfrac{\pi}{3}\right) + i\sin\left(x + \tfrac{\pi}{3}\right) = \left(\tfrac{1}{2}\cos x - \tfrac{\sqrt{3}}{2}\sin x\right)$$
$$+ i\left(\tfrac{1}{2}\sin x + \tfrac{\sqrt{3}}{2}\cos x\right)$$

then the real parts are equal, so

$$\cos\left(x + \tfrac{\pi}{3}\right) = \tfrac{1}{2}\cos x - \tfrac{\sqrt{3}}{2}\sin x$$

Likewise, the imaginary parts are also equal, so

$$\sin\left(x + \tfrac{\pi}{3}\right) = \tfrac{1}{2}\sin x + \tfrac{\sqrt{3}}{2}\cos x$$

For You to Do

1. Use the Multiplication Law to write a formula for $\sin(x + \pi)$.

The Multiplication Law makes it easy to prove two of the most useful trigonometric identities.

Theorem 2.3   *The Angle-Sum Formulas*

The following two equations are true for all values of α and β.

$$\cos(\alpha + \beta) = \cos\alpha\,\cos\beta - \sin\alpha\,\sin\beta$$
$$\sin(\alpha + \beta) = \sin\alpha\,\cos\beta + \cos\alpha\,\sin\beta$$

For practice with angle-sum identities, go to
Web Code: bge-9031

Proof
$$\mathrm{cis}(\alpha + \beta) = (\mathrm{cis}\,\alpha)(\mathrm{cis}\,\beta)$$
$$= (\cos\alpha + i\sin\alpha)(\cos\beta + i\sin\beta)$$
$$= (\cos\alpha\cos\beta + i^2\sin\alpha\sin\beta) + (i\sin\alpha\cos\beta + i\cos\alpha\sin\beta)$$
$$= (\cos\alpha\cos\beta - \sin\alpha\sin\beta) + i\,(\sin\alpha\cos\beta + \cos\alpha\sin\beta)$$

Recall that $a + bi = c + di \Leftrightarrow a = c$ and $b = d$. So if

$$\cos(\alpha + \beta) + i\sin(\alpha + \beta) = (\cos\alpha\cos\beta - \sin\alpha\sin\beta)$$
$$+ i(\sin\alpha\cos\beta + \cos\alpha\sin\beta)$$

then

$$\cos(\alpha + \beta) = \cos\alpha\cos\beta - \sin\alpha\sin\beta$$

and

$$\sin(\alpha + \beta) = \sin\alpha\cos\beta + \cos\alpha\sin\beta$$

The Angle-Sum Formulas lead directly to four more identities.

Corollary 2.3.1   The Angle-Difference Formulas

The following two equations are true for all values of α and β.

$$\cos(\alpha - \beta) = \cos\alpha\cos\beta + \sin\alpha\sin\beta$$
$$\sin(\alpha - \beta) = \sin\alpha\cos\beta - \cos\alpha\sin\beta$$

For You to Do

2. Prove the Angle-Difference Formulas.

Use the relationship
$\alpha - \beta = \alpha + (-\beta)$.

Corollary 2.3.2   The Double-Angle Formulas

The following two equations are true for all values of θ.

$$\cos 2\theta = \cos^2\theta - \sin^2\theta$$
$$\sin 2\theta = 2\sin\theta\cos\theta$$

For Discussion

3. a. If $z = \cos\theta + i\sin\theta$, show that

$$z^2 = (\cos^2\theta - \sin^2\theta) + (2\sin\theta\cos\theta)i$$

b. Explain how the result from part (a) leads to the Double-Angle Formulas.

Developing Habits of Mind

Prove a special case. Remember that corollaries are typically statements that follow directly from a previous theorem. In this case, the formulas for $\cos(\alpha - \beta)$, $\sin(\alpha - \beta)$, $\cos(2\theta)$, and $\sin(2\theta)$ all follow directly from the Angle-Sum Formulas for cosine and sine. You do not really have to memorize six formulas. You can quickly derive the Angle-Difference Formulas and the Double-Angle Formulas from the Angle-Sum Formulas.

In fact, you do not even need to memorize the Angle-Sum Formulas! The fact that

$$(\cos\alpha + i\sin\alpha)(\cos\beta + i\sin\beta) = \cos(\alpha + \beta) + i\sin(\alpha + \beta)$$

means you can always perform the arithmetic on the left side to rebuild the Angle-Sum Formulas. So here, you get six formulas for the price of one.

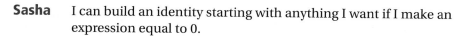

Minds in Action   episode 4

Sasha says she has a way of building identities.

Sasha   I can build an identity starting with anything I want if I make an expression equal to 0.

Derman What? How can you make something zero?

Sasha   I multiply what I start with by zero, then the product is zero.

Derman But if you multiply by zero, there won't be any expression to see! It'll just say "0".

Sasha   I will show you what I mean. Start with cosecant of x and multiply it by something equal to zero.

$$(\csc x)(\cos^2 x + \sin^2 x - 1) = 0$$

That's an identity. The left side is always zero, right?

Derman Well yeah, since $\cos^2 x + \sin^2 x = 1$.

Sasha   Now expand the left side.

$$\csc x \cos^2 x + \sin x - \csc x = 0$$

That's still an identity. If I know an equation is always true, I can use the basic rules to make new equations that are also always true. I can add csc x to each side to get another identity.

$$\csc x \cos^2 x + \sin x = \csc x$$

Derman Clever. Maybe they used your idea when writing this book.

For You to Do

4. Show how you can build the identity

$$2\cos x - 2\sec x + \sec^2 x = 1 + \tan^2 x - 2\sin x \tan x$$

by starting from the identity

$$(2\cos x - 1)(1 + \tan^2 x - \sec^2 x) = 0$$

Exercises Practicing Habits of Mind

Check Your Understanding

1. Find formulas for $\cos 3x$ and $\sin 3x$ in terms of $\cos x$ and $\sin x$.

2. **a.** Find two "nice" complex numbers that have a product with argument 75°.

   b. Use the complex numbers you found in part (a) to get exact values for $\cos 75°$ and $\sin 75°$.

   c. Find the value of $2 \sin 75° \cos 75°$.

3. **a.** Evaluate the product.
$$\left(\tfrac{3}{5} + \tfrac{4}{5}i \right)\left(\tfrac{12}{13} + \tfrac{5}{13}i \right)$$

   b. If α and β are in Quadrant I and $\cos \alpha = \tfrac{3}{5}$ and $\sin \beta = \tfrac{5}{13}$, find the value of $\sin (\alpha + \beta)$.

4. **a.** Show that this equation is an identity by using the Angle-Sum and Angle-Difference Formulas on the left side.
$$\cos (\alpha + \beta) + \cos (\alpha - \beta) = 2 \cos \alpha \cos \beta$$

   b. Determine a similar identity for $\sin (\alpha + \beta) + \sin (\alpha - \beta)$.

5. **Write About It** Use Sasha's method in episode 4 to write your own identity.

6. Write a formula for $\tan (\alpha + \beta)$ that includes only $\tan \alpha$ and $\tan \beta$.

7. **Take It Further** Determine formulas for $\cos (\alpha + \beta + \gamma)$ and $\sin (\alpha + \beta + \gamma)$. ($\gamma$ is the Greek letter *gamma*.)

Remember...

Arguments add, so you need to find two complex numbers with "nice" arguments that add to 75°.

On Your Own

8. **a.** Find the magnitude and argument of the complex number $\tfrac{\sqrt{2}}{2} + \tfrac{\sqrt{2}}{2} i$.

   b. Evaluate the product $(\cos x + i \sin x)\left(\tfrac{\sqrt{2}}{2} + \tfrac{\sqrt{2}}{2} i \right)$.

   c. Write a rule for $\cos \left(x + \tfrac{\pi}{4} \right)$ and for $\sin \left(x + \tfrac{\pi}{4} \right)$.

9. Use the Angle-Sum and Angle-Difference Formulas for cosine and sine to prove each of these identities.

   a. $\cos (x + \pi) = -\cos x$

   b. $\sin \left(\tfrac{\pi}{2} - x \right) = \cos x$

   c. $\cos \left(x + \tfrac{\pi}{2} \right) = -\sin x$

   d. $\cos (x + 2\pi) = \cos x$

   e. $\tan \left(x + \tfrac{\pi}{2} \right) = -\tfrac{1}{\tan x}$

   f. **Take It Further** Prove $\tan \left(x + \tfrac{\pi}{4} \right) = \tfrac{\cos x + \sin x}{\cos x - \sin x}$.

Go Online
PHSchool.com

For additional practice, go to **Web Code:** bga-0206

10. a. What do you get if you use the Angle-Difference Formula to expand the expression $\cos(x - x)$?

b. What is the value of $\cos(x - x)$?

11. a. Write a formula for $\tan 2x$ in terms of $\tan x$.

b. Write a formula for $\tan 3x$ in terms of $\tan x$.

12. Is this equation an identity? Justify your answer.

$$\cos 5x + \cos 3x = 2 \cos x \cos 4x$$

13. a. Calculate this product: $\left(\frac{2}{3} + \frac{\sqrt{5}}{3} i\right)\left(\frac{3}{4} + \frac{\sqrt{7}}{4} i\right)$

b. If α and β are in Quadrant I and $\cos \alpha = \frac{3}{5}$ and $\sin \beta = \frac{5}{13}$, find the value of $\cos(\alpha + \beta)$.

14. Verify the Angle-Difference Formulas by expanding this complex number multiplication.

$$(\cos \alpha + i \sin \alpha)(\cos(-\beta) + i \sin(-\beta))$$

15. Show that this equation is an identity.

$$\sin(\alpha + \beta) \sin(\alpha - \beta) = \sin^2 \alpha - \sin^2 \beta$$

16. Take it Further The Angle-Sum Formulas for cosine and sine show that, in general,

$$\cos(\alpha + \beta) \neq \cos \alpha + \cos \beta$$

Are the two expressions ever equal? Explain.

17. Standardized Test Prep Which of the following is equal to $\cos\left(x - \frac{\pi}{2}\right)$?

A. $\sin x$ **B.** $-\sin x$ **C.** $\cos^2 x - \sin^2 x$ **D.** $\cos\left(x + \frac{\pi}{2}\right)$

> **Habits of Mind**
>
> **Use facts you know.**
> First express $\tan 2x$ and $\tan 3x$ in terms of cosine and sine.

> Cosine is an even function, and sine is an odd function.

Maintain Your Skills

18. Suppose θ is the measure of an angle in Quadrant I.

a. If $\cos \theta = \cos 40° + \cos 80°$, find θ.

b. If $\cos \theta = \cos 50° + \cos 70°$, find θ.

c. If $\cos \theta = \cos 55° + \cos 65°$, find θ.

d. If $\cos \theta = \cos 57° + \cos 63°$, find θ.

e. Write a general rule suggested by the pattern above.

f. Use the identities from this lesson to prove your rule.

2.7 Proving Identities

In Chapter 1, you proved geometrically one of the key trigonometric identities, the Pythagorean identity.

$$\cos^2 x + \sin^2 x = 1$$

Two identities that follow directly from the one above are

$$1 + \tan^2 x = \sec^2 x \quad \text{and} \quad \cot^2 x + 1 = \csc^2 x$$

These two identities differ slightly from the first one since there are values of x where their expressions are not defined. But it is true that the two sides are equal wherever the expressions are defined.

One way to build these identities is to start with a known identity and then transform it using the basic rules of algebra. But how would you proceed if you wanted to consider

$$\csc x \cos^2 x + \sin x = \csc x$$

as a possible identity? A first step is to gather evidence to decide whether the equation might indeed be an identity. Lesson 2.5 suggested two ways to gather such evidence:

- substituting some values for x, and

- comparing graphs.

> You proved both of these identities in Chapter 1 as well. How do they relate to $\cos^2 x + \sin^2 x = 1$?

Example 1

Problem Determine whether $\cos\left(\frac{\pi}{2} - x\right) = \sin x$ is an identity.

Solution Gather some evidence.

- Try some values of x

  a. Let $x = 0$.

  $$\cos\left(\frac{\pi}{2} - 0\right) = \cos\frac{\pi}{2} = 0$$

  $$\sin 0 = 0$$

  The equation is true when $x = 0$.

  b. Let $x = \frac{\pi}{2}$.

  $$\cos\left(\frac{\pi}{2} - \frac{\pi}{2}\right) = \cos 0 = 1$$

  $$\sin\frac{\pi}{2} = 1$$

  The equation is true when $x = \frac{\pi}{2}$.

  c. Let $x = \pi$.

  $$\cos\left(\frac{\pi}{2} - \pi\right) = \cos\left(-\frac{\pi}{2}\right) = 0$$

  $$\sin \pi = 0$$

  The equation is true when $x = \pi$.

> Start by picking numbers for x that make the calculations easy. But be careful. Some expressions are equal for the "easy" numbers, but equal elsewhere.

These results support the idea that the equation is an identity.

- Graph $y = \cos\left(\frac{\pi}{2} - x\right)$ and $y = \sin x$.

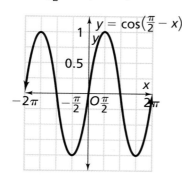 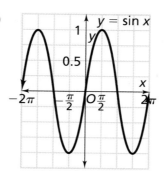

Always have the graphs of cosine and sine handy.

Both graphs look identical. If you graph them on the same axes on your calculator, they look like just one graph. So it is a good bet that the equation is an identity.

Keep in mind that evidence is not proof. Just because the two sides agree on lots of inputs and their graphs look the same, you cannot conclude that you have an identity. This first step can help you decide to try to prove the identity. But it does not constitute a proof.

One way to prove an identity is to use the basic rules of algebra, along with any other theorems you know, to transform one side of the equation into the other.

Minds in Action   episode 5

Tony and Derman are working to prove that $\cos\left(\frac{\pi}{2} - x\right) = \sin x$ is an identity.

Tony   I remember this identity from Geometry class.

Derman Of course, then we were only talking angles in triangles, and we worked with degrees.

Tony   Yeah, it was $\cos(90° - \theta) = \sin\theta$. The sine of an angle is equal to the cosine of its complement.

Derman Right, because the leg opposite one angle is the leg adjacent to the other one. But θ has values between $0°$ and $90°$, and we want to prove the identity for any value of x.

Tony   Well, we can use the Angle-Difference Formulas, right?

Derman Great idea.

After all, the *co* in *cosine* stands for *complement*.

Tony writes on his paper.

$$\cos(A - B) = \cos A \cos B + \sin A \sin B$$

$$\cos\left(\frac{\pi}{2} - x\right) = \cos\frac{\pi}{2}\cos x + \sin\frac{\pi}{2}\sin x$$

$$= 0 \cdot \cos x + 1 \cdot \sin x$$

$$= \sin x$$

Tony   And there it is!

For You to Do

1. Prove that the following equation is an identity.

$$\sin\left(x + \frac{\pi}{3}\right) = \cos\left(x - \frac{\pi}{6}\right)$$

You graphed the left and right sides of this identity in Exercise 9 of Lesson 2.5.

The idea of proving identities is to show that two expressions are identically equal. In other words, you can transform one expression to the other using

- the basic rules of algebra (the commutative, associative, and distributive properties, the additive and multiplicative identities, and additive and multiplicative inverses)
- substitution
- proven theorems

In the Minds in Action above, Tony started with one side of the identity, and showed each step he took to end up with the other side of the identity.

For some identities, like $\csc x \cos^2 x + \sin x = \csc x$, the steps may not be as apparent as in Tony's example. To prove this identity, treat it like an equation.

There are three types of equations: those with one solution, no solution, or those with all real numbers as a solution. Equations with all real numbers as a solution are identities. They are always true no matter the value of the variable.

You saw in Chapter 1 that you can solve trigonometric equations much as you do any other equations. In fact, if you try to solve a trigonometric equation and the resulting statement is always true, then the original equation is an identity.

You may find it easier to prove some trigonometric identities by trying to solve them as you would any equation, looking for an equation that you know is true. Make sure that each step you take is reversible.

There are many routes from Point A to Point B. Some are shorter while others are more scenic. Proving an identity is similar. The important thing is arriving at the goal.

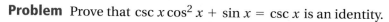

Example 2

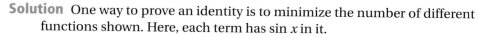

Problem Prove that $\csc x \cos^2 x + \sin x = \csc x$ is an identity.

Solution One way to prove an identity is to minimize the number of different functions shown. Here, each term has $\sin x$ in it.

$$\frac{1}{\sin x}(1 - \sin^2 x) + \sin x = \frac{1}{\sin x}$$

$$\frac{1 - \sin^2 x}{\sin x} + \frac{\sin^2 x}{\sin x} = \frac{1}{\sin x}$$

$$\frac{(1 - \sin^2 x) + \sin^2 x}{\sin x} = \frac{1}{\sin x}$$

$$\frac{1}{\sin x} = \frac{1}{\sin x} ✔$$

You may have recognized this identity. Sasha built it in Lesson 2.6. So another way to prove the identity is to reverse Sasha's steps. To show $\csc x \cos^2 x + \sin x = \csc x$, show $\csc x \cos^2 x + \sin x - \csc x = 0$.

You could make some progress by factoring out $\csc x$ from the expression on the left side, but the second term does not have a factor of $\csc x$. But notice that, since $\csc x = \frac{1}{\sin x}$, then $\csc x \sin x = 1$, so you can multiply the second term, $\sin x$, by $\sin x \csc x$.

$$\csc x \cos^2 x + \sin x - \csc x = 0$$

$$\csc x \cos^2 x + \sin x \sin x \csc x - \csc x = 0$$

$$\csc x \cos^2 x + \sin^2 x \csc x - \csc x = 0$$

$$\csc x(\cos^2 x + \sin^2 x - 1) = 0$$

$$\csc x \cdot 0 = 0$$

$$0 = 0 ✔$$

In each method, your steps are reversible, so you are done. Notice that the two methods are quite similar. In fact, you could combine ideas from both methods to write a very simple formal proof.

$$\csc x \cos^2 x + \sin x = \csc x \cos^2 x + \sin^2 x \csc x \qquad \text{(since } \sin x \csc x = 1\text{)}$$

$$= \csc x(\cos^2 x + \sin^2 x) \qquad \text{(by factoring out } \csc x\text{)}$$

$$= \csc x ✔ \qquad \text{(since } \cos^2 x + \sin^2 x = 1\text{)}$$

For You to Do

2. Prove that the following equation is an identity.

$$\frac{\sin^2 y}{1 - \cos y} - 1 = \cos y$$

Exercises *Practicing Habits of Mind*

Check Your Understanding

1. Prove each of these identities.

   a. $\tan^2 x \sin^2 x = \tan^2 x - \sin^2 x$ **b.** $\dfrac{\cos x}{1 - \sin x} = \dfrac{1 + \sin x}{\cos x}$

   c. $\cot^2 x \cos^2 x = \cot^2 x - \cos^2 x$ **d.** $\dfrac{\sin x}{1 - \cos x} = \dfrac{1 + \cos x}{\sin x}$

2. Only one of these two equations is an identity. Find and prove the identity.

   $$\cos 2x + 1 = \tfrac{1}{2} \cos^2 x$$
   $$\sin 2x + 1 = (\cos x + \sin x)^2$$

   > Use the identity from Exercise 4a in Lesson 2.6.

3. Prove this identity.

   $$\cos 5x = 2 \cos x \cos 4x - \cos 3x$$

4. Show that, for any integer $n > 1$,

   $$\cos((n + 1)x) = 2 \cos x \cos nx - \cos((n - 1)x)$$

   > Exercise 3 showed a specific case of this identity, with $n = 4$. Perhaps you could use the same method to prove this identity?

5. **a.** Show that this expression is equal to zero.

   $$(\sec x \sin x)^2 - (\sec x + 1)(\sec x - 1)$$

   b. Explain how to use the results from part (a) to justify this identity.

   $$(\sec x \sin x)^2 = (\sec x + 1)(\sec x - 1)$$

On Your Own

6. **a.** Show that you can use the result in Exercise 4 to get a formula for $\cos 2x$.

   $$\cos 2x = 2 \cos^2 x - 1$$

   b. Use the result in Exercise 4 to find a formula for $\cos 3x$.

7. One of these two equations is an identity. Find and prove the identity.

   $$\tan^2 x - \cos^2 x = (\sec x - \sin x)^2$$
   $$\tan^2 x - \sin^2 x = (\sec x - \cos x)^2$$

8. Provide explicit steps to transform the expression

$$\frac{1 - \tan x}{\sec x} + \frac{\sec x}{\tan x} \text{ into } \frac{1 + \tan x}{\sec x \tan x}$$

9. Peter has an idea for proving the identity

$$\frac{\sec x + 1}{\tan x} = \frac{\tan x}{\sec x - 1}$$

Peter says, "The right side of the identity has $\sec x - 1$ in the denominator. Maybe I should try to get $\sec x - 1$ in the denominator of the left side, too. I can do this by multiplying both the numerator and denominator of the left side by $\sec x - 1$, since that's the same thing as multiplying by 1."

a. Prove the identity using Peter's idea.

b. Use Peter's method to prove this identity.

$$\frac{\cot x}{\csc x - 1} = \frac{\csc x + 1}{\cot x}$$

10. Show that each of these equations is an identity.

a. $\sin 2x = \dfrac{2 \tan x}{1 + \tan^2 x}$　　**b.** $\cos 2x = \dfrac{1 - \tan^2 x}{1 + \tan^2 x}$

c. $\tan 2x = \dfrac{2 \tan x}{1 - \tan^2 x}$

It might help to rewrite $1 + \tan^2 x$ using an identity.

11. **Take It Further** Prove each of these identities.

a. $\cos^6 x + \sin^6 x = 3 \cos^4 x - 3 \cos^2 x + 1$

b. $\dfrac{1 + \cos x}{\sin x} = \dfrac{1 + \cos x + \sin x}{1 - \cos x + \sin x}$

12. **Standardized Test Prep** Which of the following equations is a trigonometric identity?

A. $\cos x + \sin x = 1$　　**B.** $\sin x = \sin (-x)$

C. $\cos x = \cos (-x)$　　**D.** $\sin^{-1} x = x$

Go Online
PHSchool.com

For additional practice, go to **Web Code:** bga-0207

Maintain Your Skills

13. Consider the identities from Exercise 10.

a. Let $\tan x = \dfrac{1}{2}$. Calculate the exact values of $\sin 2x$, $\cos 2x$, and $\tan 2x$.

b. Let $\tan x = \dfrac{2}{3}$. Calculate $\sin 2x$, $\cos 2x$, and $\tan 2x$.

c. Let $\tan x = \dfrac{1}{4}$. Calculate $\sin 2x$, $\cos 2x$, and $\tan 2x$.

d. Let $\tan x = \dfrac{3}{4}$. Calculate $\sin 2x$, $\cos 2x$, and $\tan 2x$.

e. Let $\tan x = \dfrac{m}{n}$. Calculate $\sin 2x$, $\cos 2x$, and $\tan 2x$ in terms of m and n.

Mathematical 2B Reflections

In this investigation, you used the Multiplication Law to prove the Angle-Sum Formulas. You used known identities to prove new trigonometric identities. The following questions will help you summarize what you have learned.

1. For which values of x is the following equation true?
$$\cos x - \cos^3 x = \cos x \sin^2 x$$

   A. $x = \frac{\pi}{3}$

   B. $x = \frac{4\pi}{3}$

   C. $x = \pi$

   D. all of the above

2. Find the pairs of expressions that are identically equal.

   $\csc^2 x$ $\cos x + \tan x \cdot \sin x$

   $(1 + \sin x)(1 - \sin x)$ $\cos^2 x$

   $1 + \cos^2 x \cdot \csc^2 x$ $\sec x$

3. **a.** Find the magnitude and argument of the complex number $\frac{1}{2} + \frac{\sqrt{3}}{2}i$.

   b. Multiply out the product $(\cos x + i \sin x)\left(\frac{1}{2} + \frac{\sqrt{3}}{2}i\right)$.

   c. Write a rule for $\cos\left(x + \frac{\pi}{3}\right)$ and another for $\sin\left(x + \frac{\pi}{3}\right)$.

4. Prove each of these identities.

   a. $\sin(x + \pi) = -\sin x$

   b. $\cos\left(\frac{\pi}{2} - x\right) = \sin x$

   c. $\cos(2\pi - x) = \cos x$

   d. $\sin(2\pi - x) = -\sin x$

5. One of these two equations is an identity and the other is not. Find and prove the identity.

   $(\cos x - \sin x)^2 = \cos 2x$ $(\cos x + \sin x)(\cos x - \sin x) = \cos 2x$

6. How can you test to see if an equation might be an identity?

7. How can you use complex numbers to find formulas for $\cos 2x$ and $\sin 2x$?

8. How can you use identities to prove other identities?

Vocabulary and Notation

In this investigation, you learned these terms. Make sure you understand what each one means and how to use it.

* **identically equal**
* **identity**

Beginning with the same set of materials, you might construct a car while your friend may build a house. Each is a personal expression. Just as two figures built with the same pieces can look quite dissimilar, two sides of a mathematical identity can look very different.

Go Online
PHSchool.com

For a mid-chapter test, go
to **Web Code:** bga-0252

Multiple Choice

1. Find $|4 - 2i|$.

   A. 2   **B.** $2\sqrt{5}$

   C. $2\sqrt{2}$ **D.** 6

2. Let $|z| = 2$ and $\arg(z) = \frac{3\pi}{2}$. Write z without using trigonometric functions.

   A. $-1 + i\sqrt{3}$ **B.** $\sqrt{3} + i$

   C. $-2i$ **D.** 2

3. If $z = -2 + i$, then find $\arg(z)$ to two decimal places (in radians).

   A. -0.46 **B.** 2.68

   C. 3.61   **D.** 153.43

4. If the magnitude of z is 4 and the magnitude of w is 9, find the magnitude of zw.

   A. 5   **B.** 6

   C. 13   **D.** 36

5. Simplify $\sin(x + \pi)$.

   A. $\sin x$ **B.** $\cos x$

   C. $-\sin x$ **D.** $-\cos x$

Open Response

6. Let z and w have the following values.
$$z = 3 - 4i$$
$$w = 2 + 2i$$

   a. In the complex plane, graph and label z, w, and zw.

   b. Copy and complete the table.

	a + bi	Magnitude	Direction (in radians)
z	3 − 4i	▦	▦
w	2 + 2i	▦	▦
zw	▦	▦	▦

   c. Write w in polar form.

7. Let z and w be complex numbers, with $|z| = 2$, $\arg(z) = 80°$, $|w| = 4$, and $\arg(w) = 200°$.

   a. Find zw

   b. Find z^2

   c. Find w^4

   d. Write z in rectangular form.

8. One of these two equations is an identity, and the other is not. Determine which equation is the identity by finding a value for x that makes one of the equations false.
$$\sin x(1 - \cos x) = \sin x - \frac{1}{2}\sin 2x$$
$$\frac{(1 - \sin x)^2}{\cos x} = \tan x$$

9. Use the Angle-Sum Formulas to find each of the following.

   a. $\cos(x + 45°)$ **b.** $\sin(\pi - x)$

   c. $\cos\left(x - \frac{5\pi}{6}\right)$ **d.** $\sin\left(x + \frac{5\pi}{3}\right)$

10. Prove the identity.
$$\cos x - \cos^3 x = \tan^2 x \cdot \cos^3 x$$

11. Use geometry to calculate the product.
$$(1 - i\sqrt{3})(-3\sqrt{3} + 3i)$$

De Moivre's Theorem

Complex numbers are rooted in algebra, but once mathematicians like Gauss and Argand had the insight to represent complex numbers geometrically, the floodgates opened. Complex numbers permeated every part of mathematics. One of the most striking applications of complex numbers is to geometry. You have already seen how beautifully the addition and multiplication of complex numbers work on the complex plane, but that is just the beginning.

In *De Moivre's Theorem,* you will peek at one of the deepest connections between geometry and algebra. It is the connection between the roots of certain equations (equations of the form $x^n - 1 = 0$, where n is a positive integer) and regular polygons. This connection is sometimes called cyclotomy ("circle division") because regular polygons divide a circle into congruent pieces.

By the end of this investigation, you will be able to answer questions like these.

1. How do you use De Moivre's Theorem to write a rule for $\cos 3x$?

2. How can you connect roots of unity to regular polygons?

3. For what values of $\cos x$ does $\cos 3x = 0$?

You will learn how to

- calculate powers of complex numbers using De Moivre's Theorem

- understand the geometry of roots of unity, and the connection to roots of equations of the form $x^n - 1 = 0$

- find exact algebraic expressions for certain trigonometric values

You will develop these habits and skills:

- Calculate with complex numbers.

- Visualize complex numbers and their arithmetic.

The design of this skylight reflects the connection between the 18 roots of unity and a regular 18-gon.

2.8 Getting Started

Activating Prior Knowledge
Exploring New Ideas

There are n complex numbers that satisfy the equation $x^n - 1 = 0$. Each is known as an **nth root of unity.** To work with roots of unity, you will have to know how to find powers of complex numbers. The following problems will help you get started.

For You to Explore

1. Play the Factor Game! It is a game for two players.

The board is all the integers from 1 to 30.

1	2	3	4	5
6	7	8	9	10
11	12	13	14	15
16	17	18	19	20
21	22	23	24	25
26	27	28	29	30

Here are the rules.

- Player 1 picks any available number on the board.
- Player 2 identifies all the remaining proper factors of that number.
- If there are no proper factors remaining on the board, Player 1 loses a turn and no points are scored.
- Remove from the board all numbers used in a turn.

In successive rounds, players alternate between picking the number and finding the factors.

Scoring.

- Player 1 scores points equal to the value of the number picked.
- For each proper factor identified, Player 2 scores points equal to the value of that factor.
- If there are no factors remaining on the board, Player 1 scores 0.
- **Bonus Points**. If Player 1 finds a factor that Player 2 missed, Player 1 scores points equal to the value of that factor.

a. Play the game a few times.

b. Describe some of the strategies a player could use in this game.

2. Find the 4 complex numbers that are solutions to the equation $x^4 - 1 = 0$. Plot them as points in the complex plane.

> For example, the proper factors of 18 are 1, 2, 3, 6, and 9.

> If the first pick is 18, that player earns 18 points while the opponent earns $1 + 2 + 3 + 6 + 9 = 21$ points. Not a great first pick!

3. Plot the first 10 powers of each complex number as points in the complex plane, starting with $z^0 = 1$.

a. $z = i$
b. $z = \frac{1}{2} + \frac{\sqrt{3}}{2}i$
c. $z = \frac{3}{5} + \frac{4}{5}i$

d. $z = \text{cis } 36°$
e. $z = 1 + i$
f. $z = \frac{1}{2} \text{ cis } \frac{\pi}{4}$

4. Describe the picture you get when you plot the powers of a complex number z (starting with z^0) given each condition.

a. $|z| = 1$
b. $|z| > 1$
c. $|z| < 1$

5. Calculate the sum

$$\sum_{k=0}^{3} \cos \frac{2\pi k}{4}$$

Remember...

You can use summation notation to describe the sum of terms. The general form is

$$\sum_{k=0}^{n} a_k = a_0 + a_1 + a_2 + \cdots + a_n$$

where k is the index variable, 0 is the starting value, and n is the final value.

6. Find the 3 complex numbers that are solutions to the equation $x^3 - 1 = 0$. Plot them as points in the complex plane.

7. Calculate the sum

$$\sum_{k=0}^{2} \sin \frac{2\pi k}{3}$$

8. Calculate the sum

$$\sum_{k=1}^{6} \cos \frac{2\pi k}{7}$$

Exercises *Practicing Habits of Mind*

On Your Own

9. For $z = \text{cis } 72°$, find each of the following.

a. $\arg(z^2)$
b. $\arg(z^3)$
c. $\arg(z^4)$
d. $\arg(z^5)$
e. $\arg(z^{10})$
f. $\arg(z^n)$

10. For each expression, write an equivalent expression that includes only $\cos x$ and $\sin x$.

a. $\cos (x + 90°)$

b. $\cos (x + x)$

c. Write $\cos 4x$ in terms of powers of $\cos x$ and $\sin x$.

d. Write $\cos 4x$ in terms of powers of $\cos x$ only.

> The identity
> $\sin 2x = 2 \sin x \cos x$
> might be helpful here.

11. The factorization of $x^6 - 1$ over $\mathbb{Z}$ is

$$x^6 - 1 = (x - 1)(x + 1)(x^2 - x + 1)(x^2 + x + 1)$$

a. Is $x^2 - 1$ a factor of $x^6 - 1$? Explain.

b. Is $x^3 - 1$ a factor of $x^6 - 1$? Explain.

c. Is $x^4 - 1$ a factor of $x^6 - 1$? Explain.

12. Find the two solutions to the equation $x^2 - 8x + 15 = 0$. Then find their sum and product.

13. Find the two solutions to the equation $x^2 - 8x + 17 = 0$. Then find their sum and product.

14. Find the five complex numbers that are solutions to the equation $x^5 - 1 = 0$. Approximate any decimal answers to four decimal places.

> See TI-Nspire Handbook on p. 704 for an example of how to solve using your calculator.

15. Plot the five complex numbers from Exercise 14 as points in the same complex plane. Compare the results to your results for Problems 2 and 6.

16. a. Approximate the value of $\cos 72°$ to four decimal places.

b. Approximate the value of $\cos \frac{4\pi}{5}$ to four decimal places.

c. Approximate the value of $\cos \frac{6\pi}{5}$ to four decimal places.

Maintain Your Skills

17. Calculate each sum.

a. $\displaystyle\sum_{k=0}^{3} \sin \frac{2\pi k}{4}$

b. $\displaystyle\sum_{k=0}^{5} \sin \frac{2\pi k}{6}$

c. $\displaystyle\sum_{k=0}^{5} \cos \frac{2\pi k}{6}$

d. $\displaystyle\sum_{k=0}^{7} \sin (45k)°$

e. $\displaystyle\sum_{k=0}^{7} \cos \frac{2\pi k}{8}$

2.9 Powers of Complex Numbers

In Lesson 2.4, you proved a theorem for the multiplication of complex numbers. A direct consequence to Theorem 2.2 lets you find a simpler way to take powers of complex numbers.

For Discussion

In Exercise 9 of Lesson 2.8, you looked at powers of $z = \text{cis } 72°$. One pattern you may have noticed is that the argument of each successive power was $72°$ greater than the argument of the argument of the previous one.

1. Use Theorem 2.2 to explain why $\arg(z^n) = n(\arg(z))$ for any $n \in \mathbb{Z}^+$.

"For any $n \in \mathbb{Z}^+$" means "for any number n contained in the positive integers."

When $|z| = 1$, you can use the statement above to determine exactly where z^n is in the complex plane. Since $|z| = 1$, $|z^n| = 1$, too. So,

$$z^n = \text{cis } \theta$$

Now the only question is, what is θ? The result stated in the discussion above suggests that $\theta = n(\arg(z))$. Theorem 2.4, first published by Abraham de Moivre (1667–1754), summarizes these ideas.

Theorem 2.4 De Moivre's Theorem

For all real θ, $(\text{cis } \theta)^n = \text{cis } n\theta$.

The argument outlined above should help you see why De Moivre's Theorem is true, but is not a solid proof.

You can use these ideas here to make a proof by induction.

Proof The proof is a repeated application of Theorem 2.2. As a first step, Theorem 2.2 states that

$$(\text{cis } \theta)(\text{cis } \alpha) = \text{cis } (\theta + \alpha)$$

So,

$$\begin{aligned}
(\text{cis } \theta)^2 &= (\text{cis } \theta)(\text{cis } \theta) \\
&= \text{cis } (\theta + \theta) \\
&= \text{cis } 2\theta
\end{aligned}$$

Similarly,

$$\begin{aligned}
(\text{cis } \theta)^2 &= (\text{cis } \theta)(\text{cis } \theta)^2 \\
&= (\text{cis } \theta)(\text{cis } 2\theta) \\
&= \text{cis } (\theta + 2\theta) \\
&= \text{cis } 3\theta
\end{aligned}$$

If you keep doing this for n steps, you have

$$\begin{aligned}
(\text{cis } \theta)^n &= (\text{cis } \theta)(\text{cis } \theta)^{n-1} \\
&= (\text{cis } \theta)(\text{cis } (n-1)\theta) \\
&= \text{cis } (\theta + (n-1)\theta) \\
&= \text{cis } n\theta
\end{aligned}$$

In Chapter 4, you will formalize and streamline this "Keep up the good work" style of proof.

De Moivre's Theorem as stated here applies only to complex numbers that fall on the unit circle. But you can generalize the theorem to include any complex number.

Corollary 2.4.1

For all real θ, $(r\,\text{cis}\,\theta)^n = r^n\text{cis}\,n\theta$.

For You to Do

2. Prove Corollary 2.4.1.

You can use De Moivre's Theorem and Corollary 2.4.1 to solve equations that involve complex numbers.

Example

Problem Find all three solutions to the equation $x^3 = 8i$.

Solution To solve this equation, first write $8i$ in "$r\,\text{cis}\,\theta$" format. Since $i = \text{cis}\,\frac{\pi}{2}$, $8i = 8\,\text{cis}\,\frac{\pi}{2}$.

Now, suppose $x = a\,\text{cis}\,\alpha$. Then you have $(a\,\text{cis}\,\alpha)^3 = 8\,\text{cis}\,\frac{\pi}{2}$. By Corollary 2.4.1, $a^3\,\text{cis}\,3\alpha = 8\,\text{cis}\,\frac{\pi}{2}$.

From there, you can say that $a^3 = 8$, so $a = 2$ since a must be a real number.

Also, you have $3\alpha = \frac{\pi}{2}$. So $\alpha = \frac{\pi}{6}$.

But recall that when you are solving for radians, you also have to consider $3\alpha = \frac{\pi}{2} + 2\pi k$ for integer values of k.

$$3\alpha = \frac{\pi}{2} + 2\pi k$$

$$\alpha = \frac{\pi}{6} + \frac{2\pi}{3}k$$

For $k = 0$, 1, and 2, you get $\alpha = \frac{\pi}{6}, \frac{5\pi}{6}$, and $\frac{3\pi}{2}$, respectively. Any other value for k gives an α value that differs from one of these three by a multiple of 2π. Since $\text{cis}\,(\alpha + 2\pi) = \text{cis}\,\alpha$, the three solutions of the equation are $x = 2\,\text{cis}\,\frac{\pi}{6}$, $x = 2\,\text{cis}\,\frac{5\pi}{6}$, and $x = 2\,\text{cis}\,\frac{3\pi}{2}$.

> In fact, in addition to $a = 2$, there are two other possible solutions to $a^3 = 8$. They are both complex numbers: $2\,\text{cis}\,\frac{2\pi}{3}$ and $2\,\text{cis}\,\frac{4\pi}{3}$.

For You to Do

3. Find all four solutions to the equation $x^4 = -16$.

Exercises Practicing Habits of Mind

Check Your Understanding

1. Let z be a complex number where $|z| = 3$ and $\arg(z) = \frac{\pi}{3}$. Find the magnitude and argument of each of the following expressions.

   a. z^2 **b.** z^3 **c.** z^5

   d. $10z$ **e.** z^0 **f.** z^{-1}

2. Suppose $z = 3 \operatorname{cis} \frac{\pi}{3}$ as in Exercise 1. If $a^2 = z$, what possible value(s) can a have?

3. Given each z, find $|z^3|$ and $\arg(z^3)$.

   a. $z = 4$ **b.** $z = 4 \operatorname{cis} 120°$

   c. $|z| = 2$ and $\arg(z) = \frac{\pi}{6}$ **d.** $z = -2i$

4. In the Example, you found three solutions to the equation $x^3 = 8i$. Find their sum and product.

5. Suppose a is a solution to the equation $x^{11} = 1$.

   a. Show that a^2 is also a solution to this equation.

   b. Show that if k is any integer, then a^k is also a solution to this equation.

On Your Own

6. Find the three solutions to the equation $x^3 + 2x^2 - 80x - 160 = 0$. Then find their sum and product.

   > One way to find the solutions is to look at the graph of $f(x) = x^3 + 2x^2 - 80x - 160$. What points on the graph correspond to solutions to the equation?

7. Expand $(\cos\theta + i\sin\theta)^2$. Use the result to generate rules for $\cos 2\theta$ and $\sin 2\theta$.

8. Find a formula for $\cos 5x$ in terms of $\cos x$ and $\sin x$.

9. Describe how to use De Moivre's Theorem to prove this fact about powers of -1.

   For integer n, $(-1)^n = -1$ if n is odd and $(-1)^n = 1$ if n is even.

10. **Write About It** Describe how to use De Moivre's Theorem to figure out whether a power of i equals i, $-i$, 1, or -1.

    > What are $|i|$ and $\arg(i)$?

11. Given the equation $x^5 - 1 = 0$, one possible solution is $x = 1$.

    a. Show that $x = \operatorname{cis} \frac{2\pi}{5}$ is also a solution to the equation $x^5 - 1 = 0$.

    b. Find all five solutions to $x^5 - 1 = 0$.

12. a. Sketch the graph of $f(x) = 4\cos^3 x - 3\cos x$ on $0 \le x < 2\pi$.

   b. Suppose $g(x) = \cos 3x$. Show that $f = g$.

13. a. Suppose $\cos 3x = 0$. What are the three possible values of $\cos x$?

   b. Find all angles on $0 \le x < 2\pi$ with $\cos 3x = 0$.

14. Find the exact value of $\cos \frac{\pi}{12}$.

15. Standardized Test Prep Which of the following is a solution to the equation $x^2 = i$?

   A. $\text{cis}\left(\frac{\pi}{6}\right)$ **B.** $\text{cis}\left(\frac{\pi}{4}\right)$ **C.** $\text{cis}\left(\frac{\pi}{3}\right)$ **D.** $\text{cis}\left(\frac{\pi}{2}\right)$

![Maintain Your Skills]

Go Online
PHSchool.com

For additional practice, go to **Web Code:** bga-0209

16. Solve each equation. Write the complete set of solutions in the form cis θ.

   a. $x^2 - 1 = 0$ **b.** $x^3 - 1 = 0$ **c.** $x^4 - 1 = 0$

   d. $x^5 - 1 = 0$ **e.** $x^6 - 1 = 0$ **f.** $x^7 - 1 = 0$

17. Approximate each sum to four decimal places.

   a. $\sum_{k=0}^{6} \sin \frac{2\pi k}{7}$ **b.** $\sum_{k=0}^{6} \cos \frac{2\pi k}{7}$ **c.** $\sum_{k=0}^{6} \cos \frac{4\pi k}{7}$

   d. $\sum_{k=0}^{8} \sin \frac{2\pi k}{9}$ **e.** $\sum_{k=0}^{8} \cos (40k)°$ **f.** $\sum_{k=0}^{10} \cos \frac{2\pi k}{12}$

Historical Perspective

Mathematicians now recognize Abraham de Moivre (1667–1754) as a genius, but this was not always the case. Despite de Moivre's mathematical talent, he did not enjoy the fame he deserved during his lifetime.

When he was 18, de Moivre moved to England because of civil and religious unrest in France. Although he had studied mathematics extensively in France, he was unable to get a job in an English university due to his status as a foreigner.

For most of his life, de Moivre's main source of income was tutoring mathematics. In his later years, he earned money by solving math puzzles in local coffee shops. He is remembered for predicting the day of his own death. He noticed he was sleeping 15 minutes longer each night and calculated he would die on the day he slept 24 hours. He was correct!

2.10 Roots of Unity

In Lesson 2.8, you played the Factor Game. Now, it is time to play the Polynomial Factor Game!

In-Class Experiment

The Polynomial Factor Game. This game is also for two players. The rules are similar to those of the Factor Game. Decide who goes first.

- Player 1 picks any available polynomial on the board.
- Player 2 identifies all polynomials on the board that are factors of that polynomial.
- If there are no factors of that polynomial remaining on the board, Player 1 loses a turn and no points are scored.
- All polynomials used in a turn are removed from the board.

For each successive round, players alternate between picking the polynomial and finding the factors.

Scoring.

- Player 1 scores points equal to the degree of the polynomial picked.
- For each factor identified, Player 2 scores points equal to the degree of that factor.
- **Bonus Points.** If Player 1 finds a factor that Player 2 missed, Player 1 scores points equal to the degree of that factor.

For example, $x - 1$ is a factor of $x^2 - 1$. So if the first pick was $x^2 - 1$, that player earns 2 points while the other player earns 1.

The board is polynomials of the form $x^n - 1$ for all integer values from 1 to a set maximum. 20 is a good maximum for this game.

$x - 1$	$x^2 - 1$	$x^3 - 1$	$x^4 - 1$	$x^5 - 1$
$x^6 - 1$	$x^7 - 1$	$x^8 - 1$	$x^9 - 1$	$x^{10} - 1$
$x^{11} - 1$	$x^{12} - 1$	$x^{13} - 1$	$x^{14} - 1$	$x^{15} - 1$
$x^{16} - 1$	$x^{17} - 1$	$x^{18} - 1$	$x^{19} - 1$	$x^{20} - 1$

For a longer game, you could use 30 as you did in the Factor Game.

Play the game a few times.

1. Describe some of the strategies a player could use in this game.

2. Compare strategies in this game with those from the Factor Game you played in Lesson 2.8.

In an earlier algebra course, you learned an important theorem regarding factors of polynomials.

Theorem 2.5 *The Factor Theorem*

Suppose $f(x)$ is a polynomial. Then $x - a$ is a factor of $f(x)$ if and only if the number a is a root of the equation $f(x) = 0$.

One strategy for finding factors in the Polynomial Factor Game is to find polynomials that have the same roots as the polynomial that the other player picked. That is, $x^n - 1$ is a factor of $x^m - 1$ if and only if every root of $x^n - 1 = 0$ is also a root of $x^m - 1 = 0$.

But what are the roots of those polynomials? You can use De Moivre's Theorem to find them. You can use geometry to get a visual idea of where those roots lie on the complex plane.

For You to Do

3. Find and plot the three roots of the equation $x^3 - 1 = 0$.

4. Find and plot the six roots of the equation $x^6 - 1 = 0$.

For Discussion

5. Explain how the results from Problems 3 and 4 show that $x^3 - 1$ is a factor of $x^6 - 1$.

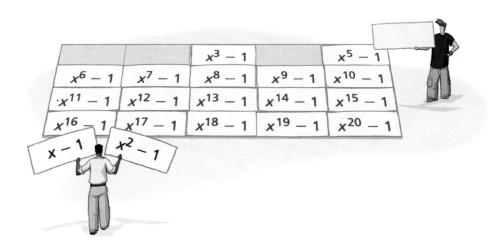

Find another way. As you saw in Lesson 2.9, you can use De Moivre's Theorem to find the roots of an equation. There is a more direct way to find all of the roots to equations of the form $x^n - 1 = 0$.

For instance, in Exercise 5 from Lesson 2.9, you supposed a was a solution of $x^{11} - 1 = 0$, and showed that a^2 was also a solution.

This fact can help you find all of the solutions to $x^{11} - 1 = 0$.

- One solution is $x = 1$, since $1^{11} = 1$.

- $x^{11} - 1 = 0 \Rightarrow x^{11} = 1$. You can find a second solution by letting $x = r \operatorname{cis} \theta$. Since $1 = \operatorname{cis} 2\pi$ you have

$$(r \operatorname{cis} \theta)^{11} = 1 \operatorname{cis} 2\pi$$
$$r^{11} \operatorname{cis} 11\theta = 1 \operatorname{cis} 2\pi$$
$$r^{11} = 1 \quad \text{and} \quad 11\theta = 2\pi$$
$$r = 1 \quad \text{and} \quad \theta = \frac{2\pi}{11}$$

So $\operatorname{cis} \frac{2\pi}{11}$ is also a solution.

- You know that if a is a solution, then a^2 is also a solution. Therefore $\left(\operatorname{cis} \frac{2\pi}{11} \right)^2$ is a solution. By De Moivre's Theorem,

$$\left(\operatorname{cis} \frac{2\pi}{11} \right)^2 = \operatorname{cis} \left(2 \cdot \frac{2\pi}{11} \right) = \operatorname{cis} \frac{4\pi}{11}$$

- In fact, any power of a is a solution because

$$(a^k)^{11} = (a^{11})^k = 1^k = 1$$

So, if $a = \operatorname{cis} \frac{2\pi}{11}$, then all of the following are solutions to $x^{11} - 1 = 0$.

$$1, a, a^2, a^3, a^4, a^5, a^6, a^7, a^8, a^9, a^{10}, a^{11}, a^{12}, a^{13}, \ldots$$

It looks like there are too many solutions. There should only be eleven. But if you plot all these on the complex plane, they repeat. For example, $a^{11} = 1$, $a^{12} = a$, $a^{13} = a^2$, and so on. There are, in fact, only eleven solutions. They are $1, a, a^2, a^3, a^4, a^5, a^6, a^7, a^8, a^9$, and a^{10}.

By De Moivre's Theorem, $a^k = \operatorname{cis} \frac{2k\pi}{11}$, since $a = \operatorname{cis} \frac{2\pi}{11}$. Thus, the complete solution set is

$$\left\{ 1, \operatorname{cis} \frac{2\pi}{11}, \operatorname{cis} \frac{4\pi}{11}, \operatorname{cis} \frac{6\pi}{11}, \operatorname{cis} \frac{8\pi}{11}, \operatorname{cis} \frac{10\pi}{11}, \operatorname{cis} \frac{12\pi}{11}, \operatorname{cis} \frac{14\pi}{11}, \operatorname{cis} \frac{16\pi}{11}, \right.$$
$$\left. \operatorname{cis} \frac{18\pi}{11}, \operatorname{cis} \frac{20\pi}{11} \right\}$$

The solutions to $x^n = 1$ are called roots of unity, so named since solving the equation involves taking a root of 1.

- A square root of unity is a root of the equation $x^2 - 1 = 0$.

- A cube root of unity is a root of the equation $x^3 - 1 = 0$.

- In general, an nth root of unity is a root of the equation $x^n - 1 = 0$.

Habits of Mind

Draw a diagram. As you work through these roots, plot each one on the complex plane.

Remember...

$A \Rightarrow B$ means "A implies B": if A is true then B is true.

So, 1 is considered "unity." And in $\mathbb{C}$, there are 2 second roots of unity, 3 third roots of unity, 4 fourth roots of unity, and in general, n nth roots of unity.

Exercises Practicing Habits of Mind

Check Your Understanding

1. Let ω be the fifth root of unity marked in this diagram.

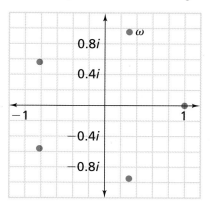

   a. Copy the diagram. Label ω^2, ω^3, ω^4, ω^5, ω^6, and ω^{13}.

   b. The product of all five fifth roots of unity is $1 \cdot \omega \cdot \omega^2 \cdot \omega^3 \cdot \omega^4$. Simplify this product as much as possible.

2. **a.** Calculate the sum of the sixth roots of unity.

   b. Evaluate the sum.

   $$\sum_{k=0}^{5} \sin \frac{2\pi k}{6}$$

   c. How are the results from parts (a) and (b) related?

3. Plot all 12 solutions to the equation $x^{12} - 1 = 0$ on the complex plane.

4. **a.** Plot all 6 solutions to the equation $x^6 - 1 = 0$ on the complex plane.

   b. Show that these 6 solutions are also solutions to the equation
   $x^{12} - 1 = 0$

   c. Show that $x^6 - 1$ is a factor of $x^{12} - 1$.

5. The fifth roots of unity appear in the diagram for Exercise 1. Find a value of n, with $n \neq 5$, such that every fifth root of unity is also an nth root of unity.

   > Your work in Exercise 3 may be helpful here.

6. Find the smallest positive integer n such that $w = \frac{1}{2} - \frac{\sqrt{3}}{2}i$ is an nth root of unity.

7. Suppose $z = \text{cis } 310°$. Can z be a root of unity? If so, find the smallest n such that z is an nth root of unity. If not, explain why z can never be a root of unity.

8. **Take It Further** Suppose z is a fifth root of unity and w is a third root of unity, as pictured.

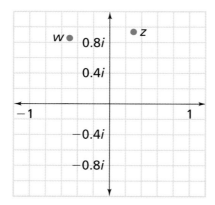

a. Find a root of unity x that lies between z and w on the unit circle.

b. Find a root of unity y that lies between z and x.

c. Given any two distinct roots of unity (of any order), can you always find another root of unity between them?

The answer might be a sixth root of unity, or seventh, or eighth. . . .

On Your Own

9. On the same axes, plot all the fifth roots of unity. Also, plot all the eighth roots of unity. Show how plotting these roots explains why $x^5 - 1$ is not a factor of $x^8 - 1$.

10. a. Find the product of all the sixth roots of unity.

b. Find the product of all the seventh roots of unity.

c. What are all possible values of the product of all the nth roots of unity? For what n do each of these results occur?

11. Describe how you can use the roots of $x^6 - 1 = 0$ to find the solutions to these equations.

a. $x^6 - 64 = 0$ b. $x^6 + 64 = 0$

Habits of Mind

Look for a pattern.
More examples may be helpful.

12. a. Calculate the sum of the eighth roots of unity.

b. Find the value of

$$\sum_{k=0}^{7} \cos \frac{2\pi k}{8}$$

c. How are the results from parts (a) and (b) related?

13. Complex number z is a ninth root of unity. Find all possible values for the magnitude and argument of z.

14. Write About It Roots of unity must lie on the unit circle. That is, they must be complex numbers with magnitude 1. Is every complex number with magnitude 1 a root of unity? Explain.

15. Suppose z is an nth root of unity.

a. Show that $\frac{1}{z} = \bar{z}$.

b. Show that $\bar{z}$ is also an nth root of unity.

16. Take It Further Consider the sixth roots of unity as labeled in this diagram.

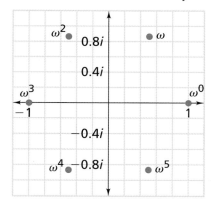

The product of all these roots is -1, but the product of the first three roots is 1.

$$\omega \cdot \omega^2 \cdot \omega^3 = \omega^6 = 1$$

a. Find another situation where the product of the first k nth roots of unity is 1, with k less than $n - 1$.

b. For what values of n will this situation occur? In other words, for what n is there a k such that the product of the first k nth roots of unity is 1 (with $k < n - 1$)?

17. Take It Further Suppose that a is an nth root of unity, and n is odd.

   a. Prove that one of the roots of $x^2 - a = 0$ is an nth root of unity.

   b. Why is this false when n is even?

18. Some roots of unity are repeats. For example, the cube roots of unity (solutions to $x^3 - 1 = 0$) are also sixth roots of unity (solutions to $x^6 - 1 = 0$). And $x = 1$ is always an nth root of unity, for any n. But some roots of unity are "new" for that power. For example, i and $-i$ are solutions to $x^4 - 1 = 0$, but not $x^3 - 1 = 0$, $x^2 - 1 = 0$, or $x^1 - 1 = 0$.

   a. Copy and complete this table with the number of new roots of unity for each equation. It may help to think of the solutions in terms of their argument.

Equation	# New Roots
$x - 1 = 0$	1
$x^2 - 1 = 0$	1
$x^3 - 1 = 0$	2
$x^4 - 1 = 0$	2
$x^5 - 1 = 0$	▪
$x^6 - 1 = 0$	▪
$x^7 - 1 = 0$	▪
$x^8 - 1 = 0$	▪
$x^9 - 1 = 0$	▪
$x^{10} - 1 = 0$	▪

   b. Describe any relationships you notice in the table. State a rule for the number of new roots of unity in terms of n.

19. Standardized Test Prep Which of the following is a factor of $x^5 - 1$?

   A. $x^4 + x^3 + x^2 + x + 1$ **B.** $x - 5$

   C. $x + 1$ **D.** $x^4 - 1$

Go **O**nline
PHSchool.com

For additional practice, go to **Web Code:** bga-0210

Maintain Your Skills

20. Evalute each sum based on what you know about roots of unity.

   a. $\displaystyle\sum_{k=0}^{2} \sin\frac{2\pi k}{4}$ **b.** $\displaystyle\sum_{k=0}^{4} \cos\frac{2\pi k}{6}$ **c.** $\displaystyle\sum_{k=0}^{4} \sin\frac{2\pi k}{6}$ **d.** $\displaystyle\sum_{k=1}^{4} \cos\frac{2\pi k}{5}$

138   **Chapter 2**   Complex Numbers and Trigonometry

Geometry of Roots of Unity

Your work in previous lessons revealed interesting geometric patterns generated by powers of complex numbers. For instance, suppose $z = \operatorname{cis} \frac{2\pi}{3}$. If you plot z^0, z^1, and z^2, you get the following picture.

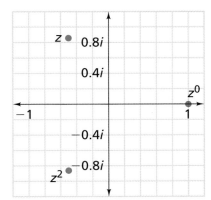

> You may recognize these numbers. They are the third roots of unity.

For You to Do

1. Prove that the three roots of $x^3 - 1 = 0$ form the vertices of an equilateral triangle.

The roots of $x^3 - 1 = 0$ and the equilateral triangle they form exemplify the remarkable connection between the algebra of $\mathbb{C}$ and the geometry of regular polygons. The following theorem generalizes this fact. It also summarizes much of the work so far in this investigation.

Theorem 2.6

If n is a positive integer, the roots of the equation

$$x^n - 1 = 0$$

are

$$1, z, z^2, z^3, \ldots, z^{n-1}$$

where

$$z = \operatorname{cis} \frac{2\pi}{n}$$

If $n \geq 3$, these roots lie on the vertices of a regular n-gon inscribed in the unit circle in the complex plane.

> One vertex of this polygon is at 1.

For You to Do

2. Prove Theorem 2.6.

You can use the theorem in two ways. If you know a simple form for the vertices of a regular n-gon in the complex plane, you can solve the equation $x^n - 1 = 0$. Conversely, if you can solve the equation, you have a simple form for the vertices of the polygon in the complex plane.

In the case $n = 5$, Theorem 2.6 says that the roots of $x^5 - 1 = 0$ are

$$1, z, z^2, z^3, z^4$$

where

$$z = \operatorname{cis} \frac{2\pi}{5}$$

These roots lie on the vertices of a regular pentagon inscribed in the unit circle on the complex plane.

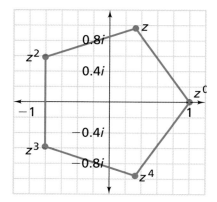

Carl Friedrich Gauss (1777–1855) was one of the greatest mathematicians of all time. He was so proud of his regular 17-sided polygon construction that he wanted it to appear on his tombstone!

Suppose you wanted exact expressions for these five roots that do not involve trigonometric functions. That is, can you express $\cos \frac{2\pi}{5}$ and $\sin \frac{2\pi}{5}$ in an algebraic form?

Earlier, you broke down angles into sums of special angles in order to use the Angle-Sum Formulas. This helped you find algebraic values of cosine and sine. For instance:

$$\cos \frac{5\pi}{12} = \cos\left(\frac{\pi}{6} + \frac{\pi}{4}\right)$$

Unfortunately, there are no convenient angles that sum to $\frac{2\pi}{5}$. But Gauss invented a method using the algebra of this problem—he focused on the roots of the equation $x^5 - 1 = 0$. Gauss started by finding as many relationships as possible among the roots. Such relationships can often be inspired by looking at the roots as vertices of a regular pentagon.

In the exercises, you will work through his method for finding the roots of $x^5 - 1 = 0$ written in the form $a + bi$, where a and b are exact, algebraic expressions.

Gauss applied the method to higher degrees. He handled the degree 17 case when he was 19 years old!

Exercises Practicing Habits of Mind

Check Your Understanding

1. Suppose $w = \text{cis } 20°$. The powers of w form the vertices of a regular polygon in the complex plane. What is the smallest number of sides that this polygon can have?

2. The graph below shows the plot of the powers (from 0 to 20) of $z = \text{cis } 17°$.

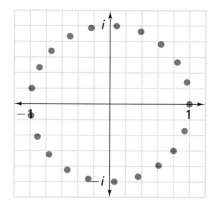

   a. Why are these powers of z not vertices of a regular polygon?

   b. Will the powers of z ever come back to 1? If so, how many times around the unit circle will it take? If not, why not?

   c. Describe all the values of θ for which the powers of $z = \text{cis } \theta$ are vertices of a regular polygon.

z^{21} does not quite make it all the way around. z^{22} would be back in the first quadrant.

For Exercises 3–7, let $z = \text{cis}\,\frac{2\pi}{5}$, one of the roots of $x^5 - 1 = 0$.

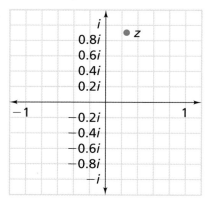

3. a. Show that $z^4 = \text{cis}\left(-\frac{2\pi}{5}\right)$.

   b. Show that $z + z^4 = 2\cos\frac{2\pi}{5}$.

4. a. Factor the expression $x^5 - 1$ into two terms.

   b. Show that $z^4 + z^3 + z^2 + z = -1$.

5. Let $a = z + z^4$ and $b = z^2 + z^3$.

   a. Explain why a is a positive real number, and b is a negative real number.

   b. Show that $a + b = -1$ using the result from Exercise 4b.

   c. Write the product ab in terms of z.

   d. Show that $ab = -1$.

6. In Exercise 5 you showed that a and b are two numbers that have a sum of -1 and a product of -1. Find exact values for a and b, given that a is positive and b is negative.

7. In Exercise 3, you found that $z + z^4 = 2\cos\frac{2\pi}{5}$.

   a. Find an exact expression for $\cos\frac{2\pi}{5}$ that does not use trigonometric functions.

   b. **Take It Further** Find an exact expression for $\sin\frac{2\pi}{5}$.

   c. **Take It Further** Write algebraic expressions for each of the roots of $x^5 - 1 = 0$ that do not involve cosine and sine.

8. Take It Further Let $\phi = \frac{1 + \sqrt{5}}{2}$. Show that the polynomial $x^5 - 1$ factors over $\mathbb{R}$ as

$$x^5 - 1 = (x - 1)(x^2 + \phi x + 1)\left(x^2 - \frac{1}{\phi}x + 1\right)$$

> **Remember...**
> z is the fifth root of unity in Quadrant I.

> **Remember...**
> The number
> $\phi = \frac{1 + \sqrt{5}}{2}$ is the
> *golden ratio*. (ϕ is the Greek letter *phi*, pronounced "fie" or "fee.")

9. Let $w = \text{cis}\, 12°$. The powers of w form the vertices of a regular polygon in the complex plane. How many sides does this polygon have?

Exercises 10–13 refer to this isosceles triangle, with each base angle measuring $72°$.

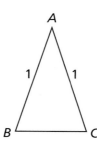

The congruent sides of the triangle have length 1.

10. Show that the third side length is $q = 2 \cos 72°$.

11. Draw $\overline{BD}$ bisecting angle ABC.

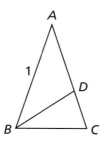

Go Online
PHSchool.com

For additional practice, go to **Web Code: bga-0211**

Show that triangle ABC is similar to triangle BCD.

12. Use the result from Exercise 11 to show the following.

a. $CD = q^2$

b. $CD = 1 - q$

13. a. Use the results from Exercise 12 to find the exact value of q without using trigonometric functions.

b. In Exercise 10 you found that $q = 2 \cos 72°$. Find the exact value of $\cos 72°$.

14. Find the exact value of $\cos 144°$.

15. Take It Further Prove the following statement.

In a regular pentagon, any diagonal drawn is exactly ϕ times as long as a side of the pentagon, where ϕ is the golden ratio $\frac{1 + \sqrt{5}}{2}$.

16. Standardized Test Prep The powers of $\text{cis}\left(\frac{3\pi}{7}\right)$ form the vertices of a regular polygon. How many sides does the polygon have?

A. 3   **B.** 7   **C.** 14   **D.** 21

17. Let $\cos \theta = 0.8$. Find the exact value of each of the following.

    a. $\cos 2\theta$

    b. $\cos 3\theta$

    c. $\cos 4\theta$

    d. $\cos 5\theta$

18. Let $z = 0.8 + 0.6i$. Calculate each of these powers of z.

    a. z^2

    b. z^3

    c. z^4

    d. z^5

19. Let $P(n, x)$ be a sequence of polynomial functions defined as follows.

$$P(n, x) = \begin{cases} 1 & \text{if } n = 0 \\ x & \text{if } n = 1 \\ 2x \cdot P(n - 1, x) - P(n - 2, x) & \text{if } n > 1 \end{cases}$$

> See TI-Nspire Handbook on p. 704 for help in defining this function on your calculator.

    a. Show that $P(0, x) = 1$ and $P(1, x) = x$.

    b. Show that $P(2, x) = 2x^2 - 1$.

    c. Show that $P(3, x) = 4x^3 - 3x$.

    d. Find $P(4, x)$ and $P(5, x)$.

    e. Let $x = 0.8$. Find $P(2, x)$, $P(3, x)$, $P(4, x)$, and $P(5, x)$.

Compare these slices of okra to the figure on p. 140. If you pay attention to detail, you will find that symmetrical patterns are common in the natural world.

Arithmetic With Roots of Unity

When you perform arithmetic with complex numbers, you likely treat expressions like $3 + 5i$ as "polynomials in i." You calculate with them using the basic rules of algebra. Then, you use one more simplification rule: you replace i^2 by -1. For example, you can reduce expressions like $3 + 2i + 4i^2 - i^3$ to something of the form $x + yi$ where x and y are real numbers.

For You to Do

1. Write $3 + 2i + 4i^2 - i^3$ in the form $x + yi$, where x and y are real numbers.

In fact, you can define the set of complex numbers by thinking of them as polynomials in i.

Definition

The set of **complex numbers** $\mathbb{C}$ consists of all expressions in the form $a + bi$ where:

- a and b are real numbers
- $i^2 = -1$
- Perform addition and multiplication as if $a + bi$ were a polynomial in i, using the new rule $i^2 = -1$.

Developing Habits of Mind

Recognize a similar process. When working on any new algebraic system, you often experiment with calculations by following the rules and practicing with examples. Eventually, the calculations begin to feel familiar, ultimately behaving like something you already know.

Working with complex numbers, they start to feel like polynomials with additional simplification rules. In fact, many algebraic systems work this way. In this lesson, you will look at examples where the new objects are expressions that involve roots of unity.

In Exercise 7 from Lesson 2.11, you found the exact value for $\cos\frac{2\pi}{5}$ by looking at the fifth roots of unity (roots of $x^5 - 1 = 0$). First, you grouped the nonreal roots into pairs, then you built a quadratic equation with one solution, $2\cos\frac{2\pi}{5}$. Following a similar technique, you can find exact values for cosines of other numbers using roots of unity. The equations will not be quadratic, but they will be polynomials.

Consider $\cos \frac{2\pi}{7}$. Does it satisfy an equation with real coefficients? You know from the last lesson that the regular 7-gon is lurking in the background. In fact, here are the roots of $x^7 - 1 = 0$ in the complex plane.

Maybe it even satisfies an equation with rational coefficients. Such numbers are called *algebraic numbers*.

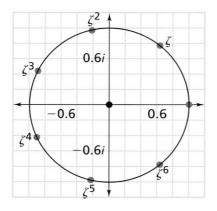

Recall Exercises 3–7 of Lesson 2.11. You know that $\zeta + \zeta^6 = 2 \cos \frac{2\pi}{7}$. If you find an algebraic expression for $\zeta + \zeta^6$, you can find an algebraic expression for $\cos \frac{2\pi}{7}$. (ζ is the Greek letter *zeta*.)

There are two other pairs of seventh roots of unity that add to real numbers.

For You to Do

2. Show that

$$\zeta^2 + \zeta^5 = 2 \cos \frac{4\pi}{7}$$

$$\zeta^3 + \zeta^4 = 2 \cos \frac{6\pi}{7}$$

You now have three pairs of roots that add to real numbers.

$$\alpha = \zeta + \zeta^6 = 2 \cos \frac{2\pi}{7}$$

$$\beta = \zeta^2 + \zeta^5 = 2 \cos \frac{4\pi}{7}$$

$$\gamma = \zeta^3 + \zeta^4 = 2 \cos \frac{6\pi}{7}$$

You can find a polynomial with roots α, β, and γ. Those roots satisfy this cubic equation.

$$(x - \alpha)(x - \beta)(x - \gamma) = x^3 - (\alpha + \beta + \gamma)x^2 + (\alpha\beta + \alpha\gamma + \beta\gamma)x - \alpha\beta\gamma$$
$$= 0 \qquad (1)$$

But are the coefficients real?

Habits of Mind

Develop your understanding. Recognize that you can evaluate trigonometric functions as sums of roots of unity and know which sums produce real results. Each pair here is a number plus its conjugate. Use the geometry of the *n*-gon to help with this.

Example

Problem

  a. Find the value of $\alpha + \beta + \gamma$.

  b. Find the value of $\alpha\beta + \alpha\gamma + \beta\gamma$.

Solution

  a. To find $\alpha + \beta + \gamma$, replace the three real numbers by their definitions to get

$$\alpha + \beta + \gamma = (\zeta + \zeta^6) + (\zeta^2 + \zeta^5) + (\zeta^3 + \zeta^4)$$

This sum includes six of the seven vertices of the 7-gon—all except for the "anchor point" 1. You worked through this sum, approximating each of the terms, using your calculator in Problem 8 of Lesson 2.8. You can also figure out the sum exactly. Try it before continuing.

You know that ζ is a root of $x^7 - 1 = 0$. The factorization

$$x^7 - 1 = (x - 1)(x^6 + x^5 + x^4 + x^3 + x^2 + 1)$$

means that ζ is a root of one of the factors on the right-hand side. But it is not a root of the first factor (why?), so it must be true that

$$\zeta^6 + \zeta^5 + \zeta^4 + \zeta^3 + \zeta^2 + \zeta + 1 = 0 \qquad (2)$$

From this identity, you can say that

$$\zeta^6 + \zeta^5 + \zeta^4 + \zeta^3 + \zeta^2 + \zeta = -1$$

But the left-hand side is just $\alpha + \beta + \gamma$, so

$$\alpha + \beta + \gamma = -1$$

  b. To find $\alpha\beta + \alpha\gamma + \beta\gamma$, again replace each of the numbers by its definition.

$$\alpha\beta + \alpha\gamma + \beta\gamma = (\zeta + \zeta^6)(\zeta^2 + \zeta^5) + (\zeta + \zeta^6)(\zeta^3 + \zeta^4) \\ + (\zeta^2 + \zeta^5)(\zeta^3 + \zeta^4)$$

Expand each product of binomials to get

$$\zeta^3 + \zeta^4 + 2\zeta^5 + 2\zeta^6 + 2\zeta^8 + 2\zeta^9 + \zeta^{10} + \zeta^{11}$$

Finally, replace ζ^7 by 1 and simplify to get

$$2\zeta + 2\zeta^2 + 2\zeta^3 + 2\zeta^4 + 2\zeta^5 + 2\zeta^6 = 2(\zeta + \zeta^2 + \zeta^3 + \zeta^4 + \zeta^5 + \zeta^6)$$

From above, you know that $\zeta + \zeta^2 + \zeta^3 + \zeta^4 + \zeta^5 + \zeta^6 = -1$, so the value of $\alpha\beta + \alpha\gamma + \beta\gamma$ is -2.

Habits of Mind

Make connections.
To calculate expressions with ζ, treat them like polynomials in ζ and use the basic rules of algebra. Then, as a last step, reduce higher powers of ζ by using the relation $\zeta^7 = 1$.

For You to Do

3. Show that $\alpha\beta\gamma = 1$.

So, the three coefficients are, in fact, real:

$$\alpha + \beta + \gamma = -1,$$

$$\alpha\beta + \alpha\gamma + \beta\gamma = -2, \quad \text{and}$$

$$\alpha\beta\gamma = 1$$

Thus, the three real numbers $2\cos\frac{2\pi}{7}$, $2\cos\frac{4\pi}{7}$, and $2\cos\frac{6\pi}{7}$ are roots of the nice cubic equation (going back to equation (1))

$$x^3 + x^2 - 2x - 1 = 0 \qquad (3)$$

From here, you could try to find an exact value of $\cos\frac{2\pi}{7}$ like you did for $\cos\frac{2\pi}{5}$. Just solve the above equation.

For the pentagon in Lesson 2.11, the resulting equation was quadratic, and the quadratic formula helps you solve quadratics easily. To solve equation (3), you need a "cubic formula." In the project for this chapter, you will derive Cardano's Formula, a formula for finding roots of cubic equations. Unfortunately, the cubic formula is not very useful for numerical calculations—the resulting solutions involve cube roots of complex numbers.

> You will apply Cardano's Formula to this equation in the project for this chapter.

For You to Do

4. Find approximate solutions to equation (3). Verify that these approximations agree with the value of $2\cos\frac{2\pi}{7}$, $2\cos\frac{4\pi}{7}$, and $2\cos\frac{6\pi}{7}$.

Developing Habits of Mind

Establish a process. When you were expanding the product

$$\alpha\beta + \alpha\gamma + \beta\gamma$$
$$= (\zeta + \zeta^6)(\zeta^2 + \zeta^5) + (\zeta + \zeta^6)(\zeta^3 + \zeta^4) + (\zeta^2 + \zeta^5)(\zeta^3 + \zeta^4)$$

did it not feel as if you were just expanding this polynomial

$$(x + x^6)(x^2 + x^5) + (x + x^6)(x^3 + x^4) + (x^2 + x^5)(x^3 + x^4)$$

to find its normal form?

You could have just entered the above expression in your CAS getting

$$x^3 + x^4 + 2x^5 + 2x^6 + 2x^8 + 2x^9 + x^{10} + x^{11}$$

replacing x by ζ in the result. Then you replaced high powers of ζ (powers 8, 9, 10, and 11) by lower ones, using the relation $\zeta^7 = 1$.

But there is an even better idea here. Suppose you take the above polynomial and divide it by $x^7 - 1$. You get:

$$x^3 + x^4 + 2x^5 + 2x^6 + 2x^8 + 2x^9 + x^{10} + x^{11}$$
$$= (x^7 - 1)(2x + 2x^2 + x^3 + x^4) + 2x + 2x^2 + 2x^3 + 2x^4 + 2x^5 + 2x^6$$

Now replace x by ζ on both sides. Since $\zeta^7 - 1 = 0$, you get

$$\zeta^3 + \zeta^4 + 2\zeta^5 + 2\zeta^6 + 2\zeta^8 + 2\zeta^9 + \zeta^{10} + \zeta^{11}$$
$$= (\zeta^7 - 1)(2\zeta + 2\zeta^2 + \zeta^3 + \zeta^4) + 2\zeta + 2\zeta^2 + 2\zeta^3 + 2\zeta^4 + 2\zeta^5 + 2\zeta^6$$
$$= 2\zeta + 2\zeta^2 + 2\zeta^3 + 2\zeta^4 + 2\zeta^5 + 2\zeta^6$$

From here, proceed as before.

If you think about it, this process amounts to

- divide the expression

$$x^3 + x^4 + 2x^5 + 2x^6 + 2x^8 + 2x^9 + x^{10} + x^{11}$$

  by $x^7 - 1$,
- take the remainder,
- replace x by ζ in this remainder, and
- simplify the result.

Most CAS systems allow you to get the remainder directly with a built in function.

See TI-Nspire Handbook on p. 704 for more about finding the remainder in polynomial division with a CAS.

For Discussion

5. Use a CAS. Find the remainder when you divide

$$(x^3 + x^4)(x^2 + x^5) + (x^3 + x^4)(x^1 + x^6) + (x^2 + x^5)(x + x^6)$$
by $x^6 + x^5 + x^4 + x^3 + x^2 + x + 1$.

Interpret the reuslt in the context of this lesson.

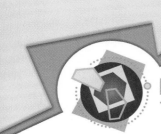 **Exercises** *Practicing Habits of Mind*

Check Your Understanding

1. For each of the following values of ζ, find the sum

$$\sum_{k=0}^{6} \zeta^{5k}$$

   a. $\zeta = \text{cis} \dfrac{2\pi}{7}$
   b. $\zeta = \text{cis} \dfrac{2\pi}{5}$
   c. $\zeta = \text{cis} \dfrac{2\pi}{10}$

2. Suppose $\alpha = \text{cis } \frac{2\pi}{6}$. Evaluate each sum.

a. $\displaystyle\sum_{k=0}^{5} \alpha^k$ **b.** $1 + \alpha^3$ **c.** $\alpha^2 + \alpha^4$

3. Suppose $\alpha = \text{cis } \frac{2\pi}{5}$. Define a function f on nonnegative integers by

$$f(n) = \sum_{k=0}^{4} \alpha^{kn}$$

Tabulate f and find a simpler way to define it.

4. Suppose $z = \text{cis } \frac{2\pi}{5}$.

a. Find $\displaystyle\sum_{k=0}^{4} z^k$ **b.** Find $\displaystyle\prod_{k=0}^{4} z^k$ **c.** Find $\displaystyle\prod_{k=1}^{4}(1 - z^k)$

> The Greek letter $\prod$ (pi) means to form a product. The following product ranges from $k = 0$ to 4:
> $$\prod_{k=0}^{4} z^k$$
> $$= z^0 \cdot z^1 \cdot z^2 \cdot z^3 \cdot z^4$$

5. Suppose $z = \text{cis } \frac{2\pi}{5}$. Find the value of
$$(z - z^2 - z^3 + z^4)^2$$

6. Suppose $z = \text{cis } \frac{2\pi}{12}$.

a. Find the value of $z + z^5 + z^7 + z^{11}$.

b. Find the value of

$$\cos \frac{\pi}{6} + \cos \frac{5\pi}{6} + \cos \frac{7\pi}{6} + \cos \frac{11\pi}{6}$$

7. a. A *primitive nth root of unity* is a solution to $x^n - 1 = 0$ that is not a solution of any equation $x^m - 1 = 0$ where $m < n$. Find all the primitive 12th roots of unity. Graph the corresponding 12-gon on the complex plane.

b. Factor $x^{12} - 1$ into irreducible polynomials over $\mathbb{Z}$. Let $\zeta = \text{cis } \frac{2\pi}{12}$. Label each vertex of the 12-gon in two ways

- as a power of ζ
- with the factor of $x^{12} - 1$ that it makes zero when you substitute it for x.

On Your Own

8. Take It Further Suppose $\alpha = \text{cis } \frac{2\pi}{6}$. Define a function f on nonnegative integers by

$$f(n) = \sum_{k=0}^{5} \alpha^{kn}$$

Tabulate f and find a simpler way to define it.

9. Suppose $z = \text{cis}\,\frac{2\pi}{7}$. Find the value of
$$(z + z^2 - z^3 + z^4 - z^5 - z^6)^2$$

10. Suppose $z = \text{cis}\,\frac{2\pi}{11}$. Let
$$\alpha_1 = z + z^3 + z^4 + z^5 + z^9 \quad \text{and}$$
$$\alpha_2 = z^2 + z^6 + z^7 + z^8 + z^{10}$$

Find a quadratic equation satisfied by α_1 and α_2.

11. Factor $x^5 - 1$ over each of the following sets.

   a. over $\mathbb{Z}$ **b.** over $\mathbb{R}$ **c.** over $\mathbb{C}$

See TI-Nspire Handbook on p. 704 to learn how to use your CAS to factor over $\mathbb{Z}$, $\mathbb{R}$, and $\mathbb{C}$.

12. Suppose that $\zeta = \text{cis}\,\frac{2\pi}{n}$. Show that ζ is a primitive nth root of unity.

13. Suppose that $\zeta = \text{cis}\,\frac{2\pi}{n}$. Show that if $\zeta^t = 1$ for some integer t, then n is a factor of t.

14. Suppose that $\zeta = \text{cis}\,\frac{2\pi}{n}$. Show that if $z = \zeta^r$ for some integer r that has no common factor with n, then z is a primitive nth root of unity.

15. **a.** Find all the primitive ninth roots of unity. Graph the corresponding 9-gon on the complex plane.

   b. Factor $x^9 - 1$ into irreducible polynomials over $\mathbb{Z}$.

     Let $\zeta = \text{cis}\,\frac{2\pi}{9}$. Label each vertex of the 9-gon in two ways
     • as a power of ζ
     • with the factor of $x^9 - 1$ that it makes zero when you substitute it for x.

16. Show that if z is an nth root of unity that is not primitive, $z^q = 1$ for some factor q of n.

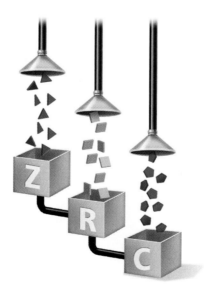

17. The polynomial that has the primitive nth roots of unity as solutions is usually denoted by $\psi_n(x)$. (ψ is the Greek letter *psi*.) Show that

$$\psi_1(x) = x - 1$$
$$\psi_2(x) = x + 1$$
$$\psi_3(x) = x^2 + x + 1$$
$$\psi_4(x) = x^2 + 1$$

18. Find $\psi_m(x)$ for $m = 5, 6, 7, 8, 9, 10, 11,$ and 12.

m	$\psi_m(x)$
5	$x^4 + x^3 + x^2 + x + 1$
6	▩
7	▩
8	▩
9	▩
10	▩
11	▩
12	▩

19. Show that $x^{12} - 1$ factors as

$$x^{12} - 1 = \psi_1(x)\,\psi_2(x)\,\psi_3(x)\,\psi_4(x)\,\psi_6(x)\,\psi_{12}(x)$$

Take It Further In Exercises 20–22, $\zeta = \operatorname{cis}\frac{2\pi}{17}$.

- Let
$$P_0 = \zeta + \zeta^9 + \zeta^{13} + \zeta^{15} + \zeta^{16} + \zeta^8 + \zeta^4 + \zeta^2 \quad \text{and}$$
$$P_1 = \zeta^3 + \zeta^{10} + \zeta^5 + \zeta^{11} + \zeta^{14} + \zeta^7 + \zeta^{12} + \zeta^6$$

- Let
$$Q_0 = \zeta + \zeta^{13} + \zeta^{16} + \zeta^4,$$
$$Q_1 = \zeta^3 + \zeta^5 + \zeta^{14} + \zeta^{12},$$
$$Q_2 = \zeta^9 + \zeta^{15} + \zeta^8 + \zeta^2, \quad \text{and}$$
$$Q_3 = \zeta^{10} + \zeta^{11} + \zeta^7 + \zeta^6$$

- And let
$$r_0 = \zeta + \zeta^{16},$$
$$r_1 = \zeta^3 + \zeta^{14},$$
$$r_2 = \zeta^9 + \zeta^8,$$
$$r_3 = \zeta^{10} + \zeta^7,$$
$$r_4 = \zeta^{13} + \zeta^4,$$
$$r_5 = \zeta^5 + \zeta^{12},$$
$$r_6 = \zeta^{15} + \zeta^2, \quad \text{and}$$
$$r_7 = \zeta^{11} + \zeta^6$$

20. Show that each of the P's, Q's, and r's are real numbers.

21. a. Show that

$$P_0 + P_1 = -1 \quad \text{and}$$
$$P_0 P_1 = -4$$

Find P_0 and P_1.

b. Show that

$$Q_0 + Q_2 = P_0 \quad \text{and}$$
$$Q_0 Q_2 = -1$$

Find Q_0 and Q_2.

c. Show that

$$Q_1 + Q_3 = P_1 \quad \text{and}$$
$$Q_1 Q_3 = -1$$

Find Q_1 and Q_3.

22. a. Show that

$$r_0 + r_4 = Q_0 \quad \text{and}$$
$$r_0 r_4 = -1$$

Find r_0 and r_4.

b. Find an exact formula for $\cos \frac{2\pi}{17}$, using only square roots and the four operations of arithmetic.

23. Standardized Test Prep Which of the following is the sum of the fourth roots of -1?

A. 0 **B.** -1 **C.** $-\frac{\sqrt{2}}{2}$ **D.** $-\frac{\sqrt{3}}{2}$

Go Online
PHSchool.com

For additional practice, go to **Web Code:** bga-0212

Maintain Your Skills

24. Find all primitive nth roots of unity if

a. $n = 3$ **b.** $n = 4$ **c.** $n = 5$ **d.** $n = 7$

e. $n = 10$ **f.** $n = 11$ **g.** $n = 24$

25. Take It Further In terms of n, how many primitive nth roots of unity are there?

Mathematical 2C Reflections

In this investigation, you learned De Moivre's Theorem for calculating powers of complex numbers. You saw how this connected to roots of unity and regular polygons in the complex plane. The following questions will help you summarize what you have learned.

1. Find all the roots of each equation.
   a. $x^6 - 1 = 0$ b. $x^8 = 1$ c. $x^8 = 256$

2. Find the exact value of the following.
   a. $\cos \frac{\pi}{12}$ b. $\cos \frac{\pi}{8}$

   c. **Take It Further** $\cos \frac{3\pi}{8}$

3. Find the exact value of the following sums.
   a. $\displaystyle\sum_{k=0}^{6} \sin \frac{2\pi k}{7}$ b. $\displaystyle\sum_{k=1}^{6} \cos \frac{2\pi k}{7}$ c. $\displaystyle\sum_{k=0}^{6} \cos \frac{(7 - 4k)\pi}{14}$

4. Suppose $\zeta = \operatorname{cis} \frac{2\pi}{12}$.
   a. Plot the distinct powers of ζ on the complex plane. Label each power with the polynomial of least degree over $\mathbb{Z}$ for which it is a zero.
   b. Find the value of
   $$(1 - \zeta)(1 - \zeta^5)(1 - \zeta^7)(1 - \zeta^{11})$$

5. Suppose $\zeta = \operatorname{cis} \frac{2\pi}{5}$.
   a. Plot the distinct powers of ζ on the complex plane.
   b. Find a quadratic equation with $\zeta + \frac{1}{\zeta}$ as a root.

   c. **Take It Further** Find the length of a side of the polygon which has the powers of ζ as vertices.

6. How do you use De Moivre's Theorem to write a rule for $\cos 3x$?

7. How can you connect roots of unity to regular polygons?

8. For what values of $\cos x$ does $\cos 3x = 0$?

Vocabulary and Notation

In this investigation, you learned these terms. Make sure you understand what each one means and how to use it.

- **algebraic numbers**
- **complex numbers**
- **primitive *n*th root of unity**
- **roots of unity**

Symmetry about the center is a familiar and attractive design element in architecture.

Project: Using Mathematical Habits

Cardano's Method

Square roots of negative numbers emerged in the first half of the sixteenth century. Many people were interested in finding a formula that would let them solve cubic equations. Girolamo Cardano (1501–1575), Rafael Bombelli (1526–1572), and others developed an algorithm for solving cubic equations. But when they applied the method to cubics that have real roots, like $x^3 - 15x - 4 = 0$, they sometimes ended up with expressions that involved square roots of negative numbers.

Cardano, Bombelli, and their contemporaries realized that the equation $x^3 - 15x - 4 = 0$ has the same form as the identity

$$(r + s)^3 - 3rs(r + s) - (r^3 + s^3) = 0$$

if you look at it like this.

$$(r \text{✋} s)^3 - 3rs(r \text{✋} s) - (r^3 + s^3) = 0$$
$$x^3 \qquad - 15 \quad x \quad - \quad 4 \quad = 0$$

So, if you can find r and s such that

$$3rs = 15 \quad \text{and} \quad r^3 + s^3 = 4$$

you could let $x = r + s$ and you would have a root. If $3rs = 15$, then $rs = 5$. Cube rs to get $r^3s^3 = 125$. Now you know the sum and product of the cubes of r and s.

$$r^3s^3 = 125 \quad \text{and} \quad r^3 + s^3 = 4$$

You now have a sum and product relationship. From this, you can say that r^3 and s^3 are the roots of the quadratic equation

$$y^2 - 4y + 125 = 0$$

which are $2 + 11i$ and $2 - 11i$. So

$$r^3 = 2 + 11i \quad \text{and} \quad s^3 = 2 - 11i$$

It is not clear how the 16th century mathematicians found values for r and s—de Moivre lived over a century later. It is likely that they just started cubing expressions until they found the correct answer. But you can use de Moivre's Theorem to solve the equations directly. First, write $2 + 11i$ in polar form

$$2 + 11i = |2 + 11i| \operatorname{cis} (\arg(2 + 11i))$$

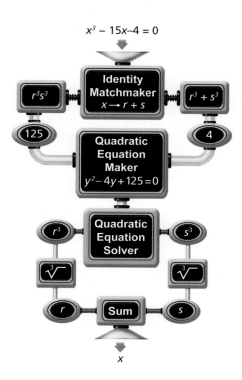

Now

$$|2 + 11i| = \sqrt{125} = (\sqrt{5})^3 \text{ and}$$

$$\arg(2 + 11i) = \tan^{-1}\frac{11}{2}$$

So, if $r^3 = 2 + 11i$, you can say that

$$|r|^3 = (\sqrt{5})^3 \text{ and}$$

$$3\arg(r) = \tan^{-1}\frac{11}{2}$$

Since z has to be a nonnegative real number, you can say $r = \sqrt{5}$. To find $\arg(r) = \theta$, use a calculator to find that if $\alpha = \tan^{-1}\frac{11}{2}$, then

$$\tan\frac{\alpha}{3} = 0.5$$

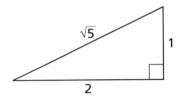

In Exercise 1, you will verify that this answer is exact. So,

$$r = \sqrt{5}(\cos\theta + i\sin\theta)$$

$$= \sqrt{5}\left(\cos\frac{\alpha}{3} + i\sin\frac{\alpha}{3}\right)$$

$$= \sqrt{5}\left(\cos\left(\tan^{-1}\frac{1}{2}\right) + i\sin\left(\tan^{-1}\frac{1}{2}\right)\right)$$

$$= \sqrt{5}\left(\frac{2}{\sqrt{5}} + i\frac{1}{\sqrt{5}}\right) = 2 + i$$

So $r = 2 + i$. You can follow the same process to find that $s = 2 - i$. Notice that $r + s = 4$ and 4 is a root of the equation $x^3 - 15x - 4 = 0$.

What about the other roots? Of course, you could just divide $x^3 - 15x - 4$ by $x - 4$, get a quadratic, and solve it. But the goal of the project (and Cardano's original goal) is to find a general method for finding all three roots of any cubic.

Go back to the equations

$$r^3 = 2 + 11i \quad \text{and} \quad s^3 = 2 - 11i$$

There are three roots to each equation. You have found one for each:

$$\alpha = 2 + i \quad \text{for the first equation, and}$$

$$\beta = 2 - i \quad \text{for the second}$$

But, from Investigation 2C, you have seen that if $\omega = \frac{-1 + i\sqrt{3}}{2}$, then ω and ω^2 are cube roots of unity so their cubes are each 1. In other words, the three roots of $r^3 = 2 + 11i$ are

$$\alpha, \ \omega\alpha, \text{ and } \omega^2\alpha$$

And the three roots of $s^3 = 2 - 11i$ are

$$\beta, \ \omega\beta, \text{ and } \omega^2\beta$$

You now have nine choices for the roots of the original equation, corresponding to the possible values for r and s.

r	s
$2 + i$	$2 - i$
$\omega(2 + i) = \dfrac{-2 - \sqrt{3}}{2} + \left(\dfrac{2\sqrt{3} - 1}{2}\right)i$	$\omega(2 - i) = \dfrac{-2 + \sqrt{3}}{2} + \left(\dfrac{2\sqrt{3} + 1}{2}\right)i$
$\omega^2(2 + i) = \dfrac{-2 + \sqrt{3}}{2} + \left(\dfrac{-2\sqrt{3} - 1}{2}\right)i$	$\omega^2(2 - i) = \dfrac{-2 - \sqrt{3}}{2} + \left(\dfrac{-2\sqrt{3} + 1}{2}\right)i$

But there are only three values of $r + s$ that work in the original cubic.

1. Find the three combinations from the nine possibilities for $r + s$ that satisfy
$$x^3 - 15x - 4 = 0$$

2. Using the formula for $\tan 3x$, show that if $\tan x = \frac{1}{2}$, then $\tan 3x = \frac{11}{2}$.

It may seem that you now have a general method of solving a cubic of the form
$$x^3 + px + q = 0$$
You will generalize the algorithm used for $x^3 - 15x - 4 = 0$ in the remaining exercises for this project. But this is a special kind of cubic—monic with no x^2 term. What about cubics like
$$x^3 + x^2 - 2x - 1 = 0$$
or even
$$8x^3 + 4x^2 - 4x - 1 = 0$$
In CME Project *Algebra 2*, you saw that you can transform any cubic, using affine transformations, to a monic cubic with no x^2 term. So, if you can solve $x^3 + px + q = 0$, you can solve any cubic.

3. Show that the roots of $x^3 - 15x - 4 = 0$ are 4, $-2 + \sqrt{3}$, and $-2 - \sqrt{3}$.

4. Solve $x^3 - 6x - 9 = 0$
   a. By any method you like
   b. By Cardano's method

5. Describe Cardano's method for solving a cubic of the form
$$x^3 + px + q = 0$$
as an algorithm

6. Consider a cubic of the form
$$x^3 + px + q = 0$$
   a. Show that if you represent a root as a sum $r + s$, then
$$r^3 + s^3 = -q$$
   and
$$rs = -\frac{p}{3}$$
   so
$$r^3 s^3 = -\frac{p^3}{27}$$
   b. Show that
$$r^3 = \frac{-q + \sqrt{q^2 + 4\frac{p^3}{27}}}{2}$$
   and
$$s^3 = \frac{-q - \sqrt{q^2 + 4\frac{p^3}{27}}}{2}.$$
   c. Explain how you can use the expressions in part (b) to find the roots of the equation.

Cardano's Formula is often stated as a theorem.

Theorem 2.7   Cardano's Formula

The roots of $x^3 + px + q = 0$ are
$$\sqrt[3]{\frac{-q + \sqrt{\frac{27q^2 + 4p^3}{27}}}{2}} + \sqrt[3]{\frac{-q - \sqrt{\frac{27q^2 + 4p^3}{27}}}{2}}$$

7. Explain how you can use the above formula to produce three roots.

8. When solving

$$x^3 + px + q = 0$$

with Cardano's method, you are led to a "reduced quadratic" that has roots r^3 and s^3.

$$x^2 + qx - \frac{p^3}{27} = 0$$

a. Show that if the discriminant of this equation is D then

$$27D = 27q^2 + 4p^3$$

b. If $27q^2 + 4p^3 > 0$, show that the cubic has one real root and two complex roots.

c. If $27q^2 + 4p^3 = 0$, show that the cubic has two real roots.

d. If $27q^2 + 4p^3 < 0$, show that the cubic has three distinct real roots.

9. a. Use scaling and translating to transform the cubic

$$8x^3 + 36x^2 + 52x + 24$$

into a monic cubic with no x^2-term.

b. Find the zeros of the cubic you found in part a.

c. Solve $8x^3 + 36x^2 + 52x + 24 = 0$.

10. In Lesson 2.12, you saw that

$$2 \cos \tfrac{2\pi}{7}, \ 2 \cos \tfrac{4\pi}{7}, \text{ and } 2 \cos \tfrac{6\pi}{7}$$

are roots of the cubic equation

$$x^3 + x^2 - 2x - 1 = 0$$

a. Transform this equation so that it has the form

$$x^3 + px + q = 0$$

b. Find the roots of the equation in part (a) in terms of

$$r = \frac{\sqrt{7}}{3} \operatorname{cis} \left(\frac{1}{3} \tan^{-1} 3\sqrt{3} \right)$$

11. a. **Take It Further** Suppose that α, β, and γ are three numbers that have a sum of 0. Show that

$$((\alpha - \beta)(\alpha - \gamma)(\beta - \gamma))^2 + 4(\alpha\beta + \alpha\gamma + \beta\gamma)^3$$
$$+ \ 27(\alpha\beta\gamma)^2 = 0$$

b. Suppose that α, β, and γ are roots of

$$x^3 + px + q = 0$$

Show that

$$-((\alpha - \beta)(\alpha - \gamma)(\beta - \gamma))^2 = 27q^2 + 4p^3$$

($27q^2 + 4p^3$ is the **discriminant** of the cubic. It is 0 if and only if the cubic has a double root. Compare with Exercise 8.)

Go Online
PHSchool.com

For vocabulary review, go
to Web Code: bgj-0251

In **Investigation 2A,** you learned to

- represent complex numbers using both rectangular coordinates and trigonometry.

- determine the magnitude and argument of any complex number.

- decide when it is best to use rectangular or polar coordinates to represent complex numbers.

The following questions will help you check your understanding.

1. **a.** Represent $-3 + 3i$ in polar form.

   b. Represent $2 \operatorname{cis} \frac{5\pi}{3}$ in rectangular form.

2. Find the magnitude and argument of each complex number z.

   a. $z = 1 - \sqrt{3}i$

   b. $z = 4$

   c. $z = -2i$

   d. $z = -1 - 3i$

   e. $z = 5 \operatorname{cis} \frac{\pi}{6}$

   f. $z = 2 \operatorname{cis} 35°$

3. Let z and w have the following values.
   $$z = 2 - 2i$$
   $$w = -4i$$

   a. Find zw.

   b. Copy and complete the following table.

	Magnitude	Argument
z	▩	▩
w	▩	▩
zw	▩	▩
z²	▩	▩
w³	▩	▩

   c. Find the magnitude of z^5.

   d. Find the argument of w^6

In **Investigation 2B,** you learned to

- test trigonometric equations to predict whether they are identities.

- show the Angle-Sum Formulas for cosine and sine using the Multiplication Law for complex numbers.

- use Pythagorean identities and algebra to prove a trigonometric equation is an identity.

The following questions will help you check your understanding.

4. One of these two equations is an identity. The other is not.
   $$1 - \cos^2 x \cdot \sin x = \sin^3 x$$
   $$\tan^2 x - \sin^2 x \cdot \tan^2 x = \sin^2 x$$

   a. Pick a value of x and test it in each equation.

   b. Which equation is the identity?

5. **a.** Write a formula for $\cos\left(x + \frac{3\pi}{4}\right)$ using
   $$\operatorname{cis}\left(x + \frac{3\pi}{4}\right) = (\operatorname{cis} x)\left(\operatorname{cis} \frac{3\pi}{4}\right)$$

   b. Write a formula for $\cos\left(x + \frac{3\pi}{4}\right)$ using an addition formula.

6. Prove that each of the following equations is an identity.

   a. $\dfrac{2}{\sec^2 x} = \cos 2x + 1$

   b. $\tan x - \sin^2 x \tan x = \frac{1}{2}\sin 2x$

In **Investigation 2C,** you learned to

- calculate powers of complex numbers using De Moivre's Theorem.
- understand the geometry of roots of unity, and the connection to roots of equations of the form $x^n - 1 = 0$.
- find exact algebraic expressions for certain trigonometric values.

The following questions will help you check your understanding.

7. Let z and w have the following values.

$$z = 2 \text{ cis } 40°$$
$$w = -2 + 2i$$

Find each of the following.

a. z^2

b. z^{10}

c. w^2

d. w^4

8. a. Find all the roots of

$$x^9 - 1 = 0$$

b. Graph the roots of $x^9 - 1 = 0$ on the complex plane.

c. Find the exact value of

$$\sum_{k=0}^{8} \sin \frac{2\pi k}{9}$$

9. Find the exact value of $\sin \frac{5\pi}{12}$.

Chapter 2 Test

For a chapter test, go
to Web Code: bga-0253

Multiple Choice

1. Find $2 \operatorname{cis} \frac{3\pi}{4}$ in rectangular form.

    A. $-1 + i$ **B.** $-\sqrt{2} + i\sqrt{2}$

    C. $\sqrt{2} - i\sqrt{2}$ **D.** $\frac{\sqrt{2}}{2} - \frac{\sqrt{2}}{2} i$

2. Let z and w have the following values.

$$z = 3 \operatorname{cis} \frac{\pi}{6}$$

$$w = 5 \operatorname{cis} \frac{2\pi}{3}$$

    Find $\arg(zw)$.

    A. 8   **B.** 15   **C.** $\frac{5\pi}{6}$ **D.** $\frac{\pi}{9}$

3. Which of the following are identically equal to $\cos 2x$?

    I. $2 \cos^2 - 1$

    II. $2 \sin x \cos x$

    III. $\cos^2 x + \sin^2 x$

    A. I only   **B.** I and II

    C. II only   **D.** I, II, and III

4. Let z be a complex number where $|z| = 4$ and $\arg(z) = \frac{\pi}{6}$. What is the magnitude of z^3?

    A. $\frac{\pi}{2}$ **B.** $\frac{\pi}{18}$ **C.** 12   **D.** 64

5. Evaluate the sum.

$$\sum_{k=0}^{4} \sin \frac{2k\pi}{5}$$

    A. -1 **B.** 0   **C.** 1   **D.** 2π

Open Response

6. Let z and w have the following values.

$$z = -2 - 2i$$

$$w = 2\sqrt{3} + 2i$$

Copy and complete the following table.

	Magnitude	Argument
z	▪	▪
w	▪	▪
zw	▪	▪
z^2	▪	▪
w^3	▪	▪

7. Use the Angle-Sum Formulas to find each of the following.

    a. $\cos\left(x + \frac{\pi}{6}\right)$ **b.** $\sin(x - 2\pi)$

    c. $\cos\left(x - \frac{\pi}{2}\right)$ **d.** $\sin\left(x + \frac{3\pi}{2}\right)$

8. Prove the identity.

$$\tan x + \cot x = \sec x \cdot \csc x$$

9. Find $|z^4|$ and $\arg(z^4)$.

    a. $z = 3$ **b.** $z = 3 \operatorname{cis} 50°$

    c. $z = -5i$ **d.** $z = \sqrt{3} - i$

10. a. Find all the roots of $x^5 - 1 = 0$.

    b. Graph the roots of $x^5 - 1 = 0$ on the complex plane.

11. How can complex numbers be used to find formulas for $\cos 2x$ and $\sin 2x$?

1. Find the value of each expression.

   a. $\tan\left(\cos^{-1}\frac{\sqrt{3}}{2} + \sin^{-1}\frac{1}{2}\right)$

   b. $\cos 0 + 3 \sin 150° - \cos\frac{\pi}{3}$

   c. $|-7 + i|$

   d. $\displaystyle\sum_{k=0}^{7} \cos\frac{2\pi k}{8}$

2. Find the solutions to each equation for $0 \le x < 2\pi$.

   a. $2 \sin x + 1 = 0$

   b. $\tan\left(2x + \frac{\pi}{6}\right) + \sqrt{3} = 0$

   c. $2\cos^2 x - \cos x = 0$

3. Simplify the expression below.

   $$\cos(\tan^{-1} 0) - \sin\left(\cos^{-1}\frac{\sqrt{3}}{2}\right)$$
   $$+ \tan\left(\sin^{-1}\frac{\sqrt{2}}{2}\right)$$

4. Find the degree measure that correspond to each of the following.

   a. $\frac{7\pi}{4}$ radians

   b. $\frac{3\pi}{2}$ radians

5. Find the period of each function.

   a. $f(t) = \sin(4t)$

   b. $h(t) = \cos\left(\frac{t}{2}\right)$

6. The temperature in an experimental chamber changes periodically as a function of time. The temperature, h, in degrees Celsius, is given by

   $$h = 25 + 8 \sin\left(\pi\left(\frac{t+1}{3}\right)\right)$$

   where t is the number of hours after the experiment begins.

   a. What is temperature when the experiment begins?

   b. What is maximum temperature during the experiment?

   c. What is minimum temperature during the experiment?

7. Evaluate the expression below, where a and b are real numbers.

   $$a^2 \sin\left(-\frac{\pi}{6}\right) + 2ab \cos\frac{3\pi}{2} + b^2 \sin\frac{3\pi}{4} \cos\frac{5\pi}{4}$$

8. Copy and complete the table.

	Amplitude	Minimum	Maximum
$f(x) = 3 \sin 2x$	▨	▨	▨
$g(x) = -\sin x + 1$	▨	▨	▨

9. Solve the equation below for $0 \le x < 2\pi$.

   $$\tan^3 x - 3 \tan x = 0$$

10. Sketch the graph of $y = -2 \sin x + 1$ on $0 \le x \le 2\pi$.

11. Where do the graphs of $y = \sin x$ and $y = \cos x$ intersect for $0 \le x < 2\pi$?

12. Find the value of each expression.

a. $\cos \frac{7\pi}{12}$

b. $\tan \left(\sin^{-1} \left(-\frac{\sqrt{3}}{2} \right) \right)$

c. $\left(\frac{\sqrt{2}}{2} + \frac{\sqrt{2}}{2}i \right)^{80}$

13. Use the Angle-Sum and Angle-Difference formulas to simplify each expression.

a. $\sin \left(x + \frac{\pi}{4} \right)$

b. $\cos \left(x + \frac{2\pi}{3} \right)$

c. $\sin \left(x - \pi \right)$

d. $\cos \left(x - \frac{\pi}{6} \right)$

14. a. Find all the roots of $x^6 - 1 = 0$.

b. Graph the roots of $x^6 - 1 = 0$ on the complex plane.

15. For $z = -1 + i\sqrt{3}$ and $w = 3 - 3i$, copy and complete the table.

Number	Magnitude	Argument
z	▪	▪
w	▪	▪
zw	▪	▪
z^4	▪	▪
w^2	▪	▪

16. Let $\omega = \frac{\sqrt{2}}{2} + \frac{i\sqrt{2}}{2}$. Simplify the expression below.

$$1 + \omega + \omega^2 + \omega^3 + \omega^4$$

17. Find the magnitude and argument (in radians) of each complex number. Approximate your answer to two decimal places.

a. $z = 5 - 5i$

b. $z = 7 \operatorname{cis} \left(\frac{2\pi}{3} \right)$

c. $z = -2\sqrt{3} + 2i$

d. $z = 3 - i$

18. Prove the identity $\frac{1}{1 + \tan x} = \frac{\cot x}{1 + \cot x}$.

19. Suppose $\sin \theta = \frac{15}{17}$ and $\cos \theta = -\frac{8}{17}$. Find the value of each expression.

a. $\tan \theta$

b. $\cos 2\theta$

c. $\sin 2\theta$

d. $\tan 2\theta$

20. Let $z = 2 - 2i\sqrt{3}$ and $w = -\sqrt{3} + i$. Graph and label z, w, and zw on the complex plane.

Analysis of Functions

The world is full of phenomena that seem to involve an abrupt change from one state to another. A balloon is whole one moment, and the next moment it has burst. A bug is sitting quietly on a branch, and an instant later a predator has eaten it. However, high-speed photography reveals that such phenomena actually involve gradual change over a period of time, albeit a very short one. The balloon that appears to burst all at once in fact tears open, with one or more rips that start out small and grow rapidly larger.

Gottfried Leibniz (1646–1716) grasped this fact, even before the invention of photography. "Nature makes no leaps," he declared, calling this the Law of Continuity. In this chapter, you will learn how to analyze continuous functions, and especially how to describe their rates of change. For instance, you will learn what it means to say that the rip in a balloon grows at a rate of about fifty feet per second. You will also learn about discontinuous functions, which (Leibniz's Law of Continuity notwithstanding) are sometimes useful for modeling real-world phenomena.

Vocabulary and Notation

- average rate of change
- continuous
- continuously compounded interest
- determinant
- e
- hole
- infinite discontinuity
- instantaneous speed
- linear fractional transformation, $\mathcal{R}_A$
- natural logarithm, $\ln x$
- power function
- removable discontinuity
- secant line
- structure-preserving map
- tangent line

Polynomial Functions

In *Polynomial Functions*, you will study the graphs of polynomial functions from various viewpoints. For each graph, you will learn the connection between the rates of change of the function and the graph's secant and tangent lines.

By the end of this investigation, you will be able to answer questions like these.

1. How can you graph a polynomial function given its factored form?

2. How can you determine a polynomial's behavior at very large or very small inputs?

3. How can you use long division to find equations of secant or tangent lines to the graph of a polynomial function?

You will learn how to
- state the Change of Sign Theorem and the Intermediate Value Theorem for Polynomials, and to use them to analyze the graphs of polynomial functions

- find the equation of a line secant to a polynomial function and the average rate of change of a function between two points

- write the Taylor expansion for a polynomial function about a point

- find the equation of the tangent to a polynomial curve at a point

You will develop these habits and skills:
- Visualize the graph of a polynomial function from its factored form.

- Use the continuity of a polynomial function to draw conclusions about the function's behavior at extreme values or about lines tangent to the graph of the function.

- Relate quotients in polynomial long division to Taylor expansions and to equations of tangent lines.

A polynomial function can describe the height, over time, of a falling object.

3.1 Getting Started

Activating Prior Knowledge
Exploring New Ideas

Polynomial functions can have all kinds of interesting graphs. Here are a few favorites:

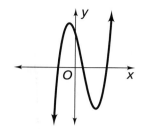

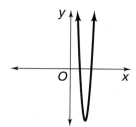

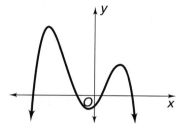

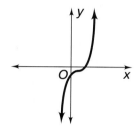

For You to Explore

1. What shapes can the graph of a cubic polynomial function have? Here are some functions to consider.

   - $f(x) = x^3 - 3x^2 - 6x - 3$
   - $g(x) = x^3 - 3x^2 + 3x + 4$

   Try other examples, too.

   > For example, the first graph shown above rises, falls, and then rises again, increasing without bound. What other shapes are possible?

2. Find, if possible, a cubic polynomial function with a graph that satisfies these conditions.

   - The graph crosses the x-axis at $(-5, 0)$, $(-1, 0)$, and somewhere on the positive x-axis.
   - From left to right, the graph rises, falls, and rises.
   - The graph crosses the y-axis at $(0, -7)$.

   Explain your work.

3. Find, if possible, a cubic polynomial function with a graph that satisfies these conditions.

   - The graph crosses the line with equation $y = 3$ at $(-5, 3)$, $(-1, 3)$, and somewhere with a positive x-coordinate.
   - From left to right, the graph rises, falls, and rises.
   - The graph crosses the y-axis at $(0, -4)$.

   Explain your work.

4. Here are some expressions that define a function f.

Expression 1: $f(x) = (x - 1)(x - 6)(x - 7)$

Expression 2: $f(x) = 24 - 2(x - 3) - 5(x - 3)^2 + (x - 3)^3$

Expression 3: $f(x) = x^3 - 14x^2 + 55x - 42$

Expression 4: $f(x) = -360 + 166(x + 3) - 23(x + 3)^2 + (x + 3)^3$

Expression 5: $f(x) = x^3\left(1 - \frac{14}{x} + \frac{55}{x^2} - \frac{42}{x^3}\right)$

a. Show that definitions 1–4 are equivalent and that definition 5 is equivalent to the others except at $x = 0$.

b. Which form is best for finding the zeros of f? What are the zeros of f?

c. Which form is best for finding $f(-3)$? What is $f(-3)$?

d. Which form is best for deciding how $f(x)$ behaves if x is a large positive number? If x is a large negative number (such as -1000)?

e. Which form is best for estimating the outputs of f for very small inputs? Estimate (without a calculator) the value of $f(0.00001)$. Explain your estimate.

f. Sketch the graph of $y = f(x)$.

Try adding a statement for the case $x = 0$ to make the last definition fully equivalent to the others. Could you model this two-part definition in your function-modeling language (FML)?

5. Sketch the graph of each function.

a. $f(x) = (x + 3)(x - 1)(x - 3)$

b. $h(x) = (x + 3)(x - 1.5)(x - 2.5)$

c. $k(x) = (x + 3)(x - 1.99)(x - 2.01)$

d. $g(x) = (x + 3)(x - 2)^2$

Habits of Mind

Make connections. The idea in Problem 5 is for you to connect what is happening with the equations to what is happening with the graphs. Use your calculator to check your sketches, but try to imagine the graphs before you use the technology.

6. Let f be the function from Problem 4. How close do you have to make a to 5 in order to be sure that the following conditions are met?

a. $|f(a) - f(5)| < 0.1$?

b. $|f(a) - f(5)| < 0.01$?

c. $|f(a) - f(5)| < 0.001$?

d. $|f(a) - f(5)| < 0.0001$?

7. The graph of the function h is at the right.

Which of these could be an equation for $h(x)$?

A. $h(x) = (x + 4)(x + 1)(x - 6)$

B. $h(x) = -(x + 4)(x + 1)(x - 6)$

C. $h(x) = (x + 1)(x - 4)(x - 6)$

D. $h(x) = -(x + 1)(x - 4)(x - 6)$

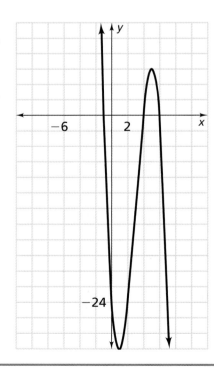

Exercises *Practicing Habits of Mind*

On Your Own

8. Find, if possible, a cubic polynomial function with a graph that satisfies these conditions:

- The graph crosses the x-axis at $(-9, 0)$, $(-5, 0)$, and somewhere on the positive x-axis.
- From left to right, the graph falls, rises, and falls.
- The graph passes through the point $(-4, -5)$.

Explain your work.

9. Sketch the graph of a function that could not possibly be a polynomial function. Explain why it could not be the graph of a polynomial.

10. Write About It Make your own polynomial function graph gallery.

- Sketch or generate 10 particularly interesting polynomial function graphs.
- Give the polynomial function for each graph.
- Describe what you find interesting about each graph.

> Make believe you are preparing a guided tour in an art museum, except the pictures are graphs of polynomial functions.

11. Draw sketches of each of these functions. A calculator should not be necessary.

a. $f_1(x) = (x - 2)(x - 4)(x - 7)$ **b.** $f_2(x) = (x - 2)(x - 4)(x - 5)$

c. $f_3(x) = (x - 2)(x - 4)(x - 4.5)$ **d.** $f_4(x) = (x - 2)(x - 4)(x - 4.1)$

e. $f_5(x) = (x - 2)(x - 4)^2$

> Do not worry about being very accurate. Is $f_1(0)$ positive or negative?

12. Suppose $f(x) = 3x^3 - 14x^2 + 15x + 9$. Find numbers A, B, C, and D if another way to write $f(x)$ is

$$f(x) = A(x - 2)^3 + B(x - 2)^2 + C(x - 2) + D$$

Maintain Your Skills

13. Sketch the graph of each of these functions.

a. $f(x) = (x - 3)^2$ **b.** $g(x) = (x + 4)^2$

c. $h(x) = -(x + 2)^2$ **d.** $j(x) = (x - 5)^3$

e. $k(x) = -(x - 5)^3$ **f.** $m(x) = x^4$

Continuity of Polynomial Functions

Graphs of polynomial functions have no breaks in them. This means that domain values that are close to each other will always have range values that are close to each other.

In-Class Experiment

Suppose $f(x) = x^3 - 2x^2 + 7$, so that $f(5) = 82$. How close must x be to 5 to meet the following conditions?

1. $|f(x) - f(5)| < 0.1$

2. $|f(x) - f(5)| < 0.01$

3. $|f(x) - f(5)| < 0.001$

4. $|f(x) - f(5)| < 10^{-6}$

In the In-Class Experiment, you saw that you could make $f(x)$ as close as you wanted to $f(5)$ by making x close enough to 5. How does the graph of $y = f(x)$ reflect this fact?

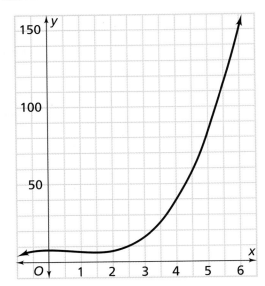

For Discussion

5. Using the graph of $y = f(x)$, explain why you can make $f(x)$ arbitrarily close to $f(5)$ by making x close enough to 5.

Definition

A function *f* is **continuous** at an input *a* if you can make *f(x)* as close as you want to *f(a)* by making *x* close enough to *a*.

You will learn a more precise definition when you take calculus.

You have seen that $f(x) = x^3 - 2x^2 + 7$ is continuous at $a = 5$. In fact, there was nothing special about the input 5. The function *f* is continuous at every real number. In this case, you say that *f* is continuous on $\mathbb{R}$, or simply that *f* is continuous.

To understand continuous functions, it helps to study functions that are not continuous. Consider a function *f* with the graph shown below.

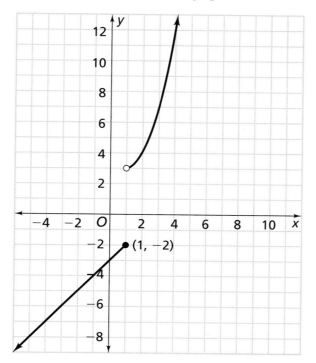

Habits of Mind

Represent a function.
Model *f* in your FML and graph it.

The graph shows that $f(1) = -2$. However, the graph also shows that the values

$$f(1.01), f(1.001), f(1.0001), f(1.00001), \ldots$$

approach 3. In other words, no matter how close you bring *x* to 1 (with $x > 1$), the distance between $f(x)$ and $f(1)$ will never be less than 5. Thus, *f* is not continuous at $x = 1$.

On the other hand, the values

$$f(0.99), f(0.999), f(0.9999), f(0.99999), \ldots$$

do approach -2. So you can make $f(x)$ as close as you want to $f(1)$ by making x close enough to 1 with the added restriction that $x < 1$. But to say that f is continuous at 1, you must be able to make $f(x)$ close to $f(1)$ from both sides of $x = 1$. In other words, you need to show it for $x > 1$ and $x < 1$.

You could say, however, that f is continuous at 1 from the left.

For You to Do

6. Name and sketch the graphs of three functions that are continuous.

7. Sketch the graphs of two functions that are not continuous.

Roughly speaking, a function is continuous if its graph has no breaks. You could trace the entire curve without picking up your pencil. Your experience tells you that polynomial functions are continuous.

Minds in Action   episode 6

Tony and Sasha are trying to show algebraically that $f(x) = 4x - 3$ is continuous at $x = 2$.

Tony   The graph of $y = 4x - 3$ is a straight line. So it obviously has no breaks, and it must be continuous everywhere.

Sasha   True, but we're suppose to show this algebraically—so no graphs allowed.

Tony   Okay, then let's go back to the definition. We need to show that we can make $f(x)$ as close as we want to $f(2)$ by making x close enough to 2.

Sasha   Well, $f(2) = 5$. And let's say we want to make $f(x)$ be within 0.01 of $f(2)$.

Tony   So we want,

$$|f(x) - f(2)| < 0.01$$

Sasha   Looks good. We can substitute for $f(x)$ and $f(2)$, too. So we have

$$|(4x - 3) - 5| < 0.01$$

or, simplifying a bit,

$$|4x - 8| < 0.01$$
$$4 \cdot |x - 2| < 0.01$$
$$|x - 2| < 0.0025$$

So if x is within 0.0025 of 2, then we're guaranteed that $f(x)$ is within 0.01 of $f(2)$.

Tony But what if we have to make $f(x)$ within 0.001 of $f(2)$? Do we have to go through this all over again?

Sasha No, you don't need to do any extra work. There was nothing special about the value 0.01 in the above calculation. So if we have to make $f(x)$ within any distance d from $f(2)$, just replace 0.01 with d and go through the same steps!

For You to Do

8. Explain what Sasha meant by saying there was nothing special about the value 0.01. Let d be any positive number. How close must x be to $a = 2$ to ensure that $f(x)$ is no more than a distance d away from $f(2)$?

A nice result of the fact that polynomial functions are continuous is that their graphs cannot get from one side of a horizontal line (such as the x-axis) to the other without crossing that line.

Theorem 3.1 The Change of Sign Theorem

Suppose f is a polynomial function and there are two numbers a and b such that $f(a) < 0$ and $f(b) > 0$. Then $f(c) = 0$ for some number c between a and b.

> This theorem is easy to believe but not so easy to prove. You will see its proof when you take calculus. The theorem is actually true for all continuous functions, not just polynomial functions.

The Change of Sign Theorem says that if a polynomial changes sign between inputs a and b, it must equal zero for some input between a and b. The number that makes it zero is a root of the equation $f(x) = 0$. The theorem says nothing about how to find the root. It just says the root exists somewhere between a and b.

A more general result, which also follows from the continuity of polynomials, is the following theorem.

Theorem 3.2 The Intermediate Value Theorem for Polynomials

Suppose f is a polynomial function and a and b are two numbers such that $f(a) < f(b)$. Then for any number c between $f(a)$ and $f(b)$, there is at least one number d between a and b such that $f(d) = c$.

For Discussion

9. Show that Theorem 3.1 implies Theorem 3.2.

10. Show that Theorem 3.2 implies Theorem 3.1.

Have you noticed that some polynomials have real roots while others do not? How can you tell which ones do and which ones do not? The Change of Sign Theorem tells you that if the graph starts out on one side of the *x*-axis and ends up on the other, there must be a real root.

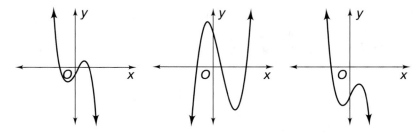

Also, the graph of a polynomial can start and end positive, or start and end negative, and still cross the *x*-axis.

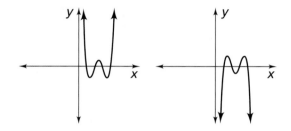

But it does not have to cross.

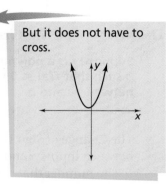

For Discussion

11. Polynomial functions with only one term, like $f(x) = 4x^3$ or $g(x) = -5x^8$, are called **power functions.** Which power functions have graphs that start on one side of the *x*-axis and end on the other?

For You to Do

12. Look at your polynomial function graph gallery (see Exercise 10 of Lesson 3.1). State a conjecture about how you can tell if a polynomial changes sign by looking at its degree. Give evidence to support your conjecture, even if you do not completely prove it.

Make strategic choices. Since they only have one term, power functions can be easier to analyze than other polynomial functions. For instance, it is clear that the function $f(x) = x^3$ increases quite quickly as x increases. But consider the polynomial

$$g(x) = x^3 - 14x^2 - 55x - 42$$

Is it equally clear what happens to the function g as x increases?

For $x \neq 0$, you can rewrite $g(x)$ like this:

$$g(x) = x^3\left(1 - \frac{14}{x} - \frac{55}{x^2} - \frac{42}{x^3}\right)$$

As $|x|$ gets large, $\frac{14}{x}$, $\frac{55}{x^2}$, and $\frac{42}{x^3}$ all get closer and closer to 0, so the values inside the parentheses get closer to 1. So when $|x|$ is large,

- $g(x) \approx x^3 = $ a large positive number, when $x > 0$.

- $g(x) \approx x^3 = $ a large negative number, when $x < 0$.

> for example $x = 10^6$ or $x = -10^6$

In other words, the graph of g starts out negative and ends positive, just as the graph of f does.

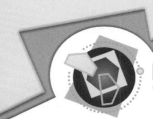

Exercises *Practicing Habits of Mind*

Check Your Understanding

1. Was there ever a time in your life when your weight in pounds was exactly equal to your height in inches? Justify your answer.

2. Consider $a(x) = 2(x - 5)(x + 3)(x - 1) = 2x^3 - 6x^2 - 26x + 30$. Give estimates for each of these values.

> An answer like "it's a really big negative number" is fine here.

   a. $a(5)$ **b.** $a(5.001)$ **c.** $a(0)$

   d. $a(0.001)$ **e.** $a(1000)$ **f.** $a(0.999)$

   g. $a(-1000)$

3. **a.** Find a polynomial function g with $g(3) = g(-7) = 0$.

   b. Find a polynomial function h with $h(5) = h(-3) = 0$ and $h(0) = 10$.

   c. Find a polynomial function j with $j(5) = j(-3) = 2$ and $j(0) = 12$.

4. Suppose $f(x) = 3x + 2$. How close must x be to 5 to meet the following conditions?

   a. $|f(x) - f(5)| < 0.1$

   b. $|f(x) - f(5)| < 0.01$

   c. $|f(x) - f(5)| < 0.001$

   d. $|f(x) - f(5)| < 10^{-6}$

5. Suppose g is a cubic polynomial and ℓ is any line in the plane. What are the maximum and minimum numbers of intersections that ℓ can have with the graph of g? Explain.

6. What shape can the graph of a fourth degree polynomial function have? Here are some functions to try:

   • $f(x) = x^4 - 3x^3 - 2x^2 + 2x + 4$

   • $g(x) = x^4 - 3x^3 - 2x^2 - 3x + 6$

   • $t(x) = x^4 + 2$

7. **Take It Further** Let f and g be arbitrary cubic polynomial functions.

   a. Must there be three real numbers x that make $f(x) = 0$? Explain.

   b. Let h be the polynomial defined as $h = f \cdot g$ (the product). Must there be a real number x for which $h(x) = 0$? Explain.

   c. Let j be the polynomial defined as $j = f^2$ (the square of function f). Must there be a real number x for which $j(x) = 0$? Explain.

   d. Let k be the polynomial defined as $k = f + g$. Must there be a real number x for which $k(x) = 0$? Explain.

   e. Let m be the polynomial defined as $m = f \circ g$. Must there be a real number x for which $m(x) = 0$? Explain.

8. Toby drives exactly 200 miles from San Jose to Morro Bay, CA. The trip takes exactly four hours. Show that at some point in the trip, Toby's speedometer indicates a speed of exactly 50 miles per hour.

9. Consider $b(x) = (x - 2)(x + 5)(x - 3) = x^3 - 19x + 30$. Give estimates for each of these values.

   a. $b(-5)$ **b.** $b(-5.001)$ **c.** $b(0)$

   d. $b(0.001)$ **e.** $b(-0.001)$ **f.** $b(1000)$

   g. $b(-1000)$

> An answer like "it's a little bit more than 10" is fine. Try to give quick answers without use of paper or calculator.

10. **Write About It** Use the Change of Sign Theorem to explain why the Odd-Degree Root Theorem is true.

Theorem 3.3 The Odd-Degree Root Theorem

A polynomial function of odd degree has at least one real root.

11. Suppose $f(x) = x^2$. How close must x be to 5 to meet the following conditions?

   a. $|f(x) - f(5)| < 0.6$ **b.** $|f(x) - f(5)| < 0.06$

   c. $|f(x) - f(5)| < 0.006$ **d.** $|f(x) - f(5)| < 6 \cdot 10^{-6}$

12. Find, if possible, a fourth degree polynomial function the graph of which satisfies these conditions:

- The graph crosses the x-axis at $(-5, 0)$, $(-1, 0)$, and intersects it somewhere on the positive x-axis.
- From left to right, the graph rises, falls, rises, and falls.
- The graph crosses the y-axis at $(0, -7)$.

Explain your work.

13. Suppose h is a degree four polynomial and ℓ is any line in the plane.

   a. What are the maximum and minimum numbers of intersections that ℓ can have with the graph of h?

   b. Can ℓ ever intersect the graph at an odd number of points? Explain.

14. Suppose g is a monic cubic polynomial.

   a. What can you say about $g(x)$ as x takes on large positive values?

   b. What can you say about $g(x)$ as x takes on large negative values?

   c. Sketch an example of what the graph of g could be.

Go **Online**
PHSchool.com

For additional practice, go to **Web Code: bga-0302**

15. **What's Wrong Here** Derman thinks there is a problem with the Odd-Degree Root Theorem.

   Derman says, "What about $\frac{1}{x}$? I can write that as x^{-1}, which has an odd exponent. And $\frac{1}{x}$ is positive if x is positive, and it's negative when x is negative, but you'll never find a number that makes $\frac{1}{x}$ equal zero."

   Why can you not apply the reasoning in this lesson to a function like $f(x) = \frac{1}{x}$?

16. **a.** What are the maximum and minimum number of real roots that a degree-4 polynomial can have? Illustrate with graphs.

   b. Can a fourth degree polynomial have exactly two real roots? Explain.

17. **Take It Further** Let $g(x) = x^3 - 3$. Show that g changes sign. Is there any rational number x such that $g(x) = 0$?

18. Is there a polynomial that fits each description? If so, find one. If not, explain why none exists.

   a. even degree, no real roots   **b.** odd degree, one real root

   c. odd degree, three real roots   **d.** odd degree, two real roots

   e. fourth degree, exactly three real roots

19. Supose that f is a polynomial function such that $f(a)$ and $f(b)$ have opposite sign for some numbers a and b. Can there be more than one value c between a and b with $f(c) = 0$? Give examples to support what you say.

20. Let $g_c(x) = x^3 - 7x^2 + 14x + c$. Find, if possible, a value of c such that $g_c(x) = 0$ has

   a. exactly one real solution   **b.** exactly two real solutions

   c. exactly three real solutions   **d.** no real solutions

21. **Take It Further** Pick any two points on the graph of $g(x) = x^3 - x$. The coordinates will be

$$(a, g(a)) \text{ and } (b, g(b))$$

   a. Write an expression for the slope of the line connecting these two points as a polynomial in a and b.

   b. Let $a = 2$ and $b = 2.01$. Calculate the slope using the new expression.

   c. Suppose a and b are very close together. Write a new expression, using only one variable, that would do a good job of approximating the slope of the line connecting these points.

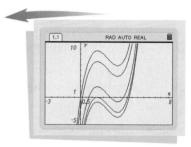

If a and b are very close to each other, you can approximate the value of the expression by assuming $a = b$.

22. **Standardized Test Prep** Which of the following functions is continuous?

A. $f(x) = -\sin\left(-\frac{x}{999}\right)$ **B.** $f(x) = \tan\frac{x}{16}$

C. $f(x) = \sec\frac{x}{16}$ **D.** $f(x) = \frac{\sin 16x}{x}$

Maintain Your Skills

If you divide $x^4 - 5x^3 + 3x - 1$ by $x - 3$, the quotient is $x^3 - 2x^2 - 6x - 15$ and the remainder is -46.

$$
\begin{array}{r}
x^3 - 2x^2 - 6x - 15 \\
x - 3 \overline{\smash{)}\, x^4 - 5x^3 + 3x - 1} \\
\underline{x^4 - 3x^3} \\
-2x^3 + 3x - 1 \\
\underline{-2x^3 + 6x^2} \\
-6x^2 + 3x - 1 \\
\underline{-6x^2 + 18x} \\
-15x - 1 \\
\underline{-15x + 45} \\
-46
\end{array}
$$

In short,

$$x^4 - 5x^3 + 3x - 1 = (x - 3)(x^3 - 2x^2 - 6x - 15) - 46$$

23. **a.** Find a number c such that

$$x^3 - 2x^2 - 6x - 15 = (x - 3)(x^2 + x - 3) + c$$

b. Find a number d such that

$$x^2 + x - 3 = (x - 3)(x + 4) + d$$

c. Find numbers A, B, C, D, and E such that

$$x^4 - 5x^3 + 3x - 1 = A + B(x - 3) + C(x - 3)^2 + D(x - 3)^3 + E(x - 3)^4$$

Habits of Mind

Reason logically.
So $f(3) = -46$. Why?

To finish the pattern, note that $x + 4 = (x - 3) \cdot 1 + 7$.

3.3 Graphs and Secant Lines

At any moment of time, you are moving at a certain speed (which could be 0). Over an interval of time, your average speed is the distance you cover divided by the time you take to do it.

In-Class Experiment

1. Below is a graph that shows how far Jerry has walked in 40 seconds. Determine his average speed between $t = 10$ and $t = 30$.

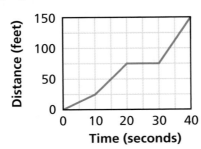

Recall that the average rate of change on a distance-time graph between two events A and B (points on the graph) is the slope $m(A, B)$ between these two points. For example, in the In-Class Experiment, the two points are $A = (10, 25)$ and $B = (30, 75)$, which give the slope

$$m(A, B) = \frac{75 - 25}{30 - 10} = \frac{5}{2}.$$

Thus, Jerry walks with an average speed of $\frac{5}{2}$ feet per second between $t = 10$ and $t = 30$.

More generally, let f be any function and let A and B be points on the graph of $y = f(x)$. The slope $m(A, B)$ is the **average rate of change** of $f(x)$ with respect to x between A and B. The line through A and B is so important that it deserves a special name.

Definition

Let f be a function and suppose A and B are distinct points on the graph of $y = f(x)$. The line passing through A and B is called a secant to the graph of $y = f(x)$. Its slope is the average rate of change of $f(x)$ with respect to x between A and B.

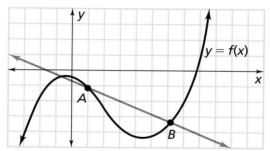

The secant to the graph between *A* and *B*

Here are three methods for finding or approximating the equations of secants to graphs of polynomial functions.

Method 1: Use Your Calculator

Some calculators can find the equation of the line through any two points on the *xy*-plane. If you choose your two points to be on the graph of some function, it will then find the equation of the secant to the graph between these points.

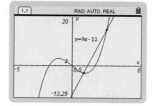

Method 2: Use the Definition of Slope

If $(a, f(a))$ and $(b, f(b))$ are points on the graph of $y = f(x)$, then the slope of the secant between them is

$$\frac{f(b) - f(a)}{b - a}$$

From here you can find the equation.

> See the TI-Nspire™ Handbook on p. 704 for details about how to set up this sketch.

Example 1

Problem Suppose $f(x) = x^3 - 4x$.

a. Find the average rate of change of *y* with respect to *x* between $x = 1$ and $x = 3$.

b. Find the equation of the secant between $(1, f(1))$ and $(3, f(3))$.

c. Find all intersections of the graph of $y = f(x)$ and the secant you found in part (b).

Solution

a. To find the average rate of change, find the slope between the points $(1, f(1))$ and $(3, f(3))$.

$$\frac{f(3) - f(1)}{3 - 1} = \frac{15 - (-3)}{3 - 1} = 9$$

b. The secant has slope 9. To find its equation, take the base point to be either $A = (1, f(1)) = (1, -3)$ or $B = (3, f(3)) = (3, 15)$.

Suppose you pick A. Then an equation of the secant is

$$\frac{y - (-3)}{x - 1} = 9 \quad \text{or} \quad 9x - y = 12$$

c. Shown below are the graphs of $y = f(x)$ and $9x - y = 12$.

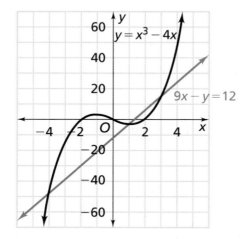

Compare this with the answer you get when you use a calculator to find the equation of the secant.

The graphs intersect at three points. You already know two of them, namely $A = (1, -3)$ and $B = (3, 15)$. To find the third, solve $9x - y = 12$ for y and set y equal to $f(x)$. Thus,

$$x^3 - 4x = 9x - 12$$

or equivalently,

$$x^3 - 13x + 12 = 0$$

Since 1 is a root of this equation, $x - 1$ is one of the factors of the cubic polynomial on the left side. Long division and factoring gives

$$x^3 - 13x + 12 = (x - 1)(x^2 + x - 12)$$
$$= (x - 1)(x - 3)(x + 4)$$

So the three roots are 1, 3, and -4. The third intersection point is $C = (-4, -48)$.

Method 3: Use the Remainder Theorem

The Remainder Theorem says that if a is any real number,

$$f(x) = (x - a)q(x) + f(a)$$

where you can find $q(x)$ and $f(a)$ by long division. You can rewrite the equation as

$$\frac{f(x) - f(a)}{x - a} = q(x)$$

This is an identity, so it is true when $x = b$.

$$\frac{f(b) - f(a)}{b - a} = q(b)$$

So $q(b)$ is the slope of the secant between $(a, f(a))$ and $(b, f(b))$. From here you can find the equation.

For a review of the Remainder Theorem, go to **Web Code: bge-9031**

Example 2

Problem Suppose $f(x) = x^3 - 4x$ again. Using the Remainder Theorem method, find the equation of the secant between $(1, f(1))$ and $(3, f(3))$.

Solution Long division gives

$$\begin{array}{r}
x^2 + x - 3 \\
x - 1 \overline{\smash{)}\, x^3 - 4x } \\
\underline{x^3 - x^2 } \\
x^2 - 4x \\
\underline{x^2 - x } \\
-3x \\
\underline{-3x + 3} \\
-3
\end{array}$$

Write this as

$$f(x) = (x - 1)(x^2 + x - 3) - 3 = (x - 1)(x^2 + x - 3) + f(1)$$

and then as

$$\frac{f(x) - f(1)}{x - 1} = x^2 + x - 3$$

Now substitute $x = 3$ to find the slope of the secant,

$$\frac{f(3) - f(1)}{3 - 1} = 3^2 + 3 - 3 = 9$$

and proceed as in part (b) of Example 1.

This approach may not seem like a time saver, but it is more general than the calculator- and definition-based methods. You can use $x^2 + x - 3$ to find the slope of the secant between $(1, f(1))$ and any point $(b, f(b))$ on the graph.

For You to Do

Let $f(x) = x^3 - 4x$.

2. By long division, you found that
$$f(x) = (x - 1)(x^2 + x - 3) - 3$$
Using this equation, explain why $f(1) = -3$.

3. Note that
$$f(x) + 3 = (x - 1)(x^2 + x - 3)$$
Since $x - 1$ is a factor of the right side, it must be a factor of the left side, which equals $x^3 - 4x + 3$. Find the other factor.

4. Find the slope of the secant through $(1, f(x))$ and $(3, f(x))$ again, but use $(3, f(3))$ as the base point. In other words, start by dividing $x^3 - 4x$ by $x - 3$ to obtain the quotient $q(x)$. Then write
$$f(x) = (x - 3)q(x) + f(3)$$

 Try long division.

Later in this chapter, you will see another way to use long division to find equations of secants. If $f(x) = (x - a)(x - b)q(x) + r(x)$, then $r(x)$ is linear and agrees with f at $x = a$ and $x = b$.

 **Exercises** *Practicing Habits of Mind*

Check Your Understanding

1. Consider $f(x) = x^2$.

a. Let $a = 2$ and $b = 5$. Find the average rate of change of $f(x)$ between $x = a$ and $x = b$.

b. Let $a = -3$ and $b = 11$. Find the equation of the secant line through $(a, f(a))$ and $(b, f(b))$.

c. Write m as a polynomial in a and b using the equation
$$m = \frac{f(b) - f(a)}{b - a}$$

2. Let $f(x) = x^3 - 2x + 1$.

    a. Find the equation of the secant through the points $(2, f(2))$ and $(2.01, f(2.01))$.

    b. Calculate, in terms of b, the equation of the secant between the points $(2, f(2))$ and $(b, f(b))$.

    c. Use geometry software to draw the graph of f. Plot the point $A(2, f(2))$. Place a moveable point B on the graph of f. Move B closer to A. What happens to the slope between A and B?

See the TI-Nspire Handbook on p. 704 for details on how set up this sketch.

3. Consider $f(x) = x^3 - 2x + 1$.

    a. Use geometry software to draw the graph of f. Plot the point $A(1, f(1))$. Place a moveable point B on the graph of f.

    b. Construct the secant line through A and B. Find the equation of this line.

    c. Let b be the x-coordinate of B. Write $m(A, B)$ as a polynomial in b, using the formula

$$m(A, B) = \frac{f(b) - f(1)}{b - 1}$$

    d. Move B closer to A. What happens to the slope of the secant line?

You denote the *limiting value* of the slope as b approaches 1 in Exercise 3d by

$$\lim_{b \to 1} \frac{f(b) - 0}{b - 1}$$

Where does the 0 come from?

4. Consider $f(x) = x^3 - 7x^2 + 3x - 2$.

    a. Use geometry software to draw the graph of f. Plot the point $A(0, f(0))$. Place a moveable point B on the graph of f.

    b. Construct the secant line through A and B. Find the equation of this line.

    c. Let b be the x-coordinate of B. Write $m(A, B)$ as a polynomial in b, using the formula

$$m(A, B) = \frac{f(b) - f(0)}{b - 0}$$

    d. Move B closer to A. What happens to the slope of the secant line?

5. Let $f(x) = 3x^2 + 5x - 7$. Find an expression in terms of a and b for the slope of the secant connecting $(a, f(a))$ and $(b, f(b))$.

6. Consider $f(x) = x^2$.

    a. Let $a = 2$ and $b = 5$. Find the y-intercept of the secant line connecting $(a, f(a))$ and $(b, f(b))$.

    b. Repeat for part (a) $a = -3$ and $b = 11$.

    c. Find and prove a general result based on parts (a) and (b).

7. **Take It Further** Show algebraically that the slope of any secant line on the graph of $y = x^3$ must be positive.

8. John leaves home at 8:00 A.M. riding his mountain bike. He pedals at a constant rate of 15 ft/s.

    a. How far has John ridden at 8:10 A.M.?

    b. How far has John ridden at 8:20 A.M.?

    c. How far has John ridden at 8:45 A.M.?

    d. Write an expression for how far John has ridden t minutes after 8:00 A.M.

9. Pete, John's older brother, leaves 10 minutes after John, heading down the same trail. He rides at 20 ft/s.

    a. How far has Pete ridden at 8:10 A.M.? Has Pete caught John?

    b. How far has Pete ridden at 8:20 A.M.? Has Pete caught John?

    c. How far has Pete ridden at 8:45 A.M.? Has Pete caught John?

    d. Write an expression for how far Pete has ridden at t minutes after 8:00 A.M.

    e. How can you find the exact time Pete caught John?

10. Demitri and Yakov are running on a track. The figure at the right shows their distance-time graphs.

    a. Who is running faster, Demitri or Yakov?

    b. When does Yakov overtake Demitri?

    c. At what distance does Yakov overtake Demitri?

    d. What is each runner's speed?

    e. Write an equation for Yakov's graph.

    f. Write an equation for Demitri's graph.

    g. Write and solve an equation for which the solution is the time at which Yakov overtakes Demitri.

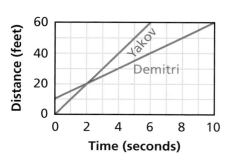

A speed of 20 feet per second is equivalent to about 13.6 miles per hour.

11. Sketch each graph.

   a. $y = x^3$ **b.** $y = x^3 - 1$

   c. $y = (x + 4)^3$ **d.** $y = (x + 4)^3 - 1$

12. Sketch the graph of each polynomial function.

   a. $a(x) = (x - 5)^3$ **b.** $b(x) = (x - 5)^3(x + 2)$

   c. $c(x) = x^3 - 4x$ **d.** $d(x) = (x - 4.9)(x - 5)(x - 5.1)$

   e. $e(x) = (x + 3)^{100}$

> **Think it through.** Try sketching the graphs first, without a calculator.

13. The graph of $g(x) = x^3 - x$ passes through the point $(2, 6)$.

   a. Use geometry software to draw the graph of f. Plot the point $A(2, f(2))$. Place a moveable point B on the graph of f.

   b. Let b be the x-coordinate of B. The slope of the line through A and B is

$$m(A, B) = \frac{f(b) - f(2)}{b - 2}$$

   Describe what happens to this slope as you move B closer to A.

14. **Take It Further** Consider a line secant to the graph of $y = x^2$, through $(3, 9)$ and a point very close to $(3, 9)$.

   a. Approximate the slope of this line.

   b. Write an equation for a line that has the slope you found in part (a) and passes through $(3, 9)$.

15. The graph of $f(x) = x^3 - 3x$ passes through the point $(-1, 2)$.

   a. Use geometry software to draw the graph of f. Plot the point $A(-1, f(-1))$. Place a moveable point B on the graph of f.

   b. Construct the secant line through A and B. Find the equation of this line.

   c. Let b be the x-coordinate of B. Write $m(A, B)$ as a polynomial in b, using the formula

$$m(A, B) = \frac{f(b) - f(-1)}{b - (-1)}$$

   d. Move B closer to A. What happens to the slope of the secant line?

Go Online
PHSchool.com

For additional practice, go to **Web Code:** bga-0303

16. Use graphs and your work from Exercise 15 to determine when $f(x) = x^3 - 3x$ is increasing.

17. **Take It Further** Let $g(x) = Ax^2 + Bx + C$. What is the slope of the secant line between $(p, g(p))$ and $(q, g(q))$?

Remember...

The slope equals the change in y divided by the change in x. You can also look back at Exercise 5 for an example using specific values of A, B, and C.

18. On the same axes, sketch the graph of each equation. Where do the graphs intersect?

   a. $y = x + (4x + 1)$ and $y = 4x + 1$

   b. $y = x^2 + (4x + 1)$ and $y = 4x + 1$

19. On the same axes, sketch the graph of each equation. Where do the graphs intersect?

   a. $y = (x - 5) + (2x - 6)$ and $y = 2x - 6$

   b. $y = (x - 5)^2 + (2x - 6)$ and $y = 2x - 6$

20. **Standardized Test Prep** What is the average rate of change of $f(x) = \dfrac{3}{x^2}$ as x goes from 1 to 3?

   A. $-\dfrac{1}{3}$ **B.** $-\dfrac{3}{2}$ **C.** $-\dfrac{3}{4}$ **D.** $-\dfrac{4}{3}$

Maintain Your Skills

21. Find a polynomial function that satisfies the conditions.

   a. $a(0) = 0$ and $a(1) = 1$

   b. $b(0) = b(1) = 0$ and $b(2) = 1$

   c. $c(0) = c(1) = c(2) = 0$ and $c(3) = 1$

   d. $d(0) = d(1) = d(2) = d(3) = 0$ and $d(4) = 1$

   e. **Take It Further** $f(0) - 0$, $f(1) = 7$, $f(2) = 10$, $f(3) = 20$, and $f(4) = 52$

22. Copy and complete this table for $f(x) = x^2 - 4x + 1$.

x	$f(x)$	Slope of secant through $(x, f(x))$ and a point near it
-1	6	▪
0	▪	▪
1	-2	▪
2	▪	0
3	▪	▪

"Near $(x, f(x))$" might mean that the x-value for the point is "within 0.01 of x."

3.4 Polynomials in Powers of $x - a$

You have a lot of experience writing expressions in different forms. Now you will learn how to write a polynomial in a form that will help you find the rate at which it is changing.

For You to Do

1. Show that

$$2(x - 3)^3 + 5(x - 3)^2 - 7(x - 3) + 14 = 2x^3 - 13x^2 + 17x + 26$$

Given a polynomial written in powers of $x - 3$, you can rewrite it as a polynomial in x, expanding it by hand or by using your calculator. The goal in this lesson, however, is to start with a polynomial in x such as

$$f(x) = 2x^3 - 13x^2 + 17x + 26$$

and rewrite it as a polynomial in powers of $x - 3$ or, in general, $x - a$.

There are at least three different methods for doing this.

Example

Problem Write $f(x) = x^4 - 5x^3 + 3x - 1$ as a polynomial in $x - 3$.

Solution Here is the first method.

Method 1: Iterated Long Division

Start with the calculation in the Maintain Your Skills section on page 179.

$$
\begin{array}{r}
x^3 - 2x^2 - 6x - 15 \\
x - 3 \overline{) x^4 - 5x^3 \qquad\quad + 3x - 1} \\
\underline{x^4 - 3x^3} \qquad\qquad\qquad \\
-2x^3 \qquad + 3x - 1 \\
\underline{-2x^3 + 6x^2} \qquad\qquad \\
-6x^2 + 3x - 1 \\
\underline{-6x^2 + 18x} \qquad \\
-15x - 1 \\
\underline{-15x + 45} \\
-46
\end{array}
$$

This says that

$$f(x) = -46 + (x - 3)\underbrace{(x^3 - 2x^2 - 6x - 15)}_{q_1(x)}$$

Let $x = 3$ to find that $f(3) = -46$.

Now work with the quotient $q_1(x) = x^3 - 2x^2 - 6x - 15$.

$$
\begin{array}{r}
x^2 + x - 3 \\
x - 3 \overline{)\; x^3 - 2x^2 - 6x - 15} \\
\underline{x^3 - 3x^2} \\
x^2 - 6x - 15 \\
\underline{x^2 - 3x} \\
-3x - 15 \\
\underline{-3x + 9} \\
-24
\end{array}
$$

This says that

$$q_1(x) = -24 + (x - 3)\underbrace{(x^2 + x - 3)}_{q_2(x)}$$

Now work with the quotient $q_2(x) = x^2 + x - 3$.

$$
\begin{array}{r}
x + 4 \\
x - 3 \overline{)\; x^2 + x - 3} \\
\underline{x^2 - 3x} \\
4x - 3 \\
\underline{4x - 12} \\
9
\end{array}
$$

This says that

$$q_2(x) = 9 + (x - 3)\underbrace{(x + 4)}_{q_3(x)}$$

Now work with the quotient $q_3(x) = x + 4$.

$$
\begin{array}{r}
1 \\
x - 3 \overline{)\; x + 4} \\
\underline{x - 3} \\
7
\end{array}
$$

This says that

$$q_3(x) = 7 + (x - 3)\underbrace{(\,1\,)}_{q_4(x)}$$

Now put it all together.

$$
\begin{aligned}
f(x) &= -46 + (x - 3)\underbrace{(x^3 - 2x^2 - 6x - 15)}_{q_1(x)} \\
&= -46 + (x - 3)(-24 + (x - 3)(x^2 + x - 3)) \\
&= -46 - 24(x - 3) + (x - 3)^2 \underbrace{(x^2 + x - 3)}_{q_2(x)} \\
&= -46 - 24(x - 3) + (x - 3)^2(9 + (x - 3)(x + 4)) \\
&= -46 - 24(x - 3) + 9(x - 3)^2 + (x - 3)^3 \underbrace{(x + 4)}_{q_3(x)} \\
&= -46 - 24(x - 3) + 9(x - 3)^2 + (x - 3)^3(7 + (x - 3)) \\
&= -46 - 24(x - 3) + 9(x - 3)^2 + 7(x - 3)^3 + (x - 3)^4
\end{aligned}
$$

The expression of $f(x)$ in terms of powers of $x - 3$ is the **Taylor expansion** for f about 3. The tools of calculus make it possible to write Taylor expansions for non-polynomial functions, as well.

For Discussion

Some older math books describe an elegant shorthand for doing polynomial division. Follow the instructions to find $(x^4 - 5x^3 + 3x - 1) \div (x - 3)$.

For a divisor $x - a$, put a in the L-shaped bracket on the left. After the bracket, write the coefficients of the dividend polynomial in descending order of degree. Leave a space, draw a line, and bring down the leading coefficient.

$$\underline{3} \; | \begin{array}{ccccc} 1 & -5 & 0 & 3 & -1 \\ \hline 1 \end{array}$$

Put in a zero if there is no term with a particular degree.

Multiply the number you just wrote under the line by the number in the bracket. Put the product under the next coefficient, and add down.

$$\underline{3} \; | \begin{array}{ccccc} 1 & -5 & 0 & 3 & -1 \\ & 3 & & & \\ \hline 1 & -2 \end{array}$$

Repeat the previous step until you reach the end.

$$\underline{3} \; | \begin{array}{ccccc} 1 & -5 & 0 & 3 & -1 \\ & 3 & -6 & -18 & -45 \\ \hline 1 & -2 & -6 & -15 & \boxed{-46} \end{array}$$

Now you have completed the first division. Look back at your long division result on page 190. You can read off the coefficients of the quotient and remainder from this shorthand. You can do repeated divisions to get the complete Taylor expansion.

$$\underline{3} \; | \begin{array}{ccccc} 1 & -5 & 0 & 3 & -1 \\ & 3 & -6 & -18 & -45 \\ \hline 1 & -2 & -6 & -15 & \boxed{-46} \\ & 3 & 3 & -9 & \\ \hline 1 & 1 & -3 & \boxed{-24} & \\ & 3 & 12 & & \\ \hline 1 & 4 & \boxed{9} & & \\ & 3 & & & \\ \hline \boxed{1} & \boxed{7} & & & \end{array}$$

This gives you $(x - 3)^4 + 7(x - 3)^3 + 9(x - 3)^2 - 24(x - 3) - 46$.

2. Use this algorithm to expand $2x^3 + 5x^2 + x - 1$ as a polynomial in $x - 2$.

3. Take It Further Why does this algorithm work?

Here is a second method for writing a polynomial in powers of $x - 3$.

Method 2: Undetermined Coefficients

Suppose

$$f(x) = x^4 - 5x^3 + 3x - 1 = A + B(x - 3) + C(x - 3)^2 + D(x - 3)^3 + E(x - 3)^4 \quad (1)$$

You need to find A, B, C, D, and E.

Why do you only need to go up to $(x - 3)^4$?

- Substitute $x = 3$ into (1) to find that $A = f(3) = -46$. Subtract -46 from each side of (1) to get

$$x^4 - 5x^3 + 3x + 45 = B(x - 3) + C(x - 3)^2 + D(x - 3)^3 + E(x - 3)^4 \quad (2)$$

The right side of (2) has $x - 3$ as a factor, and the left side does, too. You can check this by noting that

$$3^4 - 5 \cdot 3^3 + 3 \cdot 3 + 45 = 0$$

That is, $x = 3$ is a zero of the left side of (2). The left side of (2) factors as

$$(x - 3)(x^3 - 2x^2 - 6x - 15)$$

- So you can write (2) as

$$(x - 3)(x^3 - 2x^2 - 6x - 15) = B(x - 3) + C(x - 3)^2 + D(x - 3)^3 + E(x - 3)^4$$

Divide each side by $x - 3$ to get

$$x^3 - 2x^2 - 6x - 15 = B + C(x - 3) + D(x - 3)^2 + E(x - 3)^3 \quad (3)$$

Since the left and right sides are equal for $x \neq 3$, they must be equal for $x = 3$, as well.

What property of polynomials justifies this statement?

- Substitute $x = 3$ into (3) to find that $B = -24$. Subtract -24 from each side of (3) to get

$$x^3 - 2x^2 - 6x + 9 = C(x - 3) + D(x - 3)^2 + E(x - 3)^3 \quad (4)$$

The right side of (4) has $x - 3$ as a factor, and thus so does the left side. Again, note that $x = 3$ is a zero of the left side, which factors as

$$(x - 3)(x^2 + x - 3)$$

- So (4) becomes

$$(x - 3)(x^2 + x - 3) = C(x - 3) + D(x - 3)^2 + E(x - 3)^3$$

Divide by $x - 3$ to get

$$x^2 + x - 3 = C + D(x - 3) + E(x - 3)^2 \quad (5)$$

Again, the equation holds both for $x \neq 3$ and for $x = 3$.

Habits of Mind

Use a consistent process. Get into the rhythm of the calculations.

- Substitute $x = 3$ into (5) to find that $C = 9$. Subtract 9 from each side of (5) to get

$$x^2 + x - 12 = D(x - 3) + E(x - 3)^2 \quad (6)$$

The right side of (6) has $x - 3$ as a factor, and so does the left side. Note that $x = 3$ is a zero of the left side, which factors as

$$(x - 3)(x + 4)$$

- So write (6) as $(x - 3)(x + 4) = D(x - 3) + E(x - 3)^2$.

Divide by $x - 3$ to get

$$x + 4 = D + E(x - 3) \tag{7}$$

- Finally, substitute $x = 3$ into (7) to find $D = 7$, and then $E = 1$.

Here is a third method for writing a polynomial in powers of $x - 3$.

Method 3: Use Your CAS

Your CAS has a built-in function that carries out the calculations you have been doing by hand. It allows you to expand a polynomial in terms of powers of $x - a$ for any number a. The function has different names in different systems, but they all work basically the same way.

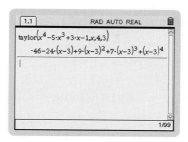

This says, "Give me the expansion of $x^4 = 5x^3 + 3x - 1$. The variable is x, give me terms up to degree is 4, and I want it in terms of $x - 3$."

$$\text{taylor} (x^4 - 5x^3 + 3x - 1, \qquad x, \qquad 4, \qquad 3)$$
$$\downarrow \qquad\qquad \downarrow \qquad \downarrow \qquad\qquad \downarrow$$
$$\text{polynomial} \qquad \text{variable} \quad \text{degree} \quad \text{in terms of } (x - 3)$$

See the TI-Nspire Handbook on p. 704 for more information about the taylor function.

For You to Do

4. Using whatever method you prefer, write
$$f(x) = 2x^3 + 5x^2 + x + 3$$
as a polynomial in $x - 1$.

Exercises *Practicing Habits of Mind*

Check Your Understanding

1. Suppose that $f(x) = 2x^3 + 5x^2 + x - 1$ and $g(x) = x^2 + 2x - 3$. Expand the following in powers of $x - 3$.

a. $f(x)$ **b.** $g(x)$ **c.** $f(x) + g(x)$

d. $4f(x)$ **e.** $4f(x) - g(x)$

2. Suppose that $f(x) = 2x^3 + 5x^2 + x - 1$ and $g(x) = x^2 + 2x - 3$. Expand the following in powers of $x - 2$.

   a. $f(x)$ **b.** $g(x)$

   c. $f(x) + g(x)$ **d.** $3f(x)$

   e. $f(x) \cdot g(x)$

3. Suppose that $g(x) = x^2 + 2x - 3$ and a is some number. Expand $g(x)$ in powers of $x - a$ as

$$g(x) = A + B(x - a) + C(x - a)^2$$

   where A, B, and C are expressions in a.

4. Expand each polynomial in powers of $x - 3$.

   a. x^3 **b.** x^2 **c.** x **d.** 1

   Sasha is thinking about Exercise 4.

   Sasha   I see an easy way to get the expansion for $f(x) = 2x^3 + 5x^2 + x - 1$ from Exercise 1 in powers of $x - 3$.

   Tony   How?

   Sasha   I use what we got from Exercise 4.

   First, we know the expansion for x^3. Since $f(x)$ starts out with $2x^3$, I multiply all the coefficients in the expansion for x^3 by 2.

   Next, we know the expansion for x^2. Since $f(x)$ has a $5x^2$ term, I multiply all the coefficients in the expansion for x^2 by 5.

   Tony   And you multiply the expansion of x by 1 and the expansion of 1 by -1, right?

   Sasha   Right, and then I add all these expressions together, making believe that the variable is $x - 3$. This will work for any cubic— I just need to know the expansions about 3 for the powers of x.

   Tony   Nice, but how do we know it works?

   Sasha   There's only one way to find out.

   > Where did Tony get the 1 and −1?

5. **Write About It**   Does Sasha's method work for $f(x) = 2x^3 + 5x^2 + x - 1$? Does it work for any cubic polynomial? Justify your answers.

On Your Own

6. Suppose that $f(x) = 2x^3 + 5x^2 + x - 1$ and $g(x) = x^2 + 2x - 3$. Expand the following in powers of $x - 5$.

   a. $f(x)$ **b.** $g(x)$ **c.** $3f(x) - 2g(x)$ **d.** $f(x) \cdot f(x)$

7. Suppose that $g(x) = rx^2 + sx + t$. Expand $g(x)$ in powers of $x - 3$.
$$g(x) = A + B(x - 3) + C(x - 3)^2$$
where, A, B, and C are in terms of r, s, and t.

8. Suppose that $g(x) = rx^2 + sx + t$ and a is a number. Expand $g(x)$ in powers of $x - a$ as
$$g(x) = A + B(x - a) + C(x - a)^2$$
where, A, B, and C are in terms of r, s, t, and a.

9. Until now, you have been dividing polynomials by a linear term. But the divisor can have any degree.

a. Find the missing numbers in this long division.

$$
\begin{array}{r}
x + \underline{} \\
x^2 - 7x + 10 \overline{)\, x^3 - 4x^2 - 10x + 31} \\
\underline{x^3 - 7x^2 + \underline{}x} \\
3x^2 + \underline{}x + 31 \\
\underline{\underline{}x^2 + \underline{}x + \underline{}} \\
\underline{}x + \underline{}
\end{array}
$$

b. How can you tell when the long division is complete?

c. Write the result as
$$x^3 - 4x^2 - 10x + 31 = (x^2 - 7x + 10)q(x) + r(x)$$
where q and r are polynomials in x.

10. Find the remainder when you divide $x^3 - 4x^2 - 10x + 31$ by

a. x **b.** x^2 **c.** x^3

11. *Derman is still reviewing his notes.*

Derman I really like the way you can write $f(x)$ in powers of $x + 3$.
$$f(x) = x^3 - 14x^2 + 55x - 42$$
$$= -360 + 166(x + 3) - 23(x + 3)^2 + (x + 3)^3$$

Tony   Why?

Derman It lets me find the remainders when I divide $f(x)$ by any power of $x + 3$.

Tony   Derman, sometimes you can be so deep.

Use Derman's idea to find the remainder when you divide $f(x)$ by

a. $x + 3$ **b.** $(x + 3)^2$ **c.** $(x + 3)^3$ **d.** $(x + 3)^8$

12. In Exercise 6, you expanded combinations of $f(x) = 2x^3 + 5x^2 + x - 1$ and $g(x) = x^2 + 2x - 3$ in powers of $x - 5$. That should make filling in this table a snap. Copy and complete the table.

	Remainder when divided by					
	$x - 5$	$(x - 5)^2$	$(x - 5)^3$	$(x - 5)^4$	$(x - 5)^5$	$(x - 5)^6$
$f(x)$	▦	▦	▦	▦	▦	▦
$g(x)$	▦	▦	▦	▦	▦	▦
$3f(x) - 2g(x)$	▦	▦	▦	▦	▦	▦
$f(x) \cdot f(x)$	▦	▦	▦	▦	▦	▦

13. Write each polynomial in the form $A + B(x - 1) + C(x)(x - 1)^2$ where $C(x)$ is a polynomial in x.

a. x^2 **b.** x^3 **c.** x^4 **d.** x^5 **e.** x^6

f. x^n (where n is a positive integer)

> While you are at it, you might as well expand 1 and x, too.

14. Take It Further Use the identity $x^n = ((x - 1) + 1)^n$ and the Binomial Theorem to write each polynomial in powers of $x - 1$.

a. x^2 **b.** x^3 **c.** x^5 **d.** x^n (n a positive integer)

15. Suppose $f(x) = x^3 - 5x^2 - 2x + 1$. Graph each of the following.

a. f

b. $x \mapsto \text{taylor}(f(x), x, 1, 2)$

c. $x \mapsto \text{taylor}(f(x), x, 2, 2)$

d. $x \mapsto \text{taylor}(f(x), x, 3, 2)$

> The taylor function on your CAS might look a bit different.

16. Standardized Test Prep What is the remainder when you divide $P(x) = 3x^5 - 5x^4 + 2x^3 - 4x^2 + x - 1$ by $x - 1$?

A. 2   **B.** −3   **C.** 4   **D.** −4

Maintain Your Skills

17. For each polynomial $f(x)$,

- Find the remainder $r(x)$ when you divide $f(x)$ by $(x - 3)^2$.
- Sketch the graphs of f and r on the same axes.

a. $f(x) = x^3 - 5x + 6$

b. $f(x) = (x - 1)(x - 5)$

c. $f(x) = x^3$

d. $f(x) = x^3 + 3x^2 - 2x + 1$

e. $f(x) = (x - 1)^3$

f. $f(x) = (x - 3)^3$

Go Online
PHSchool.com

For additional practice, go to **Web Code:** bga-0304

3.5 Secants and Tangents

You know how to find the average rate of change between two points in time. This lesson will help you find the rate of change at a particular instant in time.

In-Class Experiment

Let $d = t^2$ denote the distance d (in feet) that Jerry has walked in t seconds. The graph of this function is shown below.

1. Determine his average speed between $t = 1$ and $t = 2$.

2. Determine his average speed between $t = 1$ and $t = 1.1$.

3. Determine his average speed between $t = 1$ and $t = 1.01$.

4. Determine his instantaneous speed at $t = 1$.

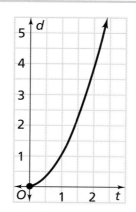

This function does not make sense as a model when t is large, but it is plausible if t is small.

To find Jerry's **instantaneous speed** at $t = 1$, you need to find the slope of the tangent to the graph of $d = t^2$ at the point $(1, 1)$.

For You to Do

5. Use geometry software to make a sketch with the graph of $y = x^2$ and a movable point (a, a^2) on the graph. Construct the tangent to the curve at the point (a, a^2).

See the TI-Nspire Handbook on p. 704 for details on how to draw tangent lines.

6. Copy the table below. Move the point along the graph and record the slope of the corresponding tangents in your table.

x	y = x²	Slope of the tangent at (x, x²)
−1	▨	▨
0	▨	▨
1	▨	▨
2	▨	▨
3	▨	▨
4	▨	▨
10	▨	▨
100	▨	▨

Given a function f and a point $A = (a, f(a))$ on the graph of $y = f(x)$, you can think of the **tangent line** at A as the secant between A and itself.

More precisely, recall Exercise 2 from Lesson 3.3, where you let $f(x) = x^3 - 2x + 1$ and used geometry software to sketch the graph of f, the base point $A = (2, f(2))$ on the graph, and a movable point $B = (b, f(b))$ on the graph.

As B moves closer to A, the secant through A and B approaches the tangent at A. The slope of the tangent at A is the "limiting value" of the slope of the secant as b approaches 2. The usual way to write this is

$$\lim_{b \to 2} \frac{f(b) - f(2)}{b - 2}$$

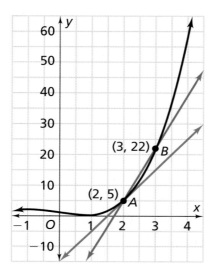

Computing the Tangent

To find the equation of a tangent line algebraically, go back to secants for a moment. Let $f(x) = x^3 - 2x + 1$. Divide $f(x)$ by $(x - 2)(x - 3) = x^2 - 5x + 6$. Using long division, you get

$$
\begin{array}{r}
x + 5 \\
x^2 - 5x + 6 \,\overline{\smash{\big)}\, x^3 \phantom{{}- 5x^2} - 2x + 1} \\
\underline{x^3 - 5x^2 + 6x \phantom{{}+ 1}} \\
5x^2 - 8x + 1 \\
\underline{5x^2 - 25x + 30} \\
17x - 29
\end{array}
$$

so you have

$$f(x) = x^3 - 2x + 1 = (x - 2)(x - 3)q(x) + r(x)$$

where $q(x) = x + 5$ and $r(x) = 17x - 29$. Substituting $x = 2$ shows that $f(2) = r(2)$. Likewise, $f(3) = r(3)$. In other words, r is a linear function that agrees with f at $x = 2$ and $x = 3$. So the graph of $y = r(x)$ must be the secant to the graph of $y = f(x)$ through the points $(2, f(2))$ and $(3, f(3))$.

Here is the generalization.

Theorem 3.4

Let $f(x)$ be a polynomial and $a, b \in \mathbb{R}$. Write

$$f(x) = (x - a)(x - b)q(x) + r(x)$$

where $r(x)$ is a linear function. Then the graph of $y = r(x)$ is the secant to the graph of $y = f(x)$ through $(a, f(a))$ and $(b, f(b))$.

In the above theorem, all you are really interested in is the remainder $r(x)$. In other words, you do not need to know what $q(x)$ is. A CAS can find this remainder easily and quickly.

How about the tangent? Let $f(x) = x^3 - 2x + 1$ again. Suppose you want to find the tangent to its graph at $A = (2, f(2))$. Consider a movable point $B = (b, f(b))$ on the graph. The secant between A and B is given by the remainder when you divide $f(x)$ by $(x - 2)(x - b)$. As point B approaches point A, the corresponding division by $(x - 2)(x - b)$ becomes division by $(x - 2)^2$.

The following theorem summarizes this result.

> See the TI-Nspire Handbook on p. 704 for details on how to use the polyremainder function to find the remainder $r(x)$ when you divide one polynomial by another.

> This type of argument works because polynomial functions are continuous.

Theorem 3.5

Let $f(x)$ be a polynomial and $a \in \mathbb{R}$. Write

$$f(x) = (x - a)^2 q(x) + r(x)$$

where $r(x)$ is a linear function. Then the graph of $y = r(x)$ is the tangent to the graph of $y = f(x)$ at $(a, f(a))$.

Example 1

Problem Suppose $f(x) = x^3 - 2x + 1$. Find the equation of the tangent to the graph of $y = f(x)$ at the point $(2, 5)$.

Solution By Theorem 3.5, the equation of the tangent is the linear function $r(x)$ where

$$f(x) = (x - 2)^2 q(x) + r(x)$$

In other words, $r(x)$ is the remainder when you divide $f(x)$ by $(x - 2)^2 = x^2 - 4x + 4$. A CAS shows that

$$r(x) = 10x - 15$$

So far, you have seen two ways to find the remainder $r(x)$:

- Using long division.
- Using a CAS.

The following technique uses methods from Lesson 3.4.

Example 2

Problem Let $f(x) = 2x^2 + 3x + 1$. Find the equation of the tangent to the graph of $y = f(x)$ at the point $(3, f(3))$.

Solution First, write $f(x)$ in powers of $x - 3$.

$$f(x) = 2x^2 + 3x + 1 = m + n(x - 3) + p(x)(x - 3)^2 \qquad (1)$$

You can read off the remainder when you divide $f(x)$ by $(x - 3)^2$—it is $m + n(x - 3)$.

See Exercise 11 from Lesson 3.4.

With $r(x) = m + n(x - 3)$, the graph of $r(x)$ is the desired tangent. So you need to solve for m and n. Substitute $x = 3$ in (1) to get

$$m = f(3) = 2 \cdot 3^2 + 3 \cdot 3 + 1 = 28$$

So

$$2x^2 + 3x + 1 = 28 + n(x - 3) + p(x)(x - 3)^2 \qquad (2)$$

Subtracting 28 from both sides of (2) gives

$$2x^2 + 3x - 27 = n(x - 3) + p(x)(x - 3)^2$$

The right side says that $x - 3$ is a factor of the left side. This makes factoring the left side easy:

$$(x - 3)(2x + 9) = n(x - 3) + p(x)(x - 3)^2$$

Dividing by $x - 3$ gives

$$2x + 9 = n + p(x)(x - 3) \qquad (3)$$

Substituting $x = 3$ into (3) gives $n = 15$. So the equation of the tangent is

$$r(x) = 28 + 15(x - 3) = 15x - 17.$$

For You to Do

7. Let $f(x) = 2x^2 + 3x + 1$ again. Using the method in Example 2, find the equation of the tangent to the graph of $y = f(x)$ at the point $(a, f(a))$. (Your equation will be in terms of a.)

Habits of Mind

You can also use a CAS to solve this, but do not let the calculator have all the fun.

Exercises *Practicing Habits of Mind*

Check Your Understanding

1. Find the equation of the line tangent to the graph of $y = x^2$ at the point $(5, 25)$.

2. Consider $f(x) = x^3 - 7x^2 + 3x - 2$. Write an equation for the line tangent to the graph of f at $(0, -2)$.

3. Generalize the result in Exercise 1 by finding the equation of the line tangent to the graph of $y = x^2$ at the point (a, a^2).

4. Copy and complete this table for $f(x) = x^2 + 1$.

x	$f(x)$	Slope of tangent at $(x, f(x))$
-1	▩	▩
0	▩	▩
1	▩	▩
2	▩	▩
3	▩	▩
4	▩	▩
10	▩	▩
100	▩	▩

5. Copy and complete this table for $f(x) = x^2 + x$.

x	$f(x)$	Slope of tangent at $(x, f(x))$
-1	▩	▩
0	▩	▩
1	▩	▩
2	▩	▩
3	▩	▩
4	▩	▩
10	▩	▩
100	▩	▩

6. Find the equation of the line tangent to the graph of each polynomial at $(1, 1)$.

    a. $f(x) = x^2$ b. $f(x) = x^3$ c. $f(x) = x^4$
    d. $f(x) = x^5$ e. $f(x) = x^6$ f. $f(x) = x$

7. Find, in terms of n, a formula for the equation of the tangent to the graph of $y = x^n$ (where n is a positive integer) at $(1, 1)$.

8. Find the slope and equation of the line tangent to the graph of
   $f(x) = x^3 - x$ at the point $(-1, 2)$.

9. Copy and complete this table for $f(x) = x^3$.

x	f(x)	Slope of tangent at (x, f(x))
−1	▨	▨
0	▨	▨
1	▨	▨
2	▨	▨
3	▨	▨
4	▨	▨
10	▨	▨
100	▨	▨

10. Find, in terms of a, the equation of the line tangent to the graph of each polynomial at $(a, f(a))$.

    a. $f(x) = x^2$ **b.** $f(x) = x^3$ **c.** $f(x) = x^4$

    d. $f(x) = x^5$ **e.** $f(x) = x^6$ **f.** $f(x) = x$

11. Find, in terms of n and a, a formula for the equation of the tangent to the graph of $f(x) = x^n$ (where n is a positive integer) at $(a, f(a))$.

12. **Take It Further** Find the equation of the line tangent to the graph of $y = \sqrt{x}$ at $(1, 1)$.

13. **Standardized Test Prep** If a function f has a well-defined slope over its entire domain, which of the following expressions gives the slope of $f(x)$ at $x = 0$?

    A. $\lim\limits_{x \to a} \dfrac{f(a) - f(0)}{x - a}$ **B.** $\lim\limits_{a \to b} \dfrac{f(b) - f(a)}{b - a}$ **C.** $\lim\limits_{b \to 0} \dfrac{f(b) - f(0)}{b}$ **D.** $\lim\limits_{x \to 0} \dfrac{f(a) - f(0)}{x}$

Maintain Your Skills

14. Find the remainder when you divide $f(x) = x^3 - 2x + 1$ by each of these linear factors.

    a. $(x + 1)$ **b.** x **c.** $(x - 1)$ **d.** $(x - 2)$

    e. $(x - 3)$ **f.** $(x - 4)$ **g.** $(x - 10)$ **h.** $(x - 100)$

Go **Online**
PHSchool.com

For additional practice, go to **Web Code:** bga-0305

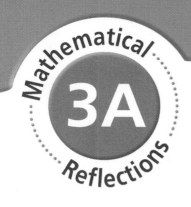

Mathematical 3A Reflections

In this investigation, you found slopes of lines secant or tangent to the graph of a polynomial function. You learned that these slopes represent, respectively, average and instantaneous rates of change of the function. The following questions will help you summarize what you have learned.

1. Here are three expressions that each define the function f.

   Expression 1: $f(x) = x^4 - 5x^3 - x^2 + 17x + 12$

   Expression 2: $f(x) = (x + 1)^2(x - 3)(x - 4)$

   Expression 3: $f(x) = (x - 1)^4 - (x - 1)^3 - 10(x - 1)^2 + 4(x - 1) + 24$

   a. Which expression would be the most useful for sketching the graph of the function? Choose an expression, use it to sketch the graph of the function, and explain how the form of the expression was helpful.

   b. Which expression is the most useful for finding the equation of the line tangent to the graph at the point $(1, 24)$? Choose an expression, use it to find the equation of the tangent, and explain how the form of the expression was helpful.

2. For each of the following numbers, sketch the graph of a third-degree polynomial which has the indicated number of x-intercepts, or explain why such a graph does not exist.

   a. 0   **b.** 1   **c.** 2   **d.** 3   **e.** 4

3. Let $f(x) = x^3 + 8x^2 + 5x - 50$.

   a. Expand the function $f(x)$ in powers of $x + 4$.

   b. Use your expansion to find the equation of the tangent to the graph of $f(x)$ at the point $(-4, f(-4))$.

4. How can you graph a polynomial function given its factored form?

5. How can you determine a polynomial's behavior at very large or very small inputs?

6. How can you use long division to find equations of secant or tangent lines to the graph of a polynomial function?

Vocabulary

In this investigation, you learned these terms. Make sure you understand what each one means and how to use it.

- **average rate of change**
- **continuous**
- **instantaneous speed**
- **power function**

- **secant line**
- **tangent line**
- **Taylor expansion**

Rational Functions

In *Rational Functions*, you will graph functions $f(x)$ that are quotients of polynomials. You will have to pay particular attention to values of x for which the denominator polynomial has value 0.

By the end of this investigation, you will be able to answer questions like these.

1. What happens to $f(x) = \frac{3x^2 + 2x - 1}{5x^2 - 3x + 10}$ as x gets larger and larger?

2. Why do the graphs of $g(x) = \frac{x^2 - 15}{x - 4}$ and $h(x) = \frac{x^2 - 16}{x - 4}$ look so different from each other?

3. How can you find tangent lines to rational functions?

You will learn how to
- sketch the graph of a rational function, including asymptotes and holes

- evaluate limits of rational expressions

- find the equation of the tangent to the graph of a rational function at a point

You will develop these habits and skills:
- Visualize different types of discontinuities, relating equations and their graphs.

- Reason logically to find limits at infinity.

- Extend the methods of Investigation 3A to find the equation of the tangent to the graph of a rational function.

Holes and vertical asymptotes represent discontinuities in the graph of a rational function.

Getting Started

In CME Project *Algebra 2*, you learned to calculate with rational expressions, expressions of the form $\frac{p}{q}$ where p and q are polynomials. The emphasis there was on the formal algebraic properties of these expressions. In this investigation, you will study **rational functions.** A rational function is a function of the form $x \mapsto \frac{p(x)}{q(x)}$, where p and q are polynomial functions of x. Rational functions have all kinds of interesting graphs. Here are some examples.

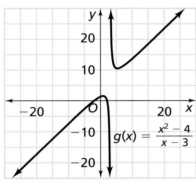

$$g(x) = \frac{x^2 - 4}{x - 3}$$

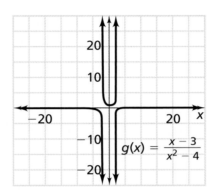

$$g(x) = \frac{x - 3}{x^2 - 4}$$

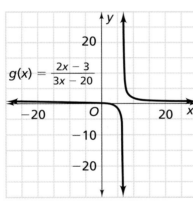

$$g(x) = \frac{2x - 3}{3x - 20}$$

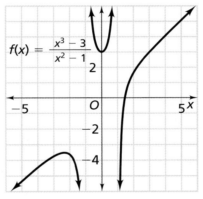

$$f(x) = \frac{x^3 - 3}{x^2 - 1}$$

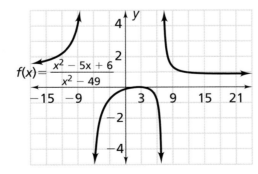

$$f(x) = \frac{x^2 - 5x + 6}{x^2 - 49}$$

For You to Explore

1. Suppose f and g are functions with the property that $g(x) = \frac{1}{f(x)}$ for any x in the domain of both functions.

a. Give an example of two functions f and g that are reciprocal functions.

b. Suppose $f(a) = 3$. What is the value of $g(a)$?

c. If $f(b)$ is very large, what can you say about $g(b)$?

d. If $f(c) = 0$, what can you say about $g(c)$?

e. If $f(5) = k$ and $g(5) = k$, what are the possible values of k?

> Functions f and g are called **reciprocal functions.** They are not inverse functions.

2. Suppose f and g are functions with $g(x) = \frac{1}{f(x)}$ for any x in the domain of both functions. Here is the graph of f:

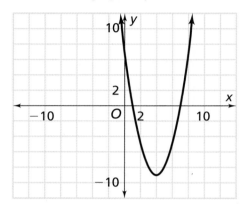

Copy the graph and, on the same axes, sketch the graph of g.

3. a. Find the domain of $g(x) = \frac{1}{x^2 - 8x + 7}$.

b. Sketch the graph of $f(x) = x^2 - 8x + 12$.

c. Use the graph of $f(x) = x^2 - 8x + 12$ to sketch the graph of $g(x) = \frac{1}{x^2 - 8x + 12}$.

d. Find the domain of $g(x) = \frac{1}{x^2 - 8x + 12}$.

4. Let

$$f(x) = \frac{x - 2}{x^2 - 9} \quad \text{and} \quad g(x) = \frac{x - 3}{x^2 - 9}$$

a. Find the domain of each function.

b. Describe the behavior of the graphs of f and g near $x = 3$.

5. Find, if possible, a rational function f that satisfies each condition.

- $f(3) = f(5) = 0$.
- The function f is undefined at 3 and 5.
- As x gets larger, $f(x)$ approaches 0.
- As x gets larger, $f(x)$ approaches 3.

6. **Write About It** Make your own rational function graph gallery.

- Sketch or generate 10 particularly interesting rational function graphs.

- Give the rational function for each graph.

- Describe what you find interesting about each graph.

7. **a.** Make an accurate sketch of

$$h(x) = \frac{|x|}{x}$$

b. What can you say about $\lim\limits_{x \to 0} h(x)$?

8. Consider $j(x) = x + \frac{1}{x}$.

a. Give estimates for $j(100)$ and $j(0.01)$.

b. What positive value of x makes $j(x)$ as small as possible?

c. **Take It Further** Show algebraically that if $x > 0$, then $j(x) \geq 2$.

$\lim\limits_{x \to 0} h(x)$ means the limit of $h(x)$ as x approaches 0.

Exercises *Practicing Habits of Mind*

On Your Own

9. If $f(x) = \frac{x+3}{2x-1}$ and $g(x) = \frac{x+1}{x-1}$, find all values of a such that
$f(a) = g(a) - \frac{4}{3}$.

10. Find, if possible, a rational function f that satisfies each condition.

a. $f(3) = 0$ and f has no other zeros.

b. The domain of f is all real numbers except for 5, and f has no zeros.

c. The domain of f is all real numbers except for 5, and $f(3) = 0$.

d. As x gets larger, the graph of f gets closer and closer to the graph of $y = x$.

11. Here is the graph of $f(x) = \sin x$. Use it to sketch the graph of $g(x) = \csc x$.

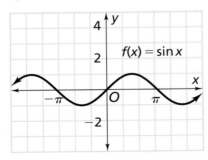

$\csc x = \dfrac{1}{\sin x}$ whenever $\sin x \neq 0$.

12. Let $k(x) = \dfrac{x^2 - x - 6}{x - 3}$.

a. Copy and complete this table for $k(x)$.

b. Use factoring to simplify the expression $\dfrac{x^2 - x - 6}{x - 3}$. Assume that $x \neq 3$.

c. Explain why k is not the same function as $m(x) = x + 2$.

d. **Write About It** In what way does the graph of k look different from the graph of m?

x	k(x)
0	2
1	▪
2	▪
3	▪
4	▪

13. Find a rational function k that is identical to $m(x) = x - 1$, except that k is undefined when $x = 4$.

14. Sketch the graphs of these three functions on the same axes.

$$f_1(x) = x$$

$$f_2(x) = \frac{1}{x}$$

$$f_3(x) = x + \frac{1}{x}$$

You should already be able to graph f_1 and f_2 without a calculator. Try graphing f_3 without a calculator, too.

Maintain Your Skills

15. Sketch the graph of each function.

a. $f(x) = \dfrac{1}{x}$

b. $f(x) = \dfrac{1}{x + 3}$

c. $f(x) = \dfrac{1}{x + 3} + 5$

d. $f(x) = \dfrac{1}{x^2}$

e. $f(x) = \dfrac{1}{(x - 4)^2}$

f. $f(x) = \dfrac{(x - 3)(x + 5)}{(x - 3)(x + 5)}$

16. Sketch the graph of each function.

a. $f(x) = \dfrac{1}{x}$

b. $f(x) = \dfrac{1}{x - 4}$

c. $f(x) = \dfrac{1}{2x - 4}$

d. $f(x) = \dfrac{x}{2x - 4}$

e. $f(x) = \dfrac{x - 3}{2x - 4}$

f. $f(x) = \dfrac{x - 3}{2x - 4} + 5$

3.7 Graphing Rational Functions

Subtle differences in functions can make their graphs look very different.

Consider the rational functions f and g from Problem 4 in Lesson 3.6:

$$f(x) = \frac{x-2}{x^2-9} \quad \text{and} \quad g(x) = \frac{x-3}{x^2-9}$$

Both have denominator $x^2 - 9 = (x+3)(x-3)$, so they are both undefined at $x = 3$. Their graphs, however, look very different. The graph of f has a vertical asymptote at $x = 3$, while the graph of g looks practically flat at $x = 3$. Why the difference?

> Of course, they are also undefined at $x = -3$.

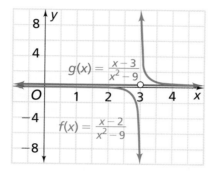

Start with f. Since $f(x) = \frac{x-2}{x^2-9}$, you can write it as

$$f(x) = m(x) \cdot \frac{1}{x-3}$$

where $m(x) = \frac{x-2}{x+3}$. Thus,

$$m(3) = \frac{3-2}{3+3} = \frac{1}{6}$$

So near $x = 3$, f behaves like the function

$$x \mapsto \frac{1}{6} \cdot \frac{1}{x-3}$$

the graph of which has a vertical asymptote at $x = 3$.

Now consider $g(x) = \frac{x-3}{x^2-9}$. For any $a \neq 3$,

$$g(a) = \frac{a-3}{(a+3)(a-3)} = \frac{1}{a+3}$$

> **Remember...**
>
> A vertical asymptote is a line that the graph of a function approaches, but does not intersect.

Since $a - 3 \neq 0$, you can cancel the term $a - 3$ from the numerator and denominator. So,

$$g(x) = \begin{cases} \frac{1}{x+3} & \text{if } x \neq 3 \\ \text{undefined} & \text{if } x = 3 \end{cases}$$

The graph of g looks just like the graph of $y = \frac{1}{x+3}$, except with a *hole* at $x = 3$.

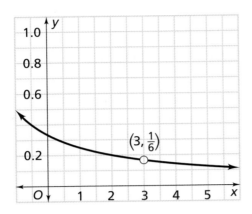

Example 1

Problem For each function below, describe the behavior of its graph near $x = 3$.

a. $f(x) = \dfrac{(x-3)^2}{(x-3)^6}$

b. $g(x) = \dfrac{(x-3)^6}{(x-3)^2}$

Solution

a. For any $a \neq 3$,

$$f(a) = \frac{(a-3)^2}{(a-3)^6} = \frac{1}{(a-3)^4}$$

Thus, as functions, the maps

$$x \mapsto f(x) \quad \text{and} \quad x \mapsto \frac{1}{(x-3)^4}$$

are equal because neither is defined at $x = 3$ and they agree on all $x \neq 3$. Their graphs are the same and so the graph of f has a vertical asymptote at $x = 3$.

b. For any $a \neq 3$,

$$g(a) = \frac{(a-3)^6}{(a-3)^2} = (a-3)^4.$$

Thus, the graph of g looks just like the graph of $y = (x-3)^4$, except with a hole at $x = 3$.

> Again, you can cancel here because $a - 3 \neq 0$.

The previous example leads to the following definition and theorem.

Definitions

Let $h(x) = \frac{f(x)}{g(x)}$ be a rational function such that

- $f(x) = (x - a)^m \cdot p(x)$
- $g(x) = (x - a)^n \cdot q(x)$

where $p(a), q(a) \neq 0$.

1. h has an **infinite discontinuity** at $x = a$ if $n > m \geq 0$.
2. h has a **removable discontinuity** at $x = a$ if $m \geq n > 0$.

> f and g are polynomials.

Theorem 3.6

Let h be a rational function.

1. If h has an infinite discontinuity at $x = a$, then the graph of h has $x = a$ as a vertical asymptote.

2. If h has a removable discontinuity at $x = a$, then the graph of h has a **hole** at $x = a$.

> Functions can also have jump discontinuities or discontinuities like $x \mapsto \sin\frac{1}{x}$ at 0, but these do not happen with rational functions.

Minds in Action   episode 7

Sasha and Tony have been discussing the function f from the start of this lesson.

Tony   Well, what's next?

Sasha   We know that the graph of $f(x) = \frac{x - 2}{x^2 - 9}$ has vertical asymptotes at $x = 3$ and $x = -3$, but I wonder if it has a horizontal asymptote.

Tony   I was looking ahead at Exercise 13 in this lesson. How about dividing every term by the highest degree?

Sasha   What do you mean?

Tony   Here, like this:

$$f(x) = \frac{x - 2}{x^2 - 9} \cdot \frac{\frac{1}{x^2}}{\frac{1}{x^2}} = \frac{\frac{1}{x} - \frac{2}{x^2}}{1 - \frac{9}{x^2}}.$$

Sasha   Wait, what if $x = 0$?

Tony   Then this new expression for f doesn't work. But I'm using it to figure out what happens when x is really big.

Sasha   Got it. And when x is big, the terms $\frac{1}{x}$, $\frac{2}{x^2}$, and $\frac{9}{x^2}$ are close to zero, and only the 1 is left.

Tony   Exactly! So if x is really big, we get

$$f(x) \approx \frac{0}{1}$$

And that means the horizontal asymptote is $y = 0$.

For You to Do

1. Use Tony's method to find the horizontal asymptote of the graph of each function.

   a. $g(x) = \dfrac{x - 3}{x^2 - 9}$ **b.** $h(x) = \dfrac{9x^3 + 5x + 1}{4x^3 - 7}$

2. Explain how Tony's method offers an explanation for why the same method works when x is a large positive or negative number.

Remember...

A large negative number is something like -1 million. Here, *large* refers to absolute value.

Consider $f(x) = \dfrac{x - 2}{x^2 - 9}$ again. Sasha and Tony showed that $f(x) \approx 0$ if x is a big number. In other words, you can make $f(x)$ as close to 0 as you want by making x large enough. To express this fact, write

$$\lim_{x \to \infty} f(x) = 0$$

As another example, you saw in the For You to Do above that

$$\lim_{x \to \infty} \frac{9x^3 + 5x + 1}{4x^3 - 7} = \frac{9}{4}$$

You will see a more precise definition when you take a course in calculus.

In fact, this limit is the same even if x becomes a large negative number. You express this fact by writing

$$\lim_{x \to -\infty} \frac{9x^3 + 5x + 1}{4x^3 - 7} = \frac{9}{4}$$

Theorem 3.7

Let $h(x) = \dfrac{f(x)}{g(x)}$ be a rational function with deg $f = m$ and deg $g = n$.

1. If $m < n$, then $\lim\limits_{x \to \infty} h(x) = 0$.

2. If $m = n$, then $\lim\limits_{x \to \infty} h(x)$ is the ratio of the leading coefficients of f and g.

   Moreover, the graph of h has a horizontal asymptote with equation $y = L$ where $L = \lim\limits_{x \to \infty} h(x)$.

deg f means the degree of the polynomial f.

You may be wondering what happens when deg f > deg g. Take a look at the following example.

Example 2

Problem Let

$$h(x) = \frac{x^3 - 4x}{x - 1}$$

Describe the behavior of h for large values of x.

Solution Using long division as shown in Method 3 from Lesson 3.3, you have

$$x^3 - 4x = (x - 1)(x^2 + x - 3) - 3$$

so that

$$h(x) = q(x) + \frac{-3}{x - 1}$$

where $q(x) = x^2 + x - 3$. Thus you can make $h(x)$ as large as you want by making x large enough. In other words,

$$\lim_{x \to \infty} h(x) = \infty$$

Furthermore,

$$\lim_{x \to \infty}(h(x) - q(x)) = \lim_{x \to \infty}\frac{-3}{x - 1} = 0$$

so that the outputs of h become arbitrarily close to the outputs of q for large positive and negative values of x. Thus, the graph of h has a nonhorizontal asymptote, namely the graph of the polynomial q.

> This limit statement says that as x increases without bound, so does $h(x)$.

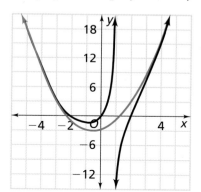

For You to Do

Let

$$k(x) = \frac{x^2 + x - 1}{3 - x}$$

3. Find $\lim_{k \to \infty} k(x)$.

4. Find all asymptotes of the graph of k.

Theorem 3.8

Let $h(x) = \dfrac{f(x)}{g(x)}$ be a rational function with deg $f >$ deg g. Then
$\lim\limits_{x\to\infty} h(x) = \infty$ or $-\infty$. Moreover, if you write

$$\frac{f(x)}{g(x)} = q(x) + \frac{r(x)}{g(x)}$$

where q and r are polynomials with deg $r <$ deg g, then the graph of q is a nonhorizontal asymptote of the graph of h.

Exercises Practicing Habits of Mind

Check Your Understanding

1. Calculate each limit.

   a. $\lim\limits_{x\to\infty} \dfrac{x-4}{x^2-4}$

   b. $\lim\limits_{x\to\infty} \dfrac{x^2-4}{x-4}$

   c. $\lim\limits_{x\to-\infty} \dfrac{x-4}{x^2-4}$

   d. $\lim\limits_{x\to-\infty} \dfrac{x^2-4}{x-4}$

2. Calculate each limit.

   a. $\lim\limits_{x\to\infty} \dfrac{3x^2-1}{5x^2+3}$

   b. $\lim\limits_{x\to\infty} \dfrac{10x^3-7}{3x^3+5}$

   c. $\lim\limits_{x\to-\infty} \dfrac{10+5x^4}{2x^4-2}$

   d. $\lim\limits_{x\to-\infty} \dfrac{7x-6x^5}{3x^5-17x}$

   e. $\lim\limits_{x\to\infty} \dfrac{10x^3-5}{4x^2+3x}$

   f. $\lim\limits_{x\to\infty} \dfrac{x^2+1}{3x^3-10}$

3. Consider $f(x) = \dfrac{x^2-3x-4}{x^2-2x-8}$.

   a. The graph of f has a horizontal asymptote. What is its equation?

   b. The graph of f has a vertical asymptote. What is its equation?

   c. The graph of f has a hole at what point?

4. Let f be a rational function.

   a. Give an example of a function f the graph of which has a horizontal asymptote with equation $y = 4$.

   b. Give an example of a function f that is undefined at $x = 2$ and $x = 5$.

   c. Give an example of a function f the graph of which has $x = -3$ as a vertical asymptote and has a hole at $x = 2$.

   d. Give an example of a function f with $f(2) = 0$, $f(1)$ undefined, and a graph with no horizontal asymptote.

5. The function $h(x) = \frac{x - 3}{x^2 - 9}$ has a removable discontinuity at $x = 3$. Define function j as

$$j(x) = \begin{cases} h(x) & \text{if } x \neq 3 \\ K & \text{if } x = 3 \end{cases}$$

What value of K would make $j(x)$ continuous at $x = 3$?

What value of K would "plug" the hole left by h at $x = 3$?

6. Consider the function $f(x) = \frac{x^2 + 1}{x}$.

a. Calculate $f(10)$ and $f(100)$.

b. What does the graph of $f(x)$ look like as x gets large?

c. Calculate $f(0.1)$ and $f(0.01)$.

d. What does the graph of $f(x)$ look like as x approaches zero?

e. Sketch the graph of f.

7. The graph of $y = \frac{x^3 + 1}{x^2 - x^4 + 1}$ looks like which of these when $x > 4$?

A. $y = x$ **B.** $y = -x$ **C.** $y = \frac{1}{x}$ **D.** $y = -\frac{1}{x}$

8. a. Sketch the graphs of $f(x) = (x - 1)(x + 3)$ and $g(x) = \frac{1}{(x - 1)(x + 3)}$ on the same axes.

b. Find the exact values of all x such that $f(x) = g(x)$.

9. Take It Further Let $d(x)$ be defined for nonnegative real numbers as the decimal part of x. For example, $d(10.63)$ is 0.63, and $d(\pi)$ starts out $0.14159\ldots$.

a. Let $x = \frac{7}{4}$. Calculate $d(x)$, $d(2x)$, $d(3x)$, and $d(4x)$.

b. Sketch a graph of d on $0 \leq x \leq 10$.

c. Sketch a graph of $r(x) = \frac{1}{d(x)}$ on $0 \leq x \leq 10$. Describe the domain and range of r.

On Your Own

10. Consider $g(x) = \frac{2x^2 - 5x + 2}{x^2 + x - 6}$.

a. The graph of g has a horizontal asymptote. What is its equation?

b. The graph of g has a vertical asymptote. What is its equation?

c. The graph of g has a hole at what point?

11. What is the domain of

a. $x \mapsto \frac{x - 4}{x^2 - 4}$?   b. $x \mapsto \frac{x - 2}{x^2 - 4}$?

12. Calculate each limit.

a. $\lim\limits_{x \to \infty} \dfrac{1 + \frac{1}{x}}{2 + \frac{1}{x}}$

b. $\lim\limits_{x \to \infty} \dfrac{x + 1}{2x + 1}$

c. $\lim\limits_{x \to \infty} \dfrac{\frac{3}{x} - \frac{4}{x^2}}{1 - \frac{5}{x} + \frac{6}{x^2}}$

d. $\lim\limits_{x \to \infty} \dfrac{3x - 4}{x^2 - 5x + 6}$

e. $\lim\limits_{x \to \infty} \dfrac{x^2 - 5x + 6}{3x - 4}$

13. a. Sketch the graphs of these three functions on the same axes with $x \geq 0$.

$$f_1(x) = \tfrac{1}{x}, \; f_2(x) = \tfrac{\sin x}{x}, \; f_3(x) = -\tfrac{1}{x}$$

b. Use the graphs to find the value of $\lim\limits_{x \to \infty} \dfrac{\sin x}{x}$.

14. Write About It Describe how you can determine the horizontal asymptote, if any, of a given rational function. Include in your explanation an example of a rational function with a horizontal asymptote $y = 0$, one with a horizontal asymptote $y = c$ (where c is a nonzero real number), and one with no horizontal asymptote at all.

15. The graphs of these two functions look identical on a graphing calculator.

$$f(x) = \dfrac{x + 11}{x^2 + 14x + 33}$$

$$g(x) = \dfrac{1}{x + 3}$$

a. Explain why they are not the same function.

b. Explain why their graphs look identical on the calculator.

16. a. Show that this equation is an identity.

$$\dfrac{1}{x + 2} - \dfrac{1}{x + 3} = \dfrac{1}{x^2 + 5x + 6}$$

b. Without using a calculator, sketch the graphs of $f(x) = \dfrac{1}{x + 2}$ and $g(x) = -\dfrac{1}{x + 3}$ on the same axes.

c. Use the graphs of f and g to make a rough sketch of $h(x) = \dfrac{1}{x^2 + 5x + 6}$. Check your work using a graphing calculator.

17. a. Find constants A and B that make this equation true.

$$\dfrac{x + 9}{x^2 - 2x - 3} = \dfrac{A}{x + 1} + \dfrac{B}{x - 3}$$

b. For the values of A and B you found, sketch the graphs of $f(x) = \dfrac{A}{x + 1}$ and $g(x) = \dfrac{B}{x - 3}$ on the same axes.

c. Use the graphs of f and g to make a rough sketch of $h(x) = \dfrac{x + 9}{x^2 - 2x - 3}$. Check your work using a graphing calculator.

18. Standardized Test Prep Let $P(x) = \dfrac{x^5}{36x^4 - 13x^2 + 1}$. If h is the number of horizontal asymptotes and v is the number of vertical asymptotes of the graph of P, what is the value of the product hv?

A. 0   **B.** 2   **C.** 4   **D.** 8

Maintain Your Skills

Go Online
PHSchool.com

For additional practice, go to **Web Code:** bga-0307

19. Sketch the graph of each function.

a. $a(x) = \dfrac{x - 2}{x - 3}$

b. $b(x) = \dfrac{2x - 5}{x - 3}$

c. $c(x) = \dfrac{3x - 8}{x - 3}$

d. $d(x) = \dfrac{4x - 11}{x - 3}$

20. For each equation, find the value of a that makes the equation true.

a. $\dfrac{2x - 5}{x - 3} = a + \dfrac{1}{x - 3}$

b. $\dfrac{3x - 8}{x - 3} = a + \dfrac{1}{x - 3}$

c. $\dfrac{4x - 11}{x - 3} = a + \dfrac{1}{x - 3}$

21. Find each value of K so the function has no removable discontinuity.

a. $f(x) = \begin{cases} \dfrac{x}{x^2 - 3x} & \text{if } x \neq 0 \\ K & \text{if } x = 0 \end{cases}$

b. $g(x) = \begin{cases} \dfrac{x^3 - 6x^2 + 11x - 6}{x - 2} & \text{if } x \neq 2 \\ K & \text{if } x = 2 \end{cases}$

c. $h(x) = \begin{cases} \dfrac{(x + 1)(x - 4)}{(x - 4)(x + 10)} & \text{if } x \neq 4 \\ K & \text{if } x = 4 \end{cases}$

d. $j(x) = \begin{cases} \dfrac{(x + 2)^2(x - 3)}{x^2 - 3x - 10} & \text{if } x \neq -2 \\ K & \text{if } x = -2 \end{cases}$

> What value of K plugs the hole in the graph?

22. Sketch the graph of each function.

a. $a(x) = \dfrac{x - 3}{(x + 1)^2}$

b. $b(x) = \dfrac{x^2 - 4}{x^2 - 1}$

c. $c(x) = \dfrac{x^2 - 6x + 5}{x^2 - 6x + 8}$

d. $d(x) = \dfrac{(x - 1)^2}{(x + 2)^2}$

e. $e(x) = \dfrac{(x - 1)^2}{(x + 2)^3}$

3.8 Revisiting Secants and Tangents

In Lesson 3.5, you saw two theorems (Theorem 3.4 and Theorem 3.5) that provided a method for finding the equations of secants and tangents to graphs of polynomial functions. In this lesson, you will see that the same method works even if f is a rational function.

> Of course, you can talk about the tangent at $(a, f(a))$ only if f is continuous at $x = a$.

Example 1

Problem Suppose $f(x) = \frac{1}{x}$. Find the equation of the tangent to the graph of $y = f(x)$ at the point $(2, \frac{1}{2})$.

Solution First, assume you can write $f(x)$ in powers of $x - 2$ up to $(x - 2)^2$ using the method of undetermined coefficients.

$$f(x) = \frac{1}{x} = m + n(x - 2) + p(x)(x - 2)^2 \tag{1}$$

Then the polynomial method indicates that the equation of the line tangent to the graph of $f(x)$ at $(2, f(2))$ is $y = m + n(x - 2)$.

Substitute $x = 2$ in (1) to get

$$m = f(2) = \frac{1}{2}$$

$$\frac{1}{x} = \frac{1}{2} + n(x - 2) + p(x)(x - 2)^2 \tag{2}$$

Subtract $\frac{1}{2}$ from each side of (2)

$$\frac{1}{x} - \frac{1}{2} = n(x - 2) + p(x)(x - 2)^2$$

Rewrite this as

$$\frac{-(x - 2)}{2x} = n(x - 2) + p(x)(x - 2)^2$$

Divide by $x - 2$ to get

$$\frac{-1}{2x} = n + p(x)(x - 2) \tag{3}$$

Now suppose p is defined and continuous at $x = 2$. Since the left and right sides of (3) are equal for $x \neq 2$, they must be equal for $x = 2$, as well. Substitute $x = 2$ in (3) to get $n = -\frac{1}{4}$.

$$\frac{1}{x} = \frac{1}{2} - \frac{1}{4}(x - 2) + p(x)(x - 2)^2$$

for some function $p(x)$. This means that the equation of the tangent at $x = 2$ is

$$r(x) = m + n(x - 2) = \frac{1}{2} - \frac{1}{4}(x - 2)$$

For You to Do

1. Find $p(x)$ if

$$\frac{1}{x} = \frac{1}{2} - \frac{1}{4}(x - 2) + p(x)(x - 2)^2$$

2. For $f(x) = \frac{1}{x}$, find an equation of the tangent to the graph of $y = f(x)$ at the point $(a, f(a))$.

$a \neq 0$, of course.

Minds in Action   episode 8

Sasha and Derman are looking at the above example.

Sasha   I'm not completely sure about this method.

Derman   What could be wrong? I write

$$\frac{1}{x} = \frac{1}{2} - \frac{1}{4}(x - 2) + p(x)(x - 2)^2$$

for some function p. Then I think about the secant becoming the tangent. The algebra says that the remainder when I divide by $(x - 2)^2$ is the equation of the tangent. The remainder when I divide the right side is $\frac{1}{2} - \frac{1}{4}(x - 2)$, so that's it.

Sasha   I'm worried about the assumption that p is continuous at $x = 2$. p is now a rational function. If its denominator had turned out to have some power of $x - 2$ as a factor, that would invalidate the reasoning by which we found p in the first place.

Derman   Well, p came out the way we needed it to in Example 1. Let's try another example and see if the same thing happens.

At the moment of takeoff, a ski jumper's skis are essentially tangent to the curve of the ramp.

Example 2

Problem Let

$$f(x) = \frac{x + 2}{2x^2 + 3x + 1}.$$

Find an equation of the tangent to the graph of $y = f(x)$ at the point $(3, f(3))$.

Solution

Write f in powers of $x - 3$.

$$f(x) = \frac{x + 2}{2x^2 + 3x + 1} = m + n(x - 3) + p(x)(x - 3)^2 \qquad (4)$$

If $r(x) = m + n(x - 3)$, then the graph of r will be the tangent.
So you need to solve for m and n. Substitute $x = 3$ in (4) and you get

$$m = f(3) = \frac{5}{28}$$

So,

$$\frac{x + 2}{2x^2 + 3x + 1} = \frac{5}{28} + n(x - 3) + p(x)(x - 3)^2 \qquad (5)$$

Subtract $\frac{5}{28}$ from each side of (5).

$$\frac{x + 2}{2x^2 + 3x + 1} - \frac{5}{28} = n(x - 3) + p(x)(x - 3)^2$$

Rewrite this as

$$\frac{-10x^2 + 13x + 51}{28(2x^2 + 3x + 1)} = n(x - 3) + p(x)(x - 3)^2$$

The right side of this equation implies that its left side has a factor of $x - 3$.
Use this fact to factor the numerator of the left side.

$$\frac{-(x - 3)(10x + 17)}{28(2x^2 + 3x + 1)} = n(x - 3) + p(x)(x - 3)^2$$

Divide each side by $x - 3$.

$$\frac{-(10x + 17)}{28(2x^2 + 3x + 1)} = n + p(x)(x - 3) \qquad (6)$$

Substitute $x = 3$ into (6) to get $n = -\frac{47}{28^2}$. The equation of the tangent at
$x = 3$ is

$$r(x) = \frac{5}{28} - \frac{47}{28^2}(x - 3)$$

For You to Do

3. Find $p(x)$ if

$$\frac{x + 2}{2x^2 + 3x + 1} = \frac{5}{28} - \frac{47}{28^2}(x - 3) + p(x)(x - 3)^2$$

4. Let

$$f(x) = \frac{2x + 5}{x + 3}$$

Find an equation of the tangent to the graph of $y = f(x)$ at the point $(1, f(1))$.

Minds in Action   episode 9

Tony, Sasha, and Derman are talking some more about the mysterious p(x).

Derman   Look, in both cases we've tried, $p(x)$ had almost the same denominator as the original function.

Tony   In fact, it was a perfect square times the denominator of the original.

Sasha   It looks too good to be true. But two examples don't make a theorem.

Tony   Here's what I think. Suppose the rational function you start with is defined at a number, say 2, and you make believe that $p(x)$ is also defined and continuous at 2. If you plow ahead and find $p(x)$ by first finding m and then n and then solving for $p(x)$, you'll see in the end that $p(x)$ is continuous at 2. I bet it's true.

Sasha   Here's what worries me. Take the $\frac{1}{x}$ example. We figured out that

$$\frac{1}{x} = \frac{1}{2} - \frac{1}{4}(x - 2) + \frac{1}{4x}(x - 2)^2$$

If I wanted to, I could write

$$\frac{1}{x} = 3 - 17(x - 2) + p(x)(x - 2)^2$$

and solve for a different $p(x)$. And I bet that one would not be continuous at 2.

> The $\frac{1}{4x}$ comes from Problem 1 on page 219.

Tony   Right, but I'm finding m and n in by a special method—our method of undetermined coefficients. Replace x by 2, find m, divide by $x - 2$, and so on.

Derman   Try another?

Tony   Or do it in general, once and for all.

Sasha   I feel some algebra coming on.

Theorem 3.9

Suppose that f is a rational function for which the denominator is not zero at $x = r$. Suppose also that you use the method of undetermined coefficients to write

$$f(x) = m + n(x - r) + p(x)(x - r)^2$$

finding first the number m and then the number n. Then p is a rational function that is defined at $x = r$.

Remember...

The Method of Undetermined Coefficients: Replace x by r, find m, subtract m from both sides, divide by $x - r$, find n, subtract n from both sides, divide by $x - r$.... When finding m and n, assume that $p(x)$ is defined and continuous at $x = r$. In the end, your assumption will be correct.

For Discussion

5. Develop a proof or a plausible argument for Theorem 3.9.

Developing Habits of Mind

Use a different process to get the same result. The Taylor expansion command in your CAS works with rational functions as well. It produces results that agree with the method of undetermined coefficients. For example, to find m and n such that

$$\frac{1}{x} = m + n(x - 2) + p(x)(x - 2)^2$$

tell the system to expand $\frac{1}{x}$ about $x = 2$ up to terms of degree 1.

See the TI-Nspire Handbook p. 704 for more information about the taylor function.

Check Your Understanding

1. Let $g(x) = -\frac{1}{x}$. Find an equation of the tangent to the graph of g at the point $(2, g(2))$.

2. In Example 1 on page 218, you saw that the tangent to the graph of $f(x) = \frac{1}{x}$ at $(2, f(2))$ has the equation

$$y = \frac{1}{2} - \frac{1}{4}(x - 2)$$

   How does this compare to the tangent of g you found in Exercise 1? Explain your answer.

3. Let $h(x) = \frac{1}{x^2}$. Find an equation of the tangent to the graph of $y = h(x)$ at the point $(a, h(a))$.

4. Copy and complete this table by finding the slope of the tangent to the graphs of $f(x) = \frac{1}{x}$ and $h(x) = \frac{1}{x^2}$ at each value of x. Explain the results using the graphs of f and h.

x	Slope of tangent to f	Slope of tangent to h
$\frac{1}{10}$	▧	▧
$\frac{1}{4}$	▧	▧
$\frac{1}{2}$	▧	▧
1	▧	▧
2	$-\frac{1}{4}$	$-\frac{1}{4}$
4	▧	▧
10	▧	▧

5. Let

$$h(x) = \frac{2x - 3}{x^2 + 4x + 5}$$

   Find an equation of the tangent to the graph of h at $x = -2$.

6. Find A and B so that

$$\frac{4x - 26}{x^2 - 7x + 10} = \frac{A}{x - 2} + \frac{B}{x - 5}$$

7. Let $f(x) = \dfrac{A}{x-2}$ and $g(x) = \dfrac{B}{x-5}$ where A and B are the values you found in Exercise 6.

   a. Graph f. Find the slope of the line tangent to f at $x = 4$.

   b. Graph g. Find the slope of the line tangent to g at $x = 4$.

   c. Graph $h(x) = \dfrac{4x-26}{x^2-7x+10}$. Find the slope of the line tangent to h at $x = 4$.

On Your Own

8. **Write About It** The function $f(x) = \frac{1}{x}$ is "decreasing everywhere." What does this mean? Give other examples of functions that are increasing everywhere, functions that are decreasing everywhere, and functions that are neither.

9. Let

$$g(x) = \frac{2x+7}{5x-2}$$

Find an equation of the tangent to the graph of g at $(3, g(3))$.

10. Copy and complete this table with the slope of the tangent to $f(x) = \frac{1}{x}$ and $g(x) = x + \frac{1}{x}$ at each value of x. Explain your answer.

x	Slope of tangent to f	Slope of tangent to g
-2	▧	▧
-1	▧	▧
$-\frac{1}{2}$	▧	▧
0	undefined	undefined
$\frac{1}{2}$	▧	▧
1	▧	▧
2	▧	▧
3	▧	▧

11. Consider the function $j(x) = \frac{1}{x^2 + 1}$.

   a. Find the slope of the tangent to j at $x = 2$.

   b. Find the slope of the tangent to j at $x = -2$.

   c. How are the answers in (a) and (b) related? Explain.

12. Let

$$f(x) = \frac{ax + b}{cx + d}$$

   Find an equation of the tangent to the graph of f at $x = 0$.

13. **Take It Further** Let $f(x) = \frac{ax + b}{cx + d}$ again, with $d \neq 0$. Write f as a power series

$$f(x) = \alpha_0 + \alpha_1 x + \alpha_2 x^2 + \alpha_3 x^3 + \alpha_4 x^4 + \cdots$$

   You saw in Exercise 12 that

$$\alpha_0 = \frac{b}{d} \text{ and } \alpha_1 = \frac{ad - bc}{d^2}$$

   Find α_n for $n \geq 2$.

14. **Standardized Test Prep** What is the slope of the tangent to the graph of $f(x) = \frac{4}{x}$ at $(3, f(3))$?

   A. $-\frac{9}{4}$ **B.** $-\frac{4}{9}$ **C.** $-\frac{4}{3}$ **D.** $-\frac{3}{4}$

Assume $d \neq 0$.

It might help to use a letter such as Δ to replace the constant value of $ad - bc$. If you do this, you can get simpler expressions, like $\alpha_1 = \frac{\Delta}{d^2}$.

Maintain Your Skills

15. Sketch the graphs of all four functions on the same axes. A graphing calculator may be helpful.

   a. $a(x) = 1 + x$

   b. $b(x) = 1 + x + \frac{x^2}{2}$

   c. $c(x) = 1 + x + \frac{x^2}{2} + \frac{x^3}{6}$

   d. $d(x) = 1 + x + \frac{x^2}{2!} + \frac{x^3}{3!} + \frac{x^4}{4!}$

16. For each of functions in Exercise 15, find the slope of the tangent line through the point $(0, 1)$.

17. **a.** Write out the first six lines of Pascal's Triangle.

   b. What is the value of $\binom{7}{3}$?

Go Online
PHSchool.com

For additional practice, go to **Web Code:** bga-0308

Case Study: $y = \dfrac{ax+b}{cx+d}$

There is a connection between the graph of $f(x) = \frac{1}{x}$ and an entire family of rational functions that have a particular form.

For You to Do

Sketch the graph of each function.

1. $f(x) = \frac{1}{x}$

2. $g(x) = \dfrac{3x+1}{5x-10}$

You have probably noticed in For You to Do that the graphs of

$$f(x) = \frac{1}{x} \text{ and } g(x) = \frac{3x+1}{5x-10}$$

look similar. Here are the graphs of a few more functions having the same form.

$m(x) = \dfrac{2x+1}{7x-10}$
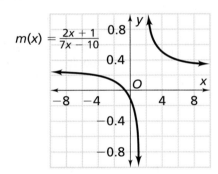

$n(x) = \dfrac{-x+5}{2x-1}$
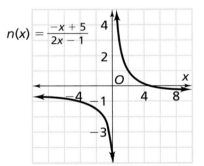

$p(x) = \dfrac{4x-1}{3x-2}$
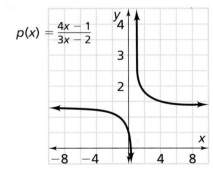

$q(x) = \dfrac{4x-1}{3x+2}$
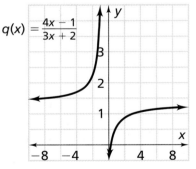

Each graph has the same general shape as the graph of $y = \frac{1}{x}$. You can transform one graph into the other through some combination of translation, scaling, and reflection. Starting with the following definition and notation, you will explore the relationship between the graphs of $y = \frac{1}{x}$ and $y = \frac{ax+b}{cx+d}$.

Definition

Let

$$A = \begin{pmatrix} a & b \\ c & d \end{pmatrix}$$

be a 2 × 2 matrix with real entries. The **linear fractional transformation** associated with A is the rational function

$$\mathcal{R}_A(x) = \frac{ax + b}{cx + d}$$

Facts and Notation

- Assume $c \neq 0$. Otherwise, $\mathcal{R}_A$ would be just a linear function.

- Recall that the **determinant** of A is $\det A = ad - bc$. In general, you may assume that $\det A \neq 0$.

You will see in the exercises what happens when $\det A = 0$.

For You to Do

For each matrix A below, find all the asymptotes of the graph of $y = \mathcal{R}_A(x)$.

3. $A = \begin{pmatrix} 1 & 2 \\ 3 & 4 \end{pmatrix}$
4. $A = \begin{pmatrix} 0 & 5 \\ 2 & 3 \end{pmatrix}$
5. $A = \begin{pmatrix} a & b \\ c & d \end{pmatrix}$

Rational functions with linear numerators and denominators typically have a "skateboard ramp" shape.

The following theorem explains why matrices can represent linear fractional transformations.

Theorem 3.10

Suppose A and B are 2×2 matrices with real coefficients. Then

$$\mathcal{R}_A \circ \mathcal{R}_B = \mathcal{R}_{AB}$$

Suppose

$$A = \begin{pmatrix} a & b \\ c & d \end{pmatrix} \text{ and } B = \begin{pmatrix} \alpha & \beta \\ \gamma & \delta \end{pmatrix}$$

To start the proof of Theorem 3.10, compute $\mathcal{R}_A \circ \mathcal{R}_B$.

$$(\mathcal{R}_A \circ \mathcal{R}_B)(x) = \mathcal{R}_A(\mathcal{R}_B(x))$$

$$= \mathcal{R}_A\left(\frac{\alpha x + \beta}{\gamma x + \delta}\right)$$

$$= \frac{a\left(\frac{\alpha x + \beta}{\gamma x + \delta}\right) + b}{c\left(\frac{\alpha x + \beta}{\gamma x + \delta}\right) + d}$$

$$= \frac{a(\alpha x + \beta) + b(\gamma x + \delta)}{c(\alpha x + \beta) + d(\gamma x + \delta)}$$

$$= \frac{(a\alpha + b\gamma)x + (a\beta + b\delta)}{(c\alpha + d\gamma)x + (c\beta + d\delta)}$$

> δ is the lower-case Greek letter delta.

For You to Do

6. Complete the proof of Theorem 3.10 by computing $\mathcal{R}_{AB}$ to obtain the same expression as you just found for $\mathcal{R}_A \circ \mathcal{R}_B$.

Theorem 3.10 says that the mapping

$$A \mapsto \mathcal{R}_A$$

from the set of 2×2 matrices to the set of linear fractional transformations is **structure preserving.** In other words, after

- multiplying matrices A and B to get AB
- composing functions $\mathcal{R}_A$ and $\mathcal{R}_B$ to get $\mathcal{R}_A \circ \mathcal{R}_B$
  the product AB still maps to the composition $\mathcal{R}_A \circ \mathcal{R}_B$ because

$$AB \mapsto \mathcal{R}_{AB} = \mathcal{R}_A \circ \mathcal{R}_B.$$

For Discussion

Discuss the following facts, using the structure-preserving nature of the map $A \mapsto \mathcal{R}_A$.

7. The multiplicative identity matrix

$$I = \begin{pmatrix} 1 & 0 \\ 0 & 1 \end{pmatrix}$$

maps to the identity function

$$\mathcal{R}_I(x) = x$$

8. The inverse matrix A^{-1} maps to the inverse function $(\mathcal{R}_A)^{-1}$. In other words,

$$(\mathcal{R}_A)^{-1} = \mathcal{R}_{A^{-1}}$$

> If A is an invertible matrix, then det $A \neq 0$.

For You to Do

9. For each matrix A below, write down the corresponding function $\mathcal{R}_A$.

a. $A = \begin{pmatrix} 1 & 2 \\ 3 & 4 \end{pmatrix}$

b. $A = \begin{pmatrix} 2 & 4 \\ 6 & 8 \end{pmatrix}$

c. $A = \begin{pmatrix} -3 & -6 \\ -9 & -12 \end{pmatrix}$

d. $A = \begin{pmatrix} a & 2a \\ 3a & 4a \end{pmatrix}$

10. Explain why

$$\mathcal{R}_{kA} = \mathcal{R}_A$$

for any nonzero real number k.

11. Is the map

$$A \mapsto \mathcal{R}_A$$

one-to-one? Explain.

You can take two approaches to examine the relationship between the graphs of $y = \frac{1}{x}$ and $y = \frac{ax + b}{cx + d}$. One involves the algebra of rational expressions. The other involves the algebra of 2×2 matrices.

Using Rational Expressions

Let

$$g(x) = \frac{3x + 1}{5x - 10}$$

as in the For You to Do section at the start of this lesson. Long division gives

$$
\begin{array}{r}
\frac{3}{5} \\
5x - 10 \overline{)\,3x + 1} \\
\underline{3x - 6} \\
7
\end{array}
$$

so that

$$3x + 1 = 7 + \frac{3}{5}(5x - 10)$$

Dividing each side by $5x - 10$ gives

$$\frac{3x + 1}{5x - 10} = \frac{7}{5x - 10} + \frac{3}{5} = \frac{1}{\frac{5}{7}(x - 2)} + \frac{3}{5}$$

Using what you have learned about transformations, you can conclude that the graph of $y = g(x)$ looks just like the graph of $y = \frac{1}{x}$, except it is

- scaled horizontally by a factor of $\frac{7}{5}$

- translated 2 units to the right

- translated $\frac{3}{5}$ units up

For You to Do

12. Using long division, show that for $\Delta = ad - bc \neq 0$,

$$\frac{ax + b}{cx + d} = \frac{1}{ex + f} + g$$

where

$$e = -\frac{c^2}{\Delta}$$

$$f = -\frac{cd}{\Delta}$$

$$g = \frac{a}{c}$$

Conclude that the graph of $y = \frac{ax + b}{cx + d}$ is the same as the graph of $y = \frac{1}{x}$ after a scaling and translation in x and a translation in y.

The skateboarder and ramp have been scaled horizontally by a factor of $-\frac{2}{3}$.

Using Matrices

First, recall affine transformations from CME Project *Algebra 2*.

$$A_{(a,b)}(x) = ax + b$$

It follows that

$$A_{(a,b)} = \mathcal{R}_A \text{ where } A = \begin{pmatrix} a & b \\ 0 & 1 \end{pmatrix}$$

Thus, you can think of linear fractional transformations as a generalization of affine transformations.

> Here, make an exception and let $c = 0$.

For ease of notation, let

$$J = \begin{pmatrix} 0 & 1 \\ 1 & 0 \end{pmatrix}$$

and note that

$$\mathcal{R}_J(x) = \frac{0 \cdot x + 1}{1 \cdot x + 0} = \frac{1}{x}$$

Let

$$A = \begin{pmatrix} a & b \\ c & d \end{pmatrix}$$

and consider

$$\mathcal{R}_A(x) = \frac{ax + b}{cx + d}$$

You have already seen that you can write

$$\frac{ax + b}{cx + d} = \frac{1}{ex + f} + g$$

for some e, f, and g. Furthermore,

$$\frac{1}{ex + f} + g = \frac{1}{A_{(e,f)}(x)} + g$$

$$= \mathcal{R}_J(A_{(e,f)}(x)) + g$$

$$= T_g(\mathcal{R}_J(A_{(e,f)}(x)))$$

So,

$$\mathcal{R}_A = T_g \circ \mathcal{R}_J \circ A_{(e,f)}$$

> Recall that T_g denotes the translation map $x \rightarrow x + g$.

which corresponds to the matrix equation

$$\begin{pmatrix} a & b \\ c & d \end{pmatrix} = \begin{pmatrix} 1 & g \\ 0 & 1 \end{pmatrix} \begin{pmatrix} 0 & 1 \\ 1 & 0 \end{pmatrix} \begin{pmatrix} e & f \\ 0 & 1 \end{pmatrix}$$

Well, not quite. The matrices determine the functions only up to a scale factor, so the equation is really

$$k \begin{pmatrix} a & b \\ c & d \end{pmatrix} = \begin{pmatrix} 1 & g \\ 0 & 1 \end{pmatrix} \begin{pmatrix} 0 & 1 \\ 1 & 0 \end{pmatrix} \begin{pmatrix} e & f \\ 0 & 1 \end{pmatrix} = \begin{pmatrix} eg & fg+1 \\ e & f \end{pmatrix}$$

This gives four equations

$$ka = eg$$
$$kb = fg + 1$$
$$kc = e$$
$$kd = f$$

with four unknowns e, f, g, and k. Solving this system, either by hand or calculator, you get

$$e = -\frac{c^2}{\Delta}$$
$$f = -\frac{cd}{\Delta}$$
$$g = \frac{a}{c}$$
$$k = -\frac{c}{\Delta}$$

where $\Delta = \det A = ad - bc$.

For You to Do

Consider the following matrices.

$$M = \begin{pmatrix} 2 & 1 \\ 7 & -10 \end{pmatrix}$$

$$N = \begin{pmatrix} -1 & 5 \\ 2 & -1 \end{pmatrix}$$

$$P = \begin{pmatrix} 4 & -1 \\ 3 & -2 \end{pmatrix}$$

$$Q = \begin{pmatrix} 4 & -1 \\ 3 & 2 \end{pmatrix}$$

13. Find the determinant of each matrix.

14. Consider the functions $\mathcal{R}_M$, $\mathcal{R}_N$, $\mathcal{R}_P$, and $\mathcal{R}_Q$. You have seen how to obtain the graphs of these functions by transforming the graph of $y = \frac{1}{x}$. Which of these transformations involve a reflection? Why? Explain your answer.

Have you seen these graphs before?

Exercises Practicing Habits of Mind

Check Your Understanding

1. Let $a(x) = \frac{3x + 5}{2x + 7}$.

   a. Find the equations of the vertical and horizontal asymptotes of the graph of a.

   b. Find all intercepts of the graph of a.

   c. Use the information about asymptotes and intercepts to sketch the graph of a.

   > Check your sketch using a graphing calculator.

2. Let $b(x) = \frac{4x + D}{x + 2}$.

   a. Sketch the graph of b for several choices of D.

   b. What value of D produces a hole in the graph of b?

   c. Calculate $\lim\limits_{x \to \infty} b(x)$.

3. Let $c(x) = \frac{Ax + B}{Cx + D}$, with $C \neq 0$.

   a. In terms of A, B, C, and D, describe when the graph of c will have a vertical asymptote and when it will have a hole.

   b. Calculate $\lim\limits_{x \to \infty} c(x)$ and explain its meaning in terms of the graph of c.

   > **Habits of Mind**
   >
   > **Look for relationships.**
   > You might try some specific cases first, then work your way up to a general fact.

4. **Write About It** Make your own linear fractional transformation function graph gallery. That is, assemble a gallery of graphs of functions of the form $f(x) = \mathcal{R}_A(x)$ for various matrices A.

   • Sketch or generate 10 particularly interesting graphs. Try to include every possible behavior.

   • Give the rational function for each graph.

   • Describe what you find interesting about each graph.

5. Suppose

   $$A = \begin{pmatrix} 3 & 5 \\ 10 & 3 \end{pmatrix} \text{ and } B = \begin{pmatrix} 1 & 3 \\ 4 & -2 \end{pmatrix}$$

   a. Sketch the graphs of $y = \mathcal{R}_A(x)$ and $y = \mathcal{R}_B(x)$.

   b. Find a matrix C so that $\mathcal{R}_A \circ \mathcal{R}_C = \mathcal{R}_B$.

   c. Find a matrix D so that $\mathcal{R}_D \circ \mathcal{R}_A = \mathcal{R}_B$.

   > Hint: $\mathcal{R}_A \circ \mathcal{R}_C = \mathcal{R}_{AC}$.

6. Suppose

$$A = \begin{pmatrix} 3 & 5 \\ 10 & 3 \end{pmatrix} \text{ and } B = \begin{pmatrix} 0 & 1 \\ 1 & 0 \end{pmatrix}$$

a. Sketch the graphs of $y = \mathcal{R}_A(x)$ and $y = \mathcal{R}_B(x)$.

b. Find a translation T_g and an affine transformation $\mathcal{A}_{(e,f)}$ such that

$$\mathcal{R}_A = T_g \circ \mathcal{R}_B \circ \mathcal{A}_{(e,f)}$$

c. Explain in words how to transform the graph of $y = \mathcal{R}_B(x)$ into the graph of $y = \mathcal{R}_A(x)$.

Habits of Mind

Recall what you know.
The graph of $y = \mathcal{R}_B(x)$ is very familiar to you.

7. Let

$$A = \begin{pmatrix} a & b \\ c & d \end{pmatrix}$$

Find conditions on a, b, c, and d so that $\mathcal{R}_A$ will have a fixed point. In other words, find a real number x such that $\mathcal{R}_A(x) = x$.

On Your Own

8. Suppose

$$A = \begin{pmatrix} 2 & 5 \\ 3 & 7 \end{pmatrix} \text{ and } B = \begin{pmatrix} 2 & -3 \\ 4 & -2 \end{pmatrix}$$

a. Sketch the graphs of $y = \mathcal{R}_A(x)$ and $y = \mathcal{R}_B(x)$.

b. Find a matrix C such that $\mathcal{R}_A \circ \mathcal{R}_C = \mathcal{R}_B$.

c. Find a matrix D such that $\mathcal{R}_D \circ \mathcal{R}_A = \mathcal{R}_B$.

9. Suppose

$$A = \begin{pmatrix} 2 & 5 \\ 3 & 7 \end{pmatrix} \text{ and } B = \begin{pmatrix} 0 & 1 \\ 1 & 0 \end{pmatrix}$$

a. Sketch the graphs of $y = \mathcal{R}_A(x)$ and $y = \mathcal{R}_B(x)$.

b. Find a translation T_g and an affine transformation $\mathcal{A}_{(e,f)}$ so that

$$\mathcal{R}_A = T_g \circ \mathcal{R}_B \circ \mathcal{A}_{(e,f)}$$

c. Explain in words how to transform the graph of $y = \mathcal{R}_B(x)$ into the graph of $y = \mathcal{R}_A(x)$.

10. Find the value of

$$1 + \frac{1}{3} + \frac{1}{9} + \frac{1}{27} + \cdots = \sum_{k=0}^{\infty} \frac{1}{3^k}$$

11. Why does the graph of $f(x) = \dfrac{1}{x^2 + 1}$ not have any vertical asymptotes?

12. Sketch the graph of this function.

$$f(x) = \frac{1}{1-x}$$

13. a. Sketch the graph of $f(x) = \frac{1}{1-x}$ and $g(x) = 1 + x$ on the same axes. In your graph, let $-2 \le x \le 2$, and $0 \le y \le 5$.

   b. Make a table of the outputs of f and g for the inputs $x = 0.1, 0.2, 0.5, 0.8$.

   c. Sketch the graph of f and $h(x) = 1 + x + x^2$ on the same axes.

   d. Make a table of the outputs of f and h for the inputs $x = 0.1, 0.2, 0.5, 0.8$.

   e. Sketch the graph of f and $j(x) = 1 + x + x^2 + x^3 + x^4 + x^5$ on the same axes.

   f. Make a table of the outputs of f and j for the inputs $x = 0.1, 0.2, 0.5, 0.8, 1.1$.

14. Take It Further Consider the function $f(x) = x + \frac{A}{x}$, with $A > 0$.

   a. In terms of A, what value of x generates the least possible output $f(x)$?

   b. Prove your result from part (a).

15. Standardized Test Prep Consider the linear fractional transformation $\mathcal{R}_A(x)$ associated with the matrix $A = \begin{pmatrix} -2 & 3 \\ 1 & 1 \end{pmatrix}$. Which of these is an asymptote of the graph of the rational function?

   A. $x = -\frac{1}{2}$ **B.** $x = -\frac{2}{3}$ **C.** $x = -\frac{1}{3}$ **D.** $x = -1$

Maintain Your Skills

Go Online
PHSchool.com

For additional practice, go to **Web Code:** bga-0309

16. For each matrix A, write $\mathcal{R}_A(x) - \mathcal{R}_A(r)$ in the form

$$(x - r)Q(x)$$

where $Q(x)$ is a rational expression in x and r.

   a. $A = \begin{pmatrix} 2 & 5 \\ 3 & 7 \end{pmatrix}$ **b.** $A = \begin{pmatrix} -2 & 5 \\ 5 & 7 \end{pmatrix}$

   c. $A = \begin{pmatrix} -\pi & 5 \\ 5 & 7 \end{pmatrix}$ **d.** $A = \begin{pmatrix} a & b \\ c & d \end{pmatrix}$

$Q(x)$ will be in terms of a, b, c, and d.

17. Calculate each sum.

   a. $\displaystyle\sum_{k=0}^{5} 2^k = 2^0 + 2^1 + 2^2 + 2^3 + 2^4 + 2^5$ **b.** $\displaystyle\sum_{k=0}^{5} 3^k$

   c. $\displaystyle\sum_{k=0}^{5} \left(\frac{1}{2}\right)^k$ **d.** $\displaystyle\sum_{k=0}^{\infty} \left(\frac{1}{2}\right)^k$

   e. $\displaystyle\sum_{k=0}^{5} \left(\frac{1}{4}\right)^k$ **f.** $\displaystyle\sum_{k=0}^{\infty} \left(\frac{1}{4}\right)^k$

In this investigation, you learned about removable continuities and infinite discontinuities. You learned the effects of these discontinuities on graphs of functions. You graphed rational functions using their horizontal and vertical asymptotes. You also found equations of lines tangent to these graphs. The following questions will help you summarize what you have learned.

1. **a.** Give an example of a rational function the graph of which has a hole at $x = 3$. Sketch its graph.

   b. Give an example of a rational function the graph of which has a vertical asymptote at $x = 3$. Sketch its graph.

2. **a.** Give an example of a rational function the graph of which has a horizontal asymptote at $y = 0$. Sketch its graph.

   b. Give an example of a rational function the graph of which has a horizontal asymptote at $y = 2$. Sketch its graph.

3. Let $f(x) = \frac{3x^2 + 10x + 8}{x - 3}$.

   a. Find all x- and y-intercepts of the graph of f.

   b. Find all asymptotes of the graph of f.

   c. Sketch the graph of f.

4. Find an equation for the tangent to the graph of $g(x) = \frac{4x + 1}{x - 3}$ at $(0, g(0))$.

5. Let $h(x) = \frac{x - 1}{x}$.

   a. Find an equation for the tangent to the graph of h at $(a, h(a))$ for $a \neq 0$.

   b. Use your answer to part (a) to find all values of x where the function h is increasing. Explain your answer.

6. What happens to $f(x) = \frac{3x^2 + 2x - 1}{5x^2 - 3x + 10}$ as x gets larger and larger?

7. Why do the graphs of $g(x) = \frac{x^2 - 15}{x - 4}$ and $h(x) = \frac{x^2 - 16}{x - 4}$ look so different from each other?

8. How can you find tangent lines to rational functions?

Vocabulary and Notation

In this investigation, you learned these terms. Make sure you understand what each one means and how to use it.

- determinant
- hole
- infinite discontinuity

- linear fractional transformation, $\mathcal{R}_A$
- removable discontinuity
- structure-preserving map

Mid-Chapter Test

 For a mid-chapter test, go to **Web Code:** bga-0352

Multiple Choice

1. Which of the following is not true of the graph of $f(x) = 2x^3 - 6x^2 - 12x + 16$?

   A. From left to right, the graph rises, falls, and rises.

   B. The graph crosses the positive x-axis at 1 and 4.

   C. The graph crosses the negative x-axis twice.

   D. The graph crosses the y-axis at $(0, 16)$.

2. Which of the following functions is continuous?

   A. Number of children enrolled in a particular school as a function of time

   B. Outdoor temperature as a function of time

   C. Cost of postage as a function of the weight of the letter

   D. Average number of soft drinks sold at a ballpark as a function of outdoor temperature

3. Calculate the average rate of change of $h(x) = x^3 - 9x$ with respect to x as x goes from 2 to 4.

   A. -19 **B.** $\frac{19}{3}$ **C.** 9 **D.** 19

4. Find the remainder when you divide $2x^4 - 7x^3 - 8x^2 + 14x + 8$ by x^3.

   A. $2x^4 - 7 - 8x^2 + 14x + 8$

   B. $2x - 7$

   C. $2x - 7 - \frac{8}{x} + \frac{14}{x^2} + \frac{8}{x^3}$

   D. $-8x^2 + 14x + 8$

5. Which function has tangent line $y = 2x - 1$ at $(1, 1)$?

   A. $a(x) = x$ **B.** $b(x) = x^2$

   C. $c(x) = x^3$ **D.** $d(x) = x^4$

Open Response

6. Suppose that $f(x) = -(x - 3)(x + 2)(x + 5)$.

   a. Where does the graph cross the x-axis?

   b. Find $f(0)$.

   c. Sketch the graph of f.

7. Consider $g(x) = x^3 - 13x - 12 = (x - 4)(x + 1)(x + 3)$. Give estimates for each of these values.

   a. $g(4)$ **b.** $g(4.001)$ **c.** $g(0)$

   d. $g(0.001)$ **e.** $g(1000)$

8. A water balloon dropped from a window will fall a distance of $s = 16t^2$ feet during the first t seconds. Find the average velocity of the balloon during the first 4 seconds of falling.

9. Expand $f(x) = x^3 - 14x^2 + 55x - 42$ in powers of $x - 4$.

10. Copy and complete this table for $f(x) = x^2 - 2x + 5$.

x	$f(x)$	Slope of the tangent at $(x, f(x))$
-1	▦	▦
0	▦	▦
1	▦	▦
2	▦	▦
3	▦	▦
4	▦	▦
10	▦	▦
100	▦	▦

Exponential and Logarithmic Functions

In earlier math courses you learned to use the constant π. In *Exponential and Logarithmic Functions*, you will learn about another important constant, *e*. You will see how it naturally appears in a variety of settings.

By the end of this investigation, you will be able to answer questions like these.

1. What happens when interest is compounded more and more frequently?

2. What are some reasons to introduce the number e?

3. How can you relate any exponential or logarithmic function to $f(x) = e^x$ and $g(x) = \ln x$?

You will learn how to
- state and use the limit and factorial definitions of e and e^x

- use the inverse relationship between e^x and $\ln x$ to solve equations

- find an equation for the line tangent to the graph of $y = e^x$ or $y = \ln x$ at a point

You will develop these habits and skills:
- Develop a definition of continuously compounded interest.

- Visualize relationships between the graphs of $f(x) = e^x$ and $g(x) = \ln x$ and the slopes of the tangents to these graphs.

- Use functional equations to recognize the ln function as a logarithm.

The same street in Shanghai, before and after several decades of essentially exponential growth.

Activating Prior Knowledge
Exploring New Ideas

A bank could compound interest every year, half year, quarter year, month, week, day, hour, or second, or over even smaller intervals. The limiting action is to compound interest continuously. For each compounding plan, a wise consumer should know how the interest grows.

For You to Explore

1. A representative of Seventh Fifth Bank offered Danielle an incredible investment, a 100% APR savings account, but only for one year. Danielle went for the offer right away, giving them all the money she had, $100.

   As she left the bank, Danielle realized she forgot to ask how often the interest was compounded. Determine, to the nearest penny, how much money Danielle will have after a year if interest is compounded on each of the following schedules.

   a. annually (once per year)

   b. semi-annually (twice per year)

   c. quarterly (four times per year)

   d. monthly (12 times per year)

2. Danielle, still thinking about her incredible offer, says, "Maybe they'll compound every day, or every minute, or every second! Then I'll really be raking it in."

   a. Is this true? How much money could Danielle have after a year if interest were compounded more frequently?

   b. If interest is compounded n times during the year, write a formula for the amount of money Danielle will have at the end of the year (in terms of n).

3. Sketch the graph of $f(x) = 2^x$.

   a. Draw a secant line connecting $(0, f(0))$ and $(2, f(2))$. Calculate its slope.

   b. Draw a secant line connecting $(0, f(0))$ and $(0.5, f(0.5))$. Calculate its slope to two decimal places.

   c. Give a good estimate for the slope of the tangent line to the graph of f at $x = 0$.

4. Sketch the graph of $g(x) = 4^x$.

   a. Draw a secant line connecting $(0, g(0))$ and $(0.25, g(0.25))$. Calculate its slope to two decimal places.

   b. Give a good estimate for the slope of the tangent line to the graph of g at $x = 0$.

As much as Danielle would like to get 100% interest every time the bank calculates it, the interest is broken up over the year. With semi-annual compounding, Danielle would earn 50% each period. With quarterly compounding, she earns 25% per quarter.

Habits of Mind

Check your results. Set up a sketch using your geometry software, similar to the sketch described in the first For You to Do section in Lesson 3.5.

5. Copy and complete this table giving the approximate slope of the tangent line at $x = 0$ for each function in the form $f(x) = b^x$.

Base b	Slope of tangent to $f(x) = b^x$ at $x = 0$
2	▪
3	▪
4	▪
5	1.609
8	▪
10	▪

6. By continuity, there must be some base b where the slope of the tangent line to the graph of $f(x) = b^x$ at $x = 0$ is exactly 1.

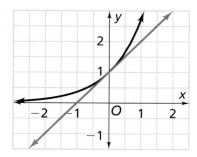

Give a good estimate for this base b.

Exercises *Practicing Habits of Mind*

On Your Own

7. Sketch the graph of $f(x) = \log_2 x$.

  a. Draw a secant line connecting $(1, f(1))$ and $(2, f(2))$. Calculate its slope.

  b. Draw a secant line connecting $(1, f(1))$ and $(1.2, f(1.2))$. Calculate its slope to two decimal places.

  c. Give a good estimate for the slope of the line tangent to the graph of f at $x = 1$.

8. Sketch the graph of $g(x) = \log_4 x$.

    a. Draw a secant line connecting $(1, g(1))$ and $(2, g(2))$. Calculate its slope.

    b. Give a good estimate for the slope of the line tangent to the graph of g at $x = 1$.

9. Copy and complete this table giving the approximate slope of the tangent line at $x = 1$ for each function in the form $f(x) = \log_b x$.

Base b	Slope of tangent to $f(x) = \log_b x$ at $x = 1$
2	▨
3	▨
4	▨
5	0.621
8	▨
10	▨

10. By continuity, there must be some base b where the slope of the tangent line to the graph of $f(x) = \log_b x$ at $x = 1$ is exactly 1.

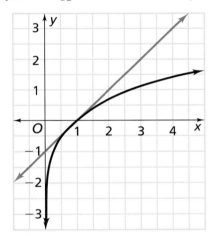

Give a good estimate for this base b.

Maintain Your Skills

11. Use the Binomial Theorem to expand each expression.

    a. $\left(1 + \frac{x}{2}\right)^2$ **b.** $\left(1 + \frac{x}{3}\right)^3$ **c.** $\left(1 + \frac{x}{4}\right)^4$

12. Let $f(x, n) = \left(1 + \frac{x}{n}\right)^n$ for any real x and positive integer n. Calculate each of the following.

    a. $f(1, n)$ for $n = 1, 2, 3, 4, 10, 100, 10000$

    b. $f(2, n)$ for $n = 1, 2, 3, 4, 10, 100, 10000$

    c. $f(0.05, n)$ for $n = 1, 4, 12, 365, 10000$

3.11   Compound Interest; the Number e

In Problems 1 and 2 from Lesson 3.10, you helped Danielle figure out how much money she would make on her $100 investment in a savings account with 100% APR, compounded at different intervals. You can write a function that takes the period as the input and outputs the balance at the end of the year.

Let $F(n)$ denote the amount of money Danielle would have after a year if interest were compounded n times during the year. Then

$$F(n) = 100\left(1 + \tfrac{1}{n}\right)^n$$

You can evaluate $F(n)$ for large values of n, rounded to six decimal places:

$$F(100) = 270.481383$$
$$F(1000) = 271.692393$$
$$F(10^4) = 271.814593$$
$$F(10^5) = 271.826824$$
$$F(10^6) = 271.828047$$
$$F(10^7) = 271.828169$$

It seems that F keeps growing as n grows, which makes sense. After all, the more compounding of the interest there is, the more money Danielle earns. But for large values of n, the rate of growth of F slows down considerably. For example, it seems unlikely that $F(n)$ will ever surpass 300, no matter how large n is.

The key point here is that

$$f(n) = \left(1 + \tfrac{1}{n}\right)^n$$

is an increasing function, but it also has an upper bound. In fact, the graph of f seems to have a horizontal asymptote at $y \approx 2.7183$.

> Assume $n > 0$.

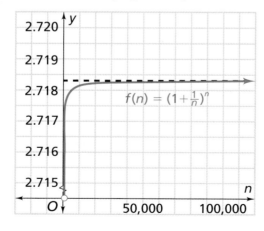

> In the context of investing money, the function $f(n)$ only makes sense for positive integers n. But you can certainly evaluate $f(n)$ at all real $n > 0$.

Historically, many people felt (as Danielle did) that more frequent compounding could lead to unbounded interest. But in the late 17th century, mathematician Jacob Bernoulli showed that there was an upper limit on the amount of money that you can earn. His proof introduced a new mathematical constant.

Definition

The number e is, by definition,

$$e = \lim_{n \to \infty} \left(1 + \frac{1}{n}\right)^n$$

The value of e is approximately e ≈ 2.71828. . . .

See the TI-Nspire Handbook on p. 704 for information about how to find e on your calculator.

Continuously compounded interest is computed by taking the limit as the frequency of compounding increases. In Danielle's case, this amounts to

$$\lim_{n \to \infty} F(n) = \lim_{n \to \infty} 100\left(1 + \frac{1}{n}\right)^n$$
$$= 100 \cdot e$$
$$\approx 271.828$$

So, rounded to the nearest penny, Danielle would have $271.83 after a year if the interest were compounded continuously.

Example 1

Problem Suppose David invests $100 at 12% APR. If the interest is compounded quarterly, how much money will he have after five years?

Solution The 12% APR means David earns 3% per quarter. Since there are 20 quarters in five years, you can calculate

$$100(1.03)^{20} \approx 180.61$$

to show that David will have $180.61 at the end of five years.

$3 = 12 \div 4$
$20 = 4 \cdot 5$

Now suppose you invest P dollars at interest rate r, compounded n times per year. Let $B(t)$ denote your balance at the end of t years. Then

An interest rate of 12% means $r = 0.12$.

$$B(t) = P\left(1 + \frac{r}{n}\right)^{nt}$$

- The interest rate in each compounding period is $\frac{r}{n}$.
- There are nt compounding periods in t years.

Example 2

Problem Suppose David invests $100 at 12% APR, but this time the interest is compounded continuously. How much money will he have after five years?

See the TI-Nspire Handbook on p. 704 to use your CAS to approximate $\lim_{n \to \infty} 100\left(1 + \frac{0.12}{n}\right)^{5n}$.

Solution Let n be the number of times the interest gets compounded per year so that:

- the interest rate in each compounding period is $\frac{0.12}{n}$.
- there are $5n$ compound periods in five years.

Thus after five years, David will have $100\left(1 + \frac{0.12}{n}\right)^{5n}$ dollars.

As n grows larger and larger, you get

$$\lim_{n \to \infty} 100\left(1 + \frac{0.12}{n}\right)^{5n} \approx 182.212$$

So David has approximately $182.21.

Exercises *Practicing Habits of Mind*

Check Your Understanding

1. Suppose Danielle could invest $100 with Seventh Fifth Bank at 100% APR for more than just a year.

   a. What would her balance be at the end of two years if compounding were annual? At the end of three years? At the end of t years?

   b. What would her balance be at the end of two years if compounding were quarterly? At the end of three years? At the end of t years?

   c. In terms of the number e, what would her balance be at the end of three years of continuous compounding? Find this value to the nearest cent.

2. Jamie says that 100% APR is totally unrealistic. "I've never seen any savings account with more than 5% or 6% interest. So could we please look at something more realistic?"

   a. If Jamie invests $100 at 6% APR, compounded annually, how much money will she have at the end of one year? At the end of two years? At the end of t years?

   b. If the 6% APR is compounded twice per year, how much money will she have at the end of one year? At the end of two years? At the end of t years?

   c. **Write About It** Danielle says that after three years of monthly compounding at 6% APR, Jamie will have $100(1.005)^{36}$ dollars in the account. Describe in detail where the values 100, 1.005, and 36 come from.

3. Jamie invests P dollars at 5% APR, compounded n times per year for t years. Find a formula for the balance of this account at the end of t years in terms of P, n, and t.

4. Jamie invests $100 at 5% APR and is looking at what happens as interest is compounded more and more often. To the nearest penny, find the balance of Jamie's account after one year if interest is compounded on each of the following schedules.

   a. quarterly   **b.** monthly

   c. daily   **d.** hourly

5. Jamie invests $100 at 5% APR, compounded continuously to earn the maximum interest. Find Jamie's balance, to the nearest penny, after each of the following time periods.

   a. 5 years   **b.** 10 years

   c. 20 years   **d.** 40 years

6. For each of the values found in Exercise 5, rewrite the result in terms of e.

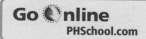

Go Online
PHSchool.com

For more information on compound interest and e, go to **Web Code:** bge-9031

7. This exercise is a proof of the fact that for $x > 0$,

$$\lim_{n \to \infty}\left(1 + \tfrac{x}{n}\right)^n = e^x$$

using the limit definition of e.

a. If $\tfrac{1}{K} = \tfrac{x}{n}$, write n in terms of x and K.

b. Rewrite the expression

$$\left(1 + \tfrac{x}{n}\right)^n$$

by making the substitution $\tfrac{1}{K} = \tfrac{x}{n}$.

c. Explain why the equation is true.

$$\lim_{n \to \infty}\left(1 + \tfrac{x}{n}\right)^n = \lim_{K \to \infty}\left(1 + \tfrac{1}{K}\right)^{Kx}$$

d. Show that

$$\lim_{K \to \infty}\left(1 + \tfrac{1}{K}\right)^{Kx} = e^x$$

using the limit definition of e.

> As n grows, what happens to K?

8. You have already seen that if you invest P dollars at an APR of r, compounded n times per year, your balance at the end of t years is

$$B(t) = P\left(1 + \tfrac{r}{n}\right)^{nt}$$

Consider the limit of the expression on the right as n gets larger and larger. Show that

$$\lim_{n \to \infty} P\left(1 + \tfrac{r}{n}\right)^{nt} = Pe^{rt}$$

On Your Own

9. Find the value of $\displaystyle\sum_{k=0}^{\infty} \tfrac{1}{k!}$ to five decimal places.

10. Suppose Danielle was able to invest $1000 instead of $100 in her Seventh Fifth Bank account.

a. What would be the effect on her balance at the end of the year?

b. What is the maximum amount of money Danielle could have at the end of a year, investing $1000 this way?

> **Remember...**
> Danielle's investment was $100 at 100% APR.

11. Jamie puts $1000 in a savings account that earns 6% APR, compounded continuously.

    a. How much money will Jamie have after 3 years? After 5 years? After t years?

    b. How long will it take for Jamie's account balance to double?

    c. How long will it take for Jamie's account to be worth $4000?

12. Which would be a better investment—an account at 6% APR compounded annually, or an account at 5.5% APR compounded continuously?

13. Sketch the graphs of these two functions on the same axes.

$$f(t) = 1.06^t, \ g(t) = e^{0.055t}$$

14. The graph of $g(t) = e^{0.055t}$ passes through the point $(0, 1)$. Find the slope of the line tangent to the graph of g at this point. Round your answer to three decimal places.

15. Rewrite $g(t)$ from Exercise 13 in the form $g(t) = b^t$ with base b accurate to four decimal places.

16. **Standardized Test Prep** Jo and Eddie each deposited $100 in a bank account paying 4% (APR) interest. Jo's bank compounds interest quarterly, while Eddie's bank compounds it continuously. What is the difference between the two account balances after one year?

    A. $0.02   **B.** $0.20   **C.** $2.00   **D.** $20.00

> Try putting the same amount of money into each account for the same time period. What does $e^{0.055}$ have to do with this exercise?

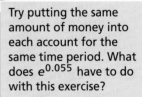

For additional practice, go to **Web Code:** bga-0311

Maintain Your Skills

17. Write the first four terms of the expansion of each expression (starting with $1 + x + \cdots$).

    a. $\left(1 + \frac{x}{3}\right)^3$ **b.** $\left(1 + \frac{x}{5}\right)^5$

    c. $\left(1 + \frac{x}{10}\right)^{10}$ **d.** $\left(1 + \frac{x}{n}\right)^n$

18. Find each limit.

    a. $\displaystyle\lim_{n\to\infty} \frac{\binom{n}{1}}{n}$ **b.** $\displaystyle\lim_{n\to\infty} \frac{\binom{n}{2}}{n^2}$ **c.** $\displaystyle\lim_{n\to\infty} \frac{\binom{n}{3}}{n^3}$

    d. $\displaystyle\lim_{n\to\infty} \frac{\binom{n}{4}}{n^4}$ **e.** $\displaystyle\lim_{n\to\infty} \frac{\binom{n}{5}}{n^5}$

> You can use most CAS software to evaluate the binomial coefficient $\binom{n}{2}$ as *nCr(n, 2)*.

3.12 Another Way to Find *e*

In Lesson 3.11, you saw the following definition for the number e.

$$e = \lim_{n \to \infty} \left(1 + \tfrac{1}{n}\right)^n \tag{1}$$

Using this definition, you proved that

$$e^x = \lim_{n \to \infty} \left(1 + \tfrac{x}{n}\right)^n \tag{2}$$

Equations (1) and (2) are the limit definitions of e and e^x, respectively. You can, however, define e and e^x another way, using the *factorial definition*. These alternatives are equivalent to the limit definitions.

> Actually, you proved this for $x > 0$ only. But (2) holds for all real x. See Exercise 12.

A Useful Lemma

Recall Exercise 18 from Lesson 3.11. In it, you saw that

$$\lim_{x \to \infty} \frac{\binom{n}{5}}{n^5} = \lim_{x \to \infty} \frac{n(n-1)(n-2)(n-3)(n-4)}{5!\,n^5}$$

$$= \tfrac{1}{5!} \lim_{n \to \infty} \left(\tfrac{n}{n} \cdot \tfrac{n-1}{n} \cdot \tfrac{n-2}{n} \cdot \tfrac{n-3}{n} \cdot \tfrac{n-4}{n} \right)$$

$$= \tfrac{1}{5!} \lim_{n \to \infty} \left(1 \cdot \left(1 - \tfrac{1}{n}\right)\left(1 - \tfrac{2}{n}\right)\left(1 - \tfrac{3}{n}\right)\left(1 - \tfrac{4}{n}\right) \right)$$

As $n \to \infty$, the terms $\tfrac{1}{n}, \tfrac{2}{n}, \tfrac{3}{n}$, and $\tfrac{4}{n}$ all go to zero, and thus

$$\lim_{x \to \infty} \frac{\binom{n}{5}}{n^5} = \frac{1}{5!}$$

You can generalize this result to state the following lemma.

Lemma 3.11

Let $k \geq 0$ be an integer. Then

$$\lim_{x \to \infty} \frac{\binom{n}{k}}{n^k} = \frac{1}{k!}$$

> It even works for $k = 0$. Remember that $0! = 1$.

Factorial Definitions of *e* and *e*ˣ

Let

$$f(n) = \sum_{k=0}^{n} \frac{1}{k!} = 1 + \frac{1}{1!} + \frac{1}{2!} + \frac{1}{3!} + \cdots + \frac{1}{n!}$$

Compute $f(n)$ for some values of n, rounded to five decimal places.

Recall Exercise 9 from Lesson 3.11.

$$f(1) = 2$$
$$f(5) = 2.71667$$
$$f(6) = 2.71806$$
$$f(7) = 2.71825$$
$$f(8) = 2.71828$$
$$f(100) = 2.71828$$

It appears that

$$\lim_{n \to \infty} f(n) = e$$

and the series seems to converge to e rather quickly.

To confirm this conclusion, start by expanding

$$\left(1 + \frac{1}{n}\right)^n$$

using the Binomial Theorem.

$$\left(1 + \frac{1}{n}\right)^n = 1 + n\left(\frac{1}{n}\right) + \binom{n}{2}\left(\frac{1}{n}\right)^2 + \binom{n}{3}\left(\frac{1}{n}\right)^3 + \cdots \qquad (3)$$

$$+ \binom{n}{2}\left(\frac{1}{n}\right)^k + \cdots + \binom{n}{n}\left(\frac{1}{n}\right)^n$$

A typical term on the right side of (3) has the form

$$\binom{n}{k}\left(\frac{1}{n}\right)^k = \frac{\binom{n}{k}}{n^k}$$

Using the lemma above,

$$\lim_{n \to \infty} \binom{n}{k}\left(\frac{1}{n}\right)^k = \lim_{n \to \infty} \frac{\binom{n}{k}}{n^k} = \frac{1}{k!}$$

Now let n get large in equation (3). The left side, by the limit definition, approaches e. And the right side looks like this:

$$1 + \frac{1}{1!} + \frac{1}{2!} + \frac{1}{3!} + \cdots + \frac{1}{k!} + \cdots$$

You can now state the following theorem.

"Letting n get large" here is actually a tricky issue involving calculus. But you should get the general gist of what is going on.

Theorem 3.12

$$\lim_{n \to \infty}\left(1 + \frac{1}{n}\right)^n = 1 + \frac{1}{1!} + \frac{1}{2!} + \frac{1}{3!} + \cdots = \sum_{k=0}^{\infty} \frac{1}{k!}$$

Theorem 3.12 states that the following definition of e is equivalent to the limit definition.

Definition

The factorial definition of e is

$$e = 1 + \frac{1}{1!} + \frac{1}{2!} + \frac{1}{3!} + \cdots = \sum_{k=0}^{\infty} \frac{1}{k!}$$

For You to Do

1. Using the limit definition of e^x,

$$e^x = \lim_{n \to \infty} \left(1 + \frac{x}{n}\right)^n$$

derive the factorial definition of e^x:

$$e^x = 1 + x + \frac{x^2}{2!} + \frac{x^3}{3!} + \cdots = \sum_{k=0}^{\infty} \frac{x^k}{k!}$$

Expand $\left(1 + \frac{x}{n}\right)^n$ using the Binomial Theorem, and let n get large.

Using the factorial definition, you can approximate e^x accurately with polynomials. For example, consider the cubic polynomial

$$c(x) = 1 + x + \frac{x^2}{2!} + \frac{x^3}{3!}$$

The graphs of $y = e^x$ and $y = c(x)$ are shown below.

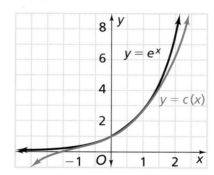

Notice how the two graphs almost agree when $-1 \le x \le 1$.

Developing Habits of Mind

Make strategic choices. Why is it useful to have different equivalent definitions of e and e^x based on factorials, when there are already ones using limits? It is useful because you can pick and choose the definition that is most convenient a given context.

For example, here is a proof that the number e is irrational, using its factorial definition. By the factorial definition of e,

$$e = 1 + \frac{1}{1!} + \frac{1}{2!} + \frac{1}{3!} + \cdots + \frac{1}{k!} + \frac{1}{(k+1)!} + \frac{1}{(k+2)!} + \cdots \qquad (4)$$

Suppose e is a rational number and write $e = \frac{p}{q}$ for some integers p and q, with $q > 0$. Choose a positive integer k such that $k > q$. Therefore,

$$k! = k(k-1)(k-2)\cdots q(q-1)(q-2)\cdots 3 \cdot 2 \cdot 1$$

We will come up with a contradiction.

and thus $\frac{k!}{q}$ is an integer. Multiply each side of (4) by $k!$ to get

$$k!e = k!\left(1 + \frac{1}{1!} + \frac{1}{2!} + \frac{1}{3!} + \cdots + \frac{1}{k!}\right) + k!\left(\frac{1}{(k+1)!} + \frac{1}{(k+2)!} + \cdots\right) \qquad (5)$$

The left side of (5) equals

$$k!e = \frac{k!}{q} \cdot p$$

which is an integer. On the right side of (5), the term

$$k!\left(1 + \frac{1}{1!} + \frac{1}{2!} + \frac{1}{3!} + \cdots + \frac{1}{k!}\right)$$

is an integer because $m!$ is a divisor of $k!$ for all m such that $0 \le m \le k$. Hence the remaining term on the right side of (5), namely

$$k!\left(\frac{1}{(k+1)!} + \frac{1}{(k+2)!} + \cdots\right)$$

must also be an integer. But

$$k!\left(\frac{1}{(k+1)!} + \frac{1}{(k+2)!} + \cdots\right) = \frac{1}{k+1} + \frac{1}{(k+2)(k+1)} + \frac{1}{(k+3)(k+2)(k+1)} + \cdots$$

Replace each term in the sum by something greater.

$$< \frac{1}{k+1} + \frac{1}{(k+1)^2} + \frac{1}{(k+1)^3} + \frac{1}{(k+1)^4} + \cdots$$

$$= \frac{1}{k+1}\left(1 + \frac{1}{k+1} + \frac{1}{(k+1)^2} + \frac{1}{(k+1)^3} + \frac{1}{(k+1)^4} + \cdots\right)$$

$$= \frac{1}{k+1}\left(\frac{1}{1 - \frac{1}{k+1}}\right)$$

$$= \frac{1}{k}$$

$$< 1$$

Therefore

$$k!\left(\frac{1}{(k+1)!} + \frac{1}{(k+2)!} + \cdots\right)$$

is a positive integer which is strictly less than 1, a contradiction. And thus, e must be irrational.

Remember...

$$\sum_{i=0}^{\infty} r^i = \frac{1}{1-r} \text{ when } |r| < 1. \text{ Here, } r = \frac{1}{k+1}.$$

Exercises Practicing Habits of Mind

Check Your Understanding

1. **a.** Use the factorial definition of e to find the value of e correctly to 10 decimal places. How many terms are necessary?

   b. Calculate $\left(1 + \frac{1}{n}\right)^n$ for $n = 10^7$. How many digits of e does this calculation correctly find?

2. The quadratic function $q(x) = 1 + x + \frac{x^2}{2}$ is a good approximation of $f(x) = e^x$ when x is near 0.

   a. Calculate $q(0.05)$ and $e^{0.05}$ to five decimal places. What is the percent error for $q(0.05)$ as an approximation to $e^{0.05}$?

   b. Calculate $q(0.5)$ and $e^{0.5}$ to five decimal places and find the percent error.

   c. Calculate $q(-1)$ and e^{-1} to five decimal places and find the percent error.

> The percent error is
> $$\frac{\text{Estimate} - \text{Actual}}{\text{Actual}} \cdot 100$$

3. Find, to three decimal places, the value of x such that $e^x = 2$.

4. In Lesson 3.10, you learned that the line tangent to the graph of $y = e^x$ at $(0,1)$ has slope 1.

   a. The graph of $y = e^x$ gets steeper as x gets larger. At some point (x, y), the tangent line has slope 2. Give a good estimate for the coordinates of this point.

   b. At some other point, the tangent line has slope 3. Give a good estimate for the coordinates of this point.

> **Habits of Mind**
>
> **Make a connection.**
> How does the graph of $y = e^x$ suggest that there is a solution to the equation $e^x = 2$?

5. **a.** Calculate this value to five decimal places.

$$\sum_{k=0}^{\infty} \frac{(-1)^k}{k!}$$

   b. Compare your results with those from Exercise 2.

> See the TI-Nspire Handbook on p. 704 for advice on how to do this on your calculator.

6. Sketch the graph of each function.

   a. $f(x) = e^{-x}$ **b.** $g(x) = -e^x$ **c.** $h(x) = \frac{1}{e^x}$

On Your Own

7. Give a good estimate for $e^{0.03}$ without using a calculator.

8. The cubic function $c(x) = 1 + x + \frac{x^2}{2} + \frac{x^3}{6}$ is a good approximation of $f(x) = e^x$ when x is small.

   a. Calculate $c(0.1)$ and $f(0.1)$, then calculate the percent error in the approximation.

   b. Repeat part (a) for $x = 0.2, 0.5, 1, 2$.

   c. Explain why $c(x)$ is a good approximation to e^x for small values of x but not for large values of x.

   d. For how many values of x does $c(x) = f(x)$ exactly?

9. Find the exact value of this infinite sum.

$$1 + 2 + \frac{4}{2} + \frac{8}{6} + \frac{16}{24} + \frac{32}{120} + \cdots + \frac{2^k}{k!} + \cdots$$

> Use the graphs of c and f to help.

10. Find the solution to each equation to three decimal places.

   a. $e^k = 3$ **b.** $e^m = 5$ **c.** $e^n = 15$

   d. $e^p = 45$ **e.** $e^r = -5$

11. Let k be the solution to $e^k = 3$, as in Exercise 10a. Sketch the graph of the function

$$f(x) = e^{kx}$$

> Is there a simpler formula for $f(x)$?

12. **Take It Further**   Use the limit definition of e.

   a. Use a substitution to show that $\lim\limits_{n \to \infty}\left(1 - \frac{1}{n}\right)^n = \frac{1}{e}$.

   b. Use your result in part (a) to show that $\lim\limits_{n \to \infty}\left(1 + \frac{x}{n}\right)^n = e^x$ for $x \le 0$.

13. **Standardized Test Prep**   Which of the following infinite series gives the exact value of e^5?

   A. $\sum\limits_{i=1}^{\infty} \frac{5^i}{i!}$ **B.** $\sum\limits_{i=0}^{\infty} \frac{5^i}{i!}$ **C.** $\sum\limits_{i=0}^{\infty} \frac{e^i}{5!}$ **D.** $\sum\limits_{i=0}^{\infty} \frac{i^5}{5^i}$

Maintain Your Skills

14. Write each of these as fractions in the form $\frac{p}{q}$ where p and q are integers. Then approximate each to four decimal places.

   a. $1 + \frac{2}{1}$

   b. $1 + \dfrac{2}{1 + \frac{1}{6}}$

   c. $1 + \dfrac{2}{1 + \dfrac{1}{6 + \frac{1}{10}}}$

   d. $1 + \dfrac{2}{1 + \dfrac{1}{6 + \dfrac{1}{10 + \frac{1}{14}}}}$

For additional practice, go to **Web Code:** bga-0312

3.13 The Natural Logarithm Function

In this In-Class Experiment, you will investigate a function on your calculator called "ln." One way to investigate a function is to tabulate it and to see if there are any familiar "functional equations" lurking in the background.

In-Class Experiment

1. Use your calculator to find the output of the ln function for each integer input from 0 to 10. Record each output to five decimal places.

2. Calculate the value of ln 2 + ln 3 to four decimal places.

3. Calculate the value of 3 ln 2 to four decimal places.

4. Find and describe some rules that appear to be true for the ln function.

5. Find x, to four decimal places, if ln $x = 1$.

6. Draw the graph of $y = \ln x$.

x	ln x
0	▧
1	▧
2	▧
3	▧
4	▧
5	▧
6	▧
7	▧
8	▧
9	▧
10	▧

It is only by convention that ln x, like sin x, is normally written without parentheses. On a calculator, parentheses are usually required.

Your table in the In-Class Experiment should show that

- ln 2 + ln 3 = ln 6
- ln 2 + ln 5 = ln 10
- ln 3 + ln 3 = ln 9

And if you extend the table, you can also see that

- ln 3 + ln 4 = ln 12
- ln 5 + ln 7 = ln 35
- ln 6 + ln 9 = ln 54

and so on. In other words, for $M, N > 0$, the function $g(x) = \ln x$ seems to satisfy the functional equation

$$\ln(MN) = \ln M + \ln N$$

But this is precisely the Fundamental Law of Logarithms.

A functional equation is an equation satisfied by a function.

For You to Do

Use your table of data from the In-Class Experiment to verify that the ln function has the following properties.

7. $\ln \frac{M}{N} = \ln M - \ln N$

8. $\ln M^p = p \ln M$

Recall that these are the corollaries to the Fundamental Law of Logarithms.

Why does the function ln behave like a logarithm? Because it is a logarithm! In other words,

$$\ln x = \log_b x$$

for some base $b > 0$. What, then, is the base?

- From the definition of the logarithm, you know that the output of $\log_b M$ is the exponent k such that $b^k = M$, that is

$$b^k = M \iff \log_b M = k \tag{1}$$

- $\log_b$ is a one-to-one function.

- It follows from equation (1) that if $\log_b x = 1$, then $x = b$, the base of the logarithm.

- In the In-Class Experiment, you found that ln e seems to be 1. If that were so, the base of ln would be e.

And in fact, the ln function built into your calculator is just the logarithm to the base e.

Definition

The **natural logarithm** function ln is the logarithm to base e:

$$\ln x = \log_e x$$

Why "natural" logarithm? You will see why in the next lesson. For an alternative approach to ln, see Chapter 8 of this book.

For You to Do

9. Copy and complete the following table.

x	e^x
0	▦
0.69315	▦
1.09861	▦
1.38629	▦
1.60944	▦
1.79176	▦
1.94591	▦
2.07944	▦
2.19722	▦
2.30259	▦

3.13 The Natural Logarithm Function **255**

From the two tables of data you have generated so far in this lesson,

- $e^{0.69315} = 2$ and $\ln 2 = 0.69315$
- $e^{1.09861} = 3$ and $\ln 3 = 1.09861$
- $e^{1.38629} = 4$ and $\ln 4 = 1.38629$

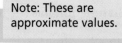

Note: These are approximate values.

and so on. And in general,

$$e^a = b \iff \ln b = a \qquad (2)$$

Statement (2) is another way of saying that the functions $x \mapsto e^x$ and $x \mapsto \ln x$ are inverses of each other. This should come as no surprise, since the logarithmic function

$$x \mapsto \log_b x$$

is the inverse of the exponential function

$$x \mapsto b^x$$

In this case, $b = e$.

For You to Do

10. Sketch the graphs of $x \mapsto e^x$ and $x \mapsto \ln x$ on the same axes.

11. Find the domain and range of each function. Do your results make sense? Explain.

12. How are the two graphs related?

13. Why is the ln function undefined for $x \le 0$?

Example

Problem Solve the equation

$$e^{x^2} = 27$$

Solution Apply the ln function to each side and use a corollary to the Law of Logarithms to proceed.

$$\ln e^{x^2} = \ln 27$$
$$x^2 \ln e = \ln 27 \qquad \ln M^p = p \ln M$$
$$x^2 = \ln 27 \qquad \ln e = 1$$
$$x^2 \approx 3.29584$$
$$x \approx \pm 1.81544$$

Exercises Practicing Habits of Mind

Check Your Understanding

1. Using only the table from the In-Class Experiment, find the value of $\ln 1024$ to three decimal places.

2. Use the fact that $\ln M^p = p \ln M$.

   a. Find values for p and M if $\ln 81 = p \ln M$.

   b. Write $\ln \sqrt[3]{2}$ as a multiple of $\ln 2$.

   c. Write $\ln \frac{1}{25}$ as a multiple of $\ln 5$.

> Indeed, for any number $b > 0$,
> $\log_b M^p = p \log_b M$.

3. Simplify each of the following.

   a. $\ln e^2$

   b. $\ln e^{10}$

   c. $\ln \frac{1}{e}$

   d. $e^{\ln 5}$

4. In Lesson 3.12, you found a number k such that $e^k = 3$.

   a. If you use a CAS to solve the equation $e^k = 3$, what answer do you get?

   b. What number m is the solution to $e^m = 5$?

   c. Show that this statement is true for any real number x.

   $$e^{x \ln 2} = 2^x$$

5. Show that you can write any exponential function $f(x) = a^x$, where $a > 0$ is real, in the form

   $$f(x) = e^{kx}$$

   for some real number k.

6. Logarithms are useful in solving equations that involve exponents.

   a. If $2^x = 7$, show that $x \ln 2 = \ln 7$. Then find x to three decimal places.

   b. Find z to three decimal places if $5^z = 123$.

   c. Use logarithms to find the one solution to $2 \cdot 6^x = 0.1$.

   d. **Take It Further** In terms of the parameters a, b, c, and d, find the solution to

   $$a \cdot b^x = c \cdot d^x$$

7. You have seen that $e^a = b$ if and only if $\ln b = a$. Here are the graphs of $y = e^x$ and $y = \ln x$ on the same axes.

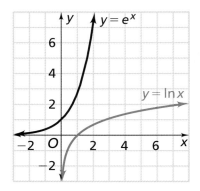

a. Exactly one point on the graph of $y = \ln x$ has x-coordinate 3. What are the coordinates of this point?

b. Exactly one point on the graph of $y = e^x$ has y-coordinate 3. What are the coordinates of this point?

c. Exactly one point on the graph of $y = e^x$ has x-coordinate 2. What are the coordinates of this point?

d. Exactly one point on the graph of $y = \ln x$ has y-coordinate 2. What are the coordinates of this point?

e. If the point $(g, 4)$ is on the graph of $y = \ln x$, find g.

f. If the point $(p, 4)$ is on the graph of $y = e^x$, find p.

On Your Own

8. Calculate each of the following to three decimal places, if possible.

a. $\ln 3$ **b.** $\ln 5$ **c.** $\ln 15$

d. $\ln 45$ **e.** $\ln \frac{5}{3}$ **f.** $\ln(-5)$

9. Jamie invests \$100 at 6% APR, compounded continuously. After t years her account balance is

$$B = 100e^{0.06t}$$

a. How much money will Jamie have in this account after 5 years? After 10 years? After 20 years?

b. How long will it take for Jamie's account to grow to exactly \$200?

c. How long will it take for Jamie's account to grow to exactly \$400?

d. Solve the equation $B = 100e^{0.06t}$ for t. Use the result to determine how long it will take for Jamie's account to grow to \$1000.

10. For each interest rate, compounded continuously, determine how long (in years) it will take for a savings account to double in value.

   a. 2% APR   **b.** 3% APR   **c.** 4% APR

   d. 5% APR   **e.** 8% APR   **f.** p% APR

11. Many financial advisors use the Rule of 72 to estimate the doubling time of an account. To find the number of years it takes to double an investment's value, divide 72 by the percent interest rate.

   a. How does the Rule of 72 compare to the results of Exercise 10?

   b. **Take It Further** Ryo jokes that it should have been called the "Rule of ln 2." Why?

If the interest rate is 6%, divide by 6.

12. **Standardized Test Prep** On the day Aaron was born, his parents deposited $24,000 into an account paying 8% (APR) interest compounded continuously. How old will Aaron be, to the nearest month, when the account balance is $100,000?

   A. 17 years, 1 month   **B.** 17 years, 10 months

   C. 18 years, 3 months   **D.** 18 years, 6 months

Maintain Your Skills

13. Find the slope of the line segment connecting each pair of points.

   a. $(3, 5)$ and $(4, 8)$ **b.** $(5, 3)$ and $(8, 4)$

   c. $(2, 1)$ and $(10, 2)$ **d.** $(1, 2)$ and $(2, 10)$

   e. $(0, 4)$ and (a, b) **f.** $(4, 0)$ and (b, a)

Go Online
PHSchool.com

For additional practice, go to **Web Code:** bga-0313

14. For parts (a) through (f), find a good estimate for the slope of the line tangent to the graph of $y = \ln x$ at each value of x.

   a. $x = 1$ **b.** $x = 2$ **c.** $x = 3$

   d. $x = 10$ **e.** $x = \frac{1}{2}$ **f.** $x = \frac{1}{3}$

   g. What relationship does the slope of the tangent have to x?

3.14 Analysis of $f(x) = e^x$ and $g(x) = \ln x$

In Exercise 14 from Lesson 3.13, you looked at the slopes of several tangents to the graph of $y = \ln x$. From your results, you might have made a conjecture that describes an interesting property of the ln function. That property is detailed in the following theorem.

Theorem 3.13

The tangent to the graph of $y = \ln x$ at the point $(a, \ln a)$ has slope $\frac{1}{a}$.

The proof of this theorem requires results from calculus. For now, you can assume it is true.

Is there a similar theorem to be found regarding tangents to $y = e^x$? You could repeat the experiment and try to find a pattern. But you can use the fact that $f(x) = e^x$ and $g(x) = \ln x$ are inverses of each other to determine a statement about tangents to f.

The figure below shows the graphs of f and g with the point $P = (2, \ln 2)$ on the graph of g and the corresponding point $Q = (\ln 2, 2)$ on the graph of f. The figure also shows the tangent to f at P, and the tangent to g at Q.

From Theorem 3.13, you know that the line tangent to g at P has slope $\frac{1}{2}$. But what is the slope of the line tangent to f at Q? From the figure, it looks as though the two tangent lines are also reflections of each other over $y = x$. The next problems help you prove this.

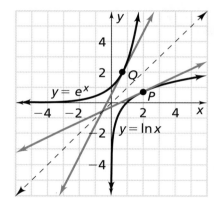

Remember...

If f and g are inverse functions, the graph of f is the reflection of the graph of g across the line $y = x$. A point (a, b) is on the graph of f if and only if (b, a) is on the graph of g.

For You to Do

Suppose h and j are inverse functions.

1. Let $R = (a, b)$ and $R' = (c, d)$ be a pair of points on the graph of h, and $S = (b, a)$ and $S' = (d, c)$ the corresponding points on the graph of j. Show that the slope of the secant between R and R' is the reciprocal of the slope of the secant between S and S'.

2. Explain why Problem 1 implies that the slope of the tangent at R is the reciprocal of the slope of the tangent at S.

If you let R' approach R, what happens to S'?

Since the slope of the line tangent to g at P is $\frac{1}{2}$, by Problem 2, the slope of the line tangent to f at Q is its reciprocal. Therefore, the line tangent to the graph of $f(x) = e^x$ at $Q = (\ln 2, 2)$ has slope 2. From this result, you can state the following theorem.

Theorem 3.14

The tangent to the graph of $y = e^x$ at the point (a, e^a) has slope e^a.

For You to Do

3. Prove Theorem 3.14.

> If you cannot see the pattern, think about a point on f such as $(4, e^4)$. What would the slope of the tangent at this point be? The corresponding point on the graph of g would be $(e^4, 4)$, which is $(e^4, \ln e^4)$. The slope of the tangent at that point would be $\frac{1}{e^4}$.

Once you know how to find the slopes of these tangent lines, you can find their equations.

Example

Problem

a. Find the equation $y = j(x)$ of the tangent to the graph of $g(x) = \ln x$ at $(3, \ln 3)$.

b. Find the equation $y = k(x)$ of the tangent to the graph of $f(x) = e^x$ at $(\ln 3, 3)$.

c. Verify that j and k are inverses of each other.

Solution

a. From Theorem 3.13, the slope of the tangent is $\frac{1}{3}$. Since the line passes through the point $(3, \ln 3)$, an equation for the line is

$$\frac{1}{3} = \frac{y - \ln 3}{x - 3}$$

and

$$j(x) = \frac{1}{3}(x - 3) + \ln 3$$

b. From Theorem 3.14, the slope of the tangent is 3. The line passes through the point $(\ln 3, 3)$, so its equation is

$$3 = \frac{y - 3}{x - \ln 3}$$

and

$$k(x) = 3(x - \ln 3) + 3$$

c. You can verify that j and k are inverses by showing that
$j(k(x)) = k(j(x)) = x$.

$$j(k(x)) = \frac{1}{3}(k(x) - 3) + \ln 3$$
$$= \frac{1}{3}([3(x - \ln 3) + 3] - 3) + \ln 3$$
$$= \frac{1}{3}(3(x - \ln 3)) + \ln 3$$
$$= (x - \ln 3) + \ln 3$$
$$= x$$

Likewise, $k(j(x)) = x$. Consequently, the graphs of j and k are reflections of each other across the line $y = x$.

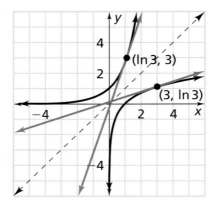

For You to Do

4. Find the equation of the line tangent to $f(x) = e^x$ at the point $\left(\frac{1}{2}, \sqrt{e}\right)$.

Exercises *Practicing Habits of Mind*

Check Your Understanding

1. In this lesson you learned that $f(x) = e^x$ has an interesting property: the slope of its tangent line at any point (x, y) is the same as the y-coordinate of that point. What can you say about the slopes of the following functions?

a. $h(x) = 3e^x$

b. $j(x) = e^{2x}$

c. $k(x) = e^{5x}$

d. $m(x) = e^{x \ln 2}$

2. Exercise 4 of Lesson 3.13 asked you to show that $e^{x \ln 2} = 2^x$ for any x. Exercise 1 of this lesson asked about the function $m(x) = e^{x \ln 2}$. You can also write this function as $m(x) = 2^x$.

   a. What is the slope of the tangent to the graph of $m(x) = 2^x$ at the point $(0, 1)$?

   b. What is the slope of the tangent to the graph of m at the point $(2, 4)$? Write your answer in terms of a logarithm.

   c. What is the slope of the tangent to the graph of $p(x) = 5^x$ at the point $(1, 5)$? Write your answer in terms of a logarithm. Verify by using a graphing calculator.

3. Look back at the table from Problem 5 of Lesson 3.10.

   a. The output for base 5 is 1.609. What expression could you use to find this number directly?

   b. Give a reason why the output for base 8 is three times the output for base 2.

   c. What base would make the slope of the tangent exactly 1?

   d. What base would make the slope of the tangent equal to zero?

4. Below is a three-step proof that

   $$\log_2 x = \frac{\ln x}{\ln 2}$$

   Justify each step.

   a. If $\log_2 x = y$, then $2^y = x$.

   b. If $2^y = x$, then $y \ln 2 = \ln x$.

   c. $\log_2 x = \dfrac{\ln x}{\ln 2}$

5. In this lesson you learned that $g(x) = \ln x$ has an interesting property: the slope of its tangent line at any point (x, y) is the reciprocal of the x-coordinate of that point. What can you say about the slopes of the following functions?

   a. $h(x) = 3 \ln x$ **b.** $j(x) = \ln 2x$

   c. $k(x) = \dfrac{\ln x}{5}$ **d.** $m(x) = \dfrac{\ln x}{\ln 2}$

> The ability to express these slopes using the logarithm to base e is a main reason to introduce the number e and the natural logarithm function. It is also one reason why $x \mapsto \ln x$ is called the *natural* logarithm. The functions $x \mapsto e^x$ and $\ln$ play a key role throughout calculus.

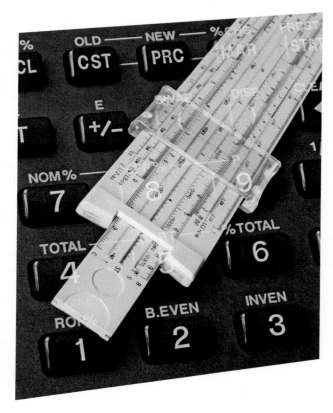

A slide rule uses logarithmic scales to perform multiplication and division by the addition and subtraction of lengths.

6. Exercise 4 asked you to show that $\log_2 x = \frac{\ln x}{\ln 2}$ for $x > 0$. Exercise 5 asked about the function $m(x) = \frac{\ln x}{\ln 2}$, which you can also write as $m(x) = \log_2 x$.

  a. What is the slope of the tangent to the graph of $m(x) = \log_2 x$ at the point $(1, 0)$?

  b. What is the slope of the tangent to the graph of m at the point $(4, 2)$? Write your answer in terms of a logarithm.

  c. What is the slope of the tangent to the graph of $p(x) = \log_5 x$ at the point $(5, 1)$? Write your answer in terms of a logarithm. Verify your answer using a graphing calculator.

7. Look back at the table from Exercise 9 of Lesson 3.10.

  a. The output given for base 5 is 0.621. What expression could you use to find this number directly?

  b. Give a reason why the output for base 8 is one-third of the output for base 2.

  c. What base would make the slope of the tangent exactly 1?

  d. What base would make the slope of the tangent equal to zero?

> Of what significance is the reciprocal of 0.621?

On Your Own

8. a. At what point does the graph of $f(x) = e^x$ have a tangent line of slope 8?

  b. What is the y-intercept of this tangent line? Is it positive or negative?

9. Exactly one line tangent to the graph of $f(x) = e^x$ passes through the origin. What is its equation? At what point is it tangent to the graph of f?

10. Find a rule that can give the slope of the line tangent to the graph of $p(x) = Ae^{bx}$ at any given point $(x, p(x))$ on the graph.

> This rule generalizes some of the results from Exercise 1.

11. Find a rule that can give the slope of the line tangent to the graph of $q(x) = A \ln Bx$ at any given point $(x, q(x))$ on the graph.

12. Find a rule that can give the slope of the line tangent to the graph of $r(x) = b^x$ at any given point $(x, r(x))$ on the graph.

13. Find a rule that can give the slope of the line tangent to the graph of $s(x) = \log_b x$ at any given point $(x, s(x))$ on the graph.

14. Write About It Compare and contrast the results from Exercises 2 and 6 from this lesson. Why are the answers similar, and in what ways do they differ?

15. Take It Further Using the rules from Exercises 10 and 11, show that if a line tangent to $p(x) = Ae^{bx}$ at (c, d) has slope m, then the line tangent to the inverse function $p^{-1}(x)$ at (d, c) has slope $\frac{1}{m}$.

16. Standardized Test Prep Which of the following is an equation of the line tangent to the graph of $f(x) = 5^x$ at $(c, 5^c)$?

A. $y = 5^c(x - c) + 5^c$

B. $y = (\ln c)(x - c) + 5^c$

C. $y = 5^c(x - c) + \ln c$

D. $y = 5^c(\ln 5)(x - c) + 5^c$

Maintain Your Skills

17. For each recursively defined function, find a closed-form definition that is equivalent for all nonnegative integers n.

For additional practice, go to **Web Code:** bga-0313

a. $a(n) = \begin{cases} 1 & \text{if } n = 0 \\ 2a(n-1) & \text{if } n > 0 \end{cases}$

b. $b(n) = \begin{cases} 0 & \text{if } n = 0 \\ b(n-1) + 2n + 4 & \text{if } n > 0 \end{cases}$

c. $c(n) = \begin{cases} 0 & \text{if } n = 0 \\ c(n-1) + n & \text{if } n > 0 \end{cases}$

d. $d(n) = \begin{cases} 1 & \text{if } n = 0 \\ 5 & \text{if } n = 1 \\ 7d(n-1) - 10d(n-2) & \text{if } n > 1 \end{cases}$

e. $f(n) = \begin{cases} 2 & \text{if } n = 0 \\ 7 & \text{if } n = 1 \\ 7f(n-1) - 10f(n-2) & \text{if } n > 1 \end{cases}$

Historical Perspective

Leonhard Euler (1707–1783) was one of the greatest mathematicians of all time. He was an extraordinary algebraist—he loved to calculate with expressions, series, and functions. He was the person who first derived the identity

$$e^x = \sum_{k=0}^{\infty} \frac{x^k}{k!}$$

Euler established hundreds of identities like this, and he found connections among many of them.

For a proof, in the style of Euler, that the graph of $y = e^x$ has slope e^a at $x = a$, go to **Web Code:** bge-8031

 Mathematical 3C Reflections

In this investigation, you saw how the constant *e* arises, and you found different ways of computing it. You studied the natural logarithm (base *e*) function and its inverse, $f(x) = e^x$. You used the ln function to solve exponential equations. The following questions will help you summarize what you have learned.

1. Adam has had $500 invested at 6% interest, compounded quarterly for 5 years. He was telling Jamie about his account, and Jamie said. "If you'd invested that money at my bank, where they compound continuously, you would have made more money." How much more would Adam have made in 5 years at the same rate of interest?

2. **a.** Approximate *e* using the first five terms of its factorial definition.

   b. What is the percent error in your estimate from part (a)?

   c. How large must *n* be for the expression $\left(1 + \frac{1}{n}\right)^n$ to give just as good an approximation?

3. If you put $5000 into an account paying 7% interest compounded continuously, when will the value of the account reach $8000?

4. Find an equation for the tangent to the graph of $y = 3 \ln x$ at the point $(2, 3 \ln 2)$.

5. Rewrite the function $g(x) = 5^x$ in terms of *e*. Find an equation for the tangent to the graph of *g* at the point $(2, 25)$.

6. What happens when interest is compounded more and more frequently?

7. What are some reasons to introduce the number *e*?

8. How can you relate any exponential or logarithmic function to $f(x) = e^x$ and $g(x) = \ln x$?

Vocabulary and Notation

In this investigation, you learned these terms. Make sure you understand what each one means and how to use it.

- **continuously compounded interest**
- **e**
- **natural logarithm, ln *x***

Project: Using Mathematical Habits

Partial Fractions

Consider the rational function

$$f(x) = \frac{1}{x^2 + 5x + 6}$$

and suppose you want to find the sum

$$\sum_{k=1}^{10} f(k) = \sum_{k=1}^{10} \frac{1}{k^2 + 5k + 6}$$

One way to do this is to compute the values

$$f(1) = \frac{1}{12}$$

$$f(2) = \frac{1}{20}$$

$$f(3) = \frac{1}{30}$$

$$\vdots$$

$$f(10) = \frac{1}{156}$$

and then add them up. But here is a more efficient approach. Note that

$$\frac{1}{x^2 + 5x + 6} = \frac{1}{x + 2} - \frac{1}{x + 3}$$

so that

$$\sum_{k=1}^{10} \frac{1}{k^2 + 5k + 6} = \sum_{k=1}^{10} \frac{1}{k + 2} - \frac{1}{k + 3} \qquad (1)$$

Now, the right side of (1) is the series

$$\underbrace{\left(\frac{1}{3} - \frac{1}{4}\right)}_{k=1} + \underbrace{\left(\frac{1}{4} - \frac{1}{5}\right)}_{k=2} + \underbrace{\left(\frac{1}{5} - \frac{1}{6}\right)}_{k=3} +$$

$$\cdots + \underbrace{\left(\frac{1}{11} - \frac{1}{12}\right)}_{k=9} + \underbrace{\left(\frac{1}{12} - \frac{1}{13}\right)}_{k=10}$$

But notice how every term except for the first $\left(\frac{1}{3}\right)$ and the last $\left(-\frac{1}{13}\right)$ cancel with an adjacent term. Thus, you get

$$\sum_{k=1}^{10} \frac{1}{k + 2} - \frac{1}{k + 3} = \frac{1}{3} - \frac{1}{13} = \frac{10}{39}$$

This canceling of adjacent terms is sometimes called "telescoping."

Writing a rational function such as $f(x)$ as a sum of simpler rational functions is a process known as *partial fraction decomposition*. (In this case, the simpler rational functions are $\frac{1}{x + 2}$ and $-\frac{1}{x + 3}$.) In this project, you will study how to decompose a rational function into partial fractions and how partial fraction decomposition can help you in computing various sums (as you have already seen) and in graphing.

1. Use partial fractions to quickly calculate this sum.

$$\sum_{k=0}^{20} \frac{1}{k^2 + 3k + 2}$$

2. Calculate this sum.

$$\sum_{k=0}^{\infty} \frac{1}{k^2 + 3k + 2}$$

3. Use telescoping to find this infinite sum.

$$\sum_{k=0}^{\infty} \frac{1}{k^2 + 7k + 12}$$

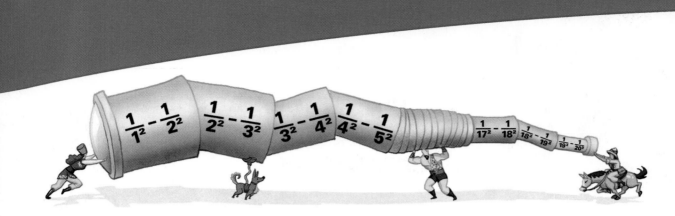

4. **a.** Show that this is an identity.

$$\frac{1}{k^2} - \frac{1}{(k+1)^2} = \frac{2k+1}{k^4 + 2k^3 + k^2}$$

b. Use telescoping to find this sum.

$$\sum_{k=1}^{19} \frac{2k+1}{k^4 + 2k^3 + k^2}$$

5. **a.** Write out the first five terms of this summation, without evaluating or simplifying anything.

$$\sum_{k=1}^{19} \frac{1}{k} - \frac{1}{k+2}$$

b. Use telescoping to find the entire sum.

6. You can break the function $f(x) = \dfrac{2x - 13}{x^2 - 7x + 10}$ into partial fractions as

$$f(x) = \frac{A}{x-2} + \frac{B}{x-5}$$

a. Write a system of two equations and two unknowns that you can solve for A and B.

b. Find A and B.

c. Sketch the graphs of $a(x) = \dfrac{A}{x-2}$ and $b(x) = \dfrac{B}{x-5}$ on the same axes.

d. Sketch the graph of f using the graphs of a and b.

7. **a.** Find values of A and B so that

$$\frac{A}{x-2} + \frac{B}{x-5} = \frac{4x+11}{x^2 - 7x + 10}$$

b. Sketch the graph of $g(x) = \dfrac{4x + 11}{x^2 - 7x + 10}$.

8. **a.** Find values of A and B so that

$$\frac{A}{x-2} + \frac{B}{x-5} = \frac{6x - 30}{x^2 - 7x + 10}$$

b. Sketch the graph of $h(x) = \dfrac{6x - 30}{x^2 - 7x + 10}$. Relate the shape of the graph to your answer in part (a).

9. Find values of A and B so that

$$\frac{A}{x-2} + \frac{B}{x-5} = \frac{px + q}{x^2 - 7x + 10}$$

Here, your answers will be in terms of p and q.

10. Suppose you want to find A and B so that

$$\frac{A}{x+5} + \frac{B}{x-2} = \frac{3x - 16}{x^2 + 3x - 10}$$

Multiplying each side by $x^2 + 3x - 10$ gives

$$A(x-2) + B(x+5) = 3x - 16 \qquad (2)$$

a. Substitute $x = -5$ into (2) and solve for A.

b. Substitute $x = 2$ into (2) and solve for B.

11. Repeat Exercise 9 using the method from Exercise 10.

12. The method of partial fractions will not work when the numerator has degree greater than or equal to the degree of the denominator, but polynomial long division can help.

   a. Find the quotient and remainder when you divide $x^3 - 4x^2 - 9x + 17$ by $x^2 - 7x + 10$.

   b. Use a graphing calculator to sketch the graph of $f(x) = \dfrac{x^3 - 4x^2 - 9x + 17}{x^2 - 7x + 10}$.

   c. Find A, B, C, and D so that

$$\frac{x^3 - 4x^2 - 9x + 17}{x^2 - 7x + 10} = Ax + B + \frac{C}{x - 2} + \frac{D}{x - 5}$$

13. Take It Further Consider the function $k(x) = \dfrac{1}{x^2 - x - 1}$. The denominator does not factor over the integers, but it does factor over the reals.

   a. Find the two roots of the polynomial

$$x^2 - x - 1$$

   b. Find A and B so you can write $k(x)$ in the form

$$k(x) = \frac{A}{x - \phi} + \frac{B}{x - \phi'}$$

   Here, ϕ is the positive root and ϕ' is the negative root of the polynomial $x^2 - x - 1$.

   c. Let $p(n) = A \cdot (\phi)^n + B \cdot (\phi')^n$ using the values from this exercise. Tabulate $p(n)$ for integers $n = 0, 1, 2, \ldots, 10$.

14. Write the rational function

$$f(x) = \frac{3x^2 + x}{x^3 - 3x^2 + x - 3}$$

as a sum of two terms with integer numerators.

15. Write the rational function

$$f(x) = \frac{5x^2 - 13x - 22}{x^3 - 19x + 30}$$

as a sum of three terms with integer numerators.

16. Consider the rational function $f(x) = \dfrac{2x - 1}{x^2 - 4x + 4}$. The denominator factors as $(x - 2)^2$.

   a. Show that $f(x)$ cannot be written in the form

$$f(x) = \frac{A}{x - 2} + \frac{B}{x - 2}$$

   with A and B real numbers.

   b. Find C and D with

$$f(x) = \frac{C}{x - 2} + \frac{D}{(x - 2)^2}$$

17. Write each of the following rational expressions as a sum,

$$\frac{A}{x - r_1} + \frac{B}{x - r_2}$$

where A, B, r_1, and r_2 are real numbers (possibly negative).

   a. $\dfrac{7x - 8}{2x^2 - 5x + 2}$

   b. $\dfrac{14x - 16}{2x^2 - 5x + 2}$

   c. $\dfrac{70x - 80}{2x^2 - 5x + 2}$

   d. $\dfrac{7x + 31}{x^2 + 5x - 14}$

   e. $\dfrac{8x + 29}{x^2 + 5x - 14}$

   f. $\dfrac{9x + 27}{x^2 + 5x - 14}$

Go Online
PHSchool.com

For vocabulary review, go
to Web Code: bgj-0351

In **Investigation 3A,** you learned to

- state the Change of Sign Theorem and the Intermediate Value Theorem for Polynomials, and to use them to analyze the graphs of polynomial functions

- find the equation of a line secant to a polynomial function and the average rate of change of a function between two points

- write the Taylor expansion for a polynomial function about a point

- find the equation of the tangent to a polynomial curve at a point

The following questions will help you check your understanding.

1. **a.** Find, if possible, a third-degree polynomial function f with a graph that satisfies the following conditions.

   - The graph of f crosses the x-axis at $(-4, 0)$ and $(-1, 0)$, and intersects it somewhere on the positive x-axis.

   - From left to right, the graph of f rises, falls, and rises.

   - The graph of f crosses the y-axis at $(0, -3)$.

   b. Can you find a polynomial that satisfies the first two conditions but crosses the y-axis at $(0, 3)$ instead of $(0, -3)$? Explain.

2. Suppose $f(x) = x^4 - x^3 - 2x^2 - 1$.

   a. Find the average rate of change of y with respect to x as x goes from -1 to 1.

   b. Find the equation of the secant line between $(-1, f(-1))$ and $(1, f(1))$.

   c. Find all intersections of the graph of $y = f(x)$ and the secant you just found. Give coordinates to the nearest thousandth.

3. Suppose that $f(x) = 4x^3 + x^2 - 3x + 5$.

   a. Expand $f(x)$ in powers of $x + 1$.

   b. Find the equation of the line tangent to the graph of $f(x)$ at the point $(-1, 5)$.

In **Investigation 3B,** you learned to

- sketch the graph of a rational function, including asymptotes and holes

- evaluate limits of rational expressions

- find the equation of the tangent to the graph of a rational function at a point

The following questions will help you check your understanding.

4. For the graph of each rational function, find, if possible,

   - the x- and y-intercepts

   - the equation of each vertical asymptote

   - the equation of each horizontal asymptote

   - the coordinates of any holes

   Then sketch the graph.

   a. $f(x) = \frac{x + 1}{x^2 - 1}$

   b. $g(x) = \frac{x - 3}{4x^2 - 9}$

   c. $h(x) = \frac{2x^2 - 5x - 12}{6x^2 + 11x + 3}$

   d. $j(x) = \frac{x^2 + 5x + 6}{x - 1}$

5. Find each limit.

   a. $\lim_{x \to \infty} \frac{3x + 1}{2x + 3}$

   b. $\lim_{x \to \infty} \frac{4x - 5}{3x^2 - x - 2}$

   c. $\lim_{x \to \infty} \frac{x^2 - 2x + 1}{x - 2}$

6. Find an equation of the line tangent to the graph of $f(x) = \dfrac{x-3}{x^2+3x-4}$ at the point $(2, f(2))$.

In **Investigation 3C,** you learned to

- state and use the limit and factorial definitions of e and e^x

- use the inverse relationship between e^x and $\ln x$ to solve equations

- find the equation for the line tangent to the graph of $y = e^x$ or $y = \ln x$ at a point

The following questions will help you check your understanding.

7. **a.** Give an estimate of $e^{0.08}$ using the first four terms of the factorial definition of e^x.

   b. Give an estimate of $e^{0.08}$ by evaluating $\left(1 + \dfrac{0.08}{n}\right)^n$ for $n = 10$.

   c. Use your calculator to find $e^{0.08}$ to five decimal places.

8. Jane invests \$1000 at 5.5% APR, compounded continuously. After t years, her account balance is

$$B = 1000e^{0.055t}$$

   a. How much money will Jane have in this account after 5 years? After 10 years?

   b. How long will it take for Jane's account to grow to \$2000? \$10,000?

9. Let $f(x) = e^x$ and $g(x) = \ln x$.

   a. Find an equation of the line tangent to the graph of f at the point $(2, f(2))$.

   b. Find an equation of the line tangent to the graph of g at the point $(2, g(2))$.

   c. At what point does the graph of f have a tangent line of slope 3?

   d. At what point does the graph of g have a tangent line of slope $\frac{1}{3}$?

Chapter 3 Test

Go Online PHSchool.com

For a chapter test, go to **Web Code:** bga-0353

Multiple Choice

1. Here is a graph of function *g*.

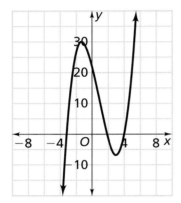

Which of these could be the equation of *g*?

A. $g(x) = (x + 4)(x + 2)(x - 3)$

B. $g(x) = -(x + 4)(x + 2)(x - 3)$

C. $g(x) = -(x - 4)(x - 2)(x + 3)$

D. $g(x) = (x - 4)(x - 2)(x + 3)$

2. Consider $f(x) = 2x^2 - 5x + 6$. What is the *y*-intercept of the line tangent to the graph of *f* at the point $(2, f(2))$?

A. -2 **B.** 2   **C.** 3   **D.** 4

3. Suppose $h(x) = x^3 - 4x^2 + 8x + 11 = A + B(x - 3) + C(x - 3)^2 + D(x - 3)^3$. Find *C*.

A. -13 **B.** -1 **C.** 5   **D.** 11

4. What is the equation of the horizontal asymptote of the function $f(x) = \dfrac{x - 1}{x^2 - x - 6}$?

A. $x = 0$ **B.** $y = 0$

C. $y = -2$ **D.** $x = 3$

5. Which of the following is an *x*-intercept of the function $f(x) = \dfrac{2x^2 - 2}{x^2 - 4}$?

A. -2 **B.** $\frac{1}{2}$ **C.** 1   **D.** 2

6. Let $h(x) = \dfrac{3x - 7}{x - 2}$. Find $\lim\limits_{x \to \infty} h(x)$.

A. ∞ **B.** 3

C. 2   **D.** $-\infty$

7. Estimate the slope of the line tangent to the graph of $g(x) = 3^x$ at $x = 0$.

A. 0.2   **B.** 0.8

C. 1.1   **D.** 2.5

8. Calculate the total value after 6 years of an initial investment of $2250 that earns 7% interest compounded quarterly.

A. $3412.00   **B.** $3424.41

C. $3472.16   **D.** $3472.27

9. Which expression could be used to directly calculate $\log_5 18$?

A. $\ln 5 - \ln 18$

B. $\ln 18 - \ln 5$

C. $\dfrac{\ln 5}{\ln 18}$

D. $\dfrac{\ln 18}{\ln 5}$

10. Which statement about the graph of $f(x) = \ln x$ is false?

A. It is symmetric about the origin.

B. It is unbounded.

C. It has a vertical asymptote.

D. It is increasing on its domain.

Open Response

11. Consider $f(x) = -(x-4)(x+2)(x+3)$.

  a. Sketch the graph of f.

  b. Identify all intercepts of the graph.

  c. Find the average rate of change of y with respect to x as x goes from 1 to 3.

  d. Write the equation of the secant between $(1, f(1))$ and $(3, f(3))$.

12. Suppose that $h(x) = x^3 - 3x^2 + 3x + 1$.

  a. Expand $h(x)$ into powers of $x - 1$.

  b. Divide the result by $x - 1$.

  c. Simplify $\dfrac{h(x)}{x-1}$.

  d. What conclusion can you draw from your answers to parts (b) and (c)?

13. A toy rocket takes off straight up in the air from level ground. The rocket's distance (in feet) above the ground at time t (in seconds) is $f(t) = 170t - 16t^2$.

  a. Find the average velocity during the first 4 seconds.

  b. Find the instantaneous velocity at $t = 2$.

14. Let $p(x) = \dfrac{2x^3 - 3x^2 - 5x - 12}{x - 3}$.

  a. Copy and complete this table for $p(x)$.

x	p(x)
0	▨
1	▨
2	▨
3	▨
4	▨

  b. Simplify the expression $\dfrac{2x^3 - 3x^2 - 5x - 12}{x - 3}$.

  c. Let $q(x) = 2x^2 + 3x + 4$. Find $\lim\limits_{x \to 3} p(x)$ and $\lim\limits_{x \to 3} q(x)$.

  d. Explain why the graph of p is not the same as q.

15. Find the limit.

  a. $\lim\limits_{x \to \infty} \dfrac{x+2}{3x+2}$ **b.** $\lim\limits_{x \to \infty} \dfrac{\cos x}{x}$ **c.** $\lim\limits_{x \to 3} \dfrac{\ln x}{\ln x^2}$

16. Let $f(x) = \dfrac{5x - 1}{x^2 - 2x - 15}$, $g(x) = \dfrac{A}{x+3}$, and $h(x) = \dfrac{B}{x-5}$, where A and B are constants.

  a. Find A and B so that $f(x) = g(x) + h(x)$.

  b. Find the slope of the line tangent to g at $x = 4$.

  c. Find the slope of the line tangent to h at $x = 4$.

  d. Find the slope of the line tangent to f at $x = 4$.

17. Copy and complete the table, using continuous compounding.

Initial Investment	APR	Time to Double	Amount in 15 years
$12,500	9%	▨	▨
$32,500	8%	▨	▨
$9,500	▨	4 years	▨
$16,800	▨	6 years	▨

18. Calculate each of the following. If necessary, round to three decimal places.

  a. $e^{2 \ln 3}$ **b.** $\ln 2 + \ln 3$

  c. $\log_2 3$ **d.** $\ln(-2)$

  e. $\ln e^{2-3}$

19. Solve for x to three decimal places.

  a. $e^x = 5$ **b.** $\ln x = 2$

20. At what point does the graph of $f(x) = \ln x$ have a tangent line of slope 5?

21. Find the polynomial function that has the following characteristics:

- Leading coefficient 2
- Degree 3
- Zeros -2, 1, and 4
- From left to right, its graph rises, falls, and rises.

Chapter 4

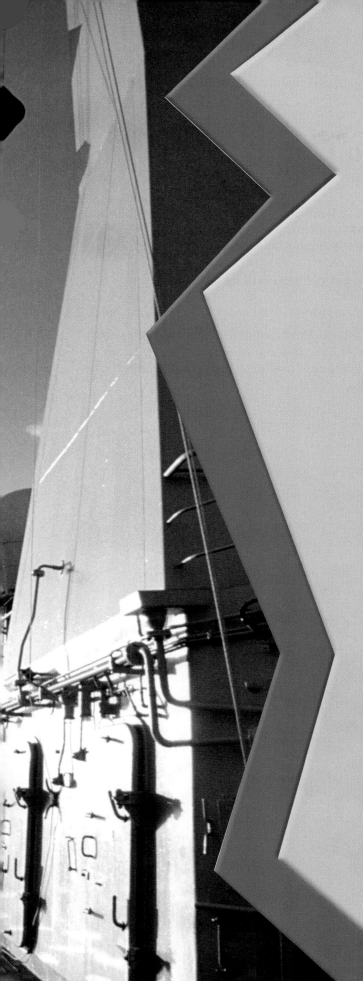

Combinatorics

Sometimes people need to know how many different ways things can happen or be combined. The mathematical study of how to count efficiently is called *combinatorics*. Some people call combinatorics "the art of counting without counting."

What sorts of things might you count? In the past, students might have counted the number of possible secret messages that four signal flags could send to a ship at sea. In the digital world of today, you might find yourself counting the number of possible secret codes to choose for your ATM card, or the ways to shuffle the songs on your favorite CD.

How might you count them? You will develop a set of tools for counting. You will explore a variety of strategies to help decide when to use each tool. As you work through the chapter, try to solve the problems in more than one way. You will be amazed to discover how many ways you can count the same thing!

Vocabulary and Notation

- anagram
- combination
- isomorphic
- permutation

- $_nC_k$, number of combinations of n objects, taken k at a time
- $_nP_k$, number of permutations of n objects, taken k at a time

Investigation 4A

Learning to Count

In *Learning to Count,* you will learn some techniques to solve counting problems. You will learn that some problems that appear different actually have the same underlying mathematical structure.

By the end of this investigation, you will be able to answer questions like these.

1. How many five-digit numbers can you make using only the digits 1 and 2?

2. In a kindergarten class, each student has four pictures: a square, a triangle, a circle, and a star. Each of the kids will make a design by gluing these four pictures in a line. There are 20 kids in the class. Can each child make a different design or will there have to be repeats?

3. What does it mean for two problems to be isomorphic?

You will learn how to

• recognize the kinds of problems that you can solve using combinatorics

• develop your own strategies for systematic counting

You will develop these habits and skills:

• Use efficient strategies for counting.

• Identify isomorphic problems.

• Apply counting strategies to functions defined on finite sets.

What does a softball team's batting order have in common with the outcome in a race of 9 horses?

4.1 Getting Started

Activating Prior Knowledge
Exploring New Ideas

Throughout this chapter, you will see three problems several times: The Same Birthday, Trains, and Pascal's Paths. You will see them for the first time in this Getting Started lesson. Try to develop your own techniques for solving them. You might not solve them all today, but you will get plenty of chances to try them during this chapter as you learn more ways to "count without counting."

For You to Explore

1. **The Same Birthday**

   In Ms. Roskam's class of 25 students, two of them have the same birthday. The students are very surprised to discover this. Ms. Roskam tells them that it is actually a good bet that, in a group of 25 people chosen at random, at least two of them will share a birthday.

   Is Ms. Roskam right? Suppose you choose 25 people at random and put them in a classroom. What is the probability that at least two of them share a birthday? If you want to ensure that the probability is more than 50%, what is the number of people you must have in that classroom?

2. **Trains**

   You can use number rods to build "trains" that all share a common length. A "train of length 5" is a row of rods that has a combined length of 5.

   | 1 | 2 | 2 |

   | 2 | 1 | 2 |

   | 1 | 3 | 1 |

   | 1 | 4 |

   | 5 |

   Notice that the 1–2–2 train and the 2–1–2 train contain the same rods. If you use identical rods in different orders, you make different trains.

   How many distinct trains of length n can you make?

   > Within a train you can repeat a length, and trains can contain different numbers of rods.

On Your Own

3. Pascal's Paths

Ms. Pascal likes to take a different route to work every day. She will quit her job the day she has to repeat a route she has already taken. The grid of streets below shows her home and her workplace. She only travels north and east and never backtracks. How many days will she work at this job?

> Two trips are different if they are not the same everywhere. They might overlap on some segments though, like the two valid paths shown below.

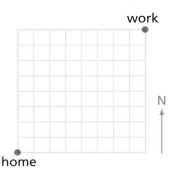

To understand the problem better, look at some possible paths on a grid of streets. Only two of the paths below are Pascal paths. The third path is not a Pascal path since Ms. Pascal never travels south or west.

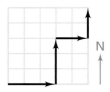   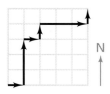   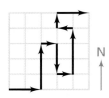

Here is a valid path.   This is also valid.   This is not a valid path.

Maintain Your Skills

4. Consider the following three games.

Game 1 Flip two coins. If you get exactly two heads, you win.

Game 2 Flip three coins. If you get exactly two heads, you win.

Game 3 Flip four coins. If you get exactly two heads, you win.

Which game gives you the greatest probability of winning?

4.2 Are They Different or the Same?

In Getting Started, you got a sense for the kinds of objects that you might count in combinatorial problems. In this lesson, you will practice counting more objects. As you work through the problems, think about how you are counting as well as what you are counting.

For You to Do

1. How many three-digit numbers can you make using only the digits 1 and 2? (In each number you may use a digit more than once.)

> Some of these numbers are 111, 112, 221.

2. In a kindergarten class, children are to color each of three different shapes either green or red. How many different colorings are possible?

3. A pizzeria has three choices of toppings: onions, mushrooms, and pepperoni. How many different kinds of pizza are possible?

> You may choose not to have any topping—this would be a plain pizza.

4. Flip a coin three times. One of the possible outcomes is *tail-head-head*, another is *head-tail-head*. How many possible outcomes are there?

Developing Habits of Mind

Be systematic. When you try to solve problems like those above, you might be tempted to list all the cases. Making a list is a good initial strategy. However, always remember

- to count every case
- not to count any case more than once

To solve a counting problem, a good strategy is to use a system to list all the cases.

Minds in Action   episode 10

Sasha and Tony are listing possible three-digit numbers while working on Problem 1 in For You to Do above.

Sasha   I'm listing numbers with no 2's, and then numbers with one 2, and then numbers with two 2's. What are you doing?

Tony   I'm listing numbers from least to greatest.

5. Make a list of possible three-digit numbers using Sasha's system.

6. Make a list of possible three-digit numbers using Tony's system.

For Discussion

7. For listing the possible cases in Problem 1, which method seems more convenient, Sasha's or Tony's? Explain your choice.

8. Did you use either of these methods when you solved the problem yourself? If not, what approach did you use and why?

What do Problems 1–4 have in common besides the answer?

Suppose you are done with Problem 1 and know exactly how many three-digit numbers are possible using only the digits 1 and 2. Now you are working on Problem 3. You are trying to list all possible pizzas by completing the following chart.

Pizza	Onions	Mushrooms	Pepperoni
First	X	X	
Second			
Third	X	X	X
⋮			

The first row is for pizza with onions and mushrooms. The second row is for plain cheese pizza.

For You to Do

9. What kind of pizza corresponds to the third row?

You could change the table a little by writing 1 if you want a certain topping on a pizza and 2 if you do not. Then, for the pizza with onions and mushrooms you write 112.

Pizza	Onions	Mushrooms	Pepperoni
First	1	1	2
⋮			

For You to Do

10. What number would you write for the second pizza? For the third pizza?

11. Does the pizza described by the number 211 have any mushrooms on it?

12. Which pizza corresponds to the number 121?

Each pizza corresponds to a three-digit number made of 1's and 2's. Also, any three-digit number made of 1's and 2's represents a type of pizza. Now you can see that the number of pizzas and the number of three-digit numbers made of 1's and 2's are the same. You do not have to solve both the pizza problem and the three-digit number problem. From a mathematical point of view, they are the same.

Definition

If two problems have the same mathematical structure then they are **isomorphic.**

> *Isomorphic* is from Greek *iso-* meaning "same," and *morphe* meaning "shape." You use this word in mathematics to refer to structures that are essentially the same.

If two problems are isomorphic then you can solve them using the same calculation, formula, or equation.

In recognizing isomorphic problems, keep the following facts in mind.

- Context does not matter.

  These problems are isomorphic:

  Problem 1 In a class of 24 students there are 2 more girls than boys. How many girls are there in this class?

  Problem 2 Tim earned $24 in two weeks. He earned $2 more during the second week than during the first week. How much did Tim earn during the second week?

  Solution In Problem 1, let x be the number of girls in the class. In Problem 2 let x be the amount Tim earned during the second week. These problems yield the same equation with the same solution.

  $$\text{Equation: } x + (x - 2) = 24$$
  $$\text{Solution: } \qquad x = 13$$

  The contexts differ, but the mathematics is the same.

- Two problems can have the same answers without being isomorphic.

  These problems involve different sorts of operations and are not isomorphic:

  Problem Jane had four apples. She ate two apples. How many apples does she have now?

  Solution $4 - 2 = 2$ (Subtraction)

  Problem Jane had four apples. She shared them equally with John. How many apples does she have now?

  Solution $4 \div 2 = 2$ (Division)

- If two problems have different numbers they are not isomorphic (even though you may be able to use the same method to solve them both).

These problems involve the same methods and operations but are not isomorphic:

Problem There were 6 chickens in a cage. Two ran away. How many are still there?

Solution $6 - 2 = 4$ (Subtraction)

Problem There were 12 eggs in a box. Eight are broken. How many remain whole?

Solution $12 - 8 = 4$ (Subtraction)

Check Your Understanding

For Exercises 1–4 decide if the two given problems are isomorphic. Explain.

1. • What is the area of a 3 meter-by-6 meter rectangle?
   • What is the perimeter of a 3 meter-by-6 meter rectangle?

2. • There are 230 pages in a book. Lisa read 45 pages yesterday and 99 pages today. How many pages does she still have to read?
   • Looking for ideas for his science project, Leo got 230 suggestions. Considering them, he found 45 too easy and 99 too difficult. How many more ideas does Leo have left to consider?

3. • Peter has twice as much money as Jack. The total is $18. How much money does each boy have?
   • Kim cuts an 18-inch long stick in two pieces. One piece is twice as long as the other. How long is each piece?

4. • Lila is organizing her 740 photos. Each of her picture albums holds 60 pictures. How many albums will she need to store all the photos?
   • What is the smallest integer n such that $60n \geq 740$?

5. Make up a problem isomorphic to each of the following.

   a. My cat is nine years old. My dog is seven years old. How much older is my cat than my dog?

   b. Cut a 12-yard long ribbon into three equal pieces. How long is each one?

6. Find a pair of isomorphic problems that you can solve using the given calculation.

   a. $40 - (3 + 7) = 30$ **b.** $7 \cdot 8 = 56$

7. Explain why Problems 2, 3, and 4 on page 279 are isomorphic to Problem 1 on that same page.

On Your Own

8. Harriet used a *tree* to solve the three-digit problem in the For You to Do section at the beginning of this lesson. This is how she started:

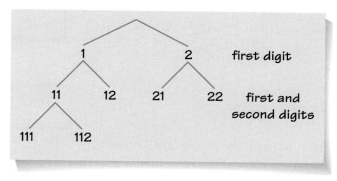

   a. Copy this tree and finish it.

   b. Does Harriet's strategy resemble either Tony's or Sasha's? If so, how?

9. How many four-digit numbers can you make with only 1's and 2's?

10. How many subsets does the set $\{A, B, C\}$ have? Count the empty set and the whole set, too.

> Any group of elements from a set is a subset. Note that $\{A, B\}$ and $\{B, A\}$ are the same subset.

For Exercises 11 and 12, decide if the two given problems are isomorphic. Explain your answers.

11. • Each of seven friends has $15. How much do they have altogether?

    • A rectangle has sides of lengths 7 inches and 15 inches. Find its area.

12. • What is $1 + 2 + 3 + \cdots + 8 + 9 + 10$?

    • On the first day of January, Jane learned one new word. Each day she learned one more word than she learned the day before. During the first ten days of January, how many words did she learn?

13. Solve the problem and then make up a problem isomorphic to it.

> In each corner of a rectangular room there is a cat. Each cat has four kittens with her. How many paws are there in the room?

Draw a picture of this room.

14. Find a pair of isomorphic problems that you can solve using the given calculation.

a. $27 \div 9 = 3$ **b.** $6 + 7 + 8 = 21$

15. **Take It Further** In class, Paul noticed something when he was working out the solution to the three-digit problem in the For You to Do section at the beginning of this lesson. First, he systematically listed all the numbers.

Then, Paul discovered a pattern. He said, "All the numbers in each column add up to 12." If you list all four-digit numbers made of 1's and 2's, will each column sum still be 12? Can you extend this pattern to five-digit numbers? To n-digit numbers? How would the pattern change if you used the digits 1, 2, and 3?

1	1	1
1	1	2
1	2	1
1	2	2
2	1	1
2	1	2
2	2	1
2	2	2

Habits of Mind

Experiment. If you make all the four-digit numbers from 1's and 2's and line them up like this, will the sum of the numbers in any column be the same? What if you use the digits 1, 2, 3?

16. **Standardized Test Prep** Given the following two problems, which sentence describes the relationship between them?

Problem I Find the area of a triangle with base 3 units and height 4 units.

Problem II Find the area of a triangle with base 6 units and height 2 units.

A. Problems I and II are isomorphic and have the same answer.

B. Problems I and II have the same answer but are not isomorphic.

C. Problems I and II are isomorphic but do not have the same answer.

D. Problems I and II are neither isomorphic nor have the same answer.

Go Online PHSchool.com

For additional practice, go to **Web Code:** bga-0402

Maintain Your Skills

17. If you expand the product, how many terms are in the resulting sum?

a. $(a + b)(c + d)$

b. $(a + b)(c + d)(e + f)$

c. $(a + b)(c + d)(e + f)(g + h)$

d. $(a + b)(c + d)(e + f) \cdots (y + z)$ (13 factors in all)

4.3 Strategies for Counting

In this lesson, you will see some strategies for counting. Students in a course just like this one developed these strategies.

For You to Do

1. How many five-digit numbers can you make using only 1's and 2's?

Minds in Action   episode 11

Sasha and Tony were working on Problem 1.

Sasha   In the last lesson, we found all the three-digit numbers we can make using only the digits 1 and 2. We can find all the four-digit numbers by attaching either 1 or 2 to the end of those. So there must be twice as many four-digit numbers as three-digit numbers. Then I can use the four-digit numbers to build the five-digit numbers in the same way.

Tony   The first digit of a number can be either 1 or 2. This gives 2 cases. In each case, the second digit can also be 1 or 2. That would give $2 \cdot 2 = 4$ cases. Then I can consider the third digit, then the fourth, and then the fifth.

For You to Do

2. Solve Problem 1 using Sasha's method.

3. Solve Problem 1 using Tony's method.

For Discussion

Using either Sasha's or Tony's method (or both!), solve the following problems.

4. How many six-digit numbers can you make using only the digits 1 and 2?

5. How many *n*-digit numbers can you make using only 1's and 2's?

Problems 6–9 are a little different from the ones you have seen before. For each new problem, think carefully about the set from which you are choosing your digits (or other objects). A counting strategy can help. The students who developed the following strategy called it "the box strategy."

For You to Do

6. Miss Rainbow has 20 hats, 30 dresses, and 10 pairs of shoes. She makes an outfit consisting of a hat, a dress, and a pair of shoes. How many outfits can she make?

Developing Habits of Mind

Recognize a similar process. Joan makes up a problem isomorphic to the problem she wants to solve. It is always about boxes with some items inside. The question is always the same—it is about the number of ways to put one item in each box.

Joan's "box problem" for Problem 6 is: "I can put any one of 20 things in the "hat" box, any one of 30 things in the "dress" box, and any one of 10 things in the "shoe" box. In how many ways can I do this?"

For You to Do

Use Joan's method to solve the following.

7. A class has 10 boys and 12 girls. You want a committee with one boy and one girl. How many possible committees are there?

8. There are four grades in a school, and 200 students in each grade. You want a committee with one representative from each grade. How many different committees are possible?

9. Suppose you want to make three-digit ATM PINs from the numbers {1, 2, 3, 4, 5}. (Numbers can be used more than once.) How many codes are there?

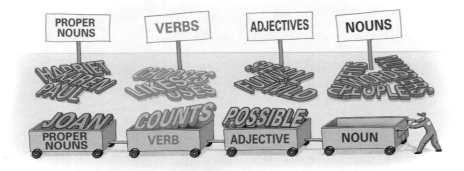

For Discussion

10. Use Problem 9 to illustrate the following theorem.

Theorem 4.1

It is possible to make m^n different strings of length n using m different symbols, if you can use a symbol more than once.

In a kindergarten class, each student has four pictures: a square, a triangle, a circle, and a star. Each of the kids will make a design by gluing these four pictures in a line. There are 20 kids in the class. Can each child make a different design or will there have to be repeats? (Note: This time unlike in Problem 9, each symbol can be used only once!)

Consider three strategies for solving this problem.

Solve a simpler problem. There are four groups of designs:

- designs that start with a square (□ ? ? ?)
- designs that start with a star (☆ ? ? ?)
- designs that start with a triangle (△ ? ? ?)
- designs that start with a circle (○ ? ? ?)

Each group has the same number of designs (why?), so you can reduce the problem to a simpler one:

> How many designs start with a square?

Then to find the total number of possible designs, multiply the result by 4.

$$? ? ? ? = 4 \cdot (□ ? ? ?)$$

Now, each design that starts with a square falls into one of three groups:

- a square then a star (□ ☆ ? ?)
- a square then a triangle (□ △ ? ?)
- a square then a circle (□ ○ ? ?)

So, here is a new, even simpler problem:

> How many designs start with a square followed by a star?

$$? ? ? ? = 4 \cdot (□ ? ? ?) = 4 \cdot 3 \cdot (□ ☆ ? ?)$$

These are two possible designs:

You could have chosen to count designs of any other single group.

You cannot reuse the square.

Use the box strategy. Think of making a design starting with four empty boxes. You fill them up, one at a time, with a picture shape. You can put any one of four shapes into the first box. For each of those choices, you can put any one of three shapes into the second box (so there are now 4 · 3 partially completed designs), and so on.

How many ways can you choose one shape to put into each box?

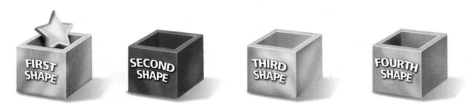

Use a tree diagram. Karen, who was trying to solve this problem, decided to list all possible designs. She arranged them in a tree. Below is the beginning of her work.

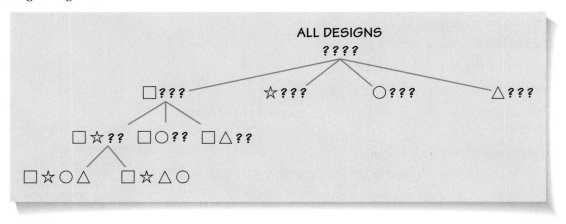

For You to Do

11. Pick one of the these three methods. Solve the problem about the kindergarten kids' designs using that method. Write up your solution in detail. Explain every step.

Check Your Understanding

1. Let $f(n)$ be the number of possible n-digit numbers consisting of only 1's and 2's.

   a. Write a recursive rule for f. **b.** Write a closed rule for f.

2. How many four-digit numbers can you make using only the digits 1, 2, and 3?

3. a. How many five-digit numbers can you make using only the digits 1, 2, and 3?

   b. How many n-digit numbers can you make using only the digits 1, 2, and 3?

4. How many n-digit numbers can you make using digits from 1 to m? Assume you can invent new digits to stand for numbers greater than 9.

5. Mr. Flyer is going to travel to Europe. He wants to visit Paris, London, Bonn, and Rome, and stay three days in each city. He can visit these cities in different orders. In how many different ways can he plan this trip?

6. In how many different ways can you arrange the letters of the word *math*?

7. How many different batting orders are possible for the nine players of a baseball team?

8. How many ways are there to line up a set of five distinct objects in a single row?

9. How many ways are there to line up a set of n distinct objects in a single row?

> **Habits of Mind**
>
> **Check extreme cases.**
> You should convince yourself that the formula you have made is correct. A good habit is to check extreme cases. What if there is just one digit to use? What if the numbers are only one digit long?

> A "batting order" is a list that shows the order in which the players will get to bat.

On Your Own

10. There are three towns in Wonderland: A, B, and C. There are six routes from A to B and three routes from B to C. No direct routes exist between A and C. How many ways are there to travel from A to C without backtracking?

11. How many four-digit numbers are there? (Hint: A number cannot start with zero.)

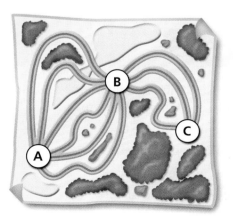

> **Habits of Mind**
>
> **Use a different process.** Another way to think about it: The largest 4-digit number is 9999. The smallest is 1000. How many numbers are between 1000 and 9999?

12. A number is *cute* if it consists of only even digits. How many cute five-digit numbers are there?

13. How many four-digit multiples of five are there?

14. Before 1995, the rules for three-digit United States telephone area codes were as follows.

- The first digit cannot be 0 or 1.
- The second digit must be 0 or 1.
- The third digit has no restriction.

How many possible area codes did the United States have before 1995?

15. Believe it or not, the United States ran out of phone numbers and had to add more area codes. The area code rules changed to these:

- The first digit cannot be 0 or 1.
- The second digit has no restriction.
- The third digit has no restriction.

How many area codes were possible using these rules?

For additional practice, go to **Web Code:** bga-0403

16. Suppose the license plate for a car must have six characters. The first three characters are digits between 0 and 9. The remaining three characters are letters from the alphabet. How many different license plates are possible?

17. A car knocked over a stop sign, but then sped off. The only information that an eyewitness remembers is that the car's license plate contains two W's and one D, but not necessarily in this order. How many license plates must the police check?

For the description of possible license plates see Exercise 16.

18. **Standardized Test Prep** Janie has *n* different coats and *n* different scarves. Katie has $n + 1$ different coats and $n - 1$ different scarves. Which statement below is true?

A. Janie has more ways to choose a coat and a scarf than Katie does.

B. Katie has more ways to choose a coat and a scarf than Jamie does.

C. Katie and Janie have the same number of choices.

D. You cannot tell who has more choices without knowing what *n* is.

Maintain Your Skills

19. A number is *wild* if it consists of different digits and does not contain zero as a digit. How many wild two-digit numbers are there?

Do you think most mathematicians would recognize this definition?

20. How many wild three-digit numbers are there?

21. How many wild six-digit numbers are there?

22. How many wild nine-digit numbers are there?

23. How many wild ten-digit numbers are there?

Counting All Functions

Another counting strategy is to translate your problem to one that counts the number of possible functions from one finite set to another.

Suppose you have a set of inputs $\{A, B, C\}$ and a set of outputs $\{1, 2, 3, 4\}$. Here is one function:

$$f(A) = 1$$
$$f(B) = 2$$
$$f(C) = 3$$

Here is another function: $f(A) = 1$
$$f(B) = 1$$
$$f(C) = 1$$

> It is easy to define a function that has only three inputs. You just list the output for each input. If there are infinitely many inputs, you could not make such a list.

Here is a third function from $\{A, B, C\}$ to $\{1, 2, 3, 4\}$:

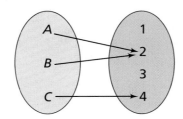

For You to Do

1. How many functions have inputs from the set $\{A, B, C\}$ and outputs from the set $\{1, 2, 3, 4\}$?

> In other words, how many functions have domain $\{A, B, C\}$ and target $\{1, 2, 3, 4\}$?

Exercises *Practicing Habits of Mind*

Check Your Understanding

1. How many functions have inputs from $\{A, B, C\}$ and outputs from $\{yes, no\}$?

2. Suppose the Martian alphabet consists of five letters. No word in the Martian language is more than four letters long. At most how many words can there be in such a language?

3. Suppose there are k letters in the alphabet of a certain language. Suppose further that no word of this language has more than n letters. At most how many words can there be in this language?

4. Write an expression for the number of functions from the set $\{1, 2, 3, 4, \ldots, 25\}$ to the set $\{1, 2, 3, 4, \ldots, 365\}$.

What is the numerical value of your expression?

5. How many functions are there from a five-element set to an eight-element set?

On Your Own

In a one-to-one function, no two inputs have the same output.

6. a. How many functions are there from a two-element set to a three-element set?

b. How many of these functions are one-to-one?

c. How many of these functions are not one-to-one?

7. How many one-to-one functions are there from a five-element set to an eight-element set?

8. How many one-to-one functions are there from an eight-element set to a five-element set?

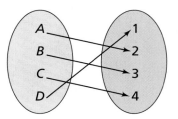
a one-to-one function

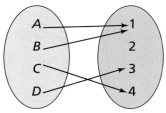
not a one-to-one function

9. Write an expression for the number of one-to-one functions from the set $\{1, 2, 3, 4, \ldots, 25\}$ to the set $\{1, 2, 3, 4, \ldots, 365\}$.

What is the numerical value of the expression?

10. Standardized Test Prep Suppose there are exactly 81 functions from a four-element set to an n-element set. What is the value of n?

A. 2 **B.** 4 **C.** 3 **D.** 9

Maintain Your Skills

11. How many wild four-digit numbers are cute?

12. How many cute five-digit numbers are wild?

Go Online
PHSchool.com

For additional practice, go to **Web Code: bga-0404**

Remember...

A number is *cute* if it consists of only even digits. A number is *wild* if it consists of different digits and does not have a zero.

Note: neither of these are official terms in mathematics. Inventing your own definitions can be fun as well as useful.

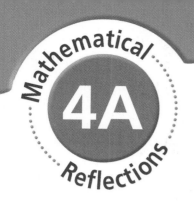

Mathematical Reflections 4A

In this investigation, you studied a variety of counting problems. Some of these appear different on the surface, but are really the same, or isomorphic. The following questions will help you summarize what you have learned.

1. How many n-digit numbers can you make using only the digits 1 through m? Assume you can invent new digits to stand for numbers greater than 9.

2. How many ways are there to line up a set of n distinct objects in a row?

3. Solve this problem and then make up a problem isomorphic to it.
   Matt is applying to four different colleges. Each application has a fee of $75. How much will Matt have to pay in application fees?

4. Andrew noticed that many of the newer license plates have six characters. The first two characters and the last two characters are digits between 0 and 9. The middle two characters are letters from the alphabet. How many different license plates are there with this format?

5. How many one-to-one functions are there from a six-element set to a ten-element set?

6. How many five-digit numbers can you make using only the digits 1 and 2?

7. In a kindergarten class, each student has four pictures: a square, a triangle, a circle, and a star. Each of the kids will make a design by gluing these four pictures in a line. There are 20 kids in the class. Can each child make a different design or will there have to be repeats?

8. What does it mean for two problems to be isomorphic?

Vocabulary

In this investigation, you learned this term. Make sure you understand what it means and how to use it.

- **isomorphic**

The number of possible batting orders for a softball team is the same as the number of possible outcomes in a race of 9 horses.

Investigation 4B

Permutations and Combinations

In *Permutations and Combinations,* you will learn more formal ways to approach counting problems. In particular, you will learn what permutations and combinations are, and how to count them.

By the end of this investigation, you will be able to answer questions like these.

1. In how many ways can you pick three objects, in order, from a set of six distinct objects?

2. How many three-digit numbers are there that have repeated digits?

3. How many five-student committees are possible in a class of 26 students?

You will learn how to

- develop and use formulas for finding the number of permutations of *n* objects, taken *k* at a time

- find a formula for the number of combinations of *n* objects, taken *k* at a time

- find the number of anagrams for a word

You will develop these habits and skills:

- Count the number of elements in a subset by counting the complement of the desired subset.

- Use appropriate counting tools and formulas.

- Relate different counting strategies to each other.

Jazz musicians often improvise by experimenting with the possible ways to choose combinations from the set of 12 notes in the diatonic scale.

Activating Prior Knowledge
Exploring New Ideas

Now that you know some different strategies for counting, you are ready for another chance at those three problems from Lesson 4.1. See if you can make more progress now that you are getting better at the art of counting! If you solved all three problems in the last investigation, try to solve them again using a different method this time.

For You to Explore

1. **The Same Birthday**

   a. In a random group of 25 people, what is the probability that at least two of them share a birthday? For the probability to be greater than 50%, how many people must there be in the group?

   b. **Take It Further** In a random group of 25 people, what is the probability that exactly two of them share a birthday?

2. **Trains**

   You can use number rods to build "trains" that all share a common length. A "train of length 5" is a row of rods that have a combined length of 5.

   | 1 | 2 | 2 |

   | 2 | 1 | 2 |

   | 1 | 3 | 1 |

   | 1 | 4 |

   | 5 |

   Notice that the 1–2–2 train and the 2–1–2 train contain the same rods. If you use identical rods in different orders, this makes different trains.

   a. How many trains of length n are possible?

   b. Describe an algorithm that will generate all trains of length n.

> Within a train you can repeat a length. Also, trains can contain different numbers of rods.

Exercises *Practicing Habits of Mind*

On Your Own

3. **Pascal's Paths**

Ms. Pascal likes to take a different route to work every day. She will quit her job the day she has to repeat a route she has already taken. The grid of streets below shows her home and her workplace. She only travels north and east and never backtracks. How many days will she work at this job?

> Two paths are different if they are not the same everywhere. They might overlap on some pieces though, like the two valid Pascal paths shown below.

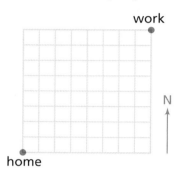

work

home

N

Again, here are some possible paths.

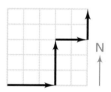

Here is a valid path.

This is also valid.

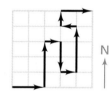

This is not a valid path.

Maintain Your Skills

4. The *Farey sequence of order n*, denoted F_n, is the set of all fractions from 0 to 1, inclusive, with denominators less than or equal to n. To write the sequence, write the fractions in lowest terms and arrange them in increasing order. For example, F_5, the Farey sequence of order 5, is

$$0, \frac{1}{5}, \frac{1}{4}, \frac{1}{3}, \frac{2}{5}, \frac{1}{2}, \frac{3}{5}, \frac{2}{3}, \frac{3}{4}, \frac{4}{5}, 1$$

a. Write out F_6, F_7, and F_8.

b. How many elements are in each of F_1 through F_8?

4.6 Permutations

In Investigation 4A, you developed your own strategies for solving counting problems. In this investigation, you will solve more complex problems, and see more formal counting methods and notations.

Do you remember the kindergarteners from Lesson 4.3? Recall that each kid was making a design by gluing four different shapes in a line. The four shapes were a square, a triangle, a circle, and a star. You counted the number of different designs possible.

Think about how to extend this problem. For instance, how many designs are possible if you could choose the four shapes from a larger set of shapes?

Go Online
PHSchool.com

For a history of combinatorics, go to **Web Code: bge-9031**

For You to Do

1. Suppose the kindergarteners are gluing pictures of four different shapes in a line. In addition to a square, a triangle, a circle, and a star, they may use a diamond and an oval. How many designs are possible?

Developing Habits of Mind

Consider more than one strategy. Here are two strategies for solving Problem 1.

- Box strategy: Think of four boxes (a box for each position in a design). You can put any one of six shapes in the first box, and any one of the five remaining shapes in the second box (which five depends on the shape you picked for the first box). This gives 6 · 5 ways to start, with two more boxes to go.

- Cut off strategy: Make all possible designs that use all six shapes. Then cut off the last two shapes to get designs with just four shapes. Of course, you will get each four-shape design more than once.

For Discussion

2. Solve Problem 1 using the box strategy.

3. Solve Problem 1 using the cut off strategy.

In Problems 1–3, you chose four shapes from a set of six possible shapes and arranged them in some order. That is, you chose a *permutation*.

Definition

A **permutation** is a one-to-one function from a set to itself.

Think of this as a linear ordering of some (or all) elements. For example, consider the following function from the set $\{A, B, C, D, E\}$ to the set $\{A, B, C, D, E\}$.

$$A \mapsto C$$
$$B \mapsto A$$
$$C \mapsto B$$
$$D \mapsto E$$
$$E \mapsto D$$

In Problems 1–3 you had 6 shapes. You selected 4 of them and glued them in a linear order. The order you put them in is one permutation of the set of 4 shapes you chose. This is because you can make a one-to-one function from the set of 4 shapes to the same set of 4 shapes to represent the ordering. A different ordering is a different permutation.

When you select 4 shapes from a group of 6, you can write the total number of designs as $_6P_4$. This is the total number of permutations of 4 objects taken from a group of 6.

> The number of different ways you can pick k things in order from a set of n distinct things is $_nP_k$.

For You to Do

4. a. What is $_6P_3$? **b.** What is $_6P_5$? **c.** What is $_6P_6$?

d. What is $_6P_k$? **e.** What is $_9P_4$? **f.** What is $_9P_5$?

g. What is $_9P_6$? **h.** What is $_9P_9$? **i.** What is $_9P_k$?

Habits of Mind

Visualize. It might help to think about lining up 6 different shapes. Line them up 3 at a time, 5 at a time, and so on.

For Discussion

5. What is a formula for $_nP_k$? Explain your answer.

Developing Habits of Mind

Think about it more than one way. Different strategies for solving the For You to Do problems lead to different (but equivalent!) formulas for $_nP_k$.

- Box strategy: You have k boxes. You can put any one of n items in the first box, any one of $(n-1)$ in the second, and so on. When you come to the kth box you must choose from the $(n - k + 1)$ items remaining.

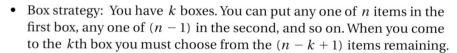

$$_nP_k = \underbrace{n \cdot (n-1) \cdot \cdots \cdot (n-k+1)}_{k \text{ factors}}$$

- Cut off strategy: There are $n!$ ways to line up all n items. If you cut off the last $(n-k)$ items, you will have repeats of each permutation of n things taken k at a time. The number of repeats will be the same as the number of ways to rearrange the tails that you cut off, $(n-k)!$. You have to divide by this number to count each permutation only once.

$$_nP_k = \frac{n!}{(n-k)!}$$

For You to Do

Show that each of the following is true.

6. $6 \cdot 5 \cdot 4 \cdot 3 = \frac{6!}{2!}$

7. $10 \cdot 9 \cdot 8 = \frac{10!}{7!}$

8. $100 \cdot 99 \cdot 98 \cdot 97 = \frac{100!}{96!}$

9. $100 \cdot 99 \cdot 98 \cdot \cdots \cdot (100 - k + 1) = \frac{100!}{(100 - k)!}$

10. $n(n - 1)(n - 2) \cdots (n - k + 1) = \frac{n!}{(n - k)!}$

Remember...

$n!$ is the product of all of the integers from 1 to n.

Extending the Factorial Function

$6!$ is defined as the descending product $6 \cdot 5 \cdot 4 \cdot 3 \cdot 2 \cdot 1$. To compute a factorial, you stop the descending products at 1. Using this definition, you cannot compute $0!$. Since picking 0 objects from a set makes sense, it would also make sense for $0!$ to have a value. Since the descending-product definition does not apply, you can define $0!$ any way you wish. How many ways can you take 0 objects from a set? Only one way—not at all. So, you can define $0! = 1$.

Definition

$$0! = 1$$

This is not a deep mathematical result. It is merely a *definition*. The factorial of 0 is 1 because it is convenient to define it that way.

Here is a summary of how to count permutation (so far).

* $_nP_k$ is the number of ways you can line up k things in order picked from a set of n things. It is the number of permutations of n things taken k at a time.

* $_nP_k = n(n - 1)(n - 2) \cdots (n - k + 1)$

* $_nP_k = \frac{n!}{(n - k)!}$

* $_nP_n = n!$

* $0! = 1$

From the third formula in the list above, $_5P_5 = n! = 5!$ For the formulas to be consistent, then, the second formula must give this same result for $_5P_5$.

$$5! = {_5P_5} = \frac{5!}{(5 - 5)!} = \frac{5!}{0!}$$

For the formulas to agree, it must be the case that $0! = 1$. So, extending the factorial function in this way not only makes sense, but it is actually necessary for the counting formulas to work together.

Habits of Mind

Make strategic choices. In other words, you can extend this definition in a way that makes sense.

Indirect Counting

Sometimes it is easier to count objects that do not have a certain property than it is to count the objects that do. Suppose you know the total number of things in a set. Take away the number of things you do not want. You are left with only the number of things that you do want. In this way you are counting indirectly.

Habits of Mind

Find another way.
Mathematicians often use clever shortcuts like this.

For You to Do

11. How many three-digit numbers are there with no repeated digits?

12. How many three-digit numbers have repeated digits?

To see what is there, artists often look at what is not there.

Developing Habits of Mind

Simplify complicated problems. Consider Problem 12. It is not obvious how to count the number of three-digit numbers with repeated digits. But you do know how to find the number of three-digit numbers with different digits. You also know how to find the total number of three-digit numbers. Using the answers to these two simpler problems, you can solve the more complicated one.

number of three-digit numbers with repeated digits =
number of all three-digit numbers −
number of those without repeated digits

Definition

An **anagram** is a rearrangement of the letters in a word or phrase.

For Discussion

13. How many different anagrams do the following words have?

a. TRIANGLE   **b.** GULLIBLE

All sequences of letters are anagrams of themselves. For example, TRIANGLE is an anagram of TRIANGLE.

In the word "TRIANGLE," as in any 8-letter word with all different letters, every rearrangement of letters is a unique anagram. There are a total of 8! anagrams.

Suppose "GULLIBLE" looked like this.

$$GUL_1L_2IBL_3E$$

Then it would have 8! anagrams. Here are a few of these anagrams.

$$L_1L_2L_3EGUBI \qquad L_2L_1L_3EGUBI \qquad L_1L_3L_2EGUBI$$

Of course, L's are not numbered, and you cannot tell these three anagrams apart without numbers. For any placement of L_1, L_2, and L_3, there are 3! ways to rearrange them without changing the placement of the other five letters. So you have to divide the number of rearrangements of 8 letters, 8!, by the number of ways to rearrange the L's. There are $\frac{8!}{3!}$ anagrams of the word "GULLIBLE."

For You to Do

14. How many different anagrams do the following words have?

    a. ANACONDA   **b.** HEDGEHOG

Exercises *Practicing Habits of Mind*

Check Your Understanding

1. Remember the factorial function.

$$n! = n(n - 1)(n - 2) \cdots 1$$

Explain why $_nP_n = n!$.

2. How many one-to-one functions from the set {place1, place2, place3, place4} to the set {a square, a triangle, a circle, a star, a diamond, an oval} are there?

3. How many one-to-one functions from the set {A, B, C, D} to the set {1, 2, 3, 4, 5, 6} are there?

4. In a class of 200 students, how many ways are there to choose a president, a vice-president, and a treasurer?

5. Consider all two-digit numbers.

    a. How many two-digit numbers have all different digits? (Call these numbers *dull*).

    b. How many two-digit numbers have repeated digits? (Call these numbers *funny*).

    c. There is a big bag, with many pieces of paper inside. On each piece of paper, there is a two-digit number. All these numbers are different, and all possible two-digit numbers are in the bag. If someone takes out one piece of paper from that bag, is it more likely to be a dull number or a funny number? Explain.

> **Remember...**
> In a one-to-one function, two different inputs cannot correspond to the same output.

6. Extend Exercise 5 and now consider all four-digit numbers.

   There is another bag, also with many pieces of paper inside. On each piece of paper, there is a four-digit number. All these numbers are different, and all possible four-digit numbers are in the bag. If someone takes out one piece of paper from that bag, is it more likely to be a dull number or a funny number? Explain your reasoning.

7. Repeat Exercise 6 with five-digit numbers.

8. Repeat Exercise 6 with ten-digit numbers.

9. How many anagrams does each word have?

   a. AGH   **b.** AHA   **c.** AAA

10. How many anagrams does each word have?

    a. JOHN   **b.** JILL   **c.** PEEP

    d. EEEK   **e.** RRRR

11. How many anagrams does each word have?

    a. BANANA   **b.** BALLOON   **c.** BORING

On Your Own

Exercises 12–17 refer to *attribute blocks*. Each block in a set of attribute blocks has

- one of two sizes (large or small)
- one of four colors (red, blue, green, or yellow)
- one of three shapes (described as square, circle, or triangle)

There is exactly one block with each combination of attributes. There is one large, green square, one small yellow circle, and so on.

12. How many pieces are there in a set of attribute blocks?

13. How many blue blocks are in a set?

14. How many large blocks are in a set?

> Use the box strategy to solve Exercise 12. How many ways are there to pick an attribute for each box?

Begin each of Exercises 15–17 with all the attribute blocks in a bucket. You are to pick one or more blocks at random from the bucket. On each pick, you are equally likely to pick any block in the bucket.

15. Pick one block from the bucket. What is the probability that it is a green square?

16. Pick two blocks from the bucket. What is the probability that they are the same size?

17. Pick three blocks from the bucket. What is the probability that they are the same color?

18. Jim rolls two number cubes. What is the probability of the same number showing on both cubes?

19. Now Jim rolls three number cubes. What is the probability that at least two of three numbers showing are the same?

20. Tom and Jerry are playing a game. Tom rolls four number cubes. If all four numbers showing on the cubes are different, he wins. Otherwise, Jerry wins. Who do you think wins more often? Why do you think so?

21. How many different anagrams are there for the word NIMBLE?

22. How many different anagrams are there for the word MUMBLE?

23. **Write About It** How are Exercises 21 and 22 similar? Are they isomorphic?

24. How many different anagrams are there for the word MISSISSIPPI?

25. **Standardized Test Prep** At dinner, Ms. Fair tries to give portions of equal size to her four sons. The kids have a theory that whoever is served last gets less. They wrote out all possible orders that their mom could use. Ms. Fair followed the list, using each possible order exactly once. How often did the youngest son get his plate last?

A. 1   **B.** 3   **C.** 4   **D.** 6

Maintain Your Skills

26. There are ten digits from 0–9. You are going to select an ATM PIN. The rules for these PINs differ from bank to bank. Assume that no valid PIN can have repeated digits. For each length given, find the number of possible ATM PINs.

In the codes, order does matter. 012 is a different code from 201.

   a. one-digit   **b.** two-digit

   c. three-digit   **d.** four-digit

   e. five-digit   **f.** ten-digit

   g. n-digit

27. There are 26 letters from A to Z. You want to select an ATM PIN consisting of these letters. Assume that no valid PIN can have repeated letters. For each length given, find the number of possible ATM PINs.

Order still matters. So GUM is a different code from MUG.

   a. one-letter   **b.** two-letter

   c. five-letter   **d.** ten-letter

   e. 26-letter   **f.** n-letter

4.7 Combinations

The game of SET® is a card game. Each card has four attributes:

shape: ovals, squiggles, or diamonds

number: one, two, or three of the shapes

color: red, green, or purple

shading: outlined, striped, or filled

The full deck has one card with each of the possible combinations of attributes. (All cards in a deck are different.)

The object of the game is to identify a SET of 3 cards from 12 cards laid out on a table.

A SET consists of three cards where each of the four attributes, looked at one by one, are either the same on each card or are different on all the cards. All the attributes must separately satisfy this rule. The shape must either be the same on the three cards of a set or all the shapes must be different on them. The colors on the three cards of a set must either be the same or all of them must be different, and so on.

For Discussion

1. How many cards are there in the whole deck?

2. In the problems below, you will need to describe different cards. It is time consuming to refer to a card as, for example, "a card with three, red, striped ovals." Think of a more efficient way to describe a card.

For You to Do

All cards in these triples are of the same color. Which ones are sets? Explain your answer.

3.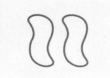

4.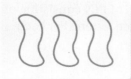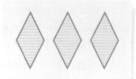

5.

6. In this array of nine cards below, find all the sets.

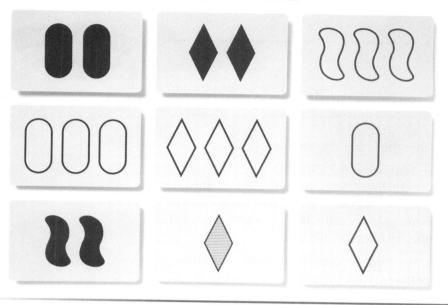

For Discussion

7. If you play SET with only the red, oval cards, then there would only be nine cards. How many different groups of three cards can you pick from nine cards?

Another question you can consider: How many of these groups of three are actually sets?

Here is a difference between objects in a group and objects in a line-up. Order does not matter for a group. Order does matter for a line-up. The number of combinations of objects in a group is less than the number of permutations of the same objects in a line-up.

Remember...

Remember, another word for "line-up" is *permutation*.

Definition

A subset of a set *S* is a **combination** of elements of *S*. You can think of a combination as being *k* things chosen from the set *S*, which itself has *n* elements.

In a combination, it does not matter how you arrange the elements.

The number of combinations of three cards from a deck of nine cards is written $_9C_3$. You say $_9C_3$ as, "9 choose 3."

For You to Do

Find each number.

8. $_9C_2$ **9.** $_9C_3$ **10.** $_{12}C_2$ **11.** $_{12}C_{10}$

In general, the number of combinations of n objects chosen k at a time is $_nC_k$. The value of k can range from 0 to n.

For You to Do

Find each number.

12. $_nC_0$ **13.** $_nC_n$ **14.** $_0C_0$

Habits of Mind

Experiment. Try it with numbers!

To find a formula for $_nC_k$, consider the following.

In one class of 200 students, elections occur the following way. First, the students choose the president. Then, out of the remaining 199 students, they choose the vice-president. Finally, out of the remaining 198 students, they choose the treasurer. There are $_{200}P_3 = 200 \cdot 199 \cdot 198$ possible ways for the class to choose these 3 officers from the 200 students.

In another class of 200 students, the students decide first to elect a three-person committee. Then they let the committee members decide who among themselves will be president, vice-president, and treasurer.

For Discussion

15. Show that both election procedures lead to the same number of possible selections of the president, vice-president, and treasurer.

16. Suppose now that another class of 200 students is going to elect a committee of three students, but each person on the committee has the same role (no president, vice-president, or treasurer). How many different committees could the class form then?

The committee {Jan, Kyle, Mena} is the same as the committee {Mena, Jan, Kyle}.

To find a formula for $_nC_k$, analyze the two different procedures of electing a president, a vice-president, and a treasurer.

The first procedure gives you $_{200}P_3$ possible choices of a president, vice-president, and treasurer.

Think, "C for Combinations and for Committees—both are unordered choices."

In the second procedure, you obtain $_{200}C_3$ possible committees with 3 members. Then the committee members decide who will play which role. Any one of the three can be the president, either of the other two can be the vice-president. There is no choice except being treasurer for the third person.

That makes $3 \cdot 2 \cdot 1 = 3!$ possibilities at the second stage. The total number of possible choices for president, vice-president, and treasurer under this second procedure is, therefore,

$$_{200}C_3 \cdot 3!$$

In the end, both procedures give the same number of possible choices for the three positions.

$$_{200}P_3 = {}_{200}C_3 \cdot 3!$$

Solving this equation for $_{200}C_3$, you arrive at the following formula.

$$_{200}C_3 = \frac{_{200}P_3}{3!} = \frac{200 \cdot 199 \cdot 198}{3 \cdot 2 \cdot 1} = 1{,}313{,}400$$

For You to Do

17. Show that the number of combinations $_nC_k$, is the number of permutations, $_nP_k$, divided by the number of permutations per combination, $_kP_k$. In other words,

$$_nC_k = \frac{_nP_k}{k!}$$

The result in Problem 17 is important enough to state as a theorem.

Theorem 4.2

$$_nC_k = \frac{_nP_k}{k!} = \frac{n!}{k!(n-k)!}$$

Proof You already proved the first part in Problem 17. The second part follows directly from the formula $_nP_k$.

$$\frac{_nP_k}{k!} = \frac{\frac{n!}{(n-k)!}}{k!}$$

$$= \frac{n!}{k!(n-k)!}$$

For Discussion

A board of directors consists of five people. They want to form a three-person subcommittee. Suppose the people on the board are

{Jason, John, Michelle, Alicia, Dan}

18. How many three-person committees include Dan?

19. How many three-person committees do not include Dan?

Sasha is working on writing a proof to show that $_5C_3 = {_4C_2} + {_4C_3}$.

Sasha   I want to show that

$$_5C_3 = {_4C_2} + {_4C_3}$$

I could use the formula for $_nC_k$, but instead I'll use a combinatorial proof. In this problem, suppose I have the 5 people in the For Discussion problem:

{Jason, John, Michelle, Alicia, Dan}

and I want to pick a committee of 3. There are $_5C_3$ different committees I could make. Every one of these committees either contains Dan or doesn't. So,

$_5C_3 =$ the number of committees that contain Dan
$+$ the number of committees that don't

But if a committee contains Dan, I have to pick 2 more people from the remaining 4, and there are $_4C_2$ ways to do that. So,

the number of committees that contain Dan $= {_4C_2}$

And, if a committee doesn't contain Dan, I have to pick all 3 people from the remaining 4, and there are $_4C_3$ ways to do that:

the number of committees that don't $= {_4C_3}$

Therefore

$$_5C_3 = {_4C_2} + {_4C_3}$$

> A combinatorial proof allows you to answer questions like these by telling a story. You can establish a formula by showing that each side of the formula represents a different way to count the same thing. You can simplify a complex algebraic identity by looking at it in the right way. Of course, finding the right way can be difficult at first, but it gets a lot easier with practice.

> There is no reason to single out Dan. Sasha could have chosen any one of the five people.

You can visualize Sasha's proof using a diagram like this.

$$
\begin{array}{c}
{_4C_2} \qquad {_4C_3} \\
6 \searrow \;+\; \swarrow 4 \\
{_5C_3} \\
10
\end{array}
$$

In fact, you could quickly create a table of the values of $_nC_k$.

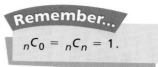
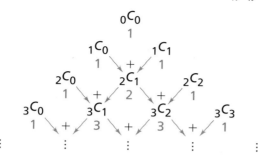

Recall Pascal's Triangle.

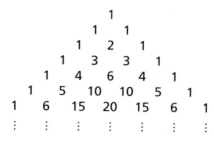

Remember that you can label an entry of Pascal's Triangle like this.

$$\binom{n}{k}$$

Remember...

Number the horizontal rows starting with 0 and number the first element in each row with a 0.

Recall that the top number n is the row number (starting with 0). The bottom number k is how far you go across in a row (starting with 0). For example, you can label the entries in the fifth row like this.

$$\binom{5}{0} \quad \binom{5}{1} \quad \binom{5}{2} \quad \binom{5}{3} \quad \binom{5}{4} \quad \binom{5}{5}$$

$$1 \quad\quad 5 \quad\quad 10 \quad\quad 10 \quad\quad 5 \quad\quad 1$$

Using this labeling method, you can see the following connection between combinations and the entries of Pascal's Triangle.

Theorem 4.3   The Pascal-Combinations Connection

For any $n \geq 0$ and all k such that $0 \leq k \leq n$,

$$\binom{n}{k} = {_nC_k}$$

You will develop more details of the Pascal-Combinations Connection Theorem as you work through the exercises. You might want to read Sasha's storytelling proof again, after working a few exercises.

Exercises *Practicing Habits of Mind*

Check Your Understanding

1. How many different committees of 4 people are possible in a class of 200 students?

2. A class of 200 students must form a committee of 4 people. Nobody wants to be elected. So instead the class is choosing $200 - 4 = 196$ students who can safely avoid serving on that committee. How many different groups of 196 students are possible out of 200 students?

3. Explain why $_{200}C_4 = {}_{200}C_{196}$.

4. Write the following using factorial notation.

   a. $_7P_3$ b. $_7C_3$

5. Consider $_7C_3$, the number of combinations of 7 things chosen 3 at a time. Show that $_7C_3$ is $_7P_3$ (the number of permutations of 3 things taken from a group of 7) divided by $_3P_3$ (the number of permutations per combination).

$$_7C_3 = \frac{_7P_3}{3!}$$

6. Show that $_nC_k = {}_nC_{n-k}$, for $0 \le k \le n$.

7. Explain why $_{10}P_3 = 6 \cdot {}_{10}C_3$.

8. Explain why $_{10}C_3 = {}_{10}C_7$.

   Tell a story that would lead to this equation. Generalize this equation to a formula.

9. **Write About It** Explain the difference between what you count to get $_nP_k$ and what you count to get $_nC_k$.

10. June wants to read four books. To keep June's taste in reading secret, you will call these books simply "book 1," "book 2," "book 3," and "book 4." June is packing for her vacation and is deciding which of these books (if any) she should take with her.

    a. June decides to take exactly two books. How many choices does she have for which two books to take?

    b. Among these two-book choices, how many include book 1?

    c. Among the two-book choices, how many do not include book 1?

11. Give a combinatorial proof that $_7C_4 = {}_6C_3 + {}_6C_4$.

Habits of Mind

Understand the problem. Do not just show that the numbers are the same. Explain why there are 6 times as many permutations as there are combinations.

12. a. Complete the statement to make it true.

$$_{10}C_6 = {}_?C_6 + {}_9C_{??}$$

b. Prove the statement.

13. Give a combinatorial proof that for $0 < k < n$

$$_nC_k = {}_{n-1}C_{k-1} + {}_{n-1}C_k$$

Why does this result not apply when $k = 0$, or when $k = n$?

14. For any $n > 1$, explain the relationship between the expressions.

a. $_nC_0$ and $_{n-1}C_0$

b. $_nC_n$ and $_{n-1}C_{n-1}$

15. Recall this table from page 309.

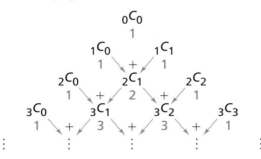

Copy the table. Then extend it by writing rows 4 through 10.

16. Explain why Theorem 4.3 is true.

17. What is a good definition of $\binom{5}{6}$? Explain your choice.

18. Wrigley High School's basketball team has ten players. The coach needs to choose five players to start in the next game. How many five-player combinations are possible?

In Exercise 18, choose the five starting players without regard to the positions they play.

19. A board of directors has eight members. They want to form several committees, but they are not sure how many members to use. The committee sizes will range from zero to eight members, inclusive. For each one of these sizes, find the number of committees possible.

20. Find a formula for the sum of the entries in any row of Pascal's Triangle.

On Your Own

21. Consider a list of ten problems. How many different assignments of exactly six problems are possible out of these ten problems?

22. In a homework set of ten problems, students can choose to skip any four. How many choices do students have for a set of four problems to omit?

23. Show that Exercises 21 and 22 are isomorphic.

24. a. How many subsets does $S = \{A, B, C, D, E\}$ have? Count the whole set and the empty set, too.

b. How many elements can a subset of S have?

c. Copy and complete the table.

Number of Elements in a Subset of S	Number of Subsets of S
0 (the empty set)	■
1	■
2	■
3	■
4	■
5 (the whole set)	■

Think of this as a "box problem." There are five boxes, one for each element of $\{A, B, C, D, E\}$. For a given subset, put a 1 in the box corresponding to an element if that element is in the subset. Put a 2 in the box if the element is not in the subset. How many ways are there to put 1's or 2's into the five boxes?

d. The sum of the numbers in the second column must be the same as the number of subsets you found in part (a). Verify that they are the same.

25. You have nine books, but there is only room for four of them on your shelf. In how many different ways can you line up four of the nine books on your shelf?

26. In how many different ways can a person choose four books from a pile of nine distinct best-sellers?

27. Consider all functions from the set $\{1, 2, 3, 4\}$ to the set $\{\text{take, leave}\}$. Two examples of such functions are shown below.

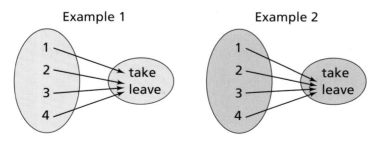

Example 1   Example 2

a. How many functions are there from the set $\{1, 2, 3, 4\}$ to the set $\{\text{take, leave}\}$?

b. How many of these functions do not have *take* as an output?

c. How many of these functions have *take* as an output for exactly one input? (Function A above is one of them.)

Habits of Mind

Make a connection.
You can think of each function as describing one of June's possible book choices. (See Exercise 10.)

Go Online
PHSchool.com

For additional practice, go to **Web Code:** bga-0407

d. How many of these functions have *take* as an output for exactly two inputs?

e. How many of these functions have *take* as an output for exactly three inputs?

f. How many of these functions have *take* as an output all four inputs?

g. You counted all functions in part (a). Then, in parts (b)–(f), you counted them again, counting by the number of times *take* is an output of the function. Check whether you got the same total number of functions.

28. Michelle, Jenn and Suzi are in a class of 21 people.

   a. How many committees of four are possible in this class?

   b. How many of those four-person committees contain Suzi?

   c. How many of those four-person committees do not contain Suzi?

   d. How many of those four-person committees do not contain Suzi, but do contain both Michelle and Jenn?

29. a. In how many ways can you choose two students out of five to write their homework solutions on the board?

   b. How many five-letter "words" are possible using two N's and three E's?

   c. In how many ways can you arrange two red chips and three blue chips in a line? (Chips of the same color are identical, so their order does not matter.)

   d. Explain why the problems in parts (a) through (c) are isomorphic.

Habits of Mind

Find another way.
Some people prefer to solve a different problem instead: In how many ways can you choose three students that will escape this duty?

30. The director of a research laboratory wants to hire 5 new workers. She will choose 2 from the 12 chemists who applied. Then she will choose 3 from the 5 physicists who applied. In how many different ways can she hire the new workers?

31. Mr. Henkle chooses five students each day (at random) to write their homework solutions on the board. There are 12 students in his class.
   a. Which entries in Pascal's Triangle will tell you how many different groups of 5 students Mr. Henkle could pick? How many groups are there?

   b. Darren is in the class. Which entries in Pascal's Triangle will tell you how many groups contain Darren? How many groups are there that contain Darren?

   c. If Darren is in class today, what is the probability that he will have to write his solution on the board?

32. Prove that

$$\binom{5}{0} + \binom{5}{1} + \binom{5}{2} + \binom{5}{3} + \binom{5}{4} + \binom{5}{5} = 2^5$$

33. Explain how can you evaluate the sum

$$\binom{6}{0} + \binom{6}{1} + \binom{6}{2} + \binom{6}{3} + \binom{6}{4} + \binom{6}{5} + \binom{6}{6}$$

by using the sum

$$\binom{5}{0} + \binom{5}{1} + \binom{5}{2} + \binom{5}{3} + \binom{5}{4} + \binom{5}{5}$$

34. Prove that for all nonnegative integers, n,

$$\binom{n}{0} + \binom{n}{1} + \binom{n}{2} + \cdots + \binom{n}{n-2} + \binom{n}{n-1} + \binom{n}{n} = 2^n$$

> This is another pattern in Pascal's Triangle. The sum of the entries in the nth row in Pascal's Triangle is 2^n. When $n = 0$, the sum is really just the single entry $\binom{0}{0}$.

35. A local high school is hosting a talent competition. A selection committee will choose three performers to perform in front of the school. The students' vote determines who wins. To choose the three performers, the selection committee will watch five auditions the first day and four auditions the second day. They will select the performers at the end of each day.

a. Suppose the selection committee rejects all five candidates the first day. How many ways can they still pick three contestants?

b. In how many ways could they pick one person from the first group and two people from the second group?

c. In how many ways could they pick two people from the first group and one person from the second group?

d. In how many ways could they pick three people from the first group and no one from the second group?

e. In how many ways are there to pick three performers from the nine candidates?

In counting the ways to choose 10 singers from 100 people, does it matter whether the auditions happen in a single day?

36. Take It Further A local high school is hosting a singing competition. A selection committee will choose four contestants to perform in front of the school. The students' vote determines who wins. To choose the four performers, the selection committee will listen to nine auditions the first day and eleven auditions the second day. They will select the performers at the end of each day. How many ways can the selection committee choose four performers?

Sasha and Derman are working on the problem above

Sasha Well, we did something exactly like this in Exercise 35. So it's going to be something like

$$\binom{9}{0}\binom{11}{4} + \binom{9}{1}\binom{11}{3} + \binom{9}{2}\binom{11}{2} + \binom{9}{3}\binom{11}{1} + \binom{9}{4}\binom{11}{0} = 4845$$

Derman Um . . . Sasha? Maybe this is crazy, but can't we just do $\binom{20}{4}$? I mean, there are twenty contestants, and the selection committee is choosing 4 . . .

Sasha That should be right, but—let's check. . . . You get the same answer. Hey! I wonder if there's an identity in here somewhere!

What's going on here?

37. Take It Further What is the sum of the squares of the entries in the nth row of Pascal's Triangle? Prove your result.

38. A four-digit number is *interesting* if it does not contain zero, and its digits are in decreasing order. For example, 9761 and 6531 are both interesting, but 9877 and 5678 are not. How many four-digit interesting numbers are there?

39. Standardized Test Prep There are 7 girls and 6 boys in a class. They want to make a committee of three students. There must be at least one boy and one girl on the committee. How many possible committees are there?

A. 126   **B.** 105   **C.** 231   **D.** 277

Habits of Mind

Look for a pattern. Try it with numbers!

Decreasing order means that each digit of a number is less than the previous one (to its left).

Maintain Your Skills

40. Suppose n is an integer with $n \geq 2$. You can define a polynomial function f with the property that f evaluated at n is $\binom{n}{2}$.

$$f(n) = \binom{n}{2} = \frac{n(n-1)}{2} = \frac{1}{2}n^2 - \frac{1}{2}n$$

a. Suppose n is an integer, with $n \geq 3$. Define a polynomial function g with the property that g evaluated at n is $\binom{n}{3}$.

b. Suppose n and k are integers, with $n \geq k$. Define a polynomial function h_k with the property that h_k evaluated at n is $\binom{n}{k}$.

4.8 Putting It Together

Here are some basic facts on combinations and permutations that you have discovered and explored so far in this chapter.

Permutations	Combinations
Order matters: Count *X, Y, Z* and *X, Z, Y* as different cases.	Order does not matter: Count *X, Y, Z* and *X, Z, Y* as the same case.
Sample problem: There are 12 people in a class. In how many different ways could the class elect a president, vice-president, and a treasurer?	Sample problem: There are 12 people in a class. In how many different ways could the class pick 3 of them to wash the chalkboard?
$_nP_k = \frac{n!}{(n-k)!}$	$_nC_k = \frac{n!}{k!(n-k)!} = \binom{n}{k}$
$_nP_k = (k!)\left(_nC_k\right)$	$_nC_k = \frac{_nP_k}{k!}$
$_nP_k = n \cdot {}_{n-1}P_{k-1},\ n > k > 0$	$_nC_k = {}_{n-1}C_{k-1} + {}_{n-1}C_k,\ n > k > 0$

Now that you have a collection of formulas, it might be difficult to choose which one to use. As you solve the next set of problems, think about which formula works best in each case.

For You to Do

1. How many four-digit numbers can you make from the digits 1, 2, 3, 4, 5, and 6 if no repeats are allowed?

2. How many four-person committees are possible in a class of 16 people?

3. There are 23 students in a class. In how many ways can Mrs. Masse pick four students in the class to carry a table to the auditorium?

Do not be too eager to use formulas. If the problem has a twist, you might not be able to just apply a formula. It is important to remember what the formulas actually mean and how you derive them.

Example

Problem In this year's student council election, there are 3 positions for junior class representatives, and 4 positions for senior class representatives. There are 25 people running for junior class representative and 32 people running for senior class representative. How many different student councils are possible?

Solution If there were only one position for the junior class and one position for the senior class, you could use the box strategy.

This is a good start for this problem. Earlier, when using the box strategy, you were choosing just one item for each box. Here you need to choose multiple items to put in the boxes.

Since the representative positions for each class are the same, order does not matter. The number of ways to elect 4 seniors from 32 candidates is $\binom{32}{4}$. For each of these outcomes there are $\binom{25}{3}$ ways to elect 3 juniors from 25 candidates. You can calculate the number of possible election results using the following formula.

$$\text{total ways} = \begin{pmatrix} \text{number of ways} \\ \text{to elect 4 seniors} \end{pmatrix} \cdot \begin{pmatrix} \text{number of ways} \\ \text{to elect 3 juniors} \end{pmatrix}$$

$$= \binom{32}{4} \cdot \binom{25}{3}$$

> The junior and senior elections need to be considered separately. You cannot just lump all 57 candidates together and choose 7 representatives from them.

The Birthday Problem

Do you remember the "birthday problem" from Getting Started?

> In Ms. Roskam's class of 25 students, two of them have the same birthday. The students are very surprised to discover this. Ms. Roskam tells them that it's actually a good bet that, in a random group of 25 students, at least two of them will share a birthday.

> Is Ms. Roskam right? Suppose you choose 25 people at random. What is the probability that at least two of them share a birthday? If you want to ensure that the probability is more than 50%, how many people must you choose?

To solve the birthday problem, consider the function

$$f(\text{person}) = \text{person's birthday}$$

- How many possible outputs does this function have?
- What does it mean for this function to be one-to-one when the domain is a class of students?

Habits of Mind

Be efficient. It is often more convenient to write out the formula for your solution, before you actually make any calculations. This is because the numbers involved in combinatorics problems can become very large very quickly!

For You to Do

4. How many functions are there from an m-element set to an n-element set?

5. How many one-to-one functions are there from an m-element set to an n-element set?

6. How many functions from an m-element set to an n-element set are not one-to-one?

7. How many functions from the set $\{1, 2, \ldots, 24, 25\}$ to the set $\{1, 2, \ldots, 364, 365\}$ are not one-to-one?

> Could you find even a single one-to-one function if n is less than m?

For Discussion

8. How do Problems 4–7 help you solve the "birthday problem"?

Number Rods

You can use number rods to build "trains" that share a common length. A "train of length 5" is a row of rods that have a combined length of 5.

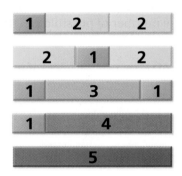

Notice that the 1–2–2 train and the 2–1–2 train contain the same rods. If you use identical rods in different orders, this makes different trains.

For You to Do

9. What are the minimum and maximum numbers of rods you can use for a train of length 3? Of length 6? Of length n?

10. Use a pile of rods to help you compile lists of all possible trains with lengths 2, 3, 4, and 5. Be sure you list each train once and only once.

For Discussion

11. Make a set of directions that explains how to list all the trains of any given length.

12. How many trains are there of length n? Write a proof to show your result is true for all integers $n > 0$.

> **Habits of Mind**
>
> **Test your directions.** Your directions should be an *algorithm*. A person (or computer) should be able to follow them without having to make any interpretations or add missing details. Test your directions by giving them to someone else. See if that person can use them to list all trains of length five.

Exercises Practicing Habits of Mind

Check Your Understanding

1. Six friends went to the school dance together. In how many ways can they line up for a photo?

2. How many ways are there to arrange the letters in the word COMBINE?

3. How many four-digit numbers can you make from the digits 0, 1, 2, 3, 4, and 5 without repeating digits?

4. A class of 16 students wants to form a four-person committee consisting of two girls and two boys. There are nine boys and seven girls in the class. How many committees are possible?

5. **Take It Further** Six friends went to the school dance together. In how many ways can they line up for a photo if two of them, June and Mark, want to stay next to each other?

6. Suppose there are five women and four men in a room. In how many ways can they do each of the following?

    a. line up to have their picture taken

    b. line up to have their picture taken, if the men and women have to alternate

    c. line up if one of them, say Harry, refuses to stand at the beginning or at the end of the line

    d. line up in two rows, with all the women in the front row and all the men in the back row

    e. line up in two rows, with five people in the front row and four people in the back row

> **Habits of Mind**
>
> **Be systematic.** First, in how many ways can you choose the five people for the front row and the four people for the back row. Then, think about how you can arrange the rows.

7. A pizzeria has 3 sizes of pizza and 12 different toppings. How many ways are there to place the following orders?

   a. a pizza with exactly two toppings

   b. a pizza with at most two toppings

   c. a pizza

   d. a pizza with mushrooms and one additional topping

8. Are there more seven-digit numbers with a 1 in them than without a 1 in them? Explain.

9. There are nine points on a paper. No three of them are on the same line. How many different triangles can you draw using these points as vertices?

10. There are 14 airports in a country. You can go from any one of them to any other airport in the country by a direct flight. How many direct flights are there?

11. How many diagonals does a 14-sided polygon have?

12. There are many ways that you can write 5 as a sum of counting numbers. Here are four:

$$5 = 1 + 4$$
$$= 5$$
$$= 2 + 1 + 1 + 1$$
$$= 1 + 2 + 1 + 1$$

How many different ways are there in all?

> *A diagonal* of a polygon is a segment that connects two of the polygon's vertices but is not a polygon's side.

13. In how many ways can you write 20 as a sum of three counting numbers?

14. In how many ways can you put 20 quarters into three colored pockets (red, green, and blue) so that there is at least one coin in each pocket?

15. The apple flats at a farmers' market hold 20 apples each. Kim wants to fill her flat with three types of apples. She selects red delicious apples, then Granny Smith apples, and then Macintosh apples. Assuming she has at least one apple of each type, how many different assortments of these apples can she make?

> **Habits of Mind**
>
> **Compare.** Does Exercise 12 remind you of the trains problem in any way? How is it similar or different from the trains problem? Are they isomorphic?

16. There are 19 people and only 2 tickets to a concert. How many ways are there to choose which two people go to the concert?

17. Explain how Exercises 13 through 16 are all isomorphic.

18. **Take It Further** Look a little more closely at the game of SET. You may want to review the rules of the game on page 304. If you lay out 3 cards from the whole deck of SET, what is the probability that the cards would be a set?

19. **Standardized Test Prep** How many "trains" of length six can you build using only three number rods?

A. 5   **B.** 9   **C.** 10   **D.** 20

Go Online
PHSchool.com

For additional practice, go to **Web Code:** bga-0408

How many different groups of three cards could you lay out from the deck? How many of them would make a set?

Maintain Your Skills

20. a. What is the coefficient of a^3b^1 in the expansion of $(a + b)^4$?

b. What other term has the same coefficient?

c. What is the coefficient of a^4b^1 in the expansion of $(a + b)^5$?

d. What other term has the same coefficient?

e. What is the coefficient of a^2b^3 in the expansion of $(a + b)^5$?

f. What other term has the same coefficient?

g. What is the coefficient of a^2b^4 in the expansion of $(a + b)^6$?

h. What other term has the same coefficient?

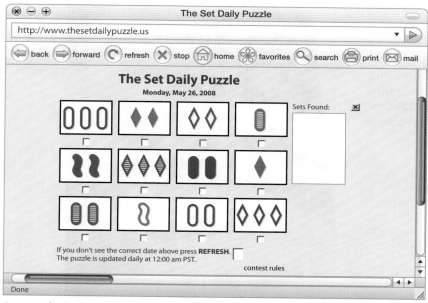

Can you find all six sets?

Mathematical 4B Reflections

In this investigation, you learned how to count permutations (ordered choices) and combinations (unordered choices). You also learned how to count anagrams (ordered choices with repetition). The following questions will help you summarize what you have learned.

1. Find the probability that in a group of 35 students, at least 2 of them have the same birthday.

2. Explain why, for any integers n and k such that $0 \leq k \leq n$, $_nC_k = \binom{n}{k}$.

3. Show that $_nC_k = {}_nC_{n-k}$ for $0 \leq k \leq n$.

4. Explain why $_{10}P_4 = 24 \cdot {}_{10}C_4$.

5. Figure out whether there are more nine-digit numbers with a 1 in them, or if there are more nine-digit numbers without a 1 in them.

6. In how many ways can you pick three objects, in order, from a set of six distinct objects?

7. How many three-digit numbers are there that have repeated digits?

8. How many five-student committees are possible in a class of 26 students?

Vocabulary and Notation

In this investigation, you learned these terms. Make sure you understand what each one means and how to use it.

- anagram
- combination
- permutation
- $_nC_k$, number of combinations of n objects, taken k at a time
- $_nP_k$, number of permutations of n objects, taken k at a time

Horns play permutations of single notes.

Mid-Chapter Test

Go Online
PHSchool.com

For a mid-chapter test, go
to Web Code: bga-0452

Multiple Choice

1. Here are three problems:

   I. Ann has saved $100. If she spends $20 on CDs, how much money does she have left?

   II. Bill earned $100 last week, but he had to pay $20 in taxes. What was the amount of Bill's paycheck?

   III. Carla took a test in history that was worth 100 points. She lost 20 points for mistakes. What was her final grade on the test?

   Which of the above problems are isomorphic?

   A. I and II only **B.** I and III only

   C. II and III only **D.** I, II, and III

2. How many three-digit numbers can you make using only the digits 1, 2, or 3?

   A. 6 **B.** 8

   C. 9 **D.** 27

3. The high school baseball team has three starting pitchers. The coach is making his pitching schedule for the first three games of the playoffs. If no pitcher can start twice, how many different options does he have?

   A. 6 **B.** 8

   C. 9 **D.** 27

4. The Town Council is going to choose two delegates. One will go to the state conference and one will go to the regional conference. There are 25 candidates for the two positions. Which expression represents the number of ways the council can choose the two delegates?

   A. 25^2 **B.** $25 + 25$

   C. $25 \cdot 24$ **D.** $25 + 24$

5. How many functions have inputs from the set $\{A, B, C, D\}$ and outputs from the set $\{1, 2, 3, 4, 5\}$?

   A. 9 **B.** 20

   C. 625 **D.** 1024

Open Response

6. Make up a problem that is isomorphic to the following problem.

   > Alice has to write a ten-page paper for her history class. So far, she has written six pages. How many more pages does she need to write?

7. How many three-digit numbers are possible with only the digits 0, 1, or 2? (Remember that the first digit of a three-digit number cannot be zero.)

8. For the early bird special at a local restaurant, you can choose one appetizer, one entree, and one dessert. There are five appetizers, six entrees, and four desserts. In how many ways can you choose your meal with the early bird special?

9. **a.** How many five-digit numbers are there?

   b. How many five-digit numbers have 3 as the final digit?

10. **a.** How many functions are there from a two-element set to a four-element set?

    b. How many of these functions are one-to-one?

    c. How many of these functions are not one-to-one?

11. Describe what it means for two problems to be isomorphic.

Making Connections

In *Making Connections*, you will develop relationships among the coefficients of binomial expansions, Pascal's Triangle, and combinations.

By the end of this investigation, you will be able to answer questions like these.

1. What is the coefficient of the $x^{13}y^{37}$ term in the expansion of $(x + y)^{50}$?

2. What is the connection between the Pascal's Paths problem and the entries in Pascal's Triangle?

3. Why is the sum of the entries in row n of Pascal's Triangle 2^n?

You will learn how to

• apply counting strategies to solve the Pascal's Paths problem

• explain why the coefficients of a binomial expansion are found in Pascal's Triangle

• see the entries of Pascal's Triangle from a variety of perspectives

You will develop these habits and skills:

• Use combinations to find binomial coefficients.

• Use combinatorics to prove the Binomial Theorem.

• Recognize isomorphic problems.

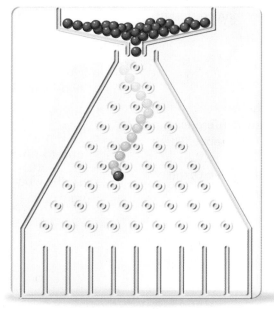

In this Galton box or "bean machine," a ball can fall to the right or left of each peg. Do you see a connection to Ms. Pascal and the routes she takes to work?

Activating Prior Knowledge
Exploring New Ideas

Recall the following problem that you have seen in the Getting Started lesson of the Investigations 4A and 4B.

Pascal's Path

Ms. Pascal likes to take a different route to work every day. She will quit her job the day she has to repeat a route she has already taken. The grid of streets below shows her home and her workplace. She only travels north or east and never back tracks. How many days will she work at this job?

> Two paths are different if they are not the same everywhere. They might overlap on some pieces though, like the two valid Pascal paths shown below.

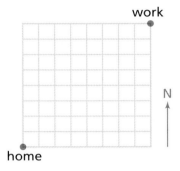

Again, here are some examples of some possible paths.

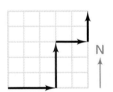

Here is a valid path.   This is also valid.   This is not a valid path.

For You to Explore

1. Jane invented a special way to describe a path. She wrote "N" if Ms. Pascal went north along a block and "E" if Ms. Pascal went east. For example, Jane wrote "EEEEEEEENNNNNNNN" to describe Ms. Pascal going eight blocks east and then eight blocks north.

   Describe how Jane could solve the Pascal's Paths problem using this approach.

2. Mark tried reasoning backward. "To get to work," Mark thought, "Ms. Pascal had to go through intersection *A* or through intersection *B*." So, Mark wanted to find the number of ways to reach *A* and the number of ways to reach *B*. Then he could add these two numbers.

   Describe how Mark could solve the Pascal's Paths problem using this approach.

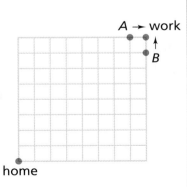

3. Eventually Mark decides to start from the very beginning. He wants to write on each street intersection the number of different ways Ms. Pascal could reach that intersection. Copy the diagram, and help him to fill at least ten more spaces.

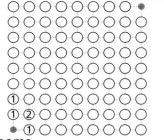

> Do the numbers in Problem 3 remind you of something?

4. **a.** If Ms. Pascal travels only two blocks, how many different places might she end up?

   b. How many different paths two blocks long are there?

   c. Write down all different paths that are two blocks long using Jane's notation.

Suppose you are expanding the square of a binomial, $(E + N)^2$. You could expand it as follows.

$$(E + N)^2 = (E + N)(E + N) = E \cdot E + E \cdot N + N \cdot E + N \cdot N$$
$$= E^2 + 2EN + N^2$$

Stop to examine the expression before combining like terms.

$$E \cdot E + E \cdot N + N \cdot E + N \cdot N$$

Ignore the multiplication and addition symbols and you will notice four strings of letters.

$$EE, EN, NE, \text{ and } NN$$

Do these strings look familiar? In Jane's notation, each of these four strings describes a valid Pascal path. Each path is two blocks long.

For You to Do

5. In expanding the square $(E + N)^2$, the monomials $E \cdot N$ and $N \cdot E$ are equal. The paths they describe bring you to the same place on the grid. Do equal monomials in the expansion of $(E + N)^k$ always describe paths that lead to the same place? Explain.

6. Expand $(E + N)^3$. How does this relate to Pascal paths of length three?

7. Expand $(E + N)^4$. How does this relate to Pascal paths of length four?

8. If you expand $(E + N)^5$ and add like terms, what is the coefficient in front of each of the following?

   a. E^5 **b.** E^4N **c.** E^3N^2

   d. E^2N^3 **e.** EN^4 **f.** N^5

   g. What is the sum of all the coefficients?

9. **a.** Show that if you expand $(E + N)^9$ and add like terms, the E^7N^2 and E^2N^7 terms have the same coefficient.

   b. What other monomials of this polynomial have equal coefficients?

> **Remember...**
>
> A monomial is a number or the product of a number and one or more variables. Any polynomial can be written as a sum of monomials.

10. a. In how many ways can Ms. Pascal reach the intersection four blocks north and three blocks east from her home?

b. Expand $(E + N)^7$. What is the coefficient of the E^3N^4 term?

c. Show that the two problems in parts (a) and (b) are isomorphic.

Exercises Practicing Habits of Mind

On Your Own

11. a. If Ms. Pascal only travels three blocks, in how many different places might she end up?

b. How many Pascal paths are three blocks long?

c. Write down all different paths three blocks long using Jane's notation.

d. In Jane's notation, how could you tell which ones lead to the same place?

12. Write About It Describe the connection between the Pascal's Paths problem and the entries in Pascal's Triangle.

13. a. How many blocks must Ms. Pascal travel to get to work?

b. How many different routes are there from Ms. Pascal's home to her workplace? You can use either Jane's or Mark's strategy to find the answer.

14. What is the sum of the coefficients of the polynomial $(E - N)^k$?

15. In how many ways can you make a string (a "word") fifteen symbols long using five U's, five F's, and five R's?

> If the answer reminds you of the total number of Pascal paths of length k, or of the number of k-digit numbers consisting of 1's and 2's—you are on the right path!

Maintain Your Skills

16. If you expand $(E + N)^2$ you'll obtain

$$(E + N)^2 = E^2 + 2EN + N^2$$

The coefficients are 1, 2, and 1. The sum of the coefficients is $1 + 2 + 1 = 4$.

a. Find the sum of coefficients of the polynomial $(E + N)^3$.

b. Find the sum of coefficients of the polynomial $(E + N)^4$.

c. Find the sum of coefficients of the polynomial $(E + N)^k$.

> **Habits of Mind**
>
> **Try a specific case.** See what happens with both sides of this identity if $N = E = 1$.

4.10 Revisiting the Binomial Theorem

In Problems 5–9 of the Getting Started lesson, you saw some rather interesting connections between the numbers in Pascal's Triangle and the coefficients of $(a + b)^n$.

$$
\begin{array}{ll}
(a + b)^0 = 1 & \qquad 1 \\
(a + b)^1 = a + b & \qquad 1 \quad 1 \\
(a + b)^2 = a^2 + 2ab + b^2 & \qquad 1 \quad 2 \quad 1 \\
(a + b)^3 = a^3 + 3a^2b + 3ab^2 + b^3 & \quad 1 \quad 3 \quad 3 \quad 1
\end{array}
$$

This may have reminded you of the Binomial Theorem.

Theorem 4.4 The Binomial Theorem

For any integers n and k with $0 \le k \le n$,

$$(a + b)^n = \binom{n}{0}a^n b^0 + \binom{n}{1}a^{n-1}b^1 + \binom{n}{2}a^{n-2}b^2 + \cdots$$

$$+ \binom{n}{k}a^{n-k}b^k + \cdots + \binom{n}{n-1}a^1 b^{n-1} + \binom{n}{n}a^0 b^n$$

Now you can use the Pascal-Combinations connection from Investigation B to understand the Binomial Theorem.

Minds in Action   episode 13

Sasha and Derman are looking at the Binomial Theorem.

Sasha   This theorem shows the connection between finding the coefficients when you expand $(a + b)^n$ and counting problems like the exercises about committees in this chapter.

Derman But how are terms of a polynomial like people on a committee? We proved the Binomial Theorem last year and our proof didn't have anything to do with committees!

Sasha   Let's look at $(a + b)^5$. It's really just

$$(a + b)(a + b)(a + b)(a + b)(a + b)$$

Derman Hold on, expanding that will take a while.

Sasha   No, just think of doing the calculation. If you multiplied all this out, you'd get a sum of terms. You get each term by taking a letter from each of the five factors and multiplying them together.

Derman You mean, for example, you could take a from factors 1, 2, and 4 and b from factors 3 and 5? That would give you an $a^3 b^2$.

Sasha   Yes, but you could also get an a^3b^2 by taking a from factors 1, 2, and 3 and b from factors 4 and 5.

Derman Oh! So the coefficient of a^3b^2 will be the number of the ways you can pick 3 factors of a and 2 factors of b.

Sasha   And that is just the number of ways you can pick three things (three a's) from five factors. It's $\binom{5}{3}$.

Derman Right! That's the connection. But couldn't we also count this as the number of ways you can pick two things (two "b"s) from five factors? That's $\binom{5}{2}$.

Sasha   Of course. But $\binom{5}{2}$ is the same as $\binom{5}{3}$ And the same idea applies to the other terms. You can pick no a's and five b's, one a and four b's, . . .

For Discussion

1. Use Sasha and Derman's argument to show that the Binomial Theorem works when applied to the expansion of $(a + b)^5$.

For You to Do

2. Explain how you could use a combinatorial proof to prove the Binomial Theorem for any $n > 0$.

Exercises *Practicing Habits of Mind*

Check Your Understanding

1. Use the Binomial Theorem to expand each of the following. Use your CAS to verify your answers.

   a. $(x + y)^7$ **b.** $(x + 2y)^5$

2. Consider the expansion of $(a + b)^{12}$.

   a. What is the coefficient of the a^5b^7 term?

   b. What other term(s) share this coefficient?

   c. Which terms do not share their coefficients with any other terms?

Go Online
PHSchool.com

For a history of the Binomial Theorem, go to Web Code: bge-9031

3. Determine the coefficient of each of the following terms in the expansion of $(x + y)^{50}$.

a. $x^{13}y^{37}$ **b.** xy^{49} **c.** $x^{25}y^{25}$

4. How could you simplify the following sum? Let $n = 5$.

$$\sum_{k=0}^{n} \binom{n}{k}(-1)^k$$

What if n were 6 instead of 5? What if n were 11 instead of 5?

5. Write a polynomial that you can factor in the form $(a + b)^n$ where:

- The constant term is not 1.
- There is exactly one variable, x.
- There are at least 5 terms.

Switch polynomials with a partner. Factor your partner's polynomial.

6. a. Factor the expression $1 + 4x + 6x^2 + 4x^3 + x^4$.

    b. Evaluate the sum (without a calculator).

$$1 + 4 \cdot 2 + 6 \cdot 2^2 + 4 \cdot 2^3 + 2^4$$

    c. Explain how the two problems in parts (a) and (b) are connected.

7. Write an equivalent expression for each of the following.

a. $(x - 1)^n$ **b.** $(a - b)^n$

8. Consider trinomial coefficients. What is the coefficient of the ab^2c term in the expansion of $(a + b + c)^4$?

9. Take It Further In the expansion of $(a + b + c + d + e)^{14}$, what is the coefficient of the $a^2b^3cd^5e^3$ term?

10. Standardized Test Prep What is the coefficient of the a^4b^3 term in the expansion of $(a - b)^7$?

A. -56 **B.** 56 **C.** 168 **D.** -280

11. Find the value of each sum. Look for shortcuts!

a. $\displaystyle\sum_{k=0}^{6} \binom{6}{k}3^{n-k}$ **b.** $\displaystyle\sum_{k=0}^{6} \binom{6}{k}(-1)^k 3^{n-k}$

Habits of Mind

Be efficient. You certainly should use your CAS to evaluate these, but do not ask your CAS to find all 51 terms! Use what you know to make the calculations easier.

Go Online
PHSchool.com

For additional practice, go to **Web Code: bga-0410**

Think about the combinatorial proof you used for the Binomial Theorem. In how many ways can you choose one a, two b's, and one c from the four factors?

You now know several ways to get the numbers in Pascal's Triangle.

- Pascal's Triangle is a recursively generated number pattern.

$$\binom{0}{0}=1$$

$$\binom{1}{0}=1 \qquad \binom{1}{1}=1$$

$$\binom{2}{0}=1 \qquad \binom{2}{1}=2 \qquad \binom{2}{2}=1$$

$$\binom{3}{0}=1 \qquad \binom{3}{1}=3 \qquad \binom{3}{2}=3 \qquad \binom{3}{3}=1$$

$$\binom{4}{0}=1 \qquad \binom{4}{1}=4 \qquad \binom{4}{2}=6 \qquad \binom{4}{3}=4 \qquad \binom{4}{4}=1$$

$$\binom{5}{0}=1 \qquad \binom{5}{1}=5 \qquad \binom{5}{2}=10 \qquad \binom{5}{3}=10 \qquad \binom{5}{4}=5 \qquad \binom{5}{5}=1$$

Notice that the numbering starts with 0. So, for example,

$$\binom{6}{0} = 1 \qquad \text{and} \qquad \binom{6}{1} = 6$$

You can write the recursive rule for generating the triangle using words.

> Each row starts and ends with a 1, and any interior element is the sum of the two above it.

You can also write this same rule using symbols.

$$\binom{n}{k} = \begin{cases} 1 & \text{if } k = 0 \text{ or if } k = n \text{ (each row starts and ends with 1)} \\ \binom{n-1}{k-1} + \binom{n-1}{k} & \text{if } 0 < k < n \text{ (an interior element is the sum of the two above it)} \end{cases}$$

See the TI-Nspire™ Handbook on p. 704 to learn how to model a recursively defined function of two variables.

- The entries in Pascal's Triangle count subsets. Suppose you have a set of five elements, say $\{A, B, C, D, E\}$. How many three-element subsets are there? There are $\binom{5}{3} = 10$. Here they are:

$$\{A, B, C\}, \{A, B, D\}, \{A, B, E\}, \{A, C, D\}, \{A, C, E\},$$
$$\{A, D, E\}, \{B, C, D\}, \{B, C, E\}, \{B, D, E\}, \{C, D, E\}$$

- The entries in Pascal's Triangle are the coefficients in $(a + b)^n$. The entries in the nth row are the coefficients in the expansion of $(a + b)^n$. More precisely,

$$(a + b)^n = \binom{n}{0}a^n + \binom{n}{1}a^{n-1}b +$$
$$\binom{n}{2}a^{n-2}b^2 + \cdots + \binom{n}{n-1}ab^{n-1} + \binom{n}{n}b^n$$

- The entries in Pascal's Triangle are quotients of factorials. Recall there is an explicit formula for $\binom{n}{k}$ in terms of factorials.

$$\binom{n}{k} = \frac{n!}{k!\,(n-k)!}$$

So, for example,

$$\binom{12}{5} = \frac{12!}{5!\,7!}$$

$$= \frac{12 \cdot 11 \cdot 10 \cdot 9 \cdot 8 \cdot 7 \cdot 6 \cdot 5 \cdot 4 \cdot 3 \cdot 2 \cdot 1}{(5 \cdot 4 \cdot 3 \cdot 2 \cdot 1)(7 \cdot 6 \cdot 5 \cdot 4 \cdot 3 \cdot 2 \cdot 1)}$$

$$= \frac{12 \cdot 11 \cdot 10 \cdot 9 \cdot 8}{5 \cdot 4 \cdot 3 \cdot 2 \cdot 1}$$

$$= 792$$

Habits of Mind

Make strategic choices. Making this factorial formula hold for the cases $k = 0$ and $k = n$ is one of the reasons for defining $0!$ to be 1.

- The entries in Pascal's Triangle are rational expressions. Sometimes it is useful to do the cancellations in the factorial expression. Then you can write $\binom{n}{k}$ as a product of fewer factors.

$$\binom{n}{k} = \frac{n(n-1)(n-2)(n-3)\cdots(n-k+1)(n-k)\cdots 1}{k!\,(n-k)!}$$

$$= \frac{n(n-1)(n-2)(n-3)\cdots(n-k+1)}{k!}$$

One advantage of this expression over all the others is that n can be any number. In a sense, this expression extends the formula for entries in Pascal's Triangle from integers to real (or even complex) numbers. This will be important in the next chapter.

In the exercises for this lesson, you will spend time developing these connections.

Habits of Mind

Extend an idea. The symbol $\binom{\pi}{3}$ doesn't make sense in the context of any of the other methods. However, using the formula for $\binom{n}{k}$ you get

$$\frac{\pi(\pi-1)(\pi-2)}{6}$$

Exercises *Practicing Habits of Mind*

Check Your Understanding

1. Explain why the sum of the entries in row n of Pascal's Triangle is 2^n. Use the fact that Pascal's Triangle is a recursively generated number pattern.

2. Explain why the sum of the entries in row n of Pascal's Triangle is 2^n. Use the fact that entries in Pascal's Triangle count subsets.

3. Using the fact that entries in Pascal's Triangle count subsets, explain why $\binom{n}{n} = 1$.

4. Using the fact that entries in Pascal's Triangle are quotients of factorials, explain why $\binom{n}{n} = 1$.

5. Using the fact that entries in Pascal's Triangle count subsets, explain why $\binom{n}{k} = \binom{n}{n-k}$.

6. Using the fact that entries in Pascal's Triangle are the coefficients in $(a + b)^n$, explain why $\binom{n}{k} = \binom{n}{n-k}$.

7. Using the fact that entries in Pascal's Triangle count subsets, explain why $\binom{n}{1} = n$.

8. Using the fact that entries in Pascal's Triangle are the coefficients in $(a + b)^n$, explain why $\binom{n}{1} = n$.

On Your Own

9. Explain why the sum of the entries in row n of Pascal's Triangle is 2^n. Use the fact that the entries in Pascal's Triangle are the coefficients in $(a + b)^n$.

10. Using the fact that entries in Pascal's Triangle are coefficients in $(a + b)^n$, explain why $\binom{n}{n} = 1$.

11. Using the fact that entries in Pascal's Triangle are quotients of factorials, explain why $\binom{n}{k} = \binom{n}{n-k}$.

12. Using the fact that entries in Pascal's Triangle are quotients of factorials, explain why $\binom{n}{1} = n$.

13. **Take It Further** Using the fact that Pascal's Triangle is a recursively generated number pattern, explain why $\binom{n}{1} = n$.

14. **Standardized Test Prep** What is the value of x if $_{2008}C_x = {}_{2008}C_{x-4}$?

   A. 1004　　　**B.** 1006　　　**C.** 1008　　　**D.** 2004

Go Online
PHSchool.com

For additional practice, go to **Web Code:** bga-0411

Maintain Your Skills

15. Let $E = \binom{n}{0} + \binom{n}{2} + \binom{n}{4} + \cdots$ (the sum of all the even-entry terms of row n), and $O = \binom{n}{1} + \binom{n}{3} + \binom{n}{5} + \cdots$ (the sum of all the odd-entry terms of row n). How do E and O compare?

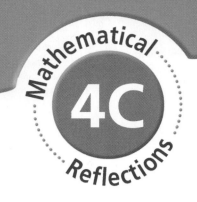
In this investigation, you learned that the coefficients in the expansion of $(a + b)^n$ are

- the numbers in the nth row of Pascal's Triangle
- the numbers of combinations when choosing from n elements

The following questions will help you summarize what you have learned.

1. Using the fact that entries in Pascal's Triangle are the coefficients in $(a + b)^n$, explain why $\binom{n}{k} = \binom{n}{n-k}$.

2. Factor the expression $1 + 4x + 6x^2 + 4x^3 + x^4$.

3. Find the sum of the coefficients of the polynomial $(E + N)^6$.

4. Find the sum of the coefficients of the polynomial $(E - N)^k$.

5. Using the fact that entries in Pascal's Triangle are quotients of factorials, explain why $\binom{n}{k} = \binom{n}{n-k}$.

6. What is the coefficient of the $x^{13}y^{37}$ term in the expansion of $(x + y)^{50}$?

7. What is the connection between the Pascal's Paths problem and the entries in Pascal's Triangle?

8. Why is the sum of the entries in row n of Pascal's Triangle 2^n?

If you overlay Pascal's Triangle, you will see the number of different paths that get to each peg. In the end, the balls will fall into the bins, approximately in a *binomial distribution*.

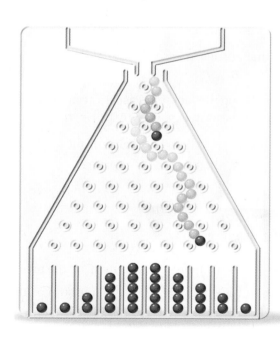

Project: Using Mathematical Habits

The Simplex® Lock

The Simplex® lock is a mechanical pushbutton lock, with five buttons. Like most keyless locks, you enter a secret code by pushing the buttons. The one code that opens the lock is called "the combination" by most people.

The Simplex lock is unusual since you can push more than one button at the same time. For example, one possible combination is "2, then 1 and 4 at the same time, then 3."

In choosing a valid combination, you must follow two rules.

Rule 1 Each button may be used at most once. For example, "2, then 2 and 3 at the same time" is not a valid combination.

Rule 2 Each push may include any number of buttons, from one to five. For example, one valid combination is "hit all five buttons at once." But hitting all five buttons cannot be part of a larger combination because of rule 1.

It follows from these rules that in a combination there can be at most five distinct pushes. (Do you see why?) The rules allow for the null combination, in which you do not have to push any buttons at all. (The door is unlocked!)

Keep in mind that when you push two or more buttons at the same time, their order does not matter. That is, you *should not* count "2 and 3 together, then 5" and "3 and 2 together, then 5" as two distinct combinations.

1. How many lock combinations are there that use all of the buttons?

2. A company that sells this lock advertises that thousands of lock combinations are possible. Are they right?

3. How many lock combinations are there that use fewer than all the buttons? (*Hint:* Use your answer from Exercise 1 to count indirectly.)

To open a door with a Simplex lock, you need the correct permutation from all of the possible codes.

Chapter 4 Review

For vocabulary review, go
to **Web Code:** bgj-0451

In **Investigation 4A,** you learned to

- become familiar with what combinatorics means and the kinds of problems that you can solve using combinatorics
- develop your own strategies for systematic counting

The following questions will help you check your understanding.

1. Make up two isomorphic problems that you can solve this way:

$$28 + 2 \cdot 3 = 34$$

2. In how many different ways can you arrange the letters of the word CUBE?

3. a. How many functions have the inputs from the set $\{A, B, C, D\}$ and outputs from the set $\{2, 4, 6\}$?

b. Are any of these functions one-to-one? Explain your answer.

In **Investigation 4B,** you learned to

- develop and use formulas for finding the number of permutations $_nP_k$, of n objects taken k at a time
- use a formula for $_nC_k$, the number of combinations of n things taken k at a time
- find the number of anagrams for a given word

The following questions will help you check your understanding.

4. Elaine has six books that she is arranging according to color on a bookshelf.

a. How many ways can she arrange the six books if they are all different colors?

b. How many ways can she arrange the six books if 4 of them are the same color?

5. The 25 students in the Student Council want to form a 5-member prom committee.

a. How many committees are possible?

b. Suppose they want to appoint one of the five members as chairperson and another as the treasurer. How many committees can they make using this method?

6. How many anagrams does each word have?

a. FRAME **b.** MIRROR **c.** PAINTING

In **Investigation 4C,** you learned to

- apply counting strategies to solve the Pascal's Paths problem
- explain why you find the coefficients of a binomial expansion in Pascal's Triangle
- See the entries of Pascal's Triangle from a variety of perspectives

The following questions will help you check your understanding.

7. a. If Ms. Pascal only travels three blocks, in how many different places might she end up?

b. How many Pascal paths are three blocks long?

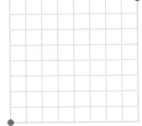

8. Consider the expansion of $(x + y)^{10}$.

a. What is the coefficient of the x^3y^7 term?

b. What is the coefficient of the x^9y term?

c. Which terms have 45 as their coefficient?

Chapter 4 Test

For a chapter test, go to Web Code: bga-0453

Multiple Choice

1. How many four-digit numbers can you make using the digits 0, 1, 2, or 3?

   A. 15 **B.** 16 **C.** 192 **D.** 256

2. Which expression is equivalent to $\frac{8!}{4!}$?

   A. 2!

   B. $8 \cdot 7 \cdot 6 \cdot 5$

   C. $8 \cdot 7 \cdot 6 \cdot 5 \cdot 4$

   D. $8 \cdot 7 \cdot 6 \cdot 5 \cdot 3 \cdot 2 \cdot 1$

3. How many anagrams does the word PEN have?

   A. 1 **B.** 3 **C.** 6 **D.** 27

4. Which of the following is not equal to $_8C_3$?

   A. $\binom{8}{3}$ **B.** $\frac{_8P_3}{3!}$ **C.** $_8C_5$ **D.** $_8P_3 \cdot 6$

5. What is the coefficient of a^9b^2 in the expansion of $(a + b)^{11}$?

   A. 9 **B.** 36 **C.** 55 **D.** 110

Open Response

6. Write the following using factorial notation and then find the value of the expression.

   a. $_6C_2$ **b.** $_6P_2$

   c. $\binom{6}{0}$ **d.** $_7P_7$

   e. $_8C_5 + \,_8C_6$

7. Ms. Smith's kindergarten class has 15 students, 8 girls and 7 boys.

   a. How many ways can the 8 girls line up for recess?

   b. How many ways can Ms. Smith choose 4 of her students to form a reading group?

   c. How many ways can she choose the reading group if there must be 2 boys and 2 girls in the group?

8. How many anagrams does each word have?

   a. EARTH

   b. MERCURY

   c. NEPTUNE

9. **a.** Write the first three terms in the expansion of $(a + b)^{24}$.

   b. Write the last three terms in the expansion of $(a + b)^{24}$.

   c. Write the term that does not share its coefficient with any other term.

10. How many three-digit numbers are there that have repeated digits?

1. For each degree measure, find the corresponding radian measure.

   a. $330°$

   b. $225°$

   c. $240°$

   d. $90°$

2. Find all solutions to the equation $4\sin^2 x - 3 = 0$ for $0 \le x \le 2\pi$.

3. Find the period of the function $g(t) = 1 + \cos(2t)$.

4. Let z be a complex number where $|z| = 3$ and $\arg(z) = \frac{\pi}{3}$. Find z^4.

5. Let $x + yi = 4\operatorname{cis}150°$. Find x and y.

6. Evaluate $(-3 + 3i\sqrt{3})^3$.

7. Examine the graph of the function g below. List all of the roots of g.

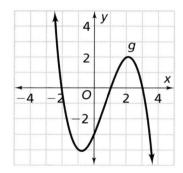

8. Consider the function $f(x) = \dfrac{x^2 - x - 12}{x^2 + x - 6}$.

   a. The graph of f has a horizontal asymptote. Find the equation of the horizontal asymptote.

   b. The graph of f has a vertical asymptote. Find the equation of the vertical asymptote.

   c. The graph of f has a hole. Find the coordinates of the hole.

9. Phoebe invests $1000 at 9% APR. She wants to determine the interest earned by different compounding methods after one year. Copy and complete the table, rounding answers to the nearest penny.

	Compounding Periods	Amount of Interest
a.	yearly	▨
b.	quarterly	▨
c.	monthly	▨
d.	daily	▨
e.	continuously	▨

10. Consider the function $f(x) = 2x^3 - 4x^2 + 1$. One point on the graph of f is $(2, 1)$.

    a. Use geometry software to draw the graph of f. Plot the point $A(2, 1)$. Place a moveable point B on the graph of f to the right of A.

    b. Construct the secant line through A and B. Find the equation of this line.

    c. Let b be the x-coordinate of B. Write $m(A, B)$ as a polynomial in b using the formula $m(A, B) = \dfrac{f(b) - f(2)}{b - 2}$.

    d. Move B closer to A. What happens to the slope of the secant line?

11. Find constants A and B such that
$$\frac{9x - 1}{x^2 - 3x - 4} = \frac{A}{x + 1} + \frac{B}{x - 4}$$

12. Suppose that $f(x) = x^3 + 4x^2 - 7x - 12$ and $g(x) = 3x^2 - 8x + 2$. Expand the following in powers of $x - 2$.

    a. $f(x)$

    b. $g(x)$

    c. $f(x) + g(x)$

    d. $5g(x)$

13. The quadratic function $q(x) = 1 - x + \frac{x^2}{2}$ is a good approximation to $f(x) = e^{-x}$ when x is near 0.

   a. Calculate $q(0.05)$ and $e^{-0.05}$ to five decimal places. What is the percent error for $q(0.05)$ as an approximation to $e^{-0.05}$?

   b. Calculate $q(0.5)$ and $e^{-0.5}$ to five decimal places. What is the percent error for $q(0.5)$ as an approximation to $e^{-0.5}$?

   c. Calculate $q(1)$ and e^{-1} to five decimal places. What is the percent error for $q(1)$ as an approximation to e^{-1}?

14. Write each of the following using factorial notation. Then find the value of the expression.

   a. $_9C_3$

   b. $_7P_2$

   c. $\binom{7}{5}$

   d. $_6C_0 + {_6C_6}$

15. For the expansion of $(u + v)^8$, find the coefficient of the specified term.

   a. the first term

   b. the last term

   c. the u^5v^3 term

   d. the u^4v^4 term

16. Find the number of anagrams that each word has.

   a. LOBSTER

   b. CHICKEN

   c. DESSERT

   d. APPETITE

17. The gymnastics team at Valley View College consists of 10 women and 8 men. The team is going to a statewide competition. Their bus can only hold twelve members of the team, so only some of them can go on the trip.

   a. How many ways can they choose 6 women and 6 men to go on the trip?

   b. How many ways can they choose 7 women and 5 men to go on the trip?

   c. Suppose the captain of the women's squad and the captain of the men's squad must go on the trip. They want 7 women and 5 men, including the captains, to make the trip. How many ways can they choose who will go?

18. Three of the following are equal to each other. The fourth is not equal to any of the others. Which one is it?

   a. $_{10}C_7$ **b.** $\binom{10}{3}$ **c.** $\frac{10!}{3!}$ **d.** $\frac{_{10}P_7}{3!}$

19. For the expansion of $(m + n)^{16}$, write the specified terms.

   a. the first three terms

   b. the last three terms

   c. the middle term

20. Darlene is planning a summer vacation to the Caribbean. She can fly from her home to Miami on any one of four different airlines. From Miami, she can then board a ship belonging to any one of two cruise lines to the Bahamas. Once in the Bahamas, she can then rent a car from one of three car rental agencies, and can stay in any one of seven different hotels. In how many ways could she select a package consisting of an airline, a cruise line, a car rental agency, and a hotel?

Chapter

5

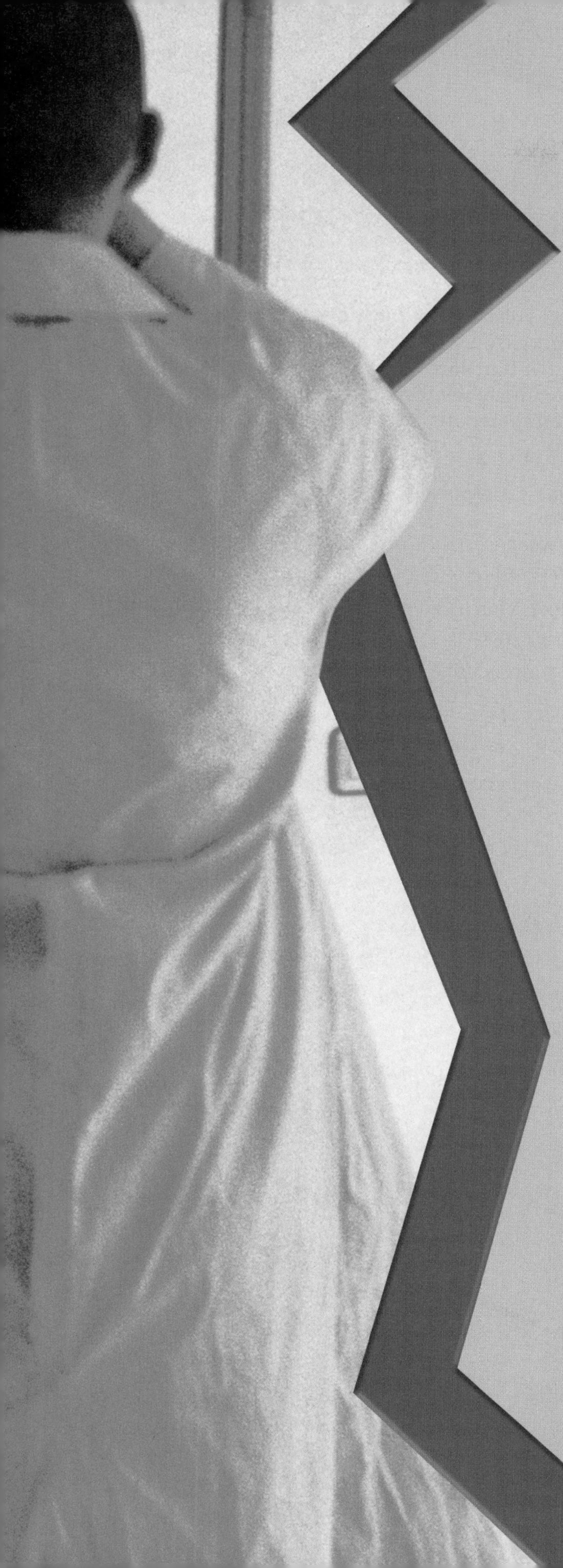

Functions and Tables

Consider the sequence

$$10, 11, 14, 19, 26, 35, \ldots$$

One person might say, "The sequence starts with 10. Then you add 1, add 3, add 5, and keep adding the odd numbers." This is a *recursive* description, one that tells you how to go from one value to the next.

A second person might say. "All the terms are 10 more than the squares of consecutive integers. Term 0 is 10, term 1 is 11, term 2 is 14, and term n is $n^2 + 10$." This is a *closed-form* description, one that tells you how to find any value directly.

Each description has its pros and cons. A recursive description is often more natural, but a closed-form description may prove more useful if you need to find a specific term.

But how might you check or prove that a recursive definition and a closed-form definition will always agree? Or, if you had only a recursive definition, how could you find a closed-form definition to directly calculate the 60th term? This chapter explores these questions.

Vocabulary

- base case
- closed-form definition
- difference table
- equilibrium point
- Fibonacci sequence
- functional equation
- hockey-stick property
- Mahler polynomials
- mathematical induction
- recurrence
- recursive definition
- two-term recurrence
- up-and-over property

A New Method of Proof

In *A New Method of Proof*, you will describe functions recursively, by relating outputs to other outputs. You will determine when a function described this way agrees with a function described by a formula, or closed-form definition, which directly relates inputs to outputs. To prove that two functions agree for all shared inputs, you will use a powerful tool known as induction.

By the end of this investigation, you will be able to answer questions like these.

1. What are the differences between a closed-form definition and a recursive definition for a function?

2. How can you prove that a closed-form and a recursive function definition agree at each of infinitely many inputs?

3. What happens to the ratio of consecutive Fibonacci numbers?

You will learn how to

• determine the domain on which two functions agree

• verify that a closed-form and a recursive function definition agree at the first few inputs in a domain

• prove by induction that two function definitions agree for all inputs in an infinite domain

You will develop these habits and skills:

• Model and work with closed-form and recursive definitions of functions.

• Determine whether two functions agree for all inputs in a given set.

• Use patterns to write function definitions.

• Prove that two functions agree for all inputs in an infinite domain.

In a match-play golf tournament, the winner of each match advances to the next round. The number of players in each round follows a recursive rule.

Activating Prior Knowledge

You already know that you can often describe a function in more than one way. On the other hand, sometimes you will be given two or more different function descriptions. If this happens, you need to be able to determine whether or not they describe the same function.

For You to Explore

Here is an input-output table for a function.

Input	Output
0	3
1	8
2	13
3	18
4	23

1. Takashi says that this table came from the function $T(n) = 5n + 3$.

   a. Does function T agree with the entire table?

   b. What does Takashi's function give for $T(20)$? For $T(500)$?

2. Christine says she has a different function for the table.

Christine: You start with 3 and keep adding 5. Each output is 5 more than the one before it. And I can write that down. It's

$$C(n) = \begin{cases} 3 & \text{if } n = 0 \\ C(n-1) + 5 & \text{if } n > 0 \end{cases}$$

Christine: I'd put this in a calculator if it was more complicated.

   a. Does function C agree with the entire table?

   b. What does Christine's function give for $C(20)$? For $C(500)$?

See the TI-Nspire™ Handbook on p. 704 for how to model this definition in your FML (function modeling language).

3. Takashi and Christine would like to know if their functions are the same.

   a. Can you find any input where the two functions from Problems 1 and 2 behave differently?

   b. What are the domains of T and C?

   c. Explain why T and C are not identical functions.

   d. Find the largest set of inputs for which the two functions agree.

   e. **Take It Further** Prove that for any number in this set, T and C must give the same output.

4. For each of the following pairs of functions, find the largest set of inputs for which the two functions agree.

a. $f(x) = \frac{1}{x} + x,$ $g(x) = \frac{1 + x^2}{x}$

b. $f(x) = 3x + 2,$ $g(x) = 5x + 1$

c. $f(x) = 3x + 2,$ $g(x) = 3x + 7$

d. $f(x) = x,$ $g(x) = |x|$

e. $f(x) = x^2,$ $g(x) = x + 2$

f. $f(x) = x + 1,$ $g(x) =$ the next integer greater than x

5. Name two functions that agree only at the inputs 1 and 4.

6. Suppose you take out a $12,000 car loan with a 6% APR compounded monthly, and your monthly payment is $300 per month. You can recursively define a function B that gives your balance after n months:

$$B(n) = \begin{cases} 12{,}000 & \text{if } n = 0 \\ B(n - 1) + \frac{0.06}{12} B(n - 1) - 300 & \text{if } n > 0 \end{cases}$$

Why do you divide the interest rate by 12?

a. Use a calculator to find $B(6)$ to the nearest cent.

b. What happens if you try to calculate $B(36)$?

c. Redefine $B(n)$ by combining like terms, then calculate $B(36)$.

d. **Take It Further** What monthly payment amount would bring the balance to exactly zero after 36 months?

Exercises *Practicing Habits of Mind*

On Your Own

7. For each of the following pairs of functions, find the largest set of inputs for which the two functions agree.

a. $f(x) = x^2 - 9,$ $g(x) = (x + 3)(x - 3)$

b. $f(x) = \frac{x^2 - 16}{x - 4},$ $g(x) = x + 4$

c. $f(x) = \sqrt{x^2},$ $g(x) = x$

d. $f(x) = 3x + 2,$ $g(x) = 3x + 2 + (x - 1)(x - 2)(x - 3)$

8. **a.** Find two functions h and k, defined on all of $\mathbb{R}$, that agree only for the set $\{1, 2, 3, 4, 5\}$.

   b. Find two functions m and n, defined on all of $\mathbb{R}$, that agree only for the set $\{6, 7, 8, 9, 10\}$.

Remember...

$\mathbb{R}$ is the set of real numbers.

9. Takashi's function for the table was $T(n) = 5n + 3$. Show that for any n, $T(n)$ satifies the condition

$$T(n) = T(n - 1) + 5$$

10. **a.** Build a model of the function C from Problem 2 in your FML. Find the greatest value of n for which the model produces an output.

    b. What is the domain of C?

    Use the form of the function in Problem 6 to answer the following questions.

11. Suppose you buy a \$10,000 car with a \$1000 down payment and take out a loan for the remaining \$9000 at 5% APR. You are to pay the loan off over 36 months. Find your monthly payment, to the nearest cent.

12. Suppose that the interest rate for the loan in Exercise 11 changes from 5% to 1.9%. How much money per month will you save? How much money will you save over the life of the loan?

Remember...

Enter 1.9% as a decimal number less than 1.

Maintain Your Skills

13. Below are recursive definitions of four functions. For each, tabulate the function using inputs from 0 to 5. Then find a closed-form definition that agrees with the table.

    a. $g(n) = \begin{cases} 5 & \text{if } n = 0 \\ g(n - 1) + 7 & \text{if } n > 0 \end{cases}$

    b. $t(n) = \begin{cases} 1 & \text{if } n = 0 \\ 2 \cdot t(n - 1) & \text{if } n > 0 \end{cases}$

    c. $k(x) = \begin{cases} -3 & \text{if } x = 0 \\ k(x - 1) + 4 & \text{if } x > 0 \end{cases}$

    d. $j(m) = \begin{cases} 0 & \text{if } m = 0 \\ j(m - 1) + m & \text{if } m > 0 \end{cases}$

Two Ways to Define a Function

When you look for a function that agrees with a table, it helps if you can see patterns in the outputs. As an example, consider this table from Lesson 5.1.

Input, n	Output, $f(n)$
0	3
1	8
2	13
3	18
4	23

You could say that each output is 3 more than 5 times the input, writing this as $n \mapsto 5n + 3$. A **closed-form definition** for a function f lets you find $f(n)$ for any input n by direct calculation.

But you might also notice that each output is 5 more than the previous output. In mathematical notation, this function f has the property that

$$f(1) = f(0) + 5 \quad (8 = 3 + 5)$$
$$f(2) = f(1) + 5 \quad (13 = 8 + 5)$$
$$f(3) = f(2) + 5 \quad (18 = 13 + 5)$$
$$f(4) = f(3) + 5 \quad (23 = 18 + 5)$$

Many people notice this pattern in the outputs before they find a function like $n \mapsto 5n + 3$.

In short, this statement is true for any n:

$$f(n) = f(n - 1) + 5$$

Developing Habits of Mind

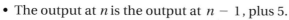

Think about it more than one way. The rule $f(n) = f(n - 1) + 5$ has many interpretations.

- The output at n is the output at $n - 1$, plus 5.
- The output at n is 5 more than the output at $n - 1$.
- The output at n is 5 more than the previous output.
- Any output is 5 more than the previous output.

For Discussion

1. Is $f(n) = 5n + 3$ the only function that makes $f(n) = f(n - 1) + 5$ true for $n = 0, 1, 2, \ldots$? Explain.

In order to produce outputs, a rule like $f(n) = f(n - 1) + 5$ has to have a place to start, called a **base case.** Once you know that f is a function for which $f(0) = 3$ and $f(n) = f(n - 1) + 5$, you can find the output for any integer input greater than 0:

$$f(n) = \begin{cases} 3 & \text{if } n = 0 \\ f(n - 1) + 5 & \text{if } n > 0 \end{cases}$$

This is called a **recursive definition** of f. It defines most of the outputs of f in terms of other outputs.

Example

Problem Suppose you know that

$$g(n) = g(n - 1) + 7$$

and $g(99) = 496$. Calculate $g(100)$ and $g(101)$.

Solution Let $n = 100$. Then

$$g(100) = g(99) + 7$$

Since $g(99) = 496$, then $g(100) = 496 + 7 = 503$. Similarly, you can use $g(100) = 503$ to find $g(101) = 510$.

If you did not have a base case you would not be able to find $g(101)$—all you would know is that it is 7 more than $g(100)$.

For You to Do

2. Find the values of $f(104)$ and $f(97)$.

Suppose you need to find a function that fits this table:

n	g(n)
0	1
1	3
2	7
3	13
4	21
5	31

One way to find a recursive definition that fits a table is to add a Δ column, containing the differences between successive outputs. For example, the first number in the difference column below is $3 - 1 = 2$.

n	g(n)	Δ
0	1	2
1	3	4
2	7	6
3	13	8
4	21	10
5	31	

The differences tell you what to add to go from one output to the next, which is perfect for defining a function recursively.

The difference table tells you that

$$g(1) = g(0) + 2$$
$$g(2) = g(1) + 4$$
$$g(3) = g(2) + 6$$
$$g(4) = g(3) + 8$$
$$g(5) = g(4) + 10$$
$$\vdots \qquad \vdots$$
$$g(n) = g(n - 1) + \text{??}$$

It appears that $g(n) = g(n - 1) + 2n$. When you combine this equation with the base case $g(0) = 1$, you obtain a recursive definition for $g(n)$:

$$g(n) = \begin{cases} 1 & \text{if } n = 0 \\ g(n - 1) + 2n & \text{if } n > 0 \end{cases}$$

This technique of using the difference column can be very helpful in finding recursive definitions.

Developing Habits of Mind

Make strategic choices. Which should you use: recursive or closed-form definitions? It depends. For some situations, such as the repayment of a loan, a recurvise definition is more natural. On the other hand, recursive definitions can really slow down a calculator or computer. In order to calculate the output at 100, it has to calculate the output at 99, and so on. A computer has to plod through all the unstacking until it gets to a base case. However, you may be able to see a pattern and write a closed-form definition that speeds up the calculation.

Exercises *Practicing Habits of Mind*

Check Your Understanding

For Exercises 1–7 find a recursive definition for a function that fits the table.

1.

n	B(n)
0	0
1	2
2	6
3	12
4	20

2.

n	G(n)
0	−7
1	−4
2	−1
3	2
4	5

3.

x	K(x)
0	1
1	2
2	5
3	10
4	17

Habits of Mind

Represent a function.
Model your functions in your FML.

4.

n	β(n)
0	0
1	1
2	3
3	6
4	10

5.

n	ε(n)
0	2
1	3
2	5
3	9
4	17

6.

n	κ(n)
0	0
1	1
2	4
3	9
4	16

Some of the functions have Greek letters as names. Here is how you say them:

β = beta
γ = gamma
ε = epsilon
κ = kappa

7.

n	γ(n)
0	0
1	1
2	4
3	10
4	20

8. Recall the example from this lesson. Given only the rule $g(n) = g(n - 1) + 7$ and the information that $g(99) = 496$, can you calculate $g(100.5)$? Explain.

9. Anna used a $500 deposit to open a savings account that earns 3% interest per year. Every year Anna deposits another $500. She makes no withdrawals. Write a recursive function definition for the balance in Anna's savings account after n years. Use the definition to calculate the balance after 5 years.

For Exercises 10–13, tabulate the function using inputs from 0 to 5. Then find a closed-form definition that agrees with the table.

10. $h(a) = \begin{cases} 3 & \text{if } a = 0 \\ h(a-1) + 8 & \text{if } a > 0 \end{cases}$

11. $f(m) = \begin{cases} 0 & \text{if } m = 0 \\ f(m-1) + 2m & \text{if } m > 0 \end{cases}$

12. $c(m) = \begin{cases} 3 & \text{if } m = 0 \\ c(m-1) + m & \text{if } m > 0 \end{cases}$

13. $j(t) = \begin{cases} -1 & \text{if } t = 0 \\ j(t-1) + 2t & \text{if } t > 0 \end{cases}$

For Exercises 14–16, find a recursive definition for a function that fits the table.

14.

n	T(n)
0	1
1	3
2	9
3	27
4	81
5	243

Go Online
PHSchool.com

For additional practice, go to Web Code: bga-0502

15.

x	Z(x)
0	3
1	10
2	21
3	36
4	55

16.

n	$\Gamma(n)$
0	1
1	1
2	2
3	6
4	24
5	120

This letter Γ is capital "gamma."

17. Standardized Test Prep Define f as

$$f(n) = \begin{cases} 5 & \text{if } n = 0 \\ f(n-1) - 6 & \text{if } n > 0 \end{cases}$$

What is $f(5)$?

A. -34 **B.** 34 **C.** -25 **D.** 5

Maintain Your Skills

18. Let $S(n)$ be the sum of the first n positive integers, with $S(0) = 0$.

a. Make a table for $S(n)$ using inputs from 0 to 6.

b. Find a recursive function definition that fits this table.

c. Find a closed-form function definition that fits this table.

19. Let $T(n)$ be the sum of the squares of the first n positive integers, with $T(0) = 0$.

a. Make a table for $T(n)$ using inputs from 0 to 6.

b. Find a recursive function definition that fits this table.

As a check, $T(5) = 55$.

c. Take It Further Find a closed-form function definition that fits this table.

5.3 Multistep Recursive Definitions

Some recursive definitions are simpler and more efficient than others.

In-Class Experiment

Exercise 9 in Lesson 5.2 asked you to find a recursive function definition for the balance in Anna's savings account. Anna deposits $500 in the account each year. She earns 3% interest on any money already in the account.

Here are two recursive definitions that should generate the same function.

$$A(n) = \begin{cases} 500 & \text{if } n = 0 \\ A(n-1) + 0.03A(n-1) + 500 & \text{if } n > 0 \end{cases}$$

$$B(n) = \begin{cases} 500 & \text{if } n = 0 \\ 1.03B(n-1) + 500 & \text{if } n > 0 \end{cases}$$

1. Enter each definition into a calculator. Use each function to calculate the balance after 1 year, 2 years, 3 years, and 10 years. Do the definitions agree? Which definition finds the outputs more quickly?

How does a calculator or computer find $A(24)$ using the recursive definition of $A(n)$? It scans the definition and notes what should be done. It sees two places where it will need to compute $A(23)$.

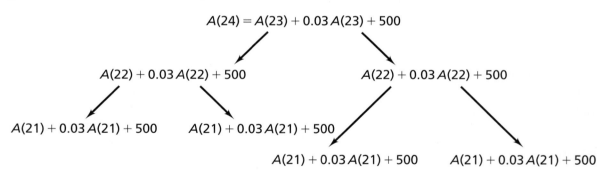

$$A(24) = A(23) + 0.03\,A(23) + 500$$

In each of the 2 computations of $A(23)$, the calculator needs to compute $A(22)$ twice, for a total of 4 times. It computes $A(21)$ 8 times, $A(20)$ 16 times, and so on. The total number of calculations required to find $A(24)$ is larger than what the calculator can handle.

The calculator will not notice that the two calculations of $A(23)$ are the same. The definition of $A(n)$ calls $A(n-1)$ twice. Combining like terms gives the $B(n)$ definition, which a calculator can use far more easily. $B(24)$ needs $B(23)$ once, which needs $B(22)$ once, and so on, until the calculator reaches $B(0)$, the base case.

For Discussion

2. Find the first integer $n > 0$ for which $B(n)$ "gives up" (returns an error). What might you do if you really needed to calculate that value of $B(n)$?

While it is sometimes possible to combine terms to simplify a recursive definition, a recursive definition may depend on more than one previous term. One famous example is the **Fibonacci sequence,** in which each term is the sum of the previous two terms:

$$F(n) = \begin{cases} 0 & \text{if } n = 0 \\ 1 & \text{if } n = 1 \\ F(n-1) + F(n-2) & \text{if } n > 1 \end{cases}$$

For You to Do

3. Use a model of F to find the value of $F(10)$. Give a value of n where you do not expect the calculator to be able to find $F(n)$.

As you can see, a recursive definition sometimes needs two or more base cases to make the definition work. If a definition referred to $F(n)$ in terms of $F(n-4)$, there would need to be four base cases.

Exercises *Practicing Habits of Mind*

Check Your Understanding

1. Louis is paying down a credit card with a $2000 balance. The credit card charges 18% annual interest, or 1.5% per month.

a. Suppose Louis makes a payment of $50 each month. Explain why this recursive function definition gives the balance on the credit card after n months.

$$B(n) = \begin{cases} 2000 & \text{if } n = 0 \\ B(n-1) - 50 + 0.015B(n-1) & \text{if } n > 0 \end{cases}$$

b. Determine the amount of money Louis will owe on this card after 6 months, 12 months, and 24 months.

c. Write a simpler recursive definition for B. Then use it to calculate $B(48)$.

2. The lesson suggests that the number of calculations required to find $A(24)$ is overwhelmingly large. How large, exactly? Remember to count all evaluations of any of $A(0)$ through $A(24)$ in your total.

Find a simpler way to obtain the sum of all of these numbers, rather than just adding them all.

3. Look at the ratios of consecutive Fibonacci numbers:

$$\frac{F(2)}{F(1)} = \frac{1}{1} = 1$$

$$\frac{F(3)}{F(2)} = \frac{2}{1} = 2$$

$$\frac{F(4)}{F(3)} = \frac{3}{2} = 1.5$$

a. For $1 \le n \le 10$, tabulate

$$\frac{F(n+1)}{F(n)}$$

b. Describe the behavior of the ratios. Are they approaching some number? Can you tell what number it might be?

4. The *Lucas numbers* use the same recursive rule as the Fibonacci numbers, but the base cases are $L(0) = 2$ and $L(1) = 1$.

a. Write the recursive definition of $L(n)$.

b. Calculate $L(10)$.

c. What happens to the ratio of consecutive Lucas numbers as n gets larger?

d. **Take It Further** Show that, in general, $L(n) = F(n-1) + F(n+1)$.

5. Here is another recursive definition with a two-term rule.

$$P(n) = \begin{cases} 2 & \text{if } n = 0 \\ 5 & \text{if } n = 1 \\ P(n-1) - P(n-2) & \text{if } n > 1 \end{cases}$$

a. Tabulate P for inputs from 0 to 10.

b. Determine the value of $P(50)$.

c. Is $P(2.5)$ defined? Why or why not?

d. What is the domain of P?

6. Here is an exponential function, the base of which is the golden ratio.

$$g(n) = \frac{1}{\sqrt{5}} \left(\frac{1 + \sqrt{5}}{2} \right)^n$$

Make a table for g using inputs 0 to 10. Approximate the outputs to four decimal places.

7. Adrian has a credit card balance of $1500 and pays $50 per month.

   a. With an APR of 18% compounded monthly, how much will Adrian owe at the end of two years?

   b. The credit card company will allow Adrian to make a minimum payment of 2.5% of the balance each month, instead of paying $50. If Adrian makes only the minimum payment, how much will he owe at the end of two years?

8. Adrian is considering switching to a credit card with an APR of 9.9% compounded monthly instead of 18%. Repeat Exercise 7 with this new interest rate. Determine how much money Adrian would save by using the card with the lower interest rate.

9. It is possible to count by 1's and 2's to any positive integer in more than one way, unless the integer is 1. For example, you can write 6 in many ways, including

$$6 = 2 + 2 + 2$$
$$6 = 2 + 1 + 1 + 1 + 1$$
$$6 = 1 + 1 + 2 + 1 + 1$$

   (Note that you count different orders of the same number of 1's and 2's.)

   a. Show that there are two ways to count to 2.

   b. How many ways are there to count to 3? to 4? to 5? to 6?

   c. Describe a pattern in your results.

   d. **Take It Further** Explain why the pattern emerges and will continue to exist for any larger number.

> **Remember...**
>
> $2 + 1$ and $1 + 2$ are different ways to count to 3.

10. Consider a new function that does a computation with three consecutive Fibonacci numbers. It takes the product of the greatest and least, and subtracts the square of the middle number:

$$s(n) = F(n + 1) \cdot F(n - 1) - (F(n))^2$$

   a. Tabulate this new function s using inputs from 1 to 10.

   b. Find a simpler function definition that agrees with your table.

11. Consider a new function that does a computation with two consecutive Fibonacci numbers. It squares the greater number, subtracts the product of the two numbers, and subtracts the square of the lesser number:

$$t(n) = (F(n + 1))^2 - F(n + 1)F(n) - (F(n))^2$$

   a. Tabulate this new function t using inputs from 1 to 10.

   b. Find a simpler function definition that agrees with your table.

> If $n = 3$, then
> $F(3) = 2$, $F(2) = 1$, and $F(4) = 3$. So
> $s(3) = 3 \cdot 1 - 2^2$
> $= -1$.

12. A function C satisfies the rule $C(n + 2) = -C(n)$

    a. If you knew that $C(2) = -1$, could you find $C(n)$ for all nonnegative integers n? Explain.

    b. If you knew that $C(2) = -1$ and $C(5) = 0$, could you find $C(n)$ for all nonnegative integers n? Explain.

    c. Take It Further Regardless of the value of $C(2)$ or $C(5)$, calculate

$$\sum_{k=0}^{15} C(k)$$

Go Online
PHSchool.com

For additional practice, go to **Web Code:** bga-0503

13. Standardized Test Prep Define C as

$$C(n) = \begin{cases} 1 & \text{if } n = 0 \\ -2 & \text{if } n = 1 \\ C(n-1) + C(n-2) & \text{if } n > 1 \end{cases}$$

What is $C(5)$?

    A. -9 **B.** -4 **C.** 0 **D.** -7

Maintain Your Skills

14. Each of these functions has the same recursive rule as the Fibonacci numbers, but they are all different functions. Tabulate each function using inputs from 0 to 7.

    a. $A(n) = \begin{cases} 0 & \text{if } n = 0 \\ 10 & \text{if } n = 1 \\ A(n-1) + A(n-2) & \text{if } n > 1 \end{cases}$

    b. $B(n) = \begin{cases} 7 & \text{if } n = 0 \\ 7 & \text{if } n = 1 \\ B(n-1) + B(n-2) & \text{if } n > 1 \end{cases}$

    c. $C(n) = \begin{cases} 7 & \text{if } n = 0 \\ 17 & \text{if } n = 1 \\ C(n-1) + C(n-2) & \text{if } n > 1 \end{cases}$

    d. $D(n) = \begin{cases} x & \text{if } n = 0 \\ y & \text{if } n = 1 \\ D(n-1) + D(n-2) & \text{if } n > 1 \end{cases}$

For the last function, each new output will be in terms of x and y.

5.4 Mathematical Induction

Here is the table from the start of Lesson 5.1.

Input	Output
0	3
1	8
2	13
3	18
4	23

You have seen two ways to define a function that could match the entries in such a table.

Closed-form definitions allow you to calculate an output directly from an input.

Recursive definitions allow you to calculate the output from some previous output.

These two functions both fit the table above, but have different definitions.

Closed form: $A(n) = 5n + 3$

Recursive:

$$B(n) = \begin{cases} 3 & \text{if } n = 0 \\ B(n-1) + 5 & \text{if } n > 0 \end{cases}$$

Minds in Action   episode 14

Tony and Derman are comparing functions A and B.

Tony   So, I entered A and B in my calculator. They have the same table for a long time.

Derman What, forever?

Tony   I'm not sure. I'll try some bigger numbers. Hey, B stopped working.

Derman Uh oh. When did that happen?

Tony   I can narrow it down. B(100) didn't work, but B(30) did. Okay, B(55) worked but B(56) won't.

Derman So the functions only agree up to 55? That seems weird.

Tony   I don't think the calculator's right. I'll bet if we used a different calculator or computer, we'd get different results.

Derman All right, maybe we can convince ourselves B will still work after it breaks on the calculator. What do we know about $B(56)$?

Tony It's five more than $B(55)$. That's what the definition says.

Derman That means it's five more than $A(55)$, since $A(55)$ and $B(55)$ were equal. The calculator said so.

Tony So now I just have to show that 5 more than $A(55)$ is $A(56)$. I think I'll need to write this down.

$$
\begin{aligned}
B(56) &= B(55) + 5 &&\text{(this is how B is defined)}\\
&= A(55) + 5 &&\text{($B(55) = A(55)$—calculator said so)}\\
&= (5 \cdot 55 + 3) + 5 &&\text{(this is how A is defined)}\\
&= (5 \cdot 55 + 5) + 3 &&\text{(basic rules of arithmetic)}\\
&= (5 \cdot 56) + 3 &&\text{(basic rules of arithmetic)}
\end{aligned}
$$

Derman Hey, I think you got it. That last thing is $A(56)$.

Tony So let's see, what did we do? If we're sure that $A(55)$ and $B(55)$ are equal, then $A(56)$ and $B(56)$ have to be equal.

Derman And $A(55)$ equals $B(55)$, because the calculator said so. What about $A(57)$ and $B(57)$?

For You to Do

1. Explain how Derman and Tony could show that $A(57) = B(57)$.

Tony I'm pretty sure there's nothing special about 55 or 56 here. If you believe me that A and B agree up to any number, I can show you that they'll agree at the next number.

Derman Okay, my favorite number is 123.

Tony Of course it is. All right, say I had a calculator that would tabulate both functions up to 123 and they agreed. But it ran out of memory at 124. I could say $A(123) = B(123)$, a fact you can check on your calculator. Then I'll show you that $A(124) = B(124)$, like this:

$$
\begin{aligned}
B(124) &= B(123) + 5\\
&= A(123) + 5\\
&= (5 \cdot 123 + 3) + 5\\
&= (5 \cdot 123 + 5) + 3\\
&= 5 \cdot 124 + 3\\
&= A(124)
\end{aligned}
$$

Derman Seems like you could do this with any number, or even a variable. Then you could prove it always works.

Tony As long as you have some starting point to work from.

Derman Very smooth.

For You to Do

2. Fill in reasons for each of the steps in Tony's calculation.

3. Repeat the argument using $A(n - 1) = B(n - 1)$ as a starting point and show that if $A(n - 1) = B(n - 1)$, then $A(n) = B(n)$.

Tony's method works for other functions. Consider this table.

n	H(n)
0	0
1	2
2	6
3	12
4	20

Here are two function definitions that fit the table, one closed-form and one recursive.

$$H(n) = n^2 + n$$

$$h(n) = \begin{cases} 0 & \text{if } n = 0 \\ h(n - 1) + 2n & \text{if } n > 0 \end{cases}$$

When entering these functions into a calculator, use different letters instead of uppercase and lowercase.

Example

Problem Suppose you know that $H(100) = h(100)$. Prove that $H(101) = h(101)$.

Solution Write $h(101)$ in terms of $h(100)$, then expand using the fact that $h(100) = H(100)$. Expand $H(101)$ as well, to show that it and $h(101)$ are equal.

$$
\begin{aligned}
h(101) &= h(100) + 2(101) \\
&= H(100) + 2(101) \\
&= (100^2 + 100) + 2(100 + 1) \\
&= 100^2 + 100 + 2 \cdot 100 + 2 \\
&= 100^2 + 3 \cdot 100 + 2
\end{aligned}
$$

$$
\begin{aligned}
H(101) &= 101^2 + 101 \\
&= (100 + 1)^2 + (100 + 1) \\
&= (100^2 + 2 \cdot 100 + 1) + (100 + 1) \\
&= 100^2 + 3 \cdot 100 + 2
\end{aligned}
$$

$h(101)$ and $H(101)$ equal the same expression, so they must be equal.

For You to Do

4. Repeat the process in the Example to show that if $h(n - 1) = H(n - 1)$, then $h(n) = H(n)$.

The statement "If $h(n - 1) = H(n - 1)$, then $h(n) = H(n)$" says that if these two functions agree at one integer, then they agree at the next one.

In the Example, the two functions are equal up to 100, so they are equal at 101, and that makes them equal at 102, and that makes them equal at 103, and so on. They are always equal for any nonnegative integer input.

This method of proof is called **mathematical induction.** You use it to show that a fact is true for some set of integers (typically positive or nonnegative ones). A proof by mathematical induction involves two parts:

Step 1 Show that the fact is true for the first few cases (often using tabulation by hand or by computer).

Step 2 Show that if the fact is true up to some integer $(n - 1)$, it must also be true for n.

This course primarily uses mathematical induction to show that a closed-form definition and a recursive definition agree for all nonnegative integers. However, you can also use induction to prove facts about summations, to prove identities and inequalities, and even to prove theorems in geometry. Induction is a key element in many proofs, such as those for the Binomial Theorem and for the *Four-Color Theorem*.

See the next lesson for some other examples of inductive proofs. See page 366 for a statement of the Four-Color Theorem.

Exercises *Practicing Habits of Mind*

Check Your Understanding

For Exercises 1–4,

- Tabulate the function for integer inputs from 0 to 5.

- Find an alternative function definition that fits the table—for example, a recursive definition for Exercise 1 and a closed-form definition for Exercise 2.

- Suppose you have checked that your two functions agree up to 1000. Explain why they will agree at 1001.

1. $M(a) = 3a + 5$

2. $k(n) = \begin{cases} 3 & \text{if } n = 0 \\ k(n - 1) + 7 & \text{if } n > 0 \end{cases}$

3. $j(n) = \begin{cases} 0 & \text{if } n = 0 \\ j(n - 1) + (2n - 1) & \text{if } n > 0 \end{cases}$

4. $f(x) = 2^x$

Exercises 5 through 8 each give two function definitions. Tabulate the functions to make sure they agree at the first few inputs. If they do, use mathematical induction to show they will agree at any nonnegative integer.

On your FML, use two different letters for the functions rather than an uppercase and lowercase letter.

5. $J(a) = 10a - 7$

$j(a) = \begin{cases} -7 & \text{if } a = 0 \\ j(a - 1) + 10 & \text{if } a > 0 \end{cases}$

6. $F(x) = x^2$

$f(x) = \begin{cases} 0 & \text{if } x = 0 \\ f(x - 1) + 2x - 1 & \text{if } x > 0 \end{cases}$

7. $G(n) = 4^n$

$g(n) = \begin{cases} 4 & \text{if } n = 0 \\ 4 \cdot g(n - 1) & \text{if } n > 0 \end{cases}$

8. Take It Further

$S(x) = \dfrac{x(x + 1)(2x + 1)}{6}$

$s(x) = \begin{cases} 0 & \text{if } x = 0 \\ s(x - 1) + x^2 & \text{if } x > 0 \end{cases}$

On Your Own

For Exercises 9–11,

- Tabulate the function for integer inputs from 0 to 5.
- Find an alternative function definition that fits the table—for example, a closed-form definition for Exercise 9.
- Suppose the two definitions agree up to 55. Explain why they will agree at 56.

9. $C(n) = \begin{cases} 4 & \text{if } n = 0 \\ C(n - 1) + 7 & \text{if } n > 0 \end{cases}$

10. $D(n) = (n - 1)^2$

11. $E(n) = \begin{cases} 0 & \text{if } n = 0 \\ E(n-1) + 4n & \text{if } n > 0 \end{cases}$

For Exercises 12–15, tabulate both functions to make sure they agree at the first few inputs. If they do, use mathematical induction to show they will always agree at any nonnegative integer.

12. $Q(a) = 3a + 2$

$q(a) = \begin{cases} 3 & \text{if } a = 0 \\ q(a-1) + 2 & \text{if } a > 0 \end{cases}$

13. $F(x) = x^2 + 3$

$f(x) = \begin{cases} 3 & \text{if } x = 0 \\ f(x-1) + 2x - 1 & \text{if } x > 0 \end{cases}$

14. $Z(n) = 2 \cdot 3^n$

$z(n) = \begin{cases} 2 & \text{if } n = 0 \\ 3 \cdot z(n-1) & \text{if } n > 0 \end{cases}$

15. Take It Further

$C(x) = \left(\dfrac{x(x+1)}{2} \right)^2$

$c(x) = \begin{cases} 0 & \text{if } x = 0 \\ c(x-1) + x^3 & \text{if } x > 0 \end{cases}$

Go Online
PHSchool.com

For additional practice, go to **Web Code:** bga-0504

16. Write About It How does a proof by mathematical induction establish that two functions agree for all nonnegative integers?

17. Standardized Test Prep Define p as

$$p(n) = \begin{cases} 1 & \text{if } n = 0 \\ p(n-1) \cdot n & \text{if } n > 0 \end{cases}$$

Which of the following agrees with p for all nonnegative integers?

A. $P(n) = n^2$ **B.** $P(n) = \dfrac{n(n-1)}{2}$

C. $P(n) = 3n - 2$ **D.** $P(n) = n!$

Maintain Your Skills

18. Calculate each sum as an expression in x. Then factor each result (if possible).

a. $\displaystyle\sum_{k=0}^{x-1} 1$ **b.** $\displaystyle\sum_{k=0}^{x-1} k$ **c.** $\displaystyle\sum_{k=0}^{x-1} \dfrac{k(k-1)}{2}$ **d.** $\displaystyle\sum_{k=0}^{x-1} \dfrac{k(k-1)(k-2)}{6}$

Yes, expression (a) is just 1 + 1 + 1... But how many 1's are there?

Ways to Think About Induction

Mathematical induction is a general method for proving a sequence of propositions—including arithmetic formulas, algebraic results, geometric facts, and more. Here is how it works.

Step 1 Set out the list of things you wish to prove.

Step 2 Show directly that the base cases are true.

Step 3 Prove that if the propositions are true for every case up to $(n - 1)$, then the nth proposition must be true.

The conclusion is that all propositions in the sequence must be true.

In your proofs so far, these steps have looked like this:

Step 1 The goal is to prove two functions agree for all integers $n \geq 0$.

Step 2 Use a table to check that the functions agree at the first few inputs, including the base cases.

Step 3 Show that if the two functions agree at $(n - 1)$, then they must agree at n.

The conclusion is that the two functions agree for all nonnegative integers.

Induction is like an infinite line of dominoes, set up so that if one falls, it will hit the next one, which will fall, and so on.

This statement is true:

> If domino $(n - 1)$ falls, it will hit domino n.
> So domino n will fall as well.

But the dominoes do not just fall automatically. To start the process, the first one must fall down. That is the base case.

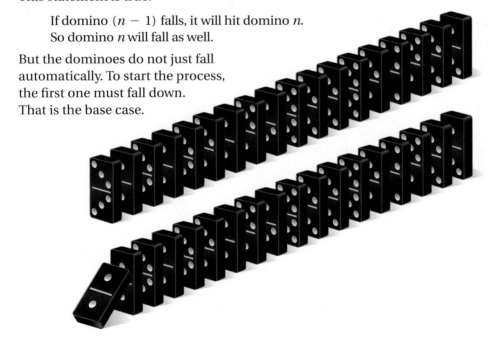

Now, this statement is true:

> If domino $(n - 1)$ falls, it will hit domino n. So domino n will fall as well. Domino 1 has fallen, so all the dominoes will fall.

Here is a geometric example. You can take a polygon and divide it into triangles by drawing diagonals, making sure none of the diagonals intersect each other.

 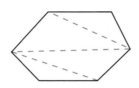 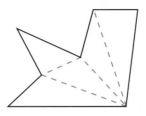

1. Copy each polygon without the diagonals, and find a different way to divide it into triangles by drawing diagonals.

2. Did you get a different number of triangles than in the example? Is it possible to get a different number of triangles?

3. Copy and complete this table. You may need to draw a few more shapes to help you fill it in.

Number of Vertices	Number of Triangles You Can Form
3	1
4	▨
5	▨
6	▨
7	▨
8	▨
9	▨

Experiments can lead you to a conjecture for the number of triangles. But how could you prove you are right? You could do it by induction.

Example

Problem Prove that for a polygon with n vertices, the number of triangles formed by drawing a set of nonintersecting diagonals is $T(n) = n - 2$.

Solution

- Your base case is $n = 3$. Here the polygon IS a triangle (you cannot draw any diagonals). $T(3) = 3 - 2 = 1$, so your formula works when $n = 3$. For another base case, consider any quadrilateral. You can form $T(4) = 4 - 2 = 2$ triangles by drawing an interior diagonal.

- You assume that your statement holds for polygons having anywhere from 3 to $(n - 1)$ vertices. You must show that this implies that your formula holds for any polygon that has n vertices.

Consider a polygon P with $n > 3$ vertices. Pick two vertices that have an interior diagonal between them. Call these vertices v and v'. Draw the diagonal.

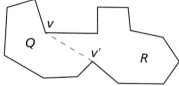

Polygon P has n vertices

This diagonal splits polygon P into two polygons, Q and R, having q and r vertices, respectively. Each of these polygons leaves out at least one vertex of P, and each has at least three vertices. So $3 \leq q \leq n - 1$ and $3 \leq r \leq n - 1$.

By assumption, Q divides into $q - 2$ triangles and R then divides into $r - 2$ triangles. Together, they make up polygon P, so

$$T(n) = (q - 2) + (r - 2) = q + r - 4$$

Now, comparing the number of vertices in Q and R to the number of vertices in P gives you

$$q + r = n + 2$$

because the vertices v and v' are counted twice (once in Q and once in R).

If you put the two equations together, you have

$$\begin{aligned} T(n) &= q + r - 4 \\ &= n + 2 - 4 \\ &= n - 2 \end{aligned}$$

This shows that if $T(k) = k - 2$ for $3 \leq k \leq n - 1$, then $T(n) = n - 2$. This completes your induction proof. You conclude:

$$T(n) = n - 2 \text{ for all integers } n \geq 3$$

The induction arguments needed to show that recursive and closed-form definitions give functions that agree are usually short and clear. Other induction proofs, however, are long and complex. The proof of the Four-Color Theorem is an example of a complicated induction. This theorem says that if you have a map of countries that are all solid areas, without holes or separated colonies, then four colors suffice to color the map so that no two countries sharing a common border have the same color.

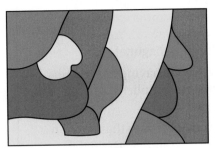

A four-color map

In 1852 Francis Guthrie, a mathematics student in England, conjectured that this was true. In 1890, Percy Heawood showed that no more than five colors are ever necessary, but the Four-Color Theorem remained unproven until 1976. Kenneth Appel and Wolfgang Haken of the University of Illinois established its truth using a computer to check over 1000 base cases. Then they proved the induction claim that if all the base cases were valid, the theorem must be true for all larger maps. As of 2008, the challenge of finding a proof that does not rely on a computer remains open.

If you try to color maps on your own, keep in mind that two regions which just meet at a point can share the same color. But regions with the same color cannot share a boundary that is a segment or curve.

Go Online
PHSchool.com

For more problems on mathematical induction, go to **Web Code: bge-9031**

Exercises *Practicing Habits of Mind*

Check Your Understanding

For Exercises 1 and 2, tabulate both functions to make sure they agree at 0. If they do, use mathematical induction to show they will agree at any nonnegative integer.

1. $P(n) = 2^n + 2$ $\qquad p(n) = \begin{cases} 3 & \text{if } n = 0 \\ 2 \cdot p(n-1) - 2 & \text{if } n > 0 \end{cases}$

2. $H(x) = \dfrac{x(x+1)}{2}$ $\qquad h(x) = \begin{cases} 0 & \text{if } x = 0 \\ h(x-1) + x & \text{if } x > 0 \end{cases}$

3. **Write About It** Explain how you can use the results from the In-Class Experiment to justify this statement:

> In a polygon with n sides, the sum of the measures of the interior angles is $(n - 2) \cdot 180°$.

4. Theorem 5.1 is the Two-Color Theorem.

Theorem 5.1

Use straight lines extending infinitely in either direction to draw a map that divides the plane into any number of regions. Two colors are enough to color the map so that no two regions with a common border have the same color.

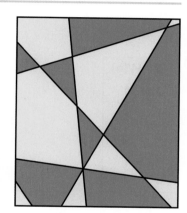

a. Check a few base cases. Do two colors suffice to color the map if you draw only one line? If you draw two parallel lines? If you draw two intersecting lines? If you draw three lines?

b. Suppose you know that up to some number $(n - 1)$ of lines, two colors will suffice. Prove that two colors suffice for n lines.

5. **What's Wrong Here?** Lester says that all sets of n horses are the same color. He offers this "proof":

Lester: I need a base case, and that's $n = 1$. Obviously, all sets of 1 horse are the same color. Now I'm going to prove that if it's true for $n - 1$, it's true for n. Show me the n horses, and I set one off to the side and look at the rest. They must be the same color, since it's true for $n - 1$. Then I bring in the one I set off to the side and send another one off. Now those $n - 1$ horses are the same color, and of course it has to be the same color as the other set, since the horses that stayed in both times did not change colors. So all n horses are the same color, and by induction this is true for any n.

What is wrong with this proof? It clearly cannot be sound, can it?

In Exercises 6–11, find a closed-form and a recursive function definition for the table. Then use mathematical induction to show that your two definitions must agree for all nonnegative integers.

6.

n	E(n)
0	2
1	4
2	6
3	8
4	10

7.

n	F(n)
0	1
1	4
2	7
3	10
4	13

8.

x	K(x)
0	1
1	2
2	5
3	10
4	17

For Exercise 6, the closed-form definition might be $E(n) = 2n + 2$. Find a recursive definition. Then use induction to prove the definitions must continue to agree for larger n.

9.

n	P(n)
0	1
1	3
2	9
3	27
4	81

10.

a	W(a)
0	1
1	$\frac{1}{2}$
2	$\frac{1}{4}$
3	$\frac{1}{8}$
4	$\frac{1}{16}$

11.

t	ε(t)
0	2
1	3
2	5
3	9
4	17

Go Online
PHSchool.com

For additional practice, go to **Web Code: bga-0505**

12. Standardized Test Prep Which of the following does NOT play a role in inductive proof?

A. assuming that the statement is true for all counting numbers through $(n - 1)$

B. verifying that the statement is true for one or more base cases

C. showing that the statement is true for all numbers between $(n - 1)$ and n

D. showing that the statement must be true for the counting number n

Maintain Your Skills

13. Show that each of these is true.

a. $\displaystyle\sum_{k=0}^{n-1} k = \frac{n(n - 1)}{2}$

b. $\displaystyle\sum_{k=0}^{n-1} \frac{k(k - 1)}{2} = \frac{n(n - 1)(n - 2)}{6}$

c. Take It Further

$\displaystyle\sum_{k=0}^{n-1} \frac{k(k - 1)(k - 2)}{6} = \frac{n(n - 1)(n - 2)(n - 3)}{4!}$

By convention,
$\displaystyle\sum_{k=0}^{-1} g(k) = 0$
for any function g.

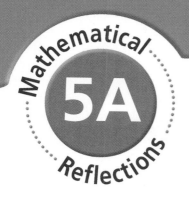
In this investigation, you looked at recursive function definitions. You learned how to use induction to prove that two functions, one with a closed-form definition and one with a recursive definition, agree for an infinite number of inputs. The following questions will help you summarize what you have learned.

1. Define f recursively by

$$f(n) = \begin{cases} k & \text{if } n = 0 \\ f(n - 1) + \frac{1}{3} & \text{if } n > 0 \end{cases}$$

If $f(20) = -3$, find the value of k.

2. Find a closed-form definition for a function that agrees with f for all integers $n \geq 0$.

$$f(n) = \begin{cases} 0 & \text{if } n = 0 \\ f(n - 1) + 4n & \text{if } n > 0 \end{cases}$$

3. Use induction to show these two functions must agree for all integers $a \geq 0$.

$$J(a) = 8a - 5$$

$$j(a) = \begin{cases} -5 & \text{if } a = 0 \\ j(a - 1) + 8 & \text{if } a > 0 \end{cases}$$

4. Derman says his calculator "broke" while finding $f(36)$ for this function:

$$f(n) = \begin{cases} 3 & \text{if } n = 0 \\ f(n - 1) + 5 - 0.2f(n - 1) & \text{if } n > 0 \end{cases}$$

What could Derman do to make it possible to calculate $f(36)$?

5. Find a recursive function definition that agrees with

$$f(n) = n^2 + 10$$

for any integer $n \geq 0$.

6. What are the differences between a closed-form definition and a recursive definition for a function?

7. How can you prove that a closed-form and a recursive function definition agree at each of infinitely many inputs?

8. What happens to the ratio of consecutive Fibonacci numbers?

Vocabulary

In this investigation, you learned these terms. Make sure you understand what each one means and how to use it.

- base case
- closed-form definition
- Fibonacci sequence
- mathematical induction
- recursive definition

Fitting Functions to Tables

In *Fitting Functions to Tables*, you will use a difference table to study a function. You will use numbers from the difference table and numbers from Pascal's Triangle to find a polynomial that fits a function table. You will use this method to find polynomials that describe sums of powers.

By the end of this investigation, you will be able to answer questions like these.

1. If the third differences in the table of a polynomial function are all 24, what can you say about that function?

2. What are the Mahler polynomials?

3. How can you use differences to find a polynomial function that fits a table?

You will learn how to

- find a polynomial function that fits a difference table

- explain how the up-and-over rule of difference tables relates to Pascal's Triangle

- quickly find rules for summations, like the sum of the first *n* squares

You will develop these habits and skills:

- Connect the properties of Pascal's Triangle with properties of difference tables.

- Construct and verify functions that fit tables.

- Work with polynomials in normal and factored form.

- Work with summations.

Charles Babbage (1791–1871) designed this difference engine, a mechanical device for using difference tables to calculate the outputs of polynomial functions.

Activating Prior Knowledge
Exploring New Ideas

In CME Project *Algebra 2*, you studied methods for fitting a function to a table. This investigation describes a method for fitting polynomials to tables where the inputs are the nonnegative integers. This method, known as Newton's Difference Formula, is more specific than some of the methods in *Algebra 2* (such as Lagrange Interpolation), but it has many theoretical applications and is closely connected to Pascal's Triangle.

For You to Explore

1. Find two different ways to fit a function to this table.

Input	Output
0	15
1	0
2	−9
3	−12
4	−9
5	0
6	15
7	36

2. **Write About It** Describe what you would do to find a polynomial function N, that fits this table.

x	$N(x)$
0	1
1	−1
2	11
3	49
4	125
5	251
6	439
7	701

3. Suppose you know that E is a quadratic function with an input-output table that starts like this.

x	$E(x)$	Δ
0	3	6
1	9	10
2	19	▦
3	33	▦
4	▦	▦
5	▦	▦
6	▦	▦
7	▦	▦
8	▦	

Without finding the formula for $E(x)$, find the value of $E(8)$.

4. Here is a table for a function f, with a lot of information missing.

n	$f(n)$	Δ	Δ^2	Δ^3
0	0	1	6	6
1	▦	▦	▦	6
2	8	▦	▦	6
3	▦	▦	▦	6
4	▦	▦	▦	6
5	▦	▦	▦	6
6	▦	▦	▦	
7	▦	▦		
8	▦			

Find the value of $f(8)$.

Remember...

The Δ column contains the differences of consecutive outputs. The first two entries are filled in: $6 = 9 - 3$ and $10 = 19 - 9$.

The Δ^2 column contains the differences of the numbers in the Δ column, not the squares of those numbers.

On Your Own

5. Calculate $f(8)$ without filling in anything else for the difference table at the right.

a	f(a)	Δ
0	17	9
1	▦	−16
2	▦	7
3	▦	2
4	▦	12
5	▦	−8
6	▦	−7
7	▦	4
8	▦	

6. The table at the right is for a cubic function P

  a. Copy and complete the table.

  b. Describe some patterns you see in the table.

x	P(x)	Δ	Δ²	Δ³
0	0	0	0	1
1	▦	▦	▦	1
2	▦	▦	▦	1
3	▦	▦	▦	1
4	▦	▦	▦	1
5	10	▦	▦	1
6	20	▦	▦	1
7	▦	▦	▦	1
8	▦	▦	▦	1

7. A cubic polynomial function P fits the input-output table from Exercise 6.

  a. What are the zeros of this polynomial?

  b. Write $P(x)$ in factored form, $P(x) = A(x - r_1)(x - r_2)(x - r_3)$.

8. Tabulate each function using inputs from 0 to 8. Then calculate difference columns until you find a constant column of differences.

  a. $f(x) = 7x - 3$ **b.** $g(x) = x^2 - 5x + 4$

  c. $h(x) = 10x^2 - 50x + 40$ **d.** $j(x) = 4x - x^2$

  e. $k(x) = 4x - x^3$ **f.** $m(x) = 5x^3 - 20x$

9. The table at the right is for N from Problem 2.

x	N(x)
0	1
1	−1
2	11
3	49
4	125
5	251
6	439
7	701

a. Build a complete difference table for N.

b. Using any method you like, find a closed-form definition for N.

Maintain Your Skills

10. For each function $f(x)$, calculate and simplify the expression

$$f(x + 1) - f(x)$$

a. $f(x) = x^2$

b. $f(x) = 7x - 3$

c. $f(x) = \dfrac{x(x - 1)}{2}$

d. $f(x) = 2^x$

11. Copy each input-output table and fill in the Δ column. Then find a function that agrees with the outputs of the Δ column.

a.

Input	Output	Δ
0	0	▪
1	1	▪
2	4	▪
3	9	▪
4	16	▪
5	25	

b.

Input	Output	Δ
0	−3	▪
1	4	▪
2	11	▪
3	18	▪
4	25	▪
5	32	

c.

Input	Output	Δ
0	0	▪
1	0	▪
2	1	▪
3	3	▪
4	6	▪
5	10	

d.

Input	Output	Δ
0	1	▪
1	2	▪
2	4	▪
3	8	▪
4	16	▪
5	32	

Properties of Difference Tables

One way to see whether a table could have come from a linear function is to compare changes in output to changes in input. If the ratio of the changes is constant, then a linear function fits the table.

Take this table, for example:

Input, x	Output, $M(x)$
0	3
1	8
2	13
3	18
4	23

$\frac{8-3}{1-0} = 5$, $\frac{13-8}{2-1} = 5$, $\frac{18-13}{3-2} = 5$, and so on. M is a linear function.

When the inputs are evenly spaced, making a **difference table** gives another way to explain whether a linear function fits the table. You can calculate differences by subtracting each output from the one before it. There are a few different possible notations, but one way is to write another column after the output and label it Δ for "difference":

x	$M(x)$	Δ
0	3	5
1	8	5
2	13	5
3	18	5
4	23	

See the TI-Nspire Handbook on p. 704 for a refresher on how to make a difference table using a spreadsheet.

Now you can describe the outputs using sums instead of ratios: $M(1)$ is $M(0) = 3$ plus the difference 5. The next output, $M(2)$, is 3 plus two 5's. You could calculate $M(4)$ as

$$3 + 5 + 5 + 5 + 5 = 3 + 4 \cdot 5$$

So $M(4)$ is 3 plus four 5's. In general, $M(n)$ is 3 plus n 5's. This general rule is written as $M(n) = 3 + 5n$.

For higher-degree polynomials, the entries in the difference column will not be constant, but there is hope—continue taking differences. The notation Δ^2 means the column of second differences, found by subtracting entries in the Δ column.

Here is a complete difference table for function N of Exercise 9 from Lesson 5.6:

x	N(x)	Δ	Δ²	Δ³	Δ⁴	Δ⁵	Δ⁶	Δ⁷
0	1	−2	14	12	0	0	0	0
1	−1	12	26	12	0	0	0	
2	11	38	38	12	0	0		
3	49	76	50	12	0			
4	125	126	62	12				
5	251	188	74					
6	439	262						
7	701							

> **Be efficient.** This table might feel a little too complete. You can stop when you reach a constant column.

The highlighted 50, for example, is $126 - 76$.

For Discussion

1. Suppose the last two rows of this table were missing. How could you use the table to determine what belongs in those rows?

2. Copy the table. Circle the number 125. Then shade five numbers in the table, including the 1 at the top of the N(x) column (the output column), that you could add to make 125.

> The five numbers to shade are near one another in a systematic way.

These two properties of difference tables are named

- **Up-and-over:** Any number in the table (other than inputs) is the sum of two numbers—the number directly above it and the number directly to the right of the one above it.

- **Hockey stick:** Any number in the table (other than inputs) is the sum of the top value in its column and all the numbers above it in the column immediately to its right.

For You to Do

3. Find the values of A, B, and C in this difference table.

Input	Output	Δ	Δ²
0	0	1	A
1	1	4	5
2	5	9	▨
3	▨	16	▨
4	▨	25	11
5	▨	B	
6	C		

Alice writes down five numbers, then adds consecutive pairs to form four numbers. She adds those four numbers in the same way. She continues adding until there is only one number left. Suppose her starting numbers are

$$1 \quad -2 \quad 14 \quad 12 \quad 0$$

Her second row reads

$$-1 \quad 12 \quad 26 \quad 12$$

4. What is Alice's final number?

5. Try the experiment with other starting numbers. How is the final number related to the original five numbers? Is there a formula?

Exercises *Practicing Habits of Mind*

Check Your Understanding

1. a. Copy and complete this table for $f(x) = ax^2 + bx + c$.

Input, x	Output, $f(x)$	Δ	Δ^2
0	c	▪	▪
1	$a + b + c$	▪	▪
2	▪	▪	▪
3	▪	▪	▪
4	▪	▪	
5	▪		

b. Use the table to write expressions for $\Delta f(x)$ and $\Delta^2 f(x)$ in terms of x. Write your expressions in normal form.

c. What does this exercise say about difference tables of quadratic functions?

2. **Take It Further**

   a. Copy and complete this difference table for the generic cubic function $f(x) = ax^3 + bx^2 + cx + d$.

Input, x	Output, $f(x)$	Δ	Δ^2	Δ^3
0	d	▦	▦	▦
1	$a + b + c + d$	▦	▦	▦
2	$8a + 4b + 2c + d$	▦	▦	▦
3	▦	▦	▦	
4	▦	▦		
5	$125a + 25b + 5c + d$			

   b. Use the table to write expresssions for $\Delta f(x)$, $\Delta^2 f(x)$ and $\Delta^3 f(x)$ in terms of x. Write your expressions in normal form.

   c. What does this exercise say about difference tables of cubic functions?

3. You have a table for an unknown function. You make a difference table, and find that all the second differences are 10.

   a. A polynomial fits the table. What is the smallest degree it could have?

   b. Is this the only kind of function that could fit the table? Explain.

   Exercises 4–6 use function N from the lesson. Here is its complete difference table.

x	$N(x)$	Δ	Δ^2	Δ^3	Δ^4	Δ^5	Δ^6	Δ^7
0	1	-2	14	12	0	0	0	0
1	-1	12	26	12	0	0	0	
2	11	38	38	12	0	0		
3	49	76	50	12	0			
4	125	126	62	12				
5	251	188	74					
6	439	262						
7	701							

4. a. Suppose you did not know that $N(4) = 125$. What two numbers in the $x = 3$ row could you add to get 125?

    b. Suppose you did not know those two numbers, either. How could you use the 11 and two 38's in the $x = 2$ row to get 125?

    c. You could also use four numbers in the $x = 1$ row to get 125. How?

    d. You could use five numbers in the $x = 0$ row to get 125. How?

5. Describe, as completely as possible, how to generate the value $N(5) = 251$ from the rows above it.

6. Without finding the closed-form definition for N, find a possible value for $N(10)$. Justify your claim. Can you write $N(10)$ in terms of the numbers in the top row?

> You can go all the way to the top, and describe $N(5)$ in terms of the numbers across the top row.

On Your Own

7. Repeating the In-Class Experiment, Alice started with the four numbers below.

$$1000 \qquad 100 \qquad 10 \qquad 1$$

She added consecutive pairs until there was only one number left.

    a. What was the final number?

    b. Repeat Alice's experiment with variable letters a, b, c, d as the starting numbers. What happens?

8. Write About It Describe, in your own words, why the up-and-over property works in a difference table. Include an example.

9. Here is a difference table with a lot of missing numbers.

Input, n	Output, $P(n)$	Δ
0	12	-5
1	▨	-5
2	▨	-5
3	▨	-5
4	▨	-5
5	▨	-5
6	▨	-5

Go Online

PHSchool.com

For additional practice, go to **Web Code:** bga-0507

    a. Calculate $P(6)$ and describe how you did it.

    b. Assuming the Δ column entries continue to be -5, what will be the value of $P(97)$?

    c. Find a closed-form definition for $P(n)$ that fits the table for $n \geq 0$.

10. According to its table, what might be the degree of the polynomial function N from Exercises 4–6. What might be its leading coefficient? Explain.

11. Here is a table for function g.

Input, n	Output, $g(n)$
0	0
1	1
2	14
3	45
4	100
5	185

a. Explain why g cannot be linear or quadratic.

b. If g is cubic, what is its leading coefficient?

12. **Take It Further**

a. Use the algebraic definition of the Δ operation, $\Delta f(x) = f(x + 1) - f(x)$, to prove that if f is a degree-n polynomial (with $n > 0$), then Δf is a polynomial with degree $n - 1$.

b. Show that if f is a degree-n polynomial, then $\Delta^n f$ must be constant and nonzero.

c. Prove that if f is a polynomial so that Δf is a polynomial with degree $n - 1$, then f has degree n.

13. **Standardized Test Prep** This is a difference table, partially filled in, for a polynomial function of degree 4.

Input	Output	Δ	Δ^2	Δ^3
0	▦	▦	−7	−2
1	▦	−7	▦	−1
2	−7	▦	▦	0
3	E	▦	▦	1
4	▦	▦	▦	2

What is the value of E?

A. 6　　　　　B. −14　　　　　C. −21　　　　　D. −23

Maintain Your Skills

14. Find a function that agrees with this difference table.

Input, x	Output, $f(x)$	Δ	Δ^2
0	3	4	2
1	▣	▣	2
2	▣	▣	2
3	▣	▣	2
4	▣	▣	
5	▣		

Start by looking at the polynomials $f(x) = x^n$.

15. Find a function that agrees with this difference table.

Input	Output	Δ	Δ^2
0	m	n	p
1	▣	▣	p
2	▣	▣	p
3	▣	▣	p
4	▣	▣	
5	▣		

You might find Exercise 1 helpful.

The Pascal Connection

There is a connection between the differences you find in a difference table and the numbers in Pascal's Triangle.

For You to Do

The difference operator Δ turns a function into another function. If f is any function, Δf is another function, defined by

$$\Delta f(x) = f(x + 1) - f(x)$$

Let $f(x) = x^2$, $g(x) = x^3$, and $h(x) = x^4$. Find a polynomial that defines each function.

1. Δf

2. Δg

3. Δh

Here is the difference table for N from the preceding lessons.

x	N(x)	Δ	Δ^2	Δ^3	Δ^4	Δ^5	Δ^6	Δ^7
0	1	−2	14	12	0	0	0	0
1	−1	12	26	12	0	0	0	
2	11	38	38	12	0	0		
3	49	76	50	12	0			
4	125	126	62	12				
5	251	188	74					
6	439	262						
7	701							

The value of $N(3)$ is given as 49. However, you can calculate $N(3)$ from the numbers above it, using the up-and-over property: $N(3) = 11 + 38$. But you can in turn calculate those numbers from the numbers above them, all the way to the top row of the table:

$$N(3) = 49$$
$$= 11 + 38$$
$$= (-1 + 12) + (12 + 26) = -1 + 2 \cdot 12 + 26$$
$$= [1 + (-2)] + 2 \cdot (-2 + 14) + (14 + 12)$$
$$= 1 + 3 \cdot (-2) + 3 \cdot 14 + 12$$

Here is the same information again, with a little more emphasis on coefficients.

$$N(3) = \mathbf{1} \cdot 49$$
$$= \mathbf{1} \cdot 11 + \mathbf{1} \cdot 38$$
$$= \mathbf{1} \cdot (-1) + \mathbf{2} \cdot 12 + \mathbf{1} \cdot 26$$
$$= \mathbf{1} \cdot 1 + \mathbf{3} \cdot (-2) + \mathbf{3} \cdot 14 + \mathbf{1} \cdot 12$$

In short, you can calculate $N(3)$ using the top row of the difference table, multiplying by coefficients from Pascal's Triangle. Here is the same process for $N(4)$, using the up-and-over property.

$$N(4) = \mathbf{1} \cdot 125$$
$$= \mathbf{1} \cdot 49 + \mathbf{1} \cdot 76$$
$$= \mathbf{1} \cdot (11 + 38) + \mathbf{1} \cdot (38 + 38)$$
$$= \mathbf{1} \cdot 11 + \mathbf{2} \cdot 38 + \mathbf{1} \cdot 38$$
$$= \mathbf{1} \cdot (-1 + 12) + \mathbf{2} \cdot (12 + 26) + \mathbf{1} \cdot (26 + 12)$$
$$= \mathbf{1} \cdot (-1) + \mathbf{3} \cdot 12 + \mathbf{3} \cdot 26 + \mathbf{1} \cdot 12$$
$$= \mathbf{1} \cdot [1 + (-2)] + \mathbf{3} \cdot (-2 + 14) + \mathbf{3} \cdot (14 + 12) + \mathbf{1} \cdot (12 + 0)$$
$$= \mathbf{1} \cdot 1 + \mathbf{4} \cdot (-2) + \mathbf{6} \cdot 14 + \mathbf{4} \cdot 12 + \mathbf{1} \cdot 0$$

Again, you can calculate the result using the top row of the difference table, multiplying by coefficients from Pascal's Triangle.

For You to Do

4. Write $N(5)$ and $N(6)$ as expressions based on the top row of the table, then verify that the values are correct.

Developing Habits of Mind

Understand the process. To find $N(10)$, you could say something like "Go to the 10th row of Pascal's Triangle and start writing out the numbers"—or you could use $\binom{n}{k}$ notation. The expression $\binom{5}{2}$, for example, designates the second number in the fifth row of Pascal's Triangle. Just remember that the top row is row number zero, and in each row the left-most entry is entry number zero.

$$\binom{0}{0} = 1$$
$$\binom{1}{0} = 1 \qquad \binom{1}{1} = 1$$
$$\binom{2}{0} = 1 \qquad \binom{2}{1} = 2 \qquad \binom{2}{2} = 1$$
$$\binom{3}{0} = 1 \qquad \binom{3}{1} = 3 \qquad \binom{3}{2} = 3 \qquad \binom{3}{3} = 1$$
$$\binom{4}{0} = 1 \qquad \binom{4}{1} = 4 \qquad \binom{4}{2} = 6 \qquad \binom{4}{3} = 4 \qquad \binom{4}{4} = 1$$
$$\binom{5}{0} = 1 \qquad \binom{5}{1} = 5 \qquad \binom{5}{2} = 10 \qquad \binom{5}{3} = 10 \qquad \binom{5}{4} = 5 \qquad \binom{5}{5} = 1$$

These binomial coefficients are named for what happens when you expand expressions like $(x + y)^5$.

So, for example, you can write $N(5)$ as

$$N(5) = \binom{5}{0} \cdot 1 + \binom{5}{1} \cdot (-2) + \binom{5}{2} \cdot 14 + \binom{5}{3} \cdot 12$$

Why stop here? Why not continue to $\binom{5}{5}$?

The notation used for binomial coefficients makes it clear how to find $N(10)$. Just replace all the 5's by 10's. You are done.

While $\binom{n}{k}$ is the standard mathematical notation, most calculators use nCr instead. For example, $nCr(5, 3)$ should return 10.

For Discussion

5. Calculate $N(10)$ and $N(20)$ using this method.

6. Are these the only possible values for $N(10)$ and $N(20)$? Explain.

Exercises *Practicing Habits of Mind*

Check Your Understanding

1. a. Copy and complete this difference table for
$a(x) = 3x^2 - 5x + 10$.

Input, x	Output, a(x)	Δ	Δ²
0	10	▪	▪
1	8	▪	▪
2	12	▪	▪
3	▪	▪	▪
4	▪	▪	▪
5	▪	▪	
6	▪		

b. Show how to find $a(5)$ from the numbers in the top row.

c. Calculate

$$10 \cdot \binom{6}{0} - 2 \cdot \binom{6}{1} + 6 \cdot \binom{6}{2}$$

Find these numbers in row 6 of Pascal's Triangle.

2. Suppose f is a polynomial function with $f(0) = f(1) = 0$ and $f(2) = 1$.

   a. What is the minimum possible degree of f?

   b. Write a closed-form definition for f

   c. Copy and complete the table of first and second differences.

Input, x	Output, $f(x)$	Δ	Δ^2
0	0	▦	▦
1	0	▦	▦
2	1	▦	▦
3	▦	▦	▦
4	▦	▦	▦
5	▦	▦	
6	▦		

3. Suppose g is a polynomial function of minimal degree with $g(x) = 0$ when $x = 0, 1, 2$ and $g(x) = 1$ when $x = 3$. Find $g(x)$ in factored form.

4. **a.** Find the values of $\binom{8}{0}$, $\binom{8}{1}$, and $\binom{8}{2}$.

   b. Copy and complete this table of differences.

n	$T(n)$	Δ	Δ^2
0	a	b	c
1	▦	▦	c
2	▦	▦	c
3	▦	▦	c
4	▦	▦	c
5	▦	▦	c
6	▦	▦	c
7	▦	▦	c
8	▦	▦	c

Evaluate these using nCr, or find row 8 of Pascal's Triangle.

5. Use your CAS to model $g(x) = \binom{x}{3}$.

a. Based on the degree of g, how many differences must you take before you arrive at a constant?

b. Copy and complete this difference table for g.

x	g(x)	Δ	Δ²	Δ³	Δ⁴
0	■	■	■	■	■
1	■	■	■	■	■
2	■	■	■	■	■
3	■	■	■	■	■
4	■	■	■	■	
5	■	■	■		
6	■	■			
7	■				

c. Locate the outputs of g in Pascal's Triangle.

d. Locate the numbers in the Δ column in Pascal's Triangle.

6. Here is a difference table for $p(x) = 2^x$, an exponential function.

x	p(x)	Δ	Δ²	Δ³	Δ⁴	Δ⁵	Δ⁶
0	1	■	■	■	■	■	■
1	2	■	■	■	■	■	
2	4	■	■	■	■		
3	8	■	■	■			
4	16	■	■				
5	32	■					
6	64						

a. Copy and complete the table.

b. Express $p(4)$ in terms of the top row of your table.

c. What is the sum of the numbers in row 6 of Pascal's Triangle?

Remember...
The 1 at the top of Pascal's Triangle is row 0.

7. A quadratic function h has a table that starts like the one at the right.

Input, x	Output, g(x)	Δ	Δ²
0	10	−18	6
1	−8	−12	6
2	−20	−6	6
3	−26	0	6
4	−26	6	6

a. Determine the value of $h(7)$.

b. Determine the value of $h(10)$.

c. Determine the value of $h(97)$.

Hint: $\binom{10}{2} = 45$.

8. Kellie says that she can use the method in Exercise 7 to find $h(x)$ for any x.

Kellie: To do $h(97)$ I have to use a calculator unless I want to spend all day filling out a difference table or making a huge Pascal's Triangle. I can type

$$10 \cdot nCr(97, 0) - 18 \cdot nCr(97, 1) + 6 \cdot nCr(97, 2)$$

Kellie: But it looks like I should be able to do this for any number. So I just enter the entire expression at once, and it seems to work for any x:

$$h(x) = 10 \cdot nCr(x, 0) - 18 \cdot nCr(x, 1) + 6 \cdot nCr(x, 2)$$

a. Calculate $h(x)$ this way. Check that it gives the correct values for $h(1)$, $h(7)$, and $h(97)$.

b. Repeat Exercise 14 from Lesson 5.7 using this method.

9. a. Find a quadratic function f with $f(0) = 5$, $f(1) = -3$, and $f(2) = -15$.

b. Find a cubic function g with $g(0) = 5$, $g(1) = -3$, $g(2) = -15$, and $g(3) = -25$.

10. a. In this table, only the Δ column is given. Copy the table and fill in the output column, in a way that makes the numbers in the Δ column valid.

b. Now, find a second way to fill in the output column that also makes the numbers in the Δ column valid.

Input	Output	Δ
0	▨	12
1	▨	−6
2	▨	−20
3	▨	0
4	▨	12
5	▨	2
6	▨	

Go Online
PHSchool.com

For additional practice, go to **Web Code: bga-0508**

11. Find a function for which the difference column is always exactly twice the function output. In algebraic terms, $\Delta f(x) = 2f(x)$ for all x.

12. **Take It Further** Find a function for which the entries in the difference column are the Fibonacci numbers: 0, 1, 1, 2, . . .

13. **Standardized Test Prep** This is the top row of the difference table for a certain cubic function.

Input, x	Output, $f(x)$	Δ	Δ^2	Δ^3
0	6	-2	3	1

What is $f(5)$?

A. 36   **B.** -36 **C.** 8   **D.** -8

Maintain Your Skills

14. a. Find the values of $\binom{7}{0}$, $\binom{7}{1}$, $\binom{7}{2}$, and $\binom{7}{3}$.

b. Copy and complete this table of differences.

n	$C(n)$	Δ	Δ^2	Δ^3
0	a	b	c	d
1	■	■	■	d
2	■	■	■	d
3	■	■	■	d
4	■	■	■	d
5	■	■	■	d
6	■	■	■	d
7	■	■	■	d

Leave room, since the expressions farther down will involve several variables.

5.9 Newton's Difference Formula

In the last lesson, you learned how to use the numbers across the top row of a difference table, along with binomial coefficients, to find the outputs of a polynomial function that fits the table. This lesson goes further, showing how to use the numbers across the top row to find an actual polynomial that defines a function that fits the table.

Example

Problem Here is a table for a cubic polynomial function *f*. Find *f*(10).

x	f(x)
0	5
1	15
2	31
3	41
4	33
5	−5

Solution Build a difference table, looking for a constant difference. Since you know *f* to be cubic, the third differences should be constant.

x	f(x)	Δ	Δ²	Δ³
0	5	10	6	−12
1	15	16	−6	−12
2	31	10	−18	−12
3	41	−8	−30	
4	33	−38		
5	−5			

Now, because of the up-and-over property, you can find *f*(10) using binomial coefficients by reading across the top row.

$$f(10) = \binom{10}{0} \cdot 5 + \binom{10}{1} \cdot 10 + \binom{10}{2} \cdot 6 + \binom{10}{3} \cdot (-12)$$

You can read the values of the binomial coefficients off of Pascal's Triangle or find them on a calculator using its *nCr* function.

$$f(10) = 1 \cdot 5 + 10 \cdot 10 + 45 \cdot 6 + 120 \cdot (-12) = -1065$$

For You to Do

1. Calculate $f(100)$, where f is the function from the Example.

You could use this method to calculate $f(n)$ for any nonnegative integer n. For example,

$$f(3) = 41 \quad = 1 \cdot 5 + 3 \cdot 10 + \ \ 3 \cdot 6 + \ \ 1 \cdot (-12)$$

$$f(4) = 33 \quad = 1 \cdot 5 + 4 \cdot 10 + \ \ 6 \cdot 6 + \ \ 4 \cdot (-12)$$

$$f(5) = -5 \quad = 1 \cdot 5 + 5 \cdot 10 + 10 \cdot 6 + 10 \cdot (-12)$$

$$f(6) = -85 \quad = 1 \cdot 5 + 6 \cdot 10 + 15 \cdot 6 + 20 \cdot (-12)$$

$$f(7) = -219 = 1 \cdot 5 + 7 \cdot 10 + 21 \cdot 6 + 35 \cdot (-12)$$

Here is a formula for $f(n)$ using binomial coefficients:

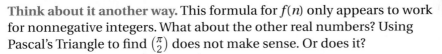

$$f(n) = \binom{n}{0} \cdot 5 + \binom{n}{1} \cdot 10 + \binom{n}{2} \cdot 6 + \binom{n}{3} \cdot (-12)$$

where 5, 10, 6, and -12 are the numbers across the top row of the difference table for f.

Developing Habits of Mind

Think about it another way. This formula for $f(n)$ only appears to work for nonnegative integers. What about the other real numbers? Using Pascal's Triangle to find $\binom{\pi}{2}$ does not make sense. Or does it?

There are several different ways to get the numbers in Pascal's Triangle. It is by no means obvious that they all produce the same numbers, but as you saw in Chapter 4, they do. Here are five ways you have used to think about the entries in Pascal's Triangle.

- *Pascal's Triangle is a recursively generated number pattern.* In words: Each row starts and ends with 1. Any interior element is the sum of the two above it.

  In symbols:

  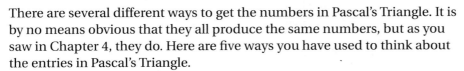

  $$\binom{n}{k} = \begin{cases} 1 & \text{if } k = 0 \text{ or if } k = n \text{ (each row starts and ends with 1)} \\ \binom{n-1}{k-1} + \binom{n-1}{k} & \text{if } 0 < k < n \text{ (an interior element is the sum of the two above it)} \end{cases}$$

- *The entries in Pascal's Triangle count subsets.* Suppose you have a set of five elements, say $\{A, B, C, D, E\}$. How many three-element subsets are there? There are $\binom{5}{3} = 10$. Here they are:

$$\{A, B, C\}, \{A, B, D\}, \{A, B, E\}, \{A, C, D\}, \{A, C, E\},$$

$$\{A, D, E\}, \{B, C, D\}, \{B, C, E\}, \{B, D, E\}, \{C, D, E\}$$

- *The entries in Pascal's Triangle are binomial coefficients.* The entries in the nth row are the coefficients in the expansion of $(a + b)^n$. More precisely,

$$(a + b)^n = \binom{n}{0}a^n + \binom{n}{1}a^{n-1}b + \binom{n}{2}a^{n-2}b^2 + \cdots + \binom{n}{n-2}a^2b^{n-2}$$

$$+ \binom{n}{n-1}ab^{n-1} + \binom{n}{n}b^n$$

$$= \sum_{k=0}^{n}\binom{n}{k}a^{n-k}b^k$$

- *The entries in Pascal's Triangle are quotients of factorials.* There is an explicit formula for $\binom{n}{k}$ in terms of factorials:

$$\binom{n}{k} = \frac{n!}{k!(n - k)!}$$

So, for example,

$$\binom{12}{5} = \frac{12!}{5!\,7!}$$

$$= \frac{12 \cdot 11 \cdot 10 \cdot 9 \cdot 8 \cdot 7 \cdot 6 \cdot 5 \cdot 4 \cdot 3 \cdot 2 \cdot 1}{5 \cdot 4 \cdot 3 \cdot 2 \cdot 1 \times 7 \cdot 6 \cdot 5 \cdot 4 \cdot 3 \cdot 2 \cdot 1}$$

$$= \frac{12 \cdot 11 \cdot 10 \cdot 9 \cdot 8}{5 \cdot 4 \cdot 3 \cdot 2 \cdot 1}$$

$$= 792$$

> Making this factorial formula hold for the cases $k = 0$ and $k = n$ is one of the reasons for defining $0!$ to be 1.

- *The entries in Pascal's Triangle are rational expressions.* Sometimes, it is useful to do the cancellations in the factorial expression and write $\binom{n}{k}$ as a product of factors:

$$\binom{n}{k} = \frac{n(n - 1)(n - 2)(n - 3) \cdots (n - k + 1)(n - k) \cdots 1}{k!(n - k)!}$$

$$= \frac{n(n - 1)(n - 2)(n - 3) \cdots (n - k + 1)}{k!}$$

One advantage of this expression over all the others is that n need not be an integer. In a sense, this expression extends the formula for entries in Pascal's triangle from integers to real (or even complex) numbers. This is the way to think about it that is most useful for this chapter.

> The symbol $\binom{\pi}{3}$ does not make sense in the context of any of the other methods. But here, it is just
>
> $$\frac{\pi(\pi - 1)(\pi - 2)}{6}$$

Definition

The **Mahler polynomials** are the set of polynomials that match the binomial coefficients. The first few Mahler polynomials are

k	$\binom{x}{k}$ (Factored)	$\binom{x}{k}$ (Expanded)
0	1	1
1	x	x
2	$\dfrac{x(x-1)}{2!}$	$\dfrac{-x+x^2}{2}$
3	$\dfrac{x(x-1)(x-2)}{3!}$	$\dfrac{2x-3x^2+x^3}{6}$
4	$\dfrac{x(x-1)(x-2)(x-3)}{4!}$	$\dfrac{-6x+11x^2-6x^3+x^4}{24}$
5	$\dfrac{x(x-1)(x-2)(x-3)(x-4)}{5!}$	$\dfrac{24x-50x^2+35x^3-10x^4+x^5}{120}$

The examples so far show how you can use the Mahler polynomials, along with the numbers in the top row of a difference table, to find a function that fits the table. This is called Newton's Difference Formula.

Theorem 5.2 *Newton's Difference Formula*

Suppose you have a table with integer inputs from 0 to m:

Input	Output	Δ	Δ^2	Δ^3	$\ldots$	Δ^m
0	a_0	a_1	a_2	a_3	$\cdots$	a_m
1						
2						
3						
4						
5						
6						
$\vdots$						
m						

A polynomial function that fits the table is

$$f(x) = \sum_{k=0}^{m} a_k \binom{x}{k}$$

Each $\binom{x}{k}$ is a Mahler polynomial.

Newton's Difference Formula explains the observations made previously about the degree and leading coefficient of a fitting polynomial. For example, consider this table for N:

x	N(x)	Δ	Δ²	Δ³	Δ⁴	Δ⁵	Δ⁶	Δ⁷
0	1	−2	14	12	0	0	0	0
1	−1	12	26	12	0	0	0	
2	11	38	38	12	0	0		
3	49	76	50	12	0			
4	125	126	62	12				
5	251	188	74					
6	439	262						
7	701							

Newton's Difference Formula says that you can find a function N that fits the table by reading across the top row of the difference table and multiplying each number by the corresponding Mahler polynomial.

$$N(x) = 1 \cdot 1 + (-2) \cdot x + 14 \cdot \frac{x(x-1)}{2} + 12 \cdot \frac{x(x-1)(x-2)}{6}$$

Without expanding, you know that this polynomial must be cubic, since it will have a nonzero x^3 term and no higher-degree term. Moreover, the coefficient of the x^3 term is $\frac{12}{6} = 2$. This term alone controls the degree and leading coefficient of N (why?).

For You to Do

2. Find the degree and leading coefficient of the lowest-degree polynomial function that fits this table.

x	p(x)
0	0
1	0
2	7
3	39
4	126
5	310
6	645
7	1197

3. Find a cubic function that matches the table from the Example in this lesson.

Check Your Understanding

1. The first few Mahler polynomials are

$$\binom{x}{0} = 1$$

$$\binom{x}{1} = x$$

$$\binom{x}{2} = \frac{x(x-1)}{2}$$

$$\binom{x}{3} = \frac{x(x-1)(x-2)}{3!}$$

   List the next three Mahler polynomials. Then write a general rule for the kth Mahler polynomial.

2. Find a polynomial function that fits this input-output table.

Input	Output
0	6
1	5
2	24
3	99
4	290
5	681

3. If you made a difference table for each of the following functions, what would the top row look like?

   a. $a(x) = x^2$ **b.** $b(x) = 2x^2$ **c.** $c(x) = x^3$

   d. $d(x) = 2x^3$ **e.** $e(x) = x^3 + x^2$

4. Derman wonders how a difference table could help if the inputs started from a different number. How might you find a function that fits this table?

Input	Output
3	3
4	−1
5	−1
6	3
7	11
8	23
9	39

5. The algebraic definition of the Δ operator is that
$$\Delta f(x) = f(x + 1) - f(x)$$

a. Show that if $f(x) = \binom{x}{3}$, then $\Delta f(x) = \binom{x}{2}$. In other words, the Δ of the third Mahler polynomial is the second Mahler polynomial.

b. **Take It Further** Show that, in general, if $f(x) = \binom{x}{k}$, then $\Delta f(x) = \binom{x}{k-1}$.

> You will need the general form for $\binom{x}{k}$ first.

6. **Take It Further** An interesting result comes from multiplying the numbers in a row of Pascal's Triangle by powers of integers. For example, take the row 1, 3, 3, 1 and multiply each number by powers of 4:

$$1 \times 1 = 1$$
$$4 \times 3 = 12$$
$$16 \times 3 = 48$$
$$64 \times 1 = 64$$

The total is $125 = 5^3$.

a. Build a difference table for $g(x) = 5^x$, and then show that you can write 125 as the sum given above.

b. Show that, in general,
$$\sum_{k=0}^{n} 4^k \binom{n}{k} = 5^k$$

c. Generalize this result to any power:
$$\sum_{k=0}^{n} p^k \binom{n}{k} = (p + 1)^k$$

7. Kei says that if the entries in the difference column of a table are all zero, the function must be constant.

Kei: If all the Δ's are 0, that means all the outputs have to be the same number. It has to be a constant function, like $f(x) = 5$.

Is he right? If so, explain why. If not, sketch the graph of a function where $f(x + 1) - f(x)$ is always zero but f is not constant.

8. Let $f(x) = 2x^3 + 5x^2 - x - 17$. Find a function for which the outputs are the fourth differences, $\Delta^4 f$.

9. The table below gives the sums of the squares of integers from 0 to n for each n.

n	Sum of Squares
0	0
1	1
2	5
3	14
4	30
5	55
6	91

Use Mahler polynomials and a difference table to find a closed-form definition for $S(n)$, the sum of the squares from 0 to n.

10. Find a closed-form definition for $C(n)$, the sum of the cubes from 0 to n.

11. **Take It Further** Find a rule for the sum of fifth powers from 0 to n.

As a challenge, try doing this without a calculator. Factoring helps.

12. Derman has a follow-up question after Exercise 4.

Derman: I changed the input numbers, but not the outputs. Is it still possible to find a function that fits this table?

Input	Output
0	3
5	−1
10	−1
15	3
20	11
25	23
30	39

You could answer this if the inputs went 0, 1, 2, 3, ..., so the question is how to change that answer so that it works for this table instead.

How could you use Mahler polynomials to find a function that fits this table?

13. Here is a function with a curious definition.

$$D(n) = \begin{cases} 1 & \text{if } n = 0 \\ 0 & \text{if } n \neq 0 \end{cases}$$

a. Explain how you know D cannot be a polynomial function.

b. Build a difference table for D and describe its top row.

14. Take It Further You can use the function D to prove an interesting fact about Pascal's Triangle:

> In any row of Pascal's Triangle, the sum of the even terms $\binom{n}{0}$, $\binom{n}{2}$, . . . is equal to the sum of the odd terms $\binom{n}{1}$, $\binom{n}{3}$, ...

Prove this using D and its difference table.

15. Standardized Test Prep Identify the next value in the row of Pascal's Triangle that begins

$$1 \quad 10 \quad 45 \ldots$$

A. 55 **B.** 80 **C.** 120 **D.** 10

Go Online
PHSchool.com

For additional practice, go to **Web Code:** bga-0509

Maintain Your Skills

16. Copy and complete this table, which gives the top row of the difference table for each polynomial from $f(x) = x^0 = 1$ to $f(x) = x^5$. You found some of the entries in Exercise 3. Describe any patterns you notice in this table.

$f(x)$	$\binom{x}{0} = 1$	$\binom{x}{1} = x$	$\binom{x}{2} = \frac{x(x-1)}{2!}$	$\binom{x}{3} = \frac{x(x-1)(x-2)}{3!}$	$\binom{x}{4}$	$\binom{x}{5}$
1	1	–	–	–	–	–
x	0	1	–	–	–	–
x^2	▦	▦	▦	–	–	–
x^3	▦	▦	▦	▦	–	–
x^4	▦	▦	▦	▦	▦	–
x^5	▦	▦	▦	▦	▦	▦

Finding a smooth function that fits a table is the mathematical equivalent of fitting a flexible plank to a rigid frame.

5.10 Sums of Powers

Recall the following sums.

$$\sum_{k=0}^{n-1} k = \frac{n(n-1)}{2}$$

$$\sum_{k=0}^{n-1} k^2 = \frac{n(n-1)(2n-1)}{6}$$

$$\sum_{k=0}^{n-1} k^3 = \frac{n^2(n-1)^2}{4}$$

$$\sum_{k=0}^{n-1} k^4 = \frac{n(n-1)(2n-1)(3n^2-3n-1)}{30}$$

$$\sum_{k=0}^{n-1} k^5 = \frac{n^2(n-1)^2(2n^2-2n-1)}{12}$$

In CME Project *Algebra 2*, the sums ran from 0 to M. Replace all the n's here by $M + 1$'s and you have sums from 0 to M.

How did anyone find these formulas? In this lesson you will use Newton's Difference Formula to find formulas for the sums of squares, cubes, or any power.

Example

Problem Find a rule for the function S defined as

$$S(n) = \sum_{k=0}^{n-1} k^2$$

Then calculate $S(101)$.

Solution Calculate $S(n)$ for the first few integers, then build a difference table.

n	S(n)	Δ	Δ²	Δ³
0	0	0	1	2
1	0	1	3	2
2	1	4	5	2
3	5	9	7	2
4	14	16	9	
5	30	25		
6	55			

Notice that the sum goes from 0 to $n - 1$. For example, $S(7) = 0^2 + 1^2 + \cdots + 6^2$. So $S(1) = 0$. Also, remember that by convention,

$$\sum_{k=0}^{-1} k^2 = 0$$

Newton's Difference Formula states that you can find a rule for S using the top row of the difference table and the Mahler polynomials:

$$S(n) = 0 \cdot 1 + 0 \cdot n + 1 \cdot \frac{n(n-1)}{2} + 2 \cdot \frac{n(n-1)(n-2)}{6}$$

$S(n)$ in expanded form is $S(n) = \frac{1}{3}n^3 - \frac{1}{2}n^2 + \frac{1}{6}n$. Then $S(101) = 338{,}350$, which is also the sum of the squares $0^2 + 1^2 + 2^2 + \cdots + 100^2$.

For Discussion

1. This function fits the table for S, but how might you prove that they will always agree?

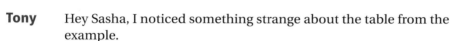

Minds in Action   episode 15

Sasha and Tony are studying the difference table for S.

Tony   Hey Sasha, I noticed something strange about the table from the example.

Sasha   What's that?

Tony   It's got the table for x^2 buried inside it.

Sasha   Huh? What do you mean?

Tony   Look. I can just cover the $S(n)$ column with my pencil. Check out what's left.

Tony covers the output column of the table for S, leaving the input and Δ columns.

n		Δ	Δ²	Δ³
0		0	1	2
1		1	3	2
2		4	5	2
3		9	7	2
4		16	9	
5		25		
6				

And what's interesting to me is the whole table comes from sums of squares.

Sasha   Wait, I think this makes sense. The Δ column should be the squares; that's just the way the function was built. It reminds me of the hockey-stick property, where you add up all the numbers.

Tony   I see what you mean. And the $n-1$ makes it line up right, otherwise there wouldn't be a zero at the top. I wonder what we could use this for.

Sasha   Well, look across the top row of the difference table you've got. The covered-up one.

Tony   0-1-2. That's the top row for x^2. We've done that before.

Sasha   Okay, now uncover that $S(n)$ column.

Tony uncovers it .

n	S(n)	Δ	Δ²	Δ³
0	0	0	1	2
1	0	1	3	2
2	1	4	5	2
3	5	9	7	2
4	14	16	9	
5	30	25		
6	55			

Tony   Ahh, 0-0-1-2. They're almost the same, except you add a zero in front. I'll bet we could do this with other functions. Do we have top rows for other functions?

Sasha   Yes, and it's not hard to make more.

You will be asked to "make more" in the exercises.

Doing It With Sums

You can use Newton's Difference Formula to find polynomial formulas for sums of powers. And you can use sums of powers to build polynomials that fit any table (in which the inputs form an arithmetic sequence). To see how, consider the mystery function g. What could a formula for g be?

n	g(n)
0	1
1	−2
2	1
3	10
4	25
5	46
6	73

Here is the table with two difference columns.

n	g(n)	Δ	Δ²
0	1	−3	6
1	−2	3	6
2	1	9	6
3	10	15	6
4	25	21	6
5	46	27	
6	73		

So there is a linear polynomial that produces the Δ column, namely $6n - 3$.

n	Δ	Δ^2
0	−3	6
1	3	6
2	9	6
3	15	6
4	21	6
5	27	

You might be able to make some progress on g, now that you are equipped with this formula for the first differences.

n	g(n)	$\Delta = 6n - 3$
0	1	$-3 = 6 \cdot 0 - 3$
1	−2	$3 = 6 \cdot 1 - 3$
2	1	$9 = 6 \cdot 2 - 3$
3	10	$15 = 6 \cdot 3 - 3$
4	25	$21 = 6 \cdot 4 - 3$
5	46	$27 = 6 \cdot 5 - 3$
6	73	

To get the entry in the Δ column for an input of n, start with −3 and add n 6's.

To see where $g(5)$ comes from, use the hockey-stick property, replacing each number in the Δ column by the calculation that led to it.

n	g(n)	$\Delta = 6n - 3$
0	1	−3
1	2	3
2	1	9
3	10	15
4	25	21
5	46	27
6	73	

$g(5) = 1 + \boxed{-3} + \boxed{3} + \boxed{9} + \boxed{15} + \boxed{21}$

$= 1 + \boxed{6 \cdot 0 - 3} + \boxed{6 \cdot 1 - 3} + \boxed{6 \cdot 2 - 3} + \boxed{6 \cdot 3 - 3} + \boxed{6 \cdot 4 - 3}$

Now, group "like terms."

$$g(5) = 1 + 6(0 + 1 + 2 + 3 + 4) + [(-3) + (-3) + (-3) + (-3) + (-3)]$$
$$= 1 + 6(0 + 1 + 2 + 3 + 4) + 5(-3)$$

Similarly,

$$g(6) = 1 + 6(0 + 1 + 2 + 3 + 4 + 5) + [(-3) + (-3) + (-3) + (-3) + (-3) + (-3)]$$
$$= 1 + 6(0 + 1 + 2 + 3 + 4 + 5) + 6(-3)$$

And, in general, a function g that agrees with the table will have the property that

$$g(n) = 1 + 6(0 + 1 + 2 + 3 + 4 + 5 + \cdots + (n - 1)) + n(-3)$$

Now, use the formula for the sum of the first n integers.

$$0 + 1 + 2 + 3 + \cdots + (n - 1) = \frac{n(n - 1)}{2}$$

So, you have

$$g(n) = 1 + 6(0 + 1 + 2 + 3 + 4 + 5 + \cdots + (n - 1)) + n(-3)$$
$$= 1 + 6\left(\frac{n(n - 1)}{2}\right) - 3n$$
$$= 3n^2 - 6n + 1$$

If you work through some more examples, it becomes clear that a constant first difference requires you to add up n identical constants. A constant second difference requires you to add up the first n integers. It turns out that a constant third difference requires you to add up the first n squares. And in general, a constant difference in the mth column requires that you are able to add up the first $n(m - 1)^{\text{st}}$ powers. This gives you another perfectly good method for "resolving" difference tables, now that you have nice formulas for sums of powers.

You can check that this fits the table.

For You to Do

2. Use this method to find a function that agrees with this table.

Input	Output
0	5
1	15
2	31
3	41
4	33
5	−5

Check Your Understanding

1. **a.** Use a difference table to show that
$$k^3 = 0\binom{k}{0} + 1\binom{k}{1} + 6\binom{k}{2} + 6\binom{k}{3}$$

 b. Find a closed form for the sum below.
$$\sum_{k=0}^{n-1} k^3$$

2. Calculate this sum as a function of n.
$$\sum_{k=0}^{n-1} 6k^2$$

 Factor the result.

3. **a.** Make a difference table for $f(x) = x^4$.

 b. Write
$$\sum_{k=0}^{n-1} k^4$$

 in terms of the Mahler polynomials.

 c. Show that
$$\sum_{k=0}^{n-1} k^4 = \frac{n(n-1)(2n-1)(3n^2 - 3n - 1)}{30}$$

4. Carlos says he found a formula for the sum of fourth powers that is different from the one in Exercise 3.

 Carlos: I searched the Internet for "sum of 4th powers," and the first hit that came back gave this formula:
$$S_4(n) = \frac{n(n+1)(2n+1)(3n^2 + 3n - 1)}{30}$$

 Carlos: It's really close to what came from Exercise 3, but it's not the same.

 a. Explain the discrepancy between Carlos' formula and the one in Exercise 3.

 b. **Take It Further** Show that
$$\frac{n(n-1)(2n-1)(3n^2 - 3n - 1)}{30} + n^4 = \frac{n(n+1)(2n+1)(3n^2 + 3n - 1)}{30}$$

5. You can model the formula for the sum of the first n squares with blocks of wood.

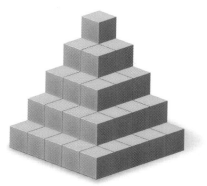

The small cube at the top of the shape is 1 inch per side.

a. Explain why the volume of the shape, in cubic inches, is
$$1^2 + 2^2 + 3^2 + 4^2 + 5^2$$

b. Show how to assemble six blocks in this shape to form a solid box (or, better yet, build it). Then, find the dimensions of the box.

c. Generalize this process to show that
$$1^2 + 2^2 + 3^2 + \cdots + n^2 = \frac{n(n + 1)(2n + 1)}{6}$$

6. **Take It Further** You can use the table in Exercise 16 of Lesson 5.9 to rewrite polynomials containing the usual powers of x ($1, x, x^2, x^3, \dots$) in terms of the Mahler polynomials $1, x, \frac{x(x - 1)}{2}, \frac{x(x - 1)(x - 2)}{6}, \dots$. But what about the other direction, converting from Mahler polynomials back to powers of x? For example,

$$\frac{x(x - 1)}{2} = \frac{1}{2}x^2 - \frac{1}{2}x$$

Copy and complete this table, which describes the conversion.

$f(x)$	1	x	x^2	x^3	x^4	x^5
$\binom{x}{0}$	1	–	–	–	–	–
$\binom{x}{1}$	0	1	–	–	–	–
$\binom{x}{2}$	0	$-\dfrac{1}{2}$	$\dfrac{1}{2}$	–	–	–
$\binom{x}{3}$	▪	▪	▪	▪	–	–
$\binom{x}{4}$	▪	▪	▪	▪	▪	–
$\binom{x}{5}$	▪	▪	▪	▪	▪	▪

Describe any patterns you find in this table, or any relationships between this table and the table for conversion to Mahler polynomials.

On Your Own

7. For each sum, find a formula in terms of n.

a. $\displaystyle\sum_{k=0}^{n-1} 3$

b. $\displaystyle\sum_{k=0}^{n-1} k$

c. $\displaystyle\sum_{k=0}^{n-1} 5k$

d. $\displaystyle\sum_{k=0}^{n-1} k^2$

e. $\displaystyle\sum_{k=0}^{n-1} (k^2 + 5k + 3)$

> How many 3's are there in part (a)?

8. The sum of cubes from 0^3 through $(n-1)^3$ is a perfect square:

$$\sum_{k=0}^{n-1} k^3 = \left(\frac{n(n-1)}{2}\right)^2$$

Interestingly, the fraction $\frac{n(n-1)}{2}$ is the sum of the integers from 0 through $(n-1)$, which means that

$$\sum_{k=0}^{n-1} k^3 = \left(\sum_{k=0}^{n-1} k\right)^2$$

Verify this claim for 0 through 10 by tabulating each sum.

9. For an ingenious proof that the sum in Exercise 8 is always a perfect square, start by actually creating the square. Here is the square for the sum $1^3 + 2^3 = (1 + 2)^2$.

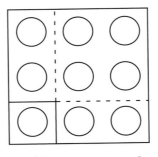

a. Show how you could add three 3-by-3 squares to this pattern to make a 6-by-6 square.

b. Show how you could add four 4-by-4 squares to the 6-by-6 square to make a 10-by-10 square. You will need to cut one of the four squares in some way.

c. Show how you could add five 5-by-5 squares to make a 15-by-15 square.

d. In general, if n is odd, show how you can add n n-by-n squares to the pattern, justifying that they fit the existing pattern.

e. In general, if n is even, show how you can also add n n-by-n squares to the pattern, cutting one of the n squares.

f. What type of proof is this? Is the proof complete based on what you have done in this exercise?

10. Define f recursively as

$$f(n) = \begin{cases} 8 & \text{if } n = 0 \\ f(n-1) + 2n + 5 & \text{if } n > 0 \end{cases}$$

Use what you have learned in this investigation to find a closed-form definition for $f(n)$ for any nonnegative integer n.

11. Generalize the result of Exercise 10 to find a closed-form equivalent for this recursive definition

$$f(n) = \begin{cases} A & \text{if } n = 0 \\ f(n-1) + Bn + C & \text{if } n > 0 \end{cases}$$

12. Standardized Test Prep In the table, output $f(n)$ is the sum of $(n + 1)$ consecutive odd numbers beginning with some number $s = f(0)$.

Input, *n*	Output, *f(n)*
0	s
1	$s + (s + 2)$
2	$s + (s + 2) + (s + 4)$
3	$s + (s + 2) + (s + 4) + (s + 6)$

Supposing s to be given, which of the following is a closed-form definition of $f(n)$, with $n \geq 0$?

A. $(n + 1)(n + s)$ **B.** $n(n + s)$ **C.** $n(n - s)$ **D.** $(n - 1)(n + s)$

Maintain Your Skills

13. For each recursively-defined function, find a value of C that makes f a constant function. (So $f(1)$ must equal $f(0)$, etc.)

a. $f(n) = \begin{cases} C & \text{if } n = 0 \\ 2f(n-1) - 3 & \text{if } n > 0 \end{cases}$

b. $f(n) = \begin{cases} C & \text{if } n = 0 \\ 4f(n-1) - 24 & \text{if } n > 0 \end{cases}$

c. $f(n) = \begin{cases} C & \text{if } n = 0 \\ 0.75f(n-1) + 3 & \text{if } n > 0 \end{cases}$

d. $f(n) = \begin{cases} C & \text{if } n = 0 \\ 1.005f(n-1) - 300 & \text{if } n > 0 \end{cases}$

Mathematical 5B Reflections

In this investigation, you studied functions with difference tables that contain a column of constants. You described any such function with a polynomial by using Newton's Difference Formula. You applied this formula to sums of powers. The following questions will help you summarize what you have learned.

1. Find a polynomial function that fits this table.

x	f(x)
0	5
1	17
2	37
3	65
4	101

2. Find a polynomial function S that satisfies

$$S(n) = \sum_{k=0}^{n-1} (k + 1)(k - 1)$$

3. Build a table that no linear, quadratic, or cubic function will fit. Explain why none of them can fit the table.

4. Find a function f for which $\Delta f(x) = 9f(x)$ for all x.

5. Let $g(x) = x^4$. Find rules for Δg and $\Delta^2 g$.

6. If the third differences in the table of a polynomial function are all 24, what can you say about that function?

7. What are the Mahler polynomials?

8. How can you use differences to find a polynomial function that fits a table?

Vocabulary

In this investigation, you learned these terms. Make sure you understand what each one means and how to use it.

- **difference table**
- **hockey-stick property**
- **Mahler polynomials**
- **up-and-over property**

Chapter 5

Mid-Chapter Test

Go Online
PHSchool.com

For a mid-chapter test, go
to Web Code: bga-0552

Multiple Choice

1. Let $f(x) = 3x - 7$. Let $g(x) = 3x - 7 - 2x(x + 1)$. What is the set of inputs for which the two functions are equal?

A. $\{-1\}$ **B.** $\{0, 1\}$

C. $\{-1, 0\}$ **D.** $\{-1, 0, \frac{7}{3}\}$

2. Let h be defined recursively by

$$h(n) = \begin{cases} a & \text{if } n = 0 \\ h(n - 1) + 2n + 5 & \text{if } n > 0 \end{cases}$$

If $h(3) = 31$, find a.

A. 1   **B.** 4   **C.** 11   **D.** 13

3. Here is a partially completed difference table for a function p.

x	$p(x)$	Δ	Δ^2	Δ^3
0	3	0	4	6
1	3	4	10	6
2	▨	B	▨	6
3	▨	▨	A	6

Find the value of $A + B$.

A. 22   **B.** 24   **C.** 36   **D.** 42

4. Let

$$S(n) = \sum_{k=0}^{n-1} k^3$$

What is $S(3)$?

A. 3   **B.** 5   **C.** 9   **D.** 36

5. Let the function f be defined by $f(x) = x^2 + x$. Which of the following is a closed-form definition for Δf?

A. $\Delta f = x^2 + x - 1$ **B.** $\Delta f = x^2 + 3x + 2$

C. $\Delta f = 2x + 2$ **D.** $\Delta f = x + 1$

Open Response

6. Find a recursively defined function that agrees with $f(n) = 2n^2 + 3$ for all nonnegative integers n.

7. Use induction to show that these two functions agree for all nonnegative integers.

$$M(n) = 3n - 2$$

$$m(n) = \begin{cases} -2 & \text{if } n = 0 \\ m(n - 1) + 3 & \text{if } n > 0 \end{cases}$$

8. A quadratic function w has a table that starts like the one below.

Input, x	Output, $w(x)$	Δ	Δ^2
0	7	2	10
1	9	12	10
2	21	22	10

a. Determine the value of $w(8)$.

b. Determine the value of $w(100)$.

9. Find a polynomial that fits the input-output table.

Input	Output
0	-5
1	-3
2	-1
3	7
4	27
5	65

10. Find a formula for each sum in terms of n.

a. $\sum_{k=0}^{n-1} 3k$ **b.** $\sum_{k=0}^{n-1} (k^2 + 1)$

Closed-Form and Recursive Definitions

In *Closed-Form and Recursive Definitions*, you will find closed-form equivalents for recursively-defined functions. You will also study relationships similar to the relationship that defines the Fibonacci numbers.

By the end of this investigation, you will be able to answer questions like these.

1. What methods are available for deciding if a linear, polynomial, or exponential rule fits a table?

2. How can you find a closed-form function definition that satisfies a two-term recurrence?

3. What is the monthly payment for a three-year car loan for $15,000, taken out at 5% APR?

You will learn how to

- find general classes of functions that fit a recurrence

- relate a solution for a two-term recurrence to a quadratic polynomial

- calculate the monthly payment for a car loan and write a general rule for all such problems

You will develop these habits and skills:

- Generalize a pattern that works for one function to a class of related functions.

- Solve linear systems.

- Decide whether you can approximate a table by a linear, polynomial, or exponential rule.

- Represent a function with a table, a graph, or an equation.

- Find equilibrium points for repeated operations.

Car dealers will arrange loans for their customers, but you can also get a car loan directly from a bank. Rates may vary, so it pays to check out all your options.

5.11 Getting Started

Activating Prior Knowledge
Exploring New Ideas

In earlier courses, you learned how to find functions with closed-form definitions that agree with functions like

$$f(n) = \begin{cases} 3 & \text{if } n = 0 \\ f(n-1) + 5 & \text{if } n > 0 \end{cases}$$

or

$$g(n) = \begin{cases} 3 & \text{if } n = 0 \\ g(n-1) + 5n + 2 & \text{if } n > 0 \end{cases}$$

or

$$h(n) = \begin{cases} 7 & \text{if } n = 0 \\ 3h(n-1) & \text{if } n > 0 \end{cases}$$

In this investigation, you will learn how to find closed-form equivalents for other kinds of recursive function definitions.

> **Habits of Mind**
>
> **Recall what you know.**
> Function f has constant first differences, so you can find a linear function that agrees with it. Function g has constant second differences, so you can find a quadratic function that agrees with it. Function h has constant ratios, so you can find an exponential function that agrees with it.

For You to Explore

1. Consider the recurrence

$$f(n) = f(n-1) + f(n-2)$$

This is not enough to define a function completely. You also need the initial terms $f(0)$ and $f(1)$.

For each pair of numbers below,

- Tabulate the function up to $f(8)$.

- Describe any patterns you find, either by examining the outputs of a single function or by comparing the functions with each other.

   a. $f(0) = 1, f(1) = 3$ **b.** $f(0) = 5, f(1) = 15$ **c.** $f(0) = 2, f(1) = -2$

   d. $f(0) = 7, f(1) = 13$ **e.** $f(0) = 3, f(1) = 17$

> An equation like $f(n) = f(n-1) + f(n-2)$ is called a *recurrence*. More about this later in the investigation.

2. Consider the recurrence

$$f(n) = 2f(n-1) + 3f(n-2)$$

Again, this is not enough to define a function. For each pair of numbers below,

- Tabulate the function up to $f(8)$.

- Describe any patterns you find, either by examining the outputs of a single function or by comparing the functions with each other.

- Find a closed-form definition for a function that fits the table.

   a. $f(0) = 1, f(1) = 3$ **b.** $f(0) = 5, f(1) = 15$ **c.** $f(0) = 2, f(1) = -2$

   d. $f(0) = 7, f(1) = 13$ **e.** $f(0) = 3, f(1) = 17$

> **Habits of Mind**
>
> **Experiment.** FML models allow you to experiment with the functions.

3. Consider a function r that satisfies the recurrence

$$r(n) = 7r(n-1) - 10r(n-2)$$

For each of the following, find a closed-form definition for a function that agrees with r. For the first two, start by tabulating the function r.

a. $r(0) = 1$, $r(1) = 5$ **b.** $r(0) = 1$, $r(1) = 2$ **c.** $r(0) = 2$, $r(1) = 7$

d. $r(0) = 0$, $r(1) = 3$ **e.** $r(0) = 5$, $r(1) = 16$ **f.** $r(0) = m$, $r(1) = n$

You might tabulate each function first, until you find a clear relationship.

4. Start with the number 1. Take its reciprocal and add 1. Take the reciprocal of the result, and add 1. Continue the process, taking the reciprocal of the result and adding 1.

a. Explain why the following definition captures the above description.

$$f(n) = \begin{cases} 1 & \text{if } n = 0 \\ \dfrac{1}{f(n-1)} + 1 & \text{if } n > 0 \end{cases}$$

b. Find the exact value of $f(n)$ for each n from 0 to 10.

c. Does $f(n)$ approach a limit as n grows without bound?

5. Define B as the 2-by-2 matrix

$$B = \begin{pmatrix} 0 & 1 \\ 1 & 1 \end{pmatrix}$$

Find B^n for $n = 1, 2, 3, 4, 5,$ and 6. Describe what is happening.

Do not let the calculator have all the fun.

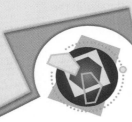

Exercises Practicing Habits of Mind

On Your Own

6. Start with the number $\frac{7}{2}$. Take its reciprocal, multiply by -10, and add 7. Take the reciprocal of the result, multiply by -10, and add 7. Continue this process, taking the reciprocal of the result, multiplying by -10, and adding 7.

a. Explain why the following definition captures the above description.

$$r(n) = \begin{cases} \dfrac{7}{2} & \text{if } n = 0 \\ \dfrac{-10}{r(n-1)} + 7 & \text{if } n > 0 \end{cases}$$

b. Find the value of $r(n)$, expressed as a fraction, for each n from 0 to 6.

c. Does $r(n)$ approach a limit as n grows without bound?

d. See if you can find other behaviors using other values for $r(0)$.

Habits of Mind

Make strategic choices. It is probably best to express $r(n)$ as an improper fraction throughout, since it is simpler to calculate the reciprocal.

7. a. Sketch the graphs of these two equations on the same axes.

$$y = x$$
$$y = -\frac{10}{x} + 7$$

b. Where do the graphs intersect?

c. What happens if, instead of $\frac{7}{2}$, you use the x-coordinate of one of the intersection points for $r(0)$ in Exercise 6?

8. Pick a number, any number. Divide it by 2 and add 1, then divide the result by 2 and add 1. Continue this process, dividing the result by 2 and adding 1.

a. What do you get after 10 iterations?

b. Do the successive outputs approach a limit?

c. Try to find other possible behaviors using different starting numbers.

9. Pick a number, any number. Multiply it by 2 and add 1, then multiply the result by 2 and add 1. Continue this process, multiplying the result by 2 and adding 1.

a. What do you get after 10 iterations?

b. Do the successive outputs approach a limit?

c. Try to find other possible behaviors using different starting numbers.

10. Find all numbers x such that

$$x^n = 7x^{n-1} - 10x^{n-2}$$

for all integers $n > 1$.

Maintain Your Skills

11. For each recurrence, find an initial value $f(0)$ that makes $f(n) = f(0)$ for all n. For example, for $f(n) = 3f(n - 1) - 12$ the value is 6, because if $f(0) = 6$, then $f(1) = 3 \cdot 6 - 12 = 6$, and then $f(2) = 6$, and so on.

a. $f(n) = 2f(n - 1)$

b. $f(n) = 2f(n - 1) + 3$

c. $f(n) = 0.5f(n - 1) + 10$

d. $f(n) = 0.8f(n - 1) + 3000$

e. $f(n) = 1.005f(n - 1) - 350$

f. $f(n) = Af(n - 1) + B$

In your studies, you have encountered recursive definitions for functions, sequences, and series. Examples include Problems 2 and 4 and Exercise 11 from Lesson 5.11. Here are some others.

- The function that gives the sum of the first n squares is

$$S(n) = \begin{cases} 0 & \text{if } n = 0 \\ S(n-1) + n^2 & \text{if } n > 0 \end{cases}$$

- The function that gives the monthly balance on a loan of \$10,000 at 5% APR with a monthly payment of \$520 is

$$b(n) = \begin{cases} 10000 & \text{if } n = 0 \\ \left(1 + \frac{0.05}{12}\right) \cdot b(n-1) - 520 & \text{if } n > 0 \end{cases}$$

- The function that gives the Fibonacci numbers is

$$F(n) = \begin{cases} 0 & \text{if } n = 0 \\ 1 & \text{if } n = 1 \\ F(n-1) + F(n-2) & \text{if } n > 1 \end{cases}$$

The goal of this investigation is to develop some general purpose tools for finding closed-from equivalents for such definitions, and for proving that the closed-form functions actually do agree with the recursively defined functions.

Facts and Notation

- A **functional equation** tells how various outputs of a function are related. For example,

$$f(2x) = (f(x))^2$$

is a functional equation. Not every function satisfies this equation. But $r(x) = 3^x$ does, because

$$r(2x) = 3x^2$$
$$= (3^x)^2$$
$$= (r(x))^2$$

- A **recurrence** is a special kind of functional equation that tells how the output of a function at integer n is related to the outputs at integers less than n. Examples include the recurrences that are satisfied by

arithmetic sequences. For example,

$$f(n) = f(n-1) + 3$$

Geometric sequences. For example,

$$f(n) = 3f(n - 1)$$

Fibonacci numbers.

$$f(n) = f(n - 1) + f(n - 2)$$

A recurrence like the last one, which defines the output at n in terms of the outputs at $n - 2$ and $n - 1$, is called a **two-term recurrence.**

As you saw in Lesson 5.1, a recurrence is not enough to define a function. You also need one or more base cases. For example, to complete the definition of an arithmetic sequence, you have to give the value for $f(0)$. See Problem 3 of Lesson 5.11 for an example of how different base cases produce different functions that satisfy the same recurrence.

The problem for this investigation is as follows.

Problem

a. Characterize all functions that satisfy a given recurrence.

b. Given base cases, find (if possible) a closed-form definition that satisfies the recurrence.

Suppose you have a recursive function definition. Here are some useful methods for finding a closed-form equivalent.

- **Model the recursive definition in your FML.** This gives you a computational model, with which you can experiment. You can look at outputs, look for patterns in the outputs, tabulate the model, graph it, and so on.

- **Tabulate the function.** Search the table for patterns. Make a difference table. If the third differences are constant, there is a cubic fit. Look at the ratios. If the successive ratios are constant, there is an exponential fit. Look at how the length of the string of digits grows. Rapid growth may point to a closed form based on an exponential function.

- **Graph the function.** For a recursively defined function, the domain is probably positive integers, in which case you will have to use a scatter plot. The shape of the plot can reveal whether the function is linear, exponential, or polynomial. A graph that looks quadratic would lead you to try a quadratic fit.

- **Use what you know from previous chapters and courses.** For example, you can write a recurrence like

$$f(n) = 3f(n - 1) + 2$$

as

$$f(n) = \mathcal{A}_{(3, 2)}(f(n - 1))$$

where $\mathcal{A}_{(a, b)}(x) = ax + b$. In *Algebra 2* you learned how to "unstack" such recurrences using the iteration formula

$$\mathcal{A}_{(a, b)}^{(n)} = \mathcal{A}\left(a^n, b\left(\frac{a^n - 1}{a - 1}\right)\right)$$

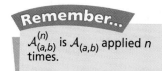

Remember...

$\mathcal{A}_{(a,b)}^{(n)}$ is $\mathcal{A}_{(a,b)}$ applied n times.

A recurrence like

$$f(n) = f(n - 1) + 5^n$$

unstacks to a geometric series. You know how to sum those.

In-Class Experiment

Use the methods above, or anything else you like, to find closed-form equivalents for the following functions.

1. $f(n) = \begin{cases} 3 & \text{if } n = 0 \\ f(n-1) + 7 & \text{if } n > 0 \end{cases}$

2. $f(n) = \begin{cases} 3 & \text{if } n = 0 \\ 7f(n-1) & \text{if } n > 0 \end{cases}$

3. $f(n) = \begin{cases} 3 & \text{if } n = 0 \\ 4f(n-1) - 6 & \text{if } n > 0 \end{cases}$

4. $f(n) = \begin{cases} 1 & \text{if } n = 0 \\ 3 & \text{if } n = 1 \\ 5f(n-1) - 6f(n-2) & \text{if } n > 1 \end{cases}$

5. $f(n) = \begin{cases} 2 & \text{if } n = 0 \\ 5 & \text{if } n = 1 \\ 5f(n-1) - 6f(n-2) & \text{if } n > 1 \end{cases}$

For Discussion

What kind of recurrence relation will each type of function satisfy?

6. linear

7. exponential

8. quadratic

9. degree-n polynomial

Computers that Prove Theorems

Babbage's difference engine performed calculations to find specific numerical outputs of polynomial functions. Today, computers can produce induction proofs of general theorems, like the identity

$$\sum_{k=1}^{n} k^4 = \frac{n^5}{5} + \frac{n^4}{2} + \frac{n^3}{3} - \frac{n}{30}$$

Even more surprisingly, computers can discover and prove new identities, ones which mathematicians had not previously suspected.

For more information on computer-based proofs, go to **Web Code:** bge-8031

Exercises Practicing Habits of Mind

1. Define function f recursively as

$$f(n) = \begin{cases} K & \text{if } n = 0 \\ 3f(n-1) & \text{if } n > 0 \end{cases}$$

Suppose also that $f(5) = 100$.

a. Calculate $f(6)$ and $f(4)$.

b. Find the value of K.

c. Find a closed-form definition for a function that agrees with f.

2. Define function g recursively, by

$$g(n) = \begin{cases} 64 & \text{if } n = 0 \\ \frac{3}{4}g(n-1) & \text{if } n > 0 \end{cases}$$

a. Calculate $g(4)$.

b. Find a closed-form definition for a function that agrees with g.

c. Find the value of this sum.

$$\sum_{j=0}^{\infty} g(j)$$

d. Approximate the value of this sum to four decimal places.

$$\sum_{j=0}^{100} g(j)$$

3. a. Find the bases for two different exponential functions $h(n) = a^n$ and $j(n) = b^n$ that satisfy the recurrence

$$f(n) = 10f(n-1) - 24f(n-2)$$

b. For your functions h and j in part (a), define

$$k(n) = 5h(n) + 8j(n)$$

Show that k also satisfies the recurrence

$$f(n) = 10f(n-1) - 24f(n-2)$$

c. Take It Further Suppose a function r satisfies the recurrence given above, and $r(0) = 3$ and $r(1) = 8$. Find a closed-form definition for a function that agrees with r.

> **Habits of Mind**
>
> **Generalize.** There is nothing special about 5 and 8 here.

4. Suppose f is a function that satisfies the recurrence $f(n) = 2f(n - 1)$.

    a. Find a value b for $f(0)$ that makes f a constant function.

    b. Judy starts with $f(0)$ a distance of 16 units away from b. That is, $|f(0) - b| = 16$. How far away from b is $f(1)$? $f(2)$?

5. Josue considers the more complicated recurrence

$$j(n) = 2j(n - 1) + 3$$

    a. What base case $j(0) = b$ makes j a constant function?

    b. Josue starts with $j(0)$ a distance of 16 units away from b. How far away from b is $j(1)$? $j(2)$?

6. Consider function g from Exercise 2.

    a. Find $\lim\limits_{n \to \infty} g(n)$.

    b. How far away from this limit is $g(0)$? $g(1)$? $g(2)$?

7. Consider the recurrence

$$r(x) = \frac{3}{4}r(x - 1) + 10$$

    a. Find a closed-form definition for a function that agrees with r if $r(0) = 40$.

    b. Copy and complete the following table for the base case $r(0) = 104$.

n	r(n)	Δ	÷
0	104	■	■
1	■	■	■
2	■	■	■
3	■	■	■
4	■	■	■
5	■	■	■
6	■	■	■
7	■	■	
8	■		

The ÷ column consists of the ratios of successive entries in the Δ column—the ratios of successive differences.

On Your Own

8. Establish the following identity.

$$(1 + r + r^2 + r^3 + \cdots + r^{n-1})(1 - r) = 1 - r^n$$

9. **Write About It** The formula for the sum of an infinite geometric series when $|r| < 1$ is

$$\sum_{k=0}^{\infty} r^k = \frac{1}{1 - r}$$

Why is $|r| < 1$ required? Why does this formula not work for $|r| \geq 1$?

> So, for any number $r \neq 1$,
> $$1 + r + r^2 + r^3 + \cdots$$
> $$+ r^{n-1} = \frac{1 - r^n}{1 - r}$$

10. Define function f recursively as

$$f(x) = 4f(x - 1)$$

with $f(0) = 3$.

a. Find a closed-form definition for a function that agrees with f.

b. Find the value of

$$\sum_{k=0}^{10} f(k)$$

11. a. Find the bases for two different exponential functions $h(n) = a^n$ and $j(n) = b^n$ that satisfy the recurrence

$$f(n) = 11f(n - 1) - 24f(n - 2)$$

b. For your functions h and j in part (a), define

$$k(n) = 7h(n) - 2j(n)$$

Show that k also satisfies the recurrence

$$f(n) = 11f(n - 1) - 24f(n - 2)$$

c. **Take It Further** Suppose a function r satisfies the recurrence given above and $r(0) = 5$ and $r(1) = 10$. Find a closed-form definition for a function that agrees with r.

Habits of Mind

Generalize. There is nothing special about 7 and −2 here.

12. Here is a recurrence.

$$f(n) = 5f(n - 1) - 6f(n - 2)$$

For each sequence below, decide whether or not the sequence could be consecutive outputs of a function that satisfies the recurrence.

a. 1, 2, 4, 8, 16, 32

b. 1, 3, 9, 27, 81, 243

c. 2, 5, 13, 35, 97, 275

d. 1, 4, 16, 64, 256, 1024

e. 0, 0, 0, 0, 0, 0

f. $a + b, 2a + 3b, 4a + 9b, 8a + 27b, 16a + 81b, 32a + 243b$

g. 7, 13, 23, 37, 47, 13

Go Online

PHSchool.com

For additional practice, go to **Web Code:** bga-0512

13. Take It Further Find a closed-form definition for a function f that generates the sequence from Exercise 12g,

$$7, 13, 23, 37, 47, 13, \ldots$$

and continues to satisfy the recurrence

$$f(n) = 5f(n - 1) - 6f(n - 2)$$

14. Standardized Test Prep This is the top row of the difference table for a polynomial function of degree 4.

Input, n	Output, $f(n)$	Δ	Δ^2	Δ^3	Δ^4
0	z	r	m	c	1

Which of the following is the $n = 3$ row?

a.

3	$z + 3r$	$r + 3m$	$m + 3c$	$c + 3$	1

b.

3	$4z + 2r + m$	$4r + 2m + c$	$4m + 2c + 1$	$4c + 2$	1

c.

3	z^3	r^3	m^3	c^3	1

d.

3	$z + 3r + 3m + c$	$r + 3m + 3c + 1$	$m + 3c + 3$	$c + 3$	1

Maintain Your Skills

15. Given each recursively-defined function,

- Tabulate t using inputs from 0 to 7.
- Describe what is happening to the ratio of consecutive terms as the input grows.
- Find a closed-form definition for a function that agrees with t.

  a. $t(n) = 5t(n - 1) - 6t(n - 2)$, with $t(0) = 2$ and $t(1) = 5$

  b. $t(n) = 3t(n - 1) + 10t(n - 2)$, with $t(0) = 2$ and $t(1) = 3$

  c. $t(n) = 13t(n - 1) - 30t(n - 2)$, with $t(0) = 2$ and $t(1) = 13$

  d. $t(n) = -7t(n - 1) - 12t(n - 2)$, with $t(0) = 2$ and $t(1) = -7$

  e. $t(n) = 7t(n - 1) - 12t(n - 2)$, with $t(0) = 2$ and $t(1) = 7$

  f. $t(n) = 6t(n - 1) + 40t(n - 2)$, with $t(0) = 2$ and $t(1) = 6$

Habits of Mind

Look for a pattern. All the closed-form definitions will be similar. If you can find one, it will be easier to find the others.

What can you say about a function that satisfies this recurrence?

$$f(n) = 7f(n-1) - 10f(n-2)$$

For the sake of illustration, try to find a closed-form definition for a function that agrees with g, which is f with base cases specified as shown:

$$g(n) = \begin{cases} 4 & \text{if } n = 0 \\ 11 & \text{if } n = 1 \\ 7g(n-1) - 10g(n-2) & \text{if } n > 1 \end{cases}$$

Start by building a model for g and tabulating it:

Habits of Mind

Use a model. Model g in your FML.

Habits of Mind

Visualize. Graph a scatter plot of $g(n)$ against n as well.

n	g(n)
0	4
1	11
2	37
3	149
4	673
5	3221
6	15,817
7	78,509
8	391,393
9	1,954,661
10	9,768,697
11	48,834,269
12	244,152,913
13	1,220,727,701
14	6,103,564,777
15	30,517,676,429
16	152,588,087,233
17	762,939,846,341
18	3,814,698,052,057
19	19,073,487,900,989
20	95,367,434,786,353

The length of the digit strings suggests exponential growth. To test this, add a column with the ratios of consecutive terms.

n	$g(n)$	$\dfrac{g(n+1)}{g(n)}$
0	4	2.75
1	11	3.36364
2	37	4.02703
3	149	4.51678
4	673	4.78603
5	3221	4.91059
6	15,817	4.96358
7	78,509	4.98533
8	391,393	4.99411
9	1,954,661	4.99764
10	9,768,697	4.99906
11	48,834,269	4.99962
12	244,152,913	4.99985
13	1,220,727,701	4.99994
14	6,103,564,777	4.99998
15	30,517,676,429	4.99999
16	152,588,087,233	5.00000
17	762,939,846,341	5.00000
18	3,814,698,052,057	5.00000
19	19,073,487,900,989	5.00000
20	95,367,434,786,353	

Depending on your system, you may get slightly different numbers for the ratios. The constant 5 is an approximation—the actual ratio is very close to 5.

It looks as if the growth is "almost exponential." In fact, it looks as if the function $n \mapsto 5^n$ is close to a solution. What is going on?

Tabulate $n \mapsto 5^n$ next to g.

The answer is hinted at in Exercise 3 in Lesson 5.12. There are exponential functions of the form $n \mapsto a^n$ that satisfy the recurrence

$$g(n) = 7g(n-1) - 10g(n-2)$$

but they do not satisfy the base cases

$$g(0) = 4 \text{ and } g(1) = 11$$

But all is not lost. By transforming the exponential solutions a little, you can get a closed-form definition for a function that agrees with g. Here is how:

Suppose $n \mapsto a^n$ satisfies the recurrence

$$g(n) = 7g(n-1) - 10g(n-2)$$

Then $a^n = 7a^{n-1} - 10a^{n-2}$ for all integers $n \geq 2$.

Since the base of an exponential function cannot be 0, you can divide both sides by a^{n-2}. You get

$$a^2 = 7a - 10$$

This is a quadratic equation. So, if $n \mapsto a^n$ satisfies the recurrence, a must be a root of the quadratic equation

$$a^2 - 7a + 10 = 0$$

The roots of this equation are 2 and 5 (there is the 5 again). Just to be sure, check it out:

> The polynomial $x^2 - 7x + 10$ is called the *characteristic polynomial* for the recurrence $g(n)$.

For You to Do

Show the following for all integers $n \geq 2$.

1. $2^n = 7 \cdot 2^{n-1} - 10 \cdot 2^{n-2}$

2. $5^n = 7 \cdot 5^{n-1} - 10 \cdot 5^{n-2}$

But not only does $n \mapsto 2^n$ satisfy the recurrence, so does the more general exponential function $n \mapsto k \cdot 2^n$, for any number k. To see this, multiply both sides of the equation

$$2^n = 7 \cdot 2^{n-1} - 10 \cdot 2^{n-2}$$

by k. If you distribute the k on the right side, you get

$$k \cdot 2^n = 7 \cdot k \cdot 2^{n-1} - 10 \cdot k \cdot 2^{n-2}$$

So, $n \mapsto k \cdot 2^n$ satisfies the recurrence

$$g(n) = 7 \cdot g(n-1) - 10 \cdot g(n-2)$$

Similarly, any function of the form $n \mapsto j \cdot 5^n$ for some constant j will also satisfy the recurrence.

Minds in Action   episode 16

Tony and Sasha are thinking about the solutions to the recurrence.

Tony We now have lots of functions that satisfy the recurrence. Things like $n \mapsto 3 \cdot 2^n$ or even $n \mapsto \pi \cdot 5^n$.

Sasha But none of them satisfy the base cases. They can't, because, for example, $j \cdot 5^n$ is j when $n = 0$, so j would have to be 4 if the first base case is true.

Tony And $j \cdot 5^n$ is $5j$ when $n = 1$, so if $j = 4$, $5j$ is 20. The second base case says it has to be 11. No good.

Enter Derman, who stares at the board.

Derman Why not do both? Do some 5^n's and some 2^n's. It would be $n \mapsto k \cdot 2^n + j \cdot 5^n$. Now you have two variables—I bet you can find k and j that make the function 4 at 0 and 11 at 1.

Sasha Two equations and two unknowns. I think he's on to something.

Tony Yes, but now it probably won't satisfy the recurrence.

Sasha Maybe it will. They each work by themselves. Look—take the two expressions and add down.

Sasha writes on the board.

$$
\begin{array}{rcl}
k \cdot 2^n & = & 7 \cdot k \cdot 2^{n-1} \quad - \quad 10 \cdot k \cdot 2^{n-2} \\
+ \quad j \cdot 5^n & = & 7 \cdot j \cdot 5^{n-1} \quad - \quad 10 \cdot j \cdot 5^{n-2} \\
\hline
k \cdot 2^n + j \cdot 5^n & = & 7(k \cdot 2^{n-1} + j \cdot 5^{n-1}) \; - \; 10(k \cdot 2^{n-2} + j \cdot 5^{n-2})
\end{array}
$$

Tony So, the sum of the two solutions will be another solution. Nice.

Derman See? I told you it would work.

Tony Don't worry, we believed you. Now we can find k and j to make the base cases work. Let's see—our closed form is $n \mapsto k \cdot 2^n + j \cdot 5^n$. If n is 0, we want this to be 4, so $k \cdot 2^0 + j \cdot 5^0 = 4$. That's just

$$k + j = 4$$

And when $n = 1$, the output is $k \cdot 2^1 + j \cdot 5^1$. We want this to be 11, so

$$2k + 5j = 11$$

Derman See? Two equations in two unknowns, like Sasha said. I told you it would work.

Sasha Fine, fine. Now we solve the system

$$
\begin{array}{rcl}
k + \; j & = & 4 \\
2k + 5j & = & 11
\end{array}
$$

and we get $k = 3$ and $j = 1$. Looks like the closed form is

$$h(n) = 3 \cdot 2^n + 5^n$$

Tony I'll check it against the table . . . It worked!

Derman No doubt!

For You to Do

3. Show that Sasha, Tony and Derman's function h and the original function g agree for the domain of g. That is, show that the two functions

$$h(n) = 3 \cdot 2^n + 5^n \text{ and } g(n) = \begin{cases} 4 & \text{if } n = 0 \\ 11 & \text{if } n = 1 \\ 7g(n-1) - 10g(n-2) & \text{if } n > 1 \end{cases}$$

agree for all nonnegative integers n.

> The natural domain of h is all of $\mathbb{R}$, while g is defined only for nonnegative integers.

Embedded in the above example is a general method for solving any two-term recurrence. You will give a precise description of the method in Exercise 6.

And Sasha's "add down" insight leads to another useful result.

Theorem 5.3   Closure of Solutions

If two functions r and s satisfy the two-term recurrence

$$f(n) = Af(n - 1) + Bf(n - 2)$$

then so does any linear combination

$$t(n) = k \cdot r(n) + j \cdot s(n)$$

where k and j are real numbers.

> **Remember...**
>
> A linear combination of x and y is $ax + by$, where a and b are real numbers.

Exercises Practicing Habits of Mind

Check Your Understanding

1. The two-term recurrence

$$f(n) = 7f(n - 1) - 10f(n - 2)$$

is satisfied by any function in the form $f(n) = A \cdot 2^n + B \cdot 5^n$. Each of the sequences below satisfies the recurrence. For each sequence, calculate the next two terms. Then find the values of A and B.

> **Habits of Mind**
>
> **Generalize.** How can you use the other sequences in this exercise to help with part (f)?

a. $4, 14, 58, \ldots$ b. $0, -3, -21, \ldots$ c. $4, 11, 37, \ldots$

d. $0, 1, 7, \ldots$ e. $1, 0, -10, \ldots$

f. **Take It Further** $x, y, -10x + 7y, \ldots$

2. Consider the two-term recurrence

$$g(n) = 13g(n-1) - 30g(n-2)$$

    a. What two numbers have a sum of 13 and a product of 30?

    b. Show that $g(n) = 10^n$ satisfies the recurrence.

    c. Show that $g(n) = 3^n$ satisfies the recurrence.

    d. Show that $g(n) = 10^n + 3^n$ satisfies the recurrence.

That is, show that $10^n = 13 \cdot 10^{n-1} - 30 \cdot 10^{n-2}$ for any integer $n \geq 2$.

3. Find a closed-form definition for a function that agrees with t.

$$t(n) = \begin{cases} 5 & \text{if } n = 0 \\ 19 & \text{if } n = 1 \\ 8t(n-1) - 15t(n-2) & \text{if } n > 1 \end{cases}$$

Habits of Mind

Make a connection.
What connection is there between this and $x^2 - 10x + 21$?

4. Define function t by

$$t(n) - 10t(n-1) + 21t(n-2) = 0$$

with $t(0) = 2$ and $t(1) = 10$. Find a closed-form equivalent for t.

5. Find different exponential functions $h(n) = a^n$ and $j(n) = b^n$ that satisfy the two-term recurrence

$$f(n) = 2f(n-1) + f(n-2)$$

Use the quadratic formula.

6. **Write About It** Describe a method for finding a closed form (in terms of A and B) for a function that satisfies the two-term recurrence

$$f(n) = Af(n-1) + Bf(n-2)$$

7. The Fibonacci numbers are the outputs of the function f defined by

$$f(n) = f(n-1) + f(n-2)$$

with the initial conditions $f(0) = 0$ and $f(1) = 1$. Find a closed-form equivalent for f.

On Your Own

8. Function f satisfies the recurrence

$$f(n) = 9f(n-1) - 20f(n-2)$$

Find a closed-form equivalent for f if

    a. $f(0) = 2$ and $f(1) = 9$

    b. $f(0) = 20$ and $f(1) = 90$

9. Consider the two-term recurrence $f(n) = 8f(n-1) - 12f(n-2)$.

   a. Why might you guess that an exponential function would satisfy the recurrence?

   b. Show that $f(n) = 6^n$ satisfies this recurrence.

   c. Find a closed-form definition for f if the initial conditions are $f(0) = 2$ and $f(1) = 8$.

   d. Find a closed-form definition for f if the initial conditions are $f(0) = 5$ and $f(1) = 26$.

10. Find a closed-form equivalent for a function f that fits this table by first determining a two-term recurrence that the function satisfies.

x	f(x)
0	2
1	10
2	36
3	152
4	592
5	2400

11. Suppose f satisfies the recurrence $f(n) = 6f(n-1) - 7f(n-2)$.

   a. Show that if $f(0) = 1$ and $f(1) = 3 + \sqrt{2}$, then $f(2) = (3 + \sqrt{2})^2$.

   b. Find both possible values of b that make $f(n) = b^n$ satisfy the recurrence.

   c. If $f(0) = 2$ and $f(1) = 6$, find a closed-form definition for f.

   d. If $f(0) = 0$ and $f(1) = 1$, find a closed-form definition for f.

12. Find a closed-form definition for the function $L(n) = L(n-1) + L(n-2)$ with $L(0) = 2$ and $L(1) = 1$. This function generates the Lucas numbers

$$2, 1, 3, 4, 7, 11, \ldots$$

13. **Take It Further** Define function f by

$$f(n) = 4f(n-1) - 13f(n-2)$$

with $f(0) = 2$ and $f(1) = 4$.

   a. Tabulate f using inputs from 0 to 8.

   b. Find a closed-form equivalent for f using the techniques from this lesson. What is different about this exercise? Does the process still work?

14. **Take It Further** Suppose f satisfies the recurrence

$$f(n) = 19f(n-2) - 30f(n-3)$$

Find a closed-form definition for f if $f(0) = 8, f(1) = 3$, and $f(2) = 79$.

Go Online
PHSchool.com

For additional practice, go to **Web Code:** bga-0513

15. Take It Further There is a special case of recurrences in the form $f(n) = Af(n-1) + Bf(n-2)$. One such recurrence is

$$f(n) = 2f(n-1) - f(n-2)$$

a. Describe the function with starting conditions $f(0) = 3$ and $f(1) = 8$.

b. Describe the function with starting conditions $f(0) = 10$ and $f(1) = 0$.

c. Describe the function in general for all functions that satisfy this recurrence.

d. Describe the function in general for all functions that satisfy the similar recurrence.

$$f(n) = 6f(n-1) - 9f(n-2)$$

16. Standardized Test Prep Consider the following function.

$$f(n) = \begin{cases} 0 & \text{if } n = 0 \\ 1 & \text{if } n = 1 \\ f(n-1) + f(n-2) & \text{if } n > 1 \end{cases}$$

Which statement is correct?

A. $f(2n) = 2(f(n-1) + f(n-2))$

B. $f(2n) = f(2(n-1)) + f(2(n-2))$

C. $f(2n) = f(2n-1) + f(2n-2)$

D. $f(2n) = f(2n-2) + f(2n-3)$

Maintain Your Skills

17. The Martinez family buys a house. They get a 15-year mortgage at a low rate of 6% APR. This means that what they owe at the end of the year is 6% more than what they owed at the start of the year. After the interest is added, the family reduces what they owe by making a payment. The family owes $200,000 to start.

a. If the Martinez family pays $12,000 every year, explain why the function B gives their balance after n years.

$$B(n) = \begin{cases} 200{,}000 & \text{if } n = 0 \\ 1.06B(n-1) - 12{,}000 & \text{if } n > 0 \end{cases}$$

For simplicity, calculate interest and payment once per year, rather than once per month.

b. If the Martinez family pays $12,000 every year, will they pay off the mortgage in 15 years? If not, how much is left at the end? What if they pay $13,000? $14,000? $15,000? Look for a pattern.

c. If the family pays D dollars every year, how much is left at the end in terms of D?

d. Determine the exact amount the Martinez family should pay per year to leave a $0 balance on the mortgage at the end.

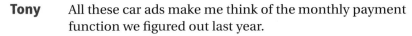

5.14 $f(n) = Af(n-1) + B$

The right strategy for solving a recurrence depends on the form of the recurrence. Lesson 5.13 showed how combining two exponential solutions to a recurrence of the form $f(n) = Af(n-1) + Bf(n-2)$ produces yet another solution. In this lesson, you will draw on skills developed earlier to solve recurrences of the form $f(n) = Af(n-1) + B$.

Minds in Action   episode 17

Sasha and Tony are looking at the newspaper.

Tony   All these car ads make me think of the monthly payment function we figured out last year.

Sasha   If you think about it, we were solving a recurrence. Remember this problem?

> Suppose you want to buy a car that costs $10,000. You can put $1000 down, so you would borrow $9000. The interest rate is 5%. The dealer wants the loan paid off in three years. Will a monthly payment of $250 pay off the loan?

Tony   Yes, I remember what we did. We figured out a function b that gave us the balance at the end of month n with a monthly payment of 250 dollars. Then we figured out $b(36)$ and saw if it was 0. The function definition was recursive:

$$b(n) = \begin{cases} 9000 & \text{if } n = 0 \\ \left(1 + \frac{0.05}{12}\right)b(n-1) - 250 & \text{if } n > 0 \end{cases}$$

We didn't get 0, but then we adjusted the monthly payment to make $b(36)$ come out to be 0.

Sasha   And later, we unstacked this and got a formula for the monthly payment. But wait. If we think about it in terms of recurrence relations, the recurrence looks like

$$b(n) = Ab(n-1) + B$$

Maybe we can use what we did for monthly payments to solve any recurrence of this form.

> **Remember...**
> What you owe at the end of the month is what you owed at the start of the month plus $\frac{1}{12}$th of the year's interest on that amount, minus the monthly payment.

> What is the actual monthly payment?

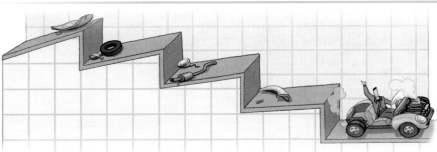

Consider more than one strategy. There are two methods from CME Project *Algebra 2* to solve the recurrence

$$f(n) = Af(n-1) + B$$

- You could use affine transformations. If $\mathcal{A}_{(a,b)}(x) = ax + b$, then the recurrence is

$$f(n) = \mathcal{A}_{(A,B)}(f(n-1))$$

But then

$$f(n-1) = \mathcal{A}_{(A,B)}(f(n-2))$$

and

$$f(n-2) = \mathcal{A}_{(A,B)}(f(n-3))$$

and so on, so that

$$f(n) = \mathcal{A}^n_{(A,B)}(f(0))$$

where $\mathcal{A}^n_{(A,B)}$ is the nth iteration of $\mathcal{A}_{(A,B)}$. In CME Project *Algebra 2*, you derived a formula for the nth iteration of an affine transformation.

> Solving a recurrence means finding a function that satisfies the recurrence at every input in the function's domain.

- If you did not want to use the language of affine transformations, you could just unstack the recurrence:

$$f(n) = Af(n-1) + B$$
$$= A(Af(n-2) + B) + B = A^2 f(n-2) + AB + B$$
$$= A^2(Af(n-3) + B) + AB + B = A^3 f(n-3) + A^2 B + AB + B$$
$$\vdots$$
$$= A^n f(0) + B(A^{n-1} + A^{n-2} + \cdots + A + 1)$$

The rightmost sum is a geometric series. You know a formula for that.

For Discussion

1. Finish one or both of these derivations to prove the following theorem.

Theorem 5.4   *Closed-form equivalent for $f(n) = Af(n-1) + B$*

Define f by

$$f(n) = \begin{cases} p & \text{if } n = 0 \\ Af(n-1) + B & \text{if } n > 0 \end{cases}$$

> Here, p is a number, the base case.

Then for nonnegative integer inputs, a closed-form equivalent for f is

$$f(n) = A^n \cdot p + B\left(\frac{A^n - 1}{A - 1}\right)$$

For You to Do

Tristen buys a car. The car costs $12,000. The financing is 6% APR, or 0.5% monthly. A car payment is due every month for 36 months.

2. Find Tristen's car payment, to the nearest cent.

3. Using the same term and interest rate, construct a function m so that $m(C)$ is the monthly payment for a car that costs C dollars.

> How could a CAS help you do this without guesswork?

Exercises *Practicing Habits of Mind*

Check Your Understanding

1. Jess invests $500 every year in a savings account. Each year she also earns 3% on the money currently invested. Find a closed-form definition for a function that gives the amount of money in Jess's account after n years.

2. Generalize the result from Exercise 1. Suppose Jess invests D dollars per year in a savings account that earns a rate of r per year (as a decimal, not a percent). Find a function B that gives the balance of Jess's account after n years.

3. A local environmental group claims that 20% of the trees in Woodville are being cut down each year. Authorities have decided to plant 3000 trees every year to try and counteract this effect.

a. Suppose there are 25,000 trees in Woodville to start. Determine how many trees there will be each year for the next seven years, rounding to the nearest tree.

b. Make a scatter plot with number of trees on the vertical axis and years on the horizontal axis.

c. Find an *equilibrium point*, the number of trees that will remain constant year-to-year after a certain number of iterations of this process.

d. How many more trees than the equilibrium point does Woodville have at the start? After one year, how many more trees than the equilibrium point are there? After two years? After three? Look for a pattern.

e. Find a closed-form definition for $T(n)$, the number of trees in Woodville after n years.

> An **equilibrium point** is a repeating value of an iteration. If $f(n) = f(n - 1) = C$, then C is an equilibrium point.

4. Define function f by the recurrence

$$f(n) = 1.065f(n - 1) + B$$

with $f(0) = 200{,}000$. Find B if $200{,}000$ is the equilibrium point for f, the value of $f(0)$ that produces a constant output.

5. Show that the equilibrium point for the recurrence

$$f(n) = Af(n - 1) + B$$

is

$$n = \frac{B}{1 - A}$$

6. **Take It Further** The general form for a car payment or mortgage comes from the recurrence

$$f(n) = (1 + r)f(n - 1) - P$$

Given $f(0) = B$ (the starting balance), the goal is to find the correct value of P so that $f(a) = 0$ where a is the length of the loan and r is the interest rate expressed as a decimal.

   a. Find the equilibrium point of f in terms of P and r.

   b. How far is the starting balance B from the equilibrium point?

   c. How far away from the equilibrium point is $f(1)$? $f(2)$? $f(n)$?

   d. Write a closed-form definition for f in terms of B, P, r, and n.

   e. Solve the equation $f(n) = 0$ to find a function for the monthly payment P in terms of the initial balance B, the rate r, and the number of payments n.

On Your Own

7. At 30 years old, Drew estimates he can save $5000 per year toward retirement. Use the result from Exercise 2 to answer these questions.

   a. How much can Drew expect to have in his retirement account at age 65 if he assumes that each year, the money in his account will grow by 10%?

   b. How much more would Drew have in his retirement account at age 65 at 12% growth instead of 10%?

   c. How much less would Drew have in his retirement account at age 65 at 8% growth instead of 10%?

10% growth per year is a reasonable average when investing in commodities such as stocks. The actual percentage varies year-to-year but a fixed percentage is usually used when estimating long-term results like this one.

8. Define f recursively as

$$f(n) = \begin{cases} P & \text{if } n = 0 \\ Af(n-1) + B & \text{if } n > 0 \end{cases}$$

a. Tabulate f for inputs from 0 to 4.

b. Find a closed-form equivalent for f.

9. Consider Tristen's situation with a \$12,000 car loan at 6% APR for 36 months. The recursive definition for Tristen's balance is

$$B(n, p) = \begin{cases} 12{,}000 & \text{if } n = 0 \\ 1005B(n-1, p) - p & \text{if } n > 0 \end{cases}$$

If 6% is the APR, what is the monthly interest rate?

a. Use the results from the previous exercise to write $f(36)$ in terms of p, the monthly payment.

b. Find the correct monthly payment to the nearest cent.

10. a. Find the correct monthly payment on a \$10,000 car loan taken at 9% APR for 48 months,

b. Find the correct monthly payment on a \$20,000 car loan with the same terms. What happens to the monthly payment?

11. Write About It Prove the following theorem.

Theorem 5.5 *Monthly Payments*

On a loan for **C** dollars taken out for **n** months with an APR of **i** percent compounded monthly, the monthly payment is **m** dollars where

$$m = \frac{q^n(q-1)}{q^n - 1} C$$

and $q = 1 + \dfrac{i}{1200}$.

12. Take It Further In this investigation you explored two-term recurrences in the form

$$f(n) = Af(n-1) + Bf(n-2)$$

A related form is

$$f(n) = Af(n-1) + Bf(n-2) + Cf(n-3)$$

Consider the three-term recurrence

$$f(n) = 10f(n-1) - 31f(n-2) + 30f(n-3)$$

a. Show that $f(n) = 2^n$ satisfies this recurrence.

b. Find two other exponential functions that satisfy the recurrence.

c. If $f(0) = 4$, $f(1) = 16$, and $f(2) = 74$, find a closed-form definition for f.

13. Take It Further Find a three-term recurrence that this sequence satisfies. Then find a closed-form definition for a function that satisfies the recurrence and agrees with the sequence.

$$1, 5, 105, 965, 10065, 99725, 1000665$$

14. Standardized Test Prep Find, to the nearest penny, the monthly payment on a $12,000 loan at 6% APR, paid off over 36 months.

A. $362.97   **B.** $365.06   **C.** $368.44   **D.** $370.60

Go Online
PHSchool.com

For additional practice, go to **Web Code:** bga-0514

Maintain Your Skills

15. Consider the recurrence

$$f(n) = 3f(n - 1) - 300$$

a. Show that 150 is an equilibrium point for f. That is, if $f(n - 1) = 150$, then $f(n) = 150$.

b. Suppose $f(0)$ is 1000 greater than the equilibrium point. How much greater than the equilibrium point is $f(1)$? $f(2)$? $f(3)$? $f(n)$?

What is the monthly payment on a $12,000 car loan at 6% APR, paid off over 36 months?

In this investigation you studied recursive relationships. You found closed polynomial and exponential forms for them. The following questions will help you summarize what you have learned.

1. Every day, Melissa takes 50 mg of prescription medication. Each day, her body metabolizes and removes 20% of the medicine present.

  a. Explain why the recurrence $f(n) = 0.8f(n-1) + 50$ models the amount of medicine in Melissa's body, day by day.

  b. Melissa begins the treatment with no medicine in her body: $f(0) = 0$. Tabulate f for days 0 through 10. Plot the results.

  c. What appears to be happening in the long run?

2. Oscar buys a house. He takes out a 15-year mortgage on the $200,000 cost of the house. The interest rate is 6.5% per year. Oscar considers an interest-only loan. In this type of loan, he would pay only the exact amount of the interest.

  a. If Oscar had an interest-only loan, how much would he pay each year?

  b. Instead, Oscar pays $16,000 per year. Write a recursive definition for the loan balance after n years. What is the balance after 15 years?

  c. Determine the annual payment Oscar should make to pay off his mortgage in 15 years.

3. The Fibonacci numbers satisfy the recurrence $f(n) = f(n-1) + f(n-2)$ with $f(0) = 0$ and $f(1) = 1$. The ratio of consecutive Fibonacci numbers approaches the golden ratio $\phi = \frac{1 + \sqrt{5}}{2}$.

  The numbers that satisfy the recurrence $g(n) = 2g(n-1) + 2g(n-2)$ with $g(0) = 0$ and $g(1) = 1$ have a similar property, but approach a different ratio. Find the exact value of this ratio.

4. What methods are available for deciding if a linear, polynomial, or exponential rule fits a table?

5. How can you find a closed-form function definition that satisfies a two-term recurrence?

6. What is the monthly payment for a three-year car loan for $15,000, taken out at 5% APR?

Vocabulary

In this investigation, you learned these terms. Make sure you understand what each one means and how to use it.

- **equilibrium point**
- **functional equation**

- **recurrence**
- **two-term recurrence**

Project: Using Mathematical Habits

Rhyme Schemes

The *rhyme scheme* of a poem dictates the pattern of rhyming lines the poem uses. For example, here is a five-line limerick:

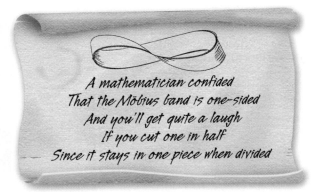

*A mathematician confided
That the Möbius band is one-sided
And you'll get quite a laugh
If you cut one in half
Since it stays in one piece when divided*

The rhyme scheme of this poem is AABBA. This means that the first, second, and fifth line all rhyme. The third and fourth line also rhyme. The letters are always assigned in alphabetical order, so it would not be correct to call this same meter BBAAB or even ZZYYZ.

Here are some other possible rhyme schemes for five-line poems:

• AAAAA. Here, all five lines rhyme.

• ABCAB. Here, lines 1 and 4 rhyme, and lines 2 and 5 rhyme. Line 3 does not rhyme with any other.

• ABCDD. Only lines 4 and 5 rhyme.

• ABCDE. No lines rhyme.

The lettering must be in alphabetical order. The first line is always A, and any time a new line does not rhyme with any other, it gets assigned the next letter in the alphabet.

1. Find or write a short poem. Detail its rhyme scheme.

2. Find all the rhyme schemes for
   a. two-line poems.
   b. three-line poems.

3. Find all the rhyme schemes for four-line poems. Think about how to organize your work to guarantee that you have found them all.

4. A five-line poem's rhyme scheme starts with ABCB. How many possible rhyme schemes are there for the entire poem?

5. Use the tactics of Exercise 4 to find the number of rhyme schemes for five-line poems.

6. Copy and complete this table with the number of different rhyme schemes of different types. (For example, the table says that there are 15 different five-line rhyme schemes that use only the two letters A and B, and 65 different six-line rhyme schemes using exactly four letters.) Look for patterns that help you extend the table.

Lines ↓ / Letters Used	1	2	3	4	5	6
1	1	–	–	–	–	–
2	1	1	–	–	–	–
3	1	3	1	–	–	–
4	▪	▪	▪	▪	–	–
5	▪	15	▪	▪	1	–
6	▪	▪	▪	65	▪	▪

7. Describe and explain some patterns found in the table of Exercise 6.

8. How many 7-line rhyme schemes are there?

9. Find a relationship between the situation in this project and the situation with the Simplex Lock in Chapter 4.

Review

Go Online
PHSchool.com

For vocabulary review, go
to **Web Code:** bga-0551

In **Investigation 5A,** you learned to

- determine the domain on which two functions agree
- verify that a closed-form and a recursive function definition agree at the first few inputs in a domain
- prove by induction that two function definitions agree for all inputs in an infinite domain

The following questions will help you check your understanding.

1. For each of the following pairs of functions, find the largest set of inputs for which the two functions are equal.

  a. $f(x) = x - \frac{1}{x}$, $g(x) = \frac{x^2 - 1}{x}$

  b. $f(x) = \frac{x^2 - 1}{x + 1}$, $g(x) = x - 1$

  c. $f(x) = 3x - 5$, $g(x) = 3x - 5 + x(x - 8)$

  d. $f(x) = |x|$, $g(x) = -|x|$

2. Tabulate each function below using inputs from 0 to 5, then find a function with a closed-form definition that agrees with the table.

  a. $f(x) = \begin{cases} 4 & \text{if } x = 0 \\ f(x - 1) + 5 & \text{if } x > 0 \end{cases}$

  b. $g(x) = \begin{cases} 5 & \text{if } x = 0 \\ 2 \cdot f(x - 1) & \text{if } x > 0 \end{cases}$

3. Define G and g as

  $$G(x) = x^2 + 2$$

  $$g(x) = \begin{cases} 2 & \text{if } x = 0 \\ g(x - 1) + 2x - 1 & \text{if } x > 0 \end{cases}$$

  a. Tabulate the functions to make sure they start out equal.

  b. Show that if $G(21) = g(21)$, then $G(22) = g(22)$.

  c. Use mathematical induction to show G and g will always agree for any nonnegative integer inputs.

In **Investigation 5B,** you learned to

- find a polynomial function that fits a difference table
- explain how the up-and-over property of difference tables relates to Pascal's Triangle
- quickly find rules for summations, like the sum of the first n squares

The following questions will help you check your understanding.

4. Find the values of A, B, and C in the difference table.

Input	Output	Δ	Δ²
0	7	−2	A
1	5	4	6
2	9	10	6
3	▨	▨	6
4	▨	▨	6
5	▨	B	
6	C		

Review continued

5. Here is a table for a function G.

x	$G(x)$
0	−4
1	0
2	22
3	74
4	168
5	316
6	530
7	822

   a. Build a complete difference table for G.

   b. Find a polynomial function that agrees with this table.

6. Use a difference table to find a closed-form equivalent for

$$S(n) = \sum_{k=0}^{n-1} (k^2 + 2)$$

In **Investigation 5C,** you learned to

- find general classes of functions that fit a recurrence

- relate a solution to a two-term recurrence to a quadratic polynomial.

- calculate the monthly payment for a car loan and write a general rule for all such problems

The following questions will help you check your understanding.

7. Define f recursively as

$$f(n) = 0.75f(n - 1) + 15$$

   with $f(0) = 10$.

   a. Tabulate f for $n = 0$ to $n = 5$.

   b. What is the equilibrium point?

   c. How far away from the equilibrium point is $f(0)$? $f(1)$? $f(2)$?

   d. Write a closed-form equivalent for f.

8. Function f satisfies the recurrence

$$f(n) = 9f(n - 1) - 14f(n - 2)$$

   a. Find both possible values of b that make $f(n) = b^n$ satisfy the recurrence.

   b. If $f(0) = 2$ and $f(1) = 9$, find a closed-form definition for f.

9. Find the correct monthly payment on a $25,000 car loan taken out at 6% APR for 60 months.

Go Online
PHSchool.com

For a chapter test, go to
Web Code: bga-0553

Multiple Choice

1. Define H recursively as

$$H(n) = \begin{cases} -3 & \text{if } n = 0 \\ 4 \cdot H(n-1) + 1 & \text{if } n > 0 \end{cases}$$

Find $H(2)$.

A. -43 **B.** -11 **C.** 13 **D.** 45

2. Define f and g as

$$f(x) = x^2 + 7$$

$$g(x) = x^2 + 7 + x(x-3)(x+5)$$

What is the largest set on which f and g agree?

A. $\{1, 3, 5\}$ **B.** $\{-5, 0, 3\}$

C. $\{-5, 3\}$ **D.** $\{-3, 0, 5\}$

3. At the right is a partial table for a function f. Use the table to find $f(4)$.

x	f(x)	Δ
0	5	2
1	▨	10
2	▨	-8
3	▨	12

A. 4 **B.** 9

C. 16 **D.** 21

4. Here is the first line of a difference table for a cubic function g.

x	g(x)	Δ	Δ²	Δ³
0	3	1	-4	6

Find $g(8)$.

A. 6 **B.** 44 **C.** 235 **D.** 249

5. Let f be a function that satisfies the recurrence.

$$f(n) = 3 \cdot f(n-1) - 4 \cdot f(n-2)$$

Which of the following cannot be a sequence of consecutive outputs of f?

A. $1, 2, 2, -2, -14, -34$ **B.** $2, 4, 4, -4, -28, -68$

C. $-1, 5, 19, 37, 37, -37$ **D.** $1, 4, 8, 8, -8, -56$

Open Response

6. Use induction to show that these two functions must agree for all integers $n \geq 0$.

$$H(n) = 5n + 2$$

$$h(n) = \begin{cases} 2 & \text{if } n = 0 \\ h(n-1) + 5 & \text{if } n > 0 \end{cases}$$

7. Find a polynomial function that fits this table.

x	m(x)
0	-1
1	-4
2	-7
3	2
4	35
5	104

8. Find a closed-form definition for

$$S(n) = \sum_{k=0}^{n-1} (k^2 + k)$$

a. by using a difference table.

b. by using the formulas for $\sum_{k=0}^{n-1} k^2$ and $\sum_{k=0}^{n-1} k$.

9. Define f recursively as

$$f(x) = 0.6f(x-1) + B$$

with $f(0) = 80$.

a. If $B = 35$, what is the equilibrium point?

b. Find the value of B if the equilibrium point is 100.

10. Find the bases for two exponential functions $h(n) = a^n$ and $j(n) = b^n$ that satisfy the recurrence

$$f(n) = 5f(n-1) - 6f(n-2)$$

11. How can differences be used to find a polynomial that matches a table?

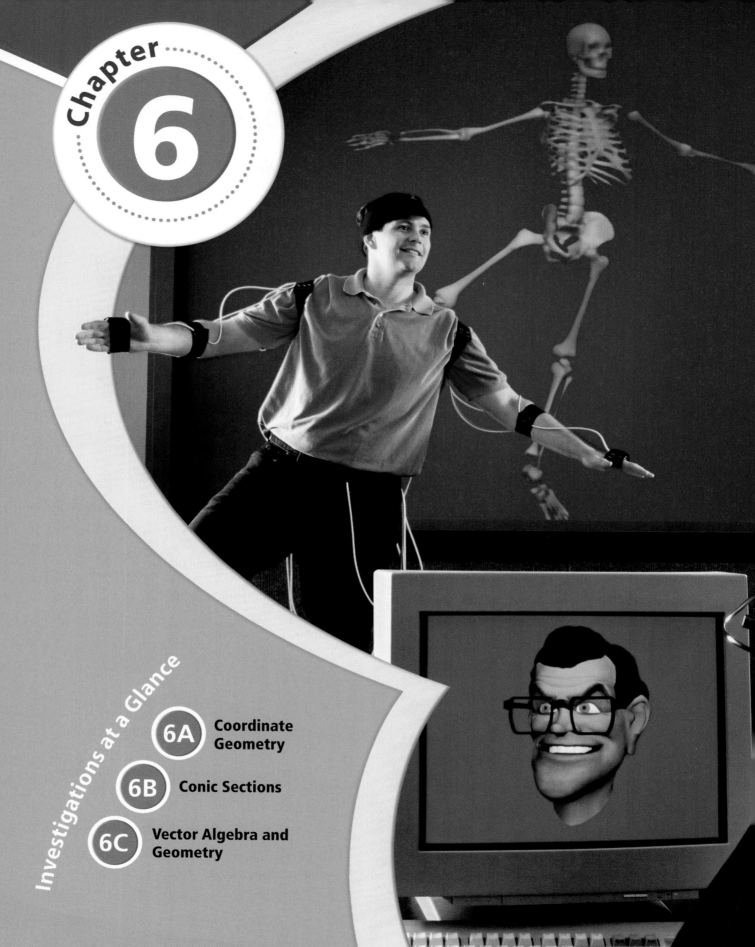

Analytic Geometry

The connections between geometry and algebra are a pathway to apply mathematics to the real world. View experimental data through a mathematical lens and you can link graphs to numerical data and see a relationship. Using this relationship, you can predict future behavior or even discover underlying physical laws of nature.

For example, tie a mass to a spring and wait until it stops moving. Displace the mass by a distance d, and use a stopwatch to find the time it takes for the mass to move through one complete oscillation (up and down and back to the starting place). You will see that this time remains constant. That is because the force on the object is always equal to kx. where k is a constant that depends on the spring you are using and x is the current distance of the object from its equilibrium position. Robert Hooke (1635–1703) discovered the law by matching an equation to the picture formed by graphing numerical data about the position of masses tied to springs.

Vocabulary and Notation

- affine combination
- centroid
- conic sections
- convex combination
- coordinatize
- Dandelin sphere
- directrix
- double cone, $z^2 = x^2 + y^2$
- eccentricity
- ellipse
- focus, foci
- head and tail of a vector
- hyperbola
- locus
- major axis
- minor axis
- parabola
- parameter
- point-tester
- power of a point, $\Pi(P)$
- signed power of a point, $\Pi_S(P)$
- vector, $\overrightarrow{AB}$

Coordinate Geometry

In *Coordinate Geometry*, you will reap the benefits of the insight of Rene Descartes. His coordinate system lets you transform geometric problems into algebraic problems. Then you will use algebra to solve those problems.

By the end of this investigation, you will be able to answer questions like these.

1. What is the set of points equidistant from the *x*-axis and the point (0, 4)?

2. How can you use coordinates to show that the diagonals of a parallelogram bisect each other?

3. How can you find the center and radius of a circle with an equation written in normal form?

You will learn how to

• sketch the graphs of equations in two variables

• use distance and slope relationships to prove geometric results

• evaluate and use the signed power of a point with respect to a circle

You will develop these habits and skills:

• Use equations as point-testers for graphs.

• Visualize collections of points that meet particular conditions—points that satisfy a distance relationship, points with the same signed power with respect to a given circle, and so on.

• Choose coordinate systems strategically to facilitate calculation and proof.

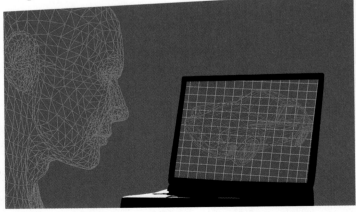

Artists and engineers employ digital wire frame models to represent three dimensional objects. The surface and underlying structure of the item is first coordinatized. Then the animator uses powerful computer software to study, manipulate, or bring the entity to virtual life.

In CME Project *Algebra 1*, you explored versions of the addition and multiplication tables placed upon a coordinate grid. Here is the multiplication table.

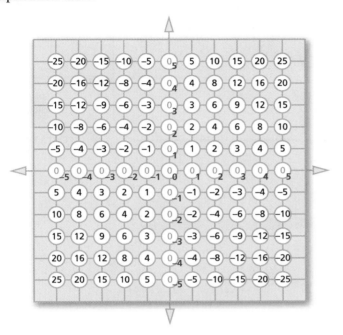

You can use the coordinate grid to visualize the outputs of any two-variable function, such as $f(x, y) = x^2 - y^2$.

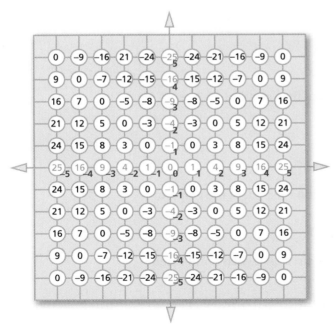

For You to Explore

1. Use the grid for f to find several solutions to the equation $x^2 - y^2 = 9$.

2. Use the grid to help draw an accurate graph of the equation $x^2 - y^2 = 9$.

   > You may need to find other points besides the ones in the grid.

3. Use the grid to help draw an accurate graph of the equation $y^2 - x^2 = 5$.

4. Find all solutions to this system of equations.
   $$x^2 - y^2 = 9$$
   $$x + y = 5$$

5. **Take It Further** Use the grid to help you draw a reasonable sketch of the graph of this equation.
   $$z = x^2 - y^2$$

   > The z-axis is perpendicular to the xy-plane, and passes through the origin.

Exercises *Practicing Habits of Mind*

On Your Own

6. Build a grid similar to the one for $f(x, y) = x^2 - y^2$ for the function g defined as
   $$g(x, y) = x^2 + y^2$$

7. Use the grid to help draw an accurate graph of the equation $x^2 + y^2 = 17$.

8. Solve this system of equations.
   $$x^2 + y^2 = 17$$
   $$x^2 - y^2 = 9$$

9. **Take It Further** Draw a rough three-dimensional sketch of the graph of this equation.
   $$z = x^2 + y^2$$

10. The graph of the equation $x^2 + y^2 = 13$ is a circle. For each point listed below, determine whether or not it is on this circle.

    a. $(3, 2)$ **b.** $(2, -3)$ **c.** $(0, 4)$ **d.** $(2\sqrt{3}, -1)$

    e. **Write About It** Describe how you would determine if any point (x, y) is on this circle.

11. Here is the graph of two chords of the circle given by the graph of the equation $x^2 + y^2 = 13$.

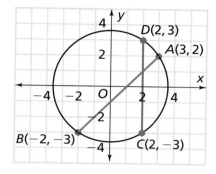

a. Find an equation for the line containing $A(3, 2)$ and $B(-2, -3)$.

b. Find an equation for the line containing $C(2, -3)$ and $D(2, 3)$.

c. Find the coordinates of the point of intersection X of the two chords.

d. Show that the following statement is true by calculating the length of each chord.

$$AX \cdot BX = CX \cdot DX$$

12. Here is the graph of two chords of the circle given by the graph of the equation $x^2 + y^2 = 25$.

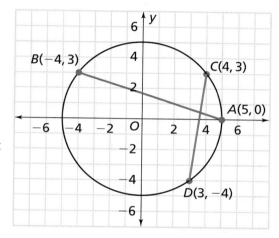

a. Find an equation for the line containing $A(5, 0)$ and $B(-4, 3)$.

b. Find an equation for the line containing $C(4, 3)$ and $D(3, -4)$.

c. Find the coordinates of the point of intersection X of the two chords.

d. Show that the following statement is true by calculating the length of each chord.

$$AX \cdot BX = CX \cdot DX$$

Maintain Your Skills

13. For each statement, write an expression that matches the description.

a. the slope between $(2, 4)$ and (x, y)

b. the distance from the origin $(0, 0)$ to (x, y)

c. the distance from $(2, 4)$ to (x, y)

d. the distance from $(3, 0)$ to (x, y), plus the distance from $(-3, 0)$ to (x, y)

e. the distance from (x, y) to the line with equation $y = -3$

f. **Take It Further** the distance from (x, y) to the line with equation $x + y = 10$

Equations as Point-Testers

In CME Project *Algebra 1*, you learned that graphs are point-testers. The graph of an equation is the set of the points on the Cartesian plane that make the equation true. Sometimes you can describe a graph using words, and sometimes by its shape and some key points. If you can write an equation that captures all the characteristics of the graph, that equation will be an equation for the graph.

For You to Do

1. Find an equation describing the points (x, y) that are 5 units away from $(3, 4)$.

2. Sketch a graph of all points (x, y) in the plane satisfying the equation $|y - 2| = 3$.

Facts and Notation

Here are some useful formulas from previous courses.

- *Distance formula*: The distance between points $A(x_1, y_1)$ and $B(x_2, y_2)$ is

$$d(A, B) = \sqrt{(x_2 - x_1)^2 + (y_2 - y_1)^2}$$

- *Midpoint formula*: The midpoint of the segment between points $A(x_1, y_1)$ and $B(x_2, y_2)$ is

$$M(A, B) = \left(\frac{x_1 + x_2}{2}, \frac{y_1 + y_2}{2} \right)$$

- *Slope formula*: The slope between points $A(x_1, y_1)$ and $B(x_2, y_2)$ is

$$m(A, B) = \frac{y_2 - y_1}{x_2 - x_1}$$

This assumes that $x_1 \neq x_2$. What happens if $x_1 = x_2$?

- *Perpendicular slopes*: Two lines in the plane are perpendicular if the product of their slopes is -1, or if one line is vertical and the other is horizontal.

Remember...

In your geometry class, you proved that if the slope of a line ℓ is m (with $m \neq 0$), then the slope of any line perpendicular to ℓ is $-\frac{1}{m}$.

Example 1

Problem Find an equation for the set of points equidistant from (5, 2) and (11, 0).

Solution

Method 1 Use the distance formula. Consider any point (x, y) on the graph. Its distance from (5, 2) must equal its distance from (11, 0).

distance from (x, y) to (5, 2) $=$ distance from (x, y) to (11, 0)

$$\sqrt{(x-5)^2 + (y-2)^2} = \sqrt{(x-11)^2 + y^2}$$

This is a valid equation but you can simplify it. Since the expressions under the radicals are nonnegative (why?), squaring both sides will not introduce any new solutions.

$$(x-5)^2 + (y-2)^2 = (x-11)^2 + y^2$$
$$x^2 - 10x + 25 + y^2 - 4y + 4 = x^2 - 22x + 121 + y^2$$
$$-10x - 4y + 29 = -22x + 121$$
$$-4y = -12x + 92$$
$$y = 3x - 23$$

Method 2 Use the geometric observation that the solution will be the equation of the perpendicular bisector of the segment connecting (5, 2) and (11, 0).

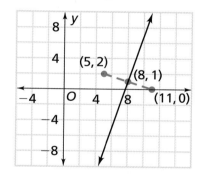

The perpendicular bisector must pass through the midpoint (8, 1) and be perpendicular to the segment. The slope between (5, 2) and (11, 0) is $-\frac{1}{3}$, so the slope of the perpendicular bisector is 3. One equation for the perpendicular bisector is $y - 1 = 3(x - 8)$. This equation is equivalent to $y = 3x - 23$ as found earlier.

> **Remember...**
> If you write the equation of a line in the form $y - k = m(x - h)$, the line passes through the point (h, k) and has slope m.

Example 2

Problem Find an equation for the set of points that are equidistant from the origin and the line with equation $y = 2$.

Solution Take an arbitrary point (x, y). Its distance to the origin is $\sqrt{x^2 + y^2}$. Its distance from the line with equation $y = 2$ is $|y - 2|$.

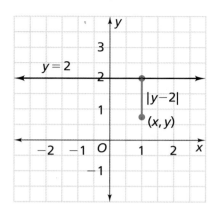

The set of points equidistant from both satisfies the equation $\sqrt{x^2 + y^2} = |y - 2|$. Simplify and solve for y.

$$\sqrt{x^2 + y^2} = |y - 2|$$
$$x^2 + y^2 = (y - 2)^2$$
$$x^2 + y^2 = y^2 - 4y + 4$$
$$x^2 + 4y = 4$$
$$y = -\frac{1}{4}x^2 + 1$$

The graph of the equation is a downward opening parabola.

Habits of Mind

Understand the process. Why is it legal to square both sides?

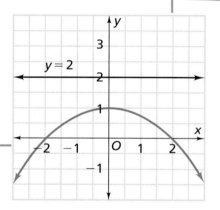

Developing Habits of Mind

Establish a process. The intersection of the graphs of two equations is the set of points that satisfies both of their equations. For example, the Getting Started lesson for this investigation asked you to find the intersection of the graphs of the equations $x^2 - y^2 = 9$ and $x + y = 5$. You can solve this algebraically. Note that you can factor $x^2 - y^2$.

$$(x + y)(x - y) = 9$$

But $x + y = 5$ is known, so $x - y$ must equal 1.8. Then a system of equations emerges.

$$x + y = 5$$
$$x - y = 1.8$$

You can solve this system of equations by many methods, including adding the two equations together. The solution $x = 3.4$, $y = 1.6$ is the only intersection of the two graphs.

Exercises Practicing Habits of Mind

Check Your Understanding

1. **a.** Write a point-tester that is true for any point (x, y) 3 units away from the line with equation $y = 2$.

   b. Sketch the graph of all points (x, y) that are 3 units away from the line with equation $y = 2$.

2. Consider the set of all points (x, y) that are the same distance away from $(4, 0)$ as they are from the y-axis.

   a. Determine whether $(3, 3)$ is in this set of points.

   b. Determine whether $(10, 8)$ is in the set.

   c. Explain why any point (a, b) with $a < 0$ cannot be in this set of points.

   d. Write a point-tester that is true for any point (x, y) equidistant from $(4, 0)$ and the y-axis.

3. You have learned that the set of points equidistant from two given points in the plane is a line. But now, consider the set of points that are twice as far away from $(15, 0)$ as they are from $(6, 0)$.

   a. Is $(5, 3)$ in this set? Justify your answer.

   b. Find the two points on the x-axis that are in this set.

   c. Write a point-tester equation that you can use to determine whether any point (x, y) is in this set.

   d. Sketch the graph of the point-tester equation.

4. A triangle has vertices $A(2, 0)$, $B(6, -2)$, and $C(8, 4)$.

   a. Find an equation for the perpendicular bisector of $\overline{AB}$.

   b. Find an equation for the perpendicular bisector of $\overline{AC}$.

   c. Find the intersection of the two perpendicular bisectors.

5. Point-testers can be useful to find equations in three-dimensional space. Consider the set of points exactly 5 units away from the point $(2, 3, 4)$.

   a. Find five points that are in this set.

   b. Find five points that are not in this set.

   c. Write a point-tester equation that you can use to determine whether any point (x, y, z) is in this set of points.

6. Consider the set of points in space that are the same distance from the origin $(0, 0, 0)$ as they are from the point $(2, 4, 6)$.

 a. In the plane, the set of points equidistant from two points would be a line. What kind of shape should it be in space?

 b. Determine whether or not $(3, 7, -1)$ is in this set of points.

 c. What equation would you use to check to see if (x, y, z) is in this set of points? Simplify the equation as much as possible.

 d. Use the point-tester from part (c) to determine whether or not the point $(15, 4, -3)$ is in this set of points.

 e. **Take It Further** Sketch the graph of all points in this set.

On Your Own

7. Exercise 4 looked at the perpendicular bisectors of $\triangle ABC$.

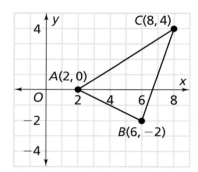

 a. Find an equation for the perpendicular bisector of $\overline{BC}$.

 b. Find an intersection for the perpendicular bisectors of $\overline{AB}$ and $\overline{BC}$.

8. Find equations for the three medians of $\triangle ABC$. Show that the three medians intersect in one point.

9. As in the Getting Started lesson, build a grid for the function h,

$$h(x, y) = x^2 + y^2 - 4x + 2y - 4$$

if $-5 \le x \le 5$, $-5 \le y \le 5$.

10. a. Use the grid from Exercise 9 to describe the graph of the equation

$$x^2 + y^2 - 4x + 2y - 4 = 0$$

 b. Prove that your description in part (a) is correct.

Remember...

A median of a triangle is a segment connecting a vertex to the midpoint of the opposite side.

You may need to add or subtract terms from each side.

11. Consider the equation in three variables

$$z^2 = x^2 + y^2$$

  a. Find several points (x, y, z) that are on the graph of this equation.

  b. Suppose $z = 5$. Describe the set of x and y values that make the equation true.

  c. Suppose $z = 11$. Describe the set of x and y values that make the equation true.

  d. Suppose $z = -11$. Describe the set of x and y values that make the equation true.

  e. Suppose $z = 0$. Describe the set of x and y values that make the equation true.

  f. Sketch the graph of $z^2 = x^2 + y^2$ as accurately as you can.

12. **Take It Further** The graph of $z^2 = x^2 + y^2$ is sometimes called a *double cone*.

  a. What kind of figure does slicing the double cone perpendicular to the z-axis (say, with the plane with equation $z = 5$) produce?

  b. What is the graph that results when the plane with equation $x = 3$ slices the double cone?

  c. Find what other shapes might be possible with other slices. Give some examples.

13. **Standardized Test Prep** Which of the following is an equation for the set of points equidistant from $(2, 3)$ and $(6, 1)$?

  A. $\sqrt{(x - 2)^2 + (y - 3)^2} = \sqrt{(x - 6)^2 + (y - 1)^2}$

  B. $\dfrac{y - 3}{x - 2} = \dfrac{y - 1}{x - 6}$

  C. $y - 3 = -\dfrac{1}{2}(x - 2)$

  D. $2x + 3y = 6x + y$

Go Online
PHSchool.com

For additional practice, go to **Web Code:** bga-0602

An equation for the plane that contains the point $(0, 0, c)$ is $z = c$. Similarly, an equation for the plane that contains the point $(a, 0, 0)$ is $x = a$.

Maintain Your Skills

14. The *centroid* of a triangle is the intersection of its medians. Given the three vertices of $\triangle ABC$, find its centroid.

  a. $A(0, 0)$, $B(10, 0)$, $C(2, 9)$

  b. $A(0, 0)$, $B(10, 0)$, $C(2, -9)$

  c. $A(0, 0)$, $B(100, 0)$, $C(20, 90)$

  d. $A(1, 2)$, $B(10, 11)$, $C(19, 5)$

  e. $A(0, 0)$, $B(3a, 0)$, $C(3b, 3c)$

  f. $A(x_1, y_1)$, $B(x_2, y_2)$, $C(x_3, y_3)$

6.3 Coordinates and Proof

In this lesson, you will learn how to use coordinate methods to prove geometric facts. For example, consider quadrilateral *ABCD* in the plane.

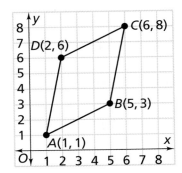

If you wanted to prove that it is a parallelogram you could use any of the following approaches.

- If a quadrilateral has pairs of opposite sides that are parallel, then it is a parallelogram.

- If a quadrilateral has pairs of opposite sides that are congruent, then it is a parallelogram.

- If a quadrilateral has one pair of opposite sides that are congruent and parallel, then it is a parallelogram.

For You to Do

1. Pick one of the three approaches above. Then use it to show that the quadrilateral *ABCD* is a parallelogram.

To prove something more generally, *coordinatize* a geometric shape by making a general version in the coordinate plane. For example, a general parallelogram might look like as follows.

If a general parallelogram lies in the plane, you can define the coordinates however you like. So, define the origin to be one of the vertices. Let one of the sides lie along the *x*-axis. But be careful not to overdefine the shape. For example, if you already defined $Q(0, a)$, point *S* in the parallelogram cannot be defined as (a, b). That assumes too much about where *S* is located. A good choice of coordinates is one that needs as few variables as possible, but does not assume any more about the shape than is necessary.

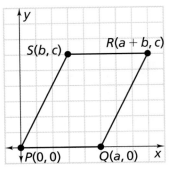

Derman and Sasha are coordinatizing △EON.

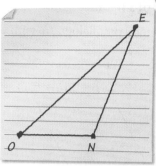

Derman What about a general triangle like this one?

Sasha So how do you want to label the points?

Derman Why not just use six letters? Make the vertices $O(a, b)$, $N(c, d)$, and $E(e, f)$.

Sasha I think we can do it with fewer variables. We can put the axes wherever we want, so let's put point O at the origin. Then we can place $\overline{ON}$ on the x-axis. Point N would have y-coordinate 0, so say its coordinates are $(c, 0)$.

Derman I can do that with the y-axis, too. Line it up with $\overline{OE}$. Then E has x-coordinate 0!

Sasha Wait a minute! If you line up $\overline{ON}$ with the x-axis and $\overline{OE}$ with the y-axis, then something is wrong. Just draw it.

Derman Okay.

Derman Oh. I get it now. I forced $\angle EON$ to be a right angle. I'll bet these would be useful coordinates for a right triangle, though.

Sasha You're right. But this is the way our general triangle should look.

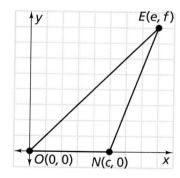

Coordinatizing lets you use formulas to obtain other information about the shape.

Example 1

Problem Show that the diagonals of a parallelogram bisect each other.

Solution Here is a diagram for a general parallelogram, with coordinates labeled.

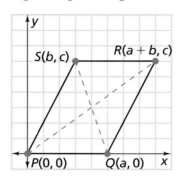

Habits of Mind

Prove. How do these coordinates guarantee that *PQRS* is a parallelogram?

The diagonals bisect each other if their midpoints are the same. So, use the midpoint formula to find the midpoint of each diagonal.

The midpoint of diagonal $\overline{PR}$ is

$$\left(\frac{0 + (a + b)}{2}, \frac{0 + c}{2} \right) = \left(\frac{a + b}{2}, \frac{c}{2} \right)$$

The midpoint of diagonal $\overline{QS}$ is

$$\left(\frac{a + b}{2}, \frac{0 + c}{2} \right) = \left(\frac{a + b}{2}, \frac{c}{2} \right)$$

The two midpoints are the same point. The diagonals must intersect at the point $\left(\frac{a + b}{2}, \frac{c}{2} \right)$. This common midpoint means that the diagonals bisect one another.

Developing Habits of Mind

Make connections. Some people like to think about points as things they can add or subtract, just like numbers. They would write

$$(3, 7) + (11, 5) = (14, 12)$$

If you think of points this way, finding a midpoint is just like averaging the points. The average of (3, 7) and (11, 5) is

$$\frac{(3, 7) + (11, 5)}{2} = (7, 6)$$

And, as you saw, (7, 6) is the midpoint of the segment from (3, 7) to (11, 5).

This algebra of points can come in handy, and matches up with the matrix concepts of addition and scalar multiplication. You will revisit these concepts in Investigation C.

For You to Do

2. Plot the points $A(3, 7)$ and $B(11, 5)$ on graph paper. Then calculate and plot $P = \frac{3}{4}(3, 7) + \frac{1}{4}(11, 5)$. How could you describe the location of P relative to points A and B?

Example 2

Problem Prove that the diagonals of a rhombus are perpendicular.

Solution A *rhombus* is a quadrilateral with four congruent sides. Start with a diagram for a general parallelogram.

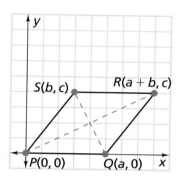

Habits of Mind

Reason logically. The fact that a rhombus has four congruent sides tells you that it is also a parallelogram. Why?

Since $PQRS$ is a rhombus, $PQ = PS$. So $a = \sqrt{b^2 + c^2}$. Or, $a^2 = b^2 + c^2$.

The slope of diagonal $\overline{PR}$ is $\frac{c}{a + b}$. The slope of diagonal $\overline{QS}$ is $\frac{-c}{a - b}$. These slopes are perpendicular if their product is -1.

$$\frac{c}{a + b} \cdot \frac{-c}{a - b} = \frac{-c^2}{a^2 - b^2}$$

Since $a^2 = b^2 + c^2$

$$\frac{-c^2}{a^2 - b^2} = \frac{-c^2}{(b^2 + c^2) - b^2} = \frac{-c^2}{c^2} = -1$$

The product of the slopes of the diagonals is -1, so they are perpendicular.

Or, relabel a as $\sqrt{b^2 + c^2}$, then continue. The proof will be messier, though.

For You to Do

The proof above only holds if neither of the diagonals is vertical (has undefined slope). However, the way you set up the coordinates means that a vertical diagonal will have interesting consequences.

3. What would the coordinates of the vertices of rhombus $PQRS$ have to be if the diagonal $\overline{QS}$ were vertical? What do these coordinates imply about $PQRS$?

4. What would the coordinates of the vertices of rhombus $PQRS$ have to be if the diagonal $\overline{PR}$ were vertical? What do these coordinates imply about $PQRS$?

Make strategic choices. The choice of coordinates is often influenced by what you are trying to prove. If you are trying to prove a statement about medians, it may make more sense to label a triangle as follows.

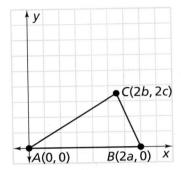

This makes working with medians a little easier, since the midpoints will not have fractional coordinates.

If your geometric shape has a line of symmetry, one choice is to place the line of symmetry on an axis. Here is one way to coordinatize an isosceles triangle.

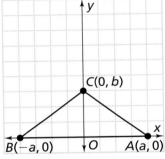

It takes some practice to develop the knack for choosing a convenient set of coordinates. You want your choice to make the calculations easier, but you do not want to introduce any extra assumptions, as Derman did in episode 18 on page 451. Try to think about what you are trying to prove and how to get there. A good choice of coordinates can reduce the work of the proof.

The massive cables of the Golden Gate Bridge, as with most suspension bridges, form parabolic arcs.

Exercises *Practicing Habits of Mind*

Check Your Understanding

1. **a.** Find four coordinate pairs to represent the vertices of a rectangle.

   b. Prove that the diagonals of a rectangle are equal in length.

2. Use coordinates to prove the *Midline Theorem*:

   The segment joining the midpoints of two sides of a triangle is parallel to the third side. Its measure is equal to half the measure of the third side.

3. Prove that if you connect the midpoints of the sides of any quadrilateral, the resulting quadrilateral is a parallelogram.

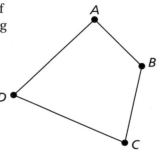

4. Determine what type of quadrilateral results when you connect the midpoints of the sides of a rectangle. Prove your result.

5. **What's Wrong Here?** Joey says that he can quickly prove that the diagonals of a rhombus are perpendicular.

   Joey: I used the symmetry of the rhombus. The diagonals ended up being right on the axes. Then of course the diagonals are perpendicular. They're the axes.

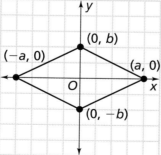

   What is wrong with Joey's reasoning?

6. **Take It Further** Prove that if the diagonals of a parallelogram are perpendicular, then the parallelogram is a rhombus.

Remember...

You first proved the Midline Theorem in your geometry course.

For additional practice, go to **Web Code:** bga-0603

On Your Own

7. Coordinatize a general square.

8. In this figure, $\triangle ABC$ is a right triangle and point D is the midpoint of hypotenuse $\overline{BC}$. Set coordinates for points B and C, then prove that $AD = BD = CD$.

9. a. Coordinatize a general equilateral triangle.

   b. Prove that in an equilateral triangle, any median is also a perpendicular bisector.

10. a. Coordinatize an *isosceles trapezoid,* a trapezoid with congruent non-parallel sides.

   b. Prove that the diagonals of an isosceles trapezoid are equal in length, but do not bisect each other.

11. Use coordinates to prove that the length of the *midline of a trapezoid* is the average of the lengths of its two bases.

12. **Take It Further** Coordinatize a regular hexagon centered at the origin. Use only one variable.

13. **Standardized Test Prep** Given a parallelogram with three of its vertices at the points $(1, 5)$, $(5, -1)$, and $(2, 2)$, which of the following could not be the fourth vertex?

A. $(6, -4)$ **B.** $(4, 2)$ **C.** $(3, 2)$ **D.** $(-2, 8)$

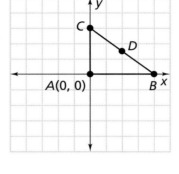

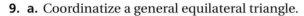

Remember...

The *midline* of a trapezoid is a segment connecting the midpoints of the two nonparallel sides. For the trapezoid given, the midline connects the midpoint of $\overline{AD}$ with the midpoint of $\overline{BC}$.

Maintain Your Skills

14. The graph of the equation

$$x^2 + y^2 - 8x + 10y + 24 = 0$$

is a circle centered at the point $(4, -5)$. For each point listed below, determine whether or not it is on the graph of the circle.

a. $(4, -1)$ **b.** $(5, -1)$ **c.** $(8, -6)$

d. $(8, 0)$ **e.** $(0, 0)$ **f.** $(3, -9)$

6.4 The Power of a Point

Consider a circle with center (h, k) and radius r. If you picked any point (x, y), how would you decide whether it was on the circle? You can find a point-tester for a circle by calculating the distance from (x, y) to the center, which must equal r.

$$\sqrt{(x - h)^2 + (y - k)^2} = r$$
$$(x - h)^2 + (y - k)^2 = r^2$$

This second equation is the *center-radius form* for a circle. Equations for circles are not always in this form. You can use the method of *completing the square* to rewrite an equation of a circle in this form.

Example 1

Problem The graph of the equation

$$x^2 + y^2 - 10x + 14y - 26 = 0$$

is a circle. Find its center and radius.

Solution You can identify the center and radius if the equation is in the form

$$(x - h)^2 + (y - k)^2 = r^2$$

Start by moving terms to make the result appear as follows.

$$(x^2 - 10x \quad) + (y^2 + 14y \quad) = 26$$

Now find constants that produce perfect square trinomials. For the first term this constant is $\left(-\frac{10}{2}\right)^2 = 25$. For the second term this constant is $\left(\frac{14}{2}\right)^2 = 49$. Add these constants to each side of the equation.

$$(x^2 - 10x + \mathbf{25}) + (y^2 + 14y + \mathbf{49}) = 26 + \mathbf{25} + \mathbf{49}$$

Factor each expression in parentheses.

$$(x - 5)^2 + (y + 7)^2 = 100$$

The center is $(5, -7)$ and the radius is $\sqrt{100} = 10$.

Remember...

This technique is called completing the square because you add the number that produces a complete perfect square trinomial.

For You to Do

1. Find the center and radius for the circle with equation
   $x^2 + y^2 + 12x - 8y + 3 = 0$.

2. Find the center for the circle with equation
   $x^2 + y^2 + 50x - 18y + 100 = 0$.

   Can you do this without completing the square? Explain.

In CME Project *Geometry*, you discovered the *Power of a Point Theorem*.

Theorem 6.1 Power of a Point

For an exploration activity on power of a point, go to **Web Code:** bge-9031

Given a point *P* and a circle, take any line through *P* that intersects the circle in two points *A* and *B*. Then *PA* · *PB* is constant, no matter what line you choose through *P*. This constant is called the power of the point *P*. The power is a function of the point, so write the power of *P* as $\Pi(P)$.

$$PA \cdot PB = PC \cdot PD = PE \cdot PF$$

Here are two corollaries.

Corollary 6.1.1

Inside a circle, the power of a point *d* units away from the center of a circle with radius *r* is $r^2 - d^2$.

Corollary 6.1.2

Outside a circle, the power of a point *d* units away from the center of a circle with radius *r* is $d^2 - r^2$.

For Discussion

3. Suppose point *P* is on the circle. What is its power?

Here is a proof of Corollary 6.1.1.

Proof The Power of a Point Theorem applies to any line through *P* that intersects the circle at two points. So, pick $\overleftrightarrow{OP}$, where *O* is the center of the circle.

This line intersects the circle at points *A* and *B*. Since *OP* = *d*, and $\overline{AB}$ is a diameter, you know the lengths *PA* and *PB*: *PA* = *r* + *d* and *PB* = *r* − *d*. The power of point *P* with respect to the circle is

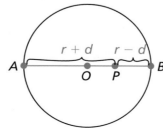

$$PA \cdot PB = (r + d)(r - d) = r^2 - d^2$$

You will prove Corollary 6.1.2 in Exercise 1 below. Note that the two rules are nearly identical. Also, the quantity $d^2 - r^2$ is invariant for any point P. This quantity is negative for points inside the circle and positive for points outside the circle. Now name this quantity.

Definition

Given point P, d units from the center of a circle of radius r. The **signed power of point** P with respect to the circle is given by

$$\Pi_S(P) = d^2 - r^2$$

Example 2

Problem Calculate the signed power of each point with respect to the circle with equation

$$x^2 + y^2 - 10x + 14y - 26 = 0$$

a. $(8, -3)$ **b.** $(-1, 1)$ **c.** $(5, -7)$

d. $(5, 18)$ **e.** (x, y)

Solution Earlier, you showed that the center of this circle is $(5, -7)$ and its radius is 10. For each point, calculate $d^2 - r^2$, where d is its distance from the center, and r is the radius (10).

a. The distance from $(8, -3)$ to $(5, -7)$ is $\sqrt{3^2 + 4^2} = 5$, so the signed power is $5^2 - 10^2 = -75$. If a chord $\overline{AB}$ of this circle passes through $P(8, -3)$, the product of PA and PB will be 75.

b. The distance from $(-1, 1)$ to $(5, -7)$ is $\sqrt{6^2 + 8^2} = 10$, so the signed power is $10^2 - 10^2 = 0$. This point is on the circle.

c. This point is the center, so its signed power is $0^2 - 10^2 = -100$.

d. The distance from $(5, 18)$ to $(5, -7)$ is 25, so the signed power is $25^2 - 10^2 = 525$.

e. The distance from (x, y) to $(5, -7)$ is

$$\sqrt{(x - 5)^2 + (y + 7)^2}$$

The signed power of point (x, y) is

$$(x - 5)^2 + (y + 7)^2 - 100$$

Expanding and collecting terms gives

$$(x^2 - 10x + 25) + (y^2 + 14y + 49) - 100$$
$$x^2 + y^2 - 10x + 14y - 26$$

Amazing! This is exactly the left side of the equation that defines the circle.

You generalize the process in Example 2.

Theorem 6.2

The signed power of point $P(x, y)$ with respect to the circle with equation $x^2 + y^2 + Cx + Dy + E = 0$ is

$$\Pi_S(P) = x^2 + y^2 + Cx + Dy + E$$

If you want to, you can write the equation that defines the circle as $\Pi_S(P) = 0$.

Developing Habits of Mind

Find another way. Given a specific circle, what is the minimum value that the signed power can have. And where does this value occur? The signed power is $d^2 - r^2$. Since r is fixed, the signed power is smallest when $d = 0$. This d is the distance to the center, so the signed power takes on its minimum value at the center of the circle. The minimum value is $-r^2$.

This gives an interesting way to find the center and radius of a circle based on its equation in normal form. For example, take the circle with equation

$$x^2 + y^2 - 16x + 22y - 344 = 0$$

If you were finding the center and radius by completing the square, you would look at the coefficients of the linear x and y terms and write an equation that looked like this:

$$(x - 8)^2 + (y + 11)^2 = \text{something}$$

The center of this circle is $(8, -11)$. You can quickly find the center for any circle this way. Then, use the signed power calculation to find the radius. The signed power of the center $(8, -11)$ is

$$\Pi_S(8, 11) = 8^2 + (-11)^2 - 16(8) + 22(-11) - 344 = -529$$

This value is equal to $-r^2$, so the radius is $\sqrt{529} = 23$. The signed power of a point allows you to find the center and radius for a circle with an equation in normal form without having to finish completing the square.

Let P be the point of intersection of the chopsticks. Can you find the power of a point P with respect to the rim of the plate?

Exercises *Practicing Habits of Mind*

Check Your Understanding

1. Prove Corollary 6.1.2.

   > Outside a circle, a point d units away from the center of a circle with radius r has power $d^2 - r^2$.

2. The graph of the equation $x^2 + y^2 + 6x - 8y - 24 = 0$ is a circle.

   a. Find the center and radius of the circle.

   b. Sketch the graph of the circle.

   c. Find the exact coordinates of all intercepts.

3. The point $P(0, 0)$ lies inside the circle from Exercise 2. Several chords of the circle defined by the graph of $x^2 + y^2 + 6x - 8y - 24 = 0$ pass through the origin.

   a. One such chord lies along the x-axis. Calculate the power of P with respect to this circle using this chord.

   b. Calculate the power of P using the chord that lies along the y-axis.

   c. Find the two intersection points of the circle with the line with equation $y = x$. Use these intersections to calculate the power of P.

4. **Write About It** The Power of a Point Theorem applies to any line drawn through a point P that intersects a circle twice. What happens when P is outside the circle and the intersection points get closer together? How could you rephrase the Power of a Point Theorem to address this situation?

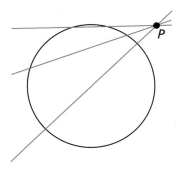

5. **Take It Further** Find the two intersection points of the circle from Exercise 3 with the line with equation $y = kx$. Then show that the power of $P(0, 0)$ with respect to this circle is independent of k.

6. Find the signed power of point $P(6, 5)$ with respect to the circle

$$(x - 3)^2 + (y + 1)^2 = 25$$

Go Online

PHSchool.com

For additional practice, go to **Web Code:** bga-0604

7. Find some other points with the same signed power as $P(6, 5)$ with respect to the circle

$$(x - 3)^2 + (y + 1)^2 = 25$$

8. Calculate the value of $f(x, y) = (x - 3)^2 + (y + 1)^2 - 25$ for each set of inputs.

  a. $x = 6, y = 5$ **b.** $x = 9, y = -4$ **c.** $x = 0, y = -7$ **d.** $x = -3, y = 2$

9. If C is the center of a circle with radius r, explain why the signed power of C with respect to the circle is $-r^2$.

10. **Take It Further** Given two circles, describe the set of points that have the same signed power with respect to both circles. Does your answer change depending on how the circles are positioned?

11. **Take It Further** Prove Theorem 6.1 in general. In other words, show that the signed power of a point $P(a, b)$ with respect to the circle with equation $x^2 + y^2 + Cx + Dy + E = 0$ is

$$\Pi_S(P) = a^2 + b^2 + aC + bD + E$$

12. **Standardized Test Prep** Which of the following is the center of the circle with equation $x^2 + y^2 + 4x - 2y = 0$?

  A. $(4, -2)$ **B.** $(-4, 2)$ **C.** $(2, -1)$ **D.** $(-2, 1)$

Maintain Your Skills

13. Let the point X be the intersection of chords $\overline{AB}$ and $\overline{CD}$ inside a circle.

  a. If $AX = 4$, $BX = 6$, $CX = 9$, find DX.
  b. If $AX = 8$, $BX = 6$, $CX = 9$, find DX.
  c. If $AX = 4$, $BX = 6$, $CX = 18$, find DX.
  d. If $AX = 4$, $BX = 6$, $CX = c$, find DX.
  e. If $AX = 4$, $BX = 6$, find the smallest possible length of chord $\overline{CD}$.

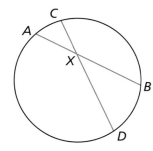

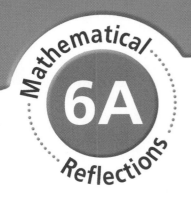

In this investigation, you found equations that characterized descriptions of various point sets. You used coordinate methods to prove geometric facts. You investigated the signed power of a point. The following questions will help you summarize what you have learned.

1. Which points with integer coordinates lie on the circle with equation $x^2 + y^2 = 25$?

2. Which of the following points lie on the ellipse with equation $\dfrac{(x-3)^2}{16} + \dfrac{(y+1)^2}{12} = 1$?

   a. $(-1, -1)$ b. $(3, -1)$ c. $(1, 2)$

3. For which values of x can the equation $\dfrac{(x-h)^2}{a^2} - \dfrac{(y-k)^2}{b^2} = 1$ be true?

4. Prove the following consequence of the Pythagorean Theorem: *The sum of the squares of the lengths of the diagonals of a parallelogram is equal to the sum of the squares of the lengths of its four sides.*

5. Determine the power of the point $(16, 6)$ with respect to the circle $(x-4)^2 + (y+3)^2 = 25$.

6. What is the set of points equidistant from the x-axis and the point $(0, 4)$?

7. How can you use coordinates to show that the diagonals of a parallelogram bisect each another?

8. How can you find the center and radius of a circle with an equation written in normal form?

Vocabulary and Notation

In this investigation, you learned these terms and symbols. Make sure you understand what each one means and how to use it.

- coordinatize
- double cone, $z^2 = x^2 + y^2$
- midline
- parallelogram
- point-tester

- perpendicular bisector
- power of a point, $\Pi(P)$
- rhombus
- signed power of a point, $\Pi_S(P)$
- trapezoid

Conic Sections

In *Conic Sections*, you will study circles, ellipses, parabolas, and hyperbolas from visual, verbal, geometrical, and analytical viewpoints.

By the end of this investigation, you will be able to answer questions like these.

1. How do you slice an infinite double cone with a plane to get a parabola?

2. What is the locus definition of a hyperbola?

3. What kind of conic section do you get when you graph $x^2 + 16y^2 - 8x + 64y + 64 = 0$? How can you identify the conic section from its equation?

You will learn how to

• visualize each of the conic sections as the intersection of a plane with an infinite double cone

• give a locus definition for each of the conic sections

• identify the equations for the graphs of the conic sections, and sketch their graphs

You will develop these habits and skills:

• Visualize the effect of different angles of intersection of a plane with an infinite double cone.

• Make connections between the different definitions of each type of conic section.

• Reason by continuity to make connections between the different types of conic section.

Parabolic curves form the surfaces of radio telescopes, freeway overpass arches, field microphones, solar ovens, and these reflectors of a solar electric generating system.

Activating Prior Knowledge
Exploring New Ideas

The intersection of a plane and a solid gives you a cross section of the solid. It is a challenging visualization habit to determine what cross section shapes are possible for different solids.

For You to Explore

1. Consider a cube.

When you take a planar slice through the cube (a smooth cut with a knife), what possible shapes could you make?

Consider the boundary of the cut as the shape of the slice. One possible shape for the slice is a square, but there are a lot more.

2. Consider a sphere.

When you take a planar slice through the sphere, what possible shapes could you make?

3. Consider a cone that extends forever from its tip.

When you take a planar slice through the cone, what possible shapes could you make?

4. Sketch the graph of each equation.

   a. $x^2 + y^2 = 16$ **b.** $x^2 - y^2 = 16$

   c. $4x^2 + y^2 = 16$ **d.** $x^2 + y = 16$

5. **Take It Further** Find and graph an equation for the set of points $\frac{4}{5}$ times as far from $(5, 2)$ as they are from the line $x = 14$.

 **Exercises** *Practicing Habits of Mind*

On Your Own

6. Find all solutions to the following equation.

$$\sqrt{x - 12} + \sqrt{x - 7} = 5$$

7. Sketch the graph of each equation.

a. $x^2 + y^2 = 25$

b. $(x - 3)^2 + y^2 = 25$

c. $(x + 3)^2 + y^2 = 25$

d. $(x - 1)^2 + (y + 4)^2 = 25$

e. $\dfrac{x^2}{5^2} + \dfrac{y^2}{5^2} = 1$

8. Sketch the graph of each equation.

a. $x^2 + y^2 = 1$

b. $\dfrac{x^2}{4^2} + \dfrac{y^2}{4^2} = 1$

c. $\dfrac{x^2}{3^2} + \dfrac{y^2}{5^2} = 1$

d. $\dfrac{x^2}{3^2} + \dfrac{y^2}{2^2} = 1$

e. $9x^2 + 25y^2 = 225$

> **Remember...**
>
> Equations are point-testers. Find some points that make the equations true.

This whispering gallery is in the Cincinnati Museum Center. To concentrate sound of one point in the hall, architects make use of the reflective properties of one of the conics. As you work through this investigation, can you guess which one?

9. You are on a camping trip. As you are returning from a hike in the woods, you see that your tent is on fire. Luckily, you are holding an empty bucket and you are near a river. You plan to run to the river to fill the bucket and then run to the tent.

Students of the CME Project curriculum always carry a bucket when hiking.

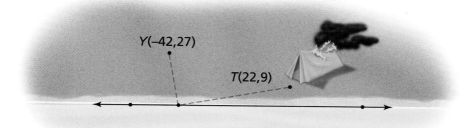

a. In CME Project *Geometry*, you found the shortest total path by reflecting your position *Y* over the line of the river's edge and connecting the reflected image *Y'* to *T* with a straight line. The intersection of that line and the river's edge is the point *P* that minimizes the path. Explain why this method produces the shortest path.

b. You also looked at contour lines for this situation. A contour line is the collection of all points *P* for which the path *Y–P–T* has the same length. What shapes are the contour lines for the burning tent problem? Why?

c. How is the contour line that contains the optimum point *P* that you found in part (a) positioned in relation to you, the river, and the tent? Why?

Maintain Your Skills

10. Find all solutions to the following equation.
$$\sqrt{x + 10} + \sqrt{x + 31} = 7$$

6.6 Slicing Cones

The theory of **conic sections** ties together algebra, geometry, and the analysis of functions. In this lesson, you start with the geometry and lay the foundations for the connections with other parts of mathematics.

Picture a line in space, fixed at one point, while another point on the line moves along a circle.

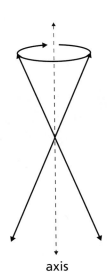

axis

The fixed point is the cone's *apex*. The rotating line is called the *generator* of the cone. The line through the apex perpendicular to the circle is the cone's *axis*.

The surface made by the moving line is an infinite double cone. Now picture a plane passing through the cone.

The plane slices the cone in a curve. That curve is a conic section. You get different kinds of curves depending on how the plane slices the cone.

In-Class Experiment

Draw sketches of the possible intersections of a plane with this infinite double cone. Classify and name your sketches. Discuss their features. Here are some questions you should answer about your intersections.

1. Is the intersection curve closed like a polygon or circle, or open like the graph of $y = x^2$?

2. Does the intersection curve have two branches like the graph of $xy = 1$ or is it a single connected curve?

3. Does the intersection curve have any symmetry?

The intersection curves look like curves you have encountered before in Algebra 1, Geometry, or Algebra 2. And it turns out that they are the same curves.

Facts and Notation

- The curve you get by slicing the cone with a plane that intersects only one branch of the cone is an **ellipse.**

- The curve you get by slicing the cone with a plane that is parallel to its generator is a **parabola.**

- The curve you get by slicing the cone with a plane that intersects both branches of the cone is a **hyperbola.**

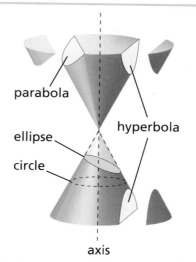

A circle is a special kind of ellipse.

Because the plane is parallel to the generator, it only slices one branch of the cone but it does not produce an ellipse. (Why?)

It should not be obvious to you that the curve you get when you slice a cone parallel to its generator is exactly the same kind curve as the one you get when you graph $y = x^2$. Or that the oval conic section is the same kind of curve as the oval you get when you graph $4x^2 + 9y^2 - 36 = 0$. Or that the conic section called "hyperbola" has the same kind of shape as the graph of $xy = 1$. One purpose of the lessons in this investigation is to see why this is the case.

Developing Habits of Mind

Visualize. Here is an interesting thought experiment: Picture a fixed line ℓ in space, outside a cone and between the apex and the base. The line ℓ is parallel to the base of the cone. Next imagine a single plane that contains ℓ and rotates around ℓ. The plane starts out perpendicular to the axis of the cone, cutting the cone in a circle. Then it rotates down, creating a family of ellipses (increasing in size) until it is parallel to the generator, producing a parabola. It continues its rotation down, creating hyperbolas until it is parallel to the generator again (now on the opposite side of the cone).

In some sense, these conic sections are all the same. You will look more carefully at this idea in Lesson 6.9.

Where did the names "ellipse," "parabola," and "hyperbola" come from? They bear a striking resemblance to the English language terms "ellipsis," "parable," and "hyperbole." This is not a coincidence—you will see the connections in Lesson 6.9.

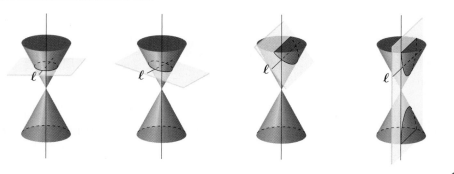

Locus Definitions for Conics: The Ellipse

In CME Project *Geometry,* you defined an ellipse with a pin and string construction. Suppose F_1 and F_2 are two fixed points—the **foci** of the ellipse—and you have a fixed length, say s. Then the ellipse with foci F_1 and F_2 and string length s is the set (locus) of all points P such that $PF_1 + PF_2 = s$.

> The singular of *foci* is *focus*.

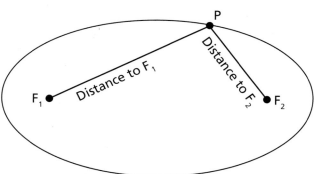

distance to F$_1$ + distance to F$_2$ = a constant

For You to Do

4. You can draw half of an ellipse by taking a string of length s and pinning its ends to F_1 and F_2. Then use a pencil to pull the string tight and trace the curve by moving the pencil, keeping tension on the string. Try it. How does the string length affect the size of the ellipse? How does the distance between the foci affect the size of the ellipse?

> See the TI-Nspire™ Handbook on p. 704 for instructions about using the pin and string idea to make an ellipse with your geometry software.

You may also have a feeling that a section of a cone sliced by a plane that only cuts one branch of the cone and is not parallel to the generator is an ellipse.

A proof by the French mathematician Germinal Dandelin shows why this is so. Begin with a cone that a plane has passed through. Now imagine placing two spheres in this cone. Put the first one into the top of the cone, big enough so it just touches the sides of the cone and just touches the plane in only one spot—it is tangent to both the cone and the plane. Then put a larger sphere into the cone under the ellipse. Again make this sphere just the right size, so it is tangent to the cone and to the plane of the ellipse.

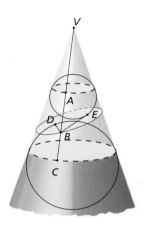

Pass a straight line down the surface of the cone, beginning at the apex V. Label the points of intersection with the smaller sphere, the plane, and the larger sphere A, B, and C in the figure above. Point D is the point where the larger sphere is tangent to the plane. Point E is the point where the smaller sphere is tangent to the plane. $BA = BE$ because $\overrightarrow{BA}$ and $\overrightarrow{BE}$ each emanates from B and are tangent to the smaller sphere.

For this same reason $BC = BD$, because both $\overrightarrow{BC}$ and $\overrightarrow{BD}$ are tangent to the larger sphere.

No matter what line you choose to draw from V, the lengths VA and VC are invariant. Note that since this is so, AC, the difference between VA and VC, is also invariant. Also note that $AC = BA + BC$. Since $BA = BE$ and $BC = BD$ then $BA + BC = BD + BE$. $BA + BC$ is constant so this means that $BD + BE$ must also be constant. So an ellipse must be a set of all points in the plane, such that the sum of the distances from two fixed points (E and D) remains constant.

Remember...

Given a circle and a point P outside the circle, the two segments from P tangent to the circle are equal in length. Rotating this gives a sphere with the same property.

Locus Definitions for Conics: The Parabola and the Hyperbola

There are similar ways to show that the other two conics have locus properties.

- A hyperbola is the set of points such that the absolute value of the difference of the distances from two fixed points is constant.

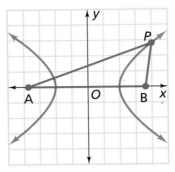

$|PA - PB|$ = **Constant**

- A parabola is the set of points equidistant from a fixed point and a line.

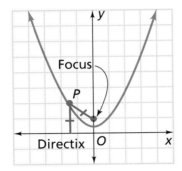

Dandelin showed that the cone slices that you call parabola and hyperbola are the same ones that satisfy the locus descriptions above, using the same idea of putting spheres around the slicing planes. The spheres are now called Dandelin spheres. The arguments are the same in spirit, but they are considerably more complicated.

See the TI-Nspire Handbook on p. 704 for instructions to use the locus definition to draw a hyperbola and a parabola in your dynamic geometry environment.

Why did you not need the absolute value in the definition of the ellipse?

A hyperbola has two foci. A parabola has only one. The fixed line in the parabola definition is called its **directrix**.

Exercises *Practicing Habits of Mind*

Check Your Understanding

1. **a.** Using the pin-and-string model, draw an ellipse that closely resembles a circle.

   b. Using the same string but different pin locations, draw an ellipse that does not resemble a circle.

   c. Where might you place the pins to draw a circle?

   The locus definition of an ellipse uses two points F_1 and F_2, the foci, and a distance s. The ellipse is the set of points P with $PF_1 + PF_2 = s$.

2. Consider foci $F_1(3, 0)$ and $F_2(-3, 0)$, and the distance $s = 10$.

   a. Find the two values of b so that $(0, b)$ is on the ellipse.

   b. Find the two values of a so that $(a, 0)$ is on the ellipse.

   c. Is the point $(2, 3)$ on the ellipse? Explain how you know.

   d. Write an equation that you could use to test whether or not any point (x, y) is on the ellipse.

3. The lesson shows what the two Dandelin spheres look like after slicing a double-cone to produce an ellipse. Suppose you slice a double cone to produce a circle. Describe what the two Dandelin spheres look like. Also, describe the points where the Dandelin spheres touch the sliced circle.

4. By its locus definition, a hyperbola is the set of points such that the absolute value of the difference of the distances from two fixed points is constant. Suppose the two points are $F_1 = (3, 0)$ and $F_2 = (-3, 0)$, with the fixed difference $d = 4$.

   a. Find five points that are on this hyperbola.

   b. Sketch a graph of the hyperbola.

   c. **Take It Further** Find an equation for the graph of the hyperbola.

5. **What's Wrong Here?** Joachim decides to make a hyperbola with fixed points $A(3, 0)$ and $B(-3, 0)$, and the fixed difference $d = 10$. But he is having trouble finding points that work. Why?

Go Online
PHSchool.com

For more information on Dandelin's spheres, go to **Web Code:** bge-9031

On Your Own

6. On the coordinate plane, a parabola has focus $(1, 0)$ and directrix with equation $x = -1$. Which of these points is on the parabola?

   A. $(1, 1.5)$ **B.** $(1.5, 2.5)$ **C.** $(2.25, 3)$ **D.** $(9, 36)$

7. Find three points on the parabola with focus $(1, 0)$ and directrix with equation $x = -1$. Do not use points listed in Exercise 6.

8. Find a given each condition.

    a. $(1, a)$ is on the parabola with focus $(1, 0)$ and directrix with equation $x = -1$.

    b. $(a, 1)$ is on the parabola with focus $(1, 0)$ and directrix with equation $x = -1$.

9. Find an equation of the parabola with focus $(1, 0)$ and directrix with equation $x = -1$.

10. One equation for an ellipse with foci $(3, 0)$ and $(-3, 0)$ and string length $s = 10$ is

$$\sqrt{(x - 3)^2 + y^2} + \sqrt{(x + 3)^2 + y^2} = 10$$

    a. Write another equation that must also be true but only involves a single square root. Proceed as follows. Move one square root to the other side. Square both sides. Simplify the equation as much as possible.

    b. Show that you can simplify the equation above to

$$\frac{x^2}{25} + \frac{y^2}{16} = 1$$

11. **Take It Further** In Exercise 2 you found an equation for an ellipse with foci $(3, 0)$ and $(-3, 0)$ and string length $s = 10$.

    a. Find an equation for the ellipse with the same foci, but leave string length as a variable s.

    b. If $s = 20$, find several points on the ellipse.

    c. Sketch the graph of the ellipse when $s = 20$.

    d. Sketch the graph of the ellipse when $s = 8$.

    e. Sketch the graph when $s = 6$.

12. **Standardized Test Prep** Which of the following points is on the parabola with focus $(3, 4)$ and directrix $y = 5$?

    A. $(-3, 4)$ **B.** $(0, 0)$ **C.** $(3, 3)$ **D.** $(5, 4)$

Go Online
PHSchool.com

For additional practice, go to **Web Code:** bga-0606

Maintain Your Skills

13. Sketch the graph of each equation.

    a. $x^2 + y^2 - 2x + 4y - 4 = 0$ **b.** $x^2 + y^2 - 2x + 4y = 0$

    c. $x^2 + y^2 - 2x + 4y + 4 = 0$ **d.** $x^2 + y^2 - 2x + 4y + 5 = 0$

    e. $x^2 + y^2 - 2x + 4y + 9 = 0$

Conics at the Origin

The words *ellipse*, *parabola*, and *hyperbola* showed up in your previous courses in another context. You gave these names to graphs of certain equations. In this lesson, you will find general forms for equations for each of the conics when you put them on the coordinate plane. These equations will connect to the curves you already know about.

Equations for Parabolas

You already found an equation for one parabola in Exercise 9 from the previous lesson. Suppose $c \neq 0$. Consider the parabola with focus $(0, c)$ and directrix with equation $y = -c$.

> In the figures that accompany this derivation, $c > 0$. The same derivation works if $c < 0$. Try it.

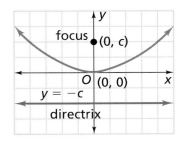

The origin is on this parabola because it is equidistant from the focus and the directrix. In fact, the parabola looks like the graph of a quadratic function with vertex $(0, 0)$.

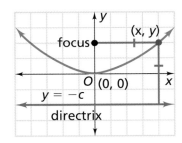

What is the point-tester for this graph? You want the distance from (x, y) to the point $(0, c)$ to be the same as the distance from (x, y) to the line $y = -c$. That gives you

$$\sqrt{x^2 + (y - c)^2} = |y + c|$$

This is fine as a point-tester. For example, $(2c, c)$ is on the graph because

$$\sqrt{(2c)^2 + (c - c)^2} = |c + c|$$

as you can check.

For You to Do

1. Find all values of x so that (x, c) is on the parabola.

You can simplify the equation in ways that will make it look familiar.

$$\sqrt{x^2 + (y - c)^2} = |y + c| \qquad \text{Square both sides.}$$
$$x^2 + (y - c)^2 = (y + c)^2 \qquad \text{Expand.}$$
$$x^2 + y^2 - 2cy + c^2 = y^2 + 2cy + c^2 \qquad \text{Cancel and simplify.}$$
$$x^2 = 4cy$$

Theorem 6.3

An equation for the parabola with focus (0, c) and directrix with equation $y = -c$ is

$$x^2 = 4cy$$

This should look familiar. In earlier courses, you wrote it as

$$y = \frac{1}{4c} x^2$$

So, your parabola is the graph of the quadratic function $f(x) = \frac{1}{4c} x^2$.

Example

Problem A favorite quadratic curve has equation $y = x^2$.

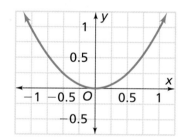

It has a focus and directrix. What are they?

Solution You can read the information from the general equation

$$x^2 = 4cy$$

In this equation, $4c = 1$ so $c = \frac{1}{4}$. Hence the focus of the standard parabola is $\left(0, \frac{1}{4}\right)$ and its directrix has equation $y = -\frac{1}{4}$.

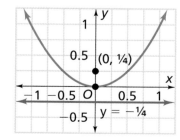

For Discussion

2. Find the equation of the parabola with focus $(c, 0)$ and directrix with equation $x = -c$.

Equations for Ellipses

Suppose an ellipse has foci $(c, 0)$ and $(-c, 0)$ and has string length is s.

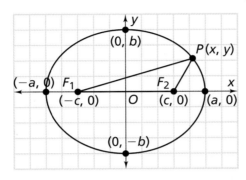

Remember...

An ellipse is the set of points such that the sum of the distances to two fixed foci is constant.

Facts and Notation

- The **center** of the ellipse is the origin.

- The ellipse has two lines of symmetry. They intersect the interior of the ellipse in two segments. The longer segment is called the **major axis** for the ellipse and the shorter segment is called the **minor axis.**

- The endpoints of the axes for the ellipse are sometimes called the **vertices** of the ellipse. Label the vertices $(a, 0)$, $(-a, 0)$, $(0, b)$ and $(0, -b)$.

- For any point P on the ellipse with foci F_1 and F_2 and string length s, $PF_1 + PF_2 = s$.

Habits of Mind

Explore the possibilities. Can an ellipse have major and minor axes of the same length?

What is the point-tester for this ellipse? The "sum of distances is constant" becomes, in this notation

$$\sqrt{(x - c)^2 + y^2} + \sqrt{(x + c)^2 + y^2} = 2a$$

This is a perfectly good point-tester, but you can simplify it. Isolate the radicals.

$$\sqrt{(x - c)^2 + y^2} = 2a - \sqrt{(x + c)^2 + y^2}$$

Square both sides.

$$(x - c)^2 + y^2 = 4a^2 - 4a\sqrt{(x + c)^2 + y^2} + (x + c)^2 + y^2$$

$s = 2a$

Expand a little and isolate again.

$$x^2 - 2cx + c^2 + y^2 = 4a^2 - 4a\sqrt{x^2 + 2cx + c^2 + y^2} + x^2 + 2cx + c^2 + y^2$$

so

$$-4cx - 4a^2 = -4a\sqrt{x^2 + 2cx + c^2 + y^2}$$

or

$$cx + a^2 = a\sqrt{x^2 + 2cx + c^2 + y^2}$$

Now square both sides once more.

$$c^2x^2 + 2a^2cx + a^4 = a^2x^2 + 2a^2cx + a^2c^2 + a^2y^2$$

The $2a^2cx$ cancels. You can rearrange terms to look like this.

$$a^4 - a^2c^2 = (a^2 - c^2)x^2 + a^2y^2$$

or

$$a^2(a^2 - c^2) = (a^2 - c^2)x^2 + a^2y^2$$

But $a^2 = b^2 + c^2$, so $a^2 - c^2 = b^2$. So the equation simplifies to

$$a^2b^2 = b^2x^2 + a^2y^2$$

It is often useful to divide both sides of this equation by a^2b^2 to get

$$1 = \frac{x^2}{a^2} + \frac{y^2}{b^2}$$

Habits of Mind

Understand the process. Each of these steps is reversible (as long as a and c are not negative). Make sure you understand why.

Theorem 6.4

The ellipse with foci $(c, 0)$ and $(-c, 0)$ and string length $2a$ has equation

$$1 = \frac{x^2}{a^2} + \frac{y^2}{b^2} \quad \text{where} \quad b^2 = a^2 - c^2.$$

Habits of Mind

Make connections. Looking at this equation, you might also recognize it as a scaling of the unit circle by a factor of a horizontally and b vertically.

Developing Habits of Mind

Understand the process. A careful proof of this theorem would require you to show that you did not gain or lose any points when you went from the raw point-tester to the equation in the theorem. There is some work to do here, because you squared both sides of the equation twice, making it possible for extra solutions to creep in. Make sure every step is reversible.

For Discussion

3. Discuss what happens to the graph of the equation $1 = \dfrac{x^2}{a^2} + \dfrac{y^2}{b^2}$ as a gets closer and closer to b.

4. Find an equation for the ellipse with foci at $(0, c)$ and $(0, -c)$ and string length $2a$.

Equations for Hyperbolas

Consider a hyperbola with foci $F_1(c, 0)$ and $F_2(-c, 0)$ defined by the condition

$$|PF_1 - PF_2| = s$$

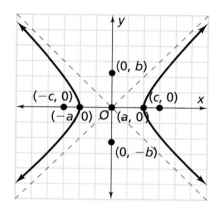

Facts and Notation

- The points $(a, 0)$ and $(-a, 0)$ are the *vertices* of the hyperbola. Therefore, $s = 2a$. The segment connecting the vertices is the hyperbola's *major axis*.

- The constant b is defined by the equation $a^2 + b^2 = c^2$.

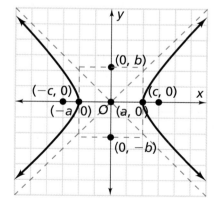

The diagonals of this little rectangle have an interesting relationship to the hyperbola. You will explore that relationship in the exercises.

You can construct b by creating a rectangle around the origin with sides parallel to the axes, one side of length $2a$, and diagonals of length $2c$. The vertical side of the rectangle is $2b$. The segment connecting $(0, b)$ to $(0, -b)$ is the hyperbola's *minor axis*.

The point-tester for the hyperbola is $|PF_1 - PF_2| = 2a$. In terms of coordinates, this translates into

$$\left| \sqrt{(x + c)^2 + y^2} - \sqrt{(x - c)^2 + y^2} \right| = 2a$$

This is a perfectly good point-tester. But you can simplify it considerably using exactly the same algebraic technique that you used to derive the equation of the ellipse. You will take care of the details in Exercise 12.

Theorem 6.5

The hyperbola with foci $(c, 0)$ and $(-c, 0)$ and constant difference $2a$ has equation

$$1 = \frac{x^2}{a^2} - \frac{y^2}{b^2}$$

where $b^2 = c^2 - a^2$.

> Well, there is one complication that you did not have with the ellipse: the absolute value. But you can avoid this by treating one branch of the hyperbola at a time. In the end, both equations come out the same.

Developing Habits of Mind

Generalize. You now have equations for all three conics, at least when they are placed on the coordinate plane in certain positions. The three equations

- $b^2x^2 + a^2y^2 = a^2b^2$,
- $b^2x^2 - a^2y^2 = a^2b^2$, and
- $x^2 = 4cy$

are all special cases of the following general quadratic equation in two variables.

$$rx^2 + sxy + ty^2 + ux + vy + w = 0$$

where $r, s, t, u, v,$ and w are real numbers. In the next lesson, you will show that if $s = 0$, the equation's graph is a conic with axis parallel to one of the coordinate axes. In fact, a very simple calculation with two numbers will tell you what kind of a conic it is. In the project for this chapter, you will show that even if $s \neq 0$, the graph is a conic, although its axis is not horizontal or vertical.

> **Habits of Mind**
>
> **Find relationships.** This predictive power—being able to tell the shape of a graph from a simple calculation—is something that mathematicians prize.

For You to Do

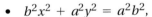

5. Find the values of $r, s, t, u, v,$ and w in each of the three equations above.

Exercises *Practicing Habits of Mind*

Check Your Understanding

1. Many different ellipses have centers at the origin and pass through the point $(0, 5)$.

   a. Show that the ellipse with equation $25x^2 + 169y^2 = 4225$ passes through $(0, 5)$.

   b. Find four other points on the ellipse from part (a).

   c. Show that the length of the major axis is 26.

   d. The foci of this ellipse are $(c, 0)$ and $(-c, 0)$. Find the value of c.

   e. Sketch a graph of this ellipse.

2. The ellipse with equation $25x^2 + 9y^2 = 225$ also has its center at the origin and passes through $(0, 5)$.

   a. Find four other points on this ellipse.

   b. Show that the length of the major axis is 10.

   c. The foci of this ellipse are $(0, c)$ and $(0, -c)$. Find the value of c.

   d. Sketch a graph of this ellipse.

3. **Write About It** Describe, as completely as possible, how to find the foci and sketch the graph of
$$1 = \frac{x^2}{a^2} + \frac{y^2}{b^2}$$

   Be careful to describe cases where $a > b$, $a = b$, and $a < b$.

4. The graph of the equation $y^2 - 9x^2 = 36$ is a hyperbola.

   a. Show that the points $(0, 6)$ and $(0, -6)$ are on the hyperbola.

   b. If $x = 1$, find approximate values of y to four decimal places.

   c. If $x = 5$, find approximate values of y to four decimal places.

   d. If $x = 100$, find approximate values of y to four decimal places.

   e. As x grows larger, what relationship is there between the x- and y-coordinates of points on the hyperbola?

5. In Exercise 4, you worked with the equation

$$y^2 - 9x^2 = 36$$

A slight change to this equation can produce very different results.

a. Sketch the graph of $y^2 - 9x^2 = 9$. How is the graph similar to the one from Exercise 4. How is it different?

b. Sketch the graph of $y^2 - 9x^2 = 1$.

c. Sketch the graph of $y^2 - 9x^2 = 0$.

6. Take It Further The following equation gives the distance from a point (x, y) to the line with equation $x + y = 10$.

$$D = \frac{|x + y - 10|}{\sqrt{2}}$$

a. Find an equation for the parabola with focus at the origin and with directrix with equation $x + y = 10$.

b. Find the two points on the graph with x-coordinate -5.

c. Sketch the graph of this parabola.

Habits of Mind

Recall what you know.
What techniques can you use when one side of an equation is set equal to zero?

Go Online

PHSchool.com

For additional practice, go to **Web Code: bga-0607**

On Your Own

7. Find an equation for the parabola with focus $(-2, 0)$ and directrix with equation $x = 2$.

8. The graph of the following equation is a hyperbola.

$$\frac{x^2}{16} - \frac{y^2}{9} = 1$$

a. If (x, y) is on this hyperbola, then so are $(-x, y)$, $(-x, -y)$ and $(x, -y)$. Explain.

b. Copy and complete this table to find the nonnegative value of y for each value of x. Approximate your results to four decimal places.

x	y
3	undefined
4	0
5	▪
6	▪
8	▪
10	▪
20	▪
40	▪
100	▪
1000	▪

c. As x grows larger, what relationship is there between the x- and y-coordinates of points on the hyperbola?

9. Show that every point on the graph of $y = x^2$ is equidistant from the focus $\left(0, \frac{1}{4}\right)$ and the directrix with equation $y = -\frac{1}{4}$.

10. Consider the equation $1 = \frac{x^2}{9} + \frac{y^2}{4}$.

 a. Find all values of x if $(x, 0)$ is on the graph of the equation.

 b. Find all values of y if $(0, y)$ is on the graph of the equation.

 c. Sketch the graph of the equation.

 d. Find all values of x if (x, x) is on the graph of the equation.

 e. Find three points that are close to being on the graph but not actually on it.

11. **Take It Further** An ellipse has foci $(8, -6)$ and $(-6, 8)$ and string length 20.

 a. Show that this ellipse passes through the origin.

 b. Find the center of the ellipse.

 c. Find the endpoints of the major axis.

 d. Find an equation of the ellipse.

 e. Sketch the graph of the ellipse.

The major axis contains the foci. It has the same length as the string length.

12. Prove Theorem 6.5, which gives an equation for a hyperbola.

13. **Standardized Test Prep** Which of the following are the foci of the ellipse with equation $\frac{x^2}{25} + \frac{y^2}{9} = 1$?

 A. $(-1, 0), (1, 0)$

 B. $(-2, 0), (2, 0)$

 C. $(-3, 0), (3, 0)$

 D. $(-4, 0), (4, 0)$

Maintain Your Skills

14. Each of these is the equation of a parabola. For each, find the coordinates of the focus and an equation of the directrix.

 a. $y = \frac{1}{4}x^2$

 b. $x = \frac{1}{4}y^2$

 c. $y = -\frac{1}{4}x^2$

 d. $x = -\frac{1}{4}y^2$

 e. $y = 2x^2$

 f. $x = 2y^2$

6.8 Conics Anywhere

In this lesson, you will look at equations for conics where the center (or vertex, for the parabola) is not at the origin.

You looked at various affine transformations of parabolas in CME Project *Algebra 2*. The ideas here are exactly the same. It is easiest to understand the general methods through examples.

Example 1

Problem Find equation of the ellipse $\mathcal{E}$ with foci at $(3, 16)$ and $(3, -8)$ and with string length 26.

Solution The situation looks like this.

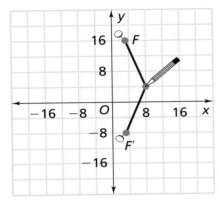

The center of an ellipse is the midpoint of the segment connecting its foci, so the center of this ellipse is $(3, 4)$. The major axis is vertical and the distance from the center to each focus is $c = 12$. Since the string length is 26, $a = 13$ and the vertices are at $(3, 4 + 13) = (3, 17)$ and $(3, 4 - 13) = (3, -9)$.

Since $a^2 = b^2 + c^2$, $b = 5$. So the minor axis connects $(-2, 4)$ to $(8, 4)$.

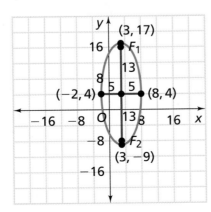

This ellipse $\mathcal{E}$ is a translation of an ellipse $\mathcal{E}'$, centered at the origin with foci located at $(0, 12)$ and $(0, -12)$ and string length 26.

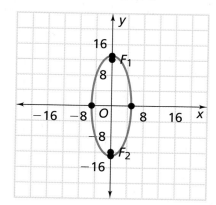

You already know how to find an equation of ellipse centered at the origin. An equation for $\mathcal{E}$ is

$$\frac{x^2}{25} + \frac{y^2}{169} = 1$$

How can you use this equation to find an equation of the ellipse centered at $(3, 4)$? Notice that the distance from any point (x, y) to $(3, 16)$ is the same as the distance from $(x - 3, y - 4)$ to $(3 - 3, 16 - 4) = (0, 12)$. (Why?) Similarly, the distance from any point (x, y) to $(3, -8)$ is the same as the distance from $(x - 3, y - 4)$ to $(3 - 3, -8 - 4) = (0, -12)$. So, the sum of the distances from (x, y) to $(3, 16)$ and $(3, -8)$ is the same as the sum of the distances from $(x - 3, y - 4)$ to $(0, 12)$ and $(0, -12)$. In particular, it follows that (x, y) is on $\mathcal{E}$ if and only if $(x - 3, y - 4)$ is on $\mathcal{E}'$.

So, the point-tester for $\mathcal{E}$ is "See if $(x - 3, y - 4)$ is on $\mathcal{E}'$." That is the same as "See if $(x - 3, y - 4)$ satisfies the equation for $\mathcal{E}'$." In other words, check to see if

$$\frac{(x - 3)^2}{25} + \frac{(y - 4)^2}{169} = 1$$

So this is an equation for the ellipse $\mathcal{E}$.

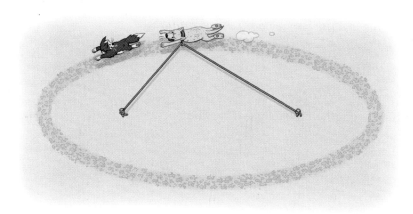

Simplify complicated problems. In the above example, you could have gone right to the locus definition. The point $P = (x, y)$ is on $\mathcal{E}$ if and only if the sum of the distances from P to the foci is 26, so the point-tester is

$$\sqrt{(x - 3)^2 + (y - 16)^2} + \sqrt{(x - 3)^2 + (y + 8)^2} = 26$$

To simplify this, you would have to face some hefty algebra (similar to what you did in the proof of Theorem 6.4). But using the translation idea reduces the problem to one you have already solved and eliminates the need for the complex calculations.

> Of course, some people love to do algebraic calculations. If you are one of them, go ahead and see if you get the same equation as you got in the example.

For Discussion

1. Suppose $F_1 = (1, 1)$ and $F_2 = (11, 1)$. Find an equation of the hyperbola defined by

$$|PF_1 - PF_2| = 8$$

Minds in Action   episode 19

Tony and Sasha are looking at the example above

Sasha   I'm one of those people who loves algebra. I think I'll see what our equation

$$\frac{(x - 3)^2}{25} + \frac{(y - 4)^2}{169} = 1$$

looks like if I expand everything and put it in normal form.

Tony   Be my guest.

Sasha pulls out some chalk and begins to write on the board. A few minutes later, she smiles at her work.

Sasha   I get

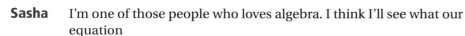

$$169x^2 - 1014x + 25y^2 - 200y - 2304 = 0$$

Tony   I wonder how we could have graphed the ellipse if we had been given this equation.

> **Habits of Mind**
>
> **Find a process.** How would you help Tony answer his question?

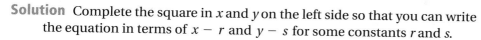
Example 2

Problem Is the graph of

$$9y^2 + 18y - 16x^2 + 64x - 199 = 0$$

a conic? If so, what kind is it?

Solution Complete the square in x and y on the left side so that you can write the equation in terms of $x - r$ and $y - s$ for some constants r and s.

See the TI-Nspire Handbook on p. 704 for ideas about how to use your calculator to graph the equation.

$$9y^2 + 18y - 16x^2 + 64x - 199 = 0$$
$$9y^2 + 18y - 16x^2 + 64x = 199$$
$$9(y^2 + 2y + \text{?}) - 16(x^2 - 4x + \text{??}) = 199 + 9 \cdot \text{?} - 16 \cdot \text{??}$$
$$9(y^2 + 2y + 1) - 16(x^2 - 4x + 4) = 199 + 9 \cdot 1 - 16 \cdot 4$$
$$9(y + 1)^2 - 16(x - 2)^2 = 199 + 9 - 64$$
$$9(y + 1)^2 - 16(x - 2)^2 = 144$$

So the equation is

$$9(y + 1)^2 - 16(x - 2)^2 = 144$$

Divide both sides by 144 to get

$$\frac{(y + 1)^2}{16} - \frac{(x - 2)^2}{9} = 1$$

The graph is a hyperbola with center $(2, -1)$.

Developing Habits of Mind

Generalize. This method will work on any equation of the form

$$rx^2 + ty^2 + ux + vy + w = 0$$

and the result will tell you what kind of a conic the graph is. When you complete the square on the left side and simplify, you will get an equation of the form

$$r(x - h)^2 + t(x - k)^2 = c$$

for constants h, k, and c.

The graph might be a degenerate conic—a point or a pair of lines, for example. See the Maintain Your Skills exercises from Lesson 6.6.

For Discussion

Suppose the conic is not degenerate. Discuss each statement.

2. If either r or t is 0, the graph is a parabola.

3. If r and t have the same sign, the graph is an ellipse.

4. If r and t have opposite signs, the graph is a hyperbola.

A little more work produces the following classification theorem.

To a mathematician a classification theorem is truly a thing of beauty.

Theorem 6.6

The graph of

$$rx^2 + ty^2 + ux + vy + w = 0$$

is a (possibly degenerate) conic. In fact, the nature of the conic is determined by the sign of rt:

• If $rt > 0$, the graph is an ellipse.

• If $rt = 0$, the graph is a parabola.

• If $rt < 0$, the graph is a hyperbola.

For You to Do

5. How can you tell from the equation if the graph is a circle?

6. How can you tell from the equation if the graph is a single point?

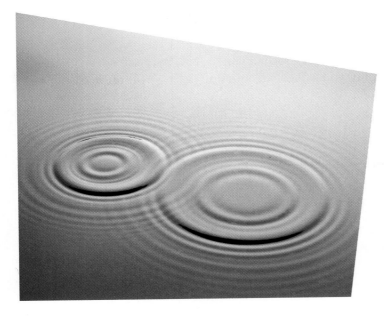

Educators and scientists use ripple tanks to discover and demonstrate the additive and subtractive properties of combinations of waves in a shallow basin of water. Here the spreading rings of drops of liquid produce interference patterns. Such patterns are the common conic sections you studied in this chapter.

Exercises *Practicing Habits of Mind*

Check Your Understanding

1. The graph of the following equation is a hyperbola.

$$\frac{(x - 3)^2}{16} - \frac{(y - 2)^2}{9} = 1$$

The hyperbola is related to the one from Exercise 8 of Lesson 6.7.

   a. What is the center of the hyperbola?

   b. Copy and complete this table to find the nonnegative value of y for each value of x. Approximate your results to four decimal places.

x	y
6	undefined
7	2
8	▨
9	▨
11	▨
13	▨
23	▨
43	▨
103	▨
1003	▨

   c. As x grows larger, what relationship is there between the x- and y-coordinates of points on the hyperbola?

2. The graph of the equation

$$9(x - 3)^2 + 16(y + 2)^2 = N$$

   depends on the value of N.

   a. Sketch the graph when $N = 144$.

   b. Does the ellipse you drew in part (a) pass through the origin?

   c. Sketch the graph when $N = 36$.

   d. Sketch the graph when $N = 0$.

   e. Sketch the graph when $N = -144$.

   f. Find all values of N such that the graph passes through the point $(13, -1)$.

3. **a.** Is the graph of $25x^2 - 4y^2 + 150x + 32y + 61 = 0$ a conic? If so, what kind is it?

   b. Sketch the graph of the equation.

4. **a.** Is the graph of $4x^2 + 25y^2 - 16x + 250y + 641 = 0$ a conic? If so, what kind is it?

   b. Sketch the graph of the equation.

5. The graph of $\dfrac{(x+3)^2}{4} - \dfrac{(y-2)^2}{16} = 1$ is not the graph of a function, but it can be the union of two function graphs.

   a. Solve the equation above for $(y-2)^2$.

   b. Why is it not possible to uniquely solve for y?

   c. Write y as two functions. Plot each function. Then combine them to sketch the entire hyperbola.

6. Sketch an accurate graph of these two equations on the same axes.
$$\frac{(x-3)^2}{16} - \frac{(y-2)^2}{9} = 1$$
$$\frac{(x-3)^2}{16} - \frac{(y-2)^2}{9} = 0$$

7. **Take It Further** Find an equation of a hyperbola that is the graph of all points P with
$$|PF_1 - PF_2| = 2\sqrt{2}$$
with foci $F_1 = (\sqrt{2}, \sqrt{2})$ and $F_2 = (-\sqrt{2}, -\sqrt{2})$.

On Your Own

8. Explain why the equation $\dfrac{(x+5)^2}{16} + \dfrac{(y-3)^2}{9} = -1$ has no graph, but the equation $\dfrac{(x+5)^2}{16} - \dfrac{(y-3)^2}{9} = -1$ does.

9. Consider the equation
$$\frac{(x-11)^2}{36} + \frac{(y+14)^2}{25} = 1$$

   a. What possible values of x could make the equation true? Explain.

   b. What possible values of y could make the equation true?

Go Online
PHSchool.com

For additional practice, go to **Web Code:** bga-0608

Try to do this without graphing the ellipse. What must be true about the entire x term?

10. Consider the equation $\dfrac{(x+9)^2}{49} - \dfrac{(y-5)^2}{16} = 1$.

a. What possible values of x could make the equation true? Explain.

b. What possible values of y could make the equation true?

11. Find the coordinates of the foci of the ellipse with equation
$$36x^2 + 11y^2 - 288x - 110y + 455 = 0$$

12. What's Wrong Here? Pam thought about stretching an ellipse.

Pam: You can stretch these ellipses in any direction, and everything moves along. If you double the length of an axis, I think you'll double the distance between the foci, too.

a. Give an example that shows Pam's conjecture is not correct.

b. Can you stretch an ellipse to double the distance? Explain.

13. An ellipse is centered at $(3, 5)$ and $(10, 5)$ is one of its foci.

a. Find the coordinates of the other focus.

b. If the point $(1, 17)$ is on the ellipse, find the length of the major and minor axes. Find an equation for the ellipse.

14. Show algebraically that the sum of the distances from (x, y) to $(3, 16)$ and $(3, -8)$ is the same as the sum of the distances from $(x - 3, y - 4)$ to $(0, 12)$ and $(0, -12)$.

15. Standardized Test Prep Which of the following is a hyperbola with foci at $(3, 4)$ and $(3, -4)$ and vertices 6 units apart?

A. $\dfrac{(x-3)^2}{9} - \dfrac{(y-4)^2}{16} = 1$

B. $\dfrac{(x-3)^2}{9} - \dfrac{y^2}{7} = 1$

C. $\dfrac{(y-4)^2}{9} - \dfrac{x^2}{16} = 1$

D. $\dfrac{y^2}{9} - \dfrac{(x-3)^2}{7} = 1$

Maintain Your Skills

16. An ellipse has center $(2, -1)$ and one vertex is $(6, -1)$.

a. Find the coordinates of the other vertex.

b. Find the foci if $(2, 0)$ is one of the endpoints of the minor axis.

c. Find the foci if $(2, 1)$ is one of the endpoints of the minor axis.

d. Find the foci if $(2, 2)$ is one of the endpoints of the minor axis.

e. Find the foci if $(2, 3)$ is one of the endpoints of the minor axis.

f. Find the foci if $(2, 4)$ is one of the endpoints of the minor axis.

They Are All the Same

In Lesson 6.6, you saw each of the conics as a planar slice of an infinite double cone. The only difference between the different types of conic was the position of the slicing plane. This lesson shows another way to see the conics as in some sense the same. All of them come from a single class of equations.

The locus definition of a parabola is the set of points that are equidistant from a point F (the focus) and a line d (the directrix).

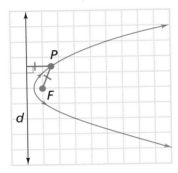

Another way to say that $PF = Pd$ is to say that $\frac{PF}{Pd} = 1$.

> Pd means the distance from P to the line d, measured along the perpendicular from P to d.

Developing Habits of Mind

Experiment. Mathematicians like to tweak definitions. What would the curve look like if $\frac{PF}{Pd}$ were 2 instead of 1? What would it look like if the ratio were $\frac{1}{2}$? Experimenting with definitions like this often leads to new connections.

You can set up an experiment in your geometry software in which you can control a slider and then produce the set of all points P so that the ratio of $\frac{PF}{Pd}$ is the length of the slider (a nonnegative real number). Here are some snapshots of such an experiment.

See the TI-Nspire Handbook on p. 704 for instructions on how to build the experiment.

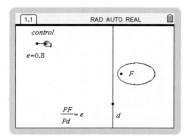

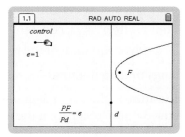

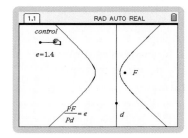

You know that when $e = 1$, the curve is a parabola. (Why?) But it sure looks as if other values of e produce conics, too. Before you see if this is so, experiment some with the sketch.

The letter e is used for the ratio for reasons that will become apparent in the exercises. But this has nothing to do with the constant e from Chapter 3.

1. For what values of e do the curves seem to be ellipses? Hyperbolas? Parabolas?

2. Experiment with the distance between the directrix and the focus. How does that affect things?

Just because something looks like a conic does not mean that it is a conic. To find out, you can use the algebra. Set up the situation on a coordinate plane. Then translate the locus definition into coordinates.

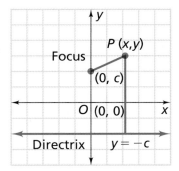

Suppose the focus is $(0, c)$ and the directrix has equation $y = -c$.

What is the point-tester? $P(x, y)$ is on the curve if and only if the distance from (x, y) to $(0, c)$ is e times the distance from (x, y) to the graph of $y = -c$.

$\frac{PF}{Pd} = e$ is the same as $PF = e \cdot Pd$.

But the distance from (x, y) to $(0, c)$ is $\sqrt{x^2 + (y - c)^2}$ and the distance from (x, y) to the graph of $y = -c$ is $|y - (-c)| = |y + c|$.

(Why?) So, the point tester is $\sqrt{x^2 + (y - c)^2} = e|y + c|$.

This is fine as a point-tester. But you can simplify the equation in ways that will make it look familiar. Remember, thanks to Theorem 6.6, if you know that the equation is a polynomial in x and y of degree 2 set equal to 0, you only need the coefficients of x^2 and y^2 to tell which conic the graph will be.

$$\sqrt{x^2 + (y - c)^2} = e|y + c| \qquad \text{Square both sides.}$$

$$x^2 + (y - c)^2 = e^2(y + c)^2 \qquad \text{Expand.}$$

$$x^2 + y^2 - 2cy + c^2 = e^2 y^2 + 2e^2 cy + e^2 c^2 \qquad \text{Cancel and simplify.}$$

$$x^2 + (1 - e^2)y^2 + \text{(things that do not matter)} = \text{a constant}$$

So, the set of all points P so that $\frac{PF}{Pd} = e$ has equation of the form

$$x^2 + (1 - e^2)y^2 + \text{(things that do not matter)} = 0$$

You know from Theorem 6.6 that the nature of the curve depends on the sign of the product of the coefficients of the x^2 and y^2 terms in the equation: $rt = 1 \cdot (1 - e^2) = 1 - e^2$. This leads to the following classification theorem.

Habits of Mind

Understand the process. $|x|^2 = x^2$ (Why?)

Theorem 6.7

> Let F be a fixed point, d be a fixed line, and e be a positive real number. The set of points P such that $\frac{PF}{Pd} = e$ is a (possibly degenerate) conic. It is an ellipse if $e < 1$, a parabola if $e = 1$, and a hyperbola if $e > 1$.

Habits of Mind

Verify a conjecture. So, what the experiment suggested was true. The curve defined by $\frac{PF}{Pd} = e$ is always a conic.

Developing Habits of Mind

Make connections. Theorem 6.7 is one reason for the names *ellipse*, *parabola*, and *hyperbola*. If you check a dictionary you will discover that the words *ellipsis*, *parable*, and *hyperbole* have roughly these meanings in English.

- **ellipsis:** fall short—something is missing
- **parable:** fall beside—usually a story that illustrates a message
- **hyperbole:** fall beyond—an exaggeration

The theorem says that the curve is

- an ellipse if e "falls short" of 1.
- a parabola if e "falls beside" 1.
- a hyperbola e "falls beyond" 1.

In English, the symbol "..." is used to denote that something is missing, usually from a quotation and it is called an *ellipsis*. For example, "Now is the winter of our discontent..." means that the writer has cut this Shakespeare quotation before the end of the sentence.

For Discussion

3. Give an example of an English sentence that exhibits ellipsis, parable, or hyperbole.

Exercises Practicing Habits of Mind

Check Your Understanding

Some ellipses are flatter than others. One way to measure this is the **eccentricity,** the ratio of the distance between the foci, called the focal distance, to the distance between the vertices. Define the eccentricity by the ratio $\frac{c}{a}$.

1. Find the eccentricity of the ellipse given by each equation.

   a. $\frac{x^2}{25} + \frac{y^2}{16} = 1$ **b.** $\frac{x^2}{25} + \frac{y^2}{9} = 1$ **c.** $\frac{x^2}{25} + \frac{y^2}{24} = 1$ **d.** $\frac{x^2}{25} + \frac{y^2}{100} = 1$

2. Find an equation of an ellipse with center $(8, 0)$, focus $(6, 0)$, and eccentricity $\frac{1}{2}$.

3. The set of points P with the ratio $\frac{PF}{Pd} = \frac{1}{2}$ using focus $F(6, 0)$ and the y-axis as directrix forms a conic section. Find its equation. Find its center.

   The definition of eccentricity given above also applies to hyperbolas. The eccentricity is still the focal distance divided by the distance between the vertices, also expressed as $\frac{c}{a}$.

4. The set of points 1.5 times as far from $(3, 5)$ as they are from the graph of $x = -2$ is a hyperbola.

   a. Find its center, vertices, and foci.

   b. Find its eccentricity.

   c. Sketch the graph of the hyperbola.

5. The set of points 3 times as far from $(-3, 4)$ as they are from the graph of $y = -4$ is a hyperbola. Find its eccentricity.

6. **Take It Further** Given focus $F(0, 1)$ and directrix d given by $x = -1$. A conic section is defined by the points P with $\frac{PF}{Pd} = e$.

   a. If $e = 1$, how do you know that the conic is a parabola?

   b. If $e < 1$ show that the conic is an ellipse with eccentricity e.

   c. If $e > 1$ show that the conic is a hyperbola with eccentricity e.

> **Remember...**
>
> For an ellipse, $a^2 = b^2 + c^2$ where a is half the major axis length, b is half the minor axis length, and c is half the distance between the foci.

7. Take It Further Graph the ellipse with a graphing window of $-5 \leq x \leq 5$, $-5 \leq y \leq 5$.

$$\frac{x^2}{49} + \frac{(y - 100)^2}{10,000} = 1$$

a. What do you notice?

b. Find another ellipse that behaves similarly.

On Your Own

8. What is the eccentricity of a circle? Explain.

9. a. Explain why the eccentricity of an ellipse must always be less than 1.

   b. Explain why the eccentricity of a hyperbola must always be greater than 1.

10. A hyperbola has foci $(5, 5)$ and $(-7, 5)$. One endpoint of the major axis is $(-2, 5)$.

    a. Find an eccentricity of this hyperbola.

    b. Find an equation of the hyperbola.

    c. Sketch the graph of the hyperbola.

11. Which of these is an equation of an ellipse?

    A. $4x^2 + 1 = 9y^2$ **B.** $4x + 6y + x^2 - y^2 = 36$

    C. $4x^2 + 9y + 8x - 36 = 0$ **D.** $-16x + 8y + 4x^2 + 8y^2 - 25 = 0$

12. The set of points that are twice as far from (3, 7) as they are from the *y*-axis is a hyperbola. Find the other focus of this hyperbola.

13. Take It Further As seen in the lesson, fix focus point *F* and directrix line *d*, then vary the ratio $\frac{PF}{Pd}$ to produce different conic sections. One focus of the conic stays in place. But ellipses and hyperbolas have two foci: what happens to the other focus?

a. As the ratio $\frac{PF}{Pd}$ approaches zero, what does the other focus move toward?

b. As the ratio $\frac{PF}{Pd}$ gets larger toward 1, what does the other focus move toward?

c. What happens when the ratio equals 1?

d. As the ratio continues to grow, what does the other focus move toward?

14. Standardized Test Prep Which of the following could be the eccentricity of an ellipse with a focus at (5, 0), vertex at (7, 0), and directrix *x* = 12?

A. $\frac{2}{5}$ **B.** $\frac{5}{7}$ **C.** $\frac{5}{12}$ **D.** $\frac{7}{12}$

Go Online
PHSchool.com

For additional practice, go to **Web Code:** bga-0609

Maintain Your Skills

15. The orbit of every planet is an ellipse. Each elliptical orbit has the sun as one focus and some eccentricity *e*. This table gives the length of the major axis and the eccentricity for each planet's orbit.

Planet	Major Axis Length (million km)	Eccentricity e
Mercury	115.8	0.2056
Venus	216.4	0.0068
Earth	299.2	0.0167
Mars	455.9	0.0934
Jupiter	1556.8	0.0484
Saturn	2853.5	0.0542
Uranus	5741.9	0.0472
Neptune	8996.5	0.0086

Kepler proved this fact about the planets in the early 17th Century. Orbits of comets may be parabolic or even hyperbolic.

a. Which planet's orbit is most like a circle? the least like a circle?

b. For each planet, determine how far away the sun is from the center of the planet's orbit.

Remember...
The sun is a focus of the ellipse. The eccentricity is known.

Mathematical 6B Reflections

In this investigation, you sliced a cone to get a conic section—a circle, an ellipse, a parabola, or a hyperbola. You described each conic section verbally as a locus of points, or algebraically by an equation. Then, given an equation, you described its graph as a conic section. The following questions will help you summarize what you have learned.

1. Determine an equation (in the form $y = a(x - h)^2 + k$) for the parabola having focus $(1, 2)$ and directrix the x-axis.

2. Find the center, foci, and the lengths of the major and minor axes of the ellipse having equation $16x^2 - 64x + 25y^2 + 50y = 311$.

3. We know from Theorem 6.6 that the graph of the equation $rx^2 + ty^2 + ux + vy + w = 0$ is a conic. In order for the conic to be a circle, what must be the relationship between r and t?

4. **a.** In order for the graph of the equation $2x^2 + cy^2 + 4x + 4cy + f = 0$ to be an ellipse, what must be true about the value of c?

   b. In order for the graph of the equation $2x^2 + cy^2 + 4x + 4cy + f = 0$ to be a nondegenerate ellipse, what must be true about the value of f?

5. Explain how you know that the graph of the equation $x^2 + y^2 - 2x + 4y + 5 = 0$ is a degenerate conic.

6. How do you slice an infinite double cone with a plane to get a parabola?

7. What is the locus definition of a hyperbola?

8. What kind of conic section do you get when you graph $x^2 + 16y^2 - 8x + 64y + 64 = 0$? How can you identify the conic section from its equation?

Vocabulary

In this investigation, you learned these terms. Make sure you understand what each one means and how to use it.

- apex
- axis
- conic sections
- Dandelin sphere
- directrix
- eccentricity
- ellipse
- focus, foci
- generator
- hyperbola
- locus
- major axis
- minor axis
- parabola
- vertex

Mid-Chapter Test

Go Online
PHSchool.com

For a mid-chapter test, go
to Web Code: bga-0652

Multiple Choice

1. The graph of $x^2 + y^2 = 53$ is a circle. Determine which point does not lie on the circle.

A. $(-1, 2\sqrt{13})$ **B.** $(-2, 7)$

C. $(-5, 3)$ **D.** $(\sqrt{8}, 3\sqrt{5})$

2. Find the equation of the line that represents the set of points that are equidistant from $(0, 6)$ and $(12, 2)$.

A. $y = -\frac{1}{3}x + 9$ **B.** $y = 3x - 14$

C. $y = -3x + \frac{9}{3}$ **D.** $y = \frac{1}{3}x + \frac{4}{3}$

3. Find an equation of a parabola with focus $(0, 8)$ and directrix $y = -8$.

A. $y = -\frac{1}{8}x^2$ **B.** $y = \frac{1}{16}x^2$

C. $y = \frac{1}{8}x^2$ **D.** $y = \frac{1}{32}x^2$

4. The graph of $9x^2 - 36x - 4y^2 + 40y - 100 = 0$ is a conic. Determine the type of conic.

A. circle   **B.** hyperbola

C. ellipse   **D.** parabola

5. Find the eccentricity of the ellipse with equation $\frac{x^2}{100} + \frac{y^2}{36} = 1$.

A. $\frac{4}{5}$ **B.** $\frac{1}{8}$ **C.** $\frac{2}{5}$ **D.** $\frac{1}{6}$

Open Response

6. A triangle has vertices at $A(-5, 2)$, $B(-1, -6)$, and $C(3, 4)$.

  a. Find the perpendicular bisector of $\overline{AB}$.

  b. Find the perpendicular bisector of $\overline{BC}$.

  c. Find the point of intersection of the two perpendicular bisectors.

7. The graph of the equation $x^2 + y^2 - 4x + 12y + 24 = 0$ is a circle.

  a. Find the center and radius of the circle.

  b. Sketch the graph of the circle.

8. The graph of $9x^2 - 16y^2 = 144$ is a hyperbola.

  a. Find the intercepts.

  b. Find the foci.

  c. Sketch the graph of the hyperbola, and label the intercepts and foci.

9. An ellipse is centered at $(1, 2)$ with one of its foci at $(13, 2)$ and one of its vertices at $(14, 2)$.

  a. Find the coordinates of the other focus.

  b. Write an equation of the ellipse.

  c. Sketch the graph of the ellipse.

10. Find the coordinates of the foci of the ellipse with equation $51x^2 + 100y^2 + 612x - 800y - 1664 = 0$.

11. The set of points twice as far from the point $(4, 6)$ as from the line $x = -2$ is a hyperbola.

  a. Find the center, foci, and vertices.

  b. Find the eccentricity.

  c. Sketch the graph of the hyperbola.

Investigation 6C

Vector Algebra and Geometry

In *Vector Algebra and Geometry*, you will study the simple but immensely useful notion of a vector. A vector, which you will define in terms of size and direction, has numerous applications in mathematics and the physical sciences. For geometry, vectors provide another vehicle for proof.

By the end of this investigation, you will be able to answer questions like these.

1. How can you interpret the matrix operations of sum and scalar product geometrically?

2. Why might it be useful to write an equation of a line in vector form?

3. How can you use vectors to prove that the medians of a triangle are concurrent?

You will learn how to

- interpret sums and scalar multiples of ordered pairs geometrically

- express lines with vector equations and solve for intersections and other useful information using these equations

- use convex and affine combinations to locate specific points, such as the midpoint and trisection points of a line segment

You will develop these habits and skills:

- Represent ordered pairs geometrically both as points and vectors, and be able to go back and forth between these representations.

- Reason logically to prove geometry theorems using vector methods.

- Look at geometric figures in a new way to see vector relationships.

A crosswind landing (Pilots refer to it as "crabbing.") vividly illustrates the vector effects of strong winds on the heading of even a large airliner.

Getting Started

Ordered pairs represent points in the coordinate plane. You first learned to calculate with points in CME Project *Geometry*. But you can also think about ordered pairs as a special type of matrix. Calculations you perform on matrices such as $2U$, $U + V$, and $V - 3U$ should have geometric meaning as well. In this investigation, you will learn how to go back and forth between the algebra and geometry of ordered pairs.

Use graph paper on these exercises. You need to plot the points accurately to see some of the patterns.

Habits of Mind

Extend the process.
These ideas can also be applied to ordered triples for three dimensions, or any number of dimensions.

For You to Explore

1. Let $U = (3, 1)$, $V = (2, 4)$. On graph paper, plot the points $(0, 0)$, U, V, and $U + V$. Connect the points with line segments. What kind of figure is it? Will a different choice for U and V produce a different kind of figure?

2. Let $U = (1, 0)$ and $V = (0, 1)$. Plot the following points, labeling each one. For each part, use a clean sheet of graph paper.

   a. U, $2U$, $3U$, $(-1)U$, $(-3)U$

   b. V, $V + U$, $V + 2U$, $V + 3U$, $V + (-1)U$, $V - 3U$

   c. U, $U + V$, $U + 2V$, $U + 3V$, $U + (-1)V$, $U - 3V$

   d. U, V, $\dfrac{U + V}{2}$, $\dfrac{1}{4}U + \dfrac{3}{4}V$, $\dfrac{2}{3}U + \dfrac{1}{3}V$

   e. U, V, $-U + 2V$, $-\dfrac{1}{2}U + \dfrac{3}{2}V$, $2U - V$, $1.5U - 0.5V$

   f. $jU + kV$ where j, k are all integer pairs with $j = 0, 1, 2, 3$ and $k = 0, 1, 2, 3$

   g. Explain why you can represent any point on the plane as $aU + bV$ for some scalars a and b.

3. Do Exercise 2, parts (a) through (e), over again, but now let $U = (3, 2)$ and $V = (-1, 3)$. Do the patterns you observed in that exercise continue to hold? What are the patterns?

Remember...

A scalar is a real number. Multiplying by a scalar is different from multiplying by a matrix.

4. Let $U = (1, 0)$, $V = (0, 1)$, and $W = (-1, -1)$. Plot all the following on the same piece of graph paper.

   a. The triangle with corners U, V, W

   b. The point $\dfrac{U + V + W}{3}$

   c. The line segment from U to $\dfrac{V + W}{2}$

   d. The line segment from V to $\dfrac{U + W}{2}$

   e. The line segment from W to $\dfrac{U + V}{2}$

   f. $\dfrac{1}{2}U + \dfrac{1}{4}V + \dfrac{1}{4}W$, $\dfrac{1}{4}U + \dfrac{1}{2}V + \dfrac{1}{4}W$

Exercises *Practicing Habits of Mind*

On Your Own

5. Let U and V be as in Exercise 4. Now let $W = (2, 5)$. Repeat the calculations of Exercise 4. Do the patterns you observed in that exercise continue to hold?

6. Consider the infinite set of points $(1, 2) + t(2, -1)$. where t is any real number.

a. Plot a few of these points for different values of t.

b. The set of points determines a geometric object. Find the object.

c. Find an equation for this geometric object in terms of x and y.

7. Consider the infinite set of points $2((1, 2) + t(2, -1))$, where t is any real number.

a. Plot a few of these points for different values of t.

b. The set of points determines a geometric object. Find the object.

c. Find an equation for this geometric object in terms of x and y.

8. Consider the quadrilateral at the right.

a. If you scale all the points on the perimeter of the figure by $\frac{1}{2}$, what figure do you get? Draw it on graph paper.

b. If, instead, you scale all the points by -1, you get another figure. Sketch the figure.

c. Draw the figure which, if you scale it by a factor of 2, you get the quadrilateral in the diagram.

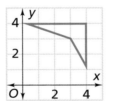

> **Remember...**
>
> Scaling a matrix M by k means multiplying each coordinate by k, to get kM. For example, scaling the ordered pair $(2, 3)$ by $\frac{1}{2}$, produces the ordered pair $\left(1, \frac{3}{2}\right)$.

Maintain Your Skills

9. Calculate the result of each matrix multiplication.

a. $\begin{pmatrix} 3 & 0 \\ 0 & 3 \end{pmatrix}\begin{pmatrix} 5 \\ 7 \end{pmatrix}$ **b.** $\begin{pmatrix} -2 & 0 \\ 0 & -2 \end{pmatrix}\begin{pmatrix} 5 \\ 7 \end{pmatrix}$ **c.** $\begin{pmatrix} 10 & 0 \\ 0 & 10 \end{pmatrix}\begin{pmatrix} 2 \\ -9 \end{pmatrix}$ **d.** $\begin{pmatrix} 1 & 0 \\ 0 & 1 \end{pmatrix}\begin{pmatrix} 13 \\ -6 \end{pmatrix}$

e. Describe the effect of multiplying any 2×1 matrix by the matrix $\begin{pmatrix} a & 0 \\ 0 & a \end{pmatrix}$.

6.11 Ordered Pairs, Points, and Vectors

There is a strong tie between algebra and geometry. In CME Project *Geometry*, you applied algebra to geometry by thinking of points as ordered pairs. Ordered pairs are just a special type of matrix, so you can apply the algebra of matrices to geometric concepts.

Remember...

You first learned about matrices in CME Project *Algebra 2*.

The main operations you learned for matrices are addition, multiplication, and scalar multiplication. You will see how to represent these operations geometrically when the matrices are ordered pairs.

Adding Points

To add two points, $A(a, b)$ and $D(c, d)$ it makes sense to simply add them the way you add two matrices—find the sum of each pair of corresponding coordinates. This gives you the sum $A + D = (a + c, b + d)$. If you look at a picture that shows A, D, $A + D$, and the origin, you can see that these four points are the vertices of a parallelogram. The sum $A + D$ completes the parallelogram determined by O, A, and D.

Remember...

In Lesson 6.3, you proved that this figure is a parallelogram.

You can also think of A as a point and D as a displacement. Then a point plus a vector equals a point.

For You to Do

A vector PQ is an arrow with tail at point P and head at point Q. Call it $\overrightarrow{PQ}$. Two vectors are equivalent if they have the same displacement $D = (c, d)$. Or they have the same displacement if they move horizontally c units and vertically d units.

1. If $\overrightarrow{AB}$ has displacement $(2, 3)$ and $A = (1, -1)$, what is B? Draw a picture, or use graph paper.

2. If $\overrightarrow{CD}$ has displacement $(2, 3)$ and $D = (-2, 5)$, what is C?

3. If $P = (0, 3)$ and $Q = (1, -2)$, find the displacement of $\overrightarrow{PQ}$. Find the displacement of $\overrightarrow{QP}$.

4. Let

$$O = (0, 0), \quad A = (1, 3), \quad B = (3, 2), \quad C = (5, 1)$$

Determine which of the following vectors are equivalent.

$$\overrightarrow{OA}, \ \overrightarrow{OB}, \ \overrightarrow{OC}, \ \overrightarrow{AB}, \ \overrightarrow{AC}, \ \overrightarrow{BC}$$

Developing Habits of Mind

Think about it more than one way. If $\overrightarrow{AB}$ and $\overrightarrow{PQ}$ have the same displacement, are they the same vector or different vectors?

In this course, they are considered to be different vectors but equivalent.

Other people say they are the same vector, because to them it is the displacement that is actually the vector. In this view, $\overrightarrow{AB}$ and $\overrightarrow{PQ}$ are just different pictures of the same thing.

You can think of it whichever way works best for you. Vectors are meant to help you locate points. So long as you have a mental picture that allows you to start with ordered pairs A and D and to get to ordered pair $A + D$, you are all set.

There is one thing everyone agrees on: If you label a vector by a single ordered pair D, that pair represents the displacement. If you label a vector by two ordered pairs A and B, they are the points at the tail and head.

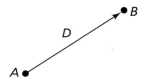

When you refer to the vector $D = (c, d)$, that means the vector displacement has c over and d up. Usually, context makes it clear which vector with that displacement you intend.

For Discussion

5. In the figure above, viewing A, B, and D as matrices that you add and subtract, find an equation that relates A, B, and D.

Scalar Multiplication

In-Class Experiment

6. On graph paper, copy the corners P, Q, and R of the figure below.

   a. Compute and mark the points $\frac{1}{2}P$, $\frac{1}{2}Q$, and $\frac{1}{2}R$.

   b. Draw the vectors from the origin to P, Q, and R.

   c. Draw the vectors from the origin to $\frac{1}{2}P$, $\frac{1}{2}Q$, and $\frac{1}{2}R$.

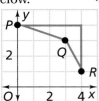

d. Compute and mark the points $(-1)P$, $(-1)Q$, and $(-1)R$.

e. Draw the vectors from the origin to $(-1)P$, $(-1)Q$, and $(-1)R$.

f. Find the relationship between A and kA when they are interpreted as points.

g. Find the relationship between A and kA when they are interpreted as displacements of vectors with tails at the origin.

You explored the effect of scaling, or dilation, in CME Project—*Geometry*. You can explain it with similar triangles. Here is the result of scaling point D and vector $\overrightarrow{OD}$ by the factor $k = 2$.

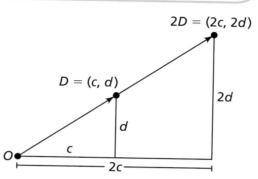

The vectors $\overrightarrow{OD}$ and $\overrightarrow{O(2D)}$ have the same slope $\frac{d}{c}$. Also, $\overrightarrow{O(2D)}$ is twice as long.

So $\overrightarrow{O(2D)} = 2\overrightarrow{OD}$.

Here is the result when using the scaling factor $k = 0.7$.

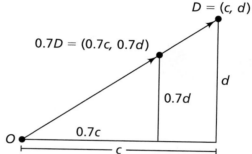

The slopes of the vectors are the same (the vectors are parallel) and the ratio of lengths is still the scaling factor (now 0.7). The resulting picture is smaller since $|k| < 1$.

Finally, here is a picture for $k = -1$. The tails of the vectors do not have to be at the origin. They can be at any point P. Then $D = (c, d)$ is the displacement and the name D appears along the vector rather than at the end.

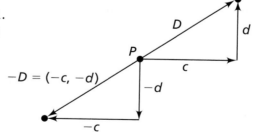

Remember…

If two vectors have the same direction, they have the same slope but they must also have the same orientation. $(1, -1)$ and $(-1, 1)$ have the same slope and length, but they point in opposite directions.

As before, the slopes of vectors D and $kD = -D$ are the same. This time the lengths are the same, but the directions are opposite. D and $-D$ are not the same vector: two vectors have the same displacement if and only if they have the same length and the same direction.

Consider a point *P* and a vector *D*.

7. Draw a sketch for all the points $P + kD$ that satisfy each of the following conditions.

a. *k* slides along from 0 to 2.

b. *k* slides along from 0 to -2.

c. *k* increases from some very large negative number to some very large positive number.

Exercises *Practicing Habits of Mind*

Check Your Understanding

1. Suppose two vectors $\vec{PQ}$ and $\vec{RS}$ are equivalent. That means that the two vectors have the same displacement, $D = (c, d)$.

a. Show that $\vec{PQ}$ and $\vec{RS}$ have the same slope.

b. Show that $\vec{PQ}$ and $\vec{RS}$ have the same length.

c. Describe how can you be sure that $\vec{PQ}$ and $\vec{RS}$ have the same direction.

Remember...

Direction includes both the slope and the orientation of the vector.

2. Suppose that $\vec{PQ}$ and $\vec{RS}$ have the same direction and length. Prove that $Q - P = S - R$.

3. Find the coordinates of the fourth point if you complete the figure at the right to form a parallelogram.

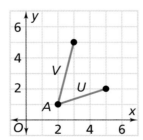

4. Find the coordinates of the fourth point if you complete the figure to form a parallelogram.

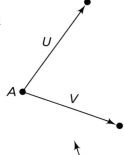

> This time there is no grid, so the answer should be in terms of *A*, *U*, and *V*.

5. This picture shows two vectors *U* and *V*. Copy and draw the sum *U* + *V*.

On Your Own

6. a. If a vector equivalent to (a_1, a_2) has its tail at the point (t_1, t_2), find the coordinates of its head.

b. If a vector equivalent to (a_1, a_2) has its head at the point (h_1, h_2), find the coordinates of its tail.

7. Consider any closed polygon, like the one at the right. View each side as a vector, with the directions shown. Find the sum of these vectors.

8. A *dilation* is any geometric transformation that expands or contracts the plane (or space) using some particular point as its center. The diagram below illustrates a dilation with center $A(1, 4)$ by a factor of 2. *S* is the figure made up of three line segments.

Use graph paper to complete the following.

a. Draw *S* and dilate it with center *A* by a factor of 3.

b. Dilate *S* with center *A* by a factor of $\frac{1}{2}$.

c. Dilate *S* with center *A* by a factor of -1.

> The vector $\overrightarrow{AB}$ is a dilation of the vector $\overrightarrow{AC}$, shown slightly offset so you can see its whole length. Actually $\overrightarrow{AC}$ goes right over the arrow $\overrightarrow{AB}$.

9. Take It Further Consider a dilation with center *A* by a factor of *k* as in Exercise 8. If you dilate point *B* to point *C*, find a formula for *C* in terms of *A*, *B*, and *k*.

10. Consider the unit cube with one corner at point $(0, 0, 0)$ and the opposite corner at point $(1, 1, 1)$. See the figure.

  a. Consider $U = (1, 0, 0)$. As a point, find where U is located on the surface of this cube.

  b. There are many vectors equivalent to U on the surface of the cube. Describe them.

  c. Now consider $V = (0, 1, 1)$. As a point, find where V is located.

  d. Describe all vectors equivalent to V lying entirely on the surface of the cube.

  e. Represent the sums $U + V$ and $V + U$ on this cube.

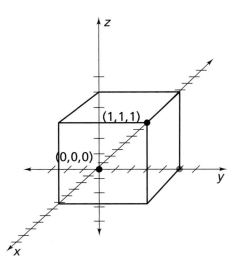

11. Find the displacements of the diagonals of the parallelogram at the right.

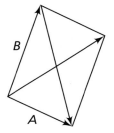

Go Online
PHSchool.com

For additional practice, go to **Web Code:** bga-0611

12. Standardized Test Prep Given U is the vector $(-3, 4)$ and V is the vector $(2, 3)$ as shown. Which of the following represents the bold vector (a, b)?

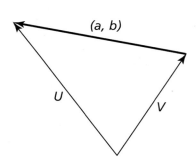

  A. $(-1, -1)$ **B.** $(3, -4)$

  C. $(-5, 1)$ **D.** $(5, -1)$

Maintain Your Skills

13. In the figure at the right, identify all vectors with the same displacement.

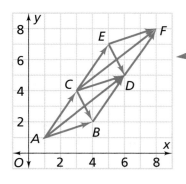

You could also phrase this question as, "Find all equivalent vectors." Some people would even say, "Find all vectors that are the same."

6.12 Vector Equations of Lines

Here is one way to think of a straight line: start at a point P and change position in some fixed direction. You can write the point P as an ordered pair. If you write the direction as a vector, you can do the same with it. This way of thinking leads to a vector equation for lines.

Minds in Action   episode 20

Tony and Sasha have been asked to figure out an equation for a typical point X on the line through point P with direction vector D.

Tony   Okay, we start at P and change position in direction D. That makes sense. Look at this picture.

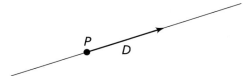

Sasha   So long as any amount can mean both positive and negative amounts. Otherwise we just get a ray.

Tony   We're supposed to write an equation for a typical point X on the line. Here it is.

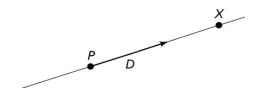

Sasha   Or it could be on the other side, like this

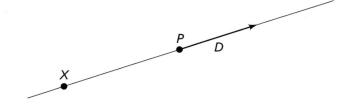

Tony   Or it could be in close, like this.

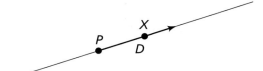

Sasha Whatever. The vector *D* just has to be scaled to get all the way from *P* to *X*. So I think it's *kD* instead of *D*.

Tony Hey, that's it, the part I was missing. From the last lesson, a point plus a vector is a point. You get from *P* to *X* by adding the vector *kD*. So $X = P + kD$. I think we're done!

Sasha Maybe. You like that point plus vector stuff, but I don't think that way. I want it to be all vectors. Plus, I like vectors from the origin, not just left out there anywhere. And I think they should be named by their tails and heads.

Tony Picky, picky. OK, let's see if we can do it that way. Maybe start with this?

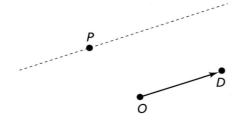

Sasha Yeah, but get some multiples *kD* in there too. I'll draw them a little to the side so I can see them.

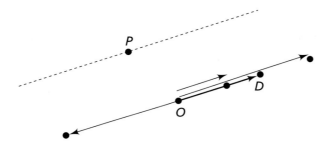

Tony OK, now we've got to translate them to *P*, draw in $\overrightarrow{OP}$, and add head to tail.

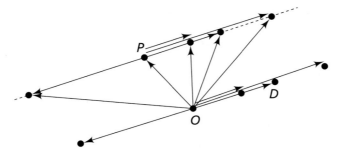

Sasha Now we're cooking. The arrows between the two lines are the sums of *P* and *kD*. The points at the ends of those arrows are the points on the line. So now it makes sense to me, $X = P + kD$.

Tony   Hey, what if we use your method, but add in the other order $kD + P$. Let's see, I think we get this.

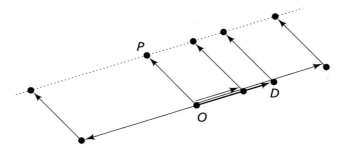

Sasha   I like that. You haven't drawn in the sum vectors, but maybe it's clearer that way. You can see that you start with a line through the origin determined by the vector D. Then you translate the whole thing by vector P, getting a new line with the same direction but through the point P.

$X = P + kD$ is called a *vector equation of a line*, or the line expressed in vector form. You may replace the scalar k by the letter t, since t usually stands for a variable while k stands for a constant.

What are good letters to use for real-number variables? The letters x and y are out since they are coordinates of X. So t is a good choice, as are s, u, and v.

For You to Do

1. How would you write a vector equation of a line through two points P and Q? What direction vector would you use? Try out your idea, by finding a vector equation for the line through $P(-1, 4)$ and $Q(2, -2)$. Make sure both of these points satisfy your equation.

Recall that equations are point-testers. This is true for vector equations of lines as well.

Example 1

Problem Consider the line with vector equation $X = (1, 3) + t(2, -3)$.

  a. Name two points on the line.

  b. Determine if $(4, -1)$ is on this line.

  c. Determine if $(-1, 6)$ is on this line.

Solution

  a. Pick t to be any real number. For example, the choice $t = 0$ gives the base point $P = (1, 3)$. The choice $t = 1$ yields $(1, 3) + (2, -3) = (3, 0)$.

  b. Substitute $(4, -1)$ for X to get the two real-number equations

$$4 = 1 + 2t$$
$$-1 = 3 - 3t$$

The first equation's solution is $t = \frac{3}{2}$. Substituting this t into the second equation does not work. So $(4, -1)$ fails the test. It is not on the line.

c. This time the two equations are

$$-1 = 1 + 2t$$
$$6 = 3 - 3t$$

The first yields $t = -1$, which does satisfy the second equation. So point $(-1, 6)$ passes the test. It is on the line.

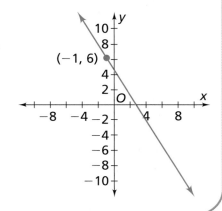

The vector form of a line has an extra variable, the t. This is called a **parameter.** It does not stand for a physical coordinate, the way x and y do. In mathematics, a parameter is a variable that does not appear in the picture but somehow determines what does appear.

So why is the vector form useful? Offhand, it seems that vector form only adds complication—the extra variable t.

The reason it is useful is that t can represent time and describe movement along the line.

> Vector equations for lines are sometimes called *parametric equations* for lines.

Example 2

Problem Two test cars start racing along straight lines in a flat desert. Suppose Car 1 starts at $(0, 0)$ and travels with constant velocity $(25, 40)$. That means, in each time unit, Car 1 travels $(25, 40)$ from where it was. (To make the speeds in this example somewhat realistic, let the units for distance be kilometers and the units for time be hours.) Suppose Car 2 starts at the same time at $(10, 25)$ and travels with velocity vector $(30, 45)$.

Do the paths of the cars intersect? Do the cars crash?

Solution At time t, Car 1 is at $(0, 0) + t(25, 40)$ and Car 2 is at $(10, 25) + t(30, 45)$.

To make sense of these equations, track Car 1's position for the first few hours. At $t = 0$, Car 1 is at $(0, 0)$. In one hour it moves along a vector equivalent to $(25, 40)$, so it reaches $(0, 0) + 1(25, 40)$. In 2 hours it has gone twice as far, so it reaches $(0, 0) + 2(25, 40)$. In general, after t hours it is at $(0, 0) + t(25, 40)$.

> t does not have to be an integer.

Set the locations of the two cars equal and solve.

$$(0, 0) + t(25, 40) = (10, 25) + t(30, 45)$$

If you write this out as two separate real-number equations, this is

$$0 + 25t = 10 + 30t$$
$$0 + 40t = 25 + 45t$$

which simplifies to

$$-5t = 10$$
$$-5t = 25$$

Clearly there is no solution that gives the same t for both equations.

But what does this mean? The two things you set equal are the positions of the cars at the same time t. No solution means there is no time t at which the cars are at the same place. So they do not crash.

How do you determine whether their paths intersect? Are there different times at which they pass through the same spot? In other words, is there a solution to

$$(0, 0) + t(25, 40) = (10, 25) + s(30, 45)$$

The expression on the left is the position of Car 1 at time t. The expression on the right is the position of Car 2 at time s. You do not know yet what these times are, or if there are times at which the location for both cars is the same, but you can solve and find out. Again, write out the real-number equations.

$$0 + 25t = 10 + 30s$$
$$0 + 40t = 25 + 45s$$

which simplifies to

$$-30s + 25t = 10$$
$$-45s + 40t = 25$$

Solve this system to give the solution $s = 3$, $t = 4$.

The paths intersect, but the cars pass through the intersection an hour apart—Car 2 at hour 3 and Car 1 at hour 4.

For You to Do

2. Find the intersection point for the cars' paths. Show that this point is on both lines according to their vector equations.

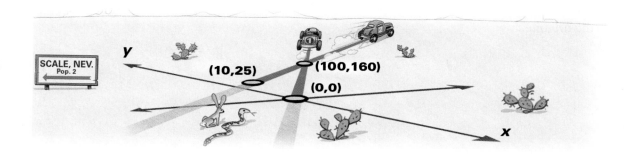

Exercises *Practicing Habits of Mind*

Check Your Understanding

1. Consider the line with vector equation $X = (1, 2) + t(3, 4)$. Test whether the points $(4, 6)$, $(-5, -5)$, and $(13, 18)$ are on the line.

2. Consider the line with parametric equation $X = (1, 0) + t(1, 2)$. Find a Cartesian equation of this line.

3. Find the slope of the line that is the graph of each of the following equations.

   a. $X = (1, 2) + t(3, 4)$ **b.** $X = (1, 2) + t(4, 3)$

   c. $X = (1, 2) + t(6, 8)$ **d.** $X = P + t(3, 4)$ for any point P

4. Find a vector equation for each of the following.

   a. the graph of $y = \frac{3}{2}x + 1$

   b. the graph of $(y - 3) = 4(x - 5)$

   c. the graph of $\frac{x}{2} + \frac{y}{3} = 1$

   d. the line through the points $(-2, 3)$ and $(3, 1)$

5. Let L be the line through $(2, 3)$ with direction vector $(3, -1)$. Find y such that $(-6, y)$ is on L.

6. Are there any lines in the plane that do not have a vector equation?

7. Give a general procedure for determining whether two vector equations

$$X = P + tD \quad \text{and} \quad X' = P' + tD'$$

describe the same line.

8. Consider the line with equation $X = (4, 3) + t(2, 1)$.

   a. Sketch the line.

   b. Now dilate all the points on the line by 2 with the origin as the center of the dilation. Sketch the result.

   c. Explain why this proves that the scaled set of points is also a line and is parallel to the original line.

On Your Own

9. Find a vector equation for the line through the points $(2, 3)$ and $(-1, 4)$.

10. A line has vector equation $X = P + tD$. Determine P and D if when $t = 0$, $X = (2, 3)$, and when $t = 1$, $X = (4, 5)$.

11. A line has vector equation $X = P + tD$. Determine P and D if when $t = 1$, $X = (2, -1)$, and when $t = 2$, $X = (4, 3)$.

12. Take It Further Consider the curve with vector equation $X = (1, 2) + t^3(2, -1)$.

  a. Find some points on this curve by using several values of t.

  b. Plot the curve. Describe the curve you graphed.

  c. Consider the curve given by the equation $X = (1, 2) + t^2(2, -1)$. Determine if this is the same set of points as $X = (1, 2) + t^3(2, -1)$.

13. Consider the two cars racing in the desert from the lesson. Recall that Car 1 starts at $(0, 0)$ and travels with velocity $(25, 40)$. That remains true in all the parts below, but the information on Car 2 changes.

  a. Suppose Car 2 starts at the same time at $(-10, -10)$ and travels with velocity vector $(30, 45)$. Determine if the paths of the cars intersect. Determine if the cars crash.

  b. Repeat part (a), except Car 2 starts at $(10, 10)$.

  c. Repeat part (a), except Car 2 has velocity $(30, 48)$.

  d. Repeat part (a), except Car 2 starts at $(30, 55)$ an hour later.

14. A vector equation of a line, $X = P + tD$, is unchanged in three dimensions. A line is still determined by a point and a direction but now X, P, D are triples. Let L' be the line through $(1, 2, 1)$ in the direction $(2, -1, 3)$. Find z such that $(5, 0, z)$ is on L'.

15. Two airplanes fly along straight lines. At time t airplane 1 is at $(75, 50, 25) + t(5, 10, 1)$ and airplane 2 is at $(60, 80, 34) + t(10, 5, -1)$.

  a. Determine if the airplanes collide.

  b. Determine if their flight paths intersect.

16. Which of the lines given by the following equations are the same? Explain.

  • $X = (1, -1) + t(3, 6)$

  • $X = (10, 17) + t(1, 3)$

  • $X = (10, 17) + s(1, 2)$

Go Online
PHSchool.com

For additional practice, go to **Web Code:** bga-0612

> The same is not true of Cartesian equations. Neither $y = mx + b$ nor $ax + by + cz = d$ is an equation of a line in three dimensions.

17. Take It Further You can think of a plane in three-space this way: You start at some base point P and move in each of two directions D_1 and D_2. Find a vector equation for a plane.

18. Standardized Test Prep Given U is the vector $(-3, 4)$ and V is the vector $(-1, 1)$. Which of the following points is on the line $U + tV$?

A. $(0, 1)$ **B.** $(-3, -4)$ **C.** $(-4, -3)$ **D.** $(-1, 1)$

Maintain Your Skills

19. Consider the line with equation $X(t) = (1, 0) + t(-1, 1)$. Now consider X as a function of t.

    a. Explain why the graph of $X(t)$ is the line through $(1, 0)$ and $(0, 1)$.

    b. Using graph paper, plot the following points, labeling them with the names given here.

$$X(0),\ X(1),\ X\left(\tfrac{1}{2}\right),\ X\left(\tfrac{1}{3}\right),\ X\left(\tfrac{2}{3}\right),\ X(2),\ X(3),\ X(-1)$$

> Writing $X(t)$, instead of just X, allows each point on the line to be identified with the value of the parameter for that point.

20. Consider the line with equation $Y(t) = (0, 1) + t(1, -1)$.

    a. Explain why this is the same line as in Exercise 19.

    b. Using graph paper, plot the following points, labeling them with the names given here.

$$Y(0),\ Y(1),\ Y\left(\tfrac{1}{2}\right),\ Y\left(\tfrac{1}{3}\right),\ Y\left(\tfrac{2}{3}\right),\ Y(2),\ Y(3),\ Y(-1)$$

21. Let P and Q be two points in the plane. Explain where each of the following points is located relative to P and Q.

    a. $\tfrac{1}{2}P + \tfrac{1}{2}Q$ **b.** $\tfrac{1}{3}P + \tfrac{2}{3}Q$

    c. $\tfrac{2}{3}P + \tfrac{1}{3}Q$ **d.** $\tfrac{4}{5}P + \tfrac{1}{5}Q$

    e. $2P - Q$ **f.** $3P - 2Q$

> If you are having trouble, pick some sample points for P and Q and calculate the others.

Even though the cars' paths intersect, the cars arrived at different times, thus avoiding a collision.

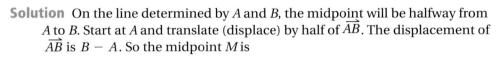

6.13 Affine Combinations and Geometry

A vector equation of a line has another advantage. You can use it to identify points in a particular position relative to given point.

Example 1

Problem Show that the midpoint of points A and B is $\frac{1}{2}(A + B)$.

Solution On the line determined by A and B, the midpoint will be halfway from A to B. Start at A and translate (displace) by half of $\overrightarrow{AB}$. The displacement of $\overrightarrow{AB}$ is $B - A$. So the midpoint M is

$$A + \tfrac{1}{2}(B - A) = A + \tfrac{1}{2}B - \tfrac{1}{2}A = \tfrac{1}{2}(A + B)$$

Remember...

If a and b are numbers, their mean is given by $\frac{1}{2}(a + b)$.

The midpoint is halfway from A to B. There is nothing special about half. What if you wanted to go $\frac{1}{3}$ of the way from A to B?

Example 2

Problem Find a formula similar to the midpoint formula, but for the *trisection* points of a segment.

Solution The trisection point of $\overline{AB}$ that is closest to A is the point that you reach when you start at A and move $\frac{1}{3}$ of the way along $\overrightarrow{AB}$. This displacement would be $\frac{1}{3}(B - A)$, so the resulting point would be $A + \frac{1}{3}(B - A) = \frac{2}{3}A + \frac{1}{3}B$.

But there are two trisection points. You also want to find the point that is $\frac{2}{3}$ of the way from A to B. That would be the same as starting at B and finding the point $\frac{1}{3}$ of the way to A, so the two endpoints change roles in the formula. The second trisection point will be $B + \frac{1}{3}(A - B) = \frac{2}{3}B + \frac{1}{3}A$.

This idea could work for any real number k between 0 and 1.

For You to Do

1. Show that, for any points A and B, the point k of the way from A to B is
$$(1 - k)A + kB$$

Actually, nothing in the algebra of this exercise requires k to be between 0 and 1. For any real number k, define *k of the way from A to B* to mean the point $A + k(B - A) = (1 - k)A + kB$. For instance, going twice the way from A to B ($k = 2$) means $A + 2(B - A) = A + (B - A) + (B - A)$, the point you get to when you go all the way from A to B and then go as far again.

For Discussion

Pick two points A and B and find the point with the following property.

2. 1.5 of the way from A to B

3. -1 of the way from A to B

4. 3 of the way from A to B

5. 0 of the way from A to B

The point $C = (1 - k)A + kB$ has a special name. If $0 \le k \le 1$, C is called a **convex combination** of A and B, because it is on the line segment between them. For any k whatsoever, C is called an **affine combination** of A and B, because C is on the line determined by A and B. Indeed,

- The line segment $\overline{AB}$ is the set of all points $(1 - k)A + kB$ for $0 \le k \le 1$.
- The line $\overleftrightarrow{AB}$ is the set of all points $(1 - k)A + kB$ for all real numbers k.

Remember...

Affine is just a fancy word for linear.

Vector Proofs of Geometry Theorems

Vector geometry, especially affine combinations, leads to algebraic proofs of many geometry theorems.

Example 3

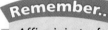

Problem Prove the Midline Theorem. Let $\triangle ABC$ be any triangle. Let P and Q be the midpoints of sides $\overline{AB}$ and $\overline{BC}$, respectively. Then $\overline{PQ}$ is parallel to $\overline{AC}$ and half as long.

Solution Show that $\overrightarrow{PQ}$ is parallel to and half as long as $\overrightarrow{AC}$ by relating their displacements. Specifically, show that $Q - P = \frac{1}{2}(C - A)$.

Use convex combinations: $P = \frac{1}{2}(A + B)$ and $Q = \frac{1}{2}(B + C)$. Then

$$Q - P = \tfrac{1}{2}(B + C) - \tfrac{1}{2}(A + B) \ = \ \tfrac{1}{2}C - \tfrac{1}{2}A \ = \ \tfrac{1}{2}(C - A)$$

Since $Q - P = \frac{1}{2}(C - A)$, $\overline{PQ}$ is half as long and in the same direction as $\overline{AC}$.

For You to Do

6. Prove: In $\triangle ABC$, if P is k of the way from A to B, and Q is k of the way from C to B, then $\overline{PQ}$ is parallel to $\overline{AC}$. Also determine the ratio of PQ and AC.

Now consider a famous theorem. A line segment from a vertex of a triangle to the midpoint of the opposite side is called a **median**. A set of lines or segments are **concurrent** if they share a common point. For two lines to be concurrent is pretty common, but for three or more lines to be concurrent is always surprising.

Theorem 6.8

In any triangle, the three medians are concurrent. Moreover, on each median the common point is $\frac{2}{3}$ the distance from the vertex to the opposite side.

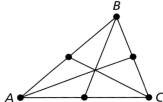

This common point is called the **centroid** of the triangle.

Proof First, mark the midpoints as convex combinations.

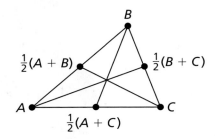

Next, compute the point $\frac{2}{3}$ of the way from A to $\frac{1}{2}(B + C)$.

$$\left(1 - \tfrac{2}{3}\right)A + \tfrac{2}{3}\left(\tfrac{1}{2}(B + C)\right) = \tfrac{1}{3}A + \tfrac{1}{3}B + \tfrac{1}{3}C$$

You can make similar computations for the other medians. The same simplified form, $\frac{1}{3}(A + B + C)$, appears for each. This is the same point for all three medians, so it is a point of concurrency.

Here is one more example. This one makes use of the assumption of parallel lines.

Remember...

The name *centroid* turns out to be doubly appropriate. It is geometrically and algebraically central. What could be more central to A, B, C than their average?

Theorem 6.9

In any parallelogram, the diagonals bisect each other.

Proof Let *ABCD* be a parallelogram, as shown.

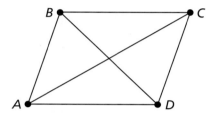

The proof requires showing that the midpoints of the diagonals are the same, so start by calculating each midpoint as an affine combination. The midpoint of $\overline{AC}$ is $\frac{1}{2}(A + C)$. The midpoint of $\overline{BD}$ is $\frac{1}{2}(B + D)$. The two expressions do not even involve the same letters.

But this is a parallelogram. In a parallelogram, opposite sides are parallel and equal in length. That means $\overrightarrow{AB}$ and $\overrightarrow{DC}$ are equivalent. So $B - A = C - D$. Add $A + D$ to both sides and divide by 2.

$$B - A = C - D$$
$$B + D = A + C$$
$$\tfrac{1}{2}(B + D) = \tfrac{1}{2}(A + C)$$

So the two midpoints are the same point, and the diagonals bisect each other.

Notice that with the vector algebra methods introduced so far, you can prove theorems about parallel lines and ratios of lengths. There are many other kinds of theorems you can prove with vector algebra, for instance, theorems about figures with right angles. But these require additional features of vector algebra that you have not seen yet.

Parallelogram faces and intersecting diagonals are conspicuous features of the remarkable Puerta de Europa office buildings in Madrid, Spain. The towers are mirror images of each other and lean at a striking 15°.

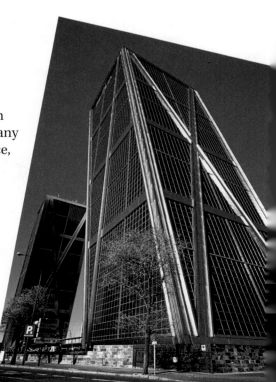

Exercises Practicing Habits of Mind

Check Your Understanding

1. **a.** Verify that the figure shown below is a parallelogram by showing that opposite sides are equivalent.

   b. Compute the midpoint of the diagonal $\overline{AC}$

   c. Compute the midpoint of the diagonal $\overline{BD}$.

   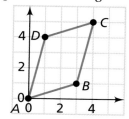

2. Consider any quadrilateral $ABCD$. Describe a method to construct the point $\dfrac{A + B + C + D}{4}$.

3. Let P, Q, R, and S be the midpoints of the sides of an arbitrary quadrilateral $ABCD$.

   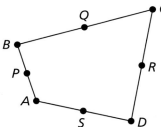

   a. Make a conjecture about the intersection of $\overline{PR}$ and $\overline{QS}$, then prove it.

   b. Make a conjecture about $\overline{PQ}$ and $\overline{RS}$, then prove it.

4. Let $A = (1, 3)$ and $B = (4, 2)$.

   a. Plot the points

   $$A, \quad B, \quad A + B, \quad A + \tfrac{1}{2}B, \quad \tfrac{3}{2}A, \quad \tfrac{3}{2}B$$

   b. Verify that $A + \tfrac{1}{2}B$ is the midpoint of the segment from A to $(A + B)$.

   c. Show that no matter how you choose A and B, $A + \tfrac{1}{2}B$ is the midpoint of the segment from A to $(A + B)$.

   d. Show that no matter how you choose A and B, $A + \tfrac{1}{2}B$ is a trisection point of the segment from $\tfrac{3}{2}A$ to $\tfrac{3}{2}B$.

5. In triangle ABC, let P be the trisection point of $\overline{AB}$ closer to A. Let Q be the trisection point of $\overline{AC}$ closer to A. Let S be the intersection point of $\overline{BQ}$ and $\overline{CP}$.

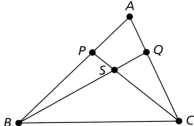

a. In what ratio does S divide $\overline{PC}$?

b. In what ratio does S divide $\overline{QB}$?

c. Prove that S is on the median from A (the line segment from A to the midpoint of $\overline{BC}$).

d. In what ratio does S divide this median line?

6. Here is another proof that the diagonals of a parallelogram bisect each other. Instead of naming the vertices A, B, C, and D, label just one point and label two different sides with their direction vectors.

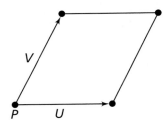

Name all the vertices of the parallelogram in terms of these labels, then compute the midpoints of the two diagonals.

7. Take It Further Prove that if both pairs of opposite sides of a quadrilateral are parallel, then both pairs are also equal in length. Explain why you can start with the following figure.

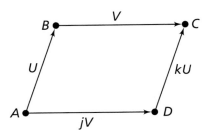

On Your Own

8. The ray $\overrightarrow{AB}$ is the infinite halfline starting at point A, going straight through B, and continuing forever. Explain why the set of points on this ray is

$$(1 - k)A + kB, \quad k \geq 0 \qquad \text{or} \qquad A + k(B - A), k \geq 0$$

9. Let A, B, and C be the vertices of a triangle.

a. Show that you can represent every point D inside the triangle is in the form $aA + bB + cC$, where a, b, $c > 0$ and $a + b + c = 1$. Such a sum is called a *three-way convex combination*.

b. Assuming the conditions in part (a), where in the triangle is $aA + bB + cC$ if exactly one of a, b, or c is 0? If exactly two of a, b, or c are 0?

10. Take It Further A *tetrahedron* is a solid in three dimensions with four vertices. See the figure. In a triangle you can draw a line from each vertex to the midpoint of the opposite side. Also, you know that the medians all intersect in a point.

In a tetrahedron you can picture drawing a line segment from each vertex to the centroid of the opposite face. Determine if these four lines also intersect in a point. Prove your result.

> If *D* is in the interior, draw a segment from some vertex, through *D*, to the opposite side. Call the intersection point with the opposite side *E*.

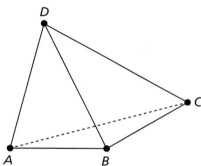

11. Start with an arbitrary triangle *ABC*. Draw the line segment from *A* to the midpoint of *BC*, but then extend it equally far outside the triangle to *P*. Locate *Q* using *B* and *R* using *C* similarly, as in the figure. Conjecture and prove a result about $\triangle PQR$.

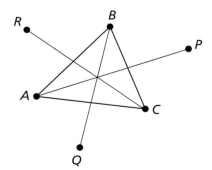

Go Online
PHSchool.com

For additional practice, go to **Web Code:** bga-0613

12. Take It Further Draw an arbitrary quadrilateral *ABCD*. Place a point *P* anywhere you like, as in the figure below. Construct a segment through *A* with *P* as an endpoint and *A* as its midpoint. Begin at the endpoint *X* of this new segment and construct another segment, this time with *B* as the midpoint. Continue doing this until you construct a segment with *D* as the midpoint. Label the finishing point *Q* in the figure.

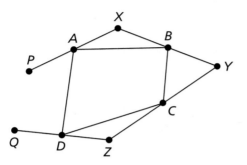

a. Draw $\overrightarrow{QP}$. If you change *P*'s location, $\overrightarrow{QP}$ changes location but not displacement. That is, $P - Q$ is constant, independent of the value of *P*. Prove this.

$P - Q$ is not independent of the values of *A, B, C,* and *D*.

b. When does $Q = P$? In light of part (a), the answer depends only on the original quadrilateral *ABCD*, not on *P*.

13. Standardized Test Prep Given the diagram as shown, which of the following represents the point $\frac{3}{7}$ of the way along the bold vector from the tip of *V* toward the tip of *U*?

A. (0, 1)   **B.** (−3, −4)

C. (−4, −3)   **D.** (−1, 1)

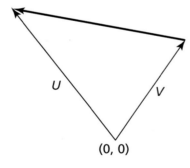

Maintain Your Skills

14. So far you have seen affine combinations of points. There are also affine combinations of sets. Let *P* be a point and *S* a set of points. Then $(1 - k)P + kS$ is the set of all points $(1 - k)P + kQ$, where $Q \in S$.

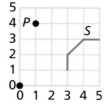

On a piece of graph paper, mark *P* and draw *S* from the following figure. Then determine the sets below.

a. $\frac{1}{2}P + \frac{1}{2}S$ (this is a convex combination of *P* and *S*)

b. $\frac{1}{4}P + \frac{3}{4}S$ **c.** $\frac{3}{2}P - \frac{1}{2}S$ **d.** $-P + 2S$

In this investigation, you expressed familiar geometric ideas in terms of vectors. You applied the basic rules of vector algebra to prove geometric facts. The following questions will help you summarize what you have learned.

1. Express the line containing the points $A(3, -1)$ and $B(5, 9)$ in vector form.

2. The vectors $U = (a, 0)$ and $V = (b, c)$ define the quadrilateral $ABCD$, with vertices $A(b, c)$, $B(a + b, c)$, $C(a, 0)$, and $D(0, 0)$. Express the diagonals of $ABCD$ in terms of vectors U and V.

3. Use vector methods to prove that quadrilateral $ABCD$ with vertices $A(0, 0)$, $B(5, 0)$, $C(8, 4)$, and $D(3, 4)$ is a rhombus. Confirm that its diagonals are perpendicular.

4. Determine which, if any, of the following vector equations have the same graph as $X = (1, -3) + t(3, 4)$.

   • $X = (1, -3) + t(6, 8)$

   • $X = (-1, 3) + t(-3, -4)$

   • $X = (7, 5) + t(3, 4)$

5. Given points $A(2, 5)$ and $B(6, -3)$, let M be the midpoint of $\overline{AB}$. Find the midpoint of $\overline{MB}$.

6. How can you interpret the matrix operations of sum and scalar product geometrically?

7. Why might it be useful to write an equation of a line in vector form?

8. How can you use vectors to prove that the medians of a triangle are concurrent?

Vocabulary

In this investigation, you learned these terms. Make sure you understand what each one means and how to use it.

• affine combination
• centroid
• concurrent
• convex combination
• dilation
• head and tail of a vector
• median
• parameter
• parametric equations
• scaling
• vector, $\overrightarrow{AB}$
• vector equations

Project: Using Mathematical Habits

The General Quadratic

In this chapter, you learned that the graph of any equation of the form

$$rx^2 + ty^2 + ux + vy + w = 0$$

is a conic. And you can tell what kind of conic you have by the sign of rt. You proved the following theorem.

Theorem 6.6

The graph of

$$rx^2 + ty^2 + ux + vy + w = 0$$

is a (possibly degenerate) conic. In fact, the nature of the conic is determined by the sign of rt:

- If $rt > 0$, the graph is an ellipse.
- If $rt = 0$, the graph is a parabola.
- If $rt < 0$, the graph is a hyperbola.

The equation

$$rx^2 + ty^2 + ux + vy + w = 0$$

is a quadratic equation in x and y. But it is not the most general one. The general quadratic in x and y is of the form

$$rx^2 + sxy + ty^2 + ux + vy + w = 0$$

The degree of each term is at most 2, the degree of each of the terms rx^2, sxy and ty^2 is 2, the degree of each of ux and vy is 1, and the degree of w is 0.

In this project, you will generalize Theorem 6.6. Start out by graphing these equations. Use any method you like. See the TI-Nspire™ Technology Handbook on page 704 for ideas about how to graph these equations.

1. $x^2 - xy + y^2 = 1$

2. $x^2 - xy + y^2 = 4$

3. $x^2 + xy + y^2 = 1$

4. $x^2 + xy + y^2 = 4$

5. $41x^2 - 24xy + 34y^2 = 51$

6. $41x^2 - 24xy + 34y^2 = 90$

7. $5x^2 + 15xy + 2y^2 = 8$

8. $5x^2 - 10xy + 5y^2 - 10y = 8$

9. $9x^2 + 24xy + 16y^2 = 49$

10. $xy = 1$

11. $xy = -1$

12. $13x^2 + 10xy + 13y^2 = 47$

13. $13x^2 + 10xy + 13y^2 = 0$

14. **Write and Reflect** Make your own quadratic equation graph gallery.

   a. Sketch or generate 10 particularly interesting graphs of quadratic equations in two variables, in addition to the ones above.

   b. Give an equation for each graph.

   c. Describe what you find interesting about each graph. Make believe you are preparing a guided tour in an art museum, except the pictures are graphs of quadratic equations in two variables. Try adding some linear terms to some of the ones you graphed above.

Graphing all these equations gives some evidence that the graph of a general quadratic is a (possibly degenerate) conic. (Can you tell what kind of conic you will get from the equation before you graph it?) For equations with a nonzero xy term, the conic seems to be rotated—its axes are not parallel to the coordinate axes.

It seems as though the graph of the general quadratic is a conic. Assume that this is true and reason from that assumption. Sometimes, when you do this, you get to a place that tells you that your assumption is, in fact, correct. And even when this does not happen, you often get to a place that shows how to refine your assumption so that it is correct.

The strategy is to start with an equation, say

$$41x^2 - 24xy + 34y^2 = 51 \qquad (1)$$

and assume that its graph is a rotated conic. If that is so, by how much should you rotate the graph so that its axes are parallel to the x and y axes? Another way to ask the question is, "How should you transform x and y to x' and y' so that the equation in x' and y' that corresponds to (1) has no xy-term?"

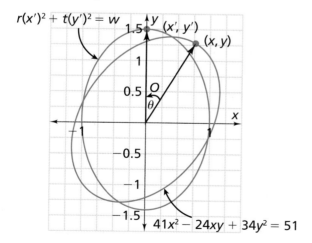

41x² − 24xy + 34y² = 51

In the picture above, you have the graph of

$$41x^2 - 24xy + 34y^2 = 51$$

The graph looks like an ellipse (see Exercise 5). If you rotate the ellipse counterclockwise about

the origin through some angle θ (that you need to find), you can turn the ellipse "upright." So, if (x, y) is any point on the original ellipse, and (x', y') is the image of (x, y) under a rotation about the origin through θ, (x', y') will satisfy an equation with no xy-term of the form

$$r(x')^2 + t(y')^2 = w$$

for numbers r, t, and w, because this is form of the equation of an upright ellipse centered at the origin. The question is how to find the precise angle θ that does the trick. This requires that you figure out how to rotate points about the origin.

15. Find x' and y' in terms of x and y if you obtain (x', y') from (x, y) by each of the given rotations.

  a. 90° counterclockwise about the origin

  b. 45° counterclockwise about the origin

  c. counterclockwise through an angle of $\cos^{-1} \frac{3}{5}$ about the origin

  d. counterclockwise through an angle of $\cos^{-1} \frac{5}{13}$ about the origin

  e. counterclockwise through an angle of θ about the origin

16. a. Show that if

$$R_\theta = \begin{pmatrix} \cos\theta & -\sin\theta \\ \sin\theta & \cos\theta \end{pmatrix}$$

   and if

$$\begin{pmatrix} x' \\ y' \end{pmatrix} = R_\theta \begin{pmatrix} x \\ y \end{pmatrix}$$

   then you can obtain (x', y') from (x, y) by a counterclockwise rotation through an angle θ about the origin.

b. Show that

$$(R_\theta)^{-1} = {}^tR_\theta = R_{-\theta}$$

(Recall that ${}^tA$ denotes the transpose of the matrix A.)

Study this example.

Problem Analyze the graph of

$$41x^2 - 24xy + 34y^2 = 51 \qquad (1)$$

Solution The equation (1) can be written as

$$(xy)\begin{pmatrix} 41 & -12 \\ -12 & 34 \end{pmatrix}\begin{pmatrix} x \\ y \end{pmatrix} = 51$$

You would like to change variables via rotation through some angle θ

$$\begin{pmatrix} x' \\ y' \end{pmatrix} = \begin{pmatrix} \cos\theta & -\sin\theta \\ \sin\theta & \cos\theta \end{pmatrix}\begin{pmatrix} x \\ y \end{pmatrix}$$

so that the resulting equation in x' and y' has no xy-term. Solve the equation

$$\begin{pmatrix} x' \\ y' \end{pmatrix} = R_\theta\begin{pmatrix} x \\ y \end{pmatrix}$$

for the old variables by multiplying both sides of this equation by the inverse of R_θ.

$$(R_\theta)^{-1}\begin{pmatrix} x' \\ y' \end{pmatrix} = \begin{pmatrix} x \\ y \end{pmatrix}$$

or

$$\begin{pmatrix} \cos\theta & \sin\theta \\ -\sin\theta & \cos\theta \end{pmatrix}\begin{pmatrix} x' \\ y' \end{pmatrix} = \begin{pmatrix} x \\ y \end{pmatrix}$$

or

$$\cos\theta x' + \sin\theta y' = x$$
$$-\sin\theta x' + \cos\theta y' = y \qquad (2)$$

Just to remove clutter, let $m = \cos\theta$ and $n = \sin\theta$. Substitute (2) in (1):

$$41(mx' + ny')^2 - 24(mx' + ny')(-nx' + my')$$
$$+ 34(-nx' + my')^2 = 51 \qquad (3)$$

Using a CAS to expand the left side, the coefficient of $x'y'$ is

$$-24m^2 + 14mn + 24n^2$$

So, you want this to be 0. That is, you want

$$-24m^2 + 14mn + 24n^2 = 0$$

One solution is $(0, 0)$, but that does not help. (Why?) So, assume $m \neq 0$ and divide both sides by m^2 to get an equation in $\frac{n}{m} = \tan\theta$.

$$-24 + 14\left(\frac{n}{m}\right) + 24\left(\frac{n}{m}\right)^2 = 0$$

Fingers crossed, hope that the roots of this are real. They are. (Is this an accident?) You find that

$$\tan\theta = \frac{3}{4} \quad \text{or}$$

$$\tan\theta = -\frac{4}{3}$$

Either will work because you can rotate in two directions to make the graph sit straight. Pick $\tan\theta = \frac{3}{4}$ so that

$$\cos\theta = \frac{4}{5}$$

and

$$\sin\theta = \frac{3}{5}$$

From here, you can get the equation of the rotated conic. It is all an algebraic calculation.

17. Find the equation of the rotated conic.

18. Carry out this analysis for the equation from Exercise 2

$$x^2 - xy + y^2 = 4$$

If you work out a few more examples, a certain rhythm develops in the calculations, one that allows you to carry out an analysis of the general quadratic, leading to a general classification theorem. The key idea is that you can write the expression

$$rx^2 + sxy + ty^2$$

as

$$(xy)\begin{pmatrix} r & \frac{s}{2} \\ \frac{s}{2} & t \end{pmatrix}\begin{pmatrix} x \\ y \end{pmatrix}$$

Through a rotation, you can transform the matrix to one of the form

$$\begin{pmatrix} r' & 0 \\ 0 & t' \end{pmatrix}$$

If you keep track of the algebra, you will find that you need to find θ so that

$$R_\theta \begin{pmatrix} r & \frac{s}{2} \\ \frac{s}{2} & t \end{pmatrix} (R_\theta)^{-1} = \begin{pmatrix} r' & 0 \\ 0 & t' \end{pmatrix}$$

You saw in the investigation that the sign of $r't'$ determines the nature of a conic. But this is the determinant of the right side. So, it is also the determinant of the left side. By a result in your earlier algebra course this determinant is the same as the determinant of the middle matrix on the left side—that is

$$rt - \left(\frac{s}{2}\right)^2$$

Technical details remain, but this is the basic idea behind the full classification theorem.

Theorem 6.10

The graph of

$$rx^2 + sxy + ty^2 + ux + vy + w = 0$$

depends only on the determinant

$$\delta = \begin{vmatrix} r & \frac{s}{2} \\ \frac{s}{2} & t \end{vmatrix} = rt - \left(\frac{s}{2}\right)^2 = \frac{4rt - s^2}{4}$$

More precisely,

- If $\delta < 0$, the graph is a (possibly degenerate) hyperbola.

- If $\delta = 0$, the graph is a (possibly degenerate) parabola.

- If $\delta > 0$, the graph is a (possibly degenerate) ellipse.

19. Verify the theorem for each of the examples in Exercises 1–13.

20. **Take It Further** Prove Theorem 6.10.

Review

For vocabulary review, go to Web Code: bgj-0651

In **Investigation 6A,** you learned to

- sketch the graphs of equations in two variables
- use distance and slope relationships to prove geometric results
- evaluate and use the signed power of a point with respect to a circle

The following questions will help you check your understanding.

1. **a.** Find an equation for the set of points equidistant from the point $(0, 2)$ and the line with equation $y = -2$.

   b. Sketch a graph of all points satisfying the equation.

2. **a.** Coordinatize a trapezoid.

   b. Prove that the midline of the trapezoid is parallel to its bases.

3. The graph of $x^2 + y^2 + 4x - 12y + 31 = 0$ is a circle.

   a. Find the center and the radius of the circle.

   b. Sketch the graph of the circle.

   c. Find the signed power of point $P(2, 3)$ with respect to the circle.

   d. Find the signed power of point $Q(-1, 7)$ with respect to the circle.

In **Investigation 6B,** you learned to

- visualize each of the conic sections as the intersection of a plane with an infinite double cone
- give a locus definition for each of the conic sections
- identify the equations for the graphs of the conic sections, and sketch their graphs

The following questions will help you check your understanding.

4. A parabola has focus $(0, 2)$ and directrix with equation $y = -2$.

   a. Find an equation of the parabola.

   b. Sketch the graph of the parabola. Graph and label the focus and the directrix.

5. An ellipse has foci $(-3, 2)$ and $(3, 2)$. One endpoint of the major axis is $(5, 2)$

   a. Find the eccentricity of the ellipse.

   b. Find the endpoints of the minor axis.

   c. Find an equation of the ellipse.

   d. Sketch the graph of the ellipse.

6. Consider the following equations.

   - $9x^2 - 4y^2 - 36x - 8y - 4 = 0$
   - $9x^2 + y^2 + 54x + 4y + 76 = 0$

   a. Identify the graph of each equation (circle, parabola, ellipse, or hyperbola).

   b. Find the coordinates of the center and foci.

   c. Find the eccentricity.

   d. Sketch the graph of the equation.

In **Investigation 6C,** you learned to

- interpret sums and scalar multiples of ordered pairs geometrically

- express lines with vector equations and solve for intersections and other useful information using these equations

- use convex and affine combinations to locate specific points, such as the midpoint and trisection points of a line segment

The following questions will help you check your understanding.

7. Let $A = (3, 4)$, $B = (-2, 0)$, and $C = (1, -4)$.

  a. Plot and label the points A, B, $A + B$, $A + 2B$, and $A - B$.

  b. Find the displacement of $\overrightarrow{AB}$. Find the displacement of $\overrightarrow{BA}$.

  c. If $\overrightarrow{CD}$ has displacement $(4, 2)$, find D.

  d. If $\overrightarrow{DC}$ has displacement of $(4, 2)$, find D.

8. a. Find a vector equation for the line through the points $(1, 3)$ and $(5, 2)$.

  b. Name two points on this line.

  c. Determine if the point $(-7, 5)$ is on this line.

  d. Find the point of intersection of this line with the graph of $X = (-2, 6) + s(1, -1)$.

9. Let $A = (-1, -4)$, $B = (9, 2)$, and $C = (1, 5)$ be the vertices of a triangle.

  a. Find the trisection points for side $\overline{AC}$.

  b. Find the centroid of the triangle.

  c. Point P is k of the way from A to B. Find P if $k = \frac{1}{4}$.

  d. Point P is k of the way from A to B. Find P if $k = 2$.

Go Online
PHSchool.com

For a chapter test, go
to **Web Code:** bga-0653

Multiple Choice

1. Determine the equation in the form
$y = a(x - h)^2 + k$ for the parabola having
focus $(3, 4)$ and directrix the x-axis.

A. $y = 8(x - 4)^2 + 3$

B. $y = \frac{1}{4}(x - 3)^2 + 4$

C. $y = \frac{1}{8}(x - 3)^2 + 2$

D. $y = 3(x - 4)^2 + \frac{1}{2}$

2. Find the type of conic given by the equation
$12x^2 + 2y^2 - 72x + 20y - 206 = 0$.

A. circle

B. ellipse

C. hyperbola

D. parabola

3. A hyperbola has foci $(4, 6)$ and $(-8, 6)$ and one
endpoint of the major axis is $(-1, 6)$. Find the
eccentricity of the hyperbola.

A. 6   **B.** $\frac{1}{8}$ **C.** 8   **D.** $\frac{1}{6}$

4. Determine which of the following is an equation
of a degenerate conic.

A. $(x - 2)^2 + (y + 5)^2 = 49$

B. $x^2 + y^2 - 4x + 14y + 53 = 0$

C. $\frac{(x - 3)^2}{16} + \frac{(y - 1)^2}{12} = 1$

D. $x^2 - 4y^2 - 6x + 40y + 18 = 0$

5. Determine which of the following points is on
the graph of $X = (-1, 4) + t(2, 6)$.

A. $(1, 8)$

B. $(5, 20)$

C. $(-1, -3)$

D. $(-5, -8)$

6. Find a vector equation for the line through the
points $(4, 7)$ and $(-3, 9)$.

A. $X = (0, 4) + t(4, 7)$

B. $X = (1, 2) + t(-7, 2)$

C. $X = (4, 7) + t(-7, 2)$

D. $X = (-3, 9) + t(4, 7)$

7. Determine which of the points would form a
parallelogram with the three points on the graph.

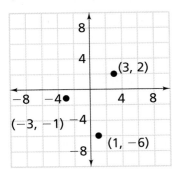

A. $(0, 2)$

B. $(-1, 6)$

C. $(-1, 7)$

D. $(-2, 4)$

8. An ellipse has foci $(10, -4)$ and $(-4, 10)$. Find
the coordinates of the center.

A. $(3, 3)$

B. $(-6, 6)$

C. $(-3, 6)$

D. $(7, 7)$

9. Consider the line with parametric equation
$X = (3, -1) + t(-1, 5)$. Which of the following is
a Cartesian equation for the line?

A. $y = \frac{1}{5}x + 3$

B. $y = -\frac{1}{5}x + 1$

C. $y = 5x + 3$

D. $y = -5x + 14$

10. A hyperbola is centered at $(-6, 4)$ and has foci $(-11, 4)$ and $(-1, 4)$. Find which of the equations gives this hyperbola.

A. $\dfrac{(x+4)^2}{16} - \dfrac{(y-6)^2}{9} = 1$

B. $\dfrac{(x+6)^2}{16} - \dfrac{(y-4)^2}{9} = 1$

C. $\dfrac{(x-6)^2}{16} - \dfrac{(y+4)^2}{9} = 1$

D. $\dfrac{(x-6)^2}{9} - \dfrac{(x+4)^2}{16} = 1$

Open Response

11. The graph of the equation

$$x^2 + y^2 + 4x - 26y - 52 = 0$$

is a circle.

  a. Find the radius and center of the circle.

  b. Calculate the signed power of the point $(1, 17)$ and describe its location with respect to the circle.

  c. Calculate the signed power of the point $(7, 25)$ and describe its location with respect to the circle.

12. Consider the equation

$$4x^2 + 9y^2 - 24x + 36y + 36 = 0$$

  a. Determine if this equation represents a conic. If it does, state what kind of conic.

  b. Sketch the graph of the equation.

13. Consider the set of points that are equidistant from the point $(6, 0)$ and the line with equation $x = -2$.

  a. Write an equation that describes this set of points.

  b. Determine what type of conic this set describes.

14. An ellipse is centered at $(-1, -3)$ with a focus at $(-1, 3)$ and eccentricity $\frac{3}{5}$.

  a. Find the major axis of the ellipse.

  b. Find the coordinates of the other focus.

  c. Find the vertices of the ellipse.

15. An ellipse has foci $(-5, 2)$ and $(7, 2)$ and string length 20.

  a. Find the center of the ellipse.

  b. Find the coordinates of the vertices.

  c. Write an equation of the ellipse.

16. Two cars drive along straight, flat lines. At time t, Car A is at $(80, 60) + t(10, 15)$ and Car B is at $(40, 15) + t(20, 25)$.

  a. Determine if the cars collide. If they do, find at what time.

  b. Determine if their paths intersect. If they do, find at what time each car passes the intersection point.

17. Consider the equation $\dfrac{(x-4)^2}{144} - \dfrac{(y+7)^2}{81} = 1$.

  a. Find what type of conic is given by the graph of this equation.

  b. Find the center and foci.

  c. Sketch the graph of the equation.

18. Let L be the line through $(4, 6)$ with direction vector $(2, -5)$. Find y so that $(-2, y)$ is on L.

19. Consider the lines given by the equations $X = (2, 5) + t(-1, -3)$ and $Y = (1, 4) + t(6, -2)$.

  a. Graph both lines.

  b. Determine if these lines are parallel, perpendicular, or neither.

1. Find all solutions to the equation $\tan^2 x - 3 = 0$ on $0 \le x \le 2\pi$.

2. A device monitors and regulates the air moisture in a greenhouse. It varies throughout the day according to the equation

$$h = 88.5 + 3.7 \sin \frac{\pi}{12}(t - 9)$$

   where h is the humidity, in percent, and t is the number of hours after midnight, $0 \le t \le 24$.

   a. Find the maximum humidity and when it occurs.

   b. Find the minimum humidity and when it occurs.

   c. Find the difference between the maximum and minimum values.

3. Simplify the expression.

$$\left(-\frac{\sqrt{2}}{2} + i\frac{\sqrt{2}}{2}\right)^5$$

4. Consider the identity $\cos(2t) = 2\cos^2 t - 1$.

   a. Let $s = 2t$ so that $t = \frac{s}{2}$. Find an identity for $\cos \frac{s}{2}$.

   b. Use your result in part (a) to find an exact value for $\cos 15°$.

   c. Use your result in part (a) to find an exact value for $\cos 22.5°$.

5. Expand each of the following in powers of $x - 2$.

   a. x^2 b. x^3 c. x^4

6. Find the solution to each equation to three decimal places using logarithms.

   a. $e^x = 5$ b. $e^x = 0.5$

   c. $e^x = 2$ d. $2^x = 5$

7. Lowe High School's student senate has 12 members.

   a. Find the number of ways the senate can choose a 6-member Activities Committee.

   b. Find the number of ways this committee can be formed if they first choose one of the six members as a chairperson.

8. Find the coefficient of the specified term in the expansion of $(a + b)^{10}$.

   a. the $a^8 b^2$ term   b. the $a^5 b^5$ term

   c. the $a^3 b^7$ term   d. the b^{10} term

9. Let h be defined recursively by

$$h(n) = \begin{cases} -2 & \text{if } n = 0 \\ 2 \cdot h(n-1) + 3n & \text{if } n > 0 \end{cases}$$

   Find each of the following values.

   a. $h(1)$ b. $h(2)$ c. $h(3)$ d. $h(4)$

10. Here is the first row of a difference table for a cubic function f. Find $f(4)$.

x	$f(x)$	Δ	Δ^2	Δ^3
0	6	2	−3	4

11. Find the set of numbers for which the functions $f(x) = -3x^2 + 2$ and $g(x) = -3x^2 + 2 + x(x-2)(x+3)$ are equal.

12. Here is a partial difference table for a function c. Find $c(4)$.

Input x	Output $c(x)$	Δ	Δ^2	Δ^3
0	−8	2	−3	4
1	▪	▪	−1	1	4
2	▪	▪	▪	5	4
3	▪	▪	▪	▪	4

13. Let the function h be defined by $h(x) = x^3 - 2x$. Find a polynomial that agrees with Δh.

14. Use mathematical induction to show that the functions G and g given here must agree for all integers $n \geq 0$.

$$G(n) = 4n - 3$$

$$g(n) = \begin{cases} -3 & \text{if } n = 0 \\ g(n-1) + 4 & \text{if } n > 0 \end{cases}$$

15. The graph of the equation

$$x^2 + y^2 - 4x + 6y - 12 = 0$$

is a circle.

a. Find the center and radius of the circle.

b. Sketch the graph of the circle.

c. Find the exact coordinates of all intercepts.

16. The point $P(0, 0)$ lies inside the circle in Exercise 15. Several chords of the circle defined by the graph of

$$x^2 + y^2 - 4x + 6y - 12 = 0$$

pass through the origin.

a. One such chord lies along the x-axis. Calculate the power of P with respect to this circle using this chord.

b. Find the two intersection points of the circle with the line with equation $y = x$.

c. Use the points found in part (b) to calculate the power of P.

17. Find an equation of the parabola with focus $(0, 2)$ and directrix with equation $y = -2$.

18. The graph of the equation

$$\frac{(x-2)^2}{4} + \frac{(y-3)^2}{k} = 1$$

depends on the value of k. Find the value of k, or the conditions for k, such that the graph of the equation is the specified conic section.

a. a circle

b. an ellipse (but not a circle)

c. a hyperbola

19. Find the eccentricity of the conic section given by each equation.

a. the hyperbola $\frac{x^2}{16} - \frac{y^2}{9} = 1$

b. the ellipse $\frac{x^2}{16} + \frac{y^2}{9} = 1$

c. the parabola $\frac{x^2}{16} - y = 0$

20. Find a vector equation for each line.

a. the graph of $y + 3 = -2(x - 1)$

b. the graph of $y = \frac{2}{5}x + 4$

c. the line through the points $(3, 2)$ and $(6, -4)$

Probability and Statistics

Although there is much variation between individuals, populations are often quite consistent. Probability and statistics allow you to quantify a population and make predictions about it.

In this picture of a school of fish, you see that this fish can be yellow or red but the yellow occurs more frequently. Is that true of this type of fish in general or just this school of fish? You can use probability and statistics to quantify this information accurately.

Vocabulary and Notation

- Bernoulli trial
- confidence interval
- cumulative density function
- event
- expected value, $E(X)$
- experimental probability
- frequency, $|A|$
- independent
- mean absolute deviation
- mean squared deviation, or variance, σ^2

- mutually exclusive
- normal distribution, $N(\mu, \sigma)$
- probability density function
- probability histogram
- random variable
- root mean squared deviation, or standard deviation, σ
- sample space
- theoretical probability
- z-score

Probability and Polynomials

In *Probability and Polynomials,* you will learn basic probability definitions and rules. You will discover connections between probability and Pascal's Triangle. You will model a variety of experiments with polynomials. You will calculate the likelihood of each outcome in an experiment, and also predict the average outcome of an experiment.

By the end of this investigation, you will be able to answer questions like these.

1. If you are to roll four number cubes, what is the probability they sum to 12?

2. What is expected value?

3. How can you use polynomials to solve probability problems?

You will learn how to
- calculate probabilities of simple random events

- build a set of equally likely outcomes for a probability experiment

- find a polynomial to model a probability experiment and interpret expansions of its powers

- calculate the expected value of a random variable

You will develop these habits and skills:
- Visualize the process of a probability experiment in order to count its outcomes.

- Reason from definitions, such as for *mutually exclusive* and *independent*, and apply them to probability situations.

- Understand the domains and ranges of various functions related to probability, including random variables, frequency, expected value, and probability functions.

Considering all possible outcomes is a good habit when calculating probabilities. If you know all possible outcomes in an experiment, you can find the likelihood of any particular outcome occurring.

For You to Explore

1. When you flip a coin three times, there are eight possible outcomes. For example, one outcome is heads-tails-heads. Write out the eight outcomes. Determine how many outcomes are in each category.

   a. no heads   **b.** one head   **c.** two heads   **d.** three heads

2. There are 16 possible outcomes when you flip a coin four times. For example, one outcome is heads-tails-heads-heads. Write out the 16 outcomes. Determine how many outcomes are in each category.

   a. no heads   **b.** one head   **c.** two heads

   d. three heads   **e.** four heads

3. You are to flip a coin five times.

   a. Write down the ten different ways you could flip two heads and three tails.

   b. What is the probability that you flip two heads and three tails?

   > One of the outcomes is "heads, tails, tails, heads, tails" but you might prefer to write it as HTTHT.

4. Expand each of these expressions.

   a. $(t + h)^2$ **b.** $(t + h)^3$ **c.** $(t + h)^4$ **d.** $(t + h)^5$

   > See the TI-Nspire™ Handbook on p. 704, for instructions on how to expand these expressions with a CAS.

If the survival rate for turtle eggs is 38%, how many are expected to hatch from a nest of 120 eggs?

On Your Own

5. Write out the first eight rows of Pascal's Triangle. Count your rows so that the third row is

1   3   3   1

6. Determine the probability that if you flip a coin eight times, you will flip exactly four heads and four tails. Explain in detail how you arrived at your answer.

7. a. Picture two spinners that are equally likely to land on any integer between 1 and 5, inclusive. List all 25 ways the spinners could land if you spin them both.

    b. Find the probability that the two numbers spun do not share a common factor greater than 1.

    c. Repeat parts (a) and (b) for two spinners that are equally likely to land on any integer between 1 and 6, inclusive. For this, there are 36 outcomes.

    d. Repeat parts (a) and (b) for two spinners that are equally likely to land on any integer between 1 and 7, inclusive.

> Here is one way: first spinner 3, second spinner 4. And here is another, different way: first spinner 4, second spinner 3.

8. a. If you flip a fair coin 240 times, how many heads would you expect?

    b. Guess the probability of getting exactly this many heads.

9. a. If you roll a fair number cube 240 times, how many ones would you expect?

    b. Guess the probability of getting exactly this many ones.

> You may assume that a number cube has the numbers 1 through 6 on its faces, unless stated otherwise.

Maintain Your Skills

10. For each value of *n*, you are to pick an integer at random from 1 to *n*. What is the probability it will be a perfect square?

    a. $n = 10$ **b.** $n = 100$ **c.** $n = 1000$ **d.** $n = 10,000$

    e. What is happening "in the long run" (as *n* grows larger without bound)?

7.2 Probability and Pascal's Triangle

In this section you will learn some basic definitions and rules of probability. If you have not done so already, start to think about how you can count the possible outcomes of experiments more efficiently.

In-Class Experiment

Here are four similar games.

Game 1: Flip two coins. If you get exactly two heads, you win.

Game 2: Flip three coins. If you get exactly two heads, you win.

Game 3: Flip four coins. If you get exactly two heads, you win.

Game 4: Flip five coins. If you get exactly two heads, you win.

1. Which game gives you the greatest probability of winning?

You can use probability theory to determine how likely it is that an event will occur. Consider a multiple-choice question with five options. Only one is right. If you guess randomly, the probability of getting the correct answer is $\frac{1}{5}$. The probability of getting an incorrect answer is $\frac{4}{5}$.

Example

Problem Roll two different-colored number cubes. Find the probability of each event.

   a. At least one number cube shows a 5.

   b. The sum of the numbers is exactly 5.

Solution One way to proceed is to write out the *sample space*, the entire list of possible outcomes. Since each number cube has 6 possible outcomes, there are 36 total outcomes for this experiment.

	1	2	3	4	5	6
1	(1,1)	(1,2)	(1,3)	(1,4)	**(1,5)**	(1,6)
2	(2,1)	(2,2)	(2,3)	(2,4)	**(2,5)**	(2,6)
3	(3,1)	(3,2)	(3,3)	(3,4)	**(3,5)**	(3,6)
4	(4,1)	(4,2)	(4,3)	(4,4)	**(4,5)**	(4,6)
5	**(5,1)**	**(5,2)**	**(5,3)**	**(5,4)**	**(5,5)**	**(5,6)**
6	(6,1)	(6,2)	(6,3)	(6,4)	**(6,5)**	(6,6)

a. The 11 highlighted outcomes have at least one 5. So, the probability of rolling at least one 5 is

$$P\text{ (at least one 5) } = \frac{\text{number of successful outcomes}}{\text{total number of outcomes}} = \frac{11}{36}$$

b. Make a second table showing the sums of the numbers on the two number cubes.

+	1	2	3	4	5	6
1	2	3	4	5	6	7
2	3	4	5	6	7	8
3	4	5	6	7	8	9
4	5	6	7	8	9	10
5	6	7	8	9	10	11
6	7	8	9	10	11	12

The 4 highlighted outcomes each show a sum of 5. So, the probability of rolling a sum of exactly 5 is $\frac{4}{36}$ or $\frac{1}{9}$.

For You to Do

2. Find the probability that when rolling two number cubes, the sum is less than or equal to 5.

Several definitions come in handy when talking about probability problems.

Definitions

The **sample space** is a set. Its elements are **outcomes.**

An **event** is a subset of the sample space, a set of outcomes. $|A|$ denotes the number of outcomes in event A.

$P(A)$, the **probability of an event** A, is the number of outcomes in A, divided by the number of outcomes in the sample space S.

$$P(A) = \frac{\text{number of outcomes in } A}{\text{total number of outcomes}} = \frac{|A|}{|S|}$$

An *outcome* could be anything, such as "rolling a 3" or "heads, heads, tails." The situation determines the appropriate outcomes.

This definition of probability depends on the assumption that all outcomes in the sample space are equally likely. You cannot use this definition when the outcomes are not equally likely.

When rolling a number cube, there are six outcomes in the sample space, all equally likely. One outcome is "roll the number 5." An event might be "roll a prime number." There are three outcomes in this event, so P(roll a prime number) $= \frac{3}{6}$ or $\frac{1}{2}$.

Often, there are shortcuts to counting either the number of outcomes in an event, or the number of outcomes in the sample space. The sample space for rolling two number cubes has $6 \times 6 = 36$ outcomes since there are six ways each number cube can land.

Derman and Sasha are working on Game 4 from the In-Class Experiment.

Derman We want to find the probability of getting exactly two heads when you flip five coins.

Sasha All right, so we need to know the number of outcomes with exactly two heads, and the total number of outcomes in the sample space.

Derman I think the probability should be 1 out of 6.

Sasha Oh?

Derman Well, you could get 0 heads, 1 head, 2, 3, 4, or 5 heads. Six ways it could happen. It's 1 out of 6.

Sasha Wait, wait, wait. That's not going to work, those things would have to be equally likely. But I'm not convinced that they are.

Derman Well, flipping a coin is equally likely: heads or tails.

Sasha Right. So start from there. Five coin flips.

Derman The total number of outcomes is . . . I think it's 32, 2 to the fifth.

Sasha That's a much better sample space. The probability's got to be something out of 32, then. Now we just have to figure out how many of those 32 outcomes have exactly two heads.

Derman I'll make a list . . .

HHTTT	TTTHH	THTHT
HTHTT	HTTTH	HTTHT
THHTT	THTTH	TTHHT

Derman Nine! It's nine out of 32.

Sasha You missed one: TTHTH. It's ten.

Derman It's hard to know the list is complete. There must be a better way to count these.

Sasha It's two H's out of a total of five spots.

Derman Ohh . . . just like a combination! From Chapter 4, I know that 10 is in Pascal's Triangle.

Sasha Hey, nice. Five flips and two H's. So the number of ways should be 5 choose 2, which is 10.

Derman So the probability is 10 out of 32. Guess it wasn't 1 out of 6 after all.

> **Remember...**
>
> The notation for "five choose 2" is $\binom{5}{2}$ or $_5C_2$. You can calculate it as $\frac{5!}{2! \cdot 3!}$.

Look for relationships. The connection to probability can also explain a property about the sum of the numbers in a row of Pascal's Triangle. Consider row 5:

$$1 \quad 5 \quad 10 \quad 10 \quad 5 \quad 1$$

When you toss five coins, these numbers show up as the number of ways to get 0 heads, 1 head, 2 heads, and so on. For example, the probability of getting no heads when you flip five coins is $\frac{1}{32}$, since there is 1 successful outcome out of 32 total. Now look at the sum of all the probabilities.

$$\frac{1}{32} + \frac{5}{32} + \frac{10}{32} + \frac{10}{32} + \frac{5}{32} + \frac{1}{32}$$

If you toss five coins, you have to get *some* number of heads from 0 to 5. If you add up the probability of getting 0 heads, 1 head, 2 heads, 3 heads, 4 heads, and 5 heads, you have covered all the possibilities. Also, there is no overlap between these events. When you count the number of heads, the answer cannot be 2 *and* 4. So, the sum of these probabilities must be 1.

$$\frac{1}{32} + \frac{5}{32} + \frac{10}{32} + \frac{10}{32} + \frac{5}{32} + \frac{1}{32} = 1$$

This happens with any row of Pascal's Triangle. The sum of the numbers in the nth row of Pascal's Triangle is 2^n, which equals the total number of outcomes when tossing n coins.

For You to Do

3. Which is more likely, flipping exactly 3 heads in 10 coin flips, or flipping exactly 4 heads in 5 coin flips?

Here are two additional terms that apply to events.

Definitions

Two events A and B are **mutually exclusive** if they do not share any outcomes in the same sample space: whenever $P(A \text{ and } B) = 0$. If A and B are mutually exclusive, then $P(A \text{ or } B) = P(A) + P(B)$.

Two events A and B are **independent** if the result from one event has no effect on the other. If A and B are independent, then $P(A \text{ and } B) = P(A) \cdot P(B)$.

Consider rolling a single number cube. Rolling a 5 and rolling a 6 are mutually exclusive: you cannot do both at once. To find the probability of rolling a 5 or 6, add the probabilities of rolling each.

$P(5 \text{ and } 6) = 0$
$P(5 \text{ or } 6) = P(5) + P(6)$

Consider rolling two number cubes. The probability of rolling a 5 on the first number cube is $\frac{1}{6}$. The probability of rolling a 6 on the second number cube is also $\frac{1}{6}$. These events are independent: the result for the second number cube does not rely in any way on the result for the first number cube. So, the probability of rolling a 5 on the first number cube and a 6 on the second number cube is $\frac{1}{6} \cdot \frac{1}{6} = \frac{1}{36}$.

Developing Habits of Mind

Extend the process. The rule for $P(A \text{ or } B)$ is slightly different when A and B share outcomes. For any events A and B,

$$P(A \text{ or } B) = P(A) + P(B) - P(A \text{ and } B)$$

One way to look at this is with a Venn diagram.

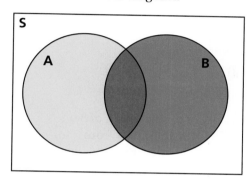

Let S be the sample space. In the diagram, the entire yellow circle represents event A. The entire blue circle represents event B. The green intersection of the two circles (where the yellow and blue overlap) represents the event $(A \text{ and } B)$. The union of the two circles represents the event $(A \text{ or } B)$.

In the diagram, this union is the part that is either yellow or blue, or is both yellow and blue. How could you compute the area of this colored region? You cannot just add the area of the entire yellow circle and the area of the entire blue circle. If you were to do this, you would double-count the middle green area, where the two circles intersect. So, subtract that green area from the sum and you will get the correct area.

Note that if A and B are mutually exclusive, $P(A \text{ and } B) = 0$. Then you do not have to take the intersection into account. This makes sense, since for mutually exclusive events $P(A \text{ or } B) = P(A) + P(B)$.

You can find probabilities for more than two overlapping events by using the inclusion-exclusion principle. For three events A, B, and C, first add the probabilities of the events. Next subtract all the intersections of pairs of events. Then add back in the intersection of *triples* of events.

$$\begin{aligned} P(A \text{ or } B \text{ or } C) = {} & P(A) + P(B) + P(C) \\ & - P(A \text{ and } B) - P(A \text{ and } C) - P(B \text{ and } C) \\ & + P(A \text{ and } B \text{ and } C) \end{aligned}$$

You can extend this principle to find probabilities for any number of overlapping events.

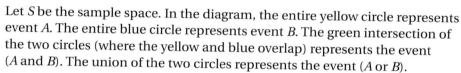

What happens if A, B, and C are mutually exclusive?

Exercises *Practicing Habits of Mind*

Check Your Understanding

1. Determine each probability.

   a. P(flip 1 coin, heads)

   b. P(flip 2 coins, both heads)

   c. P(roll a number cube and get an odd number)

   d. P(roll a number cube and get an even number)

   e. P(roll a number cube and get a negative number)

   f. P(roll two number cubes and get a sum of 2)

   g. P(roll two number cubes and get a sum greater than 2)

2. **What's Wrong Here?** Russ says that the probability of rolling a sum of 8 on two number cubes should be $\frac{1}{11}$, since there are 11 possible sums from 2 to 12. "It works for one number cube, so it should work for two." Explain what is wrong with his reasoning, and find the correct probability.

3. If you flip a coin six times, how many different ways are there for the result to be 2 heads and 4 tails? Write them out.

4. Calculate the value of $\binom{6}{2}$. Explain how your result relates to the work in Exercise 3.

5. Use the expansion of $(t + h)^6$ to find the total number of ways you could flip 3 heads and 3 tails in a sequence of six coin tosses.

6. **Take It Further** Suppose you are to roll a number cube three times. Find the probability that the sum of the numbers will be 8.

On Your Own

7. Make a game where the probability of winning is about $\frac{1}{3}$. Explain clearly how the game is played, and what the winning condition is. The best games are simple to play but complex in their potential outcomes.

> So, one game would be "Roll a number cube. If it comes up 1 or 2, you win." But you can make something more interesting!

8. You flip a coin eight times.

   a. Explain why there are 256 outcomes in the sample space.

   b. What is the most likely number of heads? How likely is it to occur?

9. Find the probability that if you flip nine coins, you will get exactly six heads and three tails.

10. In a carnival game, you roll a standard number cube and flip a coin. The coin has a 0 on one side, and a 5 on the other side. Your score is the sum of the values that appear on the number cube and the coin.

    a. You win the game if you score 10 points or more. Find the probability that you win the game.

    b. The man running the carnival says that every score from 1 to 11 is equally likely. Is he right? Explain.

11. Consider the set S of ordered pairs (x, y) such that x and y are both integers between 1 and 8, inclusive, and $x \geq y$.

    a. How many such ordered pairs are there?

    b. If you are to pick an ordered pair (x, y) at random, what is the probability that x and y do not have any common factor greater than 1?

    c. In the coordinate plane, plot all the ordered pairs (x, y) in S that do not have any common factor greater than 1.

> $(7, 3)$ is in this set, but $(3, 7)$ is not, since $x \geq y$ is required.

12. Repeat Exercise 11 with the integer pairs satisfying $1 \leq y \leq x \leq 9$.

13. **Take It Further** Flip a coin 10 times, keeping score as follows. If you flip heads, you get one point. If you flip tails, you are in "danger." If you flip tails twice in a row, you "bust," lose all your points, and the game ends.

    a. What is the probability you survive all ten flips without busting?

    b. What is the average score players achieve in this game?

14. **Standardized Test Prep** In the sample space for rolling two number cubes, how many outcomes will have neither a one nor a two on either cube?

    A. 16   **B.** 18   **C.** 20   **D.** 24

Go Online
PHSchool.com

For additional practice, go to **Web Code:** bga-0702

Maintain Your Skills

15. This is F_5, the *Farey sequence* of order 5:

$$\frac{0}{1}, \frac{1}{5}, \frac{1}{4}, \frac{1}{3}, \frac{2}{5}, \frac{1}{2}, \frac{3}{5}, \frac{2}{3}, \frac{3}{4}, \frac{4}{5}, \frac{1}{1}$$

F_5 is all fractions from 0 to 1, inclusive, with denominators less than or equal to 5. It is written in increasing order with fractions in lowest terms.

Find the number of elements in F_n. Copy and complete the table for n from 1 to 10, inclusive. Describe any patterns you find.

n	Number of elements in F_n
1	2
2	3
3	▨
4	▨
5	11

7.3 Polynomial Powers

You can use Pascal's Triangle to quickly count the number of each type of outcome for coin-flip experiments. But what about other experiments, like rolling a number cube or answering multiple-choice questions? This lesson explores the use of polynomials to solve probability problems.

For You to Do

1. Copy and complete the expansion box below to find the expanded form of $(x + x^2 + x^3 + x^4 + x^5 + x^6)^2$.

   Write the result in ascending powers of x.

$\cdot$	x	x^2	x^3	x^4	x^5	x^6
x	▪	▪	▪	▪	▪	▪
x^2	▪	▪	x^5	▪	▪	▪
x^3	▪	▪	▪	▪	▪	▪
x^4	▪	▪	▪	▪	▪	▪
x^5	▪	x^7	▪	▪	▪	▪
x^6	▪	▪	▪	▪	▪	x^{12}

2. When you roll two number cubes, what is the probability that the sum of the numbers will be exactly 5?

> **Remember...**
>
> You first used expansion boxes in CME Project *Algebra 1* as a way to keep track of all the terms when you were multiplying two expressions.

Developing Habits of Mind

Recognize a similar process. Consider the table from Lesson 7.2, with the 36 possible outcomes for the sum when rolling two number cubes.

+	1	2	3	4	5	6
1	2	3	4	5	6	7
2	3	4	5	6	7	8
3	4	5	6	7	8	9
4	5	6	7	8	9	10
5	6	7	8	9	10	11
6	7	8	9	10	11	12

This table and the one from For You To Do are nearly identical, and they should be! Think about how you might get an x^5 in the expansion: multiply two terms like x^2 and x^3, or x^4 and x^1. In all, there are four ways to do this. Now think about how you get a 5 from the sum of the numbers on two cubes: roll a 2 and a 3, or a 4 and a 1. There are four ways to do this, too. It works because when you multiply polynomials, you are adding exponents.

So, you can use the polynomial $(x + x^2 + x^3 + x^4 + x^5 + x^6)$ to model the results when rolling a number cube with the numbers 1 through 6 on it.

Consider this frequency chart, listing the number of ways to get each sum when rolling two number cubes:

Roll	2	3	4	5	6	7	8	9	10	11	12
Frequency	1	2	3	4	5	6	5	4	3	2	1

Compare it to the result when squaring the polynomial that models a number cube roll:

$$(x + x^2 + x^3 + x^4 + x^5 + x^6)^2 =$$

$$1x^2 + 2x^3 + 3x^4 + 4x^5 + 5x^6 + 6x^7 + 5x^8 + 4x^9 + 3x^{10} + 2x^{11} + 1x^{12}$$

The expansion gives the same frequency information. There is one way to make x^2, two ways to make x^3, and so on. The table analyzing the sample space is really the same as the expansion box multiplying the polynomials.

The **frequency** of an event A is the number of outcomes in A. The frequency of the event "roll a sum of 10 on two number cubes" is 3, since there are 3 different outcomes with sum 10. In shorthand, $|A| = 3$.

Polynomials come in handy when exploring sample spaces that are too complex to list by hand. The sample space for rolling two number cubes has 36 outcomes, but the sample space for rolling four number cubes has $6^4 = 1296$ outcomes. This is tough to build by hand, but a CAS can quickly perform the corresponding polynomial expansion.

$$(x + x^2 + x^3 + x^4 + x^5 + x^6)^4 =$$
$$x^{24} + 4x^{23} + 10x^{22} + 20x^{21} + 35x^{20} + 56x^{19}$$
$$+ 80x^{18} + 104x^{17} + 125x^{16} + 140x^{15} + 146x^{14} + 140x^{13}$$
$$+ 125x^{12} + 104x^{11} + 80x^{10} + 56x^9 + 35x^8 + 20x^7 + 10x^6 + 4x^5 + x^4$$

See the TI-Nspire Handbook on p. 704, for details on how to expand polynomials.

This expansion gives a lot of information. For example, there are exactly 80 ways to roll a sum of 18 on four number cubes. Since there are $6^4 = 1296$ outcomes, $P(\text{rolling a sum of 18}) = \frac{80}{1296}$.

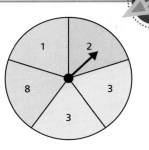

Example

A spinner has five wedges of equal area. The wedges are labeled with the numbers 1, 2, 3, 3, and 8.

Problem What is the most likely sum of the numbers from four spins. How likely is it?

Solution First, model the spinner using the polynomial $(x + x^2 + x^3 + x^3 + x^8)$, matching the five possible outcomes from one spin. With five outcomes on each spin, there will be a total of $5^4 = 625$ outcomes from four spins.

Expand the polynomial to the fourth power.

$(x + x^2 + x^3 + x^3 + x^8)^4 =$
$x^{32} + 8x^{27} + 4x^{26} + 4x^{25} + 24x^{22} + 24x^{21} + 30x^{20}$
$+ 12x^{19} + 6x^{18} + 32x^{17} + 48x^{16} + 72x^{15} + 52x^{14} + 36x^{13}$
$+ 28x^{12} + 36x^{11} + 56x^{10} + 56x^9 + 49x^8 + 28x^7 + 14x^6 + 4x^5 + x^4$

Each coefficient is the frequency for a specific sum, indicated by the exponent. The greatest coefficient is 72. There are 72 ways to make a sum of 15. The probability of this sum occuring is $\frac{72}{625}$, since there are $5^4 = 625$ total outcomes.

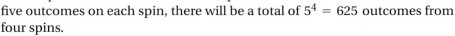

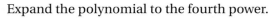

Habits of Mind

Look for a relationship. You could also write the polynomial as $(x + x^2 + 2x^3 + x^8)$. What does the coefficient 2 mean here?

For You to Do

3. A second similar spinner has the numbers 2, 4, 6, 6, 16. What is the most likely sum from four spins?

4. Let $f(x) = (x + x^2 + x^3 + x^3 + x^8)^4$. What is the value of $f(1)$?

You can model other situations using polynomials as well. To model a coin flip, use the polynomial $(t + h)$ as seen in Lesson 7.1. Look at this expansion:

$$(t + h)^5 = t^5 + 5t^4h + 10t^3h^2 + 10t^2h^3 + 5th^4 + h^5$$

You can interpret this as, "There is one way to get five tails, then five ways to get four tails and one head, then ten ways to get three tails and two heads . . ."

To model a multiple-choice question with one right answer and three wrong answers use the polynomial $(r + w + w + w)$, or $(r + 3w)$. Here is another expansion:

$$(r + 3w)^5 = r^5 + 15r^4w + 90r^3w^2 + 270r^2w^3 + 405rw^4 + 243w^5$$

Habits of Mind

Represent the situation. An appropriate choice of letters can be helpful. Here, you use t and h for tails and heads. You use r and w for right and wrong answers.

You can use the expression to show that on five questions, there are 270 different ways to get exactly two right and three wrong answers. The total number of outcomes in the sample space is the sum of the coefficients.

$$1 + 15 + 90 + 270 + 405 + 243 = 1024 = 4^5$$

So, $P(2 \text{ right and 3 wrong}) = \frac{270}{1024} \approx 0.2637$.

Developing Habits of Mind

Extend the process. The polynomials you have seen so far are helpful in counting outcomes, but you can use a variation to calculate the probability directly. For example, by raising $(r + 3w)$ to powers, you can see how many ways there are to get right and wrong answers to a multiple-choice test. But the probability of getting a question right is $\frac{1}{4} = 0.25$ and the probability of getting it wrong is $\frac{3}{4} = 0.75$.

By raising $(0.25r + 0.75w)$ to the nth power, you can see the probabilities of the different events when guessing at n questions.

Consider the expansion of $(0.25r + 0.75w)^5$.

$$0.000977r^5 + 0.014648r^4w + 0.087891r^3w^2 + 0.263672r^2w^3$$
$$+ 0.395508rw^4 + 0.237305w^5$$

> Expand using the Binomial Theorem or a CAS.

Now each coefficient gives the probability of each event occurring, rather than its frequency. The probability of getting 2 right and 3 wrong is the coefficient of the r^2w^3 term.

You can also obtain more information by evaluating the polynomial. For example, take the polynomial for rolling a number cube, $p(x) = x + x^2 + x^3 + x^4 + x^5 + x^6$. The output $p(1) = 6$ gives the total number of outcomes. Also, $(p(1))^3$ equals $6^3 = 216$. This is the total number of outcomes when rolling three number cubes.

But consider $p(-1) = 0$ and how it is built term by term. Let $x = -1$. Then $x^k = 1$ if k is even and $x^k = -1$ if k is odd. So, $p(-1) = 0$ means there are just as many even numbers on a number cube as odd numbers.

Now look at $(p(-1))^4$. It also equals zero, but models the sum of four number cubes. So, there are just as many ways to roll an odd sum from four number cubes as an even sum. This is pretty surprising, but you can verify it using the expansion on page 549. In fact, it must be true no matter how many number cubes are thrown.

One important thing to remember is that the method of polynomial powers is useful when performing the same experiment several times. Experiments involving coins, number cubes, and spinners are good examples. Picking a committee or drawing balls out of a bingo machine are not good examples, since the experiment changes over time. To see this, think about drawing a bingo number. When you draw that number, you remove it from the machine. You have fewer numbers for the next draw.

Exercises *Practicing Habits of Mind*

Check Your Understanding

1. The polynomial on page 549 gives the distribution of possible sums for rolling four number cubes.

   a. Build a histogram showing the frequency for each outcome, from 4 to 24.

   b. Explain why there are exactly as many ways to roll a sum of 5 as there are ways to roll a sum of 23.

2. Suppose you roll three number cubes. Calculate the probability that the sum of the numbers will be greater than 10.

3. On an unusual number cube the "1" face has a 10 instead.

   a. Find a polynomial that models one roll of this number cube.

   b. In four rolls, what is the most likely sum? How likely is it?

   > The six faces on this number cube have the numbers 2, 3, 4, 5, 6, and 10.

4. On another number cube the "6" face has a 5 instead.

   a. Explain why the polynomial $p(x) = x + x^2 + x^3 + x^4 + 2x^5$ models one roll of this number cube.

   b. In four rolls, what is the most likely sum? How likely is it?

   > The six faces on this number cube have the numbers 1, 2, 3, 4, 5, and 5.

5. Consider the number cube from Exercise 4 and its corresponding polynomial p.

   a. Expand $q(x) = (p(x))^2$. What does q represent?

   b. Find the value of $q(1)$.

   c. There are 36 outcomes when rolling this number cube twice. How many more ways are there to roll an even sum than an odd sum?

   d. Find the value of $q(-1)$.

6. A board game has a spinner with the numbers 1 through 10 on it. All numbers are equally likely. As you near the end of the game, you have 18 spaces left to move.

   a. Find the probability that you spin a total of *at least* 18 on just two spins.

   b. Find the probability that you spin a total of *at least* 18 on three spins.

   c. Find the probability that you spin a total of *at least* 18 on four spins.

On Your Own

7. A spinner has the five numbers 0, 1, 2, 2, and 7.

   a. Find a polynomial to model one spin.

   b. What is the most likely sum of the numbers from four spins. How likely is it?

8. Avery takes a multiple-choice test with six questions. There are five choices per question. He guesses at each question.

   a. What is the probability that Avery guesses correctly on the first question? on the second question?

   b. What is the probability that Avery guesses correctly on all six questions?

   c. Write a polynomial expansion to model this situation.

   d. Find the probability that Avery guesses correctly on exactly two of the six questions.

9. A local market has a prize wheel. Lucky customers can spin the wheel to win free fish. On one spin, it is possible to win 1 fish, 2 fish, 3 fish, or 10 fish.

   a. What is the average number of fish the market can expect to give away, per spin?

   b. Three customers spin the wheel. What is the most likely total number of fish that they win? How likely is this?

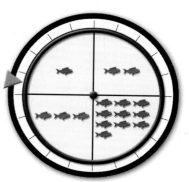

10. **Take It Further** Ten customers spin the Wheel of Fish from Exercise 9. Find the probability that the total number of fish they win is even.

11. Use a coordinate grid with $1 \leq x \leq 10$, $1 \leq y \leq 10$. Plot all 55 points with integer coordinates (x, y) in this range with $x \geq y$. Use one color if the two numbers share a common factor greater than 1. Use a second color if they do not.

12. You are to choose two integers x and y between 1 and 10, inclusive, with $x \geq y$. Use your plot from Exercise 11. Determine the probability that the pair of integers will have no common factor greater than 1.

13. **Standardized Test Prep** Which of the following is the sum of the entries in the 12th row of Pascal's Triangle?

   A. $12!$ **B.** 6^6 **C.** 2^{12} **D.** $_{12}P_2$

Maintain Your Skills

14. Write out F_{10}, the Farey sequence of order 10.

15. Take a coordinate grid with $0 \leq x \leq 10$, $0 \leq y \leq 10$. Plot all points (x, y) in this range where the fraction $\frac{y}{x}$ is in F_{10}, the Farey sequence of order 10. Compare the results to Exercise 11.

> **Remember...**
> The *Farey sequence* of order n is all fractions between 0 and 1 in lowest terms with denominators less than or equal to n, written from least to greatest.

The expected value for a game is how much you could expect to win per game, on average. It is not necessarily the most likely amount you would win in any one game. Instead, if you played many times over, your average score would approach this expected value in the long run.

In-Class Experiment

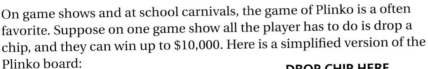

On game shows and at school carnivals, the game of Plinko is a often favorite. Suppose on one game show all the player has to do is drop a chip, and they can win up to $10,000. Here is a simplified version of the Plinko board:

Whenever the chip hits a peg, it has a 50-50 chance of going left or right as it falls. After the chip has hit eight pegs and gone left or right eight times, it falls into one of nine slots with dollar amounts on them, from $0 to $10,000.

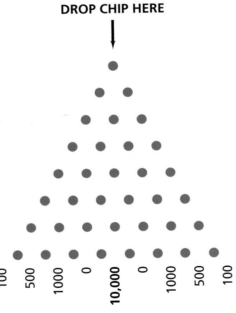

DROP CHIP HERE

100   500   1000   0   10,000   0   1000   500   100

1. Describe the relationship between the falling chip and coin flipping.

2. Write a polynomial, raised to a power, to model this game.

3. Find the probability that the chip falls into the center slot for a $10,000 win.

4. Find the probability that the chip falls into a $0 slot. Note there are two such slots.

5. What is the probability of winning $1000? $500? $100?

6. How much, on average, would you win per chip if you were to keep playing this game for a long, long time?

The sample space here has 256 outcomes. Why?

A student is thinking about the last problem from the In-Class Experiment.

Wendy   Let me answer a simpler question first: let's say you paid me $10,000 if I flip a coin heads, and $0 if it's tails. I've got a $\frac{1}{2}$ chance to make heads, so it should be $5000 per flip, on average.

So now let me look at this bigger problem. I'll focus on the $10,000 first. Every time I drop a chip, there's a $\frac{70}{256}$ chance of getting the 10 grand. If you sat me there all day dropping chips, I can find the average by multiplying.

$$\$10{,}000 \cdot \frac{70}{256} \approx \$2734$$

So if everything else was zeros, that would be my average.

But I could win some smaller amounts of money. There's a $\frac{56}{256}$ chance of hitting $1000. I'll do the same thing:

$$\$1000 \cdot \frac{56}{256} \approx \$219$$

So, I'll build a table for all the options.

Win	Probability	Win × Probability
$10,000	$\frac{70}{256}$	$2734
$1000	$\frac{56}{256}$	$219
$500	$\frac{16}{256}$	$31
$100	$\frac{2}{256}$	$1
$0	whatever	$0

I'm not sure what to do now, I think I'll just add the dollar values. On average, I'd expect to win around $2985 per chip, if you let me sit there all day and drop chips. Not a bad day's work.

Often, it makes sense to assign a number to each outcome of an experiment, such as "3" instead of "rolling a 3 on the number cube," or "2" instead of "heads, tails, heads, tails, tails" or "10,000" instead of "the chip falls in the middle slot." Each set of these numerical assignments is a random variable, and typically uses a capital letter like X or Y.

Wendy's method calculates the *expected value* of a random variable.

> A **random variable** is a function whose inputs are outcomes, and whose outputs are numbers.

Definition

The **expected value** of a random variable X is the sum when each value of X multiplied by its probability. The typical notation is $E(X)$.

$$E(X) = \sum_i x_i \cdot p_i$$

where the x_i are the values of the random variable, and the p_i are the probabilities of the values, respectively. An alternative notation is

$$E(X) = \sum_i s_i \cdot P(X = s_i)$$

where $P(X = s_i)$ is the probability that the random variable X takes on the value s_i.

Remember...

$\sum_i x_i \cdot p_i$ means to add the products of all the different possible x's and their corresponding p's. It is the same as writing $\sum_{i=1}^{n} x_i \cdot p_i$ There are n different outcomes, so there are n products to add.

The definition is a mouthful, but the Plinko game is a good example. For the Plinko board, each x_i is a dollar value. Each p_i is the probability of hitting that value.

Example

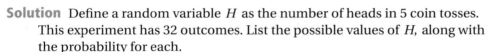

Problem Toss five coins. What is the expected value for the number of heads?

Solution Define a random variable H as the number of heads in 5 coin tosses. This experiment has 32 outcomes. List the possible values of H, along with the probability for each.

Remember...

A random variable takes in outcomes and returns numbers. For example, one outcome is $a =$ "heads, tails, heads, tails, tails." The random variable H takes in that outcome and returns the number 2, $H(a) = 2$.

Number of Heads	Probability
0	$\frac{1}{32}$
1	$\frac{5}{32}$
2	$\frac{10}{32}$
3	$\frac{10}{32}$
4	$\frac{5}{32}$
5	$\frac{1}{32}$

Calculate expected value. Multiply each value of H by its probability. Then add the results.

Number of Heads	Probability	Product
0	$\frac{1}{32}$	0/32
1	$\frac{5}{32}$	5/32
2	$\frac{10}{32}$	20/32
3	$\frac{10}{32}$	30/32
4	$\frac{5}{32}$	20/32
5	$\frac{1}{32}$	5/32
Total		80/32

The expected value is $\frac{80}{32}$, which simplifies to $\frac{5}{2}$.

Habits of Mind

Check the result. Does $\frac{5}{2}$ make sense as the average number of heads when flipping five coins?

Developing Habits of Mind

Use a different process. You might have thought about the Plinko game in a different way. You could add up all the money you would win from each path. There are 2 ways to win $100, 16 ways to win $500, 56 ways to win $1000, and 70 ways to win $10,000. The total winnings from all the different paths is

$$2 \cdot \$100 + 16 \cdot \$500 + 56 \cdot \$1000 + 70 \cdot \$10,000 = \$764,200$$

This is the total value for all 256 paths, so the average would have to be

$$\frac{\$764,200}{256} \approx \$2985.16$$

This gives the correct result! Both methods are valid. It comes down to whether you prefer to count probabilities or frequencies. The result Wendy comes up with is

$$\frac{2}{256} \cdot \$100 + \frac{16}{256} \cdot \$500 + \frac{56}{256} \cdot \$1000 + \frac{70}{256} \cdot \$10,000$$

The distributive law shows that both these results must be identical. So, you can also calculate the expected value by taking the sum of all the outputs from the random variable, then dividing by the total number of outcomes. The expected value is the mean result from the random variable.

For example, the expected value of the numeric result when rolling one number cube is the mean of the numbers on the six faces.

$$\frac{1 + 2 + 3 + 4 + 5 + 6}{6} = 3.5$$

Tony and Derman look at Exercise 9 from Lesson 7.3.

Tony   So, it's a wheel with 1, 2, 3, and 10 fish on it. And we want to know the average from one spin.

Derman   I'll just add and divide. The sum is . . . 16. So the average is 4.

Tony   Sounds good. Now what about two spins?

Derman   I think it's going to be 8. Two times four. Two spins, 4 fish each?

Tony   I'm not sure it works that way. Let's just write out the sample space. There are only 16 ways it can go.

Derman   A table it is.

+	1	2	3	10
1	2	3	4	11
2	3	4	5	12
3	4	5	6	13
10	11	12	13	20

Tony   Cool. I'm going to add all these numbers then divide by 16. Since the sample space is small, I won't bother making a frequency table.

The sum is 128. So, the expected value for two spins is 128 over 16 . . . hey, you were right! It is 8.

Derman   It was bound to happen sometime. If I'm right, for three spins the expected value should be 12. The table's going to be a mess!

Tony   Well, we should use a polynomial power instead. The outcomes are 1, 2, 3, and 10, so the polynomial for one spin should be

$$(x^1 + x^2 + x^3 + x^{10})$$

Derman   Isn't x^1 just x?

Tony   I like writing x^1, it makes it more clear where it came from. I'd do that for x^0 instead of writing 1.

Derman   Fair enough. And we raise that to the third power, since it's three spins. Expand that and . . .

Tony   Let's write that out.

For You to Do

7. Complete the work from the dialog. Write out the expansion of $(x^1 + x^2 + x^3 + x^{10})^3$, then use it to show that the expected value for three spins is 12.

Check Your Understanding

Alice, Bev, Craig, and Dawn sit at a table for four in no particular order. Rey, the host of the party, tells them their seats are assigned at the table and shows them the chart.

1. a. What is the probability that all four of them are already in the right seat?

b. What is the probability that all four of them are in the *wrong* seat?

2. On average, how many of the four will be sitting in the right seat?

3. Suppose a Plinko board has a center hole worth $20,000.

Find the average amount a player will win, per chip, in the long run.

4. What's Wrong Here? Daisuke had trouble calculating the expected number of heads when tossing three coins.

Daisuke: I built the table with each outcome and its probability, then added it up. I got the probabilities from the Getting Started lesson. I could use Pascal's Triangle to get them, too.

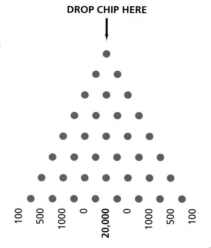

DROP CHIP HERE

100 500 1000 0 20,000 0 1000 500 100

> **Habits of Mind**
>
> **Make a list.** There are 24 possible ways for the four guests to sit down. Do you see why there are 24 possible outcomes? Try listing them.

> This is another way to say, "Calculate the expected value" for this new version of the game.

Number of Heads	Probability	Product
0	$\frac{1}{8}$	$\frac{0}{8}$
1	$\frac{3}{8}$	$\frac{3}{8}$
2	$\frac{3}{8}$	$\frac{6}{8}$
3	$\frac{1}{8}$	$\frac{3}{8}$
Total		$\frac{12}{8}$

Daisuke: But it doesn't make sense to me to get $\frac{12}{8}$ as the answer: that's one and a half, and I thought probability was never supposed to be more than one.

What would you say to Daisuke? Has he made a mistake in the calculation?

5. Avery is taking a six-question multiple choice test, with five choices for each question. He guesses at each question.

 a. Expand the polynomial $(0.2r + 0.8w)^6$. What do the results represent?

 b. Find the expected value for the number of questions Avery gets right when taking the test.

6. Three customers spin the Wheel of Fish as seen in Exercise 9 on page 553.

 a. Use a polynomial expansion to find the frequency of each outcome.

 b. Find the probability that the market will give away fewer than 10 total fish to these three customers.

On one spin, the possible outcomes are 1, 2, 3, and 10 fish.

7. Find the expected value for the total number of fish the market gives away when four customers spin the Wheel of Fish.

On Your Own

8. In this lesson's In-Class Experiment, you calculated the expected value for dropping one Plinko chip. Now suppose you drop five chips.

 a. What is the expected value, in dollars, for the first chip? the second chip? the third chip?

 b. What is the expected value for the total earned from all five chips?

For additional practice, go to **Web Code:** bga-0704

9. Find the expected value for the number of heads when tossing six coins.

10. a. Find the expected value for the sum when rolling two number cubes.

 b. Find the expected value for the sum when rolling three number cubes.

11. **Take It Further**

 a. Find the expected value for the *product* when rolling two number cubes.

 b. Find the expected value for the product when rolling three number cubes. How could you use a polynomial here?

Be efficient. Use a polynomial power!

Suppose a friend gives you five envelopes, each with a different address on it. You are to put one of five different letters in each envelope. But you have no idea which letter is for which person, so you stuff them in at random.

12. What is the probability that all five envelopes contain the right letter?

13. What is the probability that exactly four envelopes contain the right letter?

14. What is the probability that all five envelopes contain the wrong letter?

15. Find the expected value for the number of letters correctly addressed.

16. **Standardized Test Prep** A student randomly guesses on a true-false combinatorics test with five questions. Which of the following is the probability that the student will score at least 80%?

A. $\frac{5}{32}$ **B.** $\frac{3}{16}$ **C.** $\frac{1}{4}$ **D.** $\frac{1}{2}$

> This exercise is in the same style as Exercises 1 and 2. You might want to think of this as five people and five seats.

Maintain Your Skills

17. Copy and complete this table using your work from previous lessons.

n	Number of Elements in F_n	Relatively Prime Pairs
1	2	
2		
3		4
4		
5	11	
6		
7		18
8		
9		
10	33	

Here, F_n is the Farey sequence of order n. *Relatively prime pairs* refers to the number of pairs that have no common factors greater than 1 as plotted in Exercise 11 on page 553.

18. **Take It Further** Find the number of elements in F_{30}, the Farey sequence of order 30. Your goal is only to find the number of elements, not list them all.

> **Habits of Mind**
> **Look for relationships.**
> Look for a simpler method than writing out the entire sequence F_{30}.

7.5 Lotteries

One application of expected value is a lottery. There are several different kinds of lotteries. In some lotteries, expected value can be directly calculated, while others require an approach based on combinations.

Scratch Tickets

State lotteries print batches of tickets, some of which are prize winners. Players pay to get a ticket. Most tickets lose, but some tickets are worth hundreds or thousands of dollars.

Here is the distribution from a scratch ticket game where each ticket costs $1.

Payout	Frequency
$1	163,500
$2	62,800
$4	20,945
$8	4,189
$12	4,189
$50	5,621
$100	128
$1,000	4
$0 (lose)	995,324
Total	**1,256,700**

Most of the tickets lose. Only a small percentage give the player more money than the price of the ticket.

How much is the average ticket worth in this game? To find this, calculate the expected value.

Payout	Frequency	Product
1	163,500	163,500
2	62,800	125,600
4	20,945	83,780
8	4,189	33,512
12	4,189	50,268
50	5,621	281,050
100	128	12,800
1,000	4	4,000
0 (lose)	995,324	0
Total	**1,256,700**	**754,510**

The random variable is the dollar value (payout) of the ticket, from 0 to 1000. The sample space is all 1,256,700 tickets. The expected value is the sum of each payout, multiplied by its probability.

The expected value is $\frac{754,510}{1,256,700}$, very close to 60 cents. This lottery ticket actually costs $1, so roughly 60% of the money paid for tickets is returned to players as prizes, while 40% is kept by the state that runs this lottery.

In a 6-ball lottery a player picks six numbers, from 1 to 42. Then a machine draws six balls at random from a set of 42 numbered balls. The order of the drawing does not matter. The amount the player wins depends on how many of the numbers match numbers on their ticket.

The sample space has $\binom{42}{6} = 5{,}245{,}786$ elements.

This table shows the possible outcomes and their frequencies.

Matches	Frequency	Payout
0 correct	1,947,792	$0 (loss)
1 correct	2,261,952	$0 (loss)
2 correct	883,575	$0 (loss)
3 correct	142,800	$1
4 correct	9,450	$75
5 correct	216	$1,500
6 correct	1	$2,000,000 jackpot
Total	**5,245,786**	

Problem A ticket in this lottery costs $1. Find the expected value for one ticket.

Solution Multiply the frequencies by the payouts.

Matches	Frequency	Payout	Product
0 correct	1,947,792	0	0
1 correct	2,261,952	0	0
2 correct	883,575	0	0
3 correct	142,800	1	142,800
4 correct	9,450	75	708,750
5 correct	216	1,500	324,000
6 correct	1	2,000,000	2,000,000
Total	**5,245,786**		**3,175,550**

Note that the majority of the payouts go to the single jackpot winner (if there is one). Overall the expected value is

$$\frac{3{,}175{,}550}{5{,}245{,}786} \approx 0.6054$$

The $1 ticket is worth just over 60 cents, so the lottery earns an average profit of nearly 40 cents per dollar played.

For You to Do

1. Suppose the lottery is considering changing the rules to give a $5 prize for 3 numbers correct. What would happen to the expected value of a ticket? Would the lottery still be profitable for whoever is running it?

Habits of Mind

Use what you know. Try modifying the information from the table.

Combinatorics and Lotteries

You can determine the frequencies in the previous example by counting combinations. Picture the 42 balls in the lottery drawing. The player picks 6 numbers, dividing the 42 balls into two categories: 6 that they want to see, and 36 others that they do not want to see.

Suppose you want to know how many different ways there are to get exactly four balls correct in the lottery drawing. Well, out of the 6 balls the player wants to see, the machine draws 4. That can happen $\binom{6}{4}$ ways. But the machine also draws 2 of the "other" balls. That can happen $\binom{36}{2}$ ways. So, the number of ways to get exactly four balls correct is

$$\binom{6}{4} \cdot \binom{36}{2} = 15 \cdot 630 = 9450$$

You can use this approach for any count between 0 and 6.

Matches	Frequency
0 correct	$\binom{6}{0} \cdot \binom{36}{6} = 1{,}947{,}792$
1 correct	$\binom{6}{1} \cdot \binom{36}{5} = 2{,}261{,}952$
2 correct	$\binom{6}{2} \cdot \binom{36}{4} = 883{,}575$
3 correct	$\binom{6}{3} \cdot \binom{36}{3} = 142{,}800$
4 correct	$\binom{6}{4} \cdot \binom{36}{2} = 9{,}450$
5 correct	$\binom{6}{5} \cdot \binom{36}{1} = 216$
6 correct	$\binom{6}{6} \cdot \binom{36}{0} = 1$

Note that the total number of outcomes is $\binom{42}{6}$ since there are 42 balls and 6 are picked. This leads to a theorem about combinations.

Remember...

You can calculate combinations like $\binom{36}{2}$ using the nCr function on a calculator, or by using the factorial formula:

$$\binom{n}{k} = \frac{n!}{k!(n-k)!}$$

Theorem 7.1 Vandermonde's Identity

Let $r \le n$ be nonnegative integers. Then

$$\binom{n}{r} = \sum_{k=0}^{r} \binom{r}{k} \cdot \binom{n-r}{r-k}$$

This method can be used to analyze most ball-drawing lottery games.

Study the difference. Larger multi-state lotteries now exist, typically using these rules:

- First, a machine draws five balls from a set.

- Second, another machine draws the sixth ball (the "bonus ball") from a second set of balls, a completely different group.

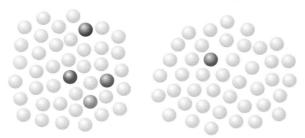

In order to win the jackpot, the player must get all five regular balls correct, plus the bonus ball. What effect does the existence of the bonus ball have on the sample space? Consider a game with 42 balls for the regular drawing, and a new set of 42 balls for the "bonus."

The size of the sample space becomes

$$\binom{42}{5} \cdot \binom{42}{1}$$

since 5 balls are chosen from the first set of 42, then 1 ball is chosen from the second set. While it may not seem like much of a difference, this has a huge effect on the size of the sample space.

$$\text{sample space for 6-ball lottery} = \binom{42}{6} = 5{,}245{,}786$$

$$\text{sample space with bonus ball} = \binom{42}{5} \cdot \binom{42}{1} = 35{,}728{,}056$$

The sample space is roughly 7 times bigger. It is much less likely a player will win. As of April 2008, one multi-state lottery had a sample space of over 146 million, while another had a sample space of over 175 million!

Think about flipping a coin 27 times in a row, and having all 27 coin flips come up heads. This would happen once every 134 million tries. In other words, flipping 27 heads in a row is *more* likely to happen than buying a winning ticket in either of these multi-state lotteries.

For Discussion

2. A multi-state lottery could increase its sample space by adding more balls to either the regular pool or the "bonus" pool. How many more regular-pool balls would be needed to double the sample space? How many more "bonus" balls would be needed to double the sample space?

Exercises *Practicing Habits of Mind*

Check Your Understanding

1. A 5-ball lottery has 55 numbered balls. A player selects five numbers. Then, five of the balls are drawn by a machine.

   Copy and complete this frequency table.

Matches	Frequency
0 correct	■
1 correct	1,151,500
2 correct	■
3 correct	■
4 correct	■
5 correct	1

2. Find the expected value for the number of balls a player will correctly match in the 5-ball lottery presented in Exercise 1.

3. Suppose an interstate lottery has a 5-ball component with 55 balls, and then a bonus ball from a separate set of 42 balls. This table lists the payouts for this lottery.

Ticket Type	Frequency	Payout
5 balls + bonus	1	Jackpot
5 balls + no bonus	41	$200,000
4 balls + bonus	250	$10,000
4 balls + no bonus	10,250	$100
3 balls + bonus	12,250	$100
3 balls + no bonus	502,250	$7
2 balls + bonus	196,000	$7
1 ball + bonus	1,151,500	$4
Bonus only	2,118,760	$3
Losing ticket	142,116,660	$0
Total outcomes	**146,107,962**	

   The base jackpot for this lottery is $16,000,000. Find the expected value of a $1 ticket in this lottery.

4. The jackpot in the game from Exercise 3 may grow as high as $100 million!

   a. Suppose the jackpot is worth m million dollars. Find the expected value of a ticket, in terms of m.

   b. If the jackpot is $100 million, what is the expected value of a ticket?

   c. How high must the jackpot be for the expected value to be greater than $1 per ticket?

5. **Take It Further** A second multistate lottery has a 5-ball component with 56 balls, and then a bonus ball from a separate set of 46 balls.

   Copy and complete this table for the frequency of each payout.

Ticket Type	Frequency	Payout
5 balls + bonus	1	Jackpot
5 balls + no bonus	▩	$250,000
4 balls + bonus	▩	$10,000
4 balls + no bonus	11,475	$150
3 balls + bonus	▩	$150
3 balls + no bonus	▩	$7
2 balls + bonus	▩	$10
1 ball + bonus	▩	$3
Bonus only	▩	$2
Losing ticket	171,306,450	$0
Total outcomes	**175,711,536**	

   Then, find the expected value of a $1 ticket at the base jackpot of $12 million.

6. A state-run raffle offers a number of prizes. A total of 500,000 tickets are available. Each ticket costs $20. These prizes are available:

Payout	Frequency
$1,000,000	4
$100,000	5
$10,000	8
$5,000	8
$1,000	500
$100	2000
$0 (lose)	497,475

   Find the expected value of a $20 raffle ticket.

The jackpots that lotteries report are actually much more than the money that they pay out or that a player would get. A player has to pay taxes on winnings. Also, the lottery pays the jackpot over many years, not all up front. In fact, it is rare for the jackpot to grow above $100 million in most lotteries.

7. Consider the 6-ball lottery with 42 balls from this lesson. Find the expected value for the number of balls that a player will correctly match.

8. Consider the following prize distribution from a large scratch ticket game.

Go Online
PHSchool.com

For additional practice, go to **Web Code:** bga-0705

Payout	Frequency
$10,000,000	10
$1,000,000	130
$25,000	130
$10,000	1,820
$1,000	33,670
$500	109,200
$200	336,700
$100	1,791,335
$50	1,310,400
$40	2,620,800
$25	7,862,400
$20	7,862,400
$0 (lose)	43,585,545
Total tickets	**65,520,000**

   a. Find the expected value of one ticket.

   b. Each ticket costs $20. If all tickets are sold, how much profit will be made by the state running this lottery?

9. A 6-ball lottery in Italy is the largest of its kind with 90 balls to pick from. A player wins a prize in this lottery if they get at least 3 of the 6 numbers right. What is the probability of winning a prize in this lottery?

10. Use the Internet to find information on a lottery or scratch ticket game. Determine the expected value on a ticket in that game.

11. Suppose a friend gives you six envelopes, each with a different address on it. You are to put one of six different letters in each envelope. But you have no idea which letter is for which person, so you stuff them in at random. You hope at least some of the envelopes contain the correct letter.

Number Correct	Frequency
0	265
1	264
2	135
3	40
4	15
5	0
6	1

This frequency table lists the number of different permutations with 0 correct envelopes, 1 correct, and so on.

a. What is the total number of outcomes in this sample space?

b. Find the expected value for the number of correct envelopes.

12. **Standardized Test Prep** A bag contains 16 red chips and 4 blue chips. Amy picks one chip. After returning the chip to the bag and remixing the chips, she reaches in a second time and picks one chip. If Amy is paid as shown in the table, what is the expected value of the amount she will win?

Outcome	Payout
Two blue	wins $10
One blue, one red	wins $1
Two red	loses $1

A. loses at least $1 **B.** loses less than $1 **C.** Breaks even

D. wins less than $1 **E.** wins at least $1

Maintain Your Skills

13. The numbers 7, 21, and 35 appear in the 7th row of Pascal's Triangle. These numbers are unusual in that they form an arithmetic sequence: add 14 to 7 to get 21, then add another 14 to get 35. Or, put another way, 21 is the mean of 7 and 35.

a. Find the next time this occurs in Pascal's Triangle.

b. **Take It Further** If $\binom{n}{k}$ is the mean of $\binom{n}{k-1}$ and $\binom{n}{k+1}$, find a relationship between n and k.

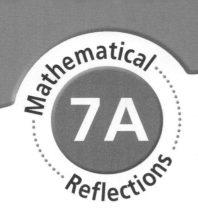
In this investigation, you calculated probabilities using Pascal's Triangle and polynomial powers. You also learned about expected value and its uses. The following questions will help you summarize what you have learned.

1. How can you use the expansion of $(t + h)^5$ to find the probability of getting exactly two heads on five coin tosses?

2. **a.** Al wins a game if he flips a coin heads, and rolls less than a six on a number cube. What is the probability that Al wins the game?

   b. Beth wins a game if she flips a coin tails, or (after flipping heads) if she rolls a six on a number cube. What is the probability that Beth wins the game?

3. A wheel has the numbers 5 through 100 on it, in multiples of 5. What is the expected value of one spin of this wheel?

4. A 5-ball state lottery uses 49 balls. What is the probability of getting exactly four of the five balls correct?

5. A wheel has the numbers 1, 2, 3, and 6 on it. After spinning the wheel four times, what is the most likely total?

6. If you are to roll four number cubes, what is the probability they sum to 12?

7. What is expected value?

8. How can you use polynomials to solve probability problems?

Vocabulary and Notation

In this investigation, you learned these terms and symbols. Make sure you understand what each one means and how to use it.

- event
- expected value, $E(X)$
- frequency, $|A|$
- independent
- mutually exclusive

- outcome
- probability of an event
- random variable
- sample space

If the survival rate for a hatchling to make it to the sea is 32%, how many in a group of 46 are expected to reach the sea?

Go Online
PHSchool.com

For a mid-chapter test, go to **Web Code: bga-0752**

Multiple Choice

1. If you flip a coin six times, how many possible outcomes are there?

A. 12   **B.** 32

C. 36   **D.** 64

2. What is the probability of flipping exactly three heads if you flip a coin six times?

A. $\frac{5}{16}$ **B.** $\frac{1}{2}$

C. $\frac{1}{6}$ **D.** $\frac{3}{64}$

3. A number cube has the numbers 2, 4, 6, 8, 10, and 12. Which polynomial models one roll of this cube?

A. $x^1 + x^2 + x^3 + x^4 + x^5 + x^6$

B. $2x^1 + 4x^2 + 6x^3 + 8x^4 + 10x^5 + 12x^6$

C. $x^2 + x^4 + x^6 + x^8 + x^{10} + x^{12}$

D. $2(x^2 + x^4 + x^6 + x^8 + x^{10} + x^{12})$

4. A spinner has four wedges of equal area with the numbers 2, 3, 5, and 6. If you spin twice, what is the probability that the sum of the spins is 8?

A. $\frac{1}{9}$ **B.** $\frac{1}{2}$

C. $\frac{1}{4}$ **D.** $\frac{1}{3}$

5. You play a game by flipping a coin three times. If you flip three heads you win $20. If you flip two heads, you win $10. If you flip only one head you win nothing. If you flip no heads you must pay $5. What is the expected value of your winnings?

A. $10   **B.** $3.50

C. $0   **D.** $6.25

6. Michaela is taking a five-question test where she is matching words with their definitions. If she just guesses, what is the probability that she gets 100%?

A. $\frac{1}{3125}$ **B.** $\frac{1}{120}$

C. $\frac{1}{25}$ **D.** $\frac{1}{5}$

Open Response

7. If you roll two number cubes, determine the following probabilities.

a. rolling a sum of 7

b. rolling a sum of 1

c. rolling a sum greater than or equal to 10

8. A box contains five coins. Two of the coins are worth $100, one of the coins is worth $50, another coin is worth $25, and the last coin is worth $5. You reach in and randomly choose a coin.

a. What is the probability of choosing a coin worth $100?

b. Calculate the expected value for this experiment.

c. Calculate the expected value if someone adds a sixth, worthless coin to the box.

9. A lottery has 36 numbered balls, and a player must select five numbers. Then, five of the balls are picked. Matching all five of the numbers wins the jackpot.

a. How many total combinations of five numbers are possible?

b. How many ways can a player match three of the five numbers?

c. What is the probability of winning the jackpot?

10. A lottery is played by choosing four numbers out of 80 numbers.

a. Copy and complete the table.

Matches	Frequency	Payout
0 correct	▦	$0
1 correct	▦	$5
2 correct	▦	$500
3 correct	▦	$5,000
4 correct	▦	$25,000

b. A ticket for this lottery costs $10. What is the expected value for one ticket?

Investigation 7B

Expectation and Variation

In *Expectation and Variation*, you will learn how to calculate an interval of values that you are likely to obtain when you perform an experiment involving data.

By the end of this investigation, you will be able to answer questions like these.

1. How can you calculate the standard deviation for a large set of data?

2. What happens to the mean, variance, and standard deviation if an experiment is repeated a second time?

3. What is the mean and standard deviation for the number of heads on 400 coin flips?

You will learn how to

- calculate expected value, mean absolute deviation, variance, and standard deviation

- calculate statistics for compound events, including repeated experiments

- identify Bernoulli trials and compute related statistics

You will develop these habits and skills:

- Interpret statistics in order to compare two data sets or make predictions.

- Understand Σ notation and apply Σ theorems.

- Reason deductively to prove relationships in statistics such as the "machine formula."

When flipping coins, you expect to get about half heads and half tails. The actual number of heads and tails cannot be predicted but the amount of variation can be calculated.

7.6 Getting Started

**Activating Prior Knowledge
Exploring New Ideas**

Here is an opportunity to explore how well you would do if you guessed at every question on a multiple-choice test.

For You to Explore

1. On a separate piece of paper, take this multiple-choice test. For each of the 20 questions, select choice A, B, C, D, or E. Only one answer is correct. After the test, your class can compile the scores and build a histogram of the data.

   Oops, the questions are missing. Good luck!

2. On average, how many questions would you expect each person in your class to get right? Explain.

3. **a.** Build a histogram for the number of questions each person in your class answered correctly.

   b. What percent of the class got between 2 and 6 correct, inclusive?

Exercises *Practicing Habits of Mind*

On Your Own

4. Bill is a contestant on a game show. On this show, Bill gets a random integer n between 1 and 75. He then guesses whether the next number (picked from the remaining numbers) will be higher or lower. If Bill is correct, he wins $100 times the new number. Bill's plan is to win as much money as possible. Determine whether Bill should pick higher or lower in each of the following cases.

a. $n = 25$ **b.** $n = 38$ **c.** $n = 39$ **d.** $n = 42$

e. Describe a strategy that maximizes Bill's winnings.

> So, he wins only $300 if a 3 comes out after a correct guess, but he wins $6,700 if a 67 comes out after a correct guess. The higher numbers are worth a lot more!

5. Nancy estimates that the books she carries to school weigh about 25 pounds. Nancy figures she is right to within 3 pounds, give or take. Nancy's dog Woody weighs about 18 pounds, give or take 2 pounds.

a. Nancy says the combined weight of the books and the dog is about 43 pounds. How accurate could this be in "give or take" terms?

b. One day, Nancy decides to bring Woody in her school bag instead of books (a lighter load!). She says the dog is about 7 pounds lighter, but how accurate could this be in "give or take" terms?

6. **Take It Further** A company has a marketing scheme to sell its new line of toy robots. You cannot see through the box, so you do not know which one of the six equally likely robots you will get. If you collect all six robots, you can connect them together to form a larger "ultimate" robot.

To collect all six robots, how many boxes will you have to buy on average?

7. **Take It Further** Bree will keep rolling a number cube until she has rolled each number (1 through 6) at least once. What is the expected value for the number of times Bree will roll?

Maintain Your Skills

8. Calculate each sum.

a. $\displaystyle\sum_{k=1}^{9} k$ **b.** $\displaystyle\sum_{k=1}^{9} k^2$ **c.** $\displaystyle\sum_{k=1}^{9} \frac{k^2}{9}$

d. $\displaystyle\sum_{k=1}^{9} \frac{(k-5)^2}{9}$ **e.** $\displaystyle\sqrt{\sum_{k=1}^{9} \frac{(k-5)^2}{9}}$

Variance and Standard Deviation

When you do an experiment repeatedly, it is likely that your results will cluster around the expected value of the experiment. You can measure how well they cluster by calculating the standard deviation.

In-Class Experiment

As the winner of a contest, you get to pick one of three spinners and spin it. You will earn $1 multiplied by the number you spin.

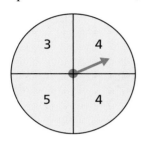 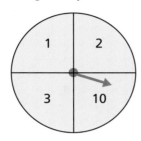 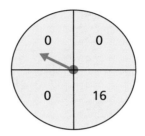

1. For each spinner, calculate the expected value of the spin. Which spinner would you choose? Explain your choice. Would your answer change if you were spinning for $10,000 multiplied by the spin?

Suppose for a random variable X, the n outputs x_1 through x_n are all equally likely. Then, as you learned in Investigation 7A, the expected value $E(X)$ is equal to the mean $\overline{x}$.

$$E(X) = \frac{x_1 + x_2 + \cdots + x_n}{n} = \frac{\sum_i x_i}{n} = \overline{x}$$

With equally likely outcomes, the expected value and the mean are interchangeable. So, both $E(Y)$ and $\overline{y}$ denote the expected value for random variable Y with equally likely outcomes.

The three spinners in the In-Class Experiment each have the same expected value. But there are major differences in the **spread** of each. Most measures of spread start by calculating the **deviation** of each result from the mean. For example, if X is the random variable corresponding to the value on one number cube roll, its possible values are 1, 2, 3, 4, 5, and 6. Its mean is $\overline{x} = 3.5$. The table at the right calculates the deviations for each result.

x	Deviation $x - \overline{x}$
1	-2.5
2	-1.5
3	-0.5
4	0.5
5	1.5
6	2.5

Deviation may be positive, negative, or zero.

For You to Do

2. For each spinner in the In-Class Experiment, calculate the deviations from the mean. Then calculate the sum of the deviations.

Three common measures of spread arise from deviations. You can use these measures to judge how wide a distribution is, or to compare distributions. A larger spread means the distribution is wider.

The first measure of spread is the **mean absolute deviation.** Calculate it by finding the absolute value of each deviation, then finding the mean of these numbers.

x	Deviation $x - \overline{x}$	$|x - \overline{x}|$
1	-2.5	2.5
2	-1.5	1.5
3	-0.5	0.5
4	0.5	0.5
5	1.5	1.5
6	2.5	2.5
	Total	**9**

The mean absolute deviation for one number cube roll is $\frac{9}{6} = \frac{3}{2} = 1.5$.

The second measure is the **mean squared deviation.** Calculate it by finding the square of each deviation, then finding the mean of these numbers.

x	Deviation $x - \overline{x}$	$(x - \overline{x})^2$
1	-2.5	6.25
2	-1.5	2.25
3	-0.5	0.25
4	0.5	0.25
5	1.5	2.25
6	2.5	6.25
	Total	**17.5**

The mean squared deviation for one number cube roll is $\frac{17.5}{6} = \frac{35}{12} \approx 2.917$. Note that you can express the mean squared deviation as

$$\frac{\sum_i (x_i - \overline{x})^2}{n}$$

The third measure is the **root mean squared deviation.** Calculate it by finding the square root of the mean squared deviation. The root mean squared deviation for one number cube roll is approximately 1.708.

Habits of Mind

Understand the process. For each of these measures of spread, the name will tell you how to calculate it.

Reason about calculations. Why would anyone use the root mean squared deviation if it is just the square root of another measure? The biggest reason is units. Squaring changes the units, so the mean squared deviation is not in the same units. Consider the second spinner from the In-Class Experiment, with outcomes 1, 2, 3, and 10 and mean 4. Include the units (dollars).

Payout x	Deviation $x - \overline{x}$	$(x - \overline{x})^2$
$1	−3 dollars	9 square dollars
$2	−2 dollars	4 square dollars
$3	−1 dollar	1 square dollar
$10	6 dollars	36 square dollars
	Total	50 square dollars

The mean squared deviation is $\frac{50}{4} = 12.5$ square dollars! By taking the square root, the result is in dollars again.

Of the three measures of spread, the last two are so common that they have shorter names. **Variance** is the shorter, more common name for mean squared deviation. **Standard deviation** is the common name for root mean squared deviation. You may want to remember the longer names, because they reveal the calculations involved and make an underlying relationship more clear:

> Standard deviation is the square root of variance

Standard deviation is a good measure of the spread of data. Most data will be within one standard deviation of the mean. For example, the mean height for adult women is 63.5 inches. The standard deviation is 2.5 inches. Most adult women are between 61 and 66 inches tall. 61 and 66 are each one standard deviation away from the mean of 63.5.

See the TI-Nspire Handbook on p. 704 for details on how to calculate variance and standard deviation.

Definitions

The *variance* σ^2 for a data set $\{x_1, x_2, \ldots, x_n\}$ is given by

$$\sigma^2 = \frac{\sum_i (x_i - \overline{x})^2}{n}$$

where $\overline{x}$ is the mean of the data set.

The *standard deviation* σ for a data set is the square root of the variance and is given by

$$\sigma = \sqrt{\frac{\sum_i (x_i - \overline{x})^2}{n}}$$

These same formulas apply when you view the data as the outputs of a random variable X (rather than as just a set of outcomes). If the outputs x_i are all equally likely, the expected value $E(X)$ is equal to the mean $\bar{x}$. So, you can write the variance as

$$V(X) = E\big((X - E(X))^2\big)$$

A short formula for variance exists: variance is "the mean of the squares minus the square of the mean." Often, this is easier to calculate. For a number cube roll of 1 through 6 consider the following calculations.

When you compute the variance using this easier calculation, you are using the "machine formula."

- The *mean of the squares* is $(1 + 4 + 9 + 16 + 25 + 36)$ divided by 6, which is $\frac{91}{6}$.

- The *square of the mean* is $\left(\frac{7}{2}\right)^2 = \frac{49}{4}$.

- The difference between these is $\frac{91}{6} - \frac{49}{4} = \frac{35}{12}$. This is the same value for the variance that you calculated using the mean squared deviation.

Below is a proof that this short formula follows from the definition of mean squared deviation, by using binomial expansion and some properties of sums.

Proof

$$\frac{\sum_i (x_i - \bar{x})^2}{n} = \frac{\sum_i (x_i^2 - 2x_i\bar{x} + \bar{x}^2)}{n}$$

$$= \sum_i \frac{x_i^2}{n} - 2\sum_i \frac{x_i\bar{x}}{n} + \sum_i \frac{\bar{x}^2}{n}$$

$$= \sum_i \frac{x_i^2}{n} - 2\bar{x}\sum_i \frac{x_i}{n} + \bar{x}^2\sum_i \frac{1}{n}$$

$$= \sum_i \frac{x_i^2}{n} - 2\bar{x}^2 + \bar{x}^2$$

$$= \sum_i \frac{x_i^2}{n} - \bar{x}^2$$

$$= \overline{x^2} - \bar{x}^2$$

For Discussion

3. For each step in the deviation of the machine formula, give a justification. Why is it okay to pull $\bar{x}$ out of the sum? Where does the $\bar{x}^2$ come from in the middle term? How does the $\sum_i \frac{1}{n}$ just disappear?

Exercises *Practicing Habits of Mind*

Check Your Understanding

A standard number cube has the numbers 1 through 6. You know from this lesson that the numbers on the faces have the following statistics.

mean $\bar{x} = 3.5$

mean absolute deviation $= 1.5$

mean squared deviation (variance) $\sigma^2 = \frac{35}{12} \approx 2.917$

root mean squared deviation (standard deviation) $\sigma = \sqrt{\frac{35}{12}} \approx 1.708$

For each nonstandard number cube listed below, calculate each of these:

a. the mean   **b.** the mean absolute deviation

c. the variance   **d.** the standard deviation

1. A number cube with the numbers 2, 3, 4, 5, 6, 7

2. A number cube with the numbers 2, 4, 6, 8, 10, 12

3. A number cube with the numbers 1, 2, 3, 4, 5, 5

4. A number cube with the numbers 3, 3, 3, 3, 3, 3

5. Write About It

   a. When you add a constant c to each element in a data set, what happens to the mean, mean absolute deviation, variance, and standard deviation? Give an additional example using a new data set.

   b. When you multiply each element of a data set by a constant k, what happens to the mean, mean absolute deviation, variance, and standard deviation? Give an additional example using a new data set.

6. This frequency table gives the results when 500 students took the 20-question multiple choice test from the Getting Started lesson.

Score	Frequency
0	5
1	34
2	74
3	100
4	100
5	85
6	59
7	29
8	10
9	4
10+	0

This is a data set with 500 elements! Think about how you might simplify the calculation. Since this is a frequency table, the mean is not the average of 5, 34, 74, . . . , but the mean of 0, 0, 0, 0, 0, 1, 1, 1, 1, . . . , 8, 9, 9, 9, 9.

Find the mean and standard deviation for this data.

7. Take It Further Use algebra and what you know about sums to prove the claims made in Exercise 5.

8. When you roll two standard number cubes, there are 36 possible outcomes. Calculate the mean, mean absolute deviation, variance, and standard deviation for the sum of the numbers rolled for all 36 possible outcomes. Compare to the results from the numbers on one number cube.

On Your Own

9. Define a random variable for a coin flip as follows. The random variable X equals 1 if the coin flip is heads. It equals 0 if the coin flip is tails.

   a. Calculate $E(X)$, the expected value for X.

   b. Calculate the deviation for X for each possible outcome.

   c. Calculate the mean absolute deviation, the variance, and the standard deviation for the number of heads on one coin flip.

How often will $X = 1$? How often will $X = 0$? Remember, deviation can be negative.

10. Define a random variable for two coin flips as follows. The random variable Y equals 2 if both coins are heads, 1 if exactly one coin is heads, and 0 if both coins are tails.

   a. Calculate $E(Y)$, the expected value for Y.

   b. Calculate the deviation for Y for each of the four outcomes.

   c. Calculate the mean absolute deviation, the variance, and the standard deviation for the number of heads on two coin flips.

11. Your class should have data for the 20-question test from the Getting Started lesson. Each element in the data set is the number of correct answers for a particular student. For your class's data, find the mean, mean absolute deviation, variance, and standard deviation.

12. Consider this set of 16 sums from Derman's table in Lesson 7.4.

+	1	2	3	10
1	2	3	4	11
2	3	4	5	12
3	4	5	6	13
10	11	12	13	20

> This might be a good place to use the machine formula for variance: the mean of the squares, minus the square of the mean.

a. Build a second table with each element's deviation from the mean.

b. Find the mean absolute deviation and the mean squared deviation for the 16 sums.

c. Which is larger, the mean absolute deviation or the standard deviation?

13. **What's Wrong Here?** Dani thinks that adding deviations is useful.

Dani: Why do we have to do absolute value or squaring? It seems like we should be able to just find the deviations from the mean, then add them up. Done, and done.

Make an argument to convince Dani that adding the deviations is not a helpful calculation.

14. Find the mean, mean absolute deviation, variance, and standard deviation for the data set {1, 2, 3, 4, 5, 6, 7, 8, 9, 10}.

15. **Take It Further** In terms of n, find formulas for the mean, mean absolute deviation, variance, and standard deviation for the data set {1, 2, 3 …, n}.

For additional practice, go to **Web Code:** bga-0707

16. **Standardized Test Prep** The table shows the frequency of each score possible in a game. Find the (mean, variance) for the score.

Score	Frequency
−5	2
0	1
1	2
2	1

A. $\left(-\frac{1}{3}, \frac{10}{3}\right)$ **B.** $\left(-\frac{1}{3}, \frac{25}{3}\right)$

C. $\left(-1, \frac{10}{3}\right)$ **D.** $\left(-1, \frac{25}{3}\right)$

Maintain Your Skills

17. Find the variance for each data set.

a. {1, 1, 1, 2, 2, 11}   **b.** {1, 1, 1, 8, 8, 11}

c. {1, 1, 1, 11, 11, 11}   **d.** {1, 1, 1, n, n, 11}

7.8 Adding Variances

You can view two separate experiments as one big experiment. If you do, there is a way to combine information about the two experiments to find the expected value and variance of the one big experiment.

In-Class Experiment

Here are two spinners. One is from the previous lesson, and the other one is a new one.

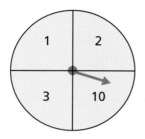
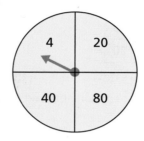

In this game, you spin each spinner once. Let Z be the random variable defined by the sum of the values on the two spinners.

1. Find the mean, mean absolute deviation, mean squared deviation, and root mean squared deviation for the values when spinning each spinner.

2. Use polynomial expansion to quickly find the 16 possible values for the random variable Z.

3. Find the mean, mean absolute deviation, mean squared deviation, and root mean squared deviation for Z.

Remember...

The mean squared deviation and the root mean squared deviation are more commonly called the *variance* and *standard deviation*.

An investment manager adds variances to find the overall risk of an investment portfolio.

Sasha and Derman are working on the In-Class Experiment.

Derman Let's start playing the game.

Sasha Derman! We can't do this by playing. We'd have to play thousands of times. This is about what will happen *on average*.

Derman So, how are we supposed to do that?

Sasha Come on, Derman. You can look back at the last lesson if you've forgotten how to find any of these things.

Derman Alright, I'm going to find the mean for each spinner by averaging. The mean for the first spinner is 4. The mean for the second spinner is 36. So, the mean for Z, when you add them, should be 40.

Sasha That seems like it makes sense.

Derman I'm making a list of the 16 possible results . . . hey, it worked!

Sasha That was a good idea.

Derman Alright, on to the next one. The mean absolute deviation for the first spinner is 3 . . . and for the second spinner is 24 . . . so for Z it should be 27.

Sasha Did you calculate it?

Derman I added 3 and 24.

Sasha Let's just check, I'm not so sure this time. Unfortunately . . . you lose. It's 24, not 27.

Derman What? It worked for the mean, it's supposed to work on everything. Do it again.

Sasha Derman. It's still 24. I think it only works for the mean. Not everything adds like that.

Derman Alright, alright, what about the variance?

Sasha The variance for the first spinner is 12.5. The variance for the second spinner is 808.

Derman So the variance for Z will be 820.5.

Sasha You wish. You can't just add these things.

Derman Au contraire. *I* win. It *is* 820.5. Exactly.

Sasha, baffled, performs the calculation.

Sasha Wow! You're kidding me. I can't believe that worked. Does that always work? That would be amazing. I've gotta see why.

Sasha and Derman suspect that mean and variance are additive.

Problem Find the mean and variance for the sum when tossing two standard number cubes. Compare to the mean and variance for the value from tossing one number cube.

Solution You calculated the mean and variance for one number cube in Lesson 7.7. The mean is 3.5. The variance is $\frac{35}{12} \approx 2.917$.

For the sum of the numbers on two number cubes, expand the polynomial $(x + x^2 + x^3 + x^4 + x^5 + x^6)^2$ or make a table of the 36 outcomes in the sample space, as you did in Investigation 7A.

+	1	2	3	4	5	6
1	2	3	4	5	6	7
2	3	4	5	6	7	8
3	4	5	6	7	8	9
4	5	6	7	8	9	10
5	6	7	8	9	10	11
6	7	8	9	10	11	12

Determine the expected value by building a frequency table as in Lesson 7.4.

Sum	Frequency	Product
2	1	2
3	2	6
4	3	12
5	4	20
6	5	30
7	6	42
8	5	40
9	4	36
10	3	30
11	2	22
12	1	12
Total	**36**	**252**

See the TI-Nspire Handbook on p. 704 for help in using a spreadsheet to perform these calculations.

The expected value is $\frac{252}{36} = 7$.

Use a similar table to calculate the mean squared deviation. Here, multiply each squared deviation by the frequency of the outcome.

Sum	Frequency	Deviation $x - \bar{x}$	Deviation^2	Freq · Dev.^{2}
2	1	−5	25	25
3	2	−4	16	32
4	3	−3	9	27
5	4	−2	4	16
6	5	−1	1	5
7	6	0	0	0
8	5	1	1	5
9	4	2	4	16
10	3	3	9	27
11	2	4	16	32
12	1	5	25	25
Total	**36**			**210**

The variance (mean squared deviation) is $\frac{210}{36} = \frac{35}{6} \approx 5.833$.

Note that both the mean and variance for the sums when rolling two number cubes are exactly double the mean and variance for the values of one number cube.

Habits of Mind

Visualize. Think about what the table might look like if it had 36 rows so each outcome had its own line. The result for ways to roll a 4 is multiplied by three, since there are three ways to roll a 4. The result for 11 is multiplied by two, since there are two ways an outcome of 11 can occur.

For You to Do

4. Take a guess at the mean and variance for the sums of the numbers when rolling three number cubes.

Proving It

The proofs that mean and variance add are complicated. Keep this picture in mind for what the combined sample space looks like when the sample spaces of two random variables X and Y are combined:

+	x_1	x_2	...	x_n
y_1	$x_1 + y_1$	$x_2 + y_1$	...	$x_n + y_1$
y_2	$x_1 + y_2$	$x_2 + y_2$	...	$x_n + y_2$
y_3	$x_1 + y_3$	$x_2 + y_3$	...	$x_n + y_3$
$\vdots$	$\vdots$	$\vdots$	$\ddots$	$\vdots$
y_m	$x_1 + y_m$	$x_2 + y_m$	...	$x_n + y_m$

Theorem 7.2

Let Z be the random variable defined by adding the results of independent random variables X and Y. Then

- The expected value, or mean, of Z is the sum of the expected values for X and Y, and

- The variance, or mean squared deviation, of Z is the sum of the variances for X and Y.

Proof First, prove the property for the mean. Let $\bar{x}$ be the mean for X with n outcomes and $\bar{y}$ be the mean for Y with m outcomes. (See the table on page 585.) Of the mn outcomes for Z, each value x_1 through x_n occurs m times, one for each y-pairing. Each value y_1 through y_m occurs n times. So, the mean for random variable Z is as follows.

$$\bar{z} = \frac{m(x_1 + x_2 + \cdots + x_n) + n(y_1 + y_2 + \cdots + y_m)}{mn}$$

$$= \frac{m(x_1 + x_2 + \cdots + x_n)}{mn} + \frac{n(y_1 + y_2 + \cdots + y_m)}{mn}$$

$$= \frac{(x_1 + x_2 + \cdots + x_n)}{n} + \frac{(y_1 + y_2 + \cdots + y_m)}{m}$$

$$= \bar{x} + \bar{y}$$

The proof for the variance uses the machine formula from Lesson 7.7. You want to show that $V(Z) = V(X) + V(Y)$. But the machine formula states that the variance is the mean of the squares less the square of the means. So, the goal is to show that

$$\overline{z^2} - \bar{z}^2 = \left(\overline{x^2} - \bar{x}^2\right) + \left(\overline{y^2} - \bar{y}^2\right)$$

Rewrite $\bar{z}$ as $\bar{x} + \bar{y}$ and expand. The left side becomes

$$\overline{z^2} - \bar{z}^2 = \overline{z^2} - (\bar{x} + \bar{y})^2$$

$$= \overline{z^2} - \left(\bar{x}^2 + 2\bar{x} \cdot \bar{y} + \bar{y}^2\right)$$

Think about how to calculate $\overline{z^2}$. First square each possible value of Z. Then add the squares and divide by mn at the end. Each value of Z is of the form $x_i + y_j$ for some i and j, so its square is $x_i^2 + 2x_iy_j + y_j^2$. Think about how many times each number appears. The number of terms is mn. Each x_i^2 appears m times, each y_j^2 appears n times, and every possible pair of x_iy_j occurs once. So,

$$\overline{z^2} = \frac{m\left(\sum_i x_i^2\right) + n\left(\sum_j y_j^2\right) + 2\sum_i \sum_j x_iy_j}{mn}$$

$$= \frac{\sum_i x_i^2}{n} + \frac{\sum_j y_j^2}{m} + 2\frac{\sum_i \sum_j x_iy_j}{mn}$$

$$= \overline{x^2} + \overline{y^2} + 2\overline{xy}$$

$$\overline{z^2} - \overline{z}^2 = \overline{x^2} + \overline{y^2} + 2\overline{xy} - \overline{x}^2 - 2\overline{x} \cdot \overline{y} - \overline{y}^2$$
$$= \left(\overline{x^2} + \overline{x}^2\right) + \left(\overline{y^2} - \overline{y}^2\right) + 2\overline{xy} - 2\overline{x} \cdot \overline{y}$$
$$= V(X) + V(Y) + 2\overline{xy} - 2\overline{x} \cdot \overline{y}$$

This is very close to what you want to show. However, you still need to show that $\overline{xy} = \overline{x} \cdot \overline{y}$ (the mean of the product is the product of the means). This is true whenever X and Y are independent random variables. The proof of this fact is left as Exercise 14. Once this is known, the proof is complete: the variance of Z is the sum of the variances of X and Y.

Exercises Practicing Habits of Mind

Check Your Understanding

1. **a.** Use a polynomial power to write a frequency table for the sums when rolling three number cubes.

   b. Find the mean for the sums when rolling three number cubes.

   c. Using the mean, find the variance and standard deviation for the sums when rolling three number cubes.

   d. How many times as large is the variance for the sums for three number cubes than the variance for one number cube?

   e. How many times as large is the standard deviation for the sums for three number cubes than the standard deviation for the values from rolling one number cube?

2. Find the mean, variance, and standard deviation for the values when spinning each spinner.

   a. Spinner A

   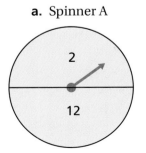

   b. Spinner B

   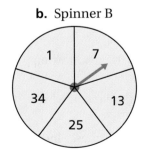

   c. Spinner C

   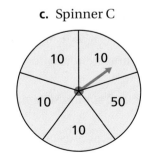

3. Consider spinners A and B from Exercise 2. Let X be the random variable defined as the sum of the values when spinning A and B once each.

   a. Build a table of the 10 possible values of X.

   b. Find the mean, variance, and standard deviation of X.

4. Consider spinners B and C from Exercise 2. Let Y be the random variable defined as the sum of the values when spinning B and C once each.

   a. Build a table of the 25 possible outcomes, and the value of Y for each.

   b. Find the mean, variance, and standard deviation for Y.

5. Suppose the values on Spinner D have standard deviation 8. Also, the values on Spinner E have standard deviation 15. Let Z be the random variable defined as the sum of the values when spinning D and E once each. What is the standard deviation for Z?

> **Remember...**
> Recall how variance is related to standard deviation.

6. a. Calculate the mean absolute deviation for each spinner A, B, and C in Exercise 2.

   b. Calculate the mean absolute deviation for X, the random variable for the resulting sum of spinning A and B.

   c. Calculate the mean absolute deviation for Y, the random variable for the resulting sum of spinning B and C.

   d. What pattern, if any, emerges for the mean absolute deviation of the combined spinners?

7. Write About It The additive property of variance is sometimes called the "Pythagorean Theorem of Statistics." Why do you suppose this is, in light of the results from Exercises 3 through 5?

On Your Own

8. Consider two number cubes with different numbers on their faces:

   Cube 1: 1, 2, 2, 3, 3, 4

   Cube 2: 1, 3, 4, 5, 6, 8

   a. Find the mean, variance, and standard deviation for the result when rolling Cube 1 once.

   b. Find the mean, variance, and standard deviation for the result when rolling Cube 2 once.

   c. If you roll both number cubes at once, there are 36 outcomes. Find the mean, variance, and standard deviation for the sum when rolling the two number cubes.

9. Here is an experiment: Roll a standard number cube. Spin Spinner A from Exercise 2. Then, add the numbers that result.

Find the mean, variance, and standard deviation for each of the 12 possible outcomes.

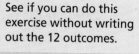

See if you can do this exercise without writing out the 12 outcomes.

10. **Take It Further** Kevin is challenged to roll a sum of 15 from standard number cubes. He can choose how many number cubes to roll. How many number cubes gives Kevin the best chance of rolling a sum of 15?

11. **What's Wrong Here?** Cayle looked at the data from Exercise 12 in Lesson 7.7:

+	1	2	3	10
1	2	3	4	11
2	3	4	5	12
3	4	5	6	13
10	11	12	13	20

Cayle: I know this data comes from two spins of that fish wheel with 1, 2, 3, 10 on it. And I know the standard deviation for one spin is about 3.54. So, the standard deviation for two spins should be 3.54 + 3.54, just over 7. But I am *not* getting that answer! I've checked it three times.

Explain what went wrong here, and how the correct standard deviation could be calculated.

12. Jane is designing a game of chance for her school's Random Fair. It costs 50 cents to play Jane's game. The player flips a coin. Then the player rolls a number cube. If the player gets heads on the coin flip, the number cube result is multiplied by 20 cents. That money is the prize. If the player gets tails on the coin flip, though, the number cube result is multiplied by 5 cents. Although everyone takes away some money, most people do not make back the price of the game.

a. List the sample space for Jane's game as a set of equally likely outcomes.

b. Calculate the expected value for Jane's game. Will Jane's game make money for the fair over time?

c. Calculate the variance and standard deviation for Jane's game.

d. **What's Wrong Here?** Jane wants to check her variance calculation by computing it two ways. In the first way, she uses the data and the machine formula. In the second way, she adds the variance for one coin flip to the variance for one number cube roll. The two methods do not give the same result. Where did Jane go wrong?

For additional practice, go to **Web Code:** bga-0708

13. The variance for one spin of the Wheel of Fish with the numbers 1, 2, 3, and 10 is 12.5.

 a. Calculate the variance and standard deviation for the sum of two spins.

 b. Calculate the variance and standard deviation for the sum of three spins.

 c. Verify that your answers to part (b) are correct by calculating the sum of three spins for all 64 outcomes, then calculating the variance for the data.

14. Consider the following table for the product of independent random variables X and Y.

$\cdot$	x_1	x_2	$\dots$	x_n
y_1	$x_1 \cdot y_1$	$x_2 \cdot y_1$	$\dots$	$x_n \cdot y_1$
y_2	$x_1 \cdot y_2$	$x_2 \cdot y_2$	$\dots$	$x_n \cdot y_2$
y_3	$x_1 \cdot y_3$	$x_2 \cdot y_3$	$\dots$	$x_n \cdot y_3$
$\vdots$	$\vdots$	$\vdots$	$\ddots$	$\vdots$
y_m	$x_1 \cdot y_m$	$x_2 \cdot y_m$	$\dots$	$x_n \cdot y_m$

Show that the mean of the products is the product of the means for the original random variables. That is,

$$\overline{xy} = \overline{x} \cdot \overline{y}$$

This completes the proof given in the lesson.

15. **Standardized Test Prep** For a random positive integer less than 1001, what is the probability that the number is neither divisible by 2 nor 5?

 A. 0.1 **B.** 0.4 **C.** 0.5 **D.** 0.6

Maintain Your Skills

16. Suppose you are to pick an integer at random. Find the probability of each event.

 a. The number is not divisible by 2.

 b. The number is not divisible by 5.

 c. The number is neither divisible by 2 nor 5.

 d. The number is divisible by 2 or 5 (or both).

17. Suppose you are to pick an integer at random. Find the probability that it is divisible by 4 or 13 (or both).

18. **Take It Further** Find some other values of p and q so that $\frac{p}{q}$ is the probability that an integer chosen at random is divisible by p or q (or both).

Repeated Experiments

Suppose you define a random variable Z as the sum of two independent random variables X and Y. In the previous lesson, you learned that the mean and variance of Z are the sum of the means and variances of X and Y. This knowledge can help you quickly calculate important statistics, especially the standard deviation for many consecutive trials of the same kind of experiment.

For Discussion

1. Suppose you flip 100 coins. What is the average number of heads you would expect? Would 40 heads seem reasonable? What about 65 heads?

In-Class Experiment

2. Flip 100 coins and count the total number of heads. Record your data along with all other data the class collects. What percent of the data was between 40 and 60 heads, inclusive? between 45 and 55 heads?

In Exercise 9 in Lesson 7.7 you found the mean, variance, and standard deviation for one coin flip. Recall for that experiment, a head counts as 1. A tail counts as 0. The mean is $\frac{1}{2}$, the variance is $\frac{1}{4}$, and the standard deviation is $\sqrt{\frac{1}{4}} = \frac{1}{2}$.

For two coin flips, there are four possible outcomes: HH, HT, TH, and TT. The mean number of heads is 1, which is twice the mean for one coin flip. This table calculates the variance:

> Here, "HT" means that the first flip is heads, and the second flip is tails. HT and TH are two different outcomes.

Outcome	Number of Heads	Deviation	Deviation²
HH	2	1	1
HT	1	0	0
TH	1	0	0
TT	0	−1	1
4 outcomes			2

The variance is $\frac{2}{4} = \frac{1}{2}$, which is twice the variance for one coin flip. The standard deviation is the square root of the variance, so it is $\sqrt{\frac{1}{2}} = \frac{\sqrt{2}}{2} \approx 0.707$.

For You to Do

3. Consider three coin flips, with eight possible outcomes. Verify that the variance of the number of heads is exactly $\frac{3}{4}$.

Each coin flip adds $\frac{1}{2}$ to the mean number of heads tossed, and $\frac{1}{4}$ to the variance. The additive rules for mean and variance give these results for the number of heads in n coin flips:

$$\text{mean: } \tfrac{1}{2}n$$

$$\text{variance: } \tfrac{1}{4}n$$

$$\text{standard deviation: } \sqrt{\tfrac{1}{4}n} = \tfrac{1}{2}\sqrt{n}$$

In Lesson 7.7, you learned that most data will be within one standard deviation of the mean.

For 100 coin flips, the standard deviation for the number of heads is $\frac{1}{2}\sqrt{100} = 5$. Most of the time you flip 100 coins, the number of heads will be between 45 and 55, one standard deviation away from the mean.

In a theoretical statistics course, you would prove that most of the data will be within one standard deviation of the mean. For now, your experiments should be enough.

> Did most of your class flip between 45 and 55 heads in the In-Class Experiment? Did everyone?

The fact that mean and variance add can help you make similar observations about other repeated experiments. While most data will fall within one standard deviation of the mean, results outside this interval are likely.

Two Kinds of Probability

As you learned in Investigation 7A, the probability of an event is the number of outcomes in that event, divided by the total number of outcomes in the sample space. This is known as **theoretical probability.** You use this kind of probability when the properties of an experiment are clear.

But many probability questions are not clear-cut. What is the probability that it will rain tomorrow? What is the probability that Teri will make her next free throw? In many cases where randomness is present, you have no way to determine the exact properties of the experiment. In these situations, experimental probability is all you can compute.

The **experimental probability** of an event is the number of times the event occurred, divided by the number of trials. If Teri has made 37 of 50 free throws, the experimental probability is $\frac{37}{50} = 0.74$. You might say that Teri has a 74% chance of making her next free throw. Experimental probability is more prone to change than theoretical probability. Maybe Teri had especially good or bad luck on her 50 shots. The greater the number of trials, the more accurate an experimental probability becomes.

For exploration of theoretical and experimental probability, go to **Web Code: bge-9031**

Make connections. The result of a random experiment is rarely exactly equal to the expected value. If you flip 100 coins, getting exactly 50 heads is pretty unlikely. But the properties of mean and standard deviation can explain an important concept. Over time, experimental probability will come closer and closer to theoretical probability.

As the number of trials grows, the mean and standard deviation are both growing, because the mean and the variance (the square of the standard deviation) are additive. But the mean grows by the factor n. Also, the standard deviation grows by the factor $\sqrt{n}$. This means that the ratio

$$\frac{\text{standard deviation}}{\text{mean}}$$

gets smaller as n grows. Consider 100 coin flips. The mean number of heads is 50. The standard deviation is 5 heads. Most of the time you flip 100 coins, the results will fall between $50 - 5 = 45$ and $50 + 5 = 55$ heads.

Now consider 2500 coin flips. The mean number of heads is 1250, and the standard deviation is 25 heads. Most of the time when you flip 2500 coins, the results will fall between $1250 - 25 = 1225$ and $1250 + 25 = 1275$ heads.

The spread is widening, but only when you consider the number of heads. If you consider the ratio of heads, the spread is narrowing. Most of the time you flip 100 coins, the ratio of heads will be between 0.45 and 0.55. But for 2500 flips, this spread narrows:

$$\frac{1225}{2500} \le \text{ratio of heads} \le \frac{1275}{2500}$$

$$0.49 \le \text{ratio of heads} \le 0.51$$

So most of the time you flip 2500 coins, you will get between 49% and 51% heads. If you continue to increase the number of coin flips, you can get the numbers as close to 50% as you like.

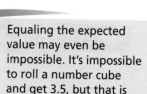

Equaling the expected value may even be impossible. It's impossible to roll a number cube and get 3.5, but that is the expected value.

Habits of Mind

Make strategic choices. Why is 2500 flips a better choice here than 1000?

For You to Do

4. What is the mean and standard deviation for the number of heads in 10,000 coin flips? Most of the time, the percentage of heads would be within what range?

Exercises *Practicing Habits of Mind*

Check Your Understanding

1. Avery answers one multiple-choice question with five options. He guesses. He scores a 1 if he is right, a 0 if he is wrong. Find the mean, variance, and standard deviation for the score on one question.

2. Avery answers two multiple-choice questions, still five options, still guessing.

   a. What is the probability that Avery scores a 2? a 1? a 0?

   b. Find the mean, variance, and standard deviation for the score on two questions.

3. Find the mean, variance, and standard deviation for the score on three multiple-choice questions with five options each.

4. A multiple-choice test has 20 questions, each with five options. Find the mean, variance, and standard deviation for the score on all 20 questions.

5. Find the variance and standard deviation for the number of heads when flipping each of the following.

   a. one coin   b. two coins

   c. four coins   d. nine coins

   e. 100 coins

6. You flip a coin 36 times. The result is 10 heads and 26 tails.

   a. Find the standard deviation for the number of heads tossed when flipping 36 coins.

   b. Is it particularly unusual to get only 10 heads? Use the standard deviation to decide.

   c. **Take It Further** Suppose you are to flip a fair coin 36 times. Find the probability that you get exactly 10 heads and 26 tails.

7. **Take It Further** An experiment has probability of success p.

   a. Find the mean, variance, and standard deviation for the number of successes in one such experiment (in terms of p).

   b. Find the mean, variance and standard deviation for the number of successes in n such experiments (in terms of n and p).

> Check that your answers are correct for $p = \frac{1}{2}$. What if $p = 0$?

8. A spinner has the numbers 25, 50, 75, and 100. Find the variance and standard deviation for the sum of each number of spins.

    a. one spin   **b.** two spins   **c.** four spins   **d.** 100 spins

9. Find the variance and standard deviation for the number of sixes you get when rolling each number of number cubes.

    a. one number cube   **b.** two number cubes

    c. four number cubes   **d.** nine number cubes

    e. n number cubes

10. You roll a number cube 50 times. The sum of the rolls is 165. Is this a particularly unusual result? Use the standard deviation to decide.

11. **Take It Further**

    a. You are to roll n number cubes and count the number of sixes. Find the smallest integer n so that the standard deviation is an integer.

    b. You are to roll n number cubes and sum the results. Find the smallest positive integer n so that the standard deviation is an integer.

12. A board game has a spinner with numbers 1 to 10.

    a. Find the mean and standard deviation when spinning this spinner 100 times.

    b. Would it be unlikely for you to get a total of 600 in 100 spins? Explain.

13. **Write About It** In a new promotion, 100 people will spin the Wheel of Fish for prizes. The manager of the market is hoping that no more than 500 fish will be given away. Is this a likely outcome? Use the standard deviation to decide.

14. **Standardized Test Prep** For each play of a game, the mean is 1 and the standard deviation is 1. Which of the following pairs of numbers represents the (mean, standard deviation) for 100 plays?

    A. (1, 100)   **B.** (10, 100)   **C.** (100, 1)   **D.** (100, 10)

Go Online
PHSchool.com

For additional practice, go to **Web Code:** bga-0709

Remember...

The Wheel of Fish has the numbers 1, 2, 3, 10 on it. The mean for one spin is 4, and the variance is 12.5.

Maintain Your Skills

15. You are to roll five number cubes. Find the probability that you roll

    a. no sixes.   **b.** exactly one six.

    c. exactly two sixes.   **e.** more than two sixes.

16. Expand $\left(\frac{1}{6}s + \frac{5}{6}n\right)^5$. How can you use this expansion to help answer the questions in Exercise 15?

7.10 Bernoulli Trials

A **Bernoulli trial** is an experiment with two outcomes, *success* and *failure*. You have seen several examples of Bernoulli trials: flipping a coin heads, answering a multiple-choice question correctly, rolling a six. A Bernoulli trial has a probability of success p, so the probability of failure is $1 - p$.

Habits of Mind

Look for a relationship. Why must the probability of failure be $1 - p$?

Example 1

Problem Consider a Bernoulli trial with probability of success $p = 0.2$. In three trials, what is the probability of exactly two successes?

Solution

Method 1 Write out all eight possible outcomes. Determine the probability of each. Then, add the probabilities that have exactly two successes. Use S for success and F for failure.

Outcome	Probability	Product
SSS	$0.2 \cdot 0.2 \cdot 0.2$	0.008
SSF	**$0.2 \cdot 0.2 \cdot 0.8$**	**0.032**
SFS	**$0.2 \cdot 0.8 \cdot 0.2$**	**0.032**
SFF	$0.2 \cdot 0.8 \cdot 0.8$	0.128
FSS	**$0.8 \cdot 0.2 \cdot 0.2$**	**0.032**
FSF	$0.8 \cdot 0.2 \cdot 0.8$	0.128
FFS	$0.8 \cdot 0.8 \cdot 0.2$	0.128
FFF	$0.8 \cdot 0.8 \cdot 0.8$	0.512

The probability is the sum for all the outcomes with exactly two successes: 0.096, or 9.6%.

Method 2 Use combinatorics to identify the number of different outcomes, with exponents that correspond to the number of successes and failures.

For this experiment, there are $\binom{3}{2} = 3$ different orderings for 2 successes and 1 failure. Each success has probability 0.2, while each failure has probability 0.8. The probability for exactly two successes is

$$\binom{3}{2} \cdot (0.2)^2 \cdot (0.8)^1 = 0.096$$

In general, the probability of exactly k successes in n trials for this experiment is given by

$$\binom{n}{k} \cdot (0.2)^k \cdot (0.8)^{n-k}$$

since there are k successes and $(n - k)$ failures.

Some examples of Bernoulli trials with probability of success 0.2: correctly answering a multiple-choice question with 5 choices, spinning a 1 or 2 on a spinner with 1–10, or a baseball player getting a hit.

Method 3 The binomial $(0.2s + 0.8f)$ models one trial. Raising this binomial to the third power gives all the probabilities:

$$(0.2s + 0.8f)^3 = 0.008s^3 + 0.096s^2f + 0.384sf^2 + 0.512f^3$$

The probability of two successes and one failure can be read by looking at the coefficient of the s^2f term. The coefficient is 0.096.

For Discussion

1. Given $p = 0.2$ as in Example 1, find the probability that there will be at least one success in the three trials. Is there more than one way to do this?

Habits of Mind

Make strategic choices. This way, the sum of the values for n trials will be the number of successes.

To calculate the mean and variance for a Bernoulli trial, assign 1 as the value of a success and 0 as the value of a failure. Using the calculation method from Lesson 7.4, find the mean by multiplying each value by its probability. The probability of a success is p. The probability of a failure is $(1 - p)$.

Value	Probability	Product
1 (success)	p	p
0 (failure)	$1 - p$	0
Total		p

The mean for a single Bernoulli trial is the probability of its success. Since the mean is additive, in n trials the expected number of successes will be np. For example, on a 20-question multiple-choice test with 5 choices per question, you would expect (on average) to get 4 out of 20 if you were completely guessing throughout the test.

$n = 20$ and $p = 0.2$, so $np = 4$.

What about variance? Variance is mean squared deviation. Here, the deviation is taken from the mean p. Each squared deviation is multiplied by its probability.

Result	Deviation	Deviation²	Probability	Product
1 (success)	$1 - p$	$(1 - p)^2$	p	$p(1 - p)^2$
0 (failure)	$-p$	p^2	$1 - p$	$p^2(1 - p)$
Total				$p(1 - p)$

This result for variance matches earlier results. For a coin flip, the variance is $0.5(1 - 0.5) = 0.25$. If an outcome is impossible ($p = 0$) or guaranteed ($p = 1$), the variance is zero.

Since variance is additive, in n trials the variance is $np(1 - p)$. As before, the standard deviation is the square root of the variance.

Facts and Notation

Consider a Bernoulli trial with probability of success p. In n trials, the mean, variance, and standard deviation for the number of successes are as follows.

$$\text{mean } \bar{x} = np$$

$$\text{variance } \sigma^2 = np(1 - p)$$

$$\text{standard deviation } \sigma = \sqrt{np(1 - p)}$$

These formulas all rely on the fact that mean and variance are additive.

Habits of Mind

Try a specific case. With $n = 20$ and $p = 0.2$ like a 20-question multiple-choice test, $\bar{x} = 4$ and $\sigma \approx 1.789$. Most people guessing on this test will get between 2 and 6 correct.

Example 2

Problem In a phone poll, 175 people out of 1200 said they were left-handed. Suppose that 10% of the population is left-handed. Is the poll result surprising, or within reasonable limits?

Solution This can be considered a Bernoulli trial with probability $p = 0.1$, tested 1200 times. Calculate the mean and standard deviation for the numbers of people expected to answer that they are left-handed.

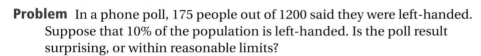

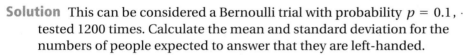

So, most of the time the poll is run, you would expect the result to be within 120 ± 10.39 because most of the data will fall within one standard deviation of the mean. The upper bound here is just over 130. But the actual poll result was 175. This is well outside the expected range, so the poll result is very surprising.

One statistic that can be useful to calculate is the **z-score,** the number of standard deviations away from the mean. For Example 2, the z-score of the phone poll is approximately

$$\frac{175 - 120}{10.39} \approx 5.29$$

Since most data fall within one standard deviation of the mean, a z-score this high is very unusual. It is more than five standard deviations from the mean. This result suggests that the premise that only 10% of people are left-handed might not be correct or that the sample in the poll was not representative of the general population.

Hypothesis testing is a branch of statistics that deals with these types of claims.

Exercises *Practicing Habits of Mind*

Check Your Understanding

1. For Exercise 8 in Lesson 7.1, you guessed the probability of tossing exactly 120 heads and 120 tails on 240 coin flips.

   a. Use the formula given in this lesson to find this probability to four decimal places.

   b. How does your answer compare to the guess you made previously?

2. For Exercise 9 in Lesson 7.1, you guessed the probability of rolling exactly 40 ones on 240 number cubes rolls.

   a. Use the formula given in this lesson to find this probability to four decimal places.

   b. How does your answer compare to the guess you made previously?

3. **a.** Find the mean and standard deviation for the number of sixes you would get when rolling 240 number cubes.

   b. If you rolled 240 number cubes and got only 20 sixes, would that be a surprising result or within reasonable limits?

4. In the Getting Started lesson, you took a 20-question multiple-choice test by guessing. Each answer had probability $p = 0.2$ of being correct.

   a. Explain why the probability of getting all 20 questions correct is $(0.2)^{20}$.

   b. Find the probability of getting all 20 questions wrong.

   c. Use the formula given in this lesson to find the probability of getting exactly 3 questions out of 20 correct.

   d. What percentage of your class actually got exactly 3 questions out of 20 correct?

5. **a.** Write the definition for a function f where the output is the probability of getting exactly n questions correct on the 20-question test from the Getting Started lesson.

   b. Copy and complete the table for n from 0 to 10.

6. Expand the polynomial $(0.2r + 0.8w)^{20}$. Find the coefficient of the r^3w^{17} term. What is its significance?

7. Show algebraically that $p(1 - p)^2 + p^2(1 - p) = p(1 - p)$.

8. **Take It Further** Consider a Bernoulli trial with probability of success p. Build tables similar to the ones on page 597 that show that the mean for the number of successes in two trials is $2p$, and the variance is $2p(1 - p)$.

n	f(n)
0	▦
1	▦
2	▦
3	▦
4	▦
5	▦
6	▦
7	▦
8	▦
9	▦
10	▦

See the TI-Nspire Handbook on p. 704 for information on how to build the table for Exercise 5.

9. Consider two independent Bernoulli trials. The first has probability of success p. The second has probability of success q.

   a. Find the probability that both trials are successful.

   b. Find the probability that neither trial is successful.

   c. Find the probability that exactly one trial is successful.

   d. **Take It Further** Find the mean and variance for the total number of successes for the two Bernoulli trials.

   Here are two carnival games involving number cubes.

Game 1	Call a number, then roll four number cubes. If the sum from the four number cubes is exactly the number you called, you win.
Game 2	Call a number, then roll 72 number cubes. If the number of sixes rolled is exactly the number you called, you win.

10. Make a quick guess: which game is easier to win, and why?

11. What number gives you the best chance to win Game 1. How likely are you to win with this number?

12. What number gives you the best chance to win Game 2. How likely are you to win with this number?

13. **Take It Further** Find the mean and standard deviation for each experiment.

   a. the sum when rolling four number cubes

   b. the number of sixes when rolling 72 number cubes

14. **Standardized Test Prep** For a Bernoulli trial with probability of success p, the variance is $p(1 - p)$. What value of p gives the maximum variance?

   A. $\frac{1}{4}$ **B.** $\frac{1}{2}$ **C.** $\frac{2}{3}$ **D.** 1

Go Online
PHSchool.com

For additional practice, go to **Web Code:** bga-0710

Maintain Your Skills

15. The mean height for an adult woman is 63.5 inches (5 feet $3\frac{1}{2}$ inches), with a standard deviation of 2.5 inches. For each height, calculate the z-score.

   a. 5 feet 6 inches   **b.** 5 feet 1 inch   **c.** 5 feet 8 inches

   d. 6 feet   **e.** 4 feet 11 inches   **f.** 7 feet

   g. x inches

   The z-score may be any real number. It can be positive, negative, or zero.

In this investigation, you calculated variance and standard deviation, which give you some sense of how much your results vary from the average outcome, or expected value, of an experiment. You then tailored these calculations to repeated experiments and Bernoulli trials. The following questions will help you summarize what you have learned.

1. If you guess on a 25-question multiple-choice test with five options, what is the expected number of correct answers? What is the standard deviation?

2. Find the variance for this set: {1, 2, 5, 7, 10, 11}.

3. A number cube has the numbers 1, 2, 2, 3, 3, and 4 on it. Find the mean, variance, and standard deviation for each random variable.

    a. the value of one roll of this number cube

    b. the sum of two rolls of this number cube

4. Find the mean and standard deviation for the number of successes in 600 Bernoulli trials with probability of success $p = 0.3$.

5. You are to roll 15 number cubes. Find the probability of getting no more than two sixes.

6. How can you calculate the standard deviation for a large set of data?

7. What happens to the mean, variance, and standard deviation if an experiment is repeated a second time?

8. What is the mean and standard deviation for the number of heads on 400 coin flips?

Vocabulary and Notation

In this investigation, you learned these terms and symbols. Make sure you understand what each one means and how to use it.

- Bernoulli trial
- experimental probability
- mean absolute deviation
- mean squared deviation, or variance, σ^2
- root mean squared deviation, or standard deviation, σ
- spread
- theoretical probability
- z-score

Investigation 7C

The Normal Distribution

In *The Normal Distribution*, you will learn that if you repeat an experiment a large number of times, the graph of the average outcomes is approximately the shape of a bell curve. You will understand Central Limit Theorem, one of the central theorems of statistics.

By the end of this investigation, you will be able to answer questions like these.

1. What is the Central Limit Theorem?

2. Why is the normal distribution so common?

3. What is the probability of rolling 10% or fewer sixes if you roll 1000 number cubes?

You will learn how to:

- make a probability histogram

- write an equation for a normal distribution given its mean and standard deviation

- use an appropriate normal distribution to find approximate probabilities

You will develop these habits and skills:

- Visualize the effect on a probability histogram of increasing the number of trials.

- Understand the consequences of the Central Limit Theorem and apply it correctly.

- Interpret and solve probability questions using appropriate normal distributions.

By design, the Empire State Building is a lightning rod. It is struck by lightning about 100 times a year. Some years lightning will strike the building fewer times and other years it will strike the building more times. The distribution of the number of lightning strikes to the building per year follows a bell curve.

A **probability histogram** is similar to a regular histogram, except each bar height (and area) is the probability of achieving each result, instead of the frequency of the result. For example, here is the probability histogram for the number of heads when tossing three coins:

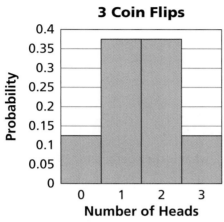

3 Coin Flips

Probability / Number of Heads

The probability of getting 1 head in 3 tosses is $\frac{3}{8} = 0.375$, so that is the height and area of the bar in the histogram. What is the probability of getting at least 1 head in 3 tosses?

Probability histograms look the same as frequency histograms, but the height of each bar must be between 0 and 1. The sum of all bars' heights (and areas) is exactly 1.

For You to Explore

1. In Exercise 1 on page 552, you made a frequency histogram for the distribution of sums when rolling four number cubes.

   Copy the diagram below. Make a probability histogram for the distribution of sums when rolling four number cubes. For example, the probability of rolling a sum of exactly 17 is $\frac{104}{1296} \approx 0.0802$.

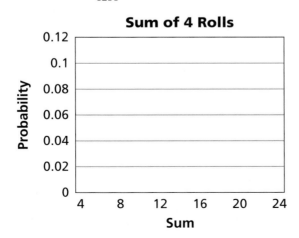

Sum of 4 Rolls

Probability / Sum

The least possible sum is 4. The greatest is 24.

2. When flipping 10 coins, there are 1024 possible outcomes.

Copy the diagram below. Make a probability histogram for the distribution of the number of heads when flipping 10 coins. For example, the probability of flipping exactly 2 heads is $\frac{45}{1024} \approx 0.0439$.

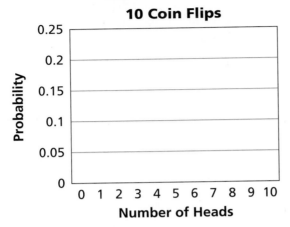

3. When the expression $(0.2r + 0.8w)^{20}$ is expanded, what is the coefficient of the $r^2 w^{18}$ term? What might this coefficient signify?

4. A multiple-choice test has 20 questions, each question with five options. Only one option is correct.

Copy the diagram below. Make a probability histogram for the distribution of the number of questions you would get correct by guessing at random. For example, the probability of getting all 20 questions wrong is about 0.0115.

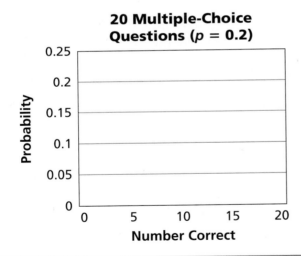

Exercises Practicing Habits of Mind

On Your Own

5. Expand the following polynomial.

$$\left(\tfrac{1}{6}x + \tfrac{1}{6}x^2 + \tfrac{1}{6}x^3 + \tfrac{1}{6}x^4 + \tfrac{1}{6}x^5 + \tfrac{1}{6}x^6\right)^4$$

   a. Find the coefficient of the x^{17} term to four decimal places.

   b. What is the sum of all the coefficients?

6. Build a probability histogram for the number of heads when flipping

   a. two coins.   b. four coins.   c. five coins.

7. Flip ten coins and write down the number of heads that result. Repeat this experiment thirty times and tabulate the results.

   Use a cup. Scoop the 10 coins into the cup, and drop them.

Number of Heads	Frequency
0	▨
1	▨
2	▨
3	▨
4	▨
5	▨
6	▨
7	▨
8	▨
9	▨
10	▨

8. a. Make a probability histogram for your data from Exercise 7.

   b. **Write About It** Compare your probability histogram to the one from Exercise 2. What might explain the differences between the two histograms?

9. The probability that Todd makes a free throw is 0.642. In a game, Todd attempts ten free throws. Assuming each free throw is an independent event, find the probability that Todd makes

   a. exactly 7 out of 10 free throws.

   b. exactly 8 out of 10 free throws.

   c. more than 8 out of 10 free throws.

10. Copy and complete this table for the function

$$f(n) = \binom{10}{n} \cdot (0.642)^n \cdot (0.358)^{10-n}$$

Give each answer to four decimal places.

n	f(n)
0	▧
1	▧
2	▧
3	▧
4	▧
5	▧
6	▧
7	▧
8	▧
9	▧
10	▧

11. When you roll five number cubes, what is the probability of each event?

a. All five number cubes show the same number.

b. All five number cubes show different numbers.

c. **Take It Further** Exactly four number cubes show the same number.

Maintain Your Skills

12. a. When rolling a number cube, there is a 1 in 6 chance of rolling a two. Find the probability, to four decimal places, that you roll the number cube six times and never get a two.

b. The spinner in a board game has numbers from 1 through 10, so there is a 1 in 10 chance of spinning a 2. Find the probability, to four decimal places, that you spin this spinner ten times and never get a 2.

c. When rolling two number cubes, there is a 1 in 36 chance of rolling a sum of two. Find the probability, to four decimal places, that you roll the pair of number cubes 36 times and never get a sum of two.

d. If an experiment with probability of success $\frac{1}{n}$ is run n times, find the probability that none of the n trials will be successful. As n increases, what happens in the long run to this probability?

The Central Limit Theorem

In the Getting Started lesson, you made the probability histogram for several different probability distributions: rolls of a number cube, coin flips, and multiple-choice tests.

A **probability distribution** is a function that assigns a probability to each numeric output of a random variable. For example, if X is the sum of four number cubes, the probability distribution gives $P(X = 17) \approx 0.0802$.

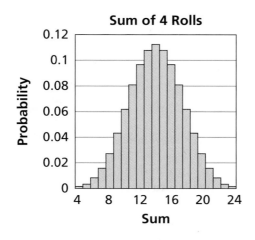

Sum of 4 Rolls

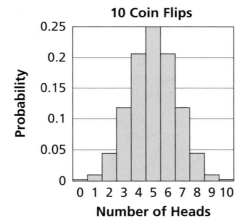

10 Coin Flips

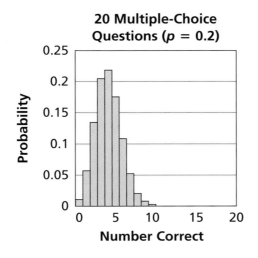

20 Multiple-Choice Questions ($p = 0.2$)

All three are the distributions of sums. The second distribution is the sum of 1's and 0's for the heads and tails of the flips. The third is the sum of 1's and 0's for the right and wrong answers.

For You to Do

1. Use the first probability histogram on the previous page to estimate the probability of rolling higher than 15 as the sum of four number cubes.

All three histograms show very similar shapes, even though the original experiments are quite different from one another. The same "bell curve" emerges, no matter what you started from. This concept forms the basis of the Central Limit Theorem, which states that the results from repeated trials of an experiment approach a specific distribution: the **normal distribution.**

Minds in Action   episode 25

Derman and Tony are comparing the three histograms shown above.

Derman I don't trust this. Sure, the number cubes picture and the coin picture look similar, but I don't feel like the picture for the multiple-choice questions looks anything like that.

Tony Really? It's a little squished to one side, but that's because the questions aren't 50–50.

Derman Maybe with more questions?

Tony Alright, let's do 50 questions instead of 20.

Derman So . . . the probability of getting *n* questions right on a 50-question test. Each question has a 20% chance of getting it right, 80% chance of getting it wrong.

Tony There was a formula for this in Lesson 7.10. For *k* successes in 50 questions it's going to be

$$\binom{50}{k} \cdot (0.2)^k \cdot (0.8)^{50-k}$$

Derman Nice, but I have to keep entering different *k* values.

Tony Then define it as a function on the calculator. For combinations, use "nCr."

Derman Oh, very nice!

Tony Now I take all these answers and plot them as a histogram. This might take a moment . . .

After some calculating . . .

Tony Check it out.

See the TI-Nspire Handbook on p. 704 for details on programming this function into your calculator.

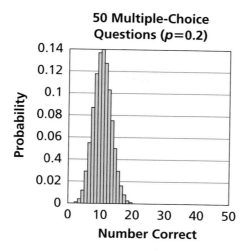

50 Multiple-Choice Questions (p=0.2)

Tony   I probably should've stopped at 20. Looks like it's really hard to get 20 out of 50 by guessing.

Derman   And the mean is 10. That looks a lot more like the others. What if I start from something else, like The Wheel of Fish? It's got 1, 2, 3, and 10 on it. That's a mess, there's no way it's going to look like this picture.

Tony   Use a polynomial. Each number is $\frac{1}{4}$ likely, so the polynomial for one spin is

$$(0.25x + 0.25x^2 + 0.25x^3 + 0.25x^{10})$$

Then raise that to some power. Might need to be a pretty high power to see a curve.

Derman   Cool, I can get all the percentages for 10 spins by raising that to the 10th power and reading off the coefficients. I'll tell you tomorrow how I did. I'm still totally unconvinced.

Tony   Good luck.

The next day ...

Derman   Look at this histogram for the 10 spins!

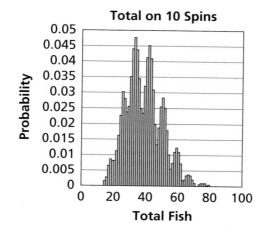

Total on 10 Spins

See the TI-Nspire Hand book on p. 704 for details on how Derman might have made this plot.

Derman It's like there's one big bell curve with the peaks. Then each peak has its own baby bell curve inside it.

Tony Wow, you've really given this a lot of thought.

Derman I know! I wasn't convinced about the overall shape for 10 spins, so I did it all again for 25 spins.

Tony And?

Derman Bam!

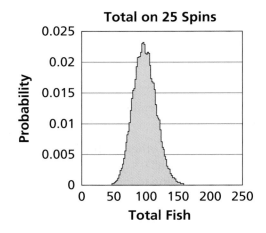

Derman And look where the biggest peak is: right at 100! Which is where it should be. The expected value is 4, times 25 spins.

Tony Hmm. That seems true for all of these. The coin flip peak is at 5 out of 10, the multiple choice peak is at 10 out of 50 . . . neat.

Derman I'm convinced. So when do we learn about this bell curve?

Developing Habits of Mind

Make a model. The histograms shown seem to be taking the shape of a bell curve like this one:

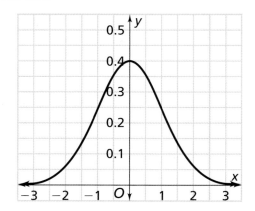

The function that defines this curve is a probability distribution called a *normal distribution*. The graph shows a normal distribution for a random variable with mean 0 and standard deviation 1. By stretching and shifting, you can construct a general normal distribution with any desired mean μ and any standard deviation σ. The notation for such a normal distribution is $N(\mu, \sigma)$.

The normal distribution gives you a close approximation for the behavior of repeated experiments. For example, on 25 spins of the spinner from the dialog, the mean is 100 and the standard deviation is $\sqrt{1250}$, or about 35. The behavior of this experiment can be approximated by $N(100, \sqrt{1250})$.

Similarly, the number of heads on 10 coin flips can be approximated by $N\left(5, \frac{\sqrt{10}}{2}\right)$ since those are the mean and standard deviation for the number of heads on 10 coin flips. Here is the probability histogram for the number of heads on 10 coin flips. It is overlaid with the graph of $N\left(5, \frac{\sqrt{10}}{2}\right)$, the corresponding normal distribution.

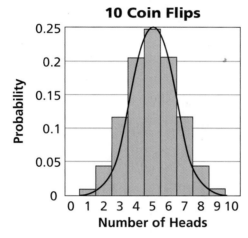

10 Coin Flips

Most calculators have a function for displaying or defining a normal distribution $N(\mu, \sigma)$.

Note that the normal distribution is an approximation of the probability histogram. The normal distribution is pretty accurate. It becomes even more accurate as the number of trials increases. In the end, the normal distribution is a single powerful tool that you can use to answer many different types of questions.

> $P(a \leq X \leq b)$ is the probability that the value of random variable X is between a and b, inclusive. This probability equals the area that is under the curve of the distribution function and is between the two vertical lines $x = a$ and $x = b$.

> See the TI-NSpire Handbook on p. 704 for details on defining normal distributions.

For You to Do

2. Find the mean and standard deviation for the sum when rolling four number cubes. Then use a calculator to display the normal distribution that has this mean and standard deviation.

Here is the Central Limit Theorem. A proof of this theorem is beyond the scope of this book. It would be part of an advanced college course in statistics.

Theorem 7.3   Central Limit Theorem

Let X be a random variable with mean μ and standard deviation σ. The distribution for the sum of the outputs of X over n experiments is more and more closely approximated by $N(\mu n, \sigma\sqrt{n})$ as n grows larger.

Often, people rephrase the Central Limit Theorem in terms of the mean of the results, rather than the sum. The statement is quite similar:

Let X be a random variable with mean μ and standard deviation σ. The distribution for the mean of the outputs of X over n experiments is more and more closely approximated by $N\left(\mu, \frac{\sigma}{\sqrt{n}}\right)$ as n grows larger.

The statement about the mean is interesting, since the standard deviation drops toward zero as n increases. As you perform an experiment many times and look at the average of the results, the observed mean should get closer and closer to the theoretically expected mean. Try rolling 100 number cubes: the average roll should be close to 3.5. Try rolling 1000 number cubes: the average roll should be even closer to 3.5. The same is true for coin flips, for spins, for any repeated experiment.

Exercises *Practicing Habits of Mind*

Check Your Understanding

1. **a.** As a class, compile the data generated from Exercise 7 from Lesson 7.11. Build a probability histogram for the class data.

   b. Write About It Compare the probability histogram for the class data to the theoretical distribution given on page 607.

   c. Take It Further Calculate the mean and standard deviation for the class data. Compare it to the theoretical prediction.

2. In this lesson, you learned that the distribution $N\left(5, \frac{\sqrt{10}}{2}\right)$ closely models the distribution for the number of heads when flipping 10 coins.

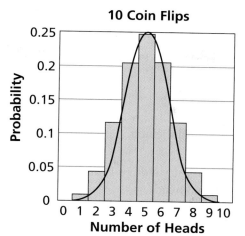

10 Coin Flips

The theoretical distribution has mean 5 and standard deviation $\frac{\sqrt{10}}{2}$.

a. Using a calculator, find the value predicted by the distribution for the probability of flipping exactly 4 heads.

b. Find the actual probability of flipping exactly 4 heads on 10 coin tosses.

c. Find the percent error between the predicted value and the actual probability of flipping 4 heads on 10 coin tosses.

d. Find the percent error between the predicted value and the experimental probability that you found for your class in Exercise 1.

On many calculators, this is normpdf $\left(4, 5, \frac{\sqrt{10}}{2}\right)$. See the TI-Nspire Handbook on p. 704 for more information.

Historical Perspective

The first person to explore the normal distribution was Abraham de Moivre, the same person whose famous theorem appears in Chapter 2 of this book. De Moivre's work is motivated by what he called "Problems of Chance."

> Altho' the Solution of Problems of Chance often require that several Terms of the Binomial $(a + b)^n$ be added together, nevertheless in very high Powers the thing appears so laborious, and of so great a difficulty, that few people have undertaken that Task . . .

De Moivre went on to determine the equation for the normal distribution, and provided some computations. The most well-known of these computations is that for a normal distribution, about 68.3% of data falls within one standard deviation from the mean. He then gives a specific example: 3600 fair "Experiments" (with 50% likelihood).

> Hence $\frac{1}{2}n$ will be 1800, and $\frac{1}{2}\sqrt{n} = 30$, then the Probability of the Event's neither appearing oftner than 1830 times, nor more rarely than 1770, will be 0.682688.

De Moivre goes on to say how his concepts could be used to decide whether a coin was fair: continue flipping it long enough, and the observed probability from its results should come closer and closer to 50–50. If not, the coin must be unfair in some way.

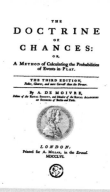

THE
DOCTRINE
OF
CHANCES:
OR,
A METHOD of Calculating the Probabilities of Events in PLAY.

THE THIRD EDITION,

By A. DE MOIVRE,

LONDON:
Printed for A. MILLAR, in the Strand.
MDCCLVI.

3. **a.** Find the mean and standard deviation for the number of heads when flipping 100 coins.

   b. Find the value predicted by the normal distribution for the probability of flipping exactly 43 heads.

   c. Use the Binomial Theorem to find the actual probability of flipping exactly 43 heads.

   d. Find the percent error between the predicted value and the actual probability of flipping exactly 43 heads.

4. De Moivre described the experiment of flipping 3600 coins and counting the number of heads. He said that roughly 68% of the time, the actual number of heads will be within one standard deviation of the mean.

   a. Find the mean and standard deviation for the number of heads when flipping 3600 coins.

   b. If the number of coins was doubled to 7200, what would happen to the mean? the standard deviation?

   c. For 7200 coin flips, find an interval that includes roughly 68% of the data.

5. A spinner has the numbers 1, 1, 2, and 4 on its four wedges.

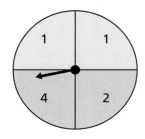

> **Habits of Mind**
>
> **Represent the situation.**
> The polynomial $0.25s^4 + 0.25s^2 + 0.5s$ might be helpful in this exercise.

   Build a probability histogram for each experiment.

   a. one spin of the spinner   **b.** sum of two spins

   c. the sum of three spins   **d.** the sum of four spins

   e. Take It Further the sum of ten spins

6. The Minds in Action dialog in this lesson refers to 25 spins of the Wheel of Fish with the numbers 1, 2, 3, and 10 on it.

   a. Find the mean and standard deviation for the sum of all 25 spins.

   b. Find a range that includes roughly 68% of the data.

> **Remember...**
>
> One spin of the Wheel of Fish has mean 4, variance 12.5, and standard deviation $\sqrt{12.5}$.

7. Suppose you flip 100 coins and count the number of heads.

   a. Using de Moivre's findings, give a range that should include roughly 68% of the data.

   b. Using the Binomial Theorem, find the actual probability that the total number of heads will be in this range.

8. One of de Moivre's other findings is that for experiments that are approximated by a bell curve, roughly 95% of the data falls within two standard deviations of the mean. The range of values within two standard deviations of the mean is the 95% **confidence interval.**

   a. Find a 95% confidence interval for the number of heads when flipping 3600 coins.

   b. Find a 95% confidence interval for the number of heads when flipping 100 coins.

   c. Find a 95% confidence interval for the total in 25 spins of the Wheel of Fish from Exercise 6.

   > If the mean is 100 and the standard deviation is 20, a 95% confidence interval is from 60 to 140. This assumes and requires that the distribution is close to a bell curve.

9. Hannah is a "300 hitter" in softball. She gets a hit on each at-bat with probability $p = 0.3$. Assume each at-bat is an independent Bernoulli trial.

   a. Find the mean and standard deviation for the numbers of hits Hannah gets in 60 at-bats.

   b. For 60 at-bats, find a 95% confidence interval for Hannah's batting average, found by dividing the number of hits by the number of at-bats.

   c. For a full season of 600 at-bats, find a 95% confidence interval for Hannah's batting average.

   > **Habits of Mind**
   >
   > **Use a different process.** You could find a confidence interval for the number of hits, then divide by 60.

10. a. Repeat Exercise 9 for Sally, a "250 hitter" who gets a hit with probability $p = 0.25$.

   b. **Write About It** Describe how your results show that Sally could outhit Hannah over a short time period, but is much less likely to do so for an entire season.

11. Todd makes free throws with probability of success $p = 0.642$.

   a. Find the mean and standard deviation for the number of successes in 100 free throws.

   b. Find a 95% confidence interval for the number of free throws Todd will make in 100 tries.

   c. Use a normal approximation to estimate, to six decimal places, the probability that Todd makes exactly 70 out of 100 free throws.

   d. Use the Binomial Theorem to find, accurate to six decimal places, the probability that Todd makes exactly 70 out of 100 free throws.

Go Online
PHSchool.com

For additional practice, go to **Web Code:** bga-0712

> On a calculator, you might do this using normpdf (70, μ, σ) where μ and σ are the mean and standard deviation you found in part (a).

12. Take It Further Use the Binomial Theorem to find the probability that Todd makes between x and y free throws in 100 tries, where x and y are the ends of the confidence interval you found in Exercise 11.

13. What's Wrong Here? Andrea said she got an unexpected result when thinking about the Central Limit Theorem.

Andrea: It says it should work for just about anything, so I picked a spinner that has 1 through 10 on it. I made a table for two spins and built the probability histogram.

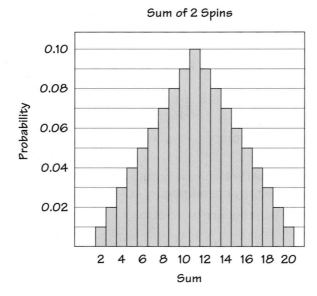

Sum of 2 Spins

But it's a triangle shape. The lesson says this is supposed to look like a bell curve, but to me it doesn't look anything like that.

What would you say to Andrea in this situation to help?

14. Standardized Test Prep A spinner with 12 has the numbers 1–12 in equal wedges. What is the probability that the sum of two spins is 13?

A. $\frac{1}{18}$ **B.** $\frac{1}{13}$ **C.** $\frac{1}{12}$ **D.** $\frac{1}{8}$

Maintain Your Skills

15. A number cube has 1, 2, 3, 4, 5, and 5 on its faces. Build a probability histogram for the sum of the number for each of the following experiments.

     a. two rolls

     b. three rolls

     c. four rolls

Remember...
You can use a polynomial power to help calculate the results.

The Normal Distribution

In Lesson 7.12, you saw the importance of the normal distribution. The heights, weights, and life expectancies of people are (typically) normally distributed. This lesson explores the graphs and properties of the normal distribution.

Each normal distribution is characterized by its mean μ and standard deviation σ. The notation for the distribution is $N(\mu, \sigma)$. The **unit normal distribution** has mean 0 and standard deviation 1.

$$N(0, 1) = \frac{1}{\sqrt{2\pi}} e^{\frac{-x^2}{2}}$$

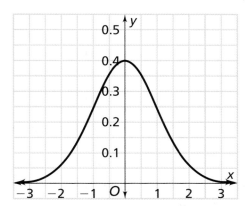

The equation for the normal distribution has the property that the total area between the curve and the x-axis is 1. This is very similar to the probability histograms in the Getting Started lesson where the total area of all the bars is exactly 1. It may help to picture many small-width bars on the above graph, between the curve and the x-axis.

In Chapter 8, you will learn some techniques for estimating an area like this.

Since the total area under the curve is 1, the unit normal distribution measures probability. Other normal distributions are shifted in ways that preserve this total area, so that they too are useful in answering questions about probability.

Consider a normal distribution with mean 0 and standard deviation σ.

$$N(0, \sigma) = \frac{1}{\sigma} \cdot \frac{1}{\sqrt{2\pi}} e^{\frac{-\left(\frac{x}{\sigma}\right)^2}{2}}$$

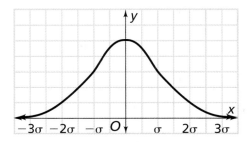

Note that this graph is σ times as wide as the unit normal distribution and x has been replaced by $\frac{x}{\sigma}$. This results in a horizontal stretch (for $\sigma < 1$). But the total area under this curve must still be equal to 1 if it is going to serve as a measure of probability. That means that a corresponding vertical shrink (also by a factor of σ) is done. The factor of $\frac{1}{\sigma}$ in front has this result. So by stretching the curve in the x direction and shrinking it in the y direction, the graph of $N(0, \sigma)$ still has a total area of 1 between its curve and the x-axis.

A horizontal shift of μ units to the right will center this graph at the mean. You can make an equation that has this kind of graph by replacing x in the previous equation by $x - \mu$. This gives you the equation for $N(\mu, \sigma)$, the normal distribution with mean μ and standard deviation σ:

$$N(\mu, \sigma) = \frac{1}{\sigma} \cdot \frac{1}{\sqrt{2\pi}} e^{-\left(\frac{x-\mu}{\sigma}\right)^2 / 2}$$

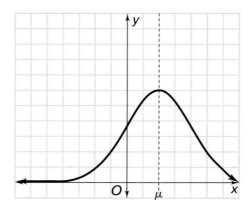

Note that the graph has shifted along the horizontal axis, but the overall shape of the bell curve has not changed.

It is possible to find the area between any two x-values under a normal curve. This graphic shows several important percents:

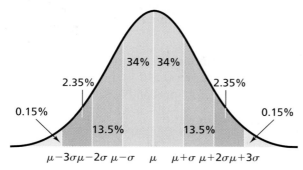

Adding these percents gives the following facts about normal distributions.

Facts and Notation

For a normal distribution, approximately

- **68% of the data lie within one standard deviation of the mean.**

- **95% of the data lie within two standard deviations of the mean.**

- **99.7% of the data lie within three standard deviations of the mean.**

For You to Do

Adult women's heights are normally distributed, with a mean of 63.5 inches and a standard deviation of 2.5 inches.

1. Approximately what percent of women have height between 61 inches and 66 inches?

2. Give a range in which approximately 99.7% of all women's heights should lie.

You can use a calculator to find the area under a normal distribution. On many calculators, the name for the function is normCdf. Its four inputs are the lower and upper boundaries, then the mean and standard deviation of the distribution. The output is a decimal between 0 and 1, giving the area under the curve.

> See the TI-Nspire Handbook p. 704 Appendix for more information.

normCdf (-2, 2, 0, 1) = 0.9545
(the 95% rule)

normCdf (60, 72, 63.5, 2.5) = 0.9189
(the percent of women with height between 5 feet and 6 feet)

Developing Habits of Mind

Explore relationships. There are two functions for working with normal distributions: normPdf and normCdf. Each has a different use.

Use the PDF, short for **probability density function,** when approximating values in a matching histogram. The approximate percentage of women with height 5 feet 5 inches is given by

> Think of this one as the height of the histogram bar at 65 inches. The normal distribution gives an approximation for what the real bar's height should be.

normPdf (65, 63.5, 2.5) = 0.13329

Approximately 13.3% of adult women have a height of 5 feet, 5 inches.

Use the CDF, short for **cumulative density function** to find the area under the normal curve between two values. It gives the percentage of values that fall within a range.

normCdf (60, 65, 63.5, 2.5) = 0.64499

> Think of this one as the total area of all the bars between 60 and 65 inches The normal distribution's CDF gives the total area under the curve in this range, which should be close to the total area of the bars in that range.

Approximately 64.5% of adult women have heights between 5 feet and 5 feet 5 inches.

You will see more about finding the area under a curve in Chapter 8. This concept, called the *integral,* is one of the foundations of calculus. The CDF is the integral of the PDF.

Problem An experiment consists of tossing a coin 10,000 times.

   a. What is the probability of getting *exactly* 5000 heads and 5000 tails?

   b. What is the probability of getting between 4900 and 5100 heads?

Solution

   a. According to the Binomial Theorem, the result should be

$$\binom{10000}{5000}(0.5)^{5000}(0.5)^{5000}$$

Most calculators cannot find the result for the binomial. It is too large a number to hold. So, approximate by using a normal curve. For one coin flip, the mean for the number of heads is $\frac{1}{2}$. The variance is $\frac{1}{4}$. For 10,000 coin flips, the mean is $10{,}000 \cdot \frac{1}{2} = 5000$ and the variance is $10{,}000 \cdot \frac{1}{4} = 2500$. The standard deviation is the square root of the variance, or 50. The 10,000 coin flips are approximated by $N(5000, 50)$.

> You could also use the formulas given in Lesson 7.10.

Use the normPdf function to approximate the probability of getting exactly 5000 heads:

normPdf(5000, 5000, 50) = 0.007979

You have about a 0.8% chance of getting exactly 5000 heads when you flip 10,000 coins.

> The actual value is about 0.00797865, while the normal approximation gives 0.00797885. Extremely close!

   b. Using the standard deviation of 50, 4900 and 5100 are exactly two standard deviations away from the mean of 5000. Apply the 68-95-99.7 rule: you have about a 95% chance of getting between 4900 and 5100 heads when you flip 10,000 coins.

Or you could use normCdf.

normCdf(4900, 5100, 5000, 50) = 0.9545

Exercises *Practicing Habits of Mind*

Check Your Understanding

1. The Intelligence Quotient, or IQ, is a score given as the result of an intelligence test. Adult IQ is normally distributed with mean 100 and standard deviation 15.

   a. About what percentage of adults have IQ between 85 and 115?

   b. About what percentage of adults have IQ between 70 and 130?

   c. About what percentage of adults have IQ above 130?

Go Online PHSchool.com

For more information on normal distribution, go to Web Code: bge-9031

2. Adult men's heights are normally distributed, with a mean of 69 inches and a standard deviation of 3 inches.

   a. Approximately what percent of men have heights between 66 and 72 inches?

   b. Give a range in which approximately 99.7% of all men's heights should lie.

3. **a.** Find the mean and standard deviation for the number of heads when tossing 2500 coins.

   b. Find the approximate probability of getting 49% or fewer heads when tossing 2500 coins.

4. Use the normal CDF to find the approximate probability of getting 49% or fewer heads when tossing each of the following.

   a. 100 coins   **b.** 400 coins   **c.** 900 coins

   d. 2500 coins   **e.** 10,000 coins   **f.** 40,000 coins

   g. 1,000,000 coins

5. Exercise 3 in Lesson 7.10 asked this question:

   > If you rolled 240 number cubes and got only 20 sixes, would that be a surprising result or within reasonable limits?

   Use a normal distribution to approximate the number of sixes when rolling 240 number cubes. Find the approximate probability that the number of sixes recorded is 20 or fewer.

6. **Take It Further** For normally distributed data, the range within two standard deviations of the mean is the 95% confidence interval. However, other confidence intervals can be calculated by changing the number of standard deviations. Determine, to two decimal places, how many standard deviations are needed for each of the following.

   a. 50% confidence interval   **b.** 68% confidence interval

   c. 90% confidence interval   **d.** 99% confidence interval

7. a. Using the values from Exercise 2, find the approximate percent of men with heights between 5 feet and 6 feet.

b. Find the approximate percent of men with height 5 feet 11 inches.

8. Revisit Exercise 13 from Lesson 7.9.

> In a new promotion, 100 people will spin the Wheel of Fish for prizes. The manager of the market is hoping that no more than 500 fish will be given away. Is this a likely outcome?

Use the normal curve's CDF to find the probability that more than 500 fish will be given away by the market.

9. It is believed that 60% of the population is now in favor of Proposition 1338. Suppose a pollster questions 500 people.

a. Find the mean and standard deviation for the number of people (out of 500) who will say they are in favor of Proposition 1338.

b. Find a 95% confidence interval for the percentage of people who will say they are in favor of Proposition 1338.

10. A wider poll of Proposition 1338 involves 2000 people. Find a 95% confidence interval for the percentage of people who will say they are in favor of Proposition 1338.

11. Show that for Bernoulli trials, when the number of trials is multiplied by 4, the 95% confidence interval is twice as wide, but is half as wide if expressing the proportion of observed successes.

12. When tossing 240 coins, find the probability that the number of heads will be between 115 and 125, inclusive.

13. Standardized Test Prep In an experiment, you are to toss 100 coins and record the proportion that land heads. What is the standard deviation of the experiment?

A. 0.025   **B.** 0.05   **C.** 0.1   **D.** 0.25

The Wheel of Fish has the values 1, 2, 3, and 10 on it. One spin has mean 4 and variance 12.5.

For additional practice, go to **Web Code:** bga-0713

Maintain Your Skills

14. A number cube has the faces 1, 3, 4, 5, 6, and 8. Build a probability histogram for the sum of the rolls in each experiment.

a. two rolls   **b.** three rolls   **c.** four rolls

Remember...

You can use a polynomial power to help calculate the results.

In this investigation, you learned about the normal distribution, $N(\mu, \sigma)$, a function that approximates the average outcomes of a large number of repeated experiments. People call it a bell curve because of the shape of its graph. The following questions will help you summarize what you have learned.

1. Make a probability histogram for the number of heads when flipping eight coins.

2. A number cube has the numbers 1, 2, 2, 3, 3, and 4 on it. Find a 95% confidence interval for the sum when rolling this number cube 132 times.

3. Give some examples of situations where a normal distribution could apply. Give some examples of where a normal distribution could not apply.

4. Approximate the probability of getting between 190 and 210 heads when flipping 400 coins.

5. Todd shoots free throws with a probability of success $p = 0.642$. In a season, Todd shoots 164 free throws. Use the normal approximation to find the probability that Todd makes at least 110 free throws in a season.

6. Approximately what percentage of women's heights are between 5 feet 3 inches and 5 feet 9 inches? Recall the mean of women's heights is 63.5 inches. The standard deviation is 2.5 inches.

7. What is the Central Limit Theorem?

8. Why is the normal distribution so common?

9. What is the probability of rolling 10% or fewer sixes if you roll 1000 number cubes?

Vocabulary and Notation

In this investigation, you learned these terms and symbols. Make sure you understand what each one means and how to use it.

- confidence interval
- cumulative density function
- normal distribution, $N(\mu, \sigma)$
- probability density function
- probability distribution
- probability histogram
- unit normal distribution, $N(0, 1)$

Project: Using Mathematical Habits

Faking the Flips

It is hard to be completely random. This project will ask you to make truly random data, but also to try to make a believable fake.

1. *Fake* the results of flipping a coin 240 times as a sequence of 1's and 0's. Write heads as 1, tails as 0, and make the order of the fake flips clear. Do not use any computer, calculator, or anything that could be used to make the random numbers.

2. Now, *make* the results of flipping a coin 240 times. Write heads as 1, tails as 0, and make the order of the real flips clear. Seriously, make it: flip a coin 240 times and write down the results as a sequence. Use the same format you used when making the fake results so that only you will know which result is real and which is fake.

3. Make a test you could use to decide whether a list someone gives you is real or fake.

4. Exchange lists with a classmate and run your test on their lists. Did your test correctly decide which was real and which was fake?

5. Use your test on each of these seven data sets to decide whether each is real or fake.

a.

```
1 0 0 1 0 1 1 1 1 0 0 0 1 1 0 1 0 0 0 1 0
1 0 1 0 0 0 0 1 1 0 1 0 0 1 0 1 0 0 0 1 1
1 0 1 0 1 1 0 1 0 1 1 0 0 0 1 1 0 1 0 0 0
1 0 0 0 1 0 1 0 0 1 0 1 1 0 0 0 0 1 0 1 1
1 0 0 0 1 0 1 1 0 0 0 1 1 1 1 0 1 0 0 1 1
1 1 1 0 0 1 1 0 0 0 0 1 1 1 1 0 0 1 1 0 0
0 0 1 1 0 0 0 1 1 1 1 0 0 0 1 1 0 1 0 1 0
0 0 0 0 1 0 1 1 0 0 0 1 1 1 1 1 1 0 0 1 0
0 1 0 0 1 1 0 0 1 1 1 0 1 0 1 1 0 0 1 0
0 1 1 0 0 1 1 0 1 0 1 0 1 1 1 0 0 0 1 0 1
1 0 1 0 0 0 1 1 1 1 0 1 0 1 1 0 0 1 1 0
1 0 0 1 1 0 1 0 0 1 1 0 0 1 0 0 1 0 0 1
```

b.

```
0 0 1 0 0 1 0 1 1 0 1 0
0 1 1 1 1 1 0 1 0 0 1 0
0 0 1 1 1 0 1 0 1 1 1 1
0 0 1 1 1 1 1 0 0 0 0 0
0 0 0 0 1 1 0 1 0 0 1 0
0 0 0 1 1 1 1 0 1 1 0 0
0 1 0 0 1 0 0 1 0 0 0 0
1 0 1 0 0 1 0 0 0 0 0 1
0 1 1 0 1 1 1 0 0 1 1 1
1 1 0 1 0 0 1 0 0 0 1 1
1 0 0 1 0 0 1 1 1 1 1 0
1 0 0 1 0 1 0 0 1 1 0 0
1 1 1 0 1 1 1 1 1 1 1 0
1 0 0 1 1 1 1 1 0 1 0 1
0 1 0 0 0 1 1 1 1 1 0 0
0 1 1 1 1 1 1 0 0 0 0 1
1 0 1 0 1 0 0 0 1 1 0 1
1 1 0 0 1 1 0 1 1 0 0 0
1 1 1 0 1 1 0 1 0 0 1 0
1 0 1 0 0 0 0 0 0 1 1 1
```

c.

```
0 0 1 0 0 1 1 0 0 0 1 1 1 1 1 0 1 0 0 1 0 1 1 0
1 1 1 0 0 1 1 0 0 0 1 1 1 0 1 1 0 1 0 1 1 0 0 1
0 1 0 1 1 1 0 1 0 0 1 1 0 1 0 1 0 1 1 0 1 0 0 0
1 0 1 1 0 1 1 0 0 1 1 1 1 1 1 0 0 1 0 1 1 0 1 0
0 0 0 0 0 0 1 0 0 1 0 1 1 0 1 1 0 1 0 0 1 1 1 1
0 1 1 0 1 0 1 1 1 0 1 0 0 0 0 1 0 1 0 1 0 1 0
0 1 0 1 0 1 0 1 0 1 1 1 0 0 0 1 0 0 1 0 1 0 0 0
1 0 0 1 1 1 0 1 1 0 1 0 1 1 0 0 1 0 1 0 0 1 0 1
0 1 0 0 1 0 0 0 1 1 1 0 1 0 0 1 0 1 0 1 0 1 1 1
1 1 0 0 1 0 0 1 1 1 0 0 0 1 0 0 0 0 0 0 1 0 1 1
```

d.

```
0 0 1 0 0 1 0 1 1 0 0 0 1 0 1 0 0 1 1 1 0 1 1 0 0 1 1 0 1 1
0 1 1 1 0 0 1 0 0 1 1 1 0 1 1 0 0 0 1 0 0 1 1 0 0 1 0 0 0 0
0 1 1 1 1 1 0 0 0 0 1 0 0 0 1 1 1 0 1 1 0 0 1 0 1 0 0 1 1 0
0 0 0 0 0 1 1 0 1 0 0 0 1 1 0 1 1 0 0 1 0 1 1 1 0 1 0 0 0 1
1 0 0 1 1 0 1 1 0 0 0 1 0 0 1 0 1 1 1 0 1 0 0 1 0 1 0 0 1 1
1 0 0 1 1 0 1 0 1 1 1 0 1 1 0 0 0 1 1 1 0 0 1 0 1 1 0 1 0 1
0 1 1 0 0 1 1 0 0 1 1 1 0 1 0 1 0 0 1 1 1 1 1 1 0 0 1 0 0 1
0 1 1 1 1 1 1 0 0 0 1 0 0 1 1 0 1 0 0 1 0 0 1 0 1 1 1 0 1 0
```

e.

```
0001  0001  0110  1100  1100  1110
0100  0010  1100  0111  0001  1111
1110  0110  0001  1000  1111  0110
0110  1000  0010  1010  0110  1001
0111  0001  0110  0000  0100  1110
0110  0010  1011  1110  0101  0100
0100  0101  0001  0010  0101  0101
0100  1010  0000  0010  0001  1010
1101  0010  0100  1011  1110  1111
1111  0011  0011  1010  1100  1000
```

g.

```
→
1 1 0 0 0 0 1 0 1 1 0 1
0 0 1 1 1 0 0 1 0 0 0 0
1 1 1 0 0 1 0 0 1 1 1 1
0 0 1 1 0 0 0 1 0 1 1 1
0 1 1 0 0 1 0 0 0 1 1 0
0 1 1 1 1 0 0 1 0 1 1 0
1 0 0 0 0 1 0 1 1 1 1 0
0 1 1 0 0 1 0 0 0 0 1 1
1 0 0 1 0 1 1 1 0 0 0 0
1 1 0 1 0 1 1 1 0 0 1 0
0 0 1 0 0 0 1 1 0 1 0 0
1 1 1 0 1 1 0 0 0 1 1 1
1 1 1 1 0 0 1 0 1 0 0 0
1 1 0 0 1 0 1 1 1 1 0 0
1 0 1 1 0 1 0 0 0 0 1 1
0 1 0 0 0 1 1 0 1 0 0
1 0 1 1 1 0 1 0 0 0 0 0
1 0 1 1 1 0 0 1 0 1 1 1
0 0 1 0 0 0 1 1 0 1 1 1
0 0 1 0 0 0 1 1 0 1 0 0
```

f.

```
1110101100110111111111101
1111111010110100010000000
0100001000001100110000010
0000110100101010101010 1011
1101010111010000010110010
1110000000001011101111101
0110110010001010101010 1001
1000001001110000110111 00
1011010110010011001110 10
1011000101001111001100000
```

6. Using what you have learned from testing real and fake data, construct a more believable fake set of 240 coin flips.

Chapter 7

Review

 Go Online
PHSchool.com

For vocabulary review go
to Web Code: bgj-0751

In **Investigation 7A,** you learned to

- calculate probabilities of simple random events.

- determine a set of equally likely outcomes for a probability experiment.

- find a polynomial to model a probability experiment and interpret expansions of its powers.

- calculate the expected value of a random variable.

The following questions will help you check your understanding.

1. In a game you are to roll a pair of regular octahedrons each with eight faces numbered 1–8.

   a. Write out the sample space for this experiment.

   b. What is the probability of rolling two 5's?

   c. What is the probability of rolling exactly one 5?

   d. What is the probability that the sum of the numbers on the faces is 9?

2. A game spinner has three colors, red, green, and blue. Each is equally likely. Expand $(r + b + g)^3$ to find the probability of getting two reds and one green when you spin three times.

3. A local high school is holding a raffle to raise money for extracurricular activities at the school. They plan to sell 1000 tickets. There will be one prize of $500, 2 prizes of $200, and 5 prizes of $100. What is the expected value of one ticket?

In **Investigation 7B,** you learned to

- calculate expected value, mean absolute deviation, variance, and standard deviation.

- calculate statistics for compound events, including repeated experiments.

- identify Bernoulli trials and compute statistics using the specialized formulas for this case.

The following questions will help you check your understanding.

4. At a recent family reunion, Carla recorded the ages of the ten children, aged 1–9, who were attending. She built the following table:

Age x	Frequency
1	2
2	1
4	3
5	1
7	2
9	1

Calculate each statistic.

   a. the mean

   b. the mean absolute deviation

   c. the variance

   d. the standard deviation

5. Karen and Joe each have a spinner. The numbers on Karen's spinner are 1, 2, 4, and 6. The numbers on Joe's spinner are 3, 5, 7, and 11. They each are to spin and then add the numbers that result. Find the mean, variance, and standard deviation for the 16 possible outcomes.

6. Using Karen's spinner from Exercise 5, find the mean, variance, and standard deviation for the sum of each number of spins.

    a. one spin

    b. four spins

    c. ten spins

    d. 100 spins

7. A local bus company advertises that your bus will be on time 85% of the time. If you are to take the bus 40 days, find the mean, variance, and standard deviation for the number of times the bus will be on time.

In **Investigation 7C,** you learned to

- make a probability histogram.

- write an equation for a normal distribution given its mean and standard deviation.

- use an appropriate normal distribution to find approximate probabilities.

The following questions will help you check your understanding.

8. Consider this experiment: Place four balls labeled with the numbers 1, 1, 2, and 3 in a bag. Draw one ball, record its number and replace it. Draw again, record the number of the ball. Add the two numbers. Make a probability histogram for the sum of the two numbers.

9. Use the container and numbered balls from Exercise 8. Make 10 draws from the container, recording the number, and replacing the ball after each draw. Find a 95% confidence interval for the sum of the 10 numbers.

10. In each at-bat, Jon has a 26% chance of getting a hit. This year, he will have approximately 180 at-bats. Use the normal approximation to find the probability that Jon will have 50 or more hits.

Multiple Choice

1. If you are to toss a coin five times, what is the expected value for the number of tails flipped?

A. 2   **B.** 2.5

C. 3   **D.** 3.5

2. Consider the following two spinners with five equal spaces.

Spinner A: 1, 3, 5, 6, 7
Spinner B: 2, 4, 5, 7, 8

What is the expected value for the sum when you spin the two spinners?

A. 10.2   **B.** 8

C. 5   **D.** 9.6

3. The probability a batter gets a hit is $p = 0.3$. What is the probability that in eight at-bats the batter will get exactly four hits? Round to two decimal places.

A. 0.14   **B.** 0.31

C. 0.01   **D.** 0.25

4. At a local dealership, the average selling prices of new cars are normally distributed. On average a new car sells for $23,000 with a standard deviation of $3500. What percent of cars sell between $25,000 and $30,000? Round to four decimal places.

A. 0.1023   **B.** 0.2157

C. 0.4772   **D.** 0.2615

5. A number cube has the numbers 2, 3, 5, 7, 8, and 11 on its faces. Calculate the mean μ and standard deviation σ for one roll, to three decimal places.

A. $\mu = 7; \sigma = 4.021$

B. $\mu = 6; \sigma = 3.055$

C. $\mu = 7; \sigma = 3.282$

D. $\mu = 6; \sigma = 3.155$

6. A multiple-choice test has 28 questions each with four choices. If you randomly guess, what is the average number of questions you expect to get correct?

A. 4   **B.** 14   **C.** 7   **D.** 10

7. Find a 95% confidence interval for the number of tails when you flip a coin 400 times.

A. (180, 220)   **B.** (190, 210)

C. (195, 205)   **D.** (200, 220)

8. A spinner contains the numbers 1, 1, 2, 2, 4, and 6 in equal wedges. Which polynomial models the sum of three spins?

A. $(x^1 + x^2 + x^4 + x^6)^3$

B. $(2x^1 + 2x^2 + x^4 + x^6)^3$

C. $(x^1 + x^2 + 2x^4 + 2x^6)^3$

D. $(3x^1 + 3x^2 + 3x^4 + 3x^6)^3$

Open Response

9. You play a game where you roll a number cube. Each time you roll a six you win. Round off answers to two decimal places.

a. What is the probability that you never win?

b. What is the probability that you win exactly twice?

c. What is the average number of wins in ten rolls?

10. A game involves rolling a standard number cube and spinning a spinner with the numbers 2, 3, and 5 in equal wedges. Then sum the two results.

a. How many equally-likely outcomes are in this sample space?

b. What is the probability of getting a sum of 7?

c. What is the probability of getting a sum of 12?

11. You have two decks of eight cards. The cards in each deck are labeled one through eight. You pick a card from each deck and find their sum.

    a. Find a polynomial to model the sum.

    b. What is the probability of getting a sum of exactly six?

    c. What is the probability of getting a sum greater than or equal to twelve?

    d. Which sum is most likely to occur?

12. To play a certain lottery, a player chooses five numbers from the numbers 1–50 and then chooses a bonus number from the numbers 1–30.

    a. How many different tickets are possible?

    b. How many ways can a player match three numbers plus the bonus number?

    c. How many ways can a player match two numbers, but not the bonus number?

13. A spinner has the numbers 1, 3, 5, and 7.

    a. Build a probability histogram for the sum of two spins.

    b. In two spins, what sum is most likely?

    c. Build a probability histogram for the sum of four spins.

    d. In four spins, what sum is most likely?

14. In a hockey shootout the probability a player will score a goal is $p = 0.25$. If the player takes 80 shots, find the following.

    a. the mean for the number of goals

    b. the standard deviation for the number of goals scored

    c. the probability that the player will score exactly 16 goals

15. Test scores from an 11th grade class are normally distributed with a mean of 77 and a standard deviation of 3.2.

    a. Approximately what percentage of students received a grade between 80 and 85?

    b. What percent of students received a grade less than 70?

    c. Give a range of scores in which approximately 99.7% of all students' scores should lie.

16. A friend tells you that his password is a five-digit number containing the digits 1, 2, 4, 5, and 8. He then asks you to guess his password.

    a. How many possible passwords are there?

    b. What is the probability that your guess has none of the digits in the correct place?

    c. What is the probability that two of the digits are in the correct place?

    d. What is the probability that you correctly guess his password?

17. A lottery is played by choosing six numbers from the set 1–42, with payouts as shown.

Matches	Frequency	Prize
0 correct	▨	$0
1 correct	▨	$0
2 correct	▨	$2
3 correct	▨	$10
4 correct	▨	$50
5 correct	▨	$20,000
6 correct	▨	$1,000,000

    a. Copy and complete the table.

    b. What is the probability of matching exactly four numbers?

    c. What is the probability of winning the million dollar prize?

    d. Find the expected value of one ticket.

Chapter 8

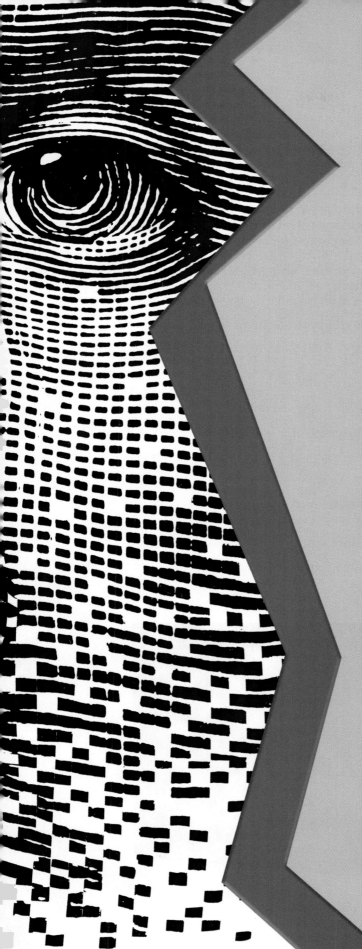

Ideas of Calculus

People have always needed to find the areas of various kinds of regions:

- Commercial builders need to know how much material a roof, wall, or foundation slab will require.

- The designers of a flood control channel need to know the rainfall area that will drain into the channel.

- Rescuers looking for a lost ship or aircraft need to know the size of the search area.

Sometimes, a common geometric formula gives the answer. More often, however, finding an area involves dividing a region into squares or rectangles of known areas that can be added together. Many small rectangles produce a more accurate result than a few large ones do.

With this method, you can do more than just find literal physical areas. Depending on your later studies, you may learn how to use the same basic method to find the following:

- the length of a stretch of road

- the strength of a load-bearing column

- the energy consumption of an appliance, a vehicle, or an entire building

Vocabulary and Notation

- Fermat lower sum, $LF_n[a, b](f(x))$
- Fermat upper sum, $UF_n[a, b](f(x))$
- lower sum, $L_n[a, b](f(x))$
- upper sum, $U_n[a, b](f(x))$
- $S[a, b](f(x))$

Finding Areas of Shapes

You already know how to find areas of lots of shapes. In *Finding Areas of Shapes*, you will look at the problem of finding areas of irregularly-shaped blobs, and you will begin to find areas under curves.

By the end of this investigation, you will be able to answer questions like these.

1. How can you find the area of an irregularly-shaped figure?

2. How can you estimate the area under a curve?

3. What is the area of the region under the graph of $y = x^2$ from $x = 0$ to $x = 1$?

You will learn how to
- estimate the areas of irregularly-shaped objects

- estimate the area under the graph of $y = x^2$ between $x = 0$ and $x = 1$

- calculate the area under the graph of $y = x^2$ between $x = 0$ and $x = 1$ exactly

You will develop these habits and skills:
- Use rectangles to estimate the areas of irregular shapes.

- Use approximation to find areas to any desired level of accuracy.

- Use the formula for the sum of squares to find areas.

By now you know how to find the areas of simple geometric shapes. But how would you find the area of a more complicated shape? How would you find the area of a piece of land with irregular boundaries? No simple formula, like $A = s^2$ or $A = \pi r^2$, will tell you the area of this island.

Activating Prior Knowledge
Exploring New Ideas

You use linear measurements to help you find areas. You can use areas of familiar shapes to help you estimate areas of other shapes.

For You to Explore

1. Copy the two shapes below. Cut them out, and without taking any measurements, decide which has the greater area.

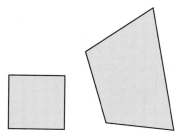

a. How did you compare the areas?   **b.** What properties of area did you use?

c. How accurate is your method?   **d.** Would it work for any two shapes?

2. Now suppose that you are allowed to measure. Then, for instance, you can find the area of a square by just measuring its side length and using the formula for the area of a square $(A = s^2)$.

Thousands of years ago, mathematicians developed formulas for the areas of simple regions, like squares, rectangles, parallelograms, and triangles.

Find the areas of the figures below.

a.

b.

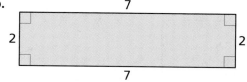

c.

d.

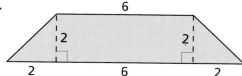

e.

f.

3. Suppose you have geometry software that can display the distance between any two selected points.

    a. Could you use this software to find the area of a square? If so, how? If not, why not?

    b. Could you use this software to find the area of a regular hexagon? If so, how? If not, why not?

    c. Could you use this software to find the area of a circle? If so, how? If not, why not?

4. For each shape, develop a formula for its area, if possible, using only the labeled measurements. Explain how you did it, or why it is not possible.

a.
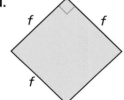

b.
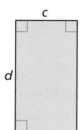

c.
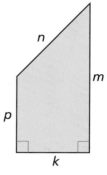

d.
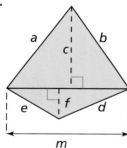

e.

f.
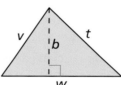

g.

h.
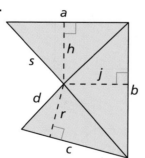

i.
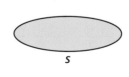

In part (i), *s* is the perimeter of the shape.

5. Write About It The palm of your hand is a nice example of an irregular shape with a curvy boundary.

    a. Think of a way to estimate the area of the palm of your hand.

    b. Explain how you came up with the estimate. How accurate do you think it is?

    c. Do you think your estimate is greater than or less than the actual area of the palm of your hand? Why do you think so?

In Exercises 6–9,

a. graph the function *f*.

Then, for each pair of lines with the given equations, find the area of the region enclosed by the lines, the graph of *f*, and the *x*-axis.

b. $x = 0$ and $x = 1$

c. $x = 0$ and $x = 2$

d. $x = 0$ and $x = 10$

e. $x = 0$ and $x = n$

6. $f(x) = x$

7. $f(x) = 2x$

8. $f(x) = 10x$

9. $f(x) = kx$, $k > 0$

10. How does the area of the region under the graph of $f(x) = kx$ between 0 and *n* compare to the area under the curve $f(x) = x$ between 0 and *n*?

> For shorthand, you may refer to the area in Problem 6b simply as "the area under the curve $y = x$ between 0 and 1."

Exercises Practicing Habits of Mind

On Your Own

11. Find the areas of these regular polygons in terms of *a* and *b*.

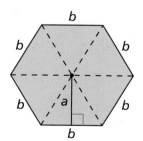
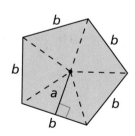

12. Prove that the area of a regular polygon is equal to half the product of its perimeter and the distance from its center to a side: $A = \frac{1}{2}Pa$.

> **Remember...**
>
> *a* is the *apothem*.

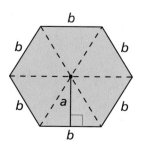

13. Below are two regular polygons with the same perimeters. Which one has the greater area? Why do you think so?

14. Graph the function defined by $f(x) = x + 1$.

a. What is the area of the region under the graph of $y = x + 1$ between 0 and 1?

b. What is the area of the region under the graph of $y = x + 1$ between 0 and 10?

c. What is the area of the region under the graph of $y = x + 1$ between 0 and n ($n \geq 0$)?

d. How does the area of the region under the graph of $y = x + 1$ between 0 and n compare to the area under the graph of $y = x$ between 0 and n ($n \geq 0$)?

Maintain Your Skills

15. Start with a blank sheet of paper.

Step 1 Tear the sheet in half. Put one half on the table in front of you.

Step 2 Tear the piece you are still holding in half on the table. Put one half on top of the piece from Step 1.

Step 3 Tear the piece you are still holding in half. Put one half on top of the piece from Step 1 and Step 2.

Step 4 Continue this process until the piece you are holding is too small to tear.

a. Let the area of the original paper be 1 and A_n the total area in your stack at Step n. Find A_n.

b. What is the area of the piece of paper in your hand at Step n?

8.2 Areas of Blobs

To find the area of any figure made only of straight lines, you can divide it into triangles and find the area of each triangle. But what if you are not dealing just with straight lines? What if you are looking for the area of an irregular shape?

In Problem 5 of Lesson 8.1, you thought about how to find the area of your hand. One common way to estimate areas of irregular figures is to "trap" the areas between inner and outer areas using the squares in a grid. The inner area is the lower approximation, A_{lower}. The outer area is the upper approximation, A_{upper}.

Here is an outline of the palm of a child's hand on a 1-inch grid.

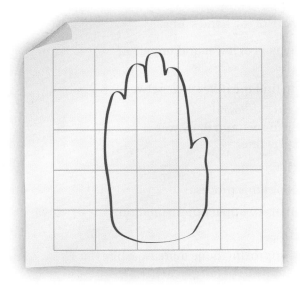

You can count the squares that are completely inside the outline. This gives a lower bound, $A_{lower} = 3$. You can also count the squares that touch the outline anywhere. This gives an upper bound, $A_{upper} = 15$.

Since each of the 1 inch-by-1 inch squares in the grid has an area of 1 square inch, you can also report your result in square inches:

$$A_{lower} = 3 \text{ in.}^2 \text{ and } A_{upper} = 15 \text{ in.}^2$$

So the area of the hand is between 3 in.^{2} and 15 in.^{2}:

$$3 \text{ in.}^2 < \text{area of hand} < 15 \text{ in.}^2$$

An estimate that the area is between 3 in.^{2} and 15 in.^{2} is not very good. How can you get a better estimate?

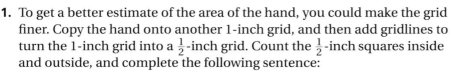

In-Class Experiment

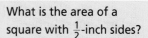

1. To get a better estimate of the area of the hand, you could make the grid finer. Copy the hand onto another 1-inch grid, and then add gridlines to turn the 1-inch grid into a $\frac{1}{2}$-inch grid. Count the $\frac{1}{2}$-inch squares inside and outside, and complete the following sentence:

   ▧ in.^{2} < area of hand < ▧ in.^{2}

   Explain why this grid gives you a better estimate for the area of the hand.

   > What is the area of a square with $\frac{1}{2}$-inch sides?

2. To get an even better estimate for the area of the hand, you could make the grid finer still. On another sheet with the hand on a 1-inch grid, make the grid into a $\frac{1}{4}$-inch grid, count the squares inside and outside, and complete the following sentence:

   ▧ in.^{2} < area of hand < ▧ in.^{2}

   Explain why this grid improves the estimate of the hand's area.

   > What is the area of a square with $\frac{1}{4}$-inch sides?

3. In the lesson so far, you have found three pairs of lower and upper approximations of the area of the hand.

   a. Which squares do you need to count to find the difference between the upper and lower approximations, $A_{\text{upper}} - A_{\text{lower}}$?

   b. Explain why the difference between the upper and the lower approximations decreases as the grid gets finer.

Here are some important observations about this process:

- Every lower approximation is less than every upper approximation.

$$A_{\text{lower}} < A_{\text{upper}}$$

- With successive refinement, the lower approximations increase while the upper approximations decrease.

- The difference between the upper approximations and the lower approximations gets smaller as the grid gets finer.

For Discussion

Here are two ways to get a single numerical estimate for the area of the hand, rather than using upper and lower estimates:

- Average the lower and upper estimates.

- For each square that is not completely inside the hand, estimate the fraction of the square that is inside the hand and add the corresponding fractional area (rather than the whole square's worth) to the running total.

> Using these methods, can you tell whether your estimate of the area is over or under the exact value?

4. Using either or both of these methods, estimate the area of the hand at the beginning of this lesson (use the finest of the grids you have already made).

Check Your Understanding

1. Below is the same hand you saw earlier in this lesson, on the same 1-inch grid, with the fingers spread. Does the area change? Does the perimeter change? Explain your answer.

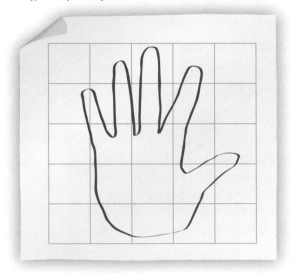

2. How would you estimate the perimeter of the hand in Exercise 1?

3. Trace your own hand on a 1-inch grid like the one you used in class, and answer the following questions. Do not spread your fingers.

    a. How many squares are totally inside your hand?

    b. How many squares touch your hand anywhere?

    c. Complete the mathematical statement.

$$\blacksquare \text{ in.}^2 < \text{area of hand} < \blacksquare \text{ in.}^2$$

    d. Estimate the area of your hand. Explain how you arrived at this estimate.

4. Change the grid used in Exercise 3 from 1-inch to $\frac{1}{2}$-inch.

    a. How many squares are totally inside your hand?

    b. How many squares touch your hand anywhere?

    c. Complete the mathematical statement.

$$\blacksquare \text{ in.}^2 < \text{area of hand} < \blacksquare \text{ in.}^2$$

    d. Estimate the area of your hand. Explain how you arrived at this estimate.

    e. Which grid, 1-inch or $\frac{1}{2}$-inch, is more useful in approximating the area of your hand? Why?

5. Use the upper and lower approximation process to estimate the area of a unit circle.

   a. Draw a circle with a 1-inch radius on a 1-inch grid. Write the upper and the lower approximations of the area. Find the average.

   b. How close to the actual area of the unit circle is the average found in part (a)?

   c. Write the upper and the lower approximations of the area, this time using a $\frac{1}{2}$-inch grid. Find the average.

   d. How close to the actual area is the average found in part (c)?

   e. What size grid would allow you to estimate the area to the nearest hundredth of a square inch? Explain.

On Your Own

6. **Take It Further** The area of a circle with radius r is πr^2, and π is an irrational number. Hippocrates of Chios was one of the first people to show that a figure bounded by curved sides could still have a rational area. One of his examples was the shape below. It is bounded by a quarter circle with radius OB and a half circle with diameter AB. It is called a *lune* because of its resemblance to a crescent moon.

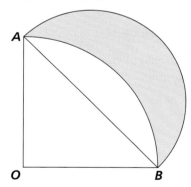

The Lune of Hippocrates

Around 430 B.C. Hippocrates showed that the area of this lune is equal to the area of triangle AOB. To do so, he first showed that the area of the circle with radius OB is twice as big as the area of the circle with diameter AB. (He did not actually find either of these areas.)

Using the area formulas you know, prove that the area of the shaded region is equal to the area of triangle AOB.

7. Suppose you have a strange dartboard, like the one shown.

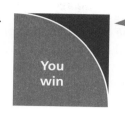

You win if your dart lands in the section of the square below the arc. You lose if it lands in the section of the square above the arc.

Assume that the arc is part of a circle of radius 1.

Suppose you throw darts so they hit the dartboard randomly.

a. In what region is the dart more likely to land? Why?

b. What is the probability of the dart landing in the "You win" region? How do you know?

8. Take It Further Write a computer program to do the following.

For some given number of trials,

- pick a random x value between 0 and 1
- pick a random y value between 0 and 1
- if $x^2 + y^2 < 1$, score a point (it is in the "You win" region of Exercise 7)

Return the total count of points divided by the total number of trials.

a. The output of this "Monte Carlo" program is a number. What does this number represent?

b. You can estimate the area of a quarter of the unit circle using this method. Explain how.

Monte Carlo is a European tourist destination, known for its casinos.

c. Can you tell if the estimate is too big or too small? Explain.

9. Standardized Test Prep An octagon is shown below, drawn on 1-cm graph paper. Using the method of complete squares, which of the following would be the upper approximation of the area of the figure?

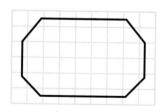

Go Online
PHSchool.com

For additional practice, go to **Web Code:** bga-0802

A. 48 cm^2 **B.** 50 cm^2 **C.** 52 cm^2 **D.** 54 cm^2

Maintain Your Skills

10. Draw a circle of radius 6 inches. Approximate its area using a grid with the following sizes.

a. 1 inch   **b.** $\frac{1}{2}$ inch   **c.** $\frac{1}{4}$ inch   **d.** $\frac{1}{8}$ inch

Describe any patterns you see in your estimates.

Finding the Area Under $y = x^2$

When you are estimating the area of a blob, usually the best you can do is to put an irregular shape on a grid and approximate the area by counting squares to get upper and lower approximations. But if you know the equations of the boundary of your region, you can sometimes use another method to do much better.

For You to Do

Look at the area of the shaded region below the graph of $y = x^2$ from $x = 0$ to $x = 1$. Call this area A.

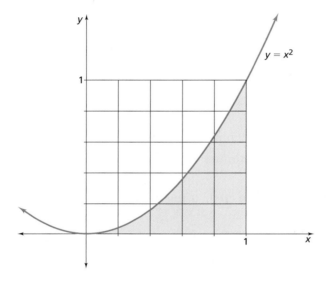

1. Write down a guess for the area of A.

2. Use the "counting squares" method from the previous lesson to estimate the area under the curve between $x = 0$ and $x = 1$. (You will need a couple of graphs of the function $y = x^2$ on graph paper for this problem.)

Sometimes A refers to a region, and sometimes it refers to the area of the region. Watch for context.

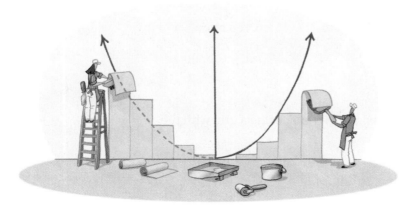

Sasha and Derman are trying to approximate the area under the graph of $y = x^2$ from $x = 0$ to $x = 1$.

Derman   Aren't you getting tired of all this square counting? I get that we keep getting better estimates with smaller and smaller grids, but it's kind of slow!

Sasha   Well, I was thinking that we haven't really used all the information we have. We actually know something about this shape—we can describe it with equations. Look at these pictures:

Sasha draws the following graphs.

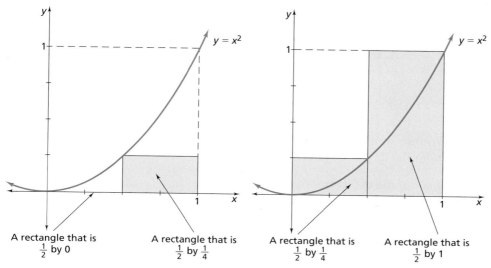

A rectangle that is $\frac{1}{2}$ by 0   A rectangle that is $\frac{1}{2}$ by $\frac{1}{4}$ A rectangle that is $\frac{1}{2}$ by $\frac{1}{4}$ A rectangle that is $\frac{1}{2}$ by 1

Sasha   I'll calculate the lower sum. There are two rectangles, even though we can't see one of them. Its area is zero, and the other rectangle has area $\frac{1}{8}$. The total area is $\frac{1}{8}$.

Derman   Oh sure, take the easy one. For the upper sum, the first rectangle has area $\frac{1}{8}$, and the second has area $\frac{1}{2}$. The total area of both rectangles is $\frac{5}{8}$.

Sasha   So we have trapped the area between $\frac{1}{8}$ and $\frac{5}{8}$. Maybe a good estimate would be the average of the two. Can we do better?

Derman   Oh, no. This is going to be like smaller and smaller grids, isn't it?

Sasha   Well, I'm guessing smaller and smaller intervals, at least.

For Discussion

The pictures below use four rectangles to give better lower and upper sums.

3. Find the lower and upper sums.

4. What is a good estimate for A, based on these sums?

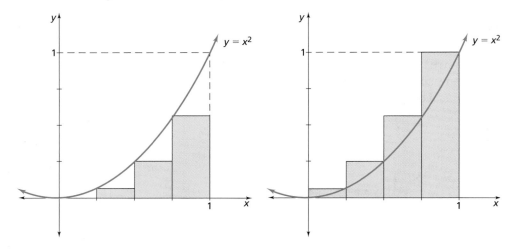

Lower sum   Upper sum

5. Does the average of the lower and upper sums give you an estimate that is too big or too small for the area under the curve? Why?

6. The pictures below say something about the difference between the upper sum and the lower sum.

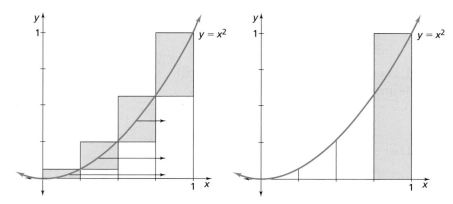

As you divide the interval $[0, 1]$ into more and more pieces (in other words, as you use more and more subdivisions), what happens to the difference between the upper sum and the lower sum? How small can you make that difference? Explain your answer.

> The notation $[0,1]$ means the interval from 0 to 1, including the endpoints.

7. The graph of $y = x^2$ is increasing on the interval $[0, 1]$. How does this relate to the x-values used to set the heights of the lower-sum rectangles? What about the upper-sum rectangles? How would you set the heights of the lower- and upper-sum rectangles for a decreasing function?

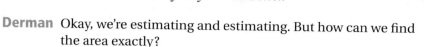
Sasha and Derman wonder if they can do better.

Derman Okay, we're estimating and estimating. But how can we find the area exactly?

Sasha We know that the exact area under the curve is somewhere between the lower sum and the upper sum:

lower sum ≤ *area under the curve* ≤ *upper sum*

Let's use the equation of the curve to write an expression for the upper and lower sums, and maybe we can make some progress.

Here is a handy notation for saying "the upper approximation of the area under the curve $y = x^2$ from $x = 0$ to $x = 1$ with 6 subdivisions."

$$U_6[0, 1](x^2)$$

Example

Problem Calculate $U_6[0, 1](x^2)$, the upper approximation for the area under $y = x^2$ from $x = 0$ to $x = 1$ with 6 subdivisions.

Solution

Start by calculating the areas of each of the 6 rectangles.

	Base	Height	Area
1st rectangle	$\frac{1}{6}$	$\left(\frac{1}{6}\right)^2$	$\frac{1}{6} \times \left(\frac{1}{6}\right)^2 = \frac{1^2}{6^3}$
2nd rectangle	$\frac{1}{6}$	$\left(\frac{2}{6}\right)^2$	$\frac{1}{6} \times \left(\frac{2}{6}\right)^2 = \frac{2^2}{6^3}$
3rd rectangle	$\frac{1}{6}$	$\left(\frac{3}{6}\right)^2$	$\frac{1}{6} \times \left(\frac{3}{6}\right)^2 = \frac{3^2}{6^3}$
4th rectangle	$\frac{1}{6}$	$\left(\frac{4}{6}\right)^2$	$\frac{1}{6} \times \left(\frac{4}{6}\right)^2 = \frac{4^2}{6^3}$
5th rectangle	$\frac{1}{6}$	$\left(\frac{5}{6}\right)^2$	$\frac{1}{6} \times \left(\frac{5}{6}\right)^2 = \frac{5^2}{6^3}$
6th rectangle	$\frac{1}{6}$	$\left(\frac{6}{6}\right)^2$	$\frac{1}{6} \times \left(\frac{6}{6}\right)^2 = \frac{6^2}{6^3}$

To obtain the expression for the upper approximation, add up the areas of all six rectangles:

$$U_6[0, 1](x^2) = \frac{1}{6^3} + \frac{2^2}{6^3} + \frac{3^2}{6^3} + \frac{4^2}{6^3} + \frac{5^2}{6^3} + \frac{6^2}{6^3}$$

$$= \frac{1}{6^3}\left(1^2 + 2^2 + 3^2 + 4^2 + 5^2 + 6^2\right)$$

Here, a formula for the sum of consecutive squares comes in handy.

$$\frac{1}{6^3}\left(1^2 + 2^2 + 3^2 + 4^2 + 5^2 + 6^2\right) = \frac{1}{6^3} \cdot \frac{6 \cdot 7 \cdot 13}{6} \approx 0.4212963$$

> **Remember...**
>
> $$\sum_{k=1}^{n} k^2 = \frac{n(n + 1)(2n + 1)}{6}$$
>
> You obtained this formula in Lesson 5.10, Exercise 5.

For You to Do

8. **a.** Write an expression for $U_7[0, 1](x^2)$, the upper sum with 7 subdivisions. Use a calculator to approximate the value of this expression.

   b. Write an expression for $U_8[0, 1](x^2)$, the upper sum with 8 subdivisions. Use a calculator to approximate the value of this expression.

9. To see how the upper sum changes when the number of subdivisions grows, copy and complete the table.

Upper Sums for Different Numbers of Subdivisions

Number of Subdivisions, n	Upper Sum, $U_n[0, 1](x^2)$	Approximate Value
6	$\frac{1}{6^3}(1^2 + 2^2 + 3^2 + 4^2 + 5^2 + 6^2)$	▓
7	$\frac{1}{7^3}(1^2 + 2^2 + 3^2 + 4^2 + 5^2 + 6^2 + 7^2)$	▓
8	▓	▓
9	▓	▓
⋮	⋮	⋮
15	▓	▓
⋮	⋮	⋮
n	▓	

10. In Problem 9, you obtained the formula for the upper sum if the number of subdivisions is n. Find a closed form for this sum.

Using the closed form you just found, you can simplify the expression for U_n:

$$U_n = \frac{1}{n^3} \cdot \frac{n(n + 1)(2n + 1)}{6}$$

$$= \frac{2n^3 + 3n^2 + n}{6n^3} \qquad \text{Multiply out the numerator.}$$

$$= \frac{2n^3}{6n^3} + \frac{3n^2}{6n^3} + \frac{n}{6n^3} \qquad \text{Break it up into a sum of 3 fractions.}$$

$$= \frac{1}{3} + \frac{1}{2n} + \frac{1}{6n^2} \qquad \text{Reduce.}$$

You can write $U_n[0, 1] (x^2)$ as U_n if the interval and function are clear from the context.

Reason about calculations. What happens to $U_n = \frac{1}{3} + \frac{1}{2n} + \frac{1}{6n^2}$ as n becomes larger and larger?

You can prove that the area under the curve $y = x^2$ between 0 and 1 is not bigger than $\frac{1}{3}$.

Method 1: $U_n[0, 1](x^2) = \frac{1}{3} + \frac{1}{2n} + \frac{1}{6n^2}$. So you can think of U_n as $\frac{1}{3}$ plus something. This "something" term is

$$\frac{1}{2n} + \frac{1}{6n^2}$$

To make U_n a more accurate approximation (closer to A), you choose more and more subdivisions. As you do this, n becomes much, much larger and the "something" term becomes much, much smaller, until it is practically 0. (Check this out for yourself.) This means that the upper sum is getting closer and closer to $\frac{1}{3}$. Since A cannot be greater than any upper sum, A can be no greater than $\frac{1}{3}$.

Method 2: Suppose that A is greater than $\frac{1}{3}$, and see what happens

- If A is greater than $\frac{1}{3}$, it must be greater than $\frac{1}{3}$ by some amount, say, 0.01.
- You can choose n big enough so that the "something" term, $\frac{1}{2n} + \frac{1}{6n^2}$, is less than 0.01.
- The n you just chose makes A greater than an upper sum.

$$A = \frac{1}{3} + 0.01$$
$$> \frac{1}{3} + \frac{1}{2n} + \frac{1}{6n^2}$$
$$= U_n[0, 1](x^2)$$

- However, this cannot be, since A is no greater than any upper sum. So, A cannot be greater than $\frac{1}{3}$.

Can the area be less than $\frac{1}{3}$? Consider the lower sums. Just as for upper sums, you can use a handy notation for "the lower approximation of the area under the curve $y = x^2$ from $x = 0$ to $x = 1$ with 6 subdivisions":

$$L_6[0, 1](x^2)$$

For You to Do

11. Just as you did for upper sums, obtain a closed form for $L_n[0, 1](x^2)$.

12. What number do the lower sums approach as n becomes very large?

13. Show that the actual area cannot be less than $\frac{1}{3}$.

To avoid cumbersome repetition, from now on the expression $S[0, 1](x^2)$ will denote the area under the curve $y = x^2$ between $x = 0$ and $x = 1$.

14. What is the exact value of $S[0, 1](x^2)$? Explain your reasoning.

Minds in Action   episode 28

Sasha and Derman reach their goal.

Derman   Isn't it kind of amazing, Sasha? We got the exact answer as a result of approximating!

Sasha   Well, it took a lot of approximating.

Exercises *Practicing Habits of Mind*

Check Your Understanding

1. Write About It   Write an algorithm so that someone, given the number of subdivisions, could calculate the lower and upper sums for $f(x) = x^2$. It might start like this:

- Divide the interval $[0, 1]$ into the specified number of equal pieces.

- First find the lower sum. On each piece, build a rectangle with that base and height equal to. . . .

2. Take It Further   Turn the algorithm you wrote in Exercise 1 into one or more programs on your graphing calculator or CAS. The programs should take an input n (the number of subdivisions) and output the lower sum, the upper sum, their average, and their difference.

   a. Test your programs with $n = 2, 4$, and 8 to make sure you get the same answers you did with your hand calculations.

   b. Run your program with several other inputs, including 10, 200, and 1000.

   c. How many subdivisions do you need to put the lower approximation within 0.01 of the actual area? Within 0.001? Remember that the actual area is $\frac{1}{3}$.

3. On page 646, you simplified and analyzed the upper sum for the area under the graph of $y = x^2$ between $x = 0$ and $x = 1$. Here is another way to simplify it:

$$\frac{1}{6} \cdot \frac{n(n+1)(2n+1)}{n^3} = \frac{1}{6} \cdot \left(1 + \frac{1}{n}\right) \cdot \left(2 + \frac{1}{n}\right)$$

a. Verify that this equation is an identity.

b. Analyze the final expression to determine what number it approaches when n becomes very large.

4. a. Using the method of Exercise 3, find the number that $L_n[0, 1](x^2)$ approaches as n becomes very large.

b. Does this method give you the same value for the area under the curve $y = x^2$ between 0 and 1 as the method described on page 646?

5. Consider the claim that it is not necessary to bother with both lower and upper sums. Someone might reason that if you know that the difference between the upper and the lower sums approaches zero, you can safely conclude that the limit of, say, the upper sum is the area you are looking for.

a. For $f(x) = x^2$, does the difference between the upper and the lower sums approach zero? How do you know?

b. Do you agree with the general claim? Explain why or why not.

Historical Perspective

Archimedes was the first to use the methods in this lesson, though he never used S for area, nor did he use U_n and L_n. Generally, if you tried to read the original works of famous mathematicians, you would find it very difficult. This is because mathematical notation has changed dramatically over the centuries. Even the way we think about things has changed. For ease of understanding, this chapter uses modern notation and, in some cases, updated presentation. However, it is faithful to the basic ideas of the early masters of mathematics, so you can enjoy and appreciate what they did.

Unlike U_n and L_n, however, S is related to a historically important mathematical symbol: $\int$, for *integral*. Around 1675, Gottfried Wilhelm Leibniz invented this symbol and used it in the very same way we are using S. The symbol $\int$ denoted the area under a curve. Leibniz had the same approach to the area problem as we are using here. In fact, $\int$ is an elongated S and stands for *sum*. The area under the curve is the limit of the sum of the areas of the ever-increasing number of ever-narrowing rectangles. Leibniz used $\int$ while laying the foundations of the branch of mathematics called *calculus*.

6. **a.** Find $S[0, 2](x^2)$.

   b. Find $S[0, a](x^2)$, where $a > 0$.

   c. Find $S[a, b](x^2)$, where $0 < a < b$.

7. **Take It Further** Prove the following result, first established by Archimedes. Draw a horizontal line that intersects the graph of $y = ax^2$ ($a > 0$) at points A and B. The area of the parabolic section (the area of the shaded region above the parabola and below $\overline{AB}$) is $\frac{4}{3}$ of the area of triangle AOB.

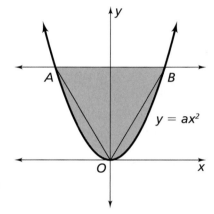

For additional practice, go to **Web Code:** bga-0803

8. In the next investigation, you will learn methods for finding areas under other curves. For each of the following, use subdivisions to find an estimate for the area under the curve between 0 and 1.

   a. $y = x^3$ **b.** $y = x^4$ **c.** $y = x^5$

9. **Standardized Test Prep** Using four equal intervals, which of the following would be the upper sum approximation of the area bounded by the graphs of $y = 0$, $y = \frac{1}{x}$, $x = 1$, and $x = 5$?

   A. $\frac{52}{25}$ **B.** $\frac{25}{12}$ **C.** $\frac{21}{10}$ **D.** $\frac{29}{20}$

Maintain Your Skills

10. Find each area.

    a. $S[0, 1](2x^2)$ **b.** $S[0, 1](3x^2)$

    c. $S[0, 1]\left(\frac{1}{2}x^2\right)$ **d.** $S[0, 1](cx^2)$, where $c > 0$

11. Find a general formula for $S[a, b](cx^2)$, where $c > 0$, and $0 < a < b$.

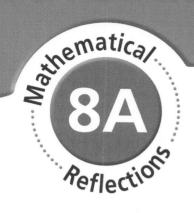

Mathematical 8A Reflections

In this investigation, you approximated the areas of irregular shapes and regions under curves by using squares or rectangles. You applied the approximation method to the area under the graph of $y = x^2$. You found better and better approximations until you were able to state the exact area. The following questions will help you summarize what you have learned.

1. Describe Archimedes' method for finding the area under the curve $y = x^2$ between 0 and 1.

2. When you use Archimedes' method, what happens to the difference between the lower and upper sums as the number of subdivisions gets bigger? Why does this happen?

3. How can you find the area of an irregularly-shaped figure?

4. How can you estimate the area under a curve?

5. What is the area of the region under the graph of $y = x^2$ from $x = 0$ to $x = 1$?

Vocabulary and Notation

In this investigation, you learned these terms and symbols. Make sure you understand what each one means and how to use it.

- lower sum, $L_n[a, b](f(x))$
- $S[a, b](f(x))$
- upper sum, $U_n[a, b](f(x))$

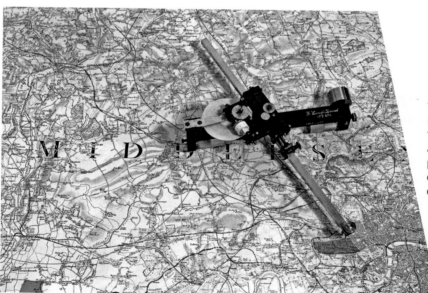

A planimeter, or mechanical integrator, is a device for measuring the area of a shape by tracing its outline. Geographers use planimeters to measure the areas of map regions. In the leather and textile industries, purchasers and production managers use planimeters to find the areas of irregularly-shaped pieces of material.

Finding Areas Under Curves

In *Finding Areas Under Curves,* you will learn how Cavalieri extended Archimedes' result to find the area under the graph of $y = x^m$, for integers $m = 2$ through 9. You will also learn Fermat's variation of this method, which allows you to find the area for any positive integer m.

By the end of this investigation, you will be able to answer questions like these.

1. What is a closed-form expression for the function defined by $F(b) = S[1, b](x^3)$, where $b > 1$?

2. What is a closed-form expression for the function defined by $F(b) = S[1, b](x^4)$, where $b > 1$?

3. What is Fermat's approach to finding the area under the graph of $y = x^m$ between $x = 0$ and $x = 1$?

You will learn how to
- find the area under the graph of $y = x^3$ between $x = 0$ and $x = 1$

- calculate the area under the graph of $y = x^m$ between $x = 0$ and $x = 1$ for any positive integer m

You will develop these habits and skills:
- Use closed forms for $\displaystyle\sum_{k=1}^{n} k^m$ to find areas.
- Use a historical perspective to make sense of the most important ideas of calculus.

- Use a CAS to make short work of complicated calculations.

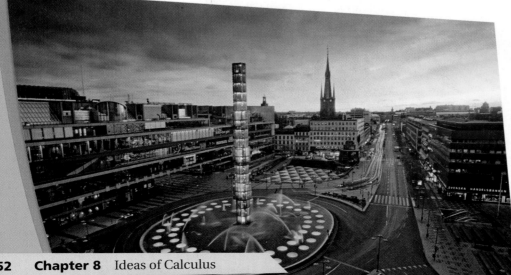

You could estimate the area of this traffic roundabout by superimposing a grid and counting squares. But as you will learn in this investigation, there is a more elegant method that gives the area exactly.

If you can find the area under the graph of $y = x^2$ so successfully, perhaps you can use the same methods on other curves. In fact, you can, and sometimes with surprising results.

For You to Explore

Start with $y = x^3$.

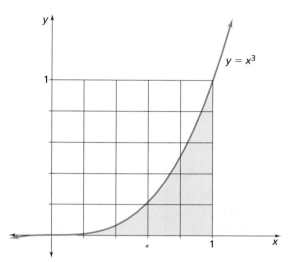

1. Before you do any calculations, how do you expect the area under the graph of $y = x^3$ to compare with the area under the graph $y = x^2$ between $x = 0$ and $x = 1$? Which is greater? Why? Write down a guess for the area under $y = x^3$, and explain your thinking.

2. Estimate $S[0, 1](x^3)$ by computing a few lower or upper approximations. Does your estimate confirm your guess from Problem 1?

To find the exact area under $y = x^2$, you wrote the expression for the upper sum with the number of subdivisions n, and you used the formula for the sum of the squares,

$$\sum_{k=1}^{n} k^2 = 1^2 + 2^2 + \cdots + n^2 = \frac{n(n+1)(2n+1)}{6}$$

You can find the areas under the other curves using the same general approach. You may need to use some of the other formulas for sums of powers, from Chapter 5.

3. Find the base, height, and area of each rectangle. Then write the expression for $U_4[0, 1](x^3)$ by adding the four areas.

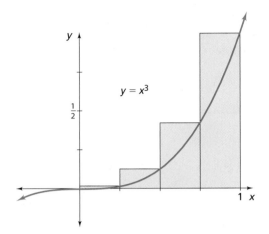

4. Write the expression for $U_5[0, 1](x^3)$, the upper approximation when the number of subdivisions is 5.

5. Copy and complete the table to see how the upper approximations change as the number of subdivisions increases.

Number of Subdivisions, n	Upper Sum Approximation for Different Numbers of Subdivisions, $U_n[0, 1](x^3)$
4	▨
5	▨
6	▨
7	▨
⋮	⋮
15	▨
⋮	⋮
n	▨

6. Find a closed form for $U_n[0, 1](x^3)$.

7. What happens to $U_n[0, 1](x^3)$ as n becomes large?

8. Find a closed form for $L_n[0, 1](x^3)$.

9. What happens to $L_n[0, 1](x^3)$ as n becomes large?

10. **Write About It** What is the exact value of $S[0, 1](x^3)$? Explain your reasoning.

Exercises *Practicing Habits of Mind*

On Your Own

11. How can you find $S[0, 1](\sqrt{x})$? The picture below may help.

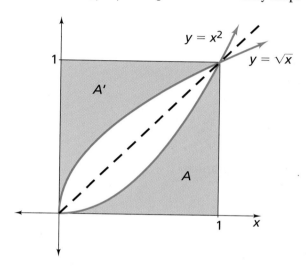

a. What is the relationship between the graphs of $y = x^2$ and $y = \sqrt{x}$?

b. How do the areas of A and A' compare? Explain your answer.

c. Find $S[0, 1](\sqrt{x})$.

12. Find $S[0, 1](\sqrt[3]{x})$.

13. In Investigation 8A, you found that $S[0, 1](x^2) = \frac{1}{3}$. Use that fact to find the following areas.

a. $S[-1, 0](x^2)$

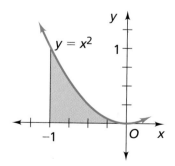

> You do not need to use upper and lower sums in any of the exercises. Drawing the graph of a function might help.

b. $S[0, 1](x^2 + 1)$ **c.** $S[-1, 1](x^2)$ **d.** $S[-1, 1](x^2 + 1)$

Use $S[0, 1](x^2) = \frac{1}{3}$ to find the areas.

e. $S[-1, 1](1 - x^2)$

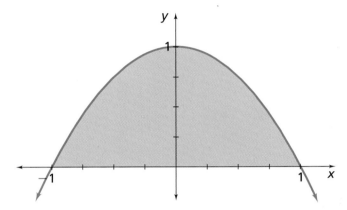

f. The area above the graph of $y = x^2$ and below the graph of $y = 1$.

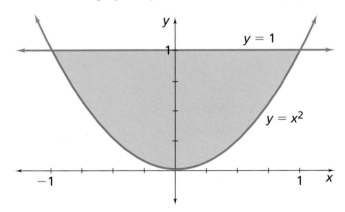

g. The area of the closed region between the x-axis and the graph of $y = x^2 - 1$.

h. The area of the closed region in the first quadrant between the graph of $y = x^2$ and $y = x^3$. (Use your answer to Problem 10 on page 654.)

Maintain Your Skills

14. Remember the identity $1 + r + r^2 + r^3 + \cdots + r^n = \frac{1 - r^{n+1}}{1 - r}$ from CME Project *Algebra 2*? Use it to find each of the following sums.

a. $1 + 5 + 5^2 + 5^3 + 5^4 + \cdots + 5^{12}$

b. $1 + \frac{1}{2} + \left(\frac{1}{2}\right)^2 + \left(\frac{1}{2}\right)^3 + \cdots + \left(\frac{1}{2}\right)^{10}$

c. $1 + 0.1 + (0.1)^2 + (0.1)^3 + \cdots + (0.1)^8$

8.5 Cavalieri's Approach

In Lesson 8.4, you found $S[0, 1](x^3)$. You also know $S[0, 1](x^2)$ from the last investigation. You can find $S[0, 1](x^m)$ for other values of m, as well.

For You to Do

1. Find $S[0, 1](x^0)$.

2. Find $S[0, 1](x)$.

3. Is $S[0, 1](x^4)$ less than or greater than $S[0, 1](x^3)$? Explain.

You are now ready to look for a pattern and come up with a conjecture about $S[0, 1](x^m)$.

For Discussion

Complete the following statements.

4. $S[0, 1](x^0) = \blacksquare$

5. $S[0, 1](x^1) = \blacksquare$

6. $S[0, 1](x^2) = \blacksquare$

7. $S[0, 1](x^3) = \blacksquare$

8. Based on the pattern, make a conjecture about $S[0, 1](x^4)$.

9. Make a conjecture about $S[0, 1](x^m)$, for any positive integer m. How would you find $S[0, 1](x^m)$? Describe what you would need to know and what you would need to do.

You have a conjecture about the area under any curve $y = x^m$. However, a conjecture and a proven theorem are not the same thing. Around 1630, Bonaventura Cavalieri (1598–1647) turned his attention to this problem, extending Archimedes' result $S[0, 1](x^2) = \frac{1}{3}$ to find $S[0, 1](x^m)$ for $m > 2$.

Cavalieri proved that

$$S[0, 1](x^2) = \frac{1}{3}$$

$$S[0, 1](x^3) = \frac{1}{4}$$

$$S[0, 1](x^4) = \frac{1}{5}$$

$$S[0, 1](x^5) = \frac{1}{6}$$

$$\vdots \qquad \vdots$$

all the way up to $S[0, 1](x^9) = \frac{1}{10}$. Then he quit.

Go Online
PHSchool.com

For more information about Cavalieri, go to
Web Code: bge-9031

To find out why Cavalieri did not go beyond the case $y = x^9$, consider what is involved in finding a general formula for $S[0, 1](x^m)$. In essence, Cavalieri tried to continue the upper- and lower-sum game that Archimedes had used so successfully to find the area under $y = x^2$, some 1800 years earlier.

For Discussion

10. Using the same methods you used for $U_n[0, 1](x^2)$ and $U_n[0, 1](x^3)$ discuss every line in this calculation.

$$U_n[0, 1](x^m) = \frac{1}{n} \cdot \left(\frac{1}{n}\right)^m + \frac{1}{n} \cdot \left(\frac{2}{n}\right)^m +$$
$$\frac{1}{n} \cdot \left(\frac{3}{n}\right)^m + \cdots + \frac{1}{n} \cdot \left(\frac{n}{n}\right)^m$$
$$= \frac{1}{n} \cdot \frac{1^m}{n^m} + \frac{1}{n} \cdot \frac{2^m}{n^m} + \frac{1}{n} \cdot \frac{3^m}{n^m} + \cdots + \frac{1}{n} \cdot \frac{n^m}{n^m}$$
$$= \frac{1^m}{n^{m+1}} + \frac{2^m}{n^{m+1}} + \frac{3^m}{n^{m+1}} + \cdots + \frac{n^m}{n^{m+1}}$$
$$= \frac{1}{n^{m+1}} (1^m + 2^m + 3^m + \cdots + n^m)$$
$$= \frac{1}{n^{m+1}} \sum_{k=1}^{n} k^m$$

> Why is it okay to pull the $\frac{1}{n^{m+1}}$ out of the sum?

So, to find a general closed form for $U_n[0, 1](x^m)$, Cavalieri needed to first find a general closed form for

$$\sum_{k=1}^{n} k^m$$

For Discussion

11. Use the general result of the last discussion and the closed forms you know for

$$\sum_{k=1}^{n} k^2 \quad \text{and} \quad \sum_{k=1}^{n} k^3$$

to find closed forms for $U_n[0, 1](x^2)$ and $U_n[0, 1](x^3)$. Check these with the closed forms you obtained earlier.

At this point, it seemed that there was nothing to stop Cavalieri from finding $S[0, 1](x^m)$ for all positive integers m. All he needed to do was to find a general closed form for $\sum_{k=1}^{n} k^m$. Unfortunately, that is easier said than done. However, Cavalieri was able to find closed forms for specific values of m.

You could go on to find $S[0, 1](x^5)$ using exactly the same method as above. But there is no need to stop there. You could calculate $S[0, 1](x^m)$, for $m = 6, 7, 8$, and so on.

As you know from Chapter 5, getting the formulas for the sums of powers involves some pretty hefty algebra, and things get more complicated quickly as powers get bigger. The fact that Cavalieri was able to work his way all the way up to $m = 9$ is a tribute to his perseverance and algebraic skills. The surprising thing is not that he quit after dealing with the case $m = 9$ (to find that $S[0, 1](x^9) = \frac{1}{10}$), but rather that he did not call it quits much earlier. Remember, Cavalieri did not have a CAS.

Developing Habits of Mind

Find another way. Cavalieri was hampered by the complicated closed forms for sums of powers. Later mathematicians paved the way for modern CAS technology, which allows one to easily generate such closed forms.

But instead of slogging through complicated algebra, why not look for a completely different way to get $S[0, 1](x^m)$, one that does not require the closed forms for sums of powers? That is exactly what another mathematician, Pierre de Fermat, did. You will look at Fermat's ideas in the next lesson.

Mathematicians love to build on what they know and to take it to another level. Now that you know how to find $S[0, 1](x^2)$, you also know how to find $S[1, 2](x^2)$, $S[1, 3](x^2)$, $S[1, 6](x^2)$, and in general, $S[1, b](x^2)$ for any integer b where $b > 1$. Mathematicians immediately see this as a function of b and start to wonder about its properties.

For You to Do

12. Copy and complete the table for the function $b \mapsto S[1, b](x^2)$.

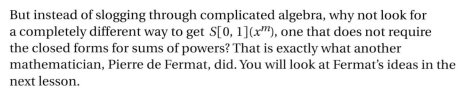

b	Area under $y = x^2$ from 1 to b, $S[1, b](x^2)$
2	▨
3	▨
4	▨
5	▨
6	▨

Think of the graph of $y = x^2$, with a point b moving along the x-axis. $S[1, b](x^2)$ is the area bounded by the graph, the x-axis, the vertical line through $(1, 0)$ and the vertical line through $(b, 0)$.

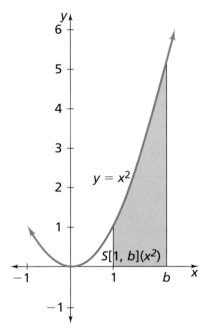

For Discussion

The table you completed in Problem 12 is for the function $G(b) = S[1, b](x^2)$.

13. Find a closed-form expression for G.

14. In the table, b takes on only positive integer values. Can b be something else, for example, 2.7 or $7\frac{1}{3}$? Explain.

15. Sketch the graph of G between 1 and 6.

Exercises Practicing Habits of Mind

Check Your Understanding

1. Even with a CAS, the algebra of sum identities is substantial. Obtain a closed-form expression for

$$U_n[0, 1](x^5)$$

and find the exact value of

$$S[0, 1](x^5)$$

2. There are at least two ways to come up with a conjecture for $S[0, 1](\sqrt[m]{x})$:

   • Use $\frac{1}{m}$ instead of m in the formula you developed in this lesson.

   • Use the symmetry of the graphs of $y = x^m$ and $y = \sqrt[m]{x}$.

   a. What formula for the upper sum do you get from each of these methods? Are the formulas equivalent?

   b. Is there any value of m for which your formula does not work?

3. Find $S[1, 2](x^4)$.

4. Make a conjecture about the value of $S[1, 2](x^m)$ where m is a positive integer.

5. Find the area of the closed region between the x-axis and the graph of $y = x^2 - 1$.

6. Find the area of the closed region between the graphs of $y = x^4$ and $y = 2 - x^2$.

7. **Take It Further** Find a value of k for which the area in the first quadrant between the graphs of $y = x^k$ and $y = x^{k+1}$ is less than 0.01.

8. Find a closed-form expression for the function $b \mapsto S[1, b](x^3)$.

9. Find a closed-form expression for the function $b \mapsto S[1, b](x^4)$.

On Your Own

10. Fill in the details for the derivation of $S[0, 1](x^4)$.

   a. Substitute $m = 4$ into the general formula for the upper sum of the area from the discussion in this lesson,

$$U_n[0, 1](x^m) = \frac{1}{n^{m+1}} \sum_{k=1}^{n} k^m$$

b. What happens to the upper sum as you increase the number of subdivisions?

c. Determine the exact value of $S[0, 1](x^4)$.

11. Find $S[1, 2](x^3)$. To do so, you could

- work out the upper and lower sums $U_n[1, 2](x^3)$ and $L_n[1, 2](x^3)$
- determine what happens to the sums, $U_n[1, 2](x^3)$ and $L_n[1, 2](x^3)$, when n becomes larger and larger
- draw a conclusion about $S[1, 2](x^3)$

Or you might use a different method.

12. Find the area of the closed region in the first quadrant between the graphs of $y = x^2$ and $y = x^3$.

13. Find the area of the closed region between the graphs of $y = x^2$ and $y = \sqrt{x}$.

Go Online
PHSchool.com

For additional practice, go to **Web Code:** bga-0805

14. Standardized Test Prep The graphs of $f(x)$ and $g(x)$ are as shown. Which of the following gives the area of the shaded region?

A. $[f(x) - g(x)](b - a)$

B. $[g(x) - f(x)](b - a)$

C. $S[a,b](f(x)) - S[a,b](g(x))$

D. $S[a,b](g(x)) - S[a,b](f(x))$

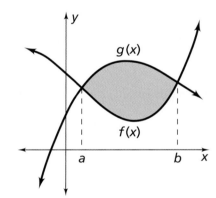

Maintain Your Skills

15. a. Draw the graphs of $y = x$, $y = 2x$, $y = 3x$ and $y = 4x$ between 0 and 1.

b. Find the area of the region above the graph of $y = x$ and below the graph of $y = 2x$ between $x = 0$ and $x = 1$.

c. Find the area of the region above the graph of $y = x$ and below the graph of $y = 3x$ between $x = 0$ and $x = 1$.

d. Find the area of the region above the graph of $y = x$ and below the graph of $y = 4x$ between $x = 0$ and $x = 1$.

e. Make a conjecture about the area between the graph of $y = x$ and the graph of $y = mx$ $(m > 1)$ between $x = 0$ and $x = 1$.

8.6 Fermat's Big Idea

Just about the time Cavalieri was patiently working his way up the curves $y = x^m$ one m at a time, Pierre de Fermat took a new and original approach to the same problem.

When Cavalieri calculated upper and lower sums, he always divided his intervals on the x-axis into equal parts. For example, the coordinates of Cavalieri's points of the interval $[1, 2]$ for 5 subdivisions would be

$$1, 1\tfrac{1}{5}, 1\tfrac{2}{5}, 1\tfrac{3}{5}, 1\tfrac{4}{5}, 2$$

Fermat's big idea was to do subdivisions with unequal intervals. He suggested dividing an interval with a geometric sequence. For the same interval $[1, 2]$ and the same number of subdivisions, Fermat would use the following points of subdivision:

$$1, r, r^2, r^3, r^4, r^5 \qquad \text{where } r^5 = 2$$

Here, r is a number between 1 and 2, such that $r^5 = 2$.

> Cavalieri divided the interval up into an arithmetic sequence. This one has first term 1 and common difference $\frac{1}{5}$.

> **Remember...**
>
> Terms in a geometric sequence have a common ratio.

For Discussion

1. Find approximate values for the above Fermat points of subdivision (the number of subdivisions is 5). Plot the points on a number line.

2. Write the sequence of Fermat points for the interval $[1, 2]$ with 6 subdivisions. Plot the points on a number line.

3. Write the sequence of Fermat points for the interval $[1, 2]$ with 10 subdivisions. Plot the points on a number line.

4. Explain how the lengths of the subintervals change as the number of subdivisions grows.

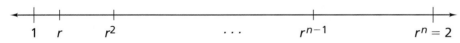

5. Write algebraic expressions and approximate values for r in the Fermat subdivision of the interval $[1, 2]$, if the number of subdivisions, n, is

   a. 20   **b.** 40   **c.** 80

6. What number does r approach as the number of subdivisions grows?

> Note that although n and r change, r^n remains equal to 2.

Fermat's method is very similar to the method of Archimedes and Cavalieri. However, Fermat could solve problems that Cavalieri and Archimedes could not.

Here is some handy notation for Fermat's method.

Fermat lower sum $= LF_n[a, b](f(x))$: the lower approximation of the area under the curve $f(x)$ from $x = a$ to $x = b$ when the number of

Fermat subdivisions is n. **Fermat upper sum** $= UF_n[a, b](f(x))$: the upper approximation of the area under the graph of the function $f(x)$ from $x = a$ to $x = b$ when the number of Fermat subdivisions is n.

You find $LF_n[a, b](f(x))$ and $UF_n[a, b](f(x))$ the same way you found $L_n[a, b](f(x))$ and $U_n[a, b](f(x))$, namely by summing the area of the n rectangles formed by subdividing the interval $[a, b]$. The difference between the method of Fermat and that of Cavalieri is that the bases of the rectangles in Fermat's method form a geometric sequence.

Say "Fermat lower sub n" and "Fermat upper sub n."

For You to Do

7. Find an estimate for the area under the graph of $y = x^2$ from 1 to 2 using Fermat's method with 3 subdivisions.

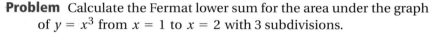 $< S[1, 2](x^2) <$ ▦

Example

Problem Calculate the Fermat lower sum for the area under the graph of $y = x^3$ from $x = 1$ to $x = 2$ with 3 subdivisions.

	Base	Height	Area
1st rectangle	$r - 1$	1	$1(r - 1)$
2nd rectangle	$r^2 - r$	r^3	$r^3(r^2 - r)$
3rd rectangle	$r^3 - r^2$	$(r^2)^3$	$r^6(r^3 - r^2)$

Solution With three subdivisions, the Fermat points will be $1, r, r^2, r^3 = 2$, and the Fermat lower sum is

$$
\begin{aligned}
LF_3[1, 2](x^3) &= 1(r - 1) + r^3(r^2 - r) + (r^2)^3(r^3 - r^2) \\
&= 1(r - 1) + r^3(r(r - 1)) + r^6(r^2(r - 1)) \\
&= 1(r - 1) + r^4(r - 1) + r^8(r - 1) \\
&= (r - 1)(1 + r^4 + r^8) \\
&= (r - 1)(1 + r^4 + (r^4)^2)
\end{aligned}
$$

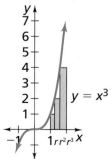

For You to Do

8. Show that when you increase the number of subdivisions to four, the Fermat points are $1, r, r^2, r^3, r^4 = 2$ and the Fermat lower sum is

$$LF_4[1, 2](x^3) = (r - 1)(1 + r^4 + (r^4)^2 + (r^4)^3)$$

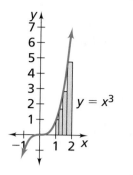

$y = x^3$

Similarly, for five subdivisions, the Fermat points are $1, r, r^2, r^3, r^4, r^5 = 2$, and the Fermat lower sum is

$$LF_5[1, 2](x^3) = (r - 1)(1 + r^4 + (r^4)^2 + (r^4)^3 + (r^4)^4)$$

Now look at the changes in $LF[1, 2](x^3)$, as you increase the number of subdivisions:

$$LF_3[1, 2](x^3) = (r - 1)(1 + r^4 + (r^4)^2)$$
$$LF_4[1, 2](x^3) = (r - 1)(1 + r^4 + (r^4)^2 + (r^4)^3)$$
$$LF_5[1, 2](x^3) = (r - 1)(1 + r^4 + (r^4)^2 + (r^4)^3 + (r^4)^4)$$

For each new subdivision, you add another term to the geometric sequence of terms. Since there is a formula for summing the terms of a geometric sequence of any length, using Fermat's method you can find a closed form for the lower sum (and the upper sum, too) for any number of subdivisions.

Note that the value of r is different in each of these.

For Discussion

9. What is $LF_n[1, 2](x^3)$?

Thus far, Fermat's method looks almost exactly like that of Cavalieri and Archimedes. Remember, their trouble was finding a closed form for the upper and lower sums when using large numbers of subdivisions for functions of the form x^m where m was bigger than 2. Fermat avoided this problem by dividing the interval with a geometric sequence. He knew that in finding the upper and lower sum he would be summing the terms of a geometric sequence. Geometric sequences are easy to sum.

$$1 + q + q^2 + \dots + q^{n-1} = \frac{q^n - 1}{q - 1}$$

This works for any ratio $q \neq 1$ and any number of terms n. In choosing this subdivision, Fermat avoided Cavalieri's difficulty finding closed forms for $\sum_{k=1}^{n} k^m$.

In Lesson 8.5, you used Archimedes' method to find that the area under the graph of $y = x^2$ from $x = 1$ to $x = 2$, $S[1, 2](x^2)$, was $\frac{7}{3}$. By first using Fermat's method on an example that you already know the answer to, you can avoid making mistakes, and you can reassure yourself that it really works.

Minds in Action   episode 29

Sasha and Derman are working on writing a general expression for the Fermat lower sum for the area under the graph of $y = x^2$ from $x = 1$ to $x = 2$, with n subdivisions, $LF_n[1, 2](x^2)$. They want to know if the lower sum approach $\frac{7}{3}$ as the number of subdivisions, n, increases.

Sasha The Fermat points are $1, r, r^2, \ldots, r^n = 2$, and the Fermat lower sum is

$$LF_n[1, 2](x^2) = 1(r - 1) + r^2(r^2 - r) + (r^2)^2(r^3 - r^2) + \ldots + (r^{n-1})^2(r^n - r^{n-1})$$

Derman Oh, not this thing again. … Didn't we just do this calculation? Now we have to do it again?

Sasha Hey, you're right! We did just do this calculation. And by the same reasoning,

$$LF_n[1, 2](x^2) = (r - 1)(1 + r^3 + r^6 + \cdots + (r^3)^{n-1})$$

Derman Can you use one of your "favorite identities"?

Sasha Of course.

$$LF_n[1, 2](x^2) = \left(\frac{(r^3)^{((n-1)+1)} - 1}{r^3 - 1}\right)(r - 1) \qquad \text{The formula for summing geometric sequences}$$

$$= \left(\frac{r^{3n} - 1}{r^3 - 1}\right)(r - 1)$$

$$= \left(\frac{2^3 - 1}{r^3 - 1}\right)(r - 1) \qquad r^n = 2$$

$$= \left(\frac{7}{r^3 - 1}\right)(r - 1)$$

$$= \left(\frac{7}{(r - 1)(r^2 + r + 1)}\right)(r - 1) \qquad \text{Factor } (r^4 - 1).$$

$$= \frac{7}{r^2 + r + 1} \qquad \begin{array}{l}(r - 1) \text{ cancels} \\ (\text{note that } r \neq 1).\end{array}$$

As n increases, r gets closer and closer to 1 but is always a little greater than 1. So as you increase the number of subdivisions, $\frac{7}{r^2 + r + 1}$ gets closer and closer to $\frac{7}{1 + 1 + 1} = \frac{7}{3}$.

Derman So as n becomes larger and larger, $LF_n[1, 2](x^2)$ gets closer and closer to $\frac{7}{3}$.

For You to Do

10. Write a general expression for $UF_n[1, 2](x^2)$.

11. What number does $UF_n[1, 2](x^2)$ approach as n becomes large? Why?

12. Use your answer to Problem 11 to find $S[1, 2](x^2)$.

So, to sum up, using Fermat's method gives $S[1, 2](x^3) = \frac{7}{3}$.
That is the same result you get using Archimedes' method.

Exercises Practicing Habits of Mind

Check Your Understanding

1. Why does Fermat's method not work for the interval $[0, 1]$?

2. Use the following steps to find the Fermat lower sum for $S[1, 2](x^m)$ for any positive integer m.

a. For n subdivisions, write down expressions for the first three and the last three Fermat points in the subdivision.

b. Copy and complete the table.

Fermat Lower Sum for $y = x^m$, $LF_n[1, 2](x^m)$

	Base	Height	Area
1st rectangle	$r - 1$	1	$1(r - 1)$
2nd rectangle	$r^2 - r = r(r - 1)$	r^m	$r^{m+1}(r - 1)$
3rd rectangle	$r^3 - r^2 = r^2(r - 1)$	$(r^2)^m = r^{2m}$	$r^{2(m+1)}(r - 1)$
4th rectangle	$r^4 - r^3 = r^3(r - 1)$	▦	▦
⋮	⋮	⋮	⋮
nth rectangle	▦	▦	▦

c. Add the areas of these rectangles to obtain an expression for the Fermat lower sum $LF_n[1, 2](x^m)$.

d. Use the formula for the geometric series to obtain the closed form.

e. What happens to $LF_n[1, 2](x^m)$ when you increase the number of subdivisions?

> As n increases, r approaches 1. Remember that $r^n = 2$.

3. Find the Fermat upper sum, $UF_n[1, 2](x^m)$, for any positive integer m.

4. Use your results from Exercises 2 and 3 to prove the general formula for all positive integers m.
$$S[1, 2](x^m) = \frac{1}{m + 1}(2^{m+1} - 1)$$

5. a. Use Fermat's method to find the formula for $LF_n[3, 6](x^m)$ by subdividing the segment $[3, 6]$ with the points $3, 3r, 3r^2, 3r^3, \ldots, 3r^n = 6$.

   b. What happens to $LF_n[3, 6](x^m)$ as you increase the number of subdivisions?

6. a. Use Fermat's method to find the formula for $LF_n[2, 3](x^m)$ by subdividing the segment $[2, 3]$ with the points $2, 2r, 2r^2, 2r^3, \ldots, 2r^n = 3$.

   b. What happens to $LF_n[2, 3](x^m)$ as you increase the number of subdivisions?

7. a. Use Fermat's method to find the formula for $LF_n[2, 6](x^m)$ by subdividing the segment $[2, 6]$ with the points $2, 2r, 2r^2, 2r^3, \ldots, 2r^n = 6$.

   b. What happens to $LF_n[2, 6](x^m)$ as you increase the number of subdivisions?

8. Write About It For each of the above exercises, you can show that the upper sum and the lower sum approach the same value, as you increase the number of subdivisions. You may have noticed that
$$S[2, 6](x^m) = S[2, 3](x^m) + S[3, 6](x^m)$$

Is it always true that
$$S[a, c](x^m) = S[a, b](x^m) + S[b, c](x^m)$$

where $0 < a < b < c$? Explain.

On Your Own

9. Copy and complete the expressions in parts (a)–(c).

   a. $LF_3[1, 2](x^5) = (r - 1)(\blacksquare)$

   b. $LF_5[1, 2](x^5) = (r - 1)(\blacksquare)$

   c. $LF_8[1, 2](x^5) = (r - 1)(\blacksquare)$

   d. In terms of r, what is the common ratio in the geometric series which you placed inside the parentheses in parts (a)–(c)?

Note that the value of r is different in each of these.

10. Justify each step in the calculations of $LF_3[1, 2](x^3)$ in the example in this lesson.

11. Use the following steps to find Fermat lower sum of $y = x^2$ from $x = 1$ to $x = 2$ with 5 subdivisions:

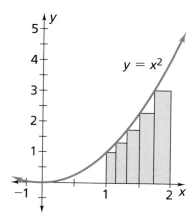

a. Write the expression for the sum of the areas of all five rectangles.

$$LF_5[1, 2](x^2) = \blacksquare$$

b. Use the formula for the geometric series to write the closed form for the Fermat lower sum.

c. Calculate r and the value of $LF_5[1, 2](x^2)$.

12. Repeat the steps of Exercise 11 for $n = 10$. Describe how the Fermat lower sum changes with this increase in the number of subdivisions.

13. Copy and complete the expressions in parts (a)–(c).

a. $LF_3[1, 2](x^4) = (r - 1)(\blacksquare)$

b. $LF_4[1, 2](x^4) = (r - 1)(\blacksquare)$

c. $LF_7[1, 2](x^4) = (r - 1)(\blacksquare)$

d. In terms of r, what is the common ratio in the geometric series which you placed inside the parentheses in parts (a)–(c)?

14. Use Fermat's method to find $S[1, 2](x^4)$.

15. Use Fermat's method to find $S[1, 3](x^4)$.

16. Find a general formula for $S[1, a](x^4)$ (where $a \geq 1$) using Fermat's method.

17. Find a general formula for $S[1, a](x^m)$ (where $a > 1$, and m is a positive integer) using Fermat's method.

> **Remember...**
>
> $1 + q + \cdots + q^{n-1}$
> $= \dfrac{q^n - 1}{q - 1}$

18. a. Use Fermat's method to find the formula for $LF_n[5, 10](x^m)$ by subdividing the segment $[5, 10]$ with the points

$$5, 5r, 5r^2, 5r^3, \ldots, 5r^n = 10$$

b. What happens to $LF_n[5, 10](x^m)$ as you increase the number of subdivisions?

19. Take It Further Derive the formula for $S[a, b](x^m)$ where $1 < a < b$, using your knowledge of $S[1, b](x^m)$.

20. a. Find $S\left[\frac{1}{a}, 1\right](x^5)$ if

- $a = 2$
- $a = 4$
- $a = 8$
- $a = 100$

b. What happens to $S\left[\frac{1}{a}, 1\right](x^5)$ as a becomes larger and larger?

c. What is the value of $S[0, 1](x^5)$? Explain.

21. Take It Further Find a general formula for $S\left[\frac{1}{a}, 1\right](x^5)$ for any integer $a > 1$, by using the Fermat points for n subdivisions of the interval $\left[\frac{1}{a}, 1\right]$.

22. Take It Further Find $S[0, 1](x^m)$ using Fermat's method.

23. Standardized Test Prep Using Fermat's geometric sequence to determine the intervals, which of the following represents the upper estimate $UF_4[1, 16]\left(\frac{1}{x}\right)$?

A. $\frac{15}{8}$ **B.** 4   **C.** 8   **D.** 15

Go Online
PHSchool.com

For additional practice, go to **Web Code:** bga-0806

Maintain Your Skills

24. Find algebraic expressions for the Fermat points for each of the following.

a. 3 subdivisions of the interval $[1, a]$

b. 6 subdivisions of the interval $[1, a]$

c. n subdivisions of the interval $[1, a]$

25. The following steps describe a method for subdividing the interval $[0, 1]$. Try it out.

> In part (c), the first 3 and last 3 points are enough.

a. Divide each of the Fermat points you found in Exercise 24c for n subdivisions of $[1, a]$ by a. This gives you the Fermat points for the interval $\left[\frac{1}{a}, 1\right]$.

b. What happens to $\frac{1}{a}$ as a becomes larger and larger? What interval does $\left[\frac{1}{a}, 1\right]$ approach, as a becomes larger and larger?

Mathematical 8B Reflections

In this investigation, you followed the historical approach taken by two mathematicians to find the areas under certain curves. The following questions will help you summarize what you have learned.

1. Calculate $S[1, a](x^m)$.

2. Find the area of the closed region between the x-axis and the graph of $y = x^2 - 1$.

3. What is a closed-form expression for the function defined by $F(b) = S[1, b](x^3)$, where $b > 1$?

4. What is a closed-form expression for the function defined by $F(b) = S[1, b](x^4)$, where $b > 1$?

5. What is Fermat's approach to finding the area under the graph of $y = x^m$ between $x = 0$ and $x = 1$?

Vocabulary and Notation

In this investigation, you learned these terms and symbols. Make sure you understand what each one means and how to use it.

- **Fermat lower sum, $LF_n[a, b](f(x))$**
- **Fermat upper sum, $UF_n[a, b](f(x))$**

In calculus, you learn to calculate the surface area of curved, three-dimensional objects like this sculpture by Piet Hein.

Multiple Choice

1. What is the value of $L_4[1, 5](x^2)$, the lower sum approximation of the area under the graph of $y = x^2$ between 1 and 5?

A. 54   **B.** 30   **C.** 7.5   **D.** 15

2. Which of the following estimates will be closest to the area under the graph of $y = \sqrt{x}$ between 0 and 4?

A. $L_4[0, 4](\sqrt{x})$

B. $U_{10}[0, 4](\sqrt{x})$

C. $L_{10}[0, 4](\sqrt{x})$

D. the average of $L_{10}[0, 4](\sqrt{x})$ and $U_{10}[0, 4](\sqrt{x})$

3. Which sum represents $L_4\left[0, \frac{\pi}{2}\right](\cos x)$, the lower sum approximation of the area under $y = \cos x$ between 0 and $\frac{\pi}{2}$ using 4 subdivisions?

A. $\frac{1}{4}\cos\frac{\pi}{8} + \frac{1}{4}\cos\frac{\pi}{4} + \frac{1}{4}\cos\frac{3\pi}{8} + \frac{1}{4}\cos\frac{\pi}{2}$

B. $\frac{\pi}{8}\cos\frac{\pi}{8} + \frac{\pi}{8}\cos\frac{\pi}{4} + \frac{\pi}{8}\cos\frac{3\pi}{8} + \frac{\pi}{8}\cos\frac{\pi}{2}$

C. $\frac{1}{4}\cos 0 + \frac{1}{4}\cos\frac{\pi}{8} + \frac{1}{4}\cos\frac{\pi}{4} + \frac{1}{4}\cos\frac{3\pi}{8}$

D. $\frac{\pi}{8}\cos 0 + \frac{\pi}{8}\cos\frac{\pi}{8} + \frac{\pi}{8}\cos\frac{\pi}{4} + \frac{\pi}{8}\cos\frac{3\pi}{8}$

4. Which sum represents $U_4\left[0, \frac{\pi}{2}\right](\cos x)$, the upper sum approximation of the area under $y = \cos x$ between 0 and $\frac{\pi}{2}$ using 4 subdivisions?

A. $\frac{1}{4}\cos\frac{\pi}{8} + \frac{1}{4}\cos\frac{\pi}{4} + \frac{1}{4}\cos\frac{3\pi}{8} + \frac{1}{4}\cos\frac{\pi}{2}$

B. $\frac{\pi}{8}\cos\frac{\pi}{8} + \frac{\pi}{8}\cos\frac{\pi}{4} + \frac{\pi}{8}\cos\frac{3\pi}{8} + \frac{\pi}{8}\cos\frac{\pi}{2}$

C. $\frac{1}{4}\cos 0 + \frac{1}{4}\cos\frac{\pi}{8} + \frac{1}{4}\cos\frac{\pi}{4} + \frac{1}{4}\cos\frac{3\pi}{8}$

D. $\frac{\pi}{8}\cos 0 + \frac{\pi}{8}\cos\frac{\pi}{8} + \frac{\pi}{8}\cos\frac{\pi}{4} + \frac{\pi}{8}\cos\frac{3\pi}{8}$

Open Response

5. a. Compute $U_2[0, 2](\sqrt{x})$, the upper sum approximation (using 2 subdivisions) of the area under $y = \sqrt{x}$ between 0 and 2. Express your answer exactly. Then approximate your answer to 3 decimal places.

  b. Compute $U_4[0, 2](\sqrt{x})$, the upper sum approximation (using 4 subdivisions) of the area under $y = \sqrt{x}$ between 0 and 2. Express your answer exactly. Then approximate your answer to 3 decimal places.

  c. Without calculating the area, which of these two approximations do you think will be closer to the exact area? Explain.

6. a. Recall that $U_4[0, 2](4 - x^2)$ is the upper sum approximation of the area under the curve $y = 4 - x^2$ between 0 and 2 using four subdivisions. Copy the graph below, and sketch the rectangles whose areas make up $U_4[0, 2](4 - x^2)$.

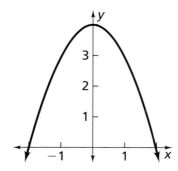

  b. Compute $U_4[0, 2](4 - x^2)$.

  c. On another copy of the same graph, sketch the rectangles the areas of which make up $L_4[0, 2](4 - x^2)$, the lower sum approximation of the area under the curve $y = 4 - x^2$ between 0 and 2 using four subdivisions.

d. Compute $L_4[0, 2](4 - x^2)$.

e. Compute the average of $L_4[0, 2](4 - x^2)$ and $L_4[0, 2](4 - x^2)$ to get a third approximation of the area.

7. The graphs of $y = x^2$ and $y = 4 - x^2$ are shown below.

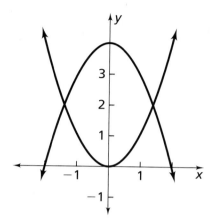

The area of the region under $y = x^2$ between -2 and 2 is $\frac{16}{3}$. Use that information to compute each of the following and explain your answers.

a. the area under $y = x^2$ between 0 and 2

b. the area under $y = 4 - x^2$ between 0 and 2

Challenge Problem

8. Using Fermat's method with n subdivisions, the endpoints of the subdivisions are $1, r, r^2, r^3, \ldots, r^n$, where $r^n = 5$.

a. Compute $UF_n[1, 5](x^3)$, the upper sum approximation.

b. What value does $UF_n[1, 5](x^3)$ approach as n becomes larger?

c. Compute $LF_n[1, 5](x^3)$, the lower sum approximation.

d. What value does $LF_n[1, 5](x^3)$ approach as n becomes larger?

e. Compute $S[1, 5](x^3)$.

A Function Emerges

In *A Function Emerges*, you will extend your work from the previous two investigations. You will learn how to calculate the area under the graph of $y = x^m$, where m can be any integer. You will also examine the area under the graph of $y = e^x$.

By the end of this investigation, you will be able to answer question like these.

1. What is the value of $S[1, 2](x^{-2})$?

2. What is the value of $S[1, 2](x^{-1})$?

3. What is the value of $S[0, 1](e^x)$?

You will learn how to

- develop formulas for calculating $S[1, a](x^m)$ where m is any integer

- investigate a mysteriously familiar function, $\mathcal{L}(a)$

- find the area under the graph of $y = e^x$ between $x = 0$ and $x = 1$

You will develop these habits and skills:

- Use properties of a mystery function to identify the function.

- Use areas under curves to gain new perspectives on familiar functions.

The mystery function in this chapter is useful in radiocarbon dating of archeological specimens.

Getting Started

In the previous investigation, you developed and proved a formula for finding the area under the graph of $y = x^m$ between $x = 1$ and $x = 2$:

$$S[1, 2](x^m) = \frac{1}{m + 1}(2^{m+1} - 1)$$

While working on this formula, you considered only nonnegative integers m. In many situations in mathematics, one of the ways to find out something new is to try to extend the result you already know.

> There is actually a more general formula, for the area on any interval $[a, b]$, $1 \leq a < b$:
> $$S[a, b](x^m) = \frac{1}{m + 1}(b^{m+1} - a^{m+1})$$

For You to Explore

1. The goal in this problem is to answer the following question:

   When $m = -2$, does the formula $S[1, 2](x^m) = \frac{1}{m + 1}(2^{m+1} - 1)$ give the correct area under the curve $y = x^{-2}$ between $x = 1$ and $x = 2$?

   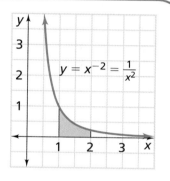

   a. What value does the formula return when $m = -2$?

   b. Copy and complete the following table.

   Habits of Mind

   Reason logically. You know from the start that there will be trouble with $\frac{1}{m + 1}(2^{m+1} - 1)$ if you try to replace m with -1. But studying the derivation shows you exactly where things go wrong.

   Fermat Upper Sum for $y = x^{-2}$, $UF_n[1, 2](x^{-2})$

	Base	Height	Area
1st rectangle	$r - 1$	1	$1(r - 1)$
2nd rectangle	$r^2 - r = r(r - 1)$	r^{-2}	$r^{-1}(r - 1)$
3rd rectangle	▩	▩	▩
4th rectangle	▩	▩	▩
⋮	⋮	⋮	⋮
nth rectangle	▩	▩	▩

   c. Why does this table give an upper sum, as opposed to a lower sum?

   d. Add the areas to find $UF_n[1, 2](x^{-2})$.

   e. What is the limit of $UF_n[1, 2](x^{-2})$ as n becomes larger and larger?

   f. Find $LF_n[1, 2](x^{-2})$.

   g. What is the limit of $LF_n[1, 2](x^{-2})$ as n becomes larger and larger?

   h. What is $S[1, 2](x^{-2})$?

2. Try to derive a general formula for $S[1, 2](x^m)$ in a way that works for all integer values (negative and nonnegative) of m. If a step of the derivation is not allowed for some value of m, explain why, and then describe all values of m for which your general formula does hold.

On Your Own

3. a. Use Fermat's method to find $S[1, 2](x^{-3})$. Do not use the general formula you found in Problem 2.

b. Does your result in part (a) agree with what you get if you replace m with -3 in

$$\frac{1}{m + 1}(2^{m+1} - 1)$$

4. Not everything that works for nonnegative exponents works for negative ones.

a. What is $S[0, 2](x^3)$?

b. Describe the difficulty in finding $S[0, 2](x^{-3})$.

5. Use Fermat's method to find $S[1, 2](x^{-4})$. Does it agree with what you get if you replace m with -4 in

$$\frac{1}{m + 1}(2^{m+1} - 1)?$$

6. Use Fermat's method to find $S[1, 3](x^{-3})$.

Maintain Your Skills

7. Find $S[1, 100](x^{-2})$.

8. Find $S[1, 200](x^{-2})$.

9. Find a closed-form expression for $S[1, b](x^{-2})$.

10. a. Does the area under the graph of $y = x^{-2}$ on the interval $[1, b]$ get gradually closer to a particular number when b becomes larger and larger?

b. What happens to $S[1, b](x^{-3})$ as b becomes very large?

8.8 The Area Under $y = \frac{1}{x}$

In the last lesson, you saw that the formula

$$S[1, 2](x^m) = \frac{1}{m+1}(2^{m+1} - 1)$$

holds for all integer exponents m, both positive and negative, with one notable exception, namely when $m = -1$. This lesson deals with that one exception.

For You to Do

1. Approximate $S[1, 2](x^{-1})$ using Fermat's method. Use your calculator to obtain approximations for 20 (or 200) subdivisions.

> In fact, the formula holds for all rational exponents, i.e., all curves of the form $y = x^{p/q}$ where p and q are integers and $q \neq 0$, so long as $\frac{p}{q} \neq -1$.

For Discussion

2. Using the graph of $y = \frac{1}{x}$, explain why

$$S[1, 10]\left(\tfrac{1}{x}\right) = S[1, 2]\left(\tfrac{1}{x}\right) + S[2, 10]\left(\tfrac{1}{x}\right)$$

3. More generally, if $1 < a < b$, explain why

$$S[1, b]\left(\tfrac{1}{x}\right) = S[1, a]\left(\tfrac{1}{x}\right) + S[a, b]\left(\tfrac{1}{x}\right)$$

Using a calculator or computer, you can approximate $S[1, 2](x^{-1})$ to any degree of accuracy you like by taking more and more subdivisions. But it turns out that the actual value of the area is irrational, just like the area of the unit circle. No fraction will ever give the exact area.

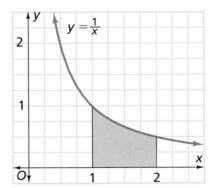

Not only is $S[1, 2](x^{-1})$ irrational, but so are $S[1, 3](x^{-1})$, $S[1, 4](x^{-1})$, and $S[1, a](x^{-1})$ where a is any integer greater than 1. In fact, the function defined for $a \geq 1$ by

$$a \mapsto S[1, a](x^{-1})$$

has no algebraic closed-form equivalent expression.

For Discussion

4. Use your calculator or computer to make a table for the function
$a \mapsto S[1, a](x^{-1})$ for integer values of a between 1 and 10. Of course, these
will be approximate values.

5. Graph this function.

Although this function, $a \mapsto S[1, a](x^{-1})$, does not have a simple algebraic
closed form, it is of central importance in mathematics. For now, call it $\mathcal{L}$.

In the early 17th century, monk Gregory of St. Vincent made a remarkable
discovery about the function $\mathcal{L}$. His idea was to compare the area under the
graph of $y = \frac{1}{x}$ between $x = a$ and $x = b$ to the area under the same curve
between $x = ta$ and $x = tb$ for positive values of t.

To begin, compare the two areas below, $A_1 = S[1, 2]\left(\frac{1}{x}\right)$ and
$A_2 = S[3, 6]\left(\frac{1}{x}\right)$.

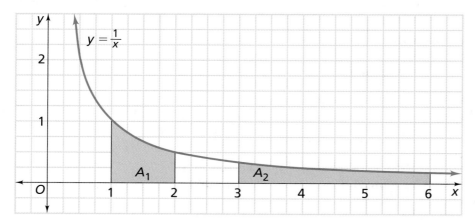

So, $a = 1$, $b = 2$, and
$t = 3$.

For Discussion

6. Which area do you think is greater?

One way to decide which is greater is to look at the upper and lower sums.
Gregory looked at the Cavalieri sums rather than the Fermat sums. He took
equal subdivisions along the x-axis.

For Discussion

7. Show that

$$U_3[1, 2]\left(\tfrac{1}{x}\right) = U_3[3, 6]\left(\tfrac{1}{x}\right)$$

by matching each rectangle in $U_3[1, 2]\left(\tfrac{1}{x}\right)$ with a rectangle in $U_3[3, 6]\left(\tfrac{1}{x}\right)$ that has the same area.

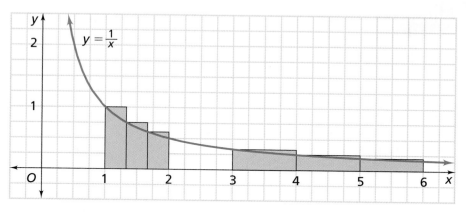

For You to Do

8. Show that

$$U_4[1, 2]\left(\tfrac{1}{x}\right) = U_4[3, 6]\left(\tfrac{1}{x}\right)$$

9. Show that

$$U_n[1, 2]\left(\tfrac{1}{x}\right) = U_n[3, 6]\left(\tfrac{1}{x}\right)$$

The upper sums are always equal. Similarly, the lower sums are always equal. It follows that

$$S[1, 2]\left(\tfrac{1}{x}\right) = S[3, 6]\left(\tfrac{1}{x}\right)$$

Actually, Gregory proved a much more general statement.

> Check the equality of the lower sums for yourself.

Theorem 8.1   Gregory of St. Vincent's Theorem

For any $t > 0$ and any real numbers a, b with $1 \le a < b$,

$$S[a, b]\left(\tfrac{1}{x}\right) = S[ta, tb]\left(\tfrac{1}{x}\right)$$

Exercises *Practicing Habits of Mind*

Check Your Understanding

1. Use your calculator to make a table for $\mathcal{L}(a)$ for values of a between 1 and 10, in increments of 0.5.

2. Suppose you allow a to take on real values between 1 and 10. Sketch the graph of $a \mapsto S[1, a](x^{-1})$ for $1 \leq a \leq 10$.

3. **Write About It** There must be a number a for which $\mathcal{L}(a) = 1$. Between what two integers is a? Explain.

4. Show that $\mathcal{L}(2^3) = 3\mathcal{L}(2)$.

5. Make a conjecture about $\mathcal{L}(r^m)$ based on Exercise 4. Are there any restrictions on r and m?

> You can use your calculator to check this numerically.

6. Prove that $\mathcal{L}(r^m) = m \cdot \mathcal{L}(r)$ if $r > 1$ and $m \geq 0$ is an integer.

7. **Take It Further** Find the approximate value of a in each of the following cases.

   a. $\mathcal{L}(a) = 1$ **b.** $\mathcal{L}(a) = 2$ **c.** $\mathcal{L}(a) = 3$

   d. $\mathcal{L}(a) = 4$ **e.** $\mathcal{L}(a) = 6$

   Exercises 8–10 will take you through a proof of Theorem 8.1.

8. **Take It Further** Suppose you are trying to compute

   $$U_n[a, b]\left(\tfrac{1}{x}\right)$$

   a. Let Δ_1 denote the width of each rectangle. Express Δ_1 in terms of a, b, and n.

   b. Find
   - the height of the first rectangle
   - the height of the second rectangle
   - the height of the third rectangle
   - the height of the ith rectangle

   c. Find
   - the area of the first rectangle
   - the area of the second rectangle
   - the area of the third rectangle
   - the area of the ith rectangle

9. Take It Further

Suppose you are trying to compute

$$U_n[ta, tb]\left(\tfrac{1}{x}\right)$$

a. Let Δ_2 denote the width of each rectangle. Express Δ_2 in terms of a, b, t, and n, How does Δ_2 relate to Δ_1 from Exercise 8?

Remember, $\Delta_2 = t\Delta_1$.

b. Find:

- the height of the first rectangle
- the height of the second rectangle
- the height of the third rectangle
- the height of the ith rectangle

c. Find

- the area of the first rectangle
- the area of the second rectangle
- the area of the third rectangle
- the area of the ith rectangle

d. Show that the area of each rectangle in $U_n[a, b]\left(\tfrac{1}{x}\right)$ is equal to the area of each rectangle in $U_n[ta, tb]\left(\tfrac{1}{x}\right)$.

e. Explain why $U_n[a, b]\left(\tfrac{1}{x}\right) = U_n[ta, tb]\left(\tfrac{1}{x}\right)$.

10. Take It Further Show that $S[a, b]\left(\tfrac{1}{x}\right) = S[ta, tb]\left(\tfrac{1}{x}\right)$.

On Your Own

11. Without using the results of Exercises 8 and 9, show that

$$U_3[1, 3]\left(\tfrac{1}{x}\right) = U_3[3, 9]\left(\tfrac{1}{x}\right)$$

by matching each rectangle in $U_3[1, 3]\left(\tfrac{1}{x}\right)$ with a rectangle in $U_3[3, 9]\left(\tfrac{1}{x}\right)$ that has the same area.

12. Without using the results of Exercises 8 and 9, show that

$$U_4[1, 5]\left(\tfrac{1}{x}\right) = U_4[3, 15]\left(\tfrac{1}{x}\right)$$

13. What do the shaded regions suggest about the relative sizes of $\mathcal{L}(m_1)$ and $\mathcal{L}(m_2)$ when $1 \le m_1 < m_2$?

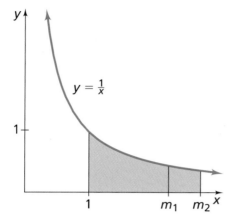

Go Online
PHSchool.com

For additional practice, go to **Web Code:** bga-0808

14. Take It Further Suppose a and b are numbers such that $\mathcal{L}(a) = 7$ and $\mathcal{L}(b) = 9$. Find each of the following.

a. $\mathcal{L}(ab)$ **b.** $\mathcal{L}(a^2)$ **c.** $\mathcal{L}(a^{10})$ **d.** $\mathcal{L}\left(\frac{b}{a}\right)$

15. Why is $\mathcal{L}(1) = 0$?

16. Standardized Test Prep Which of the following is equal to $U_7[1, 3]\left(\frac{1}{x}\right)$?

A. $L_7[1, 3]\left(\frac{1}{x}\right)$

B. $U_7[2, 4]\left(\frac{1}{x}\right)$

C. $U_7[3, 6]\left(\frac{1}{x}\right)$

D. $U_7[4, 12]\left(\frac{1}{x}\right)$

Maintain Your Skills

17. a. Without using the results of Exercises 8 and 9, show that

$$U_n[1, 4]\left(\tfrac{1}{x}\right) = U_n[3, 12]\left(\tfrac{1}{x}\right)$$

b. Show that

$$U_6[1, 3]\left(\tfrac{1}{x}\right) = U_6[3, 9]\left(\tfrac{1}{x}\right)$$

c. Show that

$$U_n[1, 3]\left(\tfrac{1}{x}\right) = U_n[3, 9]\left(\tfrac{1}{x}\right)$$

Remember...

Theorem 8.1 is a theorem about $S[a, b]\left(\frac{1}{x}\right)$, and not about $U_n[a, b]\left(\frac{1}{x}\right)$.

The function $\mathcal{L}$ defined in Lesson 8.8 is really a familiar function in disguise. You will unmask the function in this lesson.

episode 30

Sasha and Derman are working on Problem 1 of the last lesson. They are approximating $S[1, 2](x^{-1})$ using Fermat's method.

Derman I found the Fermat Upper Sum by making another table.

Fermat Upper Sum for $y = x^{-1}$ on [1, 2]

	Base	Height	Area
1st rectangle	$r - 1$	1	$1(r - 1)$
2nd rectangle	$r^2 - r$	r^{-1}	$\dfrac{r^2 - r}{r} = r - 1$
3rd rectangle	$r^3 - r^2$	$(r^2)^{-1} = r^{-2}$	$r - 1$
4th rectangle	$r^4 - r^3$	$(r^3)^{-1} = r^{-3}$	$r - 1$
$\vdots$	$\vdots$	$\vdots$	$\vdots$
nth rectangle	$r^n - r^{n-1}$	$(r^{n-1})^{-1} = r^{-(n-1)}$	$r - 1$

Derman But how do I add up all those $(r - 1)$'s?

Sasha This is the easiest addition we've done so far! There are n of them, so we get $n(r - 1)$. And in this case, $r = \sqrt[n]{2}$, so the Fermat upper sum is $n(\sqrt[n]{2} - 1)$. So if we let $n = 200$, then we get an approximation of 0.6943497.

And it gets better. Look at our table—we could replace r^n with whatever we needed. The lower sum works pretty much the same way. We can approximate $\mathcal{L}(a)$ using $n(\sqrt[n]{a} - 1)$ as long as we make n big enough.

Derman Now, this is the kind of calculation I can get into!

You will do this in the upcoming Check Your Understanding.

Derman is excited because he and Sasha found a quick way of approximating $\mathcal{L}(a)$. $\mathcal{L}$ has lots of interesting properties, which you can derive using the definition $\mathcal{L}(a) = S[1, a]\left(\frac{1}{x}\right)$ and Theorem 8.1.

Problem Show that $\mathcal{L}(6) = \mathcal{L}(2 \cdot 3) = \mathcal{L}(2) + \mathcal{L}(3)$.

Solution

$$\mathcal{L}(6) = S[1, 6]\left(\tfrac{1}{x}\right)$$

$$= S[1, 2]\left(\tfrac{1}{x}\right) + S[2, 6]\left(\tfrac{1}{x}\right)$$

$$= S[1, 2]\left(\tfrac{1}{x}\right) + S[1, 3]\left(\tfrac{1}{x}\right) \quad \text{by Theorem 8.1}$$

$$= \mathcal{L}(2) + \mathcal{L}(3)$$

There is nothing special about 2 and 3 (except that $6 = 2 \cdot 3$).

For You to Do

1. Show that $\mathcal{L}(12) = \mathcal{L}(3) + \mathcal{L}(4)$.

2. Show that $\mathcal{L}(rs) = \mathcal{L}(r) + \mathcal{L}(s)$, if r and s are greater than 1.

Minds in Action episode 31

Sasha and Derman are looking at properties of the function $\mathcal{L}$.

Sasha This function seems familiar. Look at its properties:

If $r > s \geq 1$ and m is a positive integer, then

$$\mathcal{L}(rs) = \mathcal{L}(r) + \mathcal{L}(s)$$

$$\mathcal{L}\left(\tfrac{r}{s}\right) = \mathcal{L}(r) - \mathcal{L}(s)$$

$$\mathcal{L}(r^m) = m\mathcal{L}(r)$$

$$\mathcal{L}(1) = 0$$

You will prove this in Exercise 5.

Derman It almost reminds me of exponential functions—or—

Sasha Logarithms! This function has exactly the same properties as a logarithmic function! Do you think this function is a logarithm?

Derman What would the base be?

Sasha Well, we could figure that out—we would just need to know what input a yields $\mathcal{L}(a) = 1$. We can use our approximation $\mathcal{L}(a) \approx n(\sqrt[n]{a} - 1)$ to get a pretty good estimate of a. Let's choose $n = 1,000,000$.

For You to Do

3. Use Sasha's approximation of $\mathcal{L}(a)$ to find a such that $\mathcal{L}(a) \approx 1$.

Minds in Action

episode 32

Sasha and Derman start looking for a value of a which makes
$f(a) = 1{,}000{,}000\left(\sqrt[1{,}000{,}000]{a} - 1\right)$ *approximately equal to* 1.

Sasha $a = 2.7$ is a little low, since $f(2.7) \approx 0.9933$.

Derman And $a = 2.75$ is a little high, since $f(2.75) \approx 1.0116$.

Sasha Wait a second—it can't be—Derman, try e.

Derman $f(e) = 1$.

Sasha It's the natural logarithm! It must be the natural log! And in fact, look: If $n\left(a^{\frac{1}{n}} - 1\right) \approx 1$, then $a^{\frac{1}{n}} - 1 \approx \frac{1}{n}$, so $a^{\frac{1}{n}} \approx \frac{1}{n} + 1$ and $a \approx \left(1 + \frac{1}{n}\right)^n$. We are assuming n to be very large, so that's just the definition of e!

Sasha and Derman are pretty confident that $\mathcal{L}(x) = \log_e(x)$, but they need a proof. They know that $\mathcal{L}(e) = 1$. They can easily use that, together with the third and fourth items of Sasha's list of properties of $\mathcal{L}$, to prove the following theorem.

Theorem 8.2

If m is a nonnegative integer,

$$\mathcal{L}(e^m) = m$$

Theorem 8.2 covers only cases where the exponent m is a nonnegative integer. You can do better, with a little formal calculation.

Habits of Mind

Understand the process. This kind of reasoning is typical when one wants to extend the applicability of an equation from integers to rational numbers. After you study this kind of argument a few times, you can do it yourself.

For Discussion

4. Suppose m is a positive integer. Prove that

$$\mathcal{L}\left(e^{\frac{1}{m}}\right) = \frac{1}{m}$$

by giving a reason for each step in this formal calculation:

$$1 = \mathcal{L}(e) = \mathcal{L}\left(e^{\frac{m}{m}}\right) \qquad m \text{ is a positive integer.}$$

$$= \mathcal{L}\left(\left(e^{\frac{1}{m}}\right)^{m}\right)$$

$$= m\,\mathcal{L}\left(e^{\frac{1}{m}}\right)$$

Divide both sides by m to conclude that

$$\frac{1}{m} = \mathcal{L}\left(e^{\frac{1}{m}}\right)$$

For You to Do

5. Use the same line of reasoning to prove that if $a \geq 1$,

$$\mathcal{L}\left(a^{\frac{1}{m}}\right) = \frac{1}{m}\mathcal{L}(a)$$

For Discussion

6. Prove that $\mathcal{L}\left(e^{\frac{q}{m}}\right) = \frac{q}{m}$ for any non-negative fraction $\frac{q}{m}$, by supplying the reasons.

$$\mathcal{L}\left(e^{\frac{q}{m}}\right) = \mathcal{L}\left((e^{q})^{\frac{1}{m}}\right)$$

$$= \frac{1}{m}\mathcal{L}(e^{q})$$

$$= \frac{1}{m}q\,\mathcal{L}(e)$$

$$= \frac{q}{m}$$

Since every real number can be approximated by fractions, the exponent rule extends even further, to real numbers. In calculus, you will prove the following result.

Theorem 8.3

If $r \geq 0$ is any real number, then

$$\mathcal{L}(e^{r}) = r$$

Theorem 8.3 makes the connection between $\mathcal{L}$ and the natural logarithm. Suppose you want to find $\mathcal{L}(a)$. Find a real number r such that $e^r = a$—that is, $r = \ln a$. Then

$$\mathcal{L}(a) = \mathcal{L}(e^r) = r = \ln a$$

So, $\mathcal{L}(a) = \ln a$.

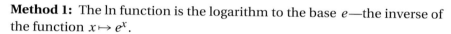

Here $a \geq 1$ and $r \geq 0$.

Theorem 8.4

If $a \geq 1$,

$$\mathcal{L}(a) = r \Leftrightarrow e^r = a$$

In other words, $\mathcal{L}$ is the natural logarithm

$$\mathcal{L}(a) = \ln a$$

Remember...

All this is still based on Sasha's convincing argument that $\mathcal{L}(e) = 1$.

Developing Habits of Mind

Think about it more than one way. You now have two ways to think about the natural logarithm function.

Method 1: The ln function is the logarithm to the base e—the inverse of the function $x \mapsto e^x$.

Method 2: The ln function is the function that gives the area under the graph of $y = \frac{1}{x}$ between $x = 1$ and $x = a$, where $a \geq 1$:

$$\ln a = S[1, a](x^{-1})$$

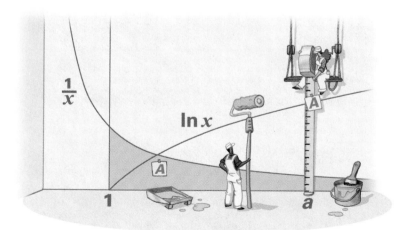

Exercises Practicing Habits of Mind

Check Your Understanding

1. In the Minds in Action episode that opens this lesson, Sasha says, "The lower sum works pretty much the same way." You will now see what she means.

   a. Copy and complete the following table.

Fermat Lower Sum for $y = x^{-1}$ on [1, 2]			
	Base	Height	Area
1st rectangle	▨	▨	▨
2nd rectangle	▨	▨	▨
3rd rectangle	▨	▨	▨
4th rectangle	▨	▨	▨
⋮	⋮	⋮	⋮
nth rectangle	▨	▨	▨

   b. Add up the areas of the rectangles.

   For Exercises 2 through 5, consider the function, g, with the following properties:

   • The domain of g is $\mathbb{R}$.

   • For all numbers x and y,
   $$g(xy) = g(x) + g(y)$$

   • $g(10) = 1$

   • g is increasing. That is, if $x < y$, then $g(x) < g(y)$ for all x and y.

2. Find each of the following.

   a. $g(10)$ b. $g(100)$ c. $g(10{,}000)$

   d. $g(10^{100})$ e. $g(1)$

3. Find each of the following.

   a. $g\left(\frac{1}{10}\right)$ b. $g\left(\frac{1}{100}\right)$ c. $g\left(\frac{1}{1000}\right)$ d. $g\left(\frac{1}{10^{100}}\right)$

4. Suppose $g(5) \approx 0.69897$. Find approximations of each of the following.

   a. $g(25)$ b. $g(2)$ c. $g(50)$ d. $g(2^4 \cdot 5^7)$

5. **a.** Show that, for all positive real numbers x and y, $g\left(\frac{x}{y}\right) = g(x) - g(y)$.

   b. What is $g(\sqrt{5})$? Why?

   c. The function g is actually a function you have seen before. Which one?

   d. Sketch the graph of $y = g(x)$.

On Your Own

6. **Write About It** The definition of $\mathcal{L}$ is $\mathcal{L}(a) = S[1, a]\left(\frac{1}{x}\right)$.

   This assumes that $a \geq 1$, and all theorems so far have retained that assumption.

   But for $a \geq 1$, $\mathcal{L}(a) = \ln a$. Describe what it might mean to extend the definition of $\mathcal{L}(a)$ to $0 < a < 1$, so that for all positive a, $\mathcal{L}(a) = \ln a$.

7. **a.** Show that $\mathcal{L}(4) = 2\mathcal{L}(2)$.   **b.** Show that $\mathcal{L}(8) = 3\mathcal{L}(2)$.

   c. Show that $\mathcal{L}(16) = 4\mathcal{L}(2)$.   **d.** Show that $\mathcal{L}(2^n) = n\mathcal{L}(2)$.

   e. Assuming only that $\mathcal{L}(rs) = \mathcal{L}(r) + \mathcal{L}(s)$, show that if $r > 1$ and m is a positive integer, then $\mathcal{L}(r^m) = m\mathcal{L}(r)$.

8. Assuming only that $\mathcal{L}(rs) = \mathcal{L}(r) + \mathcal{L}(s)$, show that if $r \geq s \geq 1$, then $\mathcal{L}\left(\frac{r}{s}\right) = \mathcal{L}(r) - \mathcal{L}(s)$.

9. Show that $\mathcal{L}(1) = 0$.

10. **Standardized Test Prep** Which of the following is a property of $\mathcal{L}(a)$?

    a. For $a \geq 1$ and $b \geq 1$, $\mathcal{L}(a) + \mathcal{L}(b) = \mathcal{L}(a + b)$

    b. For $a \geq 1$ and $b \geq 1$, $\mathcal{L}(a) + \mathcal{L}(b) = \mathcal{L}(ab)$

    c. For $a \geq 1$ and $b \geq 1$, $\mathcal{L}(ab) \geq \mathcal{L}(a + b)$

    d. For $a \geq 1$ and $b \geq 1$, $\mathcal{L}(a) \cdot (b) \geq \mathcal{L}(ab)$

> For this definition to make sense, *a* must be greater than or equal to 1.

Go Online
PHSchool.com

For additional practice, go to **Web Code:** bga-0809

Maintain Your Skills

11. **a.** Find a such that $\mathcal{L}(a) = 2$.   **b.** Find a such that $\mathcal{L}(a) = 3$.

    c. Find a such that $\mathcal{L}(a) = z$.

8.10 The Area Under $f(x) = e^x$

Take a closer look at the graph of the function $f(x) = e^x$.

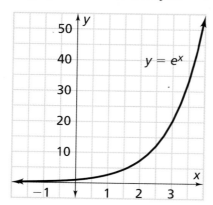

For Discussion

Analyze the graph of $f(x) = e^x$ by answering the following questions.

1. Does the graph cross the y-axis? If so, where? If not, why not?

2. Does the graph cross the x-axis? If so, where? If not, why not?

3. What happens as the x-values become larger and larger positive numbers?

4. What happens as the x-values become larger and larger negative numbers?

The focus of the chapter has been on finding the areas under curves. What is the area under the graph of $y = e^x$, from $x = a$ to $x = b$? To begin to answer this question, consider first the interval $[0, 1]$

For Discussion

5. Approximate the area under the graph of $y = e^x$ from 0 to 1, $S[0, 1](e^x)$.

If you tried to use the method of Fermat in Problem 5, you probably got stuck. Fermat designed his method to result in a sum of a geometric sequence. Since $f(x) = e^x$ is an exponential function, and not a power function like $f(x) = x^m$, the resulting sum is not that of a geometric sequence.

That is, in $f(x) = e^x$ the x is in the exponent, not used as the base.

Problem Find the area under the curve $f(x) = e^x$ from $x = 0$ to $x = 1$.

Solution First, find the lower sum $L_n[0, 1](e^x)$ using Cavalieri's method.

	Base	Height	Area
1st rectangle	$\frac{1}{n}$	$e^0 = 1$	$\frac{1}{n} \cdot 1 = \frac{1}{n}$
2nd rectangle	$\frac{1}{n}$	$e^{\frac{1}{n}}$	$\frac{1}{n} \cdot e^{\frac{1}{n}} = \frac{e^{\frac{1}{n}}}{n}$
3rd rectangle	$\frac{1}{n}$	$e^{\frac{2}{n}}$	$\frac{1}{n} \cdot e^{\frac{2}{n}} = \frac{e^{\frac{2}{n}}}{n}$
4th rectangle	$\frac{1}{n}$	$e^{\frac{3}{n}}$	$\frac{1}{n} \cdot e^{\frac{3}{n}} = \frac{e^{\frac{3}{n}}}{n}$
$\vdots$	$\vdots$	$\vdots$	$\vdots$
nth rectangle	$\frac{1}{n}$	$e^{\frac{n-1}{n}}$	$\frac{1}{n} \cdot e^{\frac{n-1}{n}} = \frac{e^{\frac{n-1}{n}}}{n}$

Add the areas of all the rectangles.

$$L_n[0, 1](e^x) = \frac{1}{n} + \frac{e^{\frac{1}{n}}}{n} + \frac{e^{\frac{2}{n}}}{n} + \frac{e^{\frac{3}{n}}}{n} + \frac{e^{\frac{4}{n}}}{n} + \cdots + \frac{e^{\frac{n-1}{n}}}{n}$$

$$= \frac{1}{n}\left(1 + e^{\frac{1}{n}} + e^{\frac{2}{n}} + e^{\frac{3}{n}} + e^{\frac{4}{n}} + \cdots + e^{\frac{n-1}{n}}\right)$$

$$= \frac{1}{n}\left(1 + e^{\frac{1}{n}} + \left(e^{\frac{1}{n}}\right)^2 + \left(e^{\frac{1}{n}}\right)^3 + \left(e^{\frac{1}{n}}\right)^4 + \cdots + \left(e^{\frac{1}{n}}\right)^{n-1}\right)$$

Use the formula for simplifying a geometric series:

$$\frac{1}{n}\left(1 + e^{\frac{1}{n}} + \left(e^{\frac{1}{n}}\right)^2 + \left(e^{\frac{1}{n}}\right)^3 + \left(e^{\frac{1}{n}}\right)^4 + \cdots + \left(e^{\frac{1}{n}}\right)^{n-1}\right)$$

$$= \frac{1}{n}\left(\frac{\left(e^{\frac{1}{n}}\right)^n - 1}{e^{\frac{1}{n}} - 1}\right)$$

$$= \frac{1}{n}\left(\frac{e - 1}{e^{\frac{1}{n}} - 1}\right)$$

$$= \frac{e - 1}{n\left(e^{\frac{1}{n}} - 1\right)}$$

> **Remember...**
>
> $$1 + q + q^2 + \cdots + q^{n-1} = \frac{q^n - 1}{q - 1}$$

Next, determine what happens to $\dfrac{e - 1}{n\left(e^{\frac{1}{n}} - 1\right)}$ as you increase the number of subdivisions, n. This is the same as calculating the value of

$$\lim_{n \to \infty} \frac{e - 1}{n\left(e^{\frac{1}{n}} - 1\right)}$$

Since $e - 1$ is a constant, you can move it out in front of the limit expression:

$$\lim_{n \to \infty} \frac{e - 1}{n\left(e^{\frac{1}{n}} - 1\right)} = (e - 1)\lim_{n \to \infty} \frac{1}{n\left(e^{\frac{1}{n}} - 1\right)}$$

Rewrite $e^{\frac{1}{n}}$ as $\sqrt[n]{e}$. Then

$$\lim_{n\to\infty} \frac{1}{n(\sqrt[n]{e}-1)} = \frac{1}{\lim\limits_{n\to\infty}[n(\sqrt[n]{e}-1)]} = \frac{1}{\mathcal{L}(e)} = \frac{1}{\ln e} = 1$$

So,

$$(e-1)\lim_{n\to\infty}\frac{1}{n\left(e^{\frac{1}{n}}-1\right)} = e-1$$

This means that the lower sum $L_n[0,1](e^x)$ approaches $e-1$ as you increase the number of subdivisions. Now, all you have to do is check that the upper sum approaches the same value. You will do this in Exercise 1.

Developing Habits of Mind

Visualize. Often, when you cannot figure out the value of a limit, you can turn to the graph for a hint of how the expression behaves. Plot the n-values on the horizontal axis and the outputs of the expression on the vertical axis. If the expression approaches one number as n grows larger, that number is *probably* the value of the limit. This does not work every time. *Sometimes* the outputs of the n-values you are looking at seem to tend towards one number, but for much much larger n-values the expression behaves differently.

Look at the graph of the expression $\dfrac{1}{n\left(e^{\frac{1}{n}}-1\right)}$.

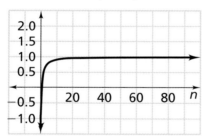

As n increases, the value of the expression becomes closer and closer to 1. This is evidence to support the conjecture that

$$\lim_{n\to\infty}\frac{1}{n\left(e^{\frac{1}{n}}-1\right)} = 1$$

Exercises Practicing Habits of Mind

Check Your Understanding

1. **a.** Find the upper sum for the curve $f(x) = e^x$ from $x = 0$ to $x = 1$ with n subdivisions, $U_n[0, 1](e^x)$.

   b. Use the fact that $\lim_{n \to \infty} L_n[0, 1](e^x) = e - 1$ and the results from part (a) to find $S[0, 1](e^x)$.

2. Find $S[a, a + 1](e^x)$ where a is any real number.

3. **Write About It** Consider the function $f(x) = e^{ax} + b$ where a and b are constants. How do a and b affect the shape of the graph?

4. Use your knowledge of $S[0, 1](e^x)$ to find each of the following.

   a. $S[0, 1](e^x + 3)$ **b.** $S[-1, 0](e^{-x})$ **c.** $S[-1, 0](e^{-x} + 7)$

5. Find the area of the shaded region.

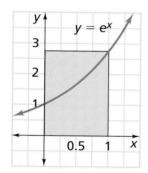

6. This is the graph of $y = \ln x$.

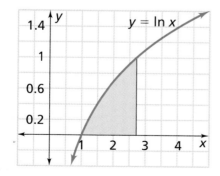

   a. Describe the relationship between the graphs of $y = \ln x$ and $y = e^x$.

   b. What is the area of the shaded region, $S[1, e](\ln x)$?

7. Take It Further Use your knowledge of $S[a, a + 1](e^x)$ from Exercise 2 to find

$$S[a, b](e^x)$$

where a and b are natural numbers with $a \leq b$.

On Your Own

8. Copy and complete the following tables.

a.

n	$\left(\dfrac{2n + 1}{2n - 1}\right)^n$
10	■
100	■
1000	■
10,000	■

b.

n	$1 + \dfrac{1}{1!} + \dfrac{1}{2!} + \cdots + \dfrac{1}{n!}$
4	■
7	■
10	■
13	■

9. Let $[a_0; a_1, a_2, a_3, \dots]$ represent the *continued fraction*

$$a_0 + \cfrac{1}{a_1 + \cfrac{1}{a_2 + \cfrac{1}{a_3 + \dots}}}$$

Find the value of each expression.

a. $[a_0; a_1, a_2, a_3] = [2; 1, 2, 1]$

b. $[a_0; a_1, a_2, a_3, a_4, a_5, a_6] = [2; 1, 2, 1, 1, 4, 1]$

c. $[a_0; a_1, a_2, a_3, a_4, a_5, a_6, a_7, a_8, a_9] = [2; 1, 2, 1, 1, 4, 1, 1, 6, 1]$

10. Do the values you found in Exercise 9 seem to approach a particular number as you add more terms a_n? If so, what is it?

11. Standardized Test Prep Which of the following is not a property of $S[r, s](e^x)$?

A. If $a < b$ then $S[a, b](e^x) = e^b - e^a$

B. If $a < b$ then $S[a, b](e^x) > 0$

C. For all $a > 0$, $S[0, a](e^x) = e^a$

D. If $a < b < c$, $S[a, b](e^x) + S[b, c](e^x) = S[a, c](e^x)$

When you get to the last term, simply stop.

$[2; 1, 2, 1]$

$= 2 + \cfrac{1}{1 + \cfrac{1}{2 + \frac{1}{1}}}$

Go Online
PHSchool.com

For additional practice, go to **Web Code:** bga-0810

Maintain Your Skills

12. In each of the tables in Exercise 8, do the values seem to approach a particular number as n becomes larger and larger? If so, what is it?

In this investigation, you found that one formula describes the area under the graph of $y = x^m$ for all values of m other than -1. You learned that the area below $y = x^{-1}$, or $y = \frac{1}{x}$, is related to the natural logarithm. You also calculated the area below $y = e^x$. The following questions will help you summarize what you have learned.

1. What is the value of $S[1, e](\ln x)$?

2. What is the value of $S[-1, 0](e^{-x} + 7)$?

3. What is the value of $S[1, 2](x^{-2})$?

4. What is the value of $S[1, 2](x^{-1})$?

5. What is the value of $S[0, 1](e^x)$?

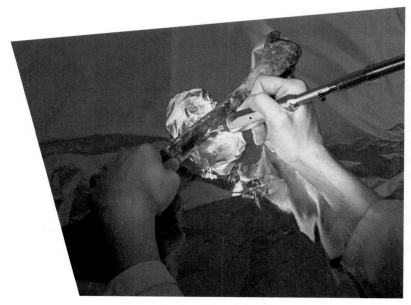

Radiocarbon dating involves using the natural logarithm function to solve an equation of the form $N = N_0 e^{-\lambda t}$.

Project: Using Mathematical Habits

A Delightful Sequence of Polynomials

In Chapter 5, you investigated function definitions with a two term recurrence like the definition of the Fibonacci numbers:

$$f(n) = \begin{cases} 0 & \text{if } n = 0 \\ 1 & \text{if } n = 1 \\ f(n-1) + f(n-2) & \text{if } n > 1 \end{cases}$$

In Chapter 5, you found a closed-form definition $f(n) = \dfrac{\left(\frac{1+\sqrt{5}}{2}\right)^n - \left(\frac{1-\sqrt{5}}{2}\right)^n}{\sqrt{5}}$ for this function. You developed methods for finding closed-form definitions for any function defined by a two-term recurrence.

The outputs of the functions in Chapter 5 are numbers, real or complex. This project is about a sequence of polynomials that show up all over mathematics and science and are defined by a similar two-term recurrence:

$$t(n, x) = \begin{cases} 1 & \text{if } n = 0 \\ x & \text{if } n = 1 \\ 2x \cdot t(n-1, x) - t(n-2, x) & \text{if } n > 1 \end{cases}$$

Here is an example.

Problem Find the normal form for the first four polynomials you get from t.

Solution The definition gives the first two polynomials.

$$t(0, x) = 1 \text{ and } t(1, x) = x$$

Use the recurrence to find $t(2, x)$.

$$\begin{aligned} t(2, x) &= 2x \cdot t(1, x) - t(0, x) \\ &= 2x \cdot x - 1 \\ &= 2x^2 - 1 \end{aligned}$$

Now that you know $t(2, x)$, you can find $t(3, x)$.

$$\begin{aligned} t(3, x) &= 2x \cdot t(2, x) - t(1, x) \\ &= 2x(2x^2 - 1) - x \\ &= 4x^3 - 3x \end{aligned}$$

1. Model the definition of $t(n, x)$ in your FML.

2. Find the normal form for $t(n, x)$ for all n from 0 through 10. Make a table of your results.

The variables n and x in the definition of t serve different purposes. The input n is a nonnegative integer—an index that tells you which polynomial you have. The input x, on the other hand, is the variable in the nth polynomial. If you were doing a strictly algebraic investigation of the function t, you would not need to include x in the definition. You could use the definition

$$s(n) = \begin{cases} 1 & \text{if } n = 0 \\ x & \text{if } n = 1 \\ 2x \cdot s(n-1) - s(n-2) & \text{if } n > 1 \end{cases}$$

If you did this, s would be a function that assigns nonnegative integers to polynomial expressions. But, in this project, you should think of $t(n, x)$ as a polynomial function of x, so that $t(3, 5)$ is a number—the third polynomial evaluated at 5. This allows you, for example, to graph the various polynomials.

Some people like to use subscripts for the index, so they write $t_n(x)$ or s_n. Making the index an input rather that a subscript helps you remember that sequences are just functions defined on non-negative integers, and it allows you to model the sequence in your CAS with exactly the same notation as you use when you write it on paper.

The project title claims that the sequence of polynomials is delightful. The rest of the project is a collection of exercises that will help you understand this claim.

3. a. Extend your table to include each polynomial $t(n, x)$ for n up through 18.

   b. Find, describe, and explain several patterns in the coefficients or the terms of the polynomials.

4. Make your own polynomial function gallery for the $t(n, x)$.

   a. Sketch the graphs of $t(n, x)$ for $0 \le n \le 10$. Draw each graph on a separate set of axes over $-1 \le x \le 1$.

   b. Describe some interesting properties of your graphs. Explain the properties and why you find them interesting.

   c. Overlay the graphs of $t(n, x)$ for $0 \le n \le 10$ on the same set of axes. Describe some interesting properties of the picture.

5. Solve each of the equations $t(n, x) = 0$ for $0 \le n \le 6$.

6. **a.** Write down the factorizations of each polynomial $t(n, x)$ over $\mathbb{Z}$ for $1 \leq n \leq 18$.

   b. For what pairs (m, n) on your list is $t(m, x)$ a factor of $t(n, x)$?

   c. Make a conjecture that describes the relation between m and n if $t(m, x)$ a factor of $t(n, x)$.

7. In Lesson 2.7, you learned that

   $$\cos 2\alpha = 2 \cos^2 \alpha - 1$$

   for all real numbers α. So, if $h(x) = 2x^2 - 1$,

   $$h(\cos \alpha) = \cos 2\alpha$$

   a. Find a polynomial function g such that

   $$g(\cos \alpha) = \cos 3\alpha$$

   b. Find a polynomial function k such that

   $$k(\cos \alpha) = \cos 4\alpha$$

8. Exercise 7 suggests that there might be a new sequence of polynomials $h(n, x)$ defined on nonnegative integers with the property that

   $$h(n, \cos \alpha) = \cos n\alpha$$

   Show that, in fact, the polynomials $t(n, x)$ do the job. That is, prove the following theorem.

Theorem 8.5

Suppose $t(n, x)$ is the sequence of polynomials defined by

$$t(n, x) = \begin{cases} 1 & \text{if } n = 0 \\ x & \text{if } n = 1 \\ 2x \cdot t(n - 1, x) - t(n - 2, x) & \text{if } n > 1 \end{cases}$$

Then, for all nonnegative integers n,

$$t(n, \cos \alpha) = \cos n\alpha$$

9. Each of the following functions has infinitely many zeros. Find formulas that describe the zeros of each.

   a. $\alpha \mapsto \cos \alpha$ **b.** $\alpha \mapsto \cos 2\alpha$ **c.** $\alpha \mapsto \cos 3\alpha$

   d. $\alpha \mapsto \cos 4\alpha$ **e.** $\alpha \mapsto \cos 5\alpha$

   f. $\alpha \mapsto \cos k\alpha$ (in terms of k)

10. Revisit Exercise 6c and prove your conjecture.

11. Suppose $f(x) = 2x - \frac{1}{x}$. Write each expression as a quotient of two polynomials in normal form.

    a. $f(x)$

    b. $2x - \dfrac{1}{f(x)}$

    c. $2x - \dfrac{1}{2x - \dfrac{1}{f(x)}}$

    d. $2x - \dfrac{1}{2x - \dfrac{1}{2x - \dfrac{1}{f(x)}}}$

    e. $2x - \dfrac{1}{2x - \dfrac{1}{2x - \dfrac{1}{2x - \dfrac{1}{f(x)}}}}$

12. **a.** Develop a conjecture about a pattern in the results of Exercise 11.

    b. Prove your conjecture.

13. This chapter was about finding areas under curves.

    a. Make a table for the area bounded by the graph of $y = t(n, x)$ between -1 and 1 for $0 \leq n \leq 10$.

    b. Make some conjectures based on patterns you see in your table.

    c. Prove as many of your conjectures as you can.

14. Use the methods of Chapter 5 to show that
    $$t(n, x) = \tfrac{1}{2}\left(\left(x + \sqrt{x^2 - 1} \right)^n + \left(x - \sqrt{x^2 - 1} \right)^n \right)$$

Go Online

PHSchool.com

For vocabulary review, go to Web Code: bgj-0851

In **Investigation 8A,** you learned how to

- estimate the areas of irregularly-shaped objects

- use a method for estimating the area under the graph of $y = x^2$ over intervals in the first quadrant

- find a surprising way to compute the area under the graph of $y = x^2$ exactly

The following questions will help you check your understanding.

1. In this exercise, you will estimate the area under $y = \sin x$ between 0 and π using the figure below.

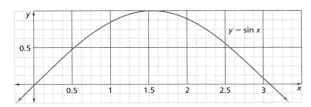

a. Using the $\frac{1}{2}$ unit grid, provide an upper bound for the area under the curve.

b. Using the $\frac{1}{2}$ unit grid, provide a lower bound for the area under the curve.

c. Using the $\frac{1}{8}$ unit grid (the smaller grid in the picture), provide an upper bound for the area under the curve.

d. Using the $\frac{1}{8}$ unit grid, provide a lower bound for the area under the curve.

e. Use the $\frac{1}{8}$ grid upper and lower estimates to find an even better estimate of the area under the curve. Explain your reasoning.

2. Compute $L_4[0, 1](x^2)$ and $U_4[0, 1](x^2)$, the lower and upper estimates of the area under the graph of $y = x^2$ between 0 and 1 with four subdivisions.

3. Compute $S[0, 1](x^2)$, the exact value of the area under the graph of $y = x^2$ between 0 and 1.

4. Compute the lower and upper estimates, $L_4\left[-\frac{\pi}{2}, 0\right](\cos x)$ and $U_4\left[-\frac{\pi}{2}, 0\right](\cos x)$, of the area under the graph of $y = \cos x$.

In **Investigation 8B,** you learned to

- compute the area under the graph of $y = x^3$ between 0 and 1

- use the closed form for $\sum\limits_{k=1}^{n} k^m$ for various values of m to compute areas

- use Fermat's method to compute the area under the graph of $y = x^m$ between 1 and 2 for any positive integer m

The following questions will help you check your understanding.

5. Cavalieri showed that

$$\sum_{k=1}^{n} k^3 = \frac{n^2(n+1)^2}{4}$$

for all positive integers n. Use this result to confirm the following identities. (You might find at least one of them useful in the next exercise.)

a. $\sum\limits_{k=1}^{n-1} k^3 = \frac{n^2(n-1)^2}{4}$
for all positive integers n.

b. $\sum\limits_{k=1}^{n} (2k)^3 = \frac{8n^2(n+1)^2}{4}$
for all positive integers n.

c. $\sum\limits_{k=1}^{n} (rk)^3 = \frac{r^3 n^2(n+1)^2}{4}$
for all positive integers n and all real numbers r.

Review continued

6. Compute the lower and upper sum estimates $L_n[0, 2](x^3)$ and $U_n[0, 2](x^3)$. Then investigate their behavior when n becomes larger and larger in order to compute the exact value of the area under the graph of $y = x^3$ between 0 and 2.

7. Use Fermat's Method to compute the area under the graph of $y = x^m$ between 1 and b where b is a positive number greater than 1.

In **Investigation 8C,** you learned to

- develop formulas for calculating $S[1, a](x^m)$ when m is a negative integer

- investigate a mysteriously familiar function $\mathcal{L}$.

- find the area under the graph of $y = e^x$

The following questions will help you check your understanding.

8. Determine the area under the graph of $y = \frac{1}{x^3}$ between 1 and 4.

9. Suppose f satisfies the property that $f(10) = 1$ and $f(xy) = f(x) + f(y)$ for all positive x and y. You proved some other properties in class and homework, but for now, just use the given information.

   a. Explain why the given information, along with the fact that $\frac{x}{y} \cdot y = x$, implies that $f(\frac{x}{y}) = f(x) - f(y)$ for all positive x and y.

   b. Explain why part (a), along with the given information, helps to show that $f(1) = 0$.

You also showed that $f(x^m) = m \cdot f(x)$ for all x when m is a positive integer. You may use this fact, along with all the other properties discussed, to make the following computations.

c. Compute $f(100,000,000)$.

d. If $f(2) \approx 0.301$, approximate $f(5)$.

e. If $f(2) \approx 0.301$, approximate $f(80)$.

f. If $f(2) \approx 0.301$, approximate $f(\frac{1}{50})$.

10. Use the method of Archimedes to compute the area under the graph of $y = e^x$ between 0 and 1. You will need to use the fact that
$$\lim_{n \to \infty} n\left(e^{\frac{1}{n}} - 1\right) = 1.$$

Go Online
PHSchool.com

For a chapter test, go
to Web Code: bga-0853

Multiple Choice

1. If T is an increasing function satisfying
   $T(xy) = T(x) + T(y)$, which of the following
   properties is also true?

   A. $T(1) = 1$

   B. $T(1) = -1$

   C. $T(1) = 0$

   D. $T(1)$ is undefined

2. Suppose T is the function defined in Exercise 1.
   Which of the following properties is also true?

   A. $T(x^3) = (T(x))^3$ for all positive real numbers x.

   B. $T(x^3) = x \cdot T(3)$ for all positive real
   numbers x.

   C. $T(x^3) = 3T(x)$ for all positive real numbers x.

   D. $T(x^3) = T(x) - T(3)$ for all positive real
   numbers x.

3. Which of the following statements is true about
   the area under $y = x^2$ between 0 and 1?

   A. The area is equal to $\frac{1}{2}$.

   B. The area is greater than $\frac{1}{2}$.

   C. The area is less than $\frac{1}{2}$.

   D. The area is infinite.

Open Response

4. Compute $LF_4[1, 3](x^2)$, the lower Fermat sum
   with 4 subdivisions, to approximate the area
   under $y = x^2$ between 1 and 3. Note that the
   points of the subdivisions are 1, r, r^2, r^3 and r^4.

5. Suppose L is an increasing function satisfying
   $L(1) = 0$, $L(10) = 1$, $L(4) \approx 0.602$, and
   $L(xy) = L(x) + L(y)$.

   a. Approximate $L(40)$.

   b. Approximate $L(2)$.

   c. Approximate $L(5)$.

   d. Explain how you know that $L(x^2) = 2L(x)$ for
   all $x > 0$.

   e. Explain how you know that $L(\frac{1}{y}) = -L(y)$ for
   all $y > 0$.

6. The area under $y = 2x^2$ between -1 and 1
   is equal to $\frac{4}{3}$. Explain how you can use this
   information to compute the area between the
   x-axis and the curve $y = 2x^2 - 2$ (region shaded
   in the figure below).

   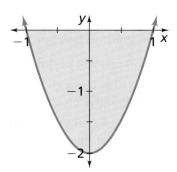

Challenge Problem

7. Use Fermat's method to compute $S[1, b](x^4)$,
   the area under $y = x^4$ between 1 and b, where
   $b > 1$.

1. Find the value of the following expression.

$$\sqrt{2} \cos 45° \sin 45° + \tan \pi - \tan 30° \tan 60° + 3\cos \frac{\pi}{3}$$

2. Solve the equation $\tan^3 x - 3\tan x = 0$ on $0 \le x \le \pi$.

3. Find the simplified form of the expression

$$\sin \frac{3\pi}{7} \cos \frac{2\pi}{7} - \cos \frac{3\pi}{7} \sin \frac{2\pi}{7}$$

4. Simplify each of the following.

   a. $\left(\frac{\sqrt{2}}{2} - \frac{\sqrt{2}}{2}i\right)^4$ b. $\left(\frac{\sqrt{3}}{2} + \frac{1}{2}i\right)^6$

5. Find the slope and the equation of the line tangent to the graph of the function $f(x) = x^3 + 2x$ at the point $(1, 3)$.

6. Sketch the graph of $y = \frac{x + 3}{x^2 + x - 6}$. Identify all asymptotes and any holes in the graph.

7. Six students will perform in a student recital.

   a. Find how many different programs are possible if each student performs once.

   b. Find how many different programs are possible if the winner and runner-up of a soloist competition perform last and next to last and the other four students can perform in any order.

8. Simplify each of the following.

   a. $\frac{_{11}P_4}{4!}$ b. $\frac{1}{5}\binom{100}{98}$

9. A quadratic function q has a difference table that begins as follows.

Input, x	Output, q(x)	Δ	Δ²
0	−1	−1	6
1	−2	5	6
2	3	11	6

Determine the value of $q(10)$.

10. Define f as

$$f(n) = \begin{cases} 2 & \text{if } n = 0 \\ 1 & \text{if } n = 1 \\ 2 \cdot f(n-1) - 3 \cdot f(n-2) & \text{if } n > 0 \end{cases}$$

Find $f(n)$ for $0 \le n \le 6$.

11. Consider the equation

$$25x^2 - 144y^2 - 3600 = 0$$

   a. Show that the graph of the equation is a hyperbola.

   b. Find the coordinates for the foci $(c, 0)$ and $(-c, 0)$.

   c. The graphs of the equations $y = \frac{b}{a}x$ and $y = -\frac{b}{a}x$ are the asymptotes of the hyperbola. Find the equations of the asymptotes for this hyperbola.

   d. Sketch the graph of the hyperbola and its asymptotes. Identify the foci and the intercepts.

12. A line has vector equation $X = P + tD$. What are the values of P and D if $t = 2$ and $X = (3, 5)$? If $t = 5$, $X = (9, -4)$?

13. A tetrahedron (a pyramid with four congruent triangular faces) has faces numbered 1 through 4. You roll it and record the number on the face not showing—the face on the bottom. You perform the experiment three times and find the sum of the three rolls.

   a. Find a polynomial that models the possible outcomes.

   b. Determine the possible sums.

   c. Determine the number of times each sum will occur.

   d. Find the sum or sums that will occur most often.

14. For the sum of the faces of the tetrahedrons in Exercise 13, calculate each of the following values.

    a. the mean

    b. the mean absolute deviation

    c. the variance

    d. the standard deviation

15. Find the expected value for the number of heads when you toss one coin five times.

16. a. Find the mean and standard deviation for the sum of the numbers showing on top of a number cube when you roll it 10 times.

    b. Using a calculator, find the value predicted by the normal distribution for the probability of a sum of 20.

    c. Using a calculator, find the value predicted by the normal distribution for the probability of a sum between 20 and 50.

17. The State Department of Agriculture has determined the size of pumpkins grown in their state is normally distributed. The mean diameter is 10.4 inches and the standard deviation is 1.3 inches.

    a. To qualify as "Grade A," a pumpkin must be within one standard deviation of the mean. Find how many pumpkins were rated Grade A if farmers harvested 2.5 million pumpkins.

    b. Give a range of diameters in which approximately 95% of all pumpkins should lie.

    c. "Mini" pumpkins are rated smaller than three standard deviations below the mean and are sold as novelties. Determine the maximum diameter for these pumpkins and the number of them in the 2.5 million pumpkin crop.

    d. Customers look for "monster" pumpkins, rated as two standard deviations or greater than the mean. Determine the minimum diameter to qualify as a "Monster" pumpkin.

18. a. Copy the graph below. Sketch the rectangles the areas of which make up $U_4[1, 3]\left(\frac{1}{x}\right)$.

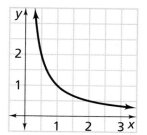

    b. Compute $U_4[1, 3]\left(\frac{1}{x}\right)$.

    c. On another copy of the same graph, sketch the rectangles the areas of which make up $L_4[1, 3]\left(\frac{1}{x}\right)$.

    d. Compute $L_4[1, 3]\left(\frac{1}{x}\right)$.

19. Consider the function $f(x) = \sqrt{x}$ on the interval $[0, 1]$.

    a. Compute $U_4[0, 1](\sqrt{x})$.

    b. Compute $L_4[0, 1](\sqrt{x})$.

    c. Compute the average of $U_4[0, 1](\sqrt{x})$ and $L_4[0, 1](\sqrt{x})$.

    d. Given that the area under the graph of $y = \sqrt{x}$ between 0 and 1 is $\frac{2}{3}$, find the percent error using the three approximations.

20. Use Fermat's method to compute $S[1, 3](x^4)$, the area under the curve $y = x^4$ between 1 and 3.

.... TI-Nspire™ Technology Handbook ....

Recognizing how to use technology to support your mathematics is an important habit of mind. Although the use of technology in this course is independent of any particular hardware or software, this handbook gives examples of how you can apply the TI-Nspire™ handheld technology.

Comparing Angle Measure and Arc Length, Lesson 1.2

1. Put the handheld in degree mode. Choose **Circle** from the **Shapes** menu. Place the cursor at the origin. Press **enter**.

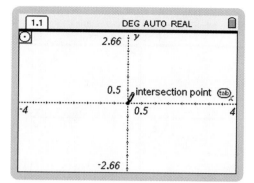

2. Place the cursor close the point (1, 0). The cursor will jump to the point (1, 0). Press **enter**. Press ⬆ Ⓐ to label the point.

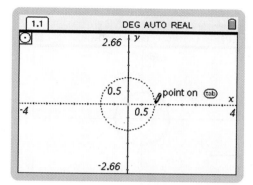

3. Choose **Segment** from the **Points & Lines** menu. Draw a segment on the screen. Press Ⓑ ● to label the end point.

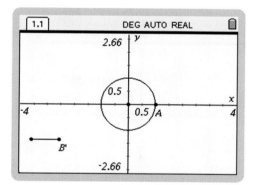

4. Choose **Length** from the **Measurement** menu. Place the cursor on the segment. Press **enter**.

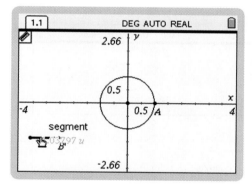

5. Move the cursor to drag the measurement to the desired location. Press **enter** to anchor it.

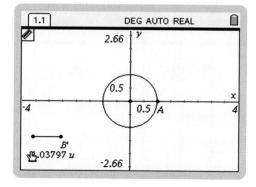

6. Choose **Measurement transfer** from the **Construction** menu. Place the cursor on the length of the segment. Press **enter**.

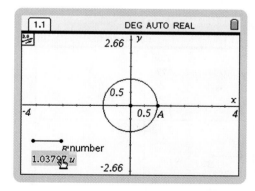

Comparing Angle Measure and Arc Length (continued)

7. Place the cursor on the circle. Press **enter**.

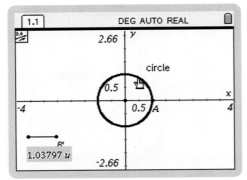

8. Place the cursor on point *A*. Press **enter**. The length of the arc from *A* to the new point that appears is equal to the length of the segment.

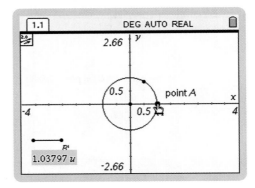

9. Use the **Text** tool from the **Actions** menu to label the new point.

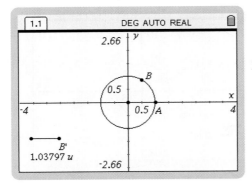

10. Choose **Coordinates and Equations** from the **Actions** menu. Place the cursor on point *B*. Press **enter**.

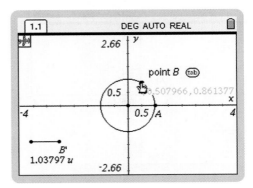

11. Move the cursor to drag the coordinates to the desired location. Press **enter** to anchor it.

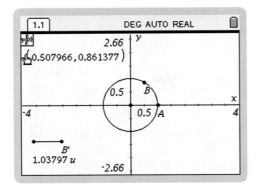

12. Choose **Angle** from the **Measurement** menu. Place the cursor on point *A*. Press **enter**.

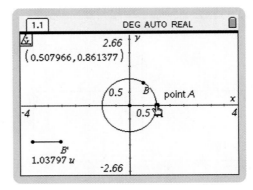

Comparing Angle Measure and Arc Length (continued)

13. Place the cursor on the origin. Press **enter**.

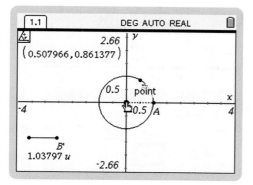

14. Place the cursor on point *B*. Press **enter**.

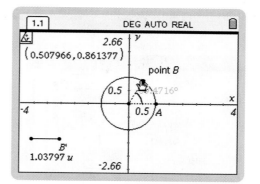

15. Move the cursor to drag the angle measurement to the desired location. Press **enter** to anchor it.

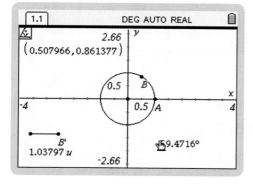

16. Move the cursor to point *B′*. Press **ctrl** ✷ to grab the point. Drag the point and observe the relationship between the length of the segment and the angle measurement.

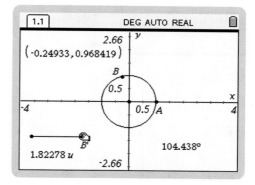

Putting the Handheld in Radian Mode, Lesson 1.2

1. Press ⌂. Choose **System Info**. Press **enter**.

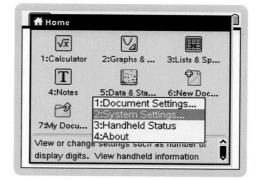

2. Choose **System Settings**. . . . Press **enter**.

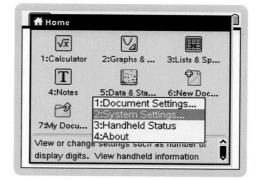

Putting the Handheld in Radian Mode (continued)

3. Press **tab** until you reach the **Angle** field. Press ▽ to open the menu. Press ▽ until **Radian** is highlighted. Press **enter** **enter**.

4. Press **enter** to confirm the change to Radian mode.

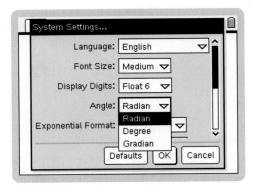

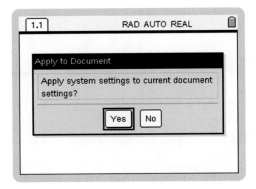

Measuring the Slope of a Line Secant to a Sine Curve, Lesson 1.5

1. Start with the graph of $y = \sin x$.

2. Choose **Point On** from the **Points & Lines** menu. Place the cursor on the curve. Press **enter**.

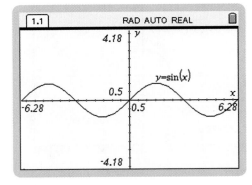

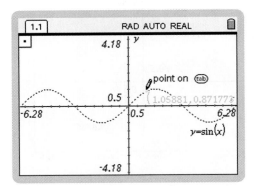

3. Press **A** to label the point.

4. Place point *B* on the curve in the same way.

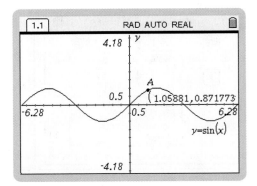

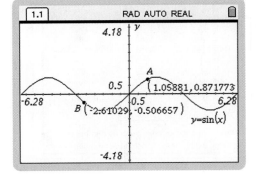

TI-Nspire™ Technology Handbook

Measuring the Slope of a Line Secant to a Sine Curve (continued)

5. Choose **Line** from the **Points & Lines** menu. Place the cursor on point *B*. Press `enter`. Place the cursor on point *A*. Press `enter`.

6. Choose **Slope** from the **Measurement** menu. Place the cursor on the line. Press `enter`.

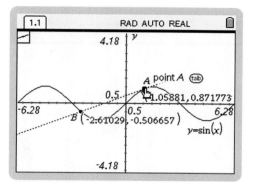

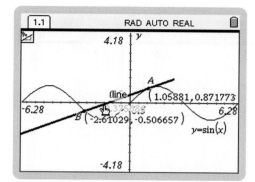

7. Move the cursor to drag the slope to the desired location. Press `enter` to anchor it.

8. Place the cursor on point *B*. Press `ctrl` `✷` to grab it. Drag point *B* along the curve. Observe how the slope changes.

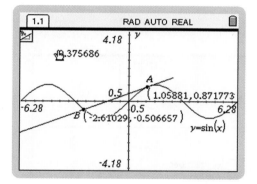

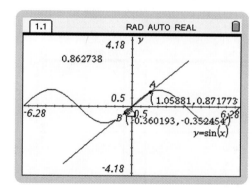

Modeling the Tangent Function, Lesson 1.7

1. Construct a circle with center at the origin that passes through the point *A*(1, 0).

2. Choose **Perpendicular** from the **Construction** menu. Place the cursor on the *x*-axis. Press `enter`.

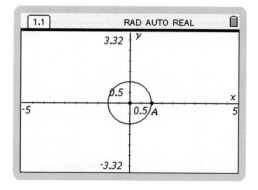

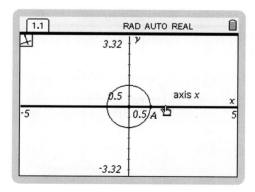

TI-Nspire™ Technology Handbook

3. Place the cursor on point *A*. Press **enter** to set the line through *A* perpendicular to the *x*-axis.

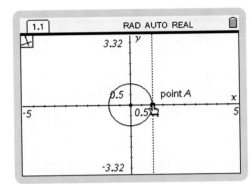

4. Choose **Segment** from the **Points & Lines** menu. Construct a segment in an open area of the screen. After setting the second endpoint, press **B** **C** to label it.

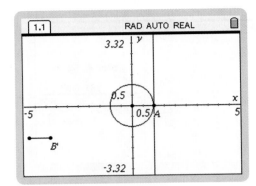

5. Choose **Length** from the **Measurement** menu. Place the cursor on the segment. Press **enter** to measure the length. Move the cursor to drag the measurement to the desired location. Press **enter** to anchor it.

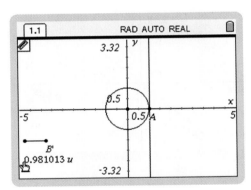

6. Choose **Measurement transfer** from the **Construction** menu. Place the cursor on the length of the segment. Press **enter**.

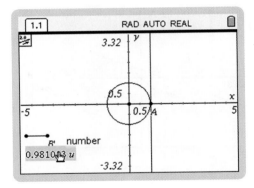

7. Place the cursor on the circle. Press **enter**.

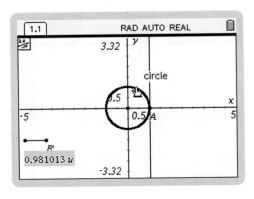

8. Place the cursor on point *A*. Press **enter**. The length of the arc from *A* to the new point that appears is equal to the length of the segment.

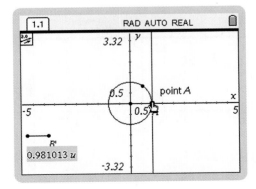

Modeling the Tangent Function (continued)

9. Use the **Text** tool in the **Actions** menu to label the new point.

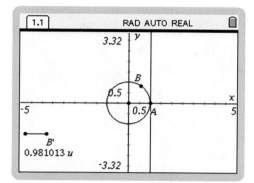

10. Choose **Line** from the **Points & Lines** menu. Place the cursor on the origin. Press ⟨**enter**⟩. Place the cursor on the point *B*. Press ⟨**enter**⟩.

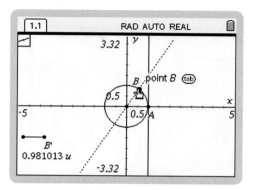

11. Choose **Intersection Point(s)** from the **Points & Lines** menu. Place the cursor on the line through the origin. Press ⟨**enter**⟩.

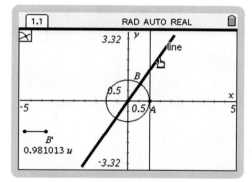

12. Place the cursor on the vertical line through the point *A*. Press ⟨**enter**⟩ to construct the intersection of the two lines.

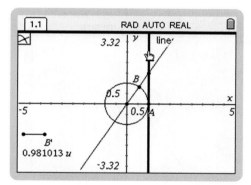

13. Use the **Text** tool in the **Actions** menu to label the new point.

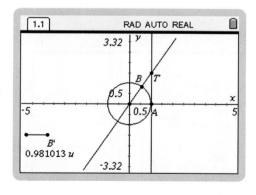

14. Choose **Coordinates and Equations** from the **Actions** menu. Place the cursor on point *T*. Press ⟨**enter**⟩.

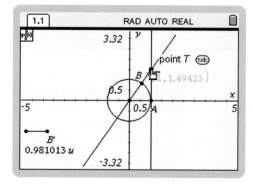

Modeling the Tangent Function (continued)

15. Move the cursor to drag the coordinates to the desired location. Press **enter** to anchor it.

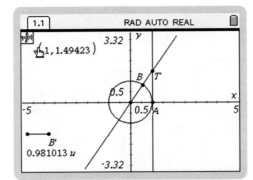

16. Choose **Text** from the **Actions** menu. Click on an empty area of the screen. Type **T** **A** **N** **(** **V** **)**. Press **enter**.

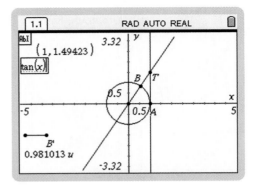

17. Choose **Calculate** from the **Actions** menu. Place the cursor on the text you wrote in step 16. Press **enter**.

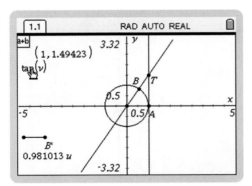

18. Place the cursor on the length of the segment. Press **enter**.

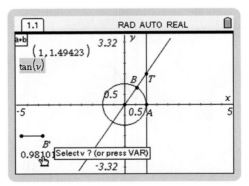

19. Move the cursor to drag the result of the calculation to the desired location. Press **enter** to anchor it.

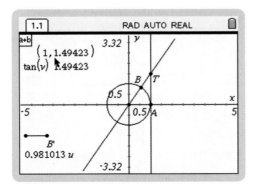

20. Place the cursor on the point *B'*. Press **ctrl** **✷** to grab it. Drag the point and observe the relationship between the coordinates of *T*, and the tangent of $m\overarc{AB}$.

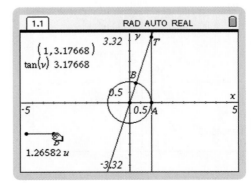

Graphing Composed Functions, Lesson 1.11

1. Choose **Define** from the **Actions** menu. Define *g* as a function of *x*.

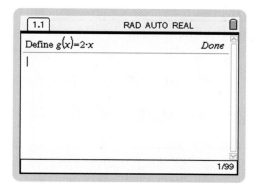

2. Press **ctrl** **⌂**. Choose the **Page Layout** menu. Choose **Layout 3** from the **Select Layout** submenu.

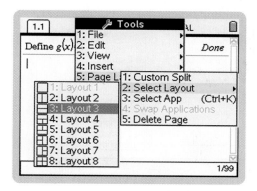

3. Press **ctrl** **tab** to highlight the new window pane.

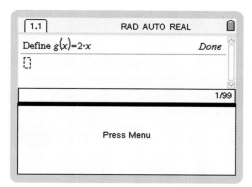

4. Add the Graphs & Geometry application. Choose **Zoom – Trig** from the Window menu. Press **ctrl** **G** to hide the function entry line.

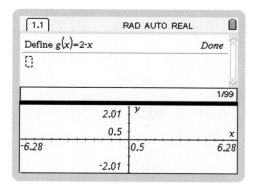

5. Use the **Text** tool in the **Actions** menu to write "*y* = sin (*g*(*x*))" on the screen. Drag the text to the axes to graph the equation.

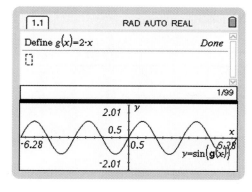

6. Press **ctrl** **tab** to switch back to the Calculator application. Redefine the function *g*. Observe the change in the graph of *y* = sin (*g*(*x*)).

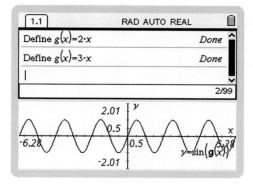

Solving Trigonometric Equations, Lesson 1.12

1. Choose **Solve** from the **Algebra** menu.

2. Type the equation, followed by a comma, then the variable. Press **enter**.

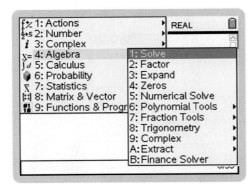

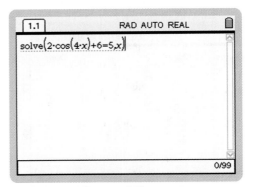

3. The general solution uses the variable *n1*, which ranges over the integers. (You may also see *n2*, *n3*, *n4*, and so on, as variables that range over the integers.)

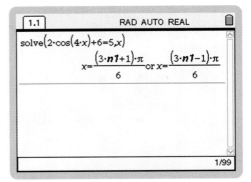

Finding the Magnitude of a Complex Number, Lesson 2.2

1. Press **ctrl** **✗** to access the templates palette. Choose |□|.

2. Type the complex number. Press **enter**.

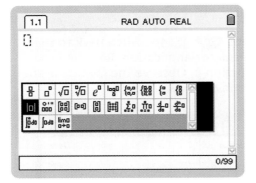

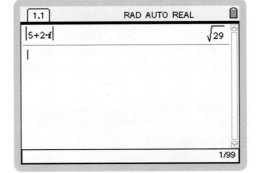

Finding Complex Solutions, Lesson 2.8

1. Type **C S O L V E (**. Then type the equation, followed by a comma, and the variable to solve for.

2. Press **enter**.

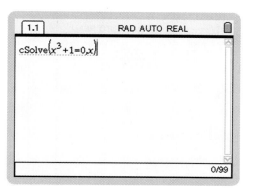

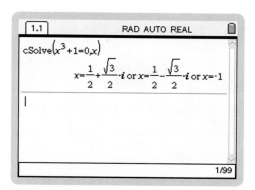

Modeling a Piecewise Defined Function, Lesson 2.11

1. Choose **Define** from the **Actions** menu. Type **P (N , X) =**. Press **ctrl X** to access the templates palette. Choose ▦.

2. Select the correct number of function pieces, 3, in the dialog box. Press **enter**.

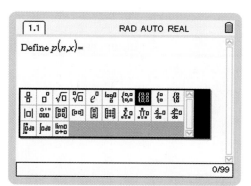

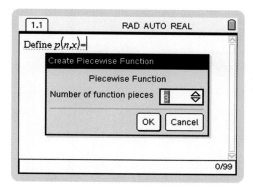

3. Press **tab** to move from box to box.

4. Complete the function definition. Press **enter**.

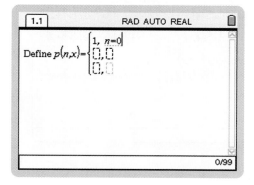

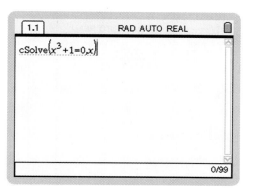

Using the polyRemainder Function, Lesson 2.12

1. Choose the **Polynomial Tools** submenu from the **Algebra** menu. Choose **Remainder of Polynomial**.

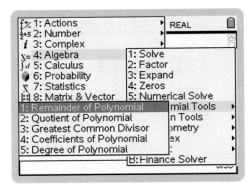

2. Enter two polynomials. The first is divided by the second. Press **enter**. The result is the remainder of the polynomial division.

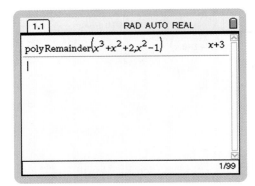

Factoring a Polynomial Over $\mathbb{Z}$, $\mathbb{R}$, and $\mathbb{C}$, Lesson 2.12

1. To factor a polynomial over $\mathbb{Z}$, press **F A C T O R (**, then type the polynomial you want to factor. Press **enter**.

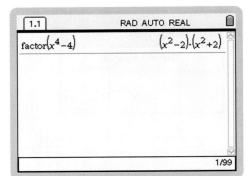

2. To factor a polynomial over $\mathbb{R}$, press **F A C T O R (**, then type the polynomial you want to factor. Press **,**, then type the variable used in the polynomial. Press **enter**.

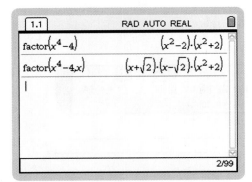

3. To factor a polynomial over $\mathbb{C}$, press **C F A C T O R (**. Then type the polynomial you want to factor. Press **,**, then type the variable used in the polynomial. Press **enter**.

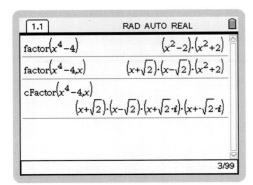

Finding the Equation of a Secant Line, Lesson 3.3

1. Graph the equation.

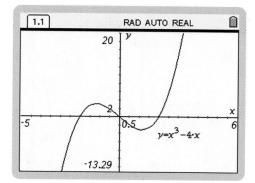

2. Follow steps 2–5 of *Finding the Slope of a Line Secant to a Sine Curve* to construct a secant line.

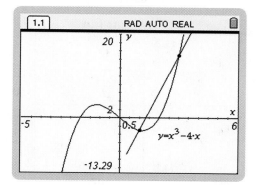

3. Choose **Coordinate and Equations** from the **Actions** menu. Place the cursor on the secant line. Press **enter**.

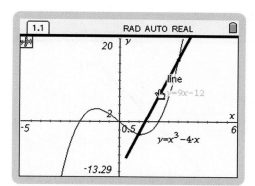

4. Move the cursor to drag the equation to the desired location. Press **enter** to anchor it.

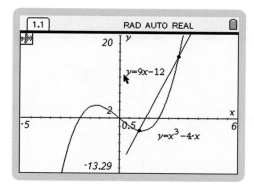

Finding the Slope of a Secant Line, Lesson 3.3

1. Graph the equation $y = x^3 - 2x + 1$.

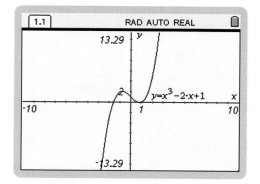

2. Choose **Point On** from the **Points & Lines** menu. Place the cursor on the curve. Press **enter**.

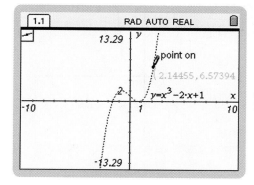

Finding the Slope of a Secant Line (continued)

3. Place the cursor on the *x*-coordinate of the new point. Press 🌀 🌀.

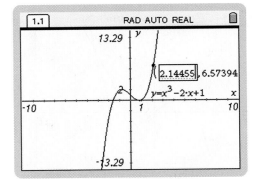

4. Press **ctrl** ⬅ to delete the *x*-coordinate. Press **2** to change the *x*-coordinate to 2. Press **enter**. The point jumps to (2, *f*(2)).

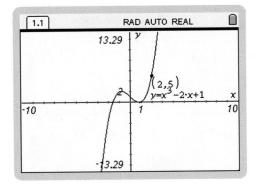

5. Construct a secant line through the point (2, 5). Label the other point the secant passes through *B*.

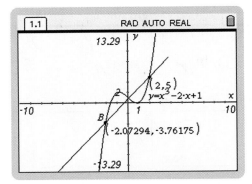

6. Choose **Slope** from the **Measurement** menu. Place the cursor on the secant line. Press **enter**.

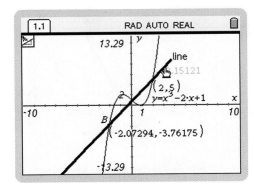

7. Move the cursor to drag the slope to the desired location. Press **enter** to anchor it.

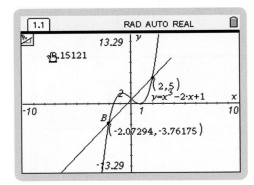

8. Place the cursor on point *B*. Press **ctrl** 🌀 to grab it. Drag point *B* and observe how the slope of the secant changes.

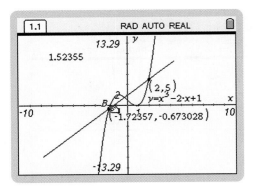

Finding a Taylor Expansion, Lesson 3.4

1. Press **Ⓣ Ⓐ Ⓨ Ⓛ Ⓞ Ⓡ Ⓒ**.

2. Enter the polynomial, the variable of the polynomial, the degree of the Taylor expansion, and the center of the expansion. Separate each with commas. Press **enter**.

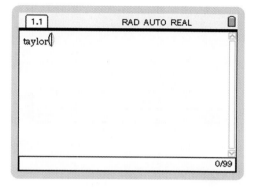

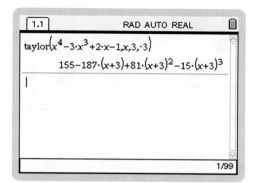

Constructing a Tangent Line, Lesson 3.5

1. Choose **Point On** from the **Points & Lines** menu. Place the cursor on the curve. Press **enter**.

2. Choose **Tangent** from the **Points & Lines** menu. Place the cursor on the point. Press **enter**.

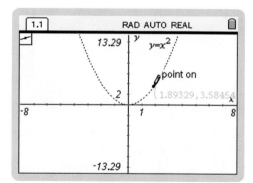

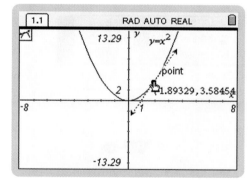

3. Place the cursor on the point. Press **ctrl** **✹** to grab it. Drag the point to the desired location. The line remains tangent to the curve at the point.

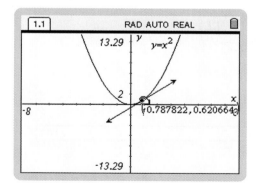

Using the number *e*, Lesson 3.11

1. Press **ctrl** **⊗** to access the templates palette. Choose *e*.

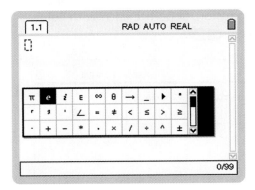

2. Press **ctrl** **enter** to find the approximate value of *e*.

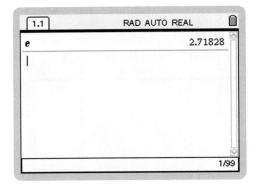

Evaluating an Infinite Sum, Lessons 3.11, 3.12

1. Press **ctrl** **⊗** to access the templates palette. Choose the summation template.

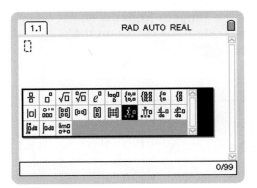

2. Press **tab** to move from box to box.

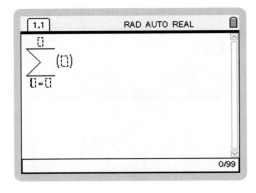

3. To enter ∞, press **ctrl** **i**.

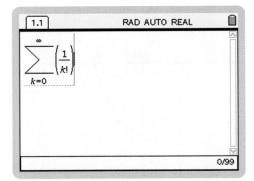

4. Press **enter** to evaluate the sum.

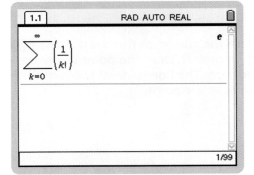

Evaluating a Limit, Lesson 3.11

1. Press **ctrl** **⊗** to access the templates palette. Choose .

2. Press **tab** to move from box to box. To enter ∞ Press **ctrl** **ⓘ**.

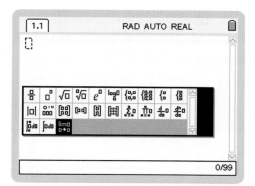

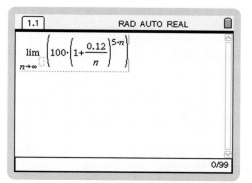

3. Press **enter** to evaluate the limit.

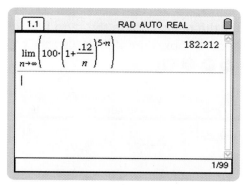

Modeling a Recursively Defined Function in Two Variables, Lesson 4.11

1. Choose **Define** from the **Actions** menu. Press **C** **(** **N** **,** **K** **)** **=**.

2. Press **ctrl** **⊗** to access the templates palette. Choose .

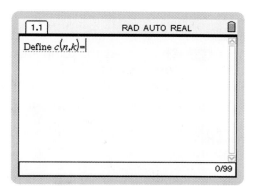

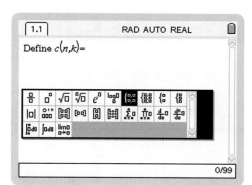

3. Press ⬭**tab** to move from box to box.

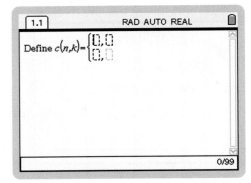

4. In the second box, type Ⓚ ⊜ ⓪ ⊜ ⓞ Ⓡ ⊜ Ⓚ ⊜ Ⓝ.

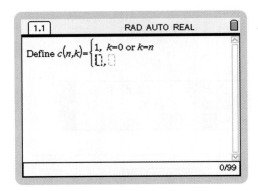

5. Enter the recurrence in the third box. In the fourth box, type ⓪ ⧀ Ⓚ ⊜ Ⓐ Ⓝ Ⓓ ⊜ Ⓚ ⧀ Ⓝ.

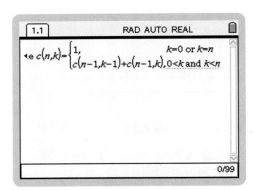

6. Press ⬭**enter** to complete the definition.

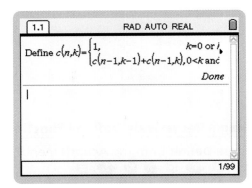

Modeling a Recursively Defined Function, Lesson 5.1

1. Choose **Define** from the **Actions** menu. Press Ⓒ ❨ Ⓝ ❩ ⊜.

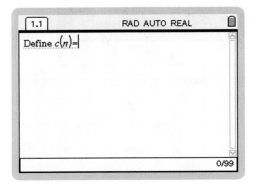

2. Press ⬭**ctrl** ⬭**✕** to access the templates palette. Choose ⊞.

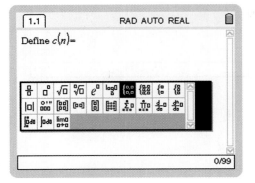

Modeling a Recursively Defined Function (continued)

3. Press **tab** to move from box to box.

4. Press **enter** to complete the definition.

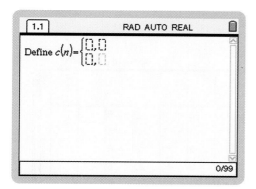

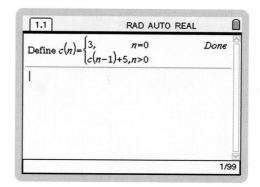

Making a Difference Table in a Spreadsheet, Lesson 5.7

1. Start with the input in column A of a spreadsheet, and the output in column B.

2. Navigate to cell C1. Type **=** **B** **2** **–** **B** **1** . Press **enter**.

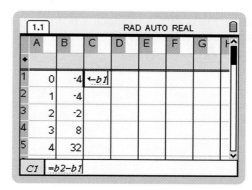

3. Navigate back to cell C1. Choose **Fill Down** from the **Data** menu.

4. Press ▽ to outline the desired area to fill down. Press **enter**.

Making a Difference Table in a Spreadsheet (continued)

5. To make a column of second differences, navigate to cell D1. Type ⊜ ⓒ ❷ ⊜ ⓒ ❶. Then proceed as in steps 3–4.

6. Make additional difference columns in a similar way.

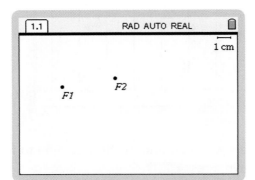

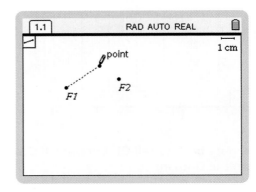

Constructing an Ellipse, Lesson 6.6

1. Choose **Point** from the **Points & Lines** menu. Press **enter** to place a point. Construct two points. Label them *F1* and *F2*.

2. Choose **Segment** from the **Points & Lines** menu. Construct a segment with one endpoint at *F1*.

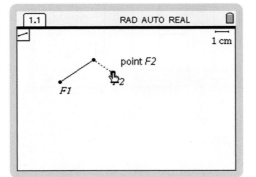

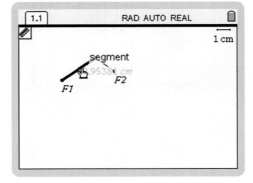

3. Construct a segment that shares an endpoint with the segment from step 2, and with the other endpoint at *F2*.

4. Choose **Length** from the **Measurement** menu. Place the cursor on the first segment. Press **enter**.

Constructing an Ellipse (continued)

5. Move the cursor to drag the length to the desired location. Press **enter** to anchor it.

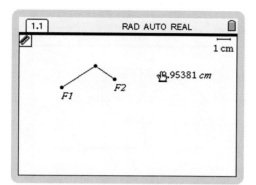

6. Measure the length of the other segment in a similar way.

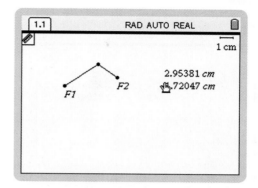

7. Choose **Text** from the **Actions** menu. Press **enter** on an open area of the screen. Press **S** **1** **+** **S** **2**. Press **enter**.

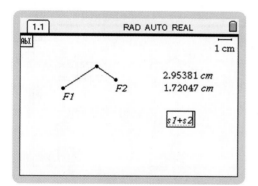

8. Choose **Calculate** from the **Actions** menu. Place the cursor on the expression $s1 + s2$. Press **enter**.

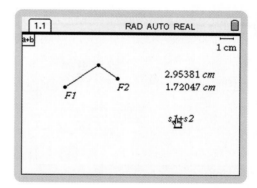

9. Place the cursor on the first segment length. Press **enter**.

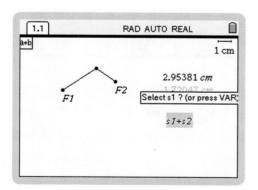

10. Place the cursor on the second segment length. Press **enter**.

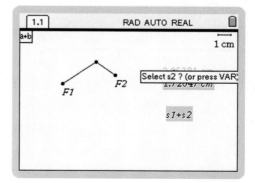

Constructing an Ellipse (continued)

11. Move the cursor to drag the result of the calculation to the desired location. Press **enter** to anchor it.

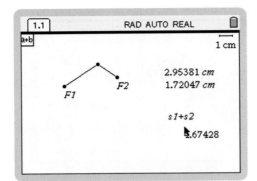

12. Place the cursor on the result of the calculation. Press **ctrl** **menu**. Choose **Attributes**.

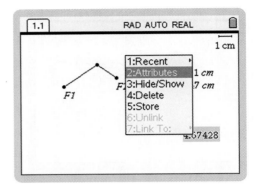

13. Press ▽ to select the Lock/Unlock attribute.

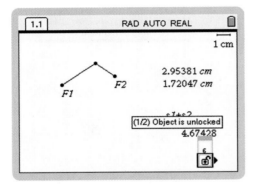

14. Press ▷ **enter** to lock the sum.

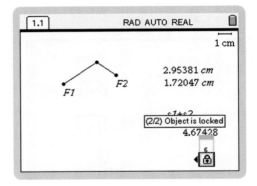

15. Choose **Geometry Trace** from the **Trace** menu. Place the cursor on the common endpoint of the two segments. Press **enter**. Press **ctrl** ✱ to grab the point.

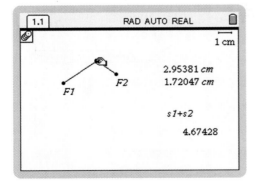

16. Drag the point. The sum of the lengths of the two segments remains constant. The point traces the path of an ellipse.

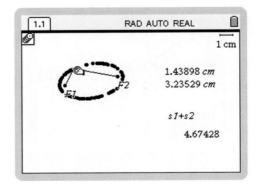

Constructing a Parabola, Lesson 6.6

1. Choose **Line** from the **Points & Lines** menu. Draw the directrix. Label the line *d*.

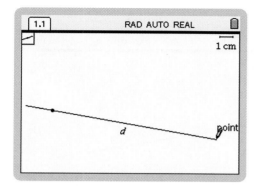

2. Choose **Point** from the **Points & Lines** menu. Place the focus on the screen. Label the point *F*.

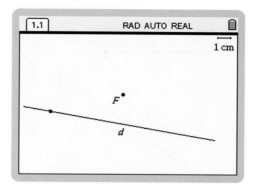

3. Choose **Segment** from the **Points & Lines** menu. Place the cursor on line *d*. Press **enter**. Place the cursor on point *F*. Press **enter**.

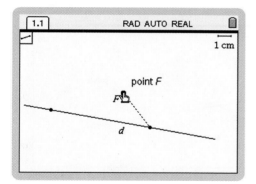

4. Choose **Perpendicular Bisector** from the **Construction** menu. Place the cursor on the segment. Press **enter**.

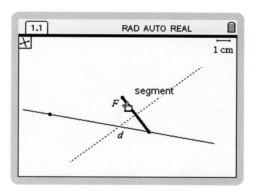

5. Choose **Perpendicular** from the **Construction** menu. Place the cursor on line *d*. Press **enter**. Place the cursor on the intersection of line *d* and the segment. Press **enter**.

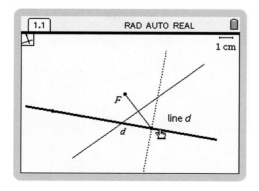

6. Choose **Intersection Point(s)** from the **Points & Lines** menu. Place the cursor on the perpendicular line you constructed in step 5. Press **enter**.

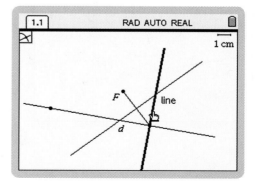

7. Place the cursor on the perpendicular bisector you constructed in step 4. Press **enter**.

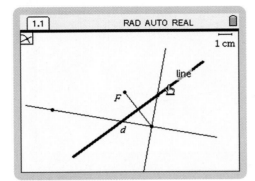

8. Choose **Hide/Show** from the **Actions** menu. Place the cursor on the perpendicular bisector from step 4. Press **enter** to hide the line.

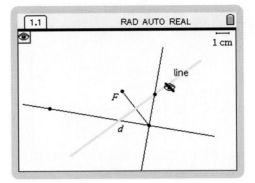

9. Hide the segment and the line perpendicular to the directrix in the same way.

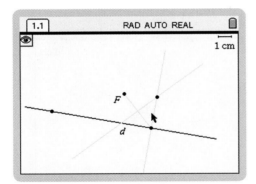

10. Choose **Locus** from the **Construction** menu. Place the cursor on the intersection point you constructed in step 7. Press **enter**.

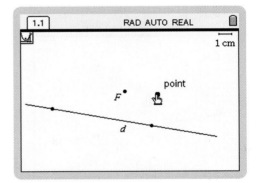

11. Place the cursor on the intersection of the directrix and the segment you constructed in step 3.

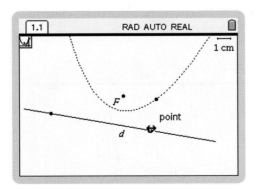

12. Press **enter** to construct the parabola.

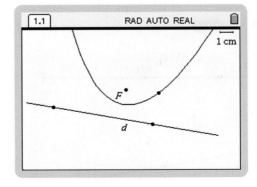

Constructing a Hyperbola, Lesson 6.6

1. Choose **Point** from the **Points & Lines** menu. Place two points on the screen. Label them *F1* and *F2*.

2. Choose **Segment** from the **Points & Lines** menu. Construct two segments with endpoints *F1* and *F2* that have a common endpoint.

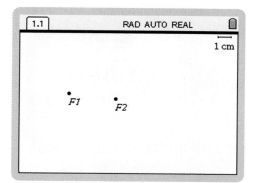

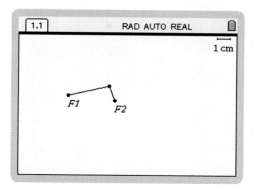

3. Choose **Length** from the **Measurement** menu. Place the cursor on the first segment. Press **enter**. Move the cursor to drag the length to the desired location. Press **enter** to anchor it.

4. Find the length of the second segment in the same way.

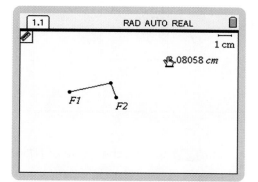

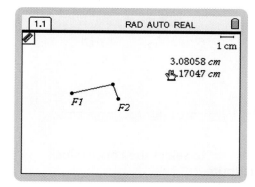

5. Choose **Text** from the **Actions** menu. Click on an open part of the screen. Type Ⓐ Ⓑ Ⓢ ❨ Ⓢ ❶ ⊖ Ⓢ ❷ ❩. Press **enter**.

6. Choose **Calculate** from the **Actions** menu. Place the cursor on the text you wrote in step 5. Press **enter**.

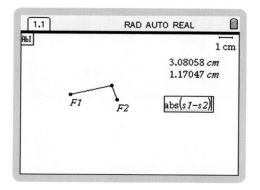

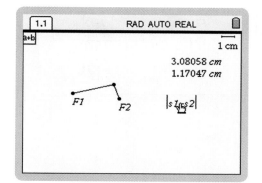

7. Place the cursor on the first length. Press **enter**.

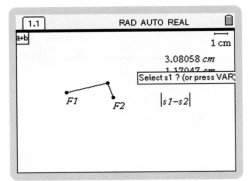

8. Place the cursor on the second length. Press **enter**.

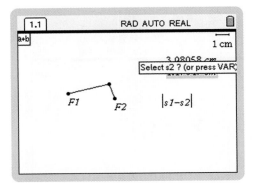

9. Move the cursor to drag the result of the calculation to the desired location. Press **enter** to anchor it.

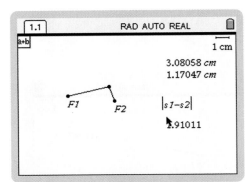

10. Place the cursor on the result of the calculation. Press **ctrl** **menu**. Choose **Attributes**.

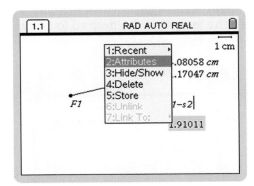

11. Press ▼ to select the Lock/Unlock attribute.

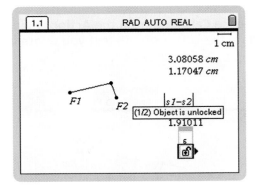

12. Press ▷ **enter** to lock the value of $|s1 - s2|$.

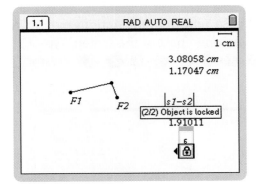

Constructing a Hyperbola (continued)

13. Choose **Geometry Trace** from the **Trace** menu. Place the cursor on the common endpoint of the two segments. Press `enter`. Press `ctrl` `✳` to grab the point.

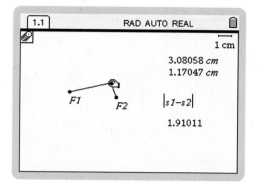

14. Drag the point. The absolute value of the difference of the lengths of the two segments remains constant. The point traces the path of an ellipse.

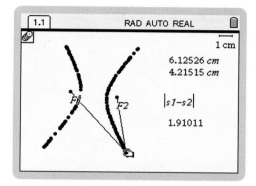

Graphing General Conic Sections, Chapter 6 Project

1. Choose **Solve** from the **Algebra** menu. Type the equation solve. Press `r`, then type the variable to solve for. Press `enter`.

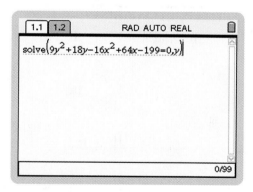

2. Define *g* and *h* using the two solutions you got in step 1.

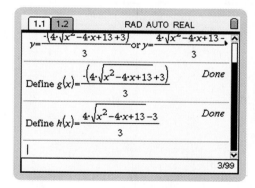

3. Navigate to the Graphs & Geometry application. Choose **Text** from the **Actions** menu. Click on an empty area of the screen. Press `Y` `=` `G` `(` `X` `)` `enter`.

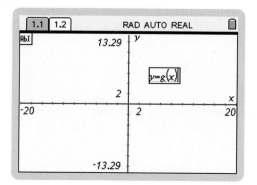

4. Place the cursor on the equation $y = g(x)$. Press `ctrl` `✳` to grab it. Drag it to an axis. Press `enter` to graph the equation.

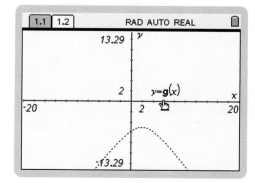

Graphing General Conic Sections (continued)

5. Choose **Text** from the **Actions** menu. Click on an empty area of the screen. Press
Ⓨ ⊜ Ⓗ ⦅ Ⓧ ⦆ ⟨enter⟩.

6. Place the cursor on the equation $y = h(x)$. Press ⟨ctrl⟩ ⊛ to grab it. Drag it to an axis. Press ⟨enter⟩ to graph the equation.

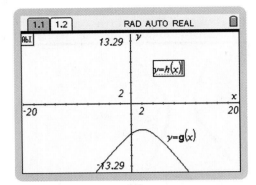

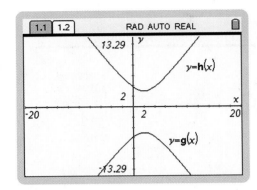

Constructing Conic Sections Using Eccentricity, Lesson 6.9

1. Draw the directrix and focus. Label them d and F respectively.

2. Draw two lines.

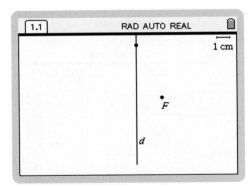

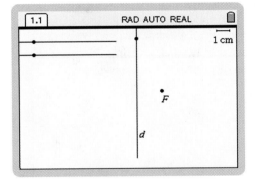

3. Construct a segment on each of the two lines you drew in step 2.

4. Use the **Hide/Show** tool to hide lines so that only the segments are visible.

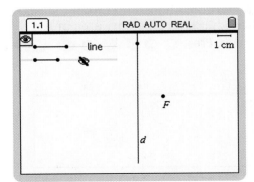

Constructing Conic Sections Using Eccentricity (continued)

5. Use the **Length** tool from the **Measurment** menu to measure the length of the bottom segment. Drag the length to an open area of the screen.

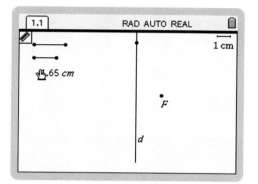

6. Double click on the length measurement. Move the cursor to the beginning of the text box. Press **E** **=** **enter**.

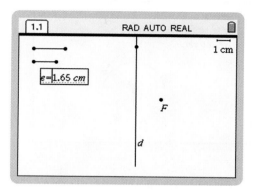

7. Choose **Dilate** from the **Transformation** menu. Place the cursor on the left endpoint of the top segment. Press **enter**.

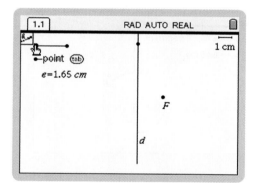

8. Place the cursor on the right endpoint of the top segment. Press **enter**.

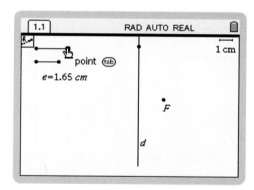

9. Place the cursor on the length measure. Press **enter**. A new point appears.

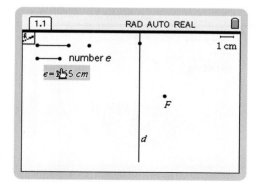

10. Choose **Compass** from the **Construction** menu. Place the cursor on the top segment. Press **enter**.

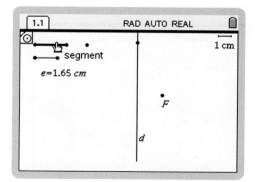

11. Place the cursor on line *d*. Press **enter**.

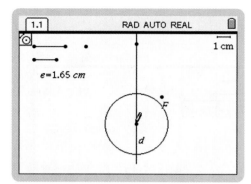

12. Use the **Hide/Show** tool to hide the top segment.

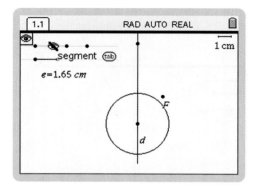

13. Construct a segment with one endpoint at the right endpoint of the segment you hid in step 12, and the other endpoint at the new point from step 9.

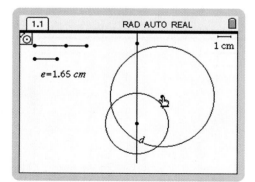

14. Choose **Compass** from the **Construction** menu. Place the cursor on the top segment. Press **enter**.

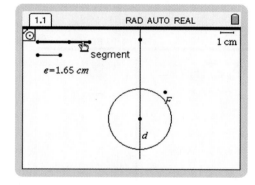

15. Place the cursor on the point *F*. Press **enter**.

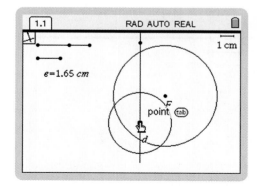

16. Choose **Perpendicular** from the **Construction** menu. Place the cursor on the center of the circle you constructed in step 11. Press **enter**.

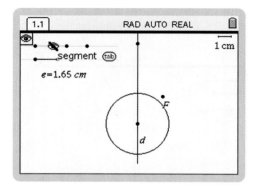

Constructing Conic Sections Using Eccentricity (continued)

17. Place the cursor on the directrix. Press **enter**.

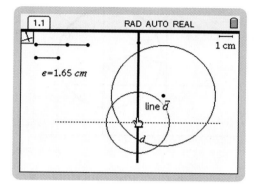

18. Choose **Intersection Point(s)** from the **Points & Lines** menu. Place the cursor on the line you constructed in step 17. Press **enter**.

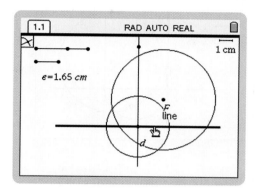

19. Place the cursor in the circle with center on the directrix. Press **enter**.

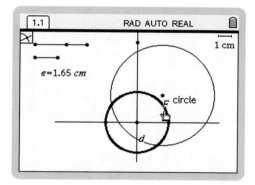

20. Construct lines through the resulting intersection points that are perpendicular to the line you constructed in step 17. Press **enter**.

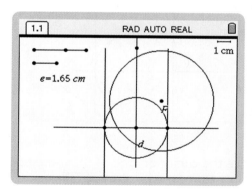

21. Choose **Intersection Point(s)** from the **Points & Lines** menu. Place the cursor on one of the lines you constructed in step 20. Press **enter**.

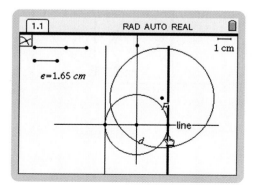

22. Place the cursor on the circle with center at *F*. Press **enter**.

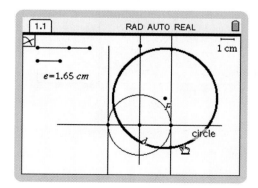

Constructing Conic Sections Using Eccentricity (continued)

23. Place the cursor on the other line you constructed in step 20. Press **enter**.

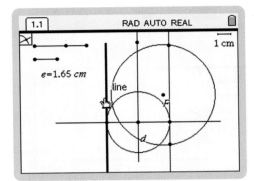

24. Place the cursor on the circle with center at *F*. Press **enter**.

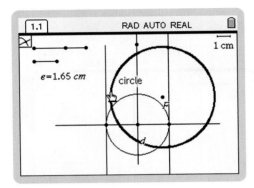

25. If there are no intersection points in step 24, drag the middle point in the top segment until intersection points appear.

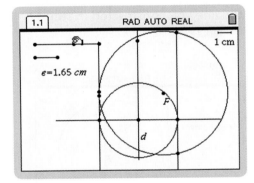

26. Choose **Locus** from the **Construction** menu. Place the cursor the middle point in the top segment. Press **enter**.

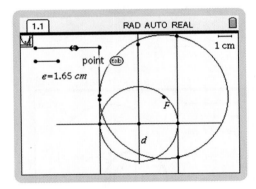

27. Place the cursor on one of the intersection points from step 22. Press **enter**.

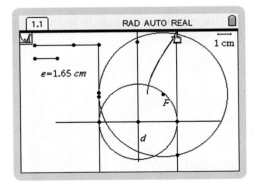

28. Construct the locus in the same way for the other intersection point.

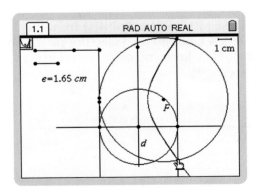

29. Construct the loci in the same way for the other pair of intersection points.

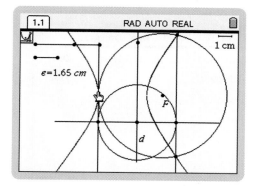

30. Use the **Hide/Show** tool from the **Actions** menu to hide the points and lines used in the construction.

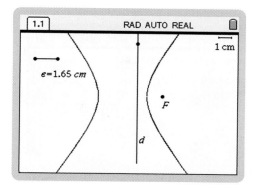

31. Drag one endpoint of the segment to change the value of e. when e = 1, the locus is a parabola.

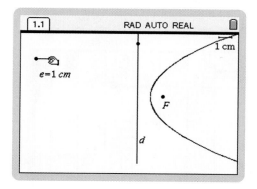

32. When e < 1, the locus is an ellipse.

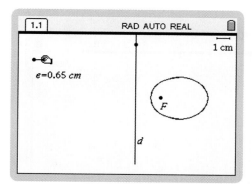

Expanding Expressions, Lessons 7.1, 7.3

1. Press **E X P A N D (**. Type an expression. Press **enter**.

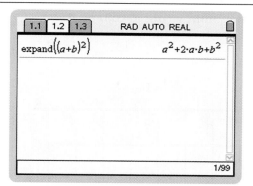

Calculating Standard Deviation and Variance, Lesson 7.7

1. Choose **List Math** from the **Statistics** menu. Choose **Population Standard Deviation**. Enter a list variable, or manually type a list in curly braces ({ and }) Press <enter>.

2. Choose **List Math** from the **Statistics** menu. Choose **Population Variance**. Enter a list variable, or manually type a list in curly braces ({ and }). Press <enter>.

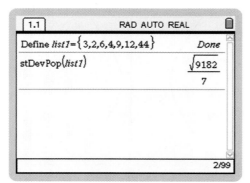

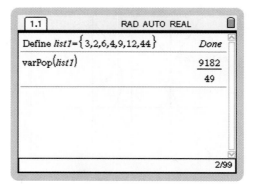

Making a Function Table, Lesson 7.10

1. Define a function *f*.

2. Navigate to the Lists & Spreadsheet application. Label the input column *n*.

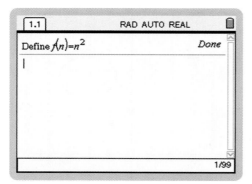

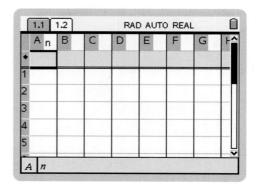

3. Enter input values in column A.

4. Navigate to the second row of the column header in column B. Press ⊜ ⒡ ⒧ ⒭ Ⓝ Ⓒⓣⓡⓛ ⒧ <enter>.

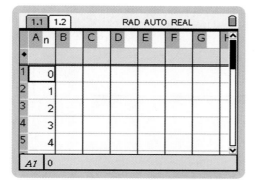

1. Column A consists of the value of *m* from 1 to 20. Column B consists of the probability of *m* successes in 20 trials, where each trial has a 0.5 probability of success.

2. Navigate to the Data & Statistics application.

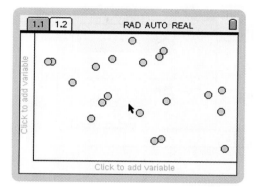

3. Click below the horizontal axis to add a variable. Choose the variable *m*.

4. Click below the vertical axis to add a variable. Choose the variable *n*.

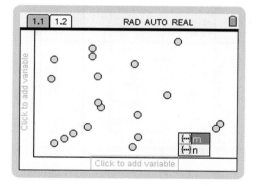

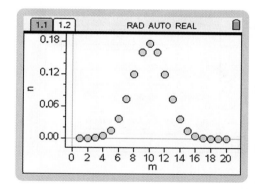

Defining a Normal Distribution, Lesson 7.12

1. Navigate to the second row of the column header in an empty column.

2. Press ⊜ Choose **Distributions** from the **Statistics** menu. Choose **Normal Pdf**.

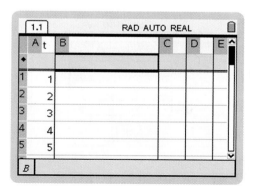

Defining a Normal Distribution (continued)

3. Choose '*t* from the drop down menu.

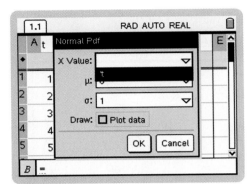

4. Press **tab** to move to the μ field. Type **M** **E** **A** **N** **(** **'** **T** **)**. Press **enter**.

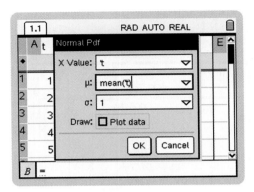

5. Press **tab** the σ field. Type **S** **T** **D** **E** **V** **P** **O** **P** **(** **'** **T** **)**. Press **enter** **enter**.

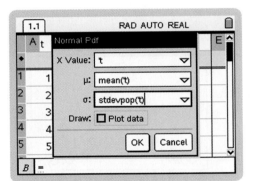

6. Press **enter** to populate the column.

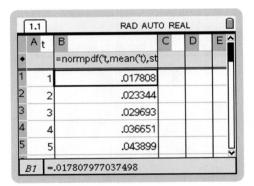

Using the normPdf command, Lesson 7.12

1. Choose **Distributions** from the **Statistics** menu. Choose **Normal Pdf**.

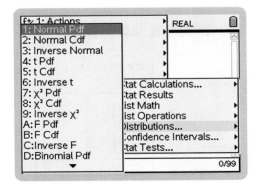

2. Press **tab** to move between the **X Value**, μ, and σ fields. Enter the appropriate values. Press **enter** **enter**.

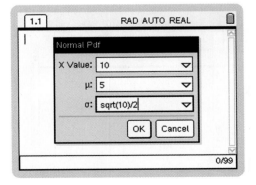

Using the normPdf command (continued)

3. Press **enter**.

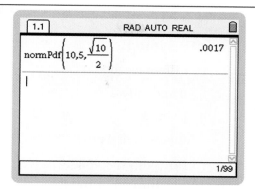

Using the normCdf Command, Lesson 7.13

1. Choose **Distributions** from the **Statistics** menu. Choose **Normal Cdf**.

2. Press **tab** to move between the **Lower Bound, Upper Bound**, μ, and σ fields. Enter the appropriate values. Press **enter enter**.

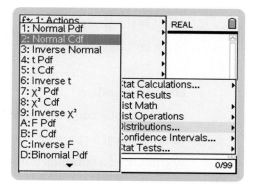

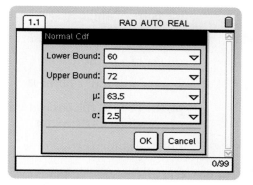

3. Press **enter**.

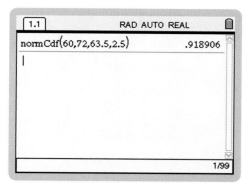

Tables

Table 1   Math Symbols

Δ	difference (delta)	$_nC_k$	number of combinations of n objects, taken k at a time
$\Leftrightarrow$	if and only if	$|A|$	frequency of event A
A	point A	$P(A)$	probability of event A
A'	image of A, A prime	$f^{-1}(x)$	inverse function of f
$\overrightarrow{AB}$	ray from A through B	$g \circ f(x)$	$g(f(x))$
$\overleftrightarrow{AB}$	line through A and B	$\displaystyle\sum_{k=1}^{n}$	summation notation
$\overline{AB}$	segment from A to B		
AB	length of $\overline{AB}$	$f^{-1}(x)$	inverse function of f
$\overrightarrow{AB}$	vector from A to B	$\mathbb{N}$	set of natural numbers
$\angle A$	angle A	$\mathbb{Z}$	set of integers
$\angle ABC$	angle with sides $\overrightarrow{BA}$ and $\overrightarrow{BC}$	$\mathbb{Q}$	set of rational numbers
$m\angle A$	measure of angle A	$\mathbb{R}$	set of real numbers
$\triangle ABC$	triangle with vertices A, B, and C	$\mathbb{C}$	set of complex numbers
$\Pi(P)$	power of a point P	i	$\sqrt{-1}$
$\Pi_S(P)$	signed power of a point P	$x + yi$	complex number
π	pi, the ratio of the circumference of a circle to its diameter	$\overline{z}$	conjugate of a complex number
		$|z|$	magnitude of a complex number
ϕ	phi, the golden ratio	$\arg(z)$	argument of a complex number
$\sin\theta$	sine of θ	$N(z)$	norm of a complex number
$\cos\theta$	cosine of θ	$\operatorname{cis}\theta$	complex number $\cos\theta + i\sin\theta$
$\tan\theta$	tangent of θ	$\overline{x}$	mean
$\sec\theta$	secant of θ	σ	standard deviation
$\csc\theta$	cosecant of θ	σ^2	variance
$\cot\theta$	cotangent of θ	$N(\mu, \sigma)$	normal distribution
$\sin^{-1}x$	inverse sine of x	$\mathcal{R}_A$	linear fractional transformation
$\cos^{-1}x$	inverse cosine of x	$\mathcal{A}_{(a,b)}$	affine transformation
$\tan^{-1}x$	inverse tangent of x	T_a	translation map
$\log_b x$	logarithm of x, base b	$L_n[a, b](f(x))$	lower sum
$\ln x$	natural logarithm of x	$U_n[a, b](f(x))$	upper sum
$n!$	n factorial	$S[a, b](f(x))$	area under curve
$\binom{n}{k}$	the nth row, kth column entry of Pascal's triangle	$LF_n[a, b](f(x))$	Fermat lower sum
		$UF_n[a, b](f(x))$	Fermat upper sum
$_nP_k$	number of permutations of n objects, taken k at a time	$\mathcal{L}$	function $a \mapsto S[1, a](x^{-1})$

Table 2 Measures

United States Customary	Metric

Length

12 inches (in.) = 1 foot (ft)	10 millimeters (mm) = 1 centimeter (cm)
36 in. = 1 yard (yd)	100 cm = 1 meter (m)
3 ft = 1 yard	1000 mm = 1 meter
5280 ft = 1 mile (mi)	1000 m = 1 kilometer (km)
1760 yd = 1 mile	

Area

144 square inches (in.^{2}) = 1 square foot (ft^2)	100 square millimeters (mm^2) = 1 square centimeter (cm^2)
9 ft^2 = 1 square yard (yd^2)	10,000 cm^2 = 1 square meter (m^2)
43,560 ft^2 = 1 acre (a)	10,000 m^2 = 1 hectare (ha)
4840 yd^2 = 1 acre	

Volume

1728 cubic inches (in.^{3}) = 1 cubic foot (ft^3)	1000 cubic millimeters (mm^3) = 1 cubic centimeter (cm^3)
27 ft^3 = 1 cubic yard (yd^3)	1,000,000 cm^3 = 1 cubic meter (m^3)

Liquid Capacity

8 fluid ounces (fl oz) = 1 cup (c)	1000 milliliters (mL) = 1 liter (L)
2 c = 1 pint (pt)	1000 L = 1 kiloliter (kL)
2 pt = 1 quart (qt)	
4 qt = 1 gallon (gal)	

Weight and Mass

16 ounces (oz) = 1 pound (lb)	1000 milligrams (mg) = 1 gram (g)
2000 pounds = 1 ton (t)	1000 g = 1 kilogram (kg)
	1000 kg = 1 metric ton

Temperature

32°F = freezing point of water	0°C = freezing point of water
98.6°F = normal body temperature	37°C = normal body temperature
212°F = boiling point of water	100°C = boiling point of water

Time

60 seconds (s) = 1 minute (min)	365 days = 1 year (yr)
60 minutes = 1 hour (h)	52 weeks (approx.) = 1 year
24 hours = 1 day (d)	12 months = 1 year
7 days = 1 week (wk)	10 years = 1 decade
4 weeks (approx.) = 1 month (mo)	100 years = 1 century

Tables

Table 3 Formulas From Geometry

You may need geometric formulas as you work through your precalculus book. Here are some perimeter, area, and volume formulas.

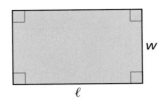

$$P = 2\ell + 2w$$
$$A = \ell w$$

Rectangle

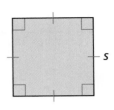

$$P = 4s$$
$$A = s^2$$

Square

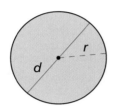

$$C = 2\pi r \ \text{ or } \ C = \pi d$$
$$A = \pi r^2$$

Circle

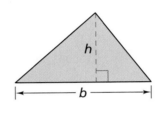

$$A = \tfrac{1}{2}bh$$

Triangle

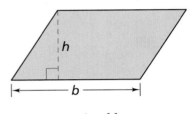

$$A = bh$$

Parallelogram

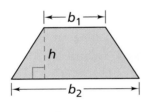

$$A = \tfrac{1}{2}(b_1 + b_2)h$$

Trapezoid

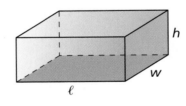

$$V = Bh$$
$$V = \ell w h$$

Rectangular Prism

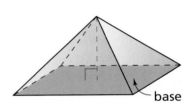

$$V = \tfrac{1}{3}Bh$$

Pyramid

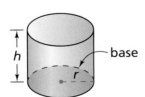

$$V = Bh$$
$$V = \pi r^2 h$$

Cylinder

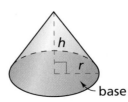

$$V = \tfrac{1}{3}Bh$$
$$V = \tfrac{1}{3}\pi r^2 h$$

Cone

$$V = \tfrac{4}{3}\pi r^3$$

Sphere

Tables

Properties and Theorems

Chapter 2

Theorem 2.1, p. 88

The absolute value of a complex number is equal to the square root of its norm.

$$|z| = \sqrt{N(z)}$$

Theorem 2.2 *The Multiplication Law*, p. 100

Given complex numbers $z = a\operatorname{cis}\alpha$ and $w = b\operatorname{cis}\beta$,

$$zw = (a\operatorname{cis}\alpha)(b\operatorname{cis}\beta) = ab\operatorname{cis}(\alpha + \beta)$$

In other words,

- $|zw| = |z| \cdot |w|$
- $\arg(zw) = \arg(z) + \arg(w)$

Theorem 2.3 *The Angle-Sum Formulas*, p. 111

The following two equations are true for all values of α and β.

$$\cos(\alpha + \beta) = \cos\alpha\cos\beta - \sin\alpha\sin\beta$$
$$\sin(\alpha + \beta) = \sin\alpha\cos\beta + \cos\alpha\sin\beta$$

Corollary 2.3.1 *The Angle-Difference Formulas*, p. 112

The following two equations are true for all values of α and β.

$$\cos(\alpha - \beta) = \cos\alpha\cos\beta + \sin\alpha\sin\beta$$
$$\sin(\alpha - \beta) = \sin\alpha\cos\beta - \cos\alpha\sin\beta$$

Corollary 2.3.2 *The Double-Angle Formulas*, p. 112

The following two equations are true for all values of θ.

$$\cos 2\theta = \cos^2\theta - \sin^2\theta$$
$$\sin 2\theta = 2\sin\theta\cos\theta$$

Theorem 2.4 *DeMoivre's Theorem*, p. 128

For all real θ, $(\operatorname{cis}\theta)^n = \operatorname{cis} n\theta$.

Corollary 2.4.1, p. 129

For all real θ, $(r\operatorname{cis}\theta)^n = r^n\operatorname{cis} n\theta$.

Theorem 2.5 *The Factor Theorem*, p. 133

Suppose $f(x)$ is a polynomial. Then $x - a$ is a factor of $f(x)$ if and only if the number a is a root of the equation $f(x) = 0$.

Theorem 2.6, p. 139

If n is a positive integer, the roots of the equation

$$x^n - 1 = 0$$

are

$$1, z, z^2, \ldots, z^{n-1}$$

where

$$z = \operatorname{cis}\frac{2\pi}{n}$$

If $n \geq 3$, these roots lie on the vertices a regular n-gon inscribed in the unit circle in the complex plane.

Theorem 2.7 *Cardano's Formula*, p. 157

The roots of $x^3 + px + q = 0$ are

$$\sqrt[3]{\frac{-q + \sqrt{\dfrac{27q^2 + 4p^3}{27}}}{2}}$$
$$+ \sqrt[3]{\frac{-q - \sqrt{\dfrac{27q^2 + 4p^3}{27}}}{2}}$$

Chapter 3

Theorem 3.1 *The Change of Sign Theorem*, p. 173

Suppose f is a polynomial function and there are two numbers a and b such that $f(a) < 0$ and $f(b) > 0$. Then, $f(c) = 0$ for some number c between a and b.

Theorem 3.2 *The Intermediate Value Theorem for Polynomials*, p. 173

Suppose f is a polynomial function and a and b are two numbers such that $f(a) < f(b)$. Then for any number c between $f(a)$ and $f(b)$ there is at least one number d between a and b such that $f(d) = c$.

Theorem 3.3 *The Odd Degree Root Theorem*, p. 177

A polynomial function of odd degree has at least one real root.

Theorem 3.4, p. 199

Let $f(x)$ be a polynomial and $a, b \in \mathbb{R}$. Write

$$f(x) = (x - a)(x - b)q(x) + r(x)$$

where $r(x)$ is a linear function. Then the graph of $y = r(x)$ is the secant to the graph of $y = f(x)$ through $(a, f(a))$ and $(b, f(b))$.

Theorem 3.5, p. 199

Let $f(x)$ be a polynomial and $a \in \mathbb{R}$. Write

$$f(x) = (x - a)^2 q(x) + r(x)$$

where $r(x)$ is a linear function. Then the graph of $y = r(x)$ is the tangent to the graph of $y = f(x)$ at $(a, f(a))$.

Theorem 3.6, p. 211

Let h be a rational function.
1. If h has an infinite discontinuity at $x = a$, then the graph of h has $x = a$ as a vertical asymptote.
2. If h has a removable discontinuity at $x = a$, then the graph of h has a hole at $x = a$.

Theorem 3.7, p. 212

Let $h(x) = \dfrac{f(x)}{g(x)}$ be a rational function with deg $f = m$ and deg $g = n$.
1. If $m < n$, then $\lim\limits_{x \to \infty} h(x) = 0$.
2. If $m = n$, then $\lim\limits_{x \to \infty} h(x)$ is the ratio of the leading coefficients of f and g.

Moreover, the graph of h has a horizontal asymptote with equation $y = L$ where $L = \lim\limits_{x \to \infty} h(x)$.

Theorem 3.8, p. 214

Let $h(x) = \dfrac{f(x)}{g(x)}$ be a rational function with deg $f >$ deg g. Then
$$\lim\limits_{x \to \infty} h(x) = \infty \text{ or } -\infty.$$
Moreover, if you write
$$\frac{f(x)}{g(x)} = q(x) + \frac{r(x)}{g(x)}$$
where q and r are polynomials with deg $r <$ deg g, then the graph of q is a nonhorizontal asymptote of the graph of h.

Theorem 3.9, p. 222

Suppose that f is a rational function for which the denominator is not zero at $x = r$. Suppose also that you use the method of undetermined coefficients to write
$$f(x) = m + n(x - r) + p(x)(x - r)^2$$
finding first the number m and then the number n. Then p is a rational function that is defined at $x = r$.

Theorem 3.10, p. 228

Suppose A and B are 2×2 matrices with real coefficients. Then
$$\mathcal{R}_A \circ \mathcal{R}_{\mathbb{B}} = \mathcal{R}_{AB}$$

Lemma 3.11, p. 248

Let $k \geq 0$ be an integer. Then
$$\lim\limits_{n \to \infty} \frac{\dbinom{n}{k}}{n^k} = \frac{1}{k!}$$

Theorem 3.12, p. 249

$$\lim\limits_{n \to \infty}(1 + \tfrac{1}{n})^n = 1 + \frac{1}{1!} + \frac{1}{2!} + \frac{1}{3!} + \cdots = \sum\limits_{k=0}^{\infty} \frac{1}{k!}$$

Theorem 3.13, p. 260

The tangent to the graph of $y = \ln x$ at the point $(a, \ln a)$ has slope $\frac{1}{a}$.

Theorem 3.14, p. 261

The tangent to the graph of $y = e^x$ at the point (a, e^a) has slope e^a.

Chapter 4

Theorem 4.1, p. 287

It is possible to make m^n different strings of length n using m different symbols, if you can use a symbol more than once.

Theorem 4.2, p. 307

$$_nC_k = \frac{_nP_k}{k!} = \frac{n!}{k!(n - k)!}$$

Theorem 4.3 *The Pascal-Combinations Connection*, p. 309

For any $n \geq 0$ and all k such that $0 \leq k \leq n$,
$$\binom{n}{k} = {_nC_k}$$

Theorem 4.4 *The Binomial Theorem*, p. 328

For any integers n and k with $0 \leq k \leq n$,
$$(a + b)^n = \binom{n}{0}a^n b^0 + \binom{n}{1}a^{n-1}b^1 + \binom{n}{2}a^{n-2}b^2 + \cdots$$
$$\cdots + \binom{n}{k}a^{n-k}b^k + \cdots + \binom{n}{n-1}a^1 b^{n-1} + \binom{n}{n}a^0 b^n$$

Chapter 5

Theorem 5.1, p. 367

Use straight lines extending infinitely in either direction to draw a map that divides the plane into any number of regions. Two colors are enough to color the map so that no two regions with a common border have the same color.

Theorem 5.2 *Newton's Difference Formula,* p. 391

Suppose you have a table with integer inputs from 0 to m:

Input	Output	Δ	Δ^2	Δ^3	$\cdots$	Δ^m
0	a_0	a_1	a_2	a_3	$\cdots$	a_m
1						
2						
3						
4						
5						
6						
$\vdots$						
m						

A polynomial function that fits the table is

$$f(x) = \sum_{k=0}^{m} a_k \binom{x}{k}$$

Theorem 5.3 *Closure of Solutions,* p. 423

If two functions r and s satisfy the two-term recurrence

$$f(n) = Af(n-1) + Bf(n-2)$$

then so does any linear combination

$$t(n) = k \cdot r(n) + j \cdot s(n)$$

where k and j are real numbers.

Theorem 5.4 *Closed-Form Equivalent for $f(n) = Af(n-1) + B$,* p. 428

Define f by

$$f(n) = \begin{cases} p & \text{if } n = 0 \\ Af(n-1) + B & \text{if } n > 0 \end{cases}$$

Then for nonnegative integer inputs, a closed-form equivalent for f is

$$f(n) = A^n \cdot p + B\left(\frac{A^n - 1}{A - 1}\right)$$

Theorem 5.5 *Monthly Payments,* p. 431

On a loan for C dollars taken out for n months with an APR of i percent compounded monthly, the monthly payment is m dollars where

$$m = \frac{q^n(q-1)}{q^n - 1} C$$

and $q = 1 + \frac{i}{1200}$.

Chapter 6

Theorem 6.1 *Power of a Point Theorem,* p. 458

Given a point P and a circle, take any line through P that intersects the circle in two points A and B. Then $PA \cdot PB$ is constant, no matter what line you choose through P. This constant is called the power of the point P. The power is a function of the point, so write the power of P as $\prod(P)$.

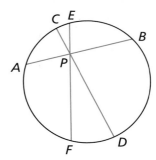

$$PA \cdot PB = PC \cdot PD = PE \cdot PF$$

Corollary 6.1.1, p. 458

Inside a circle, the power of a point d units away from the center of a circle with radius r is $r^2 - d^2$.

Corollary 6.1.2, p. 459

Outside a circle, the power of a point d units away from the center of a circle with radius r is $d^2 - r^2$.

Theorem 6.2, p. 460

The signed power of point $P(x, y)$ with respect to the circle with equation $x^2 + y^2 + Cx + Dy + E = 0$ is

$$\prod_S (P) = x^2 + y^2 + Cx + Dy + E$$

Theorem 6.3, p. 476

An equation for the parabola with focus $(0, c)$ and directrix with equation $y = -c$ is

$$x^2 = 4cy$$

Theorem 6.4, p. 478

The ellipse with foci $(c, 0)$ and $(-c, 0)$ and string length $2a$ has equation

$$1 = \frac{x^2}{a^2} + \frac{y^2}{b^2}$$

where $b^2 = a^2 - c^2$.

Theorem 6.5, p. 480

The hyperbola with foci $(c, 0)$ and $(-c, 0)$ and constant difference $2a$ has equation

$$1 = \frac{x^2}{a^2} - \frac{y^2}{b^2}$$

where $b^2 = c^2 - a^2$.

Theorem 6.6, p. 488

The graph of
$$rx^2 + ty^2 + ux + vy + w = 0$$
is a (possibly degenerate) conic. In fact, the nature of the conic is determined by the sign of rt:
- If $rt > 0$, the graph is an ellipse.
- If $rt = 0$, the graph is a parabola.
- If $rt < 0$, the graph is a hyperbola.

Theorem 6.7, p. 494

Let F be a fixed point, d be a fixed line, and e be a positive real number. The set of points P such that $\frac{PF}{Pd} = e$ is a (possibly degenerate) conic. It is an ellipse if $e < 1$, a parabola if $e = 1$, and a hyperbola if $e > 1$.

Theorem 6.8, p. 519

In any triangle, the three medians are concurrent. Moreover, on each median the common point is $\frac{2}{3}$ the distance from the vertex to the opposite side.

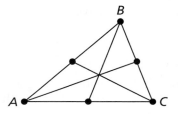

This common point is called the centroid of the triangle.

Theorem 6.9, p. 520

In any parallelogram, the diagonals bisect each other.

Theorem 6.10, p. 529

The graph of
$$rx^2 + sxy + ty^2 + ux + vy + w = 0$$
depends only on the determinant
$$\delta = \begin{vmatrix} r & \frac{s}{2} \\ \frac{s}{2} & t \end{vmatrix} = rt - \left(\frac{s}{2}\right)^2 = \frac{4rt - s^2}{4}$$
More precisely,
- If $\delta < 0$, the gr aph is a (possibly degenerate) hyperbola.
- If $\delta = 0$, the graph is a (possibly degenerate) parabola.
- If $\delta > 0$, the graph is a (possibly degenerate) ellipse.

Chapter 7

Theorem 7.1 *Vandermonde's Identity*, p. 564

Let $r \leq n$ be nonnegative integers. Then
$$\binom{n}{r} = \sum_{k=0}^{r} \binom{n}{k} \cdot \binom{n-r}{r-k}$$

Theorem 7.2, p. 586

Let Z be the random variable defined by adding the results of independent random variables X and Y. Then
- The expected value, or mean, of Z is the sum of the expected values for X and Y, and
- The variance, or mean squared deviation, of Z is the sum of the variances X and Y.

Theorem 7.3 *Central Limit Theorem*, p. 612

Let X be a random variable with mean μ and standard deviation σ. The distribution for the sum of the outputs of X over n experiments is more and more closely approximated by $N(\mu n, \sigma \sqrt{n})$ as n grows larger.

Chapter 8

Theorem 8.1 *Gregory of St. Vincent's Theorem*, p. 679

For any $t > 0$ and any real numbers a, b with $1 \leq a < b$,
$$S[a, b]\left(\tfrac{1}{x}\right) = S[ta, tab]\left(\tfrac{1}{x}\right)$$

Theorem 8.2, p. 685

If m is a nonnegative integer, then
$$\mathcal{L}(e^m) = m$$

Theorem 8.3, p. 687

If $r \geq 0$ is any real number, then
$$\mathcal{L}(e^r) = r$$

Theorem 8.4, p. 687

If $a \geq 1$,
$$\mathcal{L}(a) = r \Leftrightarrow e^r = a$$
In other words, $\mathcal{L}$ is the natural logarithm
$$\mathcal{L}(a) = \ln a$$

Theorem 8.5, p. 698

Suppose $t(n, x)$ is the sequence of polynomials defined by
$$t(n, x) = \begin{cases} 1 & \text{if } n = 0 \\ x & \text{if } n = 1 \\ 2x \cdot t(n-1, x) - t(n-2, x) & \text{if } n > 1 \end{cases}$$
Then, for all nonnegative integers n,
$$t(n, \cos \alpha) = \cos n\alpha$$

Glossary

A

affine combination (p. 518) A point C is an affine combination of points A and B if C is on the line determined by A and B. C can expressed as $C = (1 - k)A + B$ for some real number k.

affine transformation (p. 231) Let a and b be real numbers with $a \neq 0$. An affine transformation by (a, b) is a transformation $\mathcal{A}_{(a, b)}$ of $\mathbb{R}$ given by $\mathcal{A}_{(a, b)}(x) = ax + b$ for any real number x.

algebraic numbers (p. 146) Algebraic numbers are numbers that satisfy an equation with rational coefficients.

amplitude (p. 62) The amplitude of a sinusoidal function f is the distance from its average value to the maximum or minimum.

anagram (p. 300) An anagram is a rearrangement of the letters in a word or phrase.

apex (p. 468) The apex of an infinite double cone is the fixed point used to generate the cone.

arc (p. 7) An arc is a set of points of a circle that lie in the interior of a particular central angle.

argument (p. 89) The argument of a complex number z, written $\arg(z)$, is the angle measured in a counterclockwise direction from the positive real axis to the ray from the origin through z.

asymptote (p. 39) An asymptote is a line that the graph of a function approaches, but does not intersect.

average rate of change (p. 180) Let f be any function and let A and B be two points on the graph of $y = f(x)$. The average rate of change of $f(x)$ with respect to x between A and B is the slope $m(A, B)$.

axis (p. 468) The axis of an infinite double cone is the line through the apex perpendicular to the circle used to make the cone.

B

base case (p. 347) A base case a is place where a rule starts.

Bernoulli trial (p. 596) A Bernoulli trial is an experiment with two outcomes—typically called success and failure.

binomial coefficients (p. 382) The binomial coefficients are the coefficients of the binomial expansion $(x + y)^n$ where the coefficient of the $x^{n-k}y^k$ term is $\binom{n}{k}$.

C

central angle (p. 7) A central angle for a circle is an angle that has its vertex at the center of the circle.

centroid (p. 449) The centroid of a triangle is the intersection of its medians.

characteristic polynomial (p. 421) Suppose a function satisfies the recurrence $f(n) = Af(n - 1) + Bf(n - 2)$. The characteristic polynomial for this recurrence is $x^2 - Ax - B$.

closed-form definition (p. 346) A closed-form definition for a function f lets you find the $f(n)$ for any input n by direct calculation.

combination (p. 305) A combination of elements a set S is a subset of S. The number of combinations of n objects, taken k at a time, is $_nC_k = \dfrac{n!}{k!(n - k)!}$.

complementary (p. 52) Two angles are complementary if they add up to 90 degrees.

complex numbers (p. 145) The set of complex numbers $\mathbb{C}$ consists of all expressions in the form $a + bi$ where:

- a and b are real numbers
- $i^2 = -1$
- Addition and multiplication are carried out as if $a + bi$ were a polynomial in i, together with the new rule $i^2 = -1$.

concurrent (p. 519) A set of lines are concurrent if they share a common point.

confidence interval (p. 615) A confidence interval is the range of values about the mean for a given percentage.

conic sections (p. 468) Conic sections are curves that result from the intersection of infinite double cones and planes.

conjugate (p. 85) The conjugate of a complex number $z = x + yi$ is the complex number $x - yi$ and is denoted by $\overline{z}$.

continuous (p. 171) A function f is continuous at an input a if you can make $f(x)$ as close as you to $f(a)$ by making x as close as you want to a.

continuously compounded interest (p. 243) Continuously compounded interest is computed by taking the limit as the frequency of compounding increases.

convex combination (p. 518) A point C is a convex combination of points A and B if C is on the line segment between A and B. C can be expressed as $C = (1 - k)A + B$ for some real number k where $0 \le k \le 1$.

coordinatize (p. 450) Coordinatize a geometric shape by making a general version in the coordinate plane.

cumulative density function (p. 619) The cumulative density function (CDF) finds the amount of area under the normal curve between two values for a given mean and standard deviation.

cycle (p. 46) One cycle of the graph of a periodic function f results as the input x ranges over one fundamental period.

cyclotomic identity (p. 145) The identity $\zeta^{n-1} + \zeta^{n-2} + \cdots + \zeta^2 + \zeta + 1 = 0$ where ζ is a primitive nth root of unity is called a cyclotomic identity.

cyclotomy (p. 124) Cyclotomy ("circle division") is the connection between the roots of equations of the form $x^n - 1 = 0$, where n is a positive integer, and regular polygons.

D

Dandelin sphere (p. 472) A Dandelin sphere is a sphere inside a double cone that is tangent to both the cone and a plane slicing the cone.

decreasing (p. 26) A function f is decreasing on an interval if for any two values in the interval a and b, $a < b$, then $f(a) > f(b)$.

determinant (p. 227) Let $A = \begin{pmatrix} a & b \\ c & d \end{pmatrix}$ be a 2×2 matrix with real entries. The determinant of A is $\det A = ad - cb$.

deviation (p. 575) The deviation of an output value of a random variable is the difference between the output value and the mean of the random variable.

diagonal (p. 320) A diagonal of a polygon is a segment which connects two to the polygon's vertices but is not a polygon's side.

difference table (p. 374) A difference table is a table of the difference of outputs when the inputs are evenly spaced.

dilation (p. 507) A dilation is any geometric transformation that expands or contracts the plane (or space) using some particular point as the center.

direction of a vector (p. 506) The direction of a vector includes both slope of a vector and orientation.

directrix (p. 472) A parabola can be defined by the set of points equidistant from a fixed point and line. The directrix of the parabola is the fixed line.

distance formula (p. 444) The distance formula between points $A(x_1, y_1)$ and $B(x_2, y_2)$ is $d(A, B) = \sqrt{(x_2 - x_1)^2 + (y_2 - y_1)^2}$

double cone (p. 449) The graph of $z^2 = x^2 + y^2$ is called a double cone.

E

e (factorial definition) (p. 250) The factorial definition of e is given by

$$e = 1 + \frac{1}{1!} + \frac{1}{2!} + \frac{1}{3!} + \cdots = \sum_{k=0}^{\infty} \frac{1}{k!}$$

e (limit definition) (p. 243) The limit definition of e is given by

$$e = \lim_{n \to \infty} \left(1 + \frac{1}{n}\right)^n$$

The value of e is approximately 2.17828.

eccentricity (p. 495) The eccentricity is the ratio of the distance between the foci to the distance between the vertices.

ellipse (p. 469) An ellipse is the curve you get by slicing an infinite double cone with a plane that intersects only one branch of the cone in a closed curve.

equilibrium point (p. 429) An equilibrium point is a repeating value of an iteration. If $f(n) = f(n - 1) = C$, then C is an equilibrium point.

even function (p. 108) A function f is an even function if it satisfies $f(-x) = f(x)$ for all numbers x in its domain. If the point (x, y) is on the graph of f, the point $(-x, y)$ is also on the graph.

event (p. 542) An event is a subset of a sample space, a set of outcomes.

expected value (p. 558) The expected value of a random variable X is the sum when each value of X is multiplied by its probability. The typical notation is

$$E(X) = \sum_i x_i \cdot p_i$$

where the x_i are the values of the random variable, and the p_i are the probabilities of each value. An alternative notation is

$$E(X) = \sum_i s_i \cdot P(X = s_i)$$

where $P(X = s_i)$ is the probability that the random variable X takes on the value s_i.

experimental probability (p. 592) The experimental probability of an event is equal to the ratio between the number of times the event occurred and the total number of trials of the experiment.

F

factorial (p. 299) The factorial of a positive integer n is defined as the descending product $n \cdot (n - 1) \cdot (n - 2) \cdot \cdots \cdot 2 \cdot 1$, stopping at 1. Denote the factorial of n by $n!$ Using this definition, 0! is not defined. Define $0! = 1$.

Farey sequence of order n (p. 296) The Farey sequence of order n, denoted F_n, is the set of all fractions from 0 to 1, inclusive, with denominators less than or equal to n.

Fermat lower sum (p. 663) The Fermat lower sum $UF_n[a, b](f(x))$ is the lower approximation of the area under the graph of the function $f(x)$ from $x = a$ to $x = b$ when the number of Fermat subdivisions is n.

Fermat upper sum (p. 664) The Fermat upper sum $UF_n[a, b](f(x))$ is the upper approximation of the area under the graph of the function $f(x)$ from $x = a$ to $x = b$ when the number of Fermat subdivisions is n.

Fibonacci sequence (p. 353) The Fibonacci sequence is a sequence in which each term is the sum of the previous two terms and the first two terms of the sequence are 0 and 1:

$$F(n) = \begin{cases} 0 & \text{if } n = 0 \\ 1 & \text{if } n = 1 \\ F(n - 1) + F(n + 2) & \text{if } n > 1 \end{cases}$$

focus, foci (p. 470) The focus of a parabola is the fixed point in the locus definition of a parabola.

The foci of an ellipse are the two fixed points used in the locus definition of an ellipse.

The foci of a hyperbola are the two fixed points used in the locus definition of a hyperbola.

Focus is the singular of foci.

Four-Color Theorem (p. 367) The Four-Color Theorem says that if you have a map of countries which are all solid areas, without holes or separated colonies, then four colors suffice to color the map so that no two countries sharing a common border have the same color.

frequency (p. 549) Let A be an event. The frequency of the event $|A|$ is the number of outcomes in A.

functional equation (p. 412) A functional equation tells how various outputs of a function are related.

G

generator (p. 468) The generator of an infinite double cone is the rotating line through the apex used to make the cone.

golden ratio (p. 142) The golden ratio is the number $\phi = \dfrac{1 + \sqrt{5}}{2}$.

H

head of a vector (p. 503) The head of a vector $\overrightarrow{PQ}$ is at point Q.

histogram (p. 554) A histogram is a graphical representation that shows frequencies as bars.

hockey-stick property (p. 375) The hockey-stick property of difference tables is that any number in the table (other than inputs) is the sum of the top value in its column and all the numbers above it in the column immediately to its right.

hole (p. 211) A hole in a graph is a point at which a graph of a function is not connected but can be made connected by adding the point.

hyperbola (p. 469) A hyperbola is the curve you get by slicing an infinite double cone with a plane that intersects both branches of the cone.

I

identically equal (p. 107) Identically equal expressions are two expressions such that one expression can be transformed to the other using the basic rules of algebra and any other proven identities or theorems.

identity (p. 107) An identity is any equation that equates two identically equal expressions.

increasing (p. 26) A function f is increasing on an interval if for any two values in the interval a and b, $a < b$, then $f(a) < f(b)$.

independent (p. 544) Two events A and B are independent if the result from one event has no effect on the other. If A and B are independent, then $P(A \text{ and } B) = P(A) \cdot P(B)$.

infinite discontinuity (p. 211) Let $h(x) = \dfrac{f(x)}{g(x)}$ be a rational function such that

- $f(x) = (x - a)^m \cdot p(x)$
- $g(x) = (x - a)^n \cdot q(x)$

where $p(a), q(a) \neq 0$. h has an infinite discontinuity at $x = a$ if $n > m \geq 0$.

infinite double cone (p. 468) An infinite double cone is the surface made by rotating a line in space fixed at one point. The line is rotated by moving another point on the line along a circle.

instantaneous speed (p. 197) Let d be the distance function of time t. The instantaneous speed of d at $t = a$ is the slope of the tangent to the graph of $y = d(t)$ at the point $(a, d(a))$.

inverse function (p. 43) Suppose a function f is a one-to-one function with domain A and range B. The inverse function f^{-1} is a function with these properties.

- f^{-1} has domain B and range A
- $f(f^{-1}(x)) = x$

isomorphic (p. 281) If two problems have the same mathematical structure, then they are isomorphic.

isosceles trapezoid (p. 456) An isosceles trapezoid is a trapezoid with opposite nonparallel sides that are congruent.

isosceles triangle (p. 454) An isosceles triangle is a triangle with at least two sides congruent.

K

k of the way from A to B (p. 518) For any points A and B and for any real number k, k of the way from A to B is the point $A + k(B - A) = (1 - k)A + kB$.

L

linear combination (p. 423) A linear combination of x and y is $ax + by$, where a and b are real numbers.

linear fractional transformation (p. 227) Let

$$A = \begin{pmatrix} a & b \\ c & d \end{pmatrix}$$

be a 2×2 matrix with real entries. The linear fractional transformation associated with A is the rational function

$$\mathcal{R}_A(x) = \frac{ax + b}{cx + d}$$

locus (p. 470) A locus is the set of all points that satisfy an equation.

M

machine formula (p. 578) The machine formula for computing the variance is the mean of the squares minus the square of the mean.

magnitude (p. 87) The modulus of a complex number z, denoted by $|z|$, is the distance between the complex number and 0 in the complex plane.

In some older texts, the magnitude of a complex number is called the modulus.

Mahler polynomials (p. 391) The Mahler polynomials are the polynomials that match the binomial coefficients. The first few Mahler polynomials are:

k	$\binom{x}{k}$ (Factored)	$\binom{x}{k}$ (Expanded)
0	1	1
1	x	x
2	$\dfrac{x(x - 1)}{2!}$	$\dfrac{-x + x^2}{2}$
3	$\dfrac{x(x - 1)(x - 2)}{3!}$	$\dfrac{2x - 3x^2 + x^3}{6}$
4	$\dfrac{x(x - 1)(x - 2)(x - 3)}{4!}$	$\dfrac{-6x + 11x^2 - 6x^3 + x^4}{24}$
5	$\dfrac{x(x - 1)(x - 2)(x - 3)(x - 4)}{5!}$	$\dfrac{24x - 50x^2 + 35x^3 - 10x^4 + x}{120}$

major axis (p. 477) The major axis of an ellipse is the longer of the two intersections of the ellipse with the axes of symmetry of the ellipse.

mathematical induction (p. 360) Mathematical induction is a method of proof used to show that a fact is true for set of integers (typically positive or nonnegative ones). A proof by mathematical induction involves two parts:

Step 1 Show that the fact is true fro the first few cases (often using tabulation by hand or by computer).

Step 2 Show that if the fact is true up to some integer $(n - 1)$, it must also be true for n.

maximum (p. 27) The maximum of a graph is the highest value achieved on the vertical axis.

mean absolute value deviation (p. 576) The mean absolute value deviation is calculated by first finding the absolute value of each deviation and then finding the mean of these numbers.

mean squared deviation (p. 576) The mean squared deviation is calculated by first finding the square of each deviation, and then finding the mean of these numbers.

median (p. 448) A median of a triangle is a segment connecting a vertex to the midpoint of the opposite side.

midline (p. 455) A midline is a segment that connects the midpoints of two sides of a triangle.

midline of a trapezoid (p. 456) The midline of a trapezoid is the segment connecting the midpoints of the two non-parallel sides.

Midline Theorem (p. 455) The Midline Theorem states that the segment joining the midpoints of two sides of a triangle is parallel to the third side and its measure is equal to half the measure of the third side.

midpoint formula (p. 444) The midpoint formula of the segment between points $A(x_1, y_1)$ and $B(x_2, y_2)$ is

$$M(A, B) = \left(\frac{x_1 + x_2}{2}, \frac{y_1 + y_2}{2} \right)$$

minimum (p. 27) The minimum of a graph is the lowest value achieved on the vertical axis.

minor axis (p. 477) The minor axis of an ellipse is the shorter of the two intersections of the ellipse with the axes of symmetry of the ellipse.

modulus (p. 87) *See* **magnitude.**

mutually exclusive (p. 544) Two events A and B are mutually exclusive if they do not share any outcomes in the same sample space: whenever $P(A \text{ and } B) = 0$. If A and B are mutually exclusive, then $P(A \text{ or } B) = P(A) + P(B)$.

N

natural logarithm function (p. 255) The natural logarithm function ln is the logarithm to the base e:

$$\ln x = \log_e x$$

norm (p. 88) The norm of a complex number z, written $N(z)$, is the product of the number and its conjugate, $z\bar{z}$.

normal distribution (p. 611) A normal distribution $N(\mu, \sigma)$ is a probability distribution determined by the values of the mean μ and standard deviation σ.

nth root of unity (p. 125) An nth root of unity is each complex number that satisfies the equation $x^n - 1 = 0$.

O

odd function (p. 108) A function f is an odd function if it satisfies $f(-x) = -f(x)$ for all numbers x in its domain. If the point (x, y) is on the graph of f, the point $(-x, -y)$ is also on the graph.

one-to-one (p. 43) A function f is one-to-one if $f(a) = f(b)$ only when $a = b$.

outcome (p. 542) An outcome is an element of a sample space.

P

parabola (p. 469) A parabola is the curve you get by slicing an infinite double cone with a plane that is parallel to its generator.

parallelogram (p. 450) A parallelogram is a quadrilateral with two pairs of parallel sides.

parameter (p. 512) In the vector form $X = P + tD$, the variable t is called a parameter.

parametric equations (p. 512) Vector equations for lines are sometimes called parametric equations for lines.

period (p. 15) The period of a periodic function is the smallest value p such that, for all x, $f(x + p) = f(x)$.

periodic (p. 15) A nonconstant function f is periodic if there exits a real number $p > 0$ such that, for all x, $f(x + p) = f(x)$.

permutation (p. 298) A permutation is a one-to-one function from a set to itself. The number of permutations of n objects, taken k at a time, is $_nP_k = \dfrac{n!}{(n - k)!}$.

perpendicular (p. 444) Two lines in the plane are perpendicular if and only if the product of their slopes is -1, or if one line is vertical and the other is horizontal.

perpendicular bisector (p. 445) A perpendicular bisector is a line that is perpendicular to a line segment at the segment's midpoint.

phase shift (p. 64) The phase shift of a sinusoidal function

$$f(x) = A \sin (ax + b) + B \text{ or}$$
$$f(x) = A \cos (ax + b) + B$$

is the amount of horizontal translation required to obtain the graph of $y = f(x)$ from the graph of

$$y = A \sin ax \text{ or } y = A \cos ax$$

respectively.

point-tester (p. 444) A point-tester is an equation used to determine whether particular points are on a graph.

polar coordinates (p. 92) Polar coordinates (r, θ) denote a direction (an angle θ counterclockwise from the reference axis) and distance r.

polar form for complex numbers (p. 93) The polar form for complex numbers is written $r(\cos \theta + i \sin \theta)$, where r is a non-negative real number and θ is a measurement either in degrees or radians.

power functions (p. 174) Power functions are polynomial functions with only one term.

power of a point (p. 458) The power of a point P, d units from the center of a circle of radius r, with respect to the circle is given by $\Pi(P) = \left| d^2 - r^2 \right|$.

primitive nth root of unity (p. 150) A primitive nth root of unity is a solution to $x^n - 1 = 0$ that is not a solution any equation $x^m - 1 = 0$ where $m < n$.

probability density function (p. 619) The probability density function (PDF) finds the height on a normal curve at a value for a given mean and standard deviation to approximate the height in the matching histogram.

probability distribution (p. 607) A probability distribution is a function that assigns a probability to each numeric output of a random variable.

probability histogram (p. 603) A probability histogram is a histogram where the heights (and areas) of the bars are probabilities instead of frequencies.

probability of an event (p. 542) The probability of an event A, denoted $P(A)$, is the number of outcomes in A, divided by the number of outcomes in the sample space S.

$$P(A) = \frac{\text{number of outcomes in } A}{\text{number of outcomes in } S} = \frac{|A|}{|S|}$$

Pythagorean identity (p. 20) $\cos^2 x + \sin^2 x = 1$

R

radian (p. 9) A radian is an arc of length 1 unit on the unit circle.

random variable (p. 555) A random variable is function whose inputs are outcomes, and whose outputs are numbers.

rational functions (p. 205) Rational functions are functions of the form $x \mapsto \frac{p(x)}{q(x)}$, where p and q are polynomial functions of x.

reciprocal functions (p. 206) Functions f and g are called reciprocal functions if they have the property that $g(x) = \frac{1}{f(x)}$ for any x in the domain of both functions.

rectangular coordinates (p. 92) Rectangular coordinates (x, y) denote distances along two axes that are perpendicular.

rectangular form for complex numbers (p. 93) The rectangular form for complex numbers is written $x + yi$, where x and y are real numbers.

recurrence (p. 412) A recurrence is a special kind of functional equation that tells how the output of function at integer n is related to the outputs at integers less than n.

recursive definition (p. 347) A recursive definition of a function f defines most of the outputs of f in terms of other outputs.

removable discontinuity (p. 211) Let $h(x) = \frac{f(x)}{g(x)}$ be a rational function such that
- $f(x) = (x - a)^m \cdot p(x)$
- $g(x) = (x - a)^n \cdot q(x)$

where $p(a), q(a) \neq 0$. h has a removable discontinuity at $x = a$ if $m \geq n > 0$.

rhombus (p. 453) A rhombus is a quadrilateral with four congruent sides.

root mean squared deviation (p. 576) The root mean squared deviation is calculated by finding the square root of the mean squared deviation.

roots of unity (p. 134) Roots of unity are solutions to $x^n = 1$.

S

sample space (p. 542) The sample space is a set.

scalar (p. 501) A scalar is a real number.

secant (p. 180) Let f be a function and suppose A and B are distinct points on the graph of $y = f(x)$. A line secant to the graph of $y = f(x)$ is the line passing through A and B.

signed power of a point (p. 459) The signed power of a point P, d units from the center of a circle of radius r, with respect to the circle is given by $\Pi_S(P) = d^2 - r^2$.

sinusoidal function (p. 60) A sinusoidal function is a function that's defined by a formula of the form

$$f(x) = A \sin(ax + b) + b \text{ or}$$
$$f(x) = A \cos(ax + b) + B$$

where A, B, a, or b are real numbers.

slope formula (p. 444) The slope formula between points $A(x_1, y_1)$ and $B(x_2, y_2)$ is

$$m(A, B) = \frac{y_2 - y_1}{x_2 - x_1}$$

slope of a vector (p. 505) The slope of a vector with displacement $D = (c, d)$ is $\frac{d}{c}$.

spread (p. 575) The spread of the output values of a random variable is the difference of the maximum output value and the minimum output value.

standard deviation (p. 577) The standard deviation σ for a data set $\{x_1, x_2, \dots, x_n\}$ is given by

$$\sigma = \sqrt{\frac{\sum_i (x_i - \bar{x})^2}{n}}$$

where $\bar{x}$ is the mean of the data set.

The standard deviation is the common name for the root mean squared deviation.

structure-preserving map (p. 228) The map $A \mapsto \mathcal{R}_A$ is said to be structure-preserving because the product AB maps to the composition $\mathcal{R}_A \circ \mathcal{R}_{B^I}$

subset (p. 283) A subset is any group of elements from a set.

T

tail of a vector (p. 503) The tail of a vector $\overrightarrow{PQ}$ is at point P.

tangent line (p. 198) Let f be a function and A is a point on the graph of $y = f(x)$. The tangent line to the graph of $y = f(x)$ at A is the line secant between A and itself.

Taylor expansion (p. 190) The Taylor expansion for a function f about c is the expression of $f(x)$ in terms of powers of $x - c$.

theoretical probability (p. 592) The theoretical probability of an event is equal to the ratio of the number of outcomes that meet the criteria for the event to the total number of possible outcomes.

translation (p. 231) A translation by a real number g is a transformation T_g of $\mathbb{R}$ given by $T_g(x) = x + g$ for any real number x.

trapezoid (p. 456) A trapezoid is a quadrilateral with one pair of parallel sides.

turning point (p. 27) A turning point for a function is an input x where the function changes from increasing to decreasing, or from decreasing to increasing. Sometimes the phrase turning point refers to the actual coordinates $(x, f(x))$ of the point where this change occurs.

two-term recurrence (p. 413) A two-term recurrence is a recurrence that depends on the two previous terms.

U

unit normal distribution (p. 617) The unit normal distribution is a normal distribution that has mean 0 and standard deviation 1. Here are it's equation and graph:

$$N(0, 1) = \frac{1}{\sqrt{2\pi}} e^{\frac{-x^2}{2}}$$

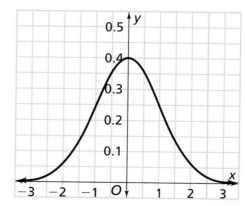

up-and-over property (p. 375) The up-and-over property of difference tables is that any number in the table (other than inputs) is the sum of two numbers—the number directly above it and the number directly to the right of the one above it.

V

variance (p. 577) The variance σ^2 for a data set $\{x_1, x_2, \ldots, x_n\}$ is given by

$$\sigma^2 = \frac{\sum\limits_{i} (x_i - \bar{x})^2}{n}$$

where $\bar{x}$ is the mean of the data set.

The variance is the common name for the mean squared deviation.

vector (p. 503) A vector $\overrightarrow{PQ}$ is an arrow with tail at point P and head at point Q.

vector equation of a line (p. 511) Let P be a point, D be a vector, and k be a scalar. Then $X = P + kD$ is called the vector equation of a line. You may replace the scalar k by the letter t.

vertical displacement (p. 62) The vertical displacement of a sinusoidal function f is its average value. More precisely, it is the average of the maximum and the minimum values of f.

vertices (p. 477) The vertices of an ellipse are the endpoints of the major and minor axes of the ellipse.

Z

z-score (p. 598) The z-score is the number of standard deviations away from the mean.

Chapter 1
Lesson 1.1
On Your Own
11. b. Start with $\frac{3\pi}{2}$ and add 2π repeatedly.
14. The maximum and minimum values for the x-coordinates are 1 and -1, respectively, and likewise for the y-coordinates. For one trip around the circle, the maximum value of the x-coordinates occurs when the distance walked is 0 m and 2π m, and the minimum value occurs when the distance walked is π m. The maximum value of the y-coordinates occurs when the distance walked is $\frac{\pi}{2}$ m, and the minimum value occurs when the distance walked is $\frac{3\pi}{2}$ m.

Lesson 1.2
Check Your Understanding
1. a. $\cos\frac{2\pi}{3} = -\frac{1}{2}$, $\sin\frac{2\pi}{3} = \frac{\sqrt{3}}{2}$ **b.** $\cos\frac{4\pi}{3} = -\frac{1}{2}$, $\sin\frac{4\pi}{3} = -\frac{\sqrt{3}}{2}$ **c.** $\cos\frac{5\pi}{3} = \frac{1}{2}$, $\sin\frac{5\pi}{3} = -\frac{\sqrt{3}}{2}$
d. $\cos\frac{6\pi}{3} = 1$, $\sin\frac{6\pi}{3} = 0$ **2.** $\cos\frac{\pi}{4} = \sin\frac{\pi}{4} = \frac{\sqrt{2}}{2}$

3.

x	$\cos x$	$\sin x$
0	1	0
$\frac{\pi}{6}$	$\frac{\sqrt{3}}{2}$	$\frac{1}{2}$
$\frac{\pi}{4}$	$\frac{\sqrt{2}}{2}$	$\frac{\sqrt{2}}{2}$
$\frac{\pi}{3}$	$\frac{1}{2}$	$\frac{\sqrt{3}}{2}$
$\frac{\pi}{2}$	0	1
$\frac{2\pi}{3}$	$-\frac{1}{2}$	$\frac{\sqrt{3}}{2}$
$\frac{3\pi}{4}$	$-\frac{\sqrt{2}}{2}$	$\frac{\sqrt{2}}{2}$
$\frac{5\pi}{6}$	$-\frac{\sqrt{3}}{2}$	$\frac{1}{2}$
π	-1	0
$\frac{7\pi}{6}$	$-\frac{\sqrt{3}}{2}$	$-\frac{1}{2}$
$\frac{5\pi}{4}$	$-\frac{\sqrt{2}}{2}$	$-\frac{\sqrt{2}}{2}$
$\frac{4\pi}{3}$	$-\frac{1}{2}$	$-\frac{\sqrt{3}}{2}$
$\frac{3\pi}{2}$	0	-1
$\frac{5\pi}{3}$	$\frac{1}{2}$	$-\frac{\sqrt{3}}{2}$
$\frac{7\pi}{4}$	$\frac{\sqrt{2}}{2}$	$-\frac{\sqrt{2}}{2}$
$\frac{11\pi}{6}$	$\frac{\sqrt{3}}{2}$	$-\frac{1}{2}$
2π	1	0
$\frac{13\pi}{6}$	$\frac{\sqrt{3}}{2}$	$\frac{1}{2}$
$\frac{9\pi}{4}$	$\frac{\sqrt{2}}{2}$	$\frac{\sqrt{2}}{2}$
$\frac{7\pi}{3}$	$\frac{1}{2}$	$\frac{\sqrt{3}}{2}$

4. $\cos^2 x + \sin^2 x = 1$ **5. a.** Yes; the vertical line through $\left(\frac{4}{5}, 0\right)$ intersects the unit circle in two points.
b. $\pm\frac{3}{5}$ **6.** B **7. a.** Yes; answers may vary. Sample: $\sin 33 \approx 0.999912$ **b.** No; if $\sin x = -1$, then x must be a number of the form $\frac{3\pi}{2} + n(2\pi)$, where n is an integer.
On Your Own
8. $\left(\frac{\sqrt{3}}{2}, \frac{1}{2}\right)$ **11. b.** negative **14.** -1

Lesson 1.3
Check Your Understanding
1. A **2. a.** 0.36; 0.64 **b.** ± 0.8
c.

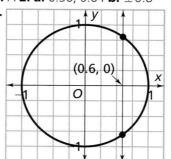

3. The solutions are approximately 0.9 and 5.4.

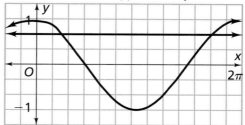

4. a. $\cos\left(-\frac{\pi}{2}\right) = 0$, $\sin\left(-\frac{\pi}{2}\right) = -1$
b. $\cos\left(-\frac{\pi}{3}\right) = \frac{1}{2}$, $\sin\left(-\frac{\pi}{3}\right) = -\frac{\sqrt{3}}{2}$
5. a. They are equal. **b.** They are opposites.
6. a. not always **b.** always **c.** always **d.** not always
On Your Own
7.

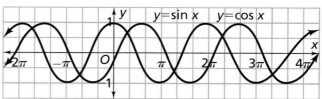

8. Quadrant IV **12. b.** The period of the new graph will be half the period of the graph in part (a).

Lesson 1.4
Check Your Understanding
1. $\frac{7\pi}{6}$ and $\frac{11\pi}{6}$ **2.** all numbers of the forms $\frac{7\pi}{6} + 2\pi n$ and $\frac{11\pi}{6} + 2\pi n$, where n is an integer **3.** -0.7599
4. all measures of the forms $50° + 360°n$ and $130° + 360°n$, where n is an integer **5.** 0.79

6. a–e. Answers may vary. Samples are given.

a. $\sin x = 1$ **b.** $\sin x = \frac{1}{2}$ **c.** $\cos x = 2$ **d.** $\sin 2x = \frac{1}{2}$

e. $\sin 3x = \frac{1}{2}$ **7.** $\alpha = 0, \theta = \frac{\pi}{6}$ or $\alpha = 0, \theta = \frac{5\pi}{6}$

On Your Own

8. -1 and $\frac{3}{5}$ **10. b.** $\cos 160° = -\cos 20°$

14. a. $\theta \approx 56.3° + 360°n$ and $\theta \approx 123.7° + 360°n$, where n is an integer **15.** $\frac{\pi}{3}, \frac{\pi}{2}, \frac{3\pi}{2}, \frac{5\pi}{3}$

Lesson 1.5

Check Your Understanding

1. The slope is 0. **2.** The maximum slope is 1, and it occurs where $x = 2\pi n$ (n an integer). The minimum slope is -1, and it occurs where $x = (2n + 1)\pi$ (n an integer). You can estimate these maximum and minimum slopes by examining the graph of $y = \sin x$.

3. a. $y = x$ **b.** 1 **4. a.** The graph should look the same as the graph of $y = \cos x$. **b.** the cosine function

5. a.

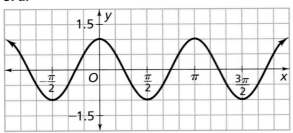

b. The functions have the same value for each value of x since $\cos^4 x - \sin^4 x = (\cos^2 x + \sin^2 x)(\cos^2 x - \sin^2 x) = 1 \cdot (\cos^2 x - \sin^2 x) = \cos^2 x - \sin^2 x$.

On Your Own

6. c. The values of x where the maximum and minimum of $y = \sin x$ occur are, respectively, $\frac{\pi}{2}$ units greater than those for $y = \cos x$. **7. a.** in intervals of the form $\left[-\frac{\pi}{2} + 2\pi n, \frac{\pi}{2} + 2\pi n\right]$, where n is an integer **11.** The graph of $c(x)$ is the same as the graph of $y = 1$.

Lesson 1.6

On Your Own

7. a. 2 **8. b.** $\sec x$ is larger for $0 < x < \frac{\pi}{2}$. By definition, $\tan x = \frac{\sin x}{\cos x}$ and $\sec x = \frac{1}{\cos x}$. For $0 < x < \frac{\pi}{2}$, we have $\frac{\sin x}{\cos x} < \frac{1}{\cos x}$ since $\sin x < 1$. Therefore $\tan x < \sec x$.

Lesson 1.7

Check Your Understanding

1. a.

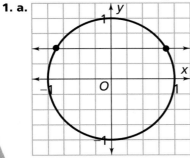

b.

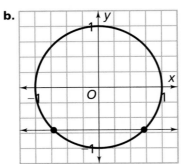

c.

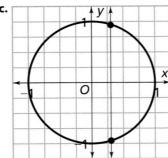

d.

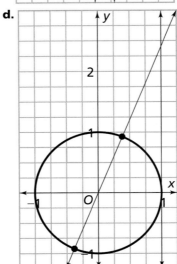

e.

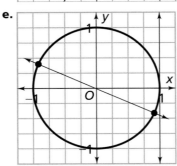

2. $\cos^2 x + \sin^2 x = 1$ for all values of x, so $\cos x = \pm\sqrt{1 - \sin^2 x}$. Since $0 < 0.38 < \frac{\pi}{2}$, $\cos 0.38 = \sqrt{1 - \sin^2 0.38}$. Therefore, use the calculator to evaluate $\frac{\sin 0.38}{\sqrt{1 - \sin^2 0.38}}$.

3. $\tan\left(\frac{\pi}{2} + x\right)$ is the opposite of the reciprocal of $\tan x$, that is, $\tan\left(\frac{\pi}{2} + x\right) = -\frac{1}{\tan x}$. **4.** Quadrants II and IV; one way: By definition, $\tan x = \frac{\sin x}{\cos x}$. So $\tan x$ is negative if and only if $\sin x$ and $\cos x$ have different signs. They have different signs if and only if x corresponds to an angle whose terminal side is in Quadrant II or Quadrant IV. Another way: We know from the In-Class Experiment that $\tan x$ is the y-coordinate of the point where the line through the origin and $(\cos x, \sin x)$ intersects the graph of $x = 1$. The line through the origin and $(\cos x, \sin x)$ intersects the graph of $x = 1$ below the x-axis if and only if $(\cos x, \sin x)$ is in Quadrant II or Quadrant IV. **5.** Yes; answers may vary. Sample: $x = 1.57$

6. a. $\tan\frac{\pi}{6} = \frac{\sqrt{3}}{3}$ and $\frac{\sqrt{3}}{3} > \frac{\pi}{6}$; $\tan\frac{\pi}{4} = 1$ and $1 > \frac{\pi}{4}$; $\tan 1 \approx 1.557$ and $1.557 > 1$. So for the three given values of x, it is true that $\tan x > x$. Other examples may vary. Samples: $\tan 0.5 \approx 0.546$ and $0.546 > 0.5$; $\tan 0.75 \approx 0.932$ and $0.932 > 0.75$; $\tan 0.1 \approx 1.0003$ and $1.0003 > 0.1$. **b.** $\frac{1}{2}\tan x$, $\frac{x}{2}$
c. The sector lies inside the triangle, so the area of the sector is less than the area of the triangle, that is, $\frac{x}{2} < \frac{1}{2}\tan x$. Therefore, $x < \tan x$.

On Your Own
9. a. Both are equal to $\frac{1}{2}$. **10.** $\tan\left(\frac{\pi}{2} - x\right) =$
$\dfrac{\sin\left(\frac{\pi}{2} - x\right)}{\cos\left(\frac{\pi}{2} - x\right)} = \dfrac{\cos x}{\sin x} = \cot x$; $\tan\left(\frac{\pi}{2} - x\right)$ and $\tan x$ are reciprocals for all values of x for which both a re defined.

Lesson 1.8
Check Your Understanding
1. a. $\frac{\pi}{2}$ **b.** 2π **2. a.** about 1.249 **b.** Infinitely many; approximately, real numbers of the form $1.249 + \pi n$ (n an integer)
3. a.

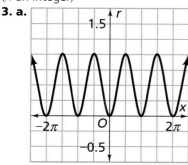

b. π **c.** Since $\sin(\pi + x) = -\sin x$, it follows that $\sin^2(\pi + x) = (-\sin x)^2 = \sin^2 x$. Hence the period of $r(x)$ is not greater than π. Since the zeros of $r(x)$ are all of the form πn (n an integer), the period of $r(x)$ is not less than π. Therefore, the period of $r(x)$ is equal to π.

4. a.

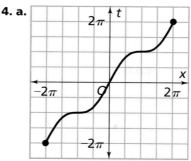

b. No; if $x > 1$, then $t(x) > \sin x + 1 \geq 0$. This means the value $t(0) = 0$ is not repeated for $x > 1$, although it would have to be repeated for $t(x)$ to be periodic. **5. a.** 4π **b.** For $B > 0$, the period of $\sin Bx$ is $\frac{2\pi}{B}$. For example, the period of $\sin 2x$ is π, and the period of $\sin\frac{1}{2}x$ is 4π.

On Your Own
8. The graphs are the same. **9.** Yes; 2π
10. c. $h(x) = 3$ for all $x \neq \frac{\pi}{2} \cdot n$ (n an integer); $h(x)$ is undefined at all the excluded values of x.

Lesson 1.9
Check Your Understanding
1. a. all the numbers $-\sin^{-1}\left(\frac{2}{3}\right) + 2n\pi$ and $\sin^{-1}\left(\frac{2}{3}\right) + (2n + 1)\pi$ (n an integer) **b.** no solutions
c. all the numbers $\tan^{-1}\left(-\frac{13}{2}\right) + n\pi$ (n an integer)
d. no solutions **2. a.** Answers may vary. Sample: $\tan^{-1}0.75 \approx 0.644$ **b.** at x-values that are $n\pi$ units (n an integer) from the solution in part (a) **c.** for the solution in part (a): $\pi + \tan^{-1}0.75 \approx 3.785$
3. a. Answers may vary. Sample: $\cos^{-1}0.8 \approx 0.644$
b. the x-values $2n\pi \pm \cos^{-1}0.8$ **c.** for the solution in part (a): $2\pi - \cos^{-1}0.8 \approx 5.640$ **4. a.** Answers may vary. Sample: $\sin^{-1}0.6 \approx 0.644$ **b.** the x-values $\sin^{-1}0.6 + 2n\pi$ and $(2n + 1)\pi - \sin^{-1}0.6$ (n an integer) **c.** for the solutions in part (a): $\pi - \sin^{-1}0.6 \approx 2.498$ **5. a.** $\frac{\pi}{6}$ **b.** $\frac{\pi}{2}$ **c.** $\frac{\pi}{4}$ **d.** $120°$
e. 2.14 **f.** $\frac{\pi}{6}$ **6. a.** $\frac{24}{25}$ **b.** $\frac{24}{25}$

On Your Own
7. c. the numbers $\frac{11}{2} + 2n$ (n an integer) **9. b.** $\frac{\pi}{2}$
12. a. Answers may vary. Sample: $t(x) = 8\sin x + 19$

Lesson 1.10
Check Your Understanding
1. a. $\frac{\pi}{6}$ and $\frac{5\pi}{6}$ **b.** $\frac{\pi}{6}$ and $\frac{7\pi}{6}$ **c.** 0, π, and 2π
d. 0, π, and 2π **2. a.** $f(30°) = \frac{16}{3}$, $g(30°) = \frac{16}{3}$
b. $f\left(\frac{\pi}{4}\right) = 4$, $g\left(\frac{\pi}{4}\right) = 4$ **c.** $f(60°) = \frac{16}{3}$, $g(60°) = \frac{16}{3}$
d. $f(120°) = \frac{16}{3}$, $g(120°) = \frac{16}{3}$ **e.** $f(2) \approx 6.9838$,
$g(2) \approx 6.9838$ **3.** $f(x) = \sec^2 x + \csc^2 x =$
$\dfrac{1}{\cos^2 x} + \dfrac{1}{\sin^2 x} = \dfrac{\sin^2 x + \cos^2 x}{(\cos^2 x)(\sin^2 x)} = \dfrac{1}{(\cos^2 x)(\sin^2 x)} =$
$\sec^2 x \cdot \csc^2 x = g(x)$

4. a. Answers may vary. Sample: Use $\theta = 60°$.
b. Answers may vary. Sample: Use $\theta = 60°$.
c. Use the equations $\cos \theta = \sin(90° - \theta)$ and $\sin \theta = \cos(90° - \theta)$.

$\tan(90° - \theta) = \dfrac{\sin(90° - \theta)}{\cos(90° - \theta)} = \dfrac{\cos \theta}{\sin \theta} = \cot \theta$

d. $\sec(90° - \theta) = \dfrac{1}{\cos(90° - \theta)} = \dfrac{1}{\sin \theta} = \csc \theta$

5. a. $\triangle OSB$ and $\triangle OAT$ are right triangles that share the acute angle with vertex O. Hence the acute angles $\angle OBS$ and $\angle OTA$ are congruent. If the angles of one triangle are congruent to those of another triangle, then the triangles are similar. So $\triangle OSB \sim \triangle OAT$.
b. By definition, $\sec \alpha = \sec \angle TOS = \dfrac{\text{hypotenuse}}{\text{adjacent}}$.
So $\sec \alpha = \dfrac{OT}{1} = OT$. **6.** D **7.** B

On Your Own
8. a. domain $= \{x \mid x \neq (2n + 1)\dfrac{\pi}{2}$ (n an integer)$\}$,
range $= \{x \mid x \leq -1 \text{ or } x \geq 1\}$
11. b. $1 + \cot^2 x = \csc^2 x$ **12.** $\triangle OAT$ is a right triangle, so $OA^2 + AT^2 = OT^2$. But $OA = 1$, $AT = \tan \alpha$, and $OT = \sec \alpha$. So $1 + \tan^2 \alpha = \sec^2 \alpha$.

Lesson 1.11
On Your Own
8. Answers may vary. Sample: $\dfrac{4}{3}$ **9. a.** 75 **11. a.** 20

Lesson 1.12
Check Your Understanding
1. a. amplitude $= 3$, vertical displacement $= 7$
b. π **c.** Answers may vary. Sample: $\dfrac{\pi}{2}$ **d.** Answers may vary. Sample: $f(x) = -3\cos 2\left(x - \dfrac{\pi}{4}\right) + 7$
2. $f(x) = -3\sin 2x + 7$ **3.** $f(x) = -3\sin 2x + 7$
4. a. Answers may vary. Sample: $\dfrac{\pi}{6}$
b.

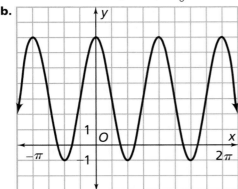

Graph $y = 4\cos 2x + 3$ and $y = 5$ on the same axes. Find the x-coordinates of the points of intersection of the graphs.
c. $\dfrac{\pi}{6} + n\pi$ and $\dfrac{5\pi}{6} + n\pi$ (n an integer)
5. a. $g(x) = 13\sin\left(4 \cdot \dfrac{\pi}{4} - \pi\right) + 10 = 13\sin 0 + 10 = 10$ **b.** amplitude $= 13$, vertical displacement $= 10$ **c.** maximum $= 23$, minimum $= -3$ **d.** $\dfrac{\pi}{2}$

e.

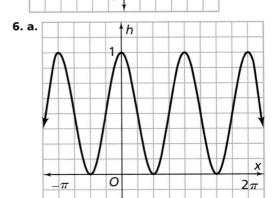

6. a.

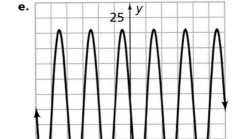

b. amplitude $= \dfrac{1}{2}$, vertical displacement $= \dfrac{1}{2}$, period $= \pi$ **7.** $\dfrac{1}{2}\cos 2x + \dfrac{1}{2}$
On Your Own
8. b. $\dfrac{2\pi}{5}$ **11.** $\dfrac{1}{2}\sin 2x$ **14.** Answers may vary. Sample: $f(x) = \sin \dfrac{2\pi}{5}x$

Lesson 1.13
Check Your Understanding
1. $H(t) = 125\cos \dfrac{2\pi}{9}t + 139$
2.

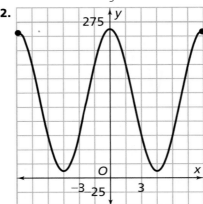

3. a. 1 min 31 s **b.** about $7\dfrac{1}{2}$ min **c.** 7 min 29 s
4. a. 8:24 P.M., 8:48 A.M. (next day) **b.** 2:12 P.M.; 2:36 A.M. (next day)

c. The numbers along the horizontal axis represent minutes.

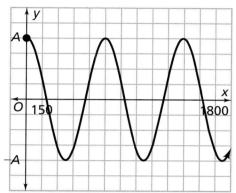

5. $H(t) = 3.5 \cos \frac{2\pi}{12.4}(t - 8) + 5.5$

6.

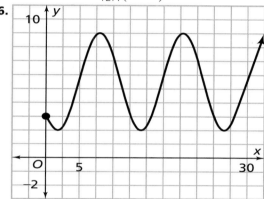

7. a. about 4 ft; about 4.6 ft **b.** about 5.5 ft
c. Answers may vary. Sample: about 11:30 P.M.
d. Answers may vary. Sample: about 10:49 A.M.
8. a. about 3.77 ft/s **b.** about 2.57 mph
c. The first two times are $t = 15$ s and $t = 45$ s.
On Your Own
10. B **13.** the Ferris wheel with radius 36 ft
14. b. about 2.99 ft

Chapter 2
Lesson 2.1
On Your Own
8. c. $f(1 + i) = (1 + i - 1)^2 + 1 = i^2 + 1 = 0$
10. d. 25 **12. b.** amplitude $= 1$, period $= \pi$

Lesson 2.2
Check Your Understanding
1. a. $\sqrt{17}$ **b.** $\sqrt{5}$ **c.** $\sqrt{13}$ **d.** $\sqrt{61}$
2. a. 17 **b.** 5 **c.** 13 **d.** 61
Each product is the square of the corresponding answer in Exercise 1.

3. a.

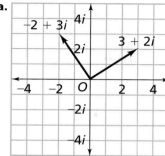

$\arg(z) \approx 0.588$, $\arg(i \cdot z) \approx 2.159$

b.

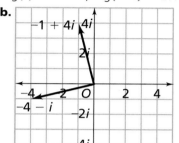

$\arg(z) \approx 1.816$, $\arg(i \cdot z) \approx 3.387$

c.

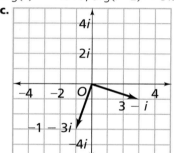

$\arg(z) \approx 4.391$, $\arg(i \cdot z) \approx 5.961$

d.

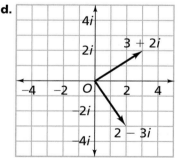

$\arg(z) \approx 5.300$, $\arg(i \cdot z) \approx 0.588$
4. a. magnitude $= 2\sqrt{2}$, argument $= \frac{\pi}{4}$

b. magnitude $= 2\sqrt{2}$, argument $= \frac{7\pi}{4}$

c. magnitude $= 2\sqrt{2}$, argument $= \frac{3\pi}{4}$

d. magnitude $= 2\sqrt{2}$, argument $= \frac{5\pi}{4}$

5. a. $|iz| = |z|$, $\arg(iz) = \arg(z) + \dfrac{\pi}{2}$
b. $|i^2 z| = |z|$, $\arg(i^2 z) = \arg(z) + \pi$
c. $|(-i)z| = |z|$, $\arg((-i)z) = \arg(z) + \dfrac{3\pi}{2}$
d. $|2z| = 2|z|$, $\arg(2z) = \arg(z)$
e. $\left|\dfrac{1}{z}\right| = \dfrac{1}{|z|}$, $\arg\left(\dfrac{1}{z}\right) = 2\pi - \arg(z)$

On Your Own
6. $|3z| = 3|z|$ and $\arg(3z) = \arg(z)$
9. a. $(\cos^2 t - \sin^2 t) + (2\sin t \cos t)i$ **13. c.** 10

Lesson 2.3
Check Your Understanding
1. a. magnitude = 5, argument = 60°
b. magnitude = $\frac{1}{5}$, argument = 300°
2. a. magnitude = 25, argument = 120°
b. magnitude = 125, argument = 180°
c. magnitude = 1, argument = 0° (or 360°)
3. a.

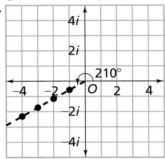

b.

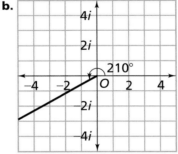

c. $-5\sqrt{3} - 5i$ **4. a.** $4\cos\dfrac{2\pi}{3} + 4i\sin\dfrac{2\pi}{3}$
b. $-2 + 2i\sqrt{3}$ **5. a.** Answers may vary. Samples:
$a = 5\text{ cis }60°$ or $a = \dfrac{5}{2} + \dfrac{5\sqrt{3}}{2}i$, $b = 3\text{ cis }30°$
or $b = \dfrac{3\sqrt{3}}{2} + \dfrac{3}{2}i$ **b.** $15i$; magnitude = 15,
argument = 90° **6. a.** Check students' work. The
values of θ will vary, but for each value of θ that is
selected, the number z should be on the ray that has
endpoint O and makes an angle of measure θ with
the positive x-axis, and z should be 3 units from O.
b. The circle with center O and radius 3; $|z| = 3$
since $z = 3\text{ cis }\theta$. Since there are no restrictions
on θ, all points 3 units from O are included.
7. a. $|\text{cis }\theta| = |\cos\theta + i\sin\theta| = $
$\sqrt{\cos^2\theta + \sin^2\theta} = 1$ **b.** $|r\text{ cis }\theta| = $
$|r| \cdot |\text{cis }\theta| = |r| \cdot 1 = |r|$

On Your Own
8. b. magnitude = 10, argument = 330°
11. b. $(\cos\alpha\cos\beta - \sin\alpha\sin\beta) + $
$(\cos\alpha\sin\beta + \sin\alpha\cos\beta)i$

Lesson 2.4
Check Your Understanding
1. a. $|z^2| = 9$, $\arg(z^2) = 240°$ **b.** Answers
may vary. Sample: $z^3 = 3^3\text{ cis }3(120°) = $
$27(\cos 360° + i\sin 360°) = 27(1 + i \cdot 0) = 27$
2. To find $|z^2|$, square $|z|$; to find $\arg(z^2)$, multiply
$\arg(z)$ by 2. To find $|z^3|$, cube $|z|$; to find $\arg(z^3)$,
multiply $\arg(z)$ by 3. In general, if n is a nonnegative
integer, to find $|z^n|$, raise $|z|$ to the nth power;
to find $\arg(z^n)$, multiply $\arg(z)$ by n. **3. a.** false
b. true; $3^3 = 27$ and $3 \cdot 40° = 120°$ **c.** false
d. true; $3^3 = 27$ and $3 \cdot 160° = 480°$ and
$480° - 360° = 120°$ **4.** Answers may vary. Sample:
$|zw| \approx 13$, $\arg(zw) \approx 160°$ **5.** To find the magnitude
of the product, multiply the magnitudes of the two
numbers. To find the argument of the product, use the
sum modulo 360° of the arguments of the numbers.
6. a.

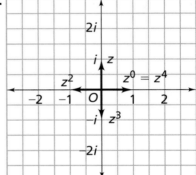

Since $|i| = 1$, all the powers have magnitude 1.
Multiplying a number by i rotates the number around
O counterclockwise by 90°. Since 360° is evenly
divisible by 90°, the set of powers consists of just
4 numbers.
b.

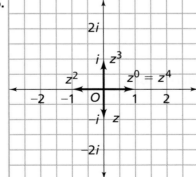

Since $|-i| = 1$, all the powers have magnitude 1.
Because of the minus sign, multiplying by $-i$ rotates
the other number not counterclockwise but clockwise

around O by 90°. Since 360° is evenly divisible by 90°, the set of powers consists of just 4 numbers.

c.

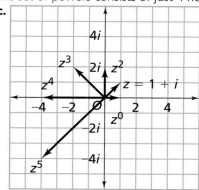

$|z| = \sqrt{2}$ and arg(z) = 45°, so for each nonnegative integer n, you can obtain z^{n+1} if you rotate z^n counterclockwise 45° and then scale by $\sqrt{2}$.

d.

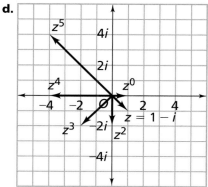

$|z| = \sqrt{2}$ and arg(z) = 315°, so for each nonnegative integer n, you can obtain z^{n+1} if you rotate z^n clockwise 45° and then scale by $\sqrt{2}$.

e.

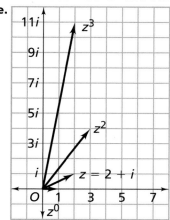

$|z| = \sqrt{5}$ and arg(z) ≈ 26.6°, so for each nonnegative integer n, you can obtain z^{n+1} if you rotate z^n counterclockwise by about 26.6° and then scale by $\sqrt{5}$.

f.

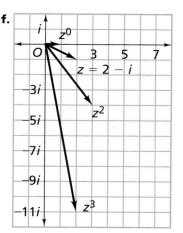

$|z| = \sqrt{5}$ and arg(z) ≈ 333.4349°, so for each nonnegative integer n, you can obtain z^{n+1} if you rotate z^n clockwise by about 26.6° and then scale by $\sqrt{5}$.

On Your Own
9. a. Answers may vary. Sample: $1 + i$ and $5 + 5i$
11. b. Quadrant I; arg(zw) is the sum of arg(z) and arg(w), or about 398°. Since 398° − 360° = 38°, the vector for zw will be in Quadrant I.
12. b. $\left|\dfrac{z}{w}\right| = \sqrt{2}$, arg$\left(\dfrac{z}{w}\right) = \tan^{-1}\left(\dfrac{1}{7}\right) \approx 8.13°$

Lesson 2.5
On Your Own
11. D **15.** cot x **18.** $\dfrac{\pi}{6}, \dfrac{5\pi}{6}, \dfrac{7\pi}{6}, \dfrac{11\pi}{6}$

Lesson 2.6
Check Your Understanding
1. Answers may vary. Sample:
cos $3x$ = cos³ x − 3 sin² x cos x,
sin $3x$ = 3 sin x cos² x − sin³ x
2. a. Answers may vary. Sample: $\dfrac{\sqrt{2}}{2} + \dfrac{\sqrt{2}}{2}i$ and
$\dfrac{\sqrt{3}}{2} + \dfrac{1}{2}i$ **b.** cos 75° = $\dfrac{\sqrt{6} - \sqrt{2}}{4}$, sin 75° =
$\dfrac{\sqrt{6} + \sqrt{2}}{4}$ **c.** $\dfrac{1}{2}$ **3. a.** $\dfrac{16}{65} + \dfrac{63}{65}i$ **b.** $\dfrac{63}{65}$
4. a. cos ($\alpha + \beta$) + cos ($\alpha - \beta$) = cos α cos β − sin α sin β + cos α cos ($-\beta$) − sin α sin ($-\beta$) = cos α cos β − sin α sin β + cos α cos β + sin α sin β = 2 cos α cos β **b.** sin ($\alpha + \beta$) + sin ($\alpha - \beta$) = 2 sin α cos β
5. Check students' work. **6.** tan($\alpha + \beta$) = $\dfrac{\tan \alpha + \tan \beta}{1 - \tan \alpha \tan \beta}$
7. cos ($\alpha + \beta + \gamma$) = cos α cos β cos γ − cos α sin β sin γ − sin α cos β sin γ − sin α sin β cos γ
sin ($\alpha + \beta + \gamma$) = cos α cos β sin γ + cos α sin β cos γ + sin α cos β cos γ − sin α sin β cos γ

On Your Own

8. c. $\cos\left(x + \frac{\pi}{4}\right) = \frac{\sqrt{2}}{2}\cos x - \frac{\sqrt{2}}{2}\sin x$,

$\sin\left(x + \frac{\pi}{4}\right) = \frac{\sqrt{2}}{2}\sin x + \frac{\sqrt{2}}{2}\cos x$

11. a. $\tan 2x = \dfrac{2\tan x}{1 - \tan^2 x}$

13. a. $\dfrac{6 - \sqrt{35}}{12} + \dfrac{2\sqrt{7} + 3\sqrt{5}}{12}\,i$

Lesson 2.7
Check Your Understanding

1. a. $\tan^2 x - \sin^2 x = \dfrac{\sin^2 x}{\cos^2 x} - \sin^2 x$

$\qquad = \left(\dfrac{1}{\cos^2 x} - 1\right)\sin^2 x$

$\qquad = \left(\dfrac{1 - \cos^2 x}{\cos^2 x}\right)\sin^2 x$

$\qquad = \dfrac{\sin^2 x}{\cos^2 x} \cdot \sin^2 x$

$\qquad = \tan^2 x \sin^2 x$

b. $\dfrac{\cos x}{1 - \sin x} = \dfrac{\cos x}{1 - \sin x} \cdot \dfrac{1 + \sin x}{1 + \sin x}$

$\qquad = \dfrac{\cos x(1 + \sin x)}{1 - \sin^2 x}$

$\qquad = \dfrac{\cos x(1 + \sin x)}{\cos^2 x}$

$\qquad = \dfrac{1 + \sin x}{\cos x}$

c. $\cot^2 x - \cos^2 x = \dfrac{\cos^2 x}{\sin^2 x} - \cos^2 x$

$\qquad = \left(\dfrac{1}{\sin^2 x} - 1\right)\cos^2 x$

$\qquad = \left(\dfrac{1 - \sin^2 x}{\sin^2 x}\right)\cos^2 x$

$\qquad = \dfrac{\cos^2 x}{\sin^2 x} \cdot \cos^2 x$

$\qquad = \cot^2 x \cos^2 x$

d. $\dfrac{\sin x}{1 - \cos x} = \dfrac{\sin x}{1 - \cos x} \cdot \dfrac{1 + \cos x}{1 + \cos x}$

$\qquad = \dfrac{\sin x(1 + \cos x)}{1 - \cos^2 x}$

$\qquad = \dfrac{\sin x(1 + \cos x)}{\sin^2 x}$

$\qquad = \dfrac{1 + \cos x}{\sin x}$

2. The second equation is an identity.
$(\cos x + \sin x)^2 = \cos^2 x + 2\cos x \sin x + \sin^2 x = 2\cos x \sin x + 1 = \sin 2x + 1$
3. Since $\cos(\alpha + \beta) + \cos(\alpha - \beta) = 2\cos\alpha\cos\beta$ is an identity, $\cos 5x + \cos 3x = 2\cos 4x\cos x$. Hence $\cos 5x = 2\cos x\cos 4x - \cos 3x$.
4. This identity follows directly from the identity $\cos(\alpha + \beta) + \cos(\alpha - \beta) = 2\cos\alpha\cos\beta$ if you let $\alpha = (n + 1)x$ and $\beta = (n - 1)x$.

5. a. $(\sec x \sin x)^2 - (\sec x + 1)(\sec x - 1)$

$\qquad = \dfrac{\sin^2 x}{\cos^2 x} - \left(\sec^2 x - 1\right)$

$\qquad = \tan^2 x - \tan^2 x$

$\qquad = 0$

b. Since $(\sec x \sin x)^2 - (\sec x + 1)(\sec x - 1) = 0$ is an identity, you obtain an identity if you add $(\sec x + 1)(\sec x - 1)$ to both sides.

On Your Own
6. b. Use the formula in Exercise 4, and let $n = 2$ to get $\cos 3x = 2\cos x\cos 2x - \cos x$. On the right side of this equation, replace $\cos 2x$ with $2\cos^2 x - 1$ and simplify to get $\cos 3x = 4\cos^3 x - 3\cos x$.

9. a. $\dfrac{\sec x + 1}{\tan x} = \dfrac{\sec x + 1}{\tan x} \cdot \dfrac{\sec x - 1}{\sec x - 1}$

$\qquad = \dfrac{\sec^2 x - 1}{\tan x(\sec x - 1)}$

$\qquad = \dfrac{\tan^2 x}{\tan x(\sec x - 1)}$

$\qquad = \dfrac{\tan x}{\sec x - 1}$

Lesson 2.8
On Your Own
9. c. $288°$ **13.** $4 + i$ and $4 - i$; sum $= 8$, product $= 17$

Lesson 2.9
Check Your Understanding
1. a. $|z^2| = 9$, $\arg(z^2) = \dfrac{2\pi}{3}$
b. $|z^3| = 27$, $\arg(z^3) = \pi$
c. $|z^5| = 243$, $\arg(z^5) = \dfrac{5\pi}{3}$
d. $|10z| = 30$, $\arg(10z) = \dfrac{\pi}{3}$
e. $|z^0| = 1$, $\arg(z^0) = 0$
f. $|z^{-1}| = \dfrac{1}{3}$, $\arg(z^{-1}) = \dfrac{5\pi}{3}$
2. $\sqrt{3}\,\text{cis}\,\dfrac{\pi}{6}$, $\sqrt{3}\,\text{cis}\,\dfrac{7\pi}{6}$
3. a. $|z^3| = 64$, $\arg(z^3) = 0$
b. $|z^3| = 64$, $\arg(z^3) = 0°$
c. $|z^3| = 8$, $\arg(z^3) = \dfrac{\pi}{2}$
d. $|z^3| = 8$, $\arg(z^3) = \dfrac{\pi}{2}$
4. sum $= 0$, product $= 8i$ **5. a.** a^2 is a solution of $x^{11} = 1$ if and only if $(a^2)^{11} = 1$. Since $(a^2)^{11} = (a^{11})^2 = 1^2 = 1$, a^2 is a solution.
b. The proof is the same as in part (a), but with 2 replaced by k.
On Your Own
6. The solutions are -2 and $\pm 4\sqrt{5}$; their sum is -2, and their product is 160. **11. b.** $\text{cis}\,0$, $\text{cis}\,\dfrac{2\pi}{5}$, $\text{cis}\,\dfrac{4\pi}{5}$, $\text{cis}\,\dfrac{6\pi}{5}$, and $\text{cis}\,\dfrac{8\pi}{5}$ **14.** $\dfrac{\sqrt{2} + \sqrt{6}}{4}$

Lesson 2.10
Check Your Understanding
1. a. The solution in Quadrant I should be labeled ω, ω^6, the solution in Quadrant II should be labeled ω^2, the solution in Quadrant III should be labeled ω^3, ω^{13}, the solution in Quadrant IV should be labeled ω^4, and the solution on the positive part of the real axis should be labeled ω^5. **b.** 1 **2. a.** 0 **b.** 0 **c.** The sum in part (b) is the sum of the imaginary parts of the six roots of $x^6 = 1$, and this sum must be 0 since the sum of the roots is 0.

3.

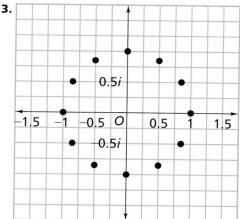

4. a.

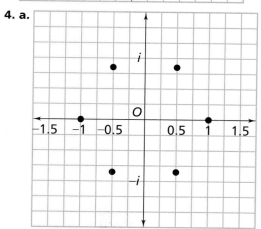

b. The plot in part (a) is part of the plot from Exercise 3, so this illustrates graphically that the solutions of $x^6 - 1 = 0$ are solutions of $x^{12} - 1 = 0$. Algebraically, the solutions of $x^6 - 1 = 0$ are the numbers $\operatorname{cis}\frac{2\pi}{6}k$ where k goes from 0 to 5. The solutions of $x^{12} - 1 = 0$ are the numbers $\operatorname{cis}\frac{2\pi}{6}n$ where n goes from 0 to 11. **c.** This result follows immediately from part (b). **5.** Every multiple of 5 greater than 5 will work. **6.** 6 **7.** Yes; $n = 36$
8. a. Answers may vary. Sample: i **b.** Answers may vary. Sample: $\operatorname{cis}\left(\frac{4\pi}{9}\right)$ **c.** yes

On Your Own
10. a. -1 **12. b.** 0 **15. a.** Suppose $z = x + yi$ and that z is a root of unity. Then $\frac{1}{z} = \frac{1}{x + yi} = \frac{x - yi}{x^2 + y^2}$.

But $x^2 + y^2 = 1$ since z is a root of unity. So $\frac{1}{z} = x - yi = \bar{z}$.

Lesson 2.11
Check Your Understanding
1. 18 **2. a.** $z^{21} = \operatorname{cis} 357°$ **b.** Yes; 360 times
c. all rational values of θ **3. a.** $z^4 = \left(\operatorname{cis}\frac{2\pi}{5}\right)^4 = \operatorname{cis}\frac{8\pi}{5} = \operatorname{cis}\left(-\frac{2\pi}{5}\right)$ **b.** Use the result from part (a).
$z + z^4 = \operatorname{cis}\frac{2\pi}{5} + \operatorname{cis}\left(-\frac{2\pi}{5}\right) = 2\cos\frac{2\pi}{5}$
4. a. $(x - 1)(x^4 + x^3 + x^2 + x + 1)$ **b.** z is a root of $(z - 1)(z^4 + z^3 + z^2 + z + 1) = 0$, and since $z \neq 1$, the value of $z^4 + z^3 + z^2 + z + 1$ must be 0. It follows that $z^4 + z^3 + z^2 + z = -1$.
5. a. From Exercise 3(b), we know that $z + z^4$ is positive, since $2\cos\frac{2\pi}{5}$ is positive. (We know this is so because $0 < \frac{2\pi}{5} < \frac{\pi}{2}$.) By Exercise 4(b), $z^2 + z^3 = -1 - (z + z^4)$, and subtracting a positive number from -1 results in a negative number.
b. This result follows immediately from Exercise 4(b).
c. $z^3 + z^4 + z^6 + z^7$, or $z + z^2 + z^3 + z^4$ (since $z^6 = z$ and $z^7 = z^2$) **d.** $ab = -1$ follows directly from part (c) and Exercise 4(b).
6. $a = \frac{-1 + \sqrt{5}}{2}$, $b = -\frac{1 + \sqrt{5}}{2}$
7. a. Use the result from Exercise 6, the fact that $a = z + z^4$, and Exercise 3(b) to obtain $2\cos 72° = \frac{-1 + \sqrt{5}}{2}$. This last equation gives $\cos 72° = \frac{-1 + \sqrt{5}}{4}$.
b. $\sin 72° = \frac{\sqrt{10 + 2\sqrt{5}}}{4}$
c. $z^0 = 1$, $z = \frac{-1 + \sqrt{5}}{4} + \frac{\sqrt{10 + 2\sqrt{5}}}{4}i$,
$z^2 = -\frac{1 + \sqrt{5}}{4} + \frac{\sqrt{10 - 2\sqrt{5}}}{4}i$,
$z^3 = -\frac{1 + \sqrt{5}}{4} - \frac{\sqrt{10 - 2\sqrt{5}}}{4}i$,
$z^4 = \frac{-1 + \sqrt{5}}{4} - \frac{\sqrt{10 + 2\sqrt{5}}}{4}i$
8. $x^5 - 1 = (x - 1)(x^4 + x^3 + x^2 + x + 1)$, so the given factorization is correct if $x^4 + x^3 + x^2 + x + 1$ equals $(x^2 + \Phi x + 1)\left(x^2 - \frac{1}{\Phi}x + 1\right)$. Expand this last expression and collect like terms to obtain $x^4 + \left(\Phi - \frac{1}{\Phi}\right)x^3 + x^2 + \left(\Phi - \frac{1}{\Phi}\right)x + 1$. Use $\Phi = \frac{1 + \sqrt{5}}{2}$ to show that $\Phi - \frac{1}{\Phi} = 1$. It follows that $x^4 + x^3 + x^2 + x + 1 = (x^2 + \Phi x + 1)\left(x^2 - \frac{1}{\Phi}x + 1\right)$.

On Your Own
9. 30 sides **10.** Let $\overline{AM}$ be the altitude to the base $\overline{BC}$ of isosceles $\triangle ABC$. Right triangle trigonometry tells you that $\cos \angle B = \cos 72° = \frac{BM}{1} = BM$. Likewise, $CM = \cos 72°$. **14.** $-\frac{\sqrt{5} + 1}{4}$

Lesson 2.12
Check Your Understanding
1. a. 0 **b.** 7 **c.** 1 **2. a.** 0 **b.** 0 **c.** -1 **3.** $f(n) = 5$ if n is a multiple of 5, otherwise $f(n) = 0$ **4. a.** 0 **b.** 1 **c.** 5

5. 5 **6. a.** 0 **b.** 0 **7. a.** $\text{cis}\left(\frac{2\pi}{12} \cdot 1\right)$, $\text{cis}\left(\frac{2\pi}{12} \cdot 5\right)$, $\text{cis}\left(\frac{2\pi}{12} \cdot 7\right)$, $\text{cis}\left(\frac{2\pi}{12} \cdot 11\right)$ **b.** $x^{12} - 1 = (x - 1) \cdot (x + 1)(x^2 + 1)(x^2 + x + 1)(x^2 - x + 1) \cdot (x^4 - x^2 + 1)$

The table shows which powers of ζ make which factors equal to 0.

Factor	Powers of ζ
$x - 1$	ζ^0
$x + 1$	ζ^6
$x^2 + 1$	ζ^3, ζ^9
$x^2 + x + 1$	ζ^4, ζ^8
$x^2 - x + 1$	ζ^2, ζ^{10}
$x^4 - x^2 + 1$	$\zeta, \zeta^5, \zeta^7, \zeta^{11}$

On Your Own
9. -7 **11. c.** $(x - 1)(x - \zeta)(x - \zeta^2)(x - \zeta^3) \cdot (x - \zeta^4)$, where $\zeta = \text{cis}\frac{2\pi}{5} = \frac{-1 + \sqrt{5}}{4} + \frac{\sqrt{10 + 2\sqrt{5}}}{4}i$ **15. a.** If $\zeta = \text{cis}\frac{2\pi}{9}$, then the primitive 9th roots of unity are $\zeta, \zeta^2, \zeta^4, \zeta^5, \zeta^7$, and ζ^8.

Chapter 3
Lesson 3.1
On Your Own
8. Not possible. For the graph to meet the first and third conditions, it would have to change directions more than just twice, as described in the second condition.

9. Answers may vary. Sample:
$f(x) = |x + 3| - 2$

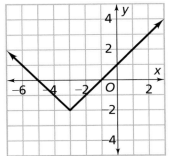

Lesson 3.2
Check Your Understanding
1. At birth, height in inches is larger; later in life, weight in pounds is larger. Since both change continuously, there must be at least one intersection.
2. a. $a(5) = 0$ **b.** $a(5.001)$ is a very small positive

number. **c.** $a(0) = 30$ **d.** $a(0.001)$ is approximately 30. **e.** $a(1000)$ is a very large positive number.
f. $a(0.999)$ is a very small positive number.
g. $a(-1000)$ is a very large negative number.
3. a. Answers may vary. Sample:
$g(x) = x^2 + 4x - 21$ **b.** Answers may vary. Sample:
$h(x) = -\frac{2}{3}x^2 + \frac{4}{3}x + 10$ **c.** Answers may vary.
Sample: $j(x) = -\frac{2}{3}x^2 + \frac{4}{3}x + 12$ **4. a.** x must be within 0.033 of 5. **b.** x must be within 0.0033 of 5.
c. x must be within 0.00033 of 5. **d.** x must be within $0.00000033 = 3.3 \cdot 10^{-7}$ of 5. **5.** The maximum number of intersections is 3 and the minimum number of intersections is 1. **6.** Consider fourth degree polynomials with a positive leading coefficient. Some possible shapes are:

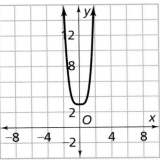

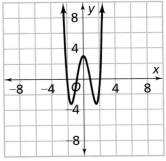

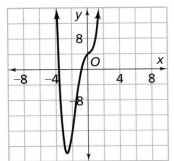

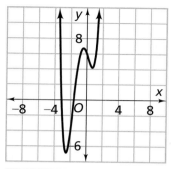

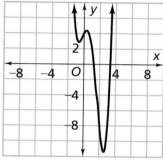

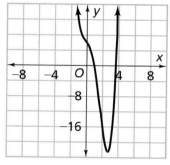

Each of these can be turned upside-down if the leading coefficient is negative.

7. a. No. For example, $f(x) = x^3$ has only one real zero. **b.** Yes. Since f has at least one real zero, $f \cdot g$ will have at least one real zero. **c.** Yes. Every zero of f is also a zero of f^2. Since f has at least one real zero, so does f^2. **d.** No. For example, $f(x) = x^3 + x^2$ and $g(x) = -x^3 + 4$ each have real zeros, but $k(x) = f(x) + g(x) = x^2 + 4$ does not. **e.** Yes. The composition of two cubic functions is a polynomial function of degree 9, and it must have at least one real zero.

On Your Own

9. a. $b(-5) = 0$ since one of the factors is zero. **b.** $b(-5.001)$ is a little bit less than 0. **c.** $b(0) = 30$ **d.** $b(0.001)$ is a little bit less than 30. **g.** $b(-1000)$ is a very large negative number. **11. a.** x must be within 0.059 of 5. **b.** x must be within 0.0059 of 5.

12. If the fourth degree polynomial rises, falls, rises, and falls and crosses the x-axis at $(-5, 0)$, $(-1, 0)$, and intersects it somewhere on the positive x-axis, it is of the form $f(x) = A(x + 5)(x + 1)(x - b)^2$ where $A < 0$ and $b > 0$. Choose some positive value for b, say $b = 1$. Then
$$f(x) = A(x + 5)(x + 1)(x - 1)^2$$
$$= A(x^4 + 4x^3 - 6x^2 - 4x + 5)$$
To find A, use the fact that $f(0) = -7$:
$$f(0) = A(5) = -7 \Rightarrow A = -\frac{7}{5}$$
A polynomial that satisfies the conditions is
$$f(x) = -\frac{7}{5}(x^4 + 4x^3 - 6x^2 - 4x + 5)$$
$$= -\frac{7}{5}x^4 - \frac{28}{5}x^3 + \frac{42}{5}x^2 + \frac{28}{5}x - 7$$

14. a. $g(x)$ takes on large positive values. **b.** $g(x)$ takes on large negative values.

18. Answers may vary. **a.** Yes; sample: $f(x) = x^4 + 1$. **b.** Yes; sample: $f(x) = x^3 + 8$. **c.** Yes; sample: $f(x) = (x - 1)(x - 2)(x - 3)$ $= x^3 - 6x^2 + 11x - 6$

19. Yes; sample: let $g(x) = x^3 - 4x + 1$. If $a = -3$, then $g(-3) = -14$ and if $b = 3$, $g(3) = 16$, but $g(x) = 0$ three times between $a = -3$ and $b = 3$. $g(x) = 0$ between $x = -3$ and $x = -2$, between $x = 0$ and $x = 1$ and between $x = 1$ and $x = 2$.

Lesson 3.3

Check Your Understanding

1. a. The average rate of change is 7. **b.** The equation of the secant is $8x - y = -33$. **c.** $m = a + b$

2. a. The equation of the secant is $\frac{y - 5}{x - 2} = 10.0601$ or $10.0601x - y = 15.1202$. **b.** The equation of the secant is $\frac{y - 5}{x - 2} = b^2 + 2b + 2$ or $(b^2 + 2b + 2)x - y = 2b^2 + 4b - 1$.

c.

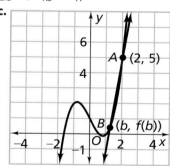

As b moves closer to 2, the slope gets closer to 10.

3. a. Answers may vary. Sample:

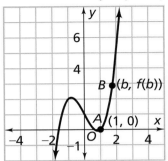

b. Answers may vary. Sample:

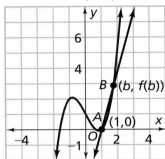

c. $m = b^2 + b - 1$ **d.** As b gets closer to 1, the slope gets closer to $1^2 + 1 - 1 = 1$.

4. a. Answers may vary. Sample:

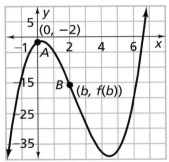

b. Answers may vary. Sample:

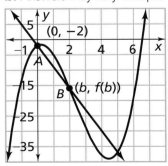

c. $m = \dfrac{f(b) - (-2)}{b}$

$= \dfrac{b^3 - 7b^2 + 3b - 2 + 2}{b}$

$= \dfrac{(b)(b^2 - 7b + 3)}{b} = b^2 - 7b + 3$

d. As b gets closer to 0, the slope gets closer to $0^2 - 7(0) + 3 = 3$. **5.** $m = 3a + 3b + 5$
6. a. $(0, -10)$ **b.** $(0, 33)$ **c.** $(0, -ab)$ **7.** The slope is $a^2 + ab + b^2 = (a - b)^2 + 3ab = (a + b)^2 - ab$. Either the second or third expression must always be positive unless $a = b = 0$, which cannot happen since $a \neq b$. **8. a.** 9000 ft or approx. 1.7 mi
b. 18,000 ft or approx. 3.4 mi **c.** 40,500 ft or approx. 7.7 mi **d.** $900t$ ft **9. a.** 0 ft; Pete has not caught John yet. **b.** 12,000 ft, or about $2\frac{1}{4}$ mi; Pete has not caught John yet. **c.** 42,000 ft, or about 8 mi; Pete has passed John. **d.** $1200(t - 10)$, where $t \geq 10$ **e.** Solve $900t = 1200(t - 10)$. **10. a.** Yakov **b.** 2 s **c.** 20 ft
d. Yakov: 10 ft/s; Demitri: 5 ft/s **e.** $y = 10x$
f. $y = 5x + 10$ **g.** $10x = 5x + 10$

On Your Own

11. a.

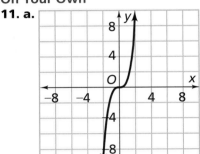

d.

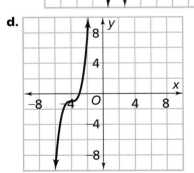

12. a.

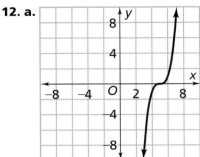

b.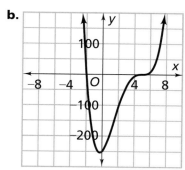

c.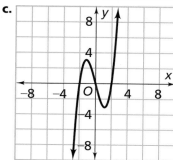

18. a. The graphs intersect at $(0, 1)$.

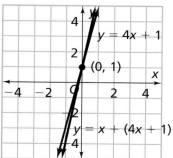

19. a. The graphs intersect at $(5, 4)$.

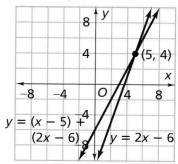

Lesson 3.4
Check Your Understanding
1. a. The expansion is $2x^3 + 5x^2 + x - 1 = 101 + 85(x - 3) + 23(x - 3)^2 + 2(x - 3)^3$.
b. The expansion is $x^2 + 2x - 3 = 12 + 8(x - 3) + (x - 3)^2$.
c. The expansion is $2x^3 + 5x^2 + x - 1 = 113 + 93(x - 3) + 24(x - 3)^2 + 2(x - 3)^3$.
d. The expansion is $8x^3 + 20x^2 + 4x - 4 = 404 + 340(x - 3) + 92(x - 3)^2 + 8(x - 3)^3$.

e. The expansion is $8x^3 + 19x^2 + 2x - 1 = 392 + 332(x - 3) + 91(x - 3)^2 + 8(x - 3)^3$.
2. a. The expansion is $2x^3 + 5x^2 + x - 1 = 37 + 45(x - 2) + 17(x - 2)^2 + 2(x - 2)^3$.
b. The expansion is $x^2 + 2x - 3 = 5 + 6(x - 2) + (x - 2)^2$.
c. The expansion is $2x^3 + 6x^2 + 3x - 4 = 42 + 51(x - 2) + 18(x - 2)^2 + 2(x - 2)^3$.
d. The expansion is $6x^3 + 15x^2 + 3x - 3 = 111 + 135(x - 2) + 51(x - 2)^2 + 6(x - 2)^3$.
e. The expansion is $2x^5 + 9x^4 + 5x^3 - 14x^2 - 5x + 3 = 185 + 447(x - 2) + 392(x - 2)^2 + 157(x - 2)^3 + 29(x - 2)^4 + 2(x - 2)^5$.
3. $x^2 + 2x - 3 = a^2 + 2a - 3 + (2a + 2)(x - a) + (x - a)^2$
4. a. $27 + 27(x - 3) + 9(x - 3)^2 + (x - 3)^3$
b. $9 + 6(x - 3) + (x - 3)^2$ **c.** $3 + (x - 3)$
d. $1 + 0(x - 3)$ **5.** Yes, it works for $f(x) = 2x^3 + 5x^2 + x - 1$. It will work for any cubic.

On Your Own
6. a. $379 + 201(x - 5) + 35(x - 5)^2 + 2(x - 5)^3$ **b.** $32 + 12(x - 5) + (x - 5)^2$
c. $1073 + 579(x - 5) + 103(x - 5)^2 + 6(x - 5)^3$ **d.** $143,641 + 152,358(x - 5) + 66,931(x - 5)^2 + 15,586(x - 5)^3 + 2029(x - 5)^4 + 140(x - 5)^5 + 4(x - 5)^6$
7. The expansion is $rx^2 + sx + t = 9r + 3s + t + (6r + s)(x - 3) + r(x - 3)^2$. **8.** The expansion is $rx^2 + sx + t = a^2r + as + t + (2ar + s)(x - a) + r(x - a)^2$. **10. a.** 31 **b.** $-10x + 31$
c. $-4x^2 - 10x + 31$ **13. a.** $x^2 = 1 + 2(x - 1) + (x - 1)^2$ **b.** $x^3 = 1 + 3(x - 1) + (x + 2)(x - 1)^2$

f. $x^n = 1 + n(x - 1) + (x - 1)^2 \sum_{k=1}^{n-1} (k \cdot x^{n-k-1})$

for positive integer n.

Lesson 3.5
Check Your Understanding
1. $y = 10x - 25$ **2.** $y = 3x - 2$ **3.** $y = 2ax - a^2$
4.

x	$f(x)$	Slope of tangent at $(x, f(x))$
-1	2	-2
0	1	0
1	2	2
2	5	4
3	10	6
4	17	8
10	101	20
100	10,001	200

5.

x	$f(x)$	Slope of tangent at $(x, f(x))$
-1	0	-1
0	0	1
1	2	3
2	6	5
3	12	7
4	20	9
10	110	21
100	10,100	201

6. a. $y = 2(x - 1) + 1 = 2x - 1$
b. $y = 3(x - 1) + 1 = 3x - 2$
c. $y = 4(x - 1) + 1 = 4x - 3$
d. $y = 5(x - 1) + 1 = 5x - 4$
e. $y = 6(x - 1) + 1 = 6x - 5$
f. $y = (x - 1) + 1 = x$
7. Using the results of Exercise 6, the tangent will be $y = n(x - 1) + 1$.

On Your Own
8. The equation of the tangent is $y = 2x + 2$; the slope of the tangent line is 2.
10. a. $y = 2a(x - a) + a^2 = 2ax - a^2$
b. $y = 3a^2(x - a) + a^3 = 3a^2x - 2a^3$
c. $y = 4a^3(x - a) + a^4 = 4a^3x - 3a^4$
11. Use your solution to Exercise 10. The equation of the tangent will be $y = na^{n-1}(x - a) + a^n = na^{n-1}x - (n - 1)a^n$.

Lesson 3.6
On Your Own
9. $x = -\frac{1}{5}$ or $x = 2$ **10. a.** Answers may vary.
Sample: $f(x) = \frac{x - 3}{x^2}$ **b.** Answers may vary.

Sample: $f(x) = \frac{1}{x - 5}$ **c.** Answers may

vary. Sample: $f(x) = \frac{x - 3}{x - 5}$ **d.** Answers

may vary. Sample: $f(x) = \frac{x^2 - 5x + 1}{x - 5}$

12. a.

x	$k(x)$
0	2
1	3
2	4
3	not defined
4	6

b. $\frac{(x - 3)(x + 2)}{x - 3} = x + 2$ **c.** $k(x)$ is *not* the same
function as $m(x) = x + 2$, because the domain of
$m(x)$ is $\mathbb{R}$, while the domain of $k(x)$ is $\{x \mid x \neq 3\}$.

Lesson 3.7
Check Your Understanding
1. a. 0 **b.** ∞ **c.** 0 **d.** $-\infty$ **2. a.** $\frac{3}{5}$ **b.** $\frac{10}{3}$ **c.** $\frac{5}{2}$ **d.** -2
e. ∞ **f.** 0 **3. a.** $y = 1$ **b.** $x = -2$ **c.** $\left(4, \frac{5}{6}\right)$

4. Answers may vary. **a.** $f(x) = \frac{4x}{x - 5}$

b. $f(x) = \frac{x}{(x - 2)(x - 5)}$ **c.** $f(x) = \frac{x - 2}{(x - 2)(x + 3)}$

d. $f(x) = \frac{x(x - 2)}{x - 1}$ **5.** $K = \frac{1}{6}$ **6. a.** $f(10) = 10.1$ and
$f(100) = 100.01$. **b.** The graph approaches the line
$y = x$. **c.** $f(0.1) = 10.1$ and $f(0.01) = 100.01$.
d. The graph of $f(x)$ as x approaches zero goes to ∞;
the function has a vertical asymptote $x = 0$.
e.

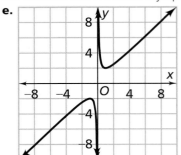

7. D
8. a.

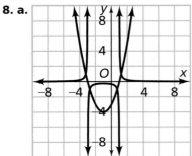

b. $-1 + \sqrt{3}$; $-1 - \sqrt{3}$; $-1 + \sqrt{5}$; $-1 - \sqrt{5}$
9. a. $d(x) = 0.75$; $d(2x) = 0.5$; $d(3x) = 0.25$;
$d(4x) = 0$

b.

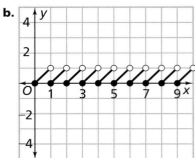

c.

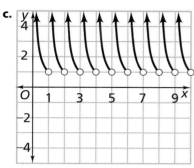

The domain of $r(x)$ is the set of all positive real numbers that are not integers. Its range is the positive real numbers.

On Your Own

10. a. $y = 2$ **b.** $x = -3$ **c.** $\left(2, \frac{3}{5}\right)$

11. a. $\{x \mid x \neq -2, 2\}$ **b.** $\{x \mid x \neq -2, 2\}$

12. a. $\frac{1}{2}$ **b.** $\frac{1}{2}$ **c.** 0 **d.** 0 **e.** ∞

15. a. $f(x) = \dfrac{x + 11}{(x + 11)(x + 3)}$ so for all $x \neq -11$
$f(x) = g(x)$. These two functions are not the same, however, because -11 does not belong to the domain of $f(x)$. **b.** The graphs look the same on the calculator because the hole is not visible, but if you look at the table you will see that the function is undefined at $x = -11$.

Lesson 3.8
Check Your Understanding

1. $y = -\frac{1}{2} + \frac{1}{4}(x - 2)$ **2.** Since $f(x) = \frac{1}{x}$ and $g(x) = -\frac{1}{x}$ are reflections of each other over the x-axis, their tangents at $x = 2$ will also be reflections of each other over the x-axis. **3.** The equation of the tangent at $(a, h(a))$ is $y = \dfrac{1}{a^2} + \dfrac{-2}{a^3}(x - a)$.

4.

x	Slope of tangent to f	Slope of tangent to h
$\frac{1}{10}$	-100	-2000
$\frac{1}{4}$	-16	-128
$\frac{1}{2}$	-4	-16
1	-1	-2
2	$-\frac{1}{4}$	$-\frac{1}{4}$
4	$-\frac{1}{16}$	$-\frac{1}{32}$
10	$-\frac{1}{100}$	$-\frac{1}{500}$

This makes sense because the slope of the tangent to the graph of f must be negative everywhere, but the slope of the tangent to the graph of h will be positive for negative x-values and negative for positive x-values.
5. $y = 2(x + 2) - 7$ **6.** $A = 6, B = -2$

7. a. The slope of the line tangent to f at $x = 4$ is $-\frac{3}{2}$.

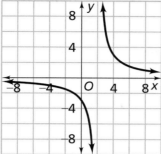

b. The slope of the line tangent to g at $x = 4$ is 2.

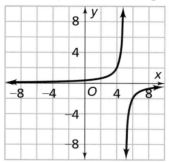

c. The slope of the line tangent to h at $x = 4$ is $\frac{1}{2}$.

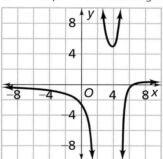

On Your Own

9. $y = 1 - \frac{3}{13}(x - 3)$

10.

x	Slope of tangent to f	Slope of tangent to g
-2	$-\frac{1}{4}$	$\frac{3}{4}$
-1	-1	0
$-\frac{1}{2}$	-4	-3
0	undefined	undefined
$\frac{1}{2}$	-4	-3
1	-1	0
2	$-\frac{1}{4}$	$\frac{3}{4}$
3	$-\frac{1}{9}$	$\frac{8}{9}$

11. a. The slope of the line tangent to $j(x)$ at $x = 2$ is $-\frac{4}{25}$. **b.** The slope of the line tangent to $j(x)$ at $x = -2$ is $\frac{4}{25}$. **c.** The answers to parts (a) and (b) are opposites, because $j(x)$ is symmetric across the y-axis.

12. $y = \frac{b}{d} + \frac{ad - bc}{d^2} x$

Lesson 3.9
Check Your Understanding
1. a. $x = -\frac{7}{2}$; $y = \frac{3}{2}$ **b.** $x = -\frac{5}{3}$; $y = \frac{5}{7}$

c.

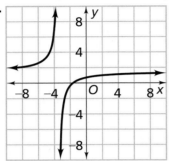

2. a.

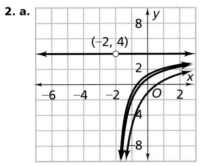

b. $D = 8$ **c.** $\lim\limits_{x \to \infty} b(x) = 4$

3. a. The graph has a vertical asymptote $x = -\frac{D}{C}$ if $AD \neq BC$; it has a hole if $AD = BC$.

b. $\lim\limits_{x \to \infty} c(x) = \lim\limits_{x \to \infty} \left(\frac{A}{C} + \frac{B - \frac{AD}{C}}{Cx + D} \right) = \frac{A}{C}$; The graph has a horizontal asymptote: $y = \frac{A}{C}$.

4. Answers may vary. Sample:

$A = \begin{pmatrix} 0 & 1 \\ 1 & 0 \end{pmatrix}$; $A = \begin{pmatrix} 0 & -1 \\ 1 & 0 \end{pmatrix}$; $A = \begin{pmatrix} 0 & 1 \\ 1 & -2 \end{pmatrix}$;

$A = \begin{pmatrix} 1 & 0 \\ 1 & -2 \end{pmatrix}$; $A = \begin{pmatrix} 1 & -1 \\ 1 & 3 \end{pmatrix}$; $A = \begin{pmatrix} 2 & 1 \\ 1 & 3 \end{pmatrix}$;

$A = \begin{pmatrix} 2 & 1 \\ 3 & -1 \end{pmatrix}$

5. a.

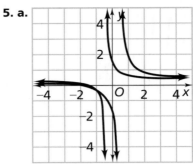

b. $C = \begin{pmatrix} \frac{17}{41} & -\frac{19}{41} \\ -\frac{2}{41} & \frac{36}{41} \end{pmatrix}$ **c.** $D = \begin{pmatrix} \frac{27}{41} & -\frac{4}{41} \\ -\frac{32}{41} & \frac{26}{41} \end{pmatrix}$

6. a.

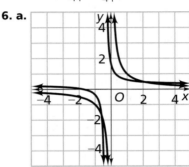

b. $T_g = T_{\frac{3}{10}}$ and $\mathcal{A}_{(e,f)} = \mathcal{A}_{\left(\frac{100}{41}, \frac{30}{41}\right)}$

c. Scale horizontally by a factor of $\frac{41}{100}$, then translate $\frac{3}{10}$ units left and $\frac{3}{10}$ units up.

7. There will be a fixed point if $(d - a)^2 + 4bc \geq 0$.
On Your Own
9. b. $T_g = T_{\frac{2}{3}}$ and $\mathcal{A}_{(e,f)} = \mathcal{A}_{(9,21)}$

c. Scale horizontally by a factor of $\frac{1}{9}$, then translate $\frac{7}{3}$ units left and $\frac{2}{3}$ units up.

10. $\frac{3}{2}$ **11.** $f(x)$ has no vertical asymptotes because its domain is $\mathbb{R}$. A necessary condition for $f(x)$ to have a vertical asymptote in $x = k$ is that $f(x) = k$ is not in the function's domain.

Lesson 3.10
On Your Own
8. a.

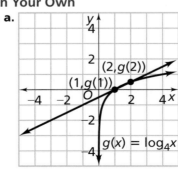

The slope of the secant is 0.5.

b. Since the slope is positive and a little more than 0.5, a good estimate might be 0.7.

9.

Base b	Slope of tangent to $f(x) = \log_b x$ at $x = 1$
2	1.443
3	0.910
4	0.721
5	0.621
8	0.481
10	0.434

Lesson 3.11
Check Your Understanding
1. a. \$400; \$800; $100(2)^t$ **b.** \$596.05; \$1455.19; $100(2.441406)^t$ **c.** \$2008.55 **2. a.** \$106.00; \$112.36; $100(1.06)^t$ **b.** \$106.09; \$112.55; $100(1.03)^{2n}$ $= 100(1.0609)^n$ **c.** The 100 is the amount Jamie invested. The 1.005 is $1 + \frac{0.06}{12}$, 0.06 is the interest rate expressed as a decimal, 12 is the number of times it is compounded in a year (monthly). $36 = 12 \cdot 3$ is (number of times compounded in a year)(number of years).

3. $B = P\left(1 + \frac{0.05}{n}\right)^{nt}$ **4. a.** \$105.09 **b.** \$105.12 **c.** \$105.13 **d.** \$105.13 **5. a.** \$128.40 **b.** \$164.87 **c.** \$271.83 **d.** \$738.91 **6. a.** $\$128.40 \approx 47.237e$ **b.** $\$164.87 \approx 60.653e$ **c.** $\$271.83 \approx 100e$ **d.** $\$738.91 \approx 271.828e$

7. a. $\frac{1}{K} = \frac{x}{n}$

$n \cdot \frac{1}{K} = n \cdot \frac{x}{n}$

$\frac{n}{K} = x$

$n = Kx$

b. $\left(1 + \frac{x}{n}\right)^n = \left(1 + \frac{1}{K}\right)^{Kx}$

c. The two limits are the same because as $n \to \infty$, $K \to \infty$.

d. $\lim\limits_{K \to \infty} \left(1 + \frac{1}{K}\right)^{Kx} = \lim\limits_{K \to \infty} \left(\left(1 + \frac{1}{K}\right)^K\right)^x$

$= \left(\lim\limits_{K \to \infty} \left(1 + \frac{1}{K}\right)^K\right)^x$

$= e^x$

8. $\lim\limits_{n \to \infty} P\left(1 + \frac{r}{n}\right)^{nt} = P\left(\lim\limits_{n \to \infty} \left(1 + \frac{r}{n}\right)^n\right)^t$

$= P(e^r)^t$

$= Pe^{rt}$

On Your Own
10. a. Her balance is \$2000; It is multiplied by a factor of 10. **b.** \$2718.28

11. a. $B(3) = \$1197.22$; $B(5) = \$1349.86$; $B(t) = 1000 \cdot e^{0.06 \cdot t}$ dollars **b.** It will take approximately 11.55 years for the balance to double. **c.** It will take approximately 23.1 years for the balance to become \$4000. **12.** The better investment is the account at 6% APR compounded annually.
14. $m = 0.055$

Lesson 3.12
Check Your Understanding
1. a. $1 + \frac{1}{1!} + \frac{1}{2!} + \frac{1}{3!} + \cdots + \frac{1}{13!} \approx$ 2.7182818285; fourteen terms ($k = 13$).

b. $\left(1 + \frac{1}{10^7}\right)^{10^7} \approx 2.71828169255$; six
2. a. $q(0.05) = 1.05125$ and $e^{0.05} = 1.05127$; approximately -0.02% **b.** $q(0.5) = 1.625$ and $e^{0.05} = 1.64872$; approximately -1.44%
c. $q(-1) = 0.5$ and $e^{-1} = 0.36788$; approximately 35.91%

3. $x \approx 0.693$ **4. a.** $(0.693, 2)$ **b.** $(1.099, 3)$

5. a. $\sum\limits_{k=0}^{\infty} \frac{(-1)^k}{k!} \approx 0.36788$ **b.** The summation gives the same rule as e^x where $x = -1$. So it should equal e^{-1}, and it does.

6. a.

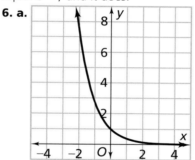

b.

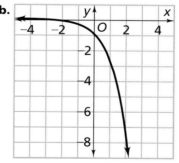

c.

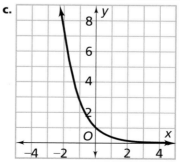

On Your Own

8. a. $c(0.1) = 1.10516666667$ and $f(0.1) = 1.10517091808$; -0.00038%

b. $c(0.2) = 1.22133333333$ and $f(0.2) = 1.22140275816$; -0.00568%
$c(0.5) = 1.64583333333$ and $f(0.5) = 1.6487212707$; -0.17516%
$c(1) = 2.666666666667$ and $f(1) = 2.71828182846$; -1.89882%
$c(2) = 6.33333333$ and $f(2) = 7.38905609893$; -14.28765%

c. The graphs are very close together for small values of x. As x gets larger, the graphs are farther apart.
d. There are two solutions: $x = -0.00017$ and $x = -0.00015$.
9. e^2 **10. a.** $k \approx 1.09861$ **c.** $n \approx 2.70805$
e. no solution

Lesson 3.13
Check Your Understanding

1. 6.931 **2. a.** $p = 4$; $M = 3$ **b.** $\frac{1}{3} \ln 2$
c. $-2 \ln 5$ **3. a.** 2 **b.** 10 **c.** -1 **d.** 5
4. a. $\ln 3$ **b.** $m = \ln 5$ **c.** $e^{x \ln 2} = e^{\ln 2^x} = 2^x$
5. $a^x = e^{\ln a^x} = e^{x \ln a} = e^{kx}$ where $k = \ln a$.
6. a. $x \approx 2.807$ **b.** $z \approx 2.990$ **c.** $x \approx -1.672$
d. $x = \dfrac{\ln c - \ln a}{\ln b - \ln d} = \dfrac{\ln \frac{c}{a}}{\ln \frac{b}{d}}$ **7. a.** $(3, \ln 3)$ **b.** $(\ln 3, 3)$
c. $(2, e^2)$ **d.** $(e^2, 2)$ **e.** $g = e^4$ **f.** $p = \ln 4$

On Your Own

8. a. 1.099 **e.** 0.511 **f.** undefined **9. a.** \$134.99;
\$182.21; \$332.01 **d.** $t = \dfrac{\ln \frac{B}{100}}{0.06}$; 38.38 years
10. a. 34.7 years **b.** 23.1 years **f.** $\dfrac{\ln 2}{0.01p}$ years

Lesson 3.14
Check Your Understanding

1. a. The slope of the tangent at any point is equal to the y-value of that point. **b.** The slope of the tangent at any point is equal to the y-value of that point times 2. **c.** The slope of the tangent at any point is equal to the y-value of that point times 5. **d.** The slope of the tangent at any point is equal to the y-value of that point times $\ln 2$.

2. a. $\ln 2$ **b.** $\ln 16$ **c.** $\ln 5^5$

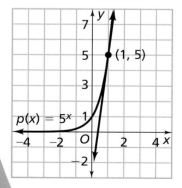

3. a. $5^0 \ln 5 = \ln 5$ **b.** $\ln 8 = \ln 2^3 = 3 \ln 2$
c. Base e, because $e^0 \ln e = 1$. **d.** $b = 1$, but this is just a horizontal line: $y = 1^x \rightarrow y = 1$. **4. a.** This is the definition of logarithm. **b.** $2^y = x \Rightarrow \ln 2^y = \ln x \Rightarrow y \ln 2 = \ln x$ **c.** Divide both sides by $\ln 2$ to get $y = \dfrac{\ln x}{\ln 2}$. Since $\log_2 x = y$, $\log_2 x = y = \dfrac{\ln x}{\ln 2}$.
5. a. The slope is 3 times the reciprocal of the x-value.
b. The slope is the reciprocal of the x-value.
c. The slope is the reciprocal of the x-value times $\frac{1}{5}$.
d. The slope is the reciprocal of the x-value times $\frac{1}{\ln 2}$.
6. a. $\dfrac{1}{\ln 2} \approx 1.443$ **b.** $\dfrac{1}{4 \ln 2} \approx 0.361$
c. $\dfrac{1}{5 \ln 5} \approx 0.124$

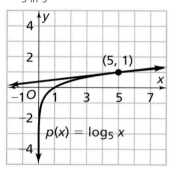

7. a. $\dfrac{1}{\ln 5} \approx 0.621$ **b.** The output for base 8 will be $\dfrac{1}{\ln 8} = \dfrac{1}{\ln 2^3} = \dfrac{1}{3 \ln 2} = \dfrac{1}{3}\left(\dfrac{1}{\ln 2}\right)$ and $\dfrac{1}{\ln 2}$ is the output for base 2. **c.** The slope of the tangent will be 1 if $\dfrac{1}{\ln b} = 1 \Rightarrow \ln b = 1 \Rightarrow b = e$. **d.** The slope of the tangent will never be zero.

On Your Own

8. a. $(\ln 8, 8)$ **b.** The y-intercept is $-8 \ln 8 + 8 \approx -8.636$, which is negative. **9.** $y = ex$; $(1, e)$
10. slope $= Abe^{bx} = b \cdot p(x)$ **11.** slope $= \dfrac{A}{x}$

Chapter 4
Lesson 4.2
Check Your Understanding

1. Not isomorphic; the area is found by using multiplication alone, but the perimeter is found using addition at least once. **2.** Isomorphic; both problems can be solved by using the same calculation of subtracting 45 and 99 from 230. **3.** Isomorphic; both problems can be solved by solving the same equation, $x + 2x = 18$. **4.** Isomorphic; both problems can be solved by using the same calculation of dividing 740 by 60 to find the smallest integer number. **5.** Answers may vary. Samples are given. **a.** The Red Sox scored nine runs and the Yankees scored seven runs in the same game. How many more runs did the Red Sox score? **b.** Three friends divide a dozen cookies equally among them. How many cookies does each friend get?

6. Answers will vary. Samples are given.

a. • Joe had $40 at the beginning of the day. He spent $3 on breakfast and $7 on lunch. How much money does he have left for dinner?

• Paula had 40 baseball cards. She gave 3 to Jesse, and 7 to Kira. How many does she have left?

b. • If seven people go out to dinner and each contributes eight dollars toward the bill, what is the total contribution?

• Mr. Hill made cookies for the 8 students on the Math Team. He made enough so that each student could have exactly 7 cookies. How many cookies did he make?

7. The text explained how Problems 1 and 3 can be viewed as essentially the same.

In Problem 2, let 1 denote the color green and 2 denote the color red. Then let the ones digit denote the color of the circle, let the tens digit denote the color of the triangle, and finally let the hundreds digit denote the color of the square. In Problem 4, let 1 denote a head and 2 to denote a tail. Then let the hundreds digit denote the first toss, let the tens digit denote the second toss, and the ones digit denote the third toss.

On Your Own

9. 16 four-digit numbers **11.** Isomorphic; both problems can be solved by using the same calculation of multiplying 15 and 7. **12.** Isomorphic; both problems can be solved using the same calculation of taking the sum of the integers from 1 to 10.

Lesson 4.3
Check Your Understanding

1. a. $f(n) = \begin{cases} 2 & \text{if } n = 1 \\ f(n-1) \cdot 2 & \text{if } n > 1 \end{cases}$ **b.** $f(n) = 2^n$

2. 81 numbers **3. a.** 243 numbers **b.** 3^n numbers **4.** m^n **5.** 24 ways **6.** 24 ways **7.** 362,880 batting orders. **8.** 120 ways **9.** $n!$ ways

On Your Own

10. 18 ways **13.** 1800 numbers. **16.** 17,576,000 license plates

Lesson 4.4
Check Your Understanding

1. 8 functions **2.** 780 words **3.** There are $k + k^2 + \cdots + k^n$ words (that is, n words if $k = 1$ and $\frac{k^{n+1} - k}{k - 1}$ words if $k > 1$) **4.** $365^{25} \approx 1.14 \times 10^{64}$ **5.** 32,768 functions

On Your Own

6. a. 9 functions **7.** 6720 functions

Lesson 4.6
Check Your Understanding

1. Answers may vary. Sample: Since $_nP_k = \frac{n!}{(n-k)!}$ when $1 \leq k \leq n$, then $_nP_n = \frac{n!}{(n-n)!} = \frac{n!}{0!} = \frac{n!}{1} = n!$ **2.** 360 functions **3.** 360 functions

4. 7,880,400 **5. a.** 81 numbers **b.** 9 numbers. **c.** Dull number; there are more dull numbers than funny numbers in the bag. **6.** dull number **7.** funny number **8.** funny number **9. a.** 6 anagrams **b.** 3 anagrams **c.** 1 anagram **10. a.** 24 anagrams **b.** 12 anagrams **c.** 6 anagrams **d.** 4 anagrams **e.** 1 anagrams **11. a.** 60 anagrams **b.** 1260 anagrams **c.** 720 anagrams

On Your Own

15. $\frac{1}{12} \approx 8.3\%$ **16.** $\frac{11}{23} \approx 47.8\%$ **21.** 720 anagrams **22.** 360 anagrams

Lesson 4.7
Check Your Understanding

1. 64,684,950 committees **2.** 64,684,950 groups **3.** For each distinct committee of 4 people you choose, you leave behind a distinct *non-committee* of 196 people. So, there are the same number of committees of 4 people and committees of 196 people. **4. a.** $_7P_3 = \frac{7!}{4!}$ **b.** $_7C_3 = \frac{7!}{4! \cdot 3!}$

5. From the previous exercise, $_7C_3 = \frac{_7P_3}{3!} = \frac{_7P_3}{_3P_3}$. This makes sense, since every combination of 3 particular objects accounts for $3! = 6$ of the permutations of 3 of the 6 objects.

6. Use the formulas for $_nC_k$ and $_nP_k$:

$$_nC_k = \frac{_nP_k}{k!}$$
$$= \frac{n!}{(n-k)! \cdot k!}$$
$$= \frac{n!}{(n-k)! \cdot [n-(n-k)]!}$$
$$= \frac{_nP_{n-k}}{(n-k)!}$$
$$= \,_nC_{n-k}$$

7. Every combination of 3 objects from a set of 10 can be arranged in $3! = 6$ ways (that is, has $3! = 6$ permutations). So, $_{10}C_3 \cdot 6$ is the number of possible permutations of 3 objects chosen from a set of 10, or $_{10}P_3$. **8.** $_{10}P_3$ represents the number of subsets of 3 cards you can make from a set of 10 cards, and $_{10}C_7$ represents the number of subsets of 7 cards you can make from a set of 10 cards. But, every time you make a different subset of 3 cards, you leave behind a different group of seven cards—that is, there are as many subsets of 7 cards as there are of 3 cards: $_{10}C_3 = \,_{10}C_7$. The same argument would hold for any subset of k cards chosen from a set of n cards: $_nC_k = \,_nC_{(n-k)}$. **9.** Answers may vary. Sample: To find $_nP_k$, you count all of the different ways you can pick k objects from a set of n objects and line them up in a row. To find $_nC_k$, you count all of the different ways you can pick k objects from a set of n objects (without lining them up). So, to find permutations, you are finding all the combinations, and then also rearranging them. Combinations do not count the rearrangements since "order doesn't matter" with combinations.

10. a. 6 choices **b.** 3 choices **c.** 3 choices

11. Suppose we have a group of 7 people, including a girl named Kira, and we want to choose a committee of 4 people from this group. There are $_7C_4$ ways to do this. Or, we can think of it in terms of the committees that contain and don't contain Kira

$$_7C_4 = \text{number of possible committees}$$
$$\text{Kira is on} + \text{number of}$$
$$\text{committee Kira is not on.}$$

If Kira is on the committee, then there are 6 people left who can fill the remaining 3 spots on the committee. So, there are $_6C_3$ different committees that can be made with Kira. If Kira is not on the committee, the entire committee needs to be chosen from the other 6 people. So, there are $_6C_4$ 4-person committees that can be made without Kira. That is,

$$_7C_4 = {}_6C_3 + {}_6C_4$$

12. a. $_{10}C_6 = {}_9C_6 + {}_9C_5$. **b.** Suppose we have a group of 10 people, including a person named Gill. We want to make a committee of 6 people from this group of 10. There are $_{10}C_6$ different committees we could make. However,

$$_{10}C_6 = \text{number of possible committees}$$
$$\text{Gill is on} + \text{number of}$$
$$\text{committees Gill is not}$$

If Gill is on a committee, then there are 9 remaining people to fill the other 5 spots on the committee. So, there are $_9C_5$ different committees that can be made

with Gill. If Gill is not on the committee, then the entire committee of 6 people needs to be chosen from the remaining 9 people. So, there are $_9C_6$ different committees that can be made without Gill. Thus:

$$_{10}C_6 = {}_9C_6 + {}_9C_5$$

13. The proof follows the same logic as Exercises 11 and 12. Suppose we have a group of n people (including Jan and at least one other person) and we would like to make a committee of k people from this group. The committee will have someone on it, and it will not have everyone on it (so $0 < k < n$). There are $_nC_k$ different possible committees that can be made. Since the committees must, have someone on them ($k > 0$), some of these committees will contain Jan. Since the committees do not contain everyone ($k < n$), some of them will not contain Jan. If Jan is on a committee, then there are $n - 1$ people remaining to fill the $k - 1$ remaining spot (and since $0 \le k - 1 < n - 1$, it is possible to make a committee of $k - 1$ people from a group of $n - 1$ people, and if $k - 1 = 0$, then there's only 1 choice: NOBODY). So, there are $_{n-1}C_{k-1}$ different committees that contain Jan. If Jan is not on the committee, then the committee of k people must made from the remaining $n - 1$ people (and since $k \le n - 1$, it is possible to make a committee of k people from a group of $n - 1$ people). So, there are $_{n-1}C_k$ different committees that do not contain Jan. Thus,

$$_nC_k = {}_{n-1}C_{k-1} + {}_{n-1}C_k.$$

14. a. $_nC_0 = {}_{n-1}C_0 = 1$ **b.** $_nC_n = {}_{n-1}C_{n-1} = 1$

15.

		$_4C_0$	$_4C_1$	$_4C_2$	$_4C_3$	$_4C_4$		
		1	4	6	4	1		

	$_5C_0$	$_5C_1$	$_5C_2$	$_5C_3$	$_5C_4$	$_5C_5$	
	1	5	10	10	5	1	

$_6C_0$ $_6C_1$ $_6C_2$ $_6C_3$ $_4C_4$ $_6C_5$ $_6C_6$
1 6 15 20 15 6 1

$_7C_0$ $_7C_1$ $_7C_2$ $_7C_3$ $_7C_4$ $_7C_5$ $_7C_6$ $_7C_7$
1 7 21 35 35 21 7 1

$_8C_0$ $_8C_1$ $_8C_2$ $_8C_3$ $_8C_4$ $_8C_5$ $_8C_6$ $_8C_7$ $_8C_8$
1 8 28 56 70 56 28 8 1

$_9C_0$ $_9C_1$ $_9C_2$ $_9C_3$ $_9C_4$ $_9C_5$ $_9C_6$ $_9C_7$ $_9C_8$ $_9C_9$
1 9 36 84 126 126 84 36 9 1

$_{10}C_0$ $_{10}C_1$ $_{10}C_2$ $_{10}C_3$ $_{10}C_4$ $_{10}C_5$ $_{10}C_6$ $_{10}C_7$ $_{10}C_8$ $_{10}C_9$ $_{10}C_{10}$
1 10 45 120 210 252 210 120 45 10 1

16. To see that $_nC_k = \binom{n}{k}$ we need to show that combinations satisfy the recursive definition of $\binom{n}{k}$:
$$\binom{n}{0} = \binom{n}{n} = 1 \quad \text{(far left and far right entries equal 1);}$$
$$\binom{n}{k} + \binom{n}{k+1} = \binom{n+1}{k+1} \quad \text{(sum of two entries is the entry is the entry below them)}$$
That is, we need to show that
$$_nC_0 = {_nC_n} = 1;$$
$$_nC_k + {_nC_{k+1}} = {_{n+1}C_{k+1}}$$
But we've already shown these statements to be true, so the theorem is true.
17. Answers may vary. Sample: Let $\binom{5}{6} = 0$, because there are 0 ways to choose six objects from a set of five.
18. 252 combinations **19.** 1; 8; 28; 56; 70; 56; 28; 8; 1
20. The sum of all the entries in row n of Pascal's triangle is 2^n.

On Your Own
21. 210 assignments **28. a.** 5985 committees
b. 1140 committees **c.** 4845 committees
31. b. $\binom{11}{4}$ or $\binom{11}{7}$; 330 groups **38.** 126 numbers

Lesson 4.8
Check Your Understanding
1. 720 ways **2.** 5040 ways **3.** 300 numbers
4. 756 committees **5.** 240 ways **6. a.** 362,880 ways
b. 2880 ways **c.** 282,240 ways **d.** 2880 ways
e. 326,880 ways
On Your Own
7. b. 237 ways **10.** 182 flights **12.** 16 ways

Lesson 4.9
On Your Own
11. b. 8 paths **13. b.** 12, 870 routes
15. 756,756 ways

Lesson 4.10
Check Your Understanding
1. a. $(x + y)^7 = x^7 + 7x^6y + 21x^5y^2 + 35x^4y^3 + 35x^3y^4 + 21x^2y^5 + 7xy^6 + y^7w$
b. $(x + 2y)^5 = x^5 + 10x^4y + 40x^3y^2 + 80x^2y^3 + 80xy^4 + 32y^5$
2. a. 792 **b.** the term containing a^7b^5 **c.** the term containing a^6b^6 **3. a.** $\binom{50}{13} = 354, 860, 518, 600$
b. $\binom{50}{1} = 50$ **c.** $\binom{50}{25} = 126, 410, 606, 437, 752$
4. All sums are equal to 0. **5.** Answers may vary. Sample: $32x^5 + 240x^4 + 720x^3 + 1080x^2 + 810x + 243$; factors as $(2x + 3)^5$

On Your Own
7. a. $\binom{n}{0}x^n - \binom{n}{1}x^{n-1} + \binom{n}{2}x^{n-2} + \cdots +$
$(-1)^k\binom{n}{k}x^{n-k} + \cdots + (-1)^{n-1}\binom{n}{n-1}x +$
$(-1)^n\binom{n}{n}$

Lesson 4.11
Check Your Understanding
1. Use mathematical induction. Since $2^0 = 1 = \binom{n}{0}$, the base case is confirmed. For good measure, notice that the sum of the entries in row 1 is $1 + 1 = 2 = 2^1$. For the induction step, suppose $m \geq 1$ and sum of the entries in row m of the triangle is 2^m. Then

$$2^{m+1} = 2^m + 2^m = \sum_{k=0}^{m}\binom{m}{k} + \sum_{k=0}^{m}\binom{m}{k}$$
$$= \left[\binom{m}{0} + \binom{m}{1} + \cdots + \binom{m}{m}\right]$$
$$+ \left[\binom{m}{0} + \binom{m}{1} + \cdots + \binom{m}{m}\right]$$
$$= \binom{m}{0} + \left[\binom{m}{0} + \binom{m}{1}\right] + \left[\binom{m}{1}\right.$$
$$\left. + \binom{m}{2}\right] + \left[\binom{m}{2} + \binom{m}{3}\right]$$
$$+ \cdots + \left[\binom{m}{m-2} + \binom{m}{m-1}\right]$$
$$+ \left[\binom{m}{m-1} + \binom{m}{m}\right] + \binom{m}{m}$$
$$= \binom{m}{0} + \binom{m+1}{1} + \binom{m+1}{2}$$
$$+ \binom{m+1}{3} + \cdots + \binom{m+1}{m-1}$$
$$+ \binom{m+1}{m} + \binom{m}{m}$$
$$= \binom{m+1}{0} + \binom{m+1}{1}$$
$$+ \cdots + \binom{m+1}{m} + \binom{m+1}{m+1}$$

The final sum is the sum of the entries in row $m + 1$ of Pascal's Triangle, so the conjecture is proved.
2. Entry k in row n of Pascal's Triangle, $_nC_k$, is the number of subsets of size k that can be made from a set with n elements. Therefore, the sum of these entries represents the number of all subsets (the subsets of each possible size from 0 to n), which we already know is 2^n. **3.** Since $\binom{n}{n}$ is the number of the subsets of the set $\{1, 2, 3, \ldots, n\}$ containing all n elements and there is only one such subset (the set itself). Therefore, $\binom{n}{n} = 1$. **4.** $\binom{n}{n} = \dfrac{n!}{n!0!} = \dfrac{n!}{n!} = 1$

5. We know that $\binom{n}{k} = {}_nC_k$ is the number of subsets of $\{1, 2, 3, \ldots, n\}$ that contain k elements. But for every k-element subset, there is a unique $n - k$ element subset consisting of the elements that are *not* included in the particular k-element subset. Also, for every $n - k$-element subset, there is a unique k-element subset (consisting of the remaining elements). But this means that ${}_nC_k = {}_nC_{n-k}$, so $\binom{n}{k} = \binom{n}{n-k}$.

6. First, notice that $(a + b)^n = (b + a)^n$. But, according to the Binomial Theorem,

$$(a + b)^n = \sum_{k=0}^{n} \binom{n}{n-k} a^{n-k}b^k \text{ and}$$

$$(b + n)^n = \sum_{k=0}^{n} \binom{n}{n-k} b^{n-k}a^k.$$

In the expansion of $(a + b)^n$, the coefficient of $a^{n-k}b^k$ is $\binom{n}{n-k}$, but in the expansion of $(b + a)^n$, the cofficient of $a^{n-k}b^k$ is $\binom{n}{k}$. Therefore, $\binom{n}{k} = \binom{n}{n-k}$.

7. $\binom{n}{1}$ is the number of 1-element subsets of a set with n elements. Since there are n 1-element subsets (containing each of the n elements individually), $\binom{n}{1} = n$. **8.** $\binom{n}{1}$ is the cofficient of ab^{n-1} in the expansion of $(a + b)^n$. Since there are n ways to choose an a from the n parentheses, $\binom{n}{1} = n$.

On Your Own

11. $\binom{n}{k} = \dfrac{n!}{k!(n-k)!} = \dfrac{n!}{(n-k)!k!} = \binom{n}{n-k}$

Chapter 5
Lesson 5.1
On Your Own
7. a. $\mathbb{R}$ **b.** $\{x \mid x \neq 4\}$ **c.** $\{x \mid x > 0\}$ **d.** $\{1, 2, 3\}$

8. a. Answers may vary. Sample answer form: $h(x) = A$, $k(x) = A + (x - 1)(x - 2)(x - 3)(x - 4)(x - 5)$
b. Answers may vary. Sample answer form: $m(x) = A$, $n(x) = A + (x - 6)(x - 7)(x - 8)(x - 9)(x - 10)$
11. $269.74

Lesson 5.2
Check Your Understanding

1. $B(n) = \begin{cases} 0 & n = 0 \\ B(n-1) + 2n & n > 0 \end{cases}$

2. $G(n) = \begin{cases} -7 & n = 0 \\ G(n-1) + 3 & n > 0 \end{cases}$

3. $K(x) = \begin{cases} 1 & x = 0 \\ K(x-1) + 2x - 1 & x > 0 \end{cases}$

4. $\beta(n) = \begin{cases} 0 & n = 0 \\ \beta(n-1) + n & n > 0 \end{cases}$

5. $\varepsilon(n) = \begin{cases} 2 & n = 0 \\ \varepsilon(n-1) + 2^{n-1} & n > 0 \end{cases}$

6. $\kappa(n) = \begin{cases} 0 & n = 0 \\ \kappa(n-1) + 2n - 1 & n > 0 \end{cases}$

7. $\gamma(n) = \begin{cases} 0 & n = 0 \\ \gamma(n-1) + \frac{1}{2}n(n-1) & n > 0 \end{cases}$

8. No. In the base case, n is an integer. Therefore, $g(n)$ is only defined for integer n.

On Your Own

9. $B(n) = \begin{cases} 0 & n = 0 \\ 1.03 \cdot B(n-1) + 500 & n > 0 \end{cases}$

$B(5) = 2654.57$

10.

a	h(a)
0	3
1	11
2	19
3	27
4	35
5	43

$h(a) = 8a + 3$

11.

m	f(m)
0	0
1	2
2	6
3	12
4	20
5	30

$f(m) = m(m + 1)$

14. $T(n) = \begin{cases} 1 & n = 0 \\ T(n-1) \cdot 3 & n > 0 \end{cases}$

Lesson 5.3
Check Your Understanding
1. a. The balance at $n = 0$ is $2000 (initial balance), and in subsequent months the balance decreases by $50 (monthly payment) and increases by 1.5% of the previous balance (monthly interest).
b. $B(6) = 1875.41$; $B(12) = 1739.18$; $B(24) = 1427.33$

c. $B(n) = \begin{cases} 2000 & n = 0 \\ 1.015 \cdot B(n-1) - 50 & n > 0 \end{cases}$

$B(48) = 608.70$

2. $2^{25} - 1 = 33{,}554{,}431$

3. a.

n	$\dfrac{F(n+1)}{F(n)}$
1	1
2	2
3	1.5
4	$1.6\bar{6}$
5	1.6
6	1.625
7	1.6154 ...
8	1.619 ...
9	1.61764 ...
10	1.61818 ...

b. The ratios approach $\dfrac{1 + \sqrt{5}}{2} \approx 1.618034$.

4. a. $L(n) = \begin{cases} 2 & n = 0 \\ 1 & n = 1 \\ L(n-1) + L(n-2) & n > 1 \end{cases}$

b. $L(10) = 123$ **c.** The ratio approaches $\dfrac{1 + \sqrt{5}}{2} \approx$ 1.618034, the golden ratio.

d. $L(n) = L(n-1) + L(n-2)$
$= F(2) \cdot L(n-1) + F(1) \cdot L(n-2)$
$= F(3) \cdot L(n-2) + F(2) \cdot L(n-3)$
$= F(4) \cdot L(n-3) + F(3) \cdot L(n-4)$
$\vdots$
$= F(n) \cdot L(1) + F(n-1) \cdot L(0)$
$= F(n) + 2F(n-1)$
$= F(n+1) + F(n-1)$

5. a.

n	P(n)
0	2
1	5
2	3
3	-2
4	-5
5	-3
6	2
7	5
8	3
9	-2
10	-5

b. $P(50) = 3$ **c.** No, because $P(1.5)$ and $P(0.5)$ are not defined. **d.** the set of nonnegative integers

6.

n	g(n)
0	0.4472
1	0.7236
2	1.1708
3	1.8944
4	3.0652
5	4.9597
6	8.0249
7	12.9846
8	21.0095
9	33.9941
10	55.0036

On Your Own
7. a. $712.58 **b.** $1178.52
8. a. $505.91 **b.** $1000.06

10. a.

n	t(n)
1	-1
2	1
3	-1
4	1
5	-1
6	1
7	-1
8	1
9	-1
10	1

b. $s(n) = (-1)^n$

11. a.

n	t(n)
1	-1
2	1
3	-1
4	1
5	-1
6	1
7	-1
8	1
9	-1
10	1

b. $t(n) = (-1)^n$

Lesson 5.4
Check Your Understanding
1.

a	M(a)
0	5
1	8
2	11
3	14
4	17
5	20

$m(a) = \begin{cases} 5 & a = 0 \\ m(a-1) + 3 & a > 0 \end{cases}$

$m(1001) = m(1000) + 3$
$= M(1000) + 3$
$= (3 \cdot 1000 + 5) + 3$
$= (3 \cdot 1000 + 3) + 5$
$= 3 \cdot 1001 + 5$
$= M(1001)$

2.

n	k(n)
0	3
1	10
2	17
3	24
4	31
5	38

$K(n) = 7n + 3$

$$\begin{aligned}k(1001) &= k(1000) + 7 \\ &= K(1000) + 7 \\ &= (7 \cdot 1000 + 3) + 7 \\ &= (7 \cdot 1000 + 7) + 3 \\ &= 7 \cdot 1001 + 3 \\ &= K(1001)\end{aligned}$$

3.

n	j(n)
0	0
1	1
2	4
3	9
4	16
5	25

$J(n) = n^2$

$$\begin{aligned}j(1001) &= j(1000) + (2 \cdot 1001) - 1 \\ &= J(1000) + (2 \cdot 1000 + 2 - 1) \\ &= 1000^2 + 2 \cdot 1000 + 1 \\ &= (1000 + 1)^2 = 1001^2 \\ &= J(1001)\end{aligned}$$

4.

x	f(x)
0	1
1	2
2	4
3	8
4	16
5	32

$$F(x) = \begin{cases} 1 & x = 0 \\ F(x - 1) \cdot 2 & x > 0 \end{cases}$$

$$\begin{aligned}f(1001) &= 2^{1001} \\ &= 2^{1000} \cdot 2 \\ &= f(1000) \cdot 2 \\ &= F(1000) \cdot 2 \\ &= F(1001)\end{aligned}$$

5.

a	J(a)	j(a)
0	−7	−7
1	3	3
2	13	13
3	23	23

$$\begin{aligned}J(n + 1) &= 10 \cdot (n + 1) - 7 \\ &= 10n + 10 - 7 \\ &= 10n - 7 + 10 \\ &= J(n) + 10 \\ &= j(n) + 10 \\ &= j(n + 1)\end{aligned}$$

6.

x	F(x)	f(x)
0	0	0
1	1	1
2	4	4
3	9	9

$$\begin{aligned}f(x + 1) &= f(x) + 2(x + 1) - 1 \\ &= F(x) + 2x + 2 - 1 \\ &= x^2 + 2x + 1 \\ &= (x + 1)^2 \\ &= F(x + 1)\end{aligned}$$

7.

n	G(n)	g(n)
0	1	4
1	4	16
2	16	64
3	64	256

$G(n) \neq g(n)$

8.

x	S(x)	s(x)
0	0	0
1	1	1
2	5	5
3	14	14

$$\begin{aligned}S(n + 1) &= \frac{(n + 1)(n + 2)(2n + 3)}{6} \\ &= \frac{1}{6}(n + 1)(2n^2 + 7n + 6) \\ &= \frac{1}{6}(n + 1)[n(2n + 1) + 6n + 6] \\ &= \frac{1}{6}n(n + 1)(2n + 1) + \frac{1}{6}(n + 1) \cdot 6(n + 1) \\ &= S(n) + (n + 1) \cdot (n + 1) \\ &= s(n) + (n + 1)^2 \\ &= s(n + 1)\end{aligned}$$

On Your Own

9.

n	$C(n)$
0	4
1	11
2	18
3	25
4	32
5	39

$c(n) = 7n + 4$

$$
\begin{aligned}
C(75) &= C(74) + 7 \\
&= c(74) + 7 \\
&= 7 \cdot 74 + 4 + 7 \\
&= 7(74 + 1) + 4 \\
&= 7 \cdot 75 + 4 \\
&= c(75)
\end{aligned}
$$

10.

n	$D(n)$
0	1
1	0
2	1
3	4
4	9
5	16

$$
d(n) = \begin{cases} 1 & n = 0 \\ d(n-1) + (2n - 3) & n > 0 \end{cases}
$$

$$
\begin{aligned}
d(75) &= d(74) + 2 \cdot 75 - 3 \\
&= D(74) + 2 \cdot 73 + 4 - 3 \\
&= 73^2 + 2 \cdot 73 + 1 \\
&= (73 + 1)^2 \\
&= 74^2 \\
&= D(75)
\end{aligned}
$$

12.

a	$Q(a)$	$q(a)$
0	2	3
1	5	5
2	8	7
3	11	9

$Q(a) \neq q(a)$

13.

x	$F(x)$	$f(x)$
0	3	3
1	4	4
2	7	7
3	12	12

$$
\begin{aligned}
F(n + 1) &= (n + 1)^2 + 3 \\
&= n^2 + 2n + 1 + 3 \\
&= (n^2 + 3) + (2n + 1) \\
&= F(n) + (2n + 1) \\
&= f(n) + 2(n + 1) - 1 \\
&= f(n + 1)
\end{aligned}
$$

Lesson 5.5
Check Your Understanding

1. $P(0) = 3 = p(0)$

$$
\begin{aligned}
P(n + 1) &= 2^{n+1} + 2 \\
&= 2 \cdot 2^n + 2 \\
&= 2 \cdot (2^n + 2) - 4 + 2 \\
&= 2 \cdot P(n) - 2 \\
&= 2 \cdot p(n) - 2 \\
&= p(n + 1)
\end{aligned}
$$

2. $H(0) = 0 = h(0)$

$$
\begin{aligned}
H(n + 1) &= \frac{(n + 2)(n + 1)}{2} \\
&= \frac{n(n + 1)}{2} + \frac{2(n + 1)}{2} \\
&= 2 \cdot (2^n + 2) - 4 + 2 \\
&= H(n) + (n + 1) \\
&= h(n) + (n + 1) \\
&= h(n + 1)
\end{aligned}
$$

3. Since a polygon containing n sides can be divided into $n - 2$ triangles, and the sum of the measures of the 3 angles of each triangle is $180°$, the sum of the interior angles of a polygon with n sides is $(n - 2) \cdot 180°$. **4. a.** In all four cases, the Two-Color Theorem would hold. **b.** Suppose you have a coloring for $(n - 1)$ lines. Then add the nth line. On one side of this line, switch the color of everything; on the other side, leave it the same. Now, nothing on either side of the new line has the same color (since you only switched one side). And the coloring you had before means that everything else is still colored properly (since switching all colors from one to the other cannot make a coloring fail). So this gives a proper coloring for n lines, completing the induction step of the proof. **5.** The "set one off to the side" argument in the inductive step assumes that the two sets of $n - 1$ horses have one or more horses in common, the horses that "stayed in both times." This assumption is false for $n = 2$, and so the claim that the $n - 1$ case implies the n case remains unproven.

On Your Own

6. $E(n) = 2n + 2$; $e(n) = \begin{cases} 2 & n = 0 \\ e(n - 1) + 2 & n > 0 \end{cases}$

$$
\begin{aligned}
E(n + 1) &= 2(n + 1) + 2 \\
&= 2n + 2 + 2 \\
&= E(n) + 2 \\
&= e(n) + 2 \\
&= e(n + 1)
\end{aligned}
$$

7. $F(n) = 3n + 1$; $f(n) = \begin{cases} 1 & n = 0 \\ f(n - 1) + 3 & n > 0 \end{cases}$

$$\begin{aligned} F(n + 1) &= 3(n + 1) + 1 \\ &= 3n + 3 + 1 \\ &= 3n + 1 + 3 \\ &= F(n) + 3 \\ &= f(n) + 3 \\ &= f(n + 1) \end{aligned}$$

8. $K(x) = x^2 + 1$;

$$k(x) = \begin{cases} 1 & x = 0 \\ k(x - 1) + 2x + 1 & x > 0 \end{cases}$$

$$\begin{aligned} K(n + 1) &= (n + 1)^2 + 1 \\ &= n^2 + 2n + 1 + 1 \\ &= K(n) + 2n + 1 \\ &= k(n) + 2(n + 1) - 1 \\ &= k(n + 1) \end{aligned}$$

Lesson 5.6
On Your Own

5. $f(8) = 20$

8. a.

x	f(x)	Δ
0	−3	7
1	4	7
2	11	7
3	18	7
4	25	7
5	32	7
6	39	7
7	46	7
8	53	

b.

x	g(x)	Δ	Δ²
0	4	−4	2
1	0	−2	2
2	−2	0	2
3	−2	2	2
4	0	4	2
5	4	6	2
6	10	8	2
7	18	10	
8	28		

e.

x	k(x)	Δ	Δ²	Δ³
0	0	3	−6	−6
1	3	−3	−12	−6
2	0	−15	−18	−6
3	−15	−33	−24	−6
4	−48	−57	−30	−6
5	−105	−87	−36	−6
6	−192	−123	−42	
7	−315	−165		
8	−480			

Lesson 5.7
Check Your Understanding

1. a.

Input, x	Output, f(x)	Δ	Δ²
0	c	a + b	2a
1	a + b + c	3a + b	2a
2	4a + 2b + c	5a + b	2a
3	9a + 3b + c	7a + b	2a
4	16a + 4b + c	9a + b	
5	25a + 5b + c		

b. $\Delta f(x) = 2ax + (a + b)$
$\Delta^2 f(x) = 2a$

c. The Δ^2 column will contain a constant equal to twice the coefficient of the x^2 term of the function.

2. a.

Input, x	Output, f(x)	Δ	Δ²	Δ³
0	d	a + b + c	6a + 2b	6a
1	a + b + c + d	7a + 3b + c	12a + 2b	6a
2	8a + 4b + 2c + d	19a + 5b + c	18a + 2b	6a
3	27a + 9b + 3c + d	37a + 7b + c	24a + 2b	
4	64a + 16b + 4c + d	61a + 9b + c		
5	125a + 25b + 5c + d			

b. $\Delta f(x) = 3ax^2 + (3a + 2b)x + (a + b + c)$
$\Delta^2 f(x) = 6ax + (6a + 2b)$
$\Delta^3 f(x) = 6a$
c. The Δ^3 column will contain a constant equal to 6 times the coefficient of the x^3 term.
3. a. degree 2 **b.** No; any function that equals zero at the x-values shown on the table could be added to a polynomial function that fits the table, and the resulting function would also fit the table.
4. a. $49 + 76$ **b.** $11 + 2 \cdot 38 + 38$
c. $-1 + 3 \cdot 12 + 3 \cdot 26 + 12$
d. $1 + 4 \cdot (-2) + 6 \cdot 14 + 4 \cdot 12 + 0$
5. Continue using the up-and-over property all the way up to the top row.
$$251 = 1 + 5(-2) + 10 \cdot 14 + 10 \cdot 12$$
$$+ 5 \cdot 0 + 1 \cdot 0$$
6. $N(10) = 2051$; $N(10)$ could be written in terms of the numbers across the top row using the numbers in the tenth row of Pascal's triangle (i.e. $N(10) = a + 10b + 45c + 120d + 210e + 252f + 210g + 120h + 45i + 10j + k$).
On Your Own
9. a. $P(n) = -18$; $P(n + 1) = P(n) + \Delta$
b. $P(97) = -473$ **c.** $P(n) = -5n + 12$
10. This table could represent a third-order polynomial (cubic function) with leading coefficient equal to one-sixth of the Δ^3 term, or 2. **11. a.** The Δ and Δ^2 columns are not constant. **b.** 1

Lesson 5.8
Check Your Understanding
1. a.

Input, x	Output, $a(x)$	Δ	Δ^2
0	10	-2	6
1	8	4	6
2	12	10	6
3	22	16	6
4	38	22	6
5	60	28	
6	88		

b. $a(5) = 1 \cdot 10 + 5 \cdot (-2) + 10 \cdot 6 = 60$ **c.** 88
2. a. 2 **b.** $f(x) = \frac{1}{2}x(x - 1)$

c.

Input, x	Output, $f(x)$	Δ	Δ^2
0	0	0	1
1	0	1	1
2	1	2	1
3	3	3	1
4	6	4	1
5	10	5	
6	15		

3. $g(x) = \dfrac{x(x - 1)(x - 2)}{6}$
4. a. $\binom{8}{0} = 1$; $\binom{8}{1} = 8$; $\binom{8}{2} = 28$

b.

n	$T(n)$	Δ	Δ^2
0	a	b	c
1	$a + b$	$b + c$	c
2	$a + 2b + c$	$b + 2c$	c
3	$a + 3b + 3c$	$b + 3c$	c
4	$a + 4b + 6c$	$b + 4c$	c
5	$a + 5b + 10c$	$b + 5c$	c
6	$a + 6b + 15c$	$b + 6c$	c
7	$a + 7b + 21c$	$b + 7c$	c
8	$a + 8b + 28c$	$b + 8c$	c

5. a. 3

b.

x	$g(x)$	Δ	Δ^2	Δ^3	Δ^4
0	0	0	0	1	0
1	0	0	1	1	0
2	0	1	2	1	0
3	1	3	3	1	0
4	4	6	4	1	
5	10	10	5		
6	20	15			
7	35				

c. These numbers are along the third diagonal in Pascal's Triangle. **d.** These numbers are along the second diagonal in Pascal's Triangle.

6. a.

x	p(x)	Δ	Δ²	Δ³	Δ⁴	Δ⁵	Δ⁶
0	1	1	1	1	1	1	1
1	2	2	2	2	2	2	
2	4	4	4	4	4		
3	8	8	8	8			
4	16	16	16				
5	32	32					
6	64						

b. $p(4) = 1 \cdot 1 + 4 \cdot 1 + 6 \cdot 1 + 4 \cdot 1 + 1 \cdot 1 = 16$

c. 64

On Your Own

7. a. $h(7) = 10$ **b.** $h(10) = 100$ **c.** $h(97) = 26{,}200$

9. a. $f(x) = -2x^2 - 6x + 5$

b. $f(x) = x^3 - 5x^2 - 4x + 5$

10. Answers may vary. Samples:

a.

Input	Output	Δ
0	0	12
1	12	−6
2	6	−20
3	−14	0
4	−14	12
5	−2	2
6	0	

b.

Input	Output	Δ
0	5	12
1	17	−6
2	11	−20
3	−9	0
4	−9	12
5	3	2
6	5	

Lesson 5.9

Check Your Understanding

1. $\dbinom{x}{4} = \dfrac{x(x-1)(x-2)(x-3)}{4!}$

$\dbinom{x}{5} = \dfrac{x(x-1)(x-2)(x-3)(x-4)}{5!}$

$\dbinom{x}{6} = \dfrac{x(x-1)(x-2)(x-3)(x-4)(x-5)}{6!}$

In general, the kth Mahler polynomial is

$\dbinom{x}{k} = \dfrac{x(x-1)(x-2)\cdots(x-k+1)}{k!}$

2. $f(n) = n^4 + 3n^2 - 5n + 6$ **3. a.** 0, 1, 2 **b.** 0, 2, 4
c. 0, 1, 6, 6 **d.** 0, 2, 12, 12 **e.** 0, 2, 8, 6

4. Method 1: Work backwards to build a difference table for all values of the function between 0 and 9, then use the top row to determine the function.

$f(x) = 39 \cdot \dbinom{x}{0} - 16 \cdot \dbinom{x}{1} + 4 \cdot \dbinom{x}{2}$

$\quad = 2x^2 - 18x + 39$

Method 2: Pretend the outputs start at 0 and find $g(x) = 2x^2 - 6x + 3$. Then replace x with $x - 3$ and expand to obtain $g(x - 3) = f(x) = 2x^2 - 18x + 39$.

5. a. If $f(x) = \dbinom{x}{3}$,

$\Delta f(x) = f(x + 1) - f(x)$

$\quad = \dbinom{x+1}{3} - \dbinom{x}{3}$

$\quad = \dfrac{(x+1)x(x-1)}{6} - \dfrac{x(x-1)(x-2)}{6}$

$\quad = \dfrac{x(x-1)}{6}[(x+1) - (x-2)]$

$\quad = \dfrac{x(x-1)}{6} \cdot 3$

$\quad = \dfrac{x(x-1)}{2}$

$\quad = \dbinom{x}{2}$

b. If $f(x) = \dbinom{x}{k}$,

$\Delta f(x) = f(x + 1) - f(x)$

$\quad = \dbinom{x+1}{k} - \dbinom{x}{k}$

$\quad = \dfrac{(x+1)x(x-1)\cdots(x-k+2)}{k!} -$
$\qquad \dfrac{x(x-1)(x-2)\cdots(x-k+1)}{k!}$

$\quad = \dfrac{x(x-1)\cdots(x-k+2)}{k!} \cdot$
$\qquad [(x+1) - (x-k+1)]$

$\quad = \dfrac{x(x-1)\cdots(x-k+2)}{k!} \cdot k$

$\quad = \dfrac{x(x-1)\cdots(x-k+2)}{(k-1)!}$

$\quad = \dbinom{x}{k-1}$

6. a.

x	g(x)	Δ	Δ²	Δ³
0	1	4	16	64
1	5	20	80	320
2	25	100	400	
3	125	500		
4	625			

$g(3) = 1 \cdot \dbinom{3}{0} + 4 \cdot \dbinom{3}{1} + 16 \cdot \dbinom{3}{2} +$

$\qquad 64 \cdot \dbinom{3}{3} = 125$

b. You can generalize the argument in part (a) for $g(n)$ for any nonnegative integer n:

$$g(n) = \sum_{k=0}^{n} 4^k \binom{n}{k} = 5^n$$

c. Let $h(x) = (p + 1)^x$.

x	h(x)	Δ	Δ²	Δ³
0	1	p	p²	p²
1	(p + 1)	p(p + 1)	p²(p + 1)	p³(p + 1)
2	(p + 1)²	p(p + 1)²	p²(p + 1)²	
3	(p + 1)³	p(p + 1)³		
4	(p + 1)⁴			

The top row of the difference table contains powers of p; therefore by the same argument made for $g(n)$,

$$h(n) = \sum_{k=0}^{n} p^k \binom{n}{k} = (p + 1)^n$$

7. Incorrect; a periodic function such as $f(x) = 5 + \sin 2\pi x$ would have a difference table with $\Delta = 0$. If f is a polynomial function, then it must be constant.

On Your Own

8. $f(x) = 2x^3 + 5x^2 - x - 17$

9. $S(n) = \dfrac{n(n + 1)(2n + 1)}{6}$ **10.** $C(n) = \dfrac{n^2(n + 1)^2}{4}$

Lesson 5.10
Check Your Understanding

1. a.

k	k³	Δ	Δ²	Δ³
0	0	1	6	6
1	1	7	12	6
2	8	19	18	6
3	27	37	24	
4	64	61		
5	125			

b. $\dfrac{n^2(n - 1)^2}{4}$ **2.** $n(n - 1)(2n - 1)$

3. a.

x	f(x)	Δ	Δ²	Δ³	Δ⁴
0	0	1	14	36	24
1	1	15	50	60	24
2	16	65	110	84	
3	81	175	194		
4	256	369			
5	625				

b. $x^4 = 0 \cdot \binom{x}{0} + 1 \cdot \binom{x}{1} + 14 \cdot \binom{x}{2} + 36 \cdot \binom{x}{3} + 24 \cdot \binom{x}{4}$

Then $\displaystyle\sum_{k=0}^{n-1} k^4 = 0 \cdot \binom{n}{1} + 1 \cdot \binom{n}{2} + 14 \cdot \binom{n}{3} + 36 \cdot \binom{n}{4} + 24 \cdot \binom{n}{5}$

c. $\displaystyle\sum_{k=0}^{n-1} k^4 = \frac{n(n - 1)}{2} + 14 \cdot \frac{n(n - 1)(n - 2)}{6} + 36 \cdot \frac{n(n - 1)(n - 2)(n - 3)}{24} + 24 \cdot \frac{n(n - 1)(n - 2)(n - 3)(n - 4)}{120}$

4. a. Substitute $(n - 1)$ for n and the formulas are the same. **b.** Write n^4 as $\frac{30n^4}{30}$ and factor both sides to demonstrate that these two expressions are equal. **5. a.** The volume is made up of five smaller shapes: $5 \times 5 \times 1$, $4 \times 4 \times 1$, $3 \times 3 \times 1$, $2 \times 2 \times 1$, and $1 \times 1 \times 1$. $V = 1^2 + 2^2 + 3^2 + 4^2 + 5^2$ **b.** $5 \times 6 \times 11$ **c.** The dimensions of the box are n by $(n + 1)$ by $(2n + 1)$. Since six congruent shapes were used to build the box, the volume of each shape is $V = \dfrac{n(n + 1)(2n + 1)}{6}$, which also equals $1^2 + 2^2 + 3^2 + 4^2 + 5^2$.

6.

f(x)	1	x	x²	x³	x⁴	x⁵
$\binom{x}{0}$	1	-	-	-	-	-
$\binom{x}{1}$	0	1	-	-	-	-
$\binom{x}{2}$	0	$-\frac{1}{2}$	$\frac{1}{2}$	-	-	-
$\binom{x}{3}$	0	$\frac{1}{3}$	$-\frac{1}{2}$	$\frac{1}{6}$	-	-
$\binom{x}{4}$	0	$-\frac{1}{4}$	$\frac{11}{24}$	$-\frac{1}{4}$	$\frac{1}{24}$	-
$\binom{x}{5}$	0	$\frac{1}{5}$	$-\frac{5}{24}$	$-\frac{7}{24}$	$\frac{1}{12}$	$\frac{1}{120}$

Patterns: Reciprocals of the factorial numbers appear along the diagonal; within each row, the terms always alternate signs; the x column contains reciprocals of all positive integers in an alternating positive/negative pattern. This matrix is the inverse of the matrix from Exercise 16 in Lesson 5.9.

On Your Own

7. a. $3n$ **b.** $\dfrac{n(n-1)}{2}$ **c.** $\dfrac{5n(n-1)}{2}$

10. $f(n) = n^2 + 6n + 8$

11. $f(n) = A + Cn + B \cdot \dfrac{n(n-1)}{2}$

Lesson 5.11

On Your Own

6. a. The function defined matches the description in the problem.

b.

n	$r(n)$
0	$\dfrac{7}{2}$
1	$\dfrac{29}{7}$
2	$\dfrac{133}{29}$
3	$\dfrac{641}{133}$
4	$\dfrac{3157}{641}$
5	$\dfrac{15{,}689}{3157}$
6	$\dfrac{78{,}253}{15{,}689}$

c. Yes, it approaches 5. **d.** Except for $r(0) = 2$, $r(n) \to 5$ as n grows without bound. $r(0) = 2$ repeatedly returns 2. **8. a.** Check students' work. **b.** The outputs appear to be approaching 2. **c.** The long-term behavior of the outputs seems independent of the starting number. They always approach 2.

Lesson 5.12

Check Your Understanding

1. a. $f(6) = 300$; $f(4) = \dfrac{100}{3}$ **b.** $K = \dfrac{100}{243}$ or $\dfrac{100}{3^5}$

c. $f(n) = 100 \cdot 3^{n-5}$ **2. a.** $g(4) = 20.25$

b. $g(n) = 64 \cdot \left(\dfrac{3}{4}\right)^n$ **c.** 256 **d.** 256.0000

3. a. $h(n) = 4^n$; $j(n) = 6^n$

b. $10k(n-1) -$
$$24k(n-2) = 10(5 \cdot 4^{n-1} + 8 \cdot 6^{n-1}) -$$
$$24(5 \cdot 4^{n-2} + 8 \cdot 6^{n-2})$$
$$= 50 \cdot 4^{n-1} + 80 \cdot 6^{n-1} -$$
$$120 \cdot 4^{n-2} - 192 \cdot 6^{n-2}$$
$$= 50 \cdot 4^{n-1} + 80 \cdot 6^{n-1} -$$
$$30 \cdot 4 \cdot 4^{n-2} -$$
$$32 \cdot 6 \cdot 6^{n-2}$$
$$= 50 \cdot 4^{n-1} + 80 \cdot 6^{n-1} -$$
$$30 \cdot 4^{n-1} - 32 \cdot 6^{n-1}$$
$$= 20 \cdot 4^{n-1} + 48 \cdot 6^{n-1}$$
$$= 5 \cdot 4 \cdot 4^{n-1} + 8 \cdot 6 \cdot 6^{n-1}$$
$$= 5 \cdot 4^n + 8 \cdot 6^n$$
$$= k(n)$$
c. $r(n) = 5 \cdot 4^n - 2 \cdot 6^n$

4. a. $b = 0$ **b.** $f(1)$ is 32 away from b and $f(2)$ is 64 away from b. **5. a.** $b = -3$ **b.** $j(1)$ is 32 away from b and $j(2)$ is 64 away from b. **6. a.** 0 **b.** $g(0)$ is 64 away from the limit; $g(1)$ is 48 away from the limit; $g(2)$ is 36 away from the limit. **7. a.** $r(x) = 40$

b.

n	$r(n)$	Δ	$\div$
0	104	-16	0.75
1	88	-12	0.75
2	76	-9	0.75
3	67	-6.75	0.75
4	60.25	-5.0625	0.75
5	55.1875	-3.7969	0.75
6	51.3906	-2.8477	0.75
7	48.5430	-2.1357	
8	46.4072		

On Your Own

8. Expand the left side to $1 + r^2 + r^3 + \cdots + r^{n-1}$, then multiply by -1 to get $-1 - r^2 - r^3 - \ldots - r^{n-1}$. Adding together these terms leaves just $(1 - r^n)$ as the result of the expansion. **10. a.** $f(n) = 3 \cdot 4^n$ **b.** 4,194,303 **12. c.** yes **d.** no **e.** yes

Lesson 5.13

Check Your Understanding

1. a. 266 and 1282; $A = 2$, $B = 2$ **b.** -117 and -609; $A = 1$, $B = -1$ **c.** 149 and 673; $A = 3$, $B = 1$ **d.** 39 and 203; $A = -\dfrac{1}{3}$, $B = \dfrac{1}{3}$ **e.** -70 and -390; $A = \dfrac{5}{3}$, $B = -\dfrac{2}{3}$ **f.** $-70x + 39y$ and $-390x + 203y$; $A = \dfrac{5x - y}{3}$, $B = \dfrac{y - 2x}{3}$ **2. a.** 10 and 3

b. $13 \cdot 10^{n-1} - 30 \cdot 10^{n-2}$
$$= 13 \cdot 10^{n-1} - 3 \cdot 10 \cdot 10^{n-2}$$
$$= 13 \cdot 10^{n-1} - 3 \cdot 10^{n-1}$$
$$= 10 \cdot 10^{n-1}$$
$$= 10^n$$

c. $13 \cdot 3^{n-1} - 30 \cdot 3^{n-2}$
$$= 13 \cdot 3^{n-1} - 10 \cdot 3 \cdot 3^{n-2}$$
$$= 13 \cdot 3^{n-1} - 10 \cdot 3^{n-1}$$
$$= 3 \cdot 3^{n-1}$$
$$= 3^n$$

d. $13(10^{n-1} + 3^{n-1}) - 30(10^{n-2} + 3^{n-2})$
$$= (13 \cdot 10^{n-1} - 30 \cdot 10^{n-2}) +$$
$$(13 \cdot 3^{n-1} - 30 \cdot 3^{n-2})$$
See proofs in parts (b) and (c) to complete the proof.
3. $t(n) = 3 \cdot 3^n + 2 \cdot 5^n$ **4.** $t(n) = 3^n + 7^n$
5. $h(n) = (1 + \sqrt{2})^n$; $j(n) = (1 - \sqrt{2})^n$
6. Answers may vary. Sample: Use the quadratic equation $x^2 = Ax + B$ to find the two roots that are used to determine the closed form. Either root of the equation $x^2 - Ax - B = 0$ can be the base.

7. $f(n) = \dfrac{\left(\frac{1 + \sqrt{5}}{2}\right)^n - \left(\frac{1 - \sqrt{5}}{2}\right)^n}{\sqrt{5}}$

On Your Own

8. a. $f(n) = 4^n + 5^n$ **b.** $f(n) = 10(4^n + 5^n)$

9. a. Answers may vary. Sample: One way would be to tabulate $f(n)$ and notice that a common ratio between terms emerges, suggesting that this ratio might fit the recurrence.

b. $8 \cdot 6^{n-1} - 12 \cdot 6^{n-2}$
$= 8 \cdot 6^{n-1} - 2 \cdot 6 \cdot 6^{n-2}$
$= 8 \cdot 6^{n-1} - 2 \cdot 6^{n-1}$
$= 6 \cdot 6^{n-1}$
$= 6^n$

c. $f(n) = 6^n + 2^n$ **d.** $f(n) = 4 \cdot 6^n + 2^n$

10. $f(n) = \dfrac{7}{3} \cdot 4^n - \dfrac{1}{3} \cdot (-2)^n$

12. $L(n) = \left(\dfrac{1 + \sqrt{5}}{2}\right)^n + \left(\dfrac{1 - \sqrt{5}}{2}\right)^n$

Lesson 5.14
Check Your Understanding

1. $B(n) = 500\left(\dfrac{1.03^n - 1}{0.03}\right)$

2. $B(n) = D\left(\dfrac{(1 + r)^n - 1}{r}\right)$

3. a.

Years n	Trees $T(n)$
0	25,000
1	23,000
2	21,400
3	20,120
4	19,096
5	18,277
6	17,621
7	17,097

b.

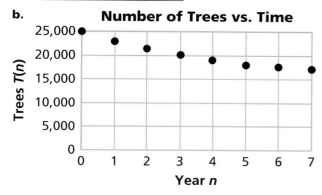

Number of Trees vs. Time

Trees $T(n)$ vs. *Year n*

c. 15,000

d.

Years n	Trees $T(n)$	$T(n) - 15{,}000$	÷
0	25,000	10,000	0.8
1	23,000	8000	0.8
2	21,400	6400	0.8
3	20,120	5120	0.8
4	19,096	4096	0.8
5	18,277	3277	0.8
6	17,621	2621	0.8
7	17,097	2097	0.8

e. $T(n) = 15{,}000 + 10{,}000 \cdot 0.8^n$

4. $B = -13{,}000$ **5.** If x is an equilibrium point, then $f(n) = x$ for all n. Therefore:

$x = Ax + B$
$x - Ax = B$
$x(1 - A) = B$
$x = \dfrac{B}{1 - A}$

6. a. $\dfrac{P}{r}$ **b.** $B - \dfrac{P}{r}$ **c.** $f(1)$ is $(1 + r)\left(B - \dfrac{P}{r}\right)$ away from the equilibrium point.

$f(2)$ is $(1 + r)^2\left(B - \dfrac{P}{r}\right)$ away from the equilibrium point.

$f(n)$ is $(1 + r)^n\left(B - \dfrac{P}{r}\right)$ away from the equilibrium point.

d. $f(n) = \dfrac{P}{r} + (1 + r)^n\left(B - \dfrac{P}{r}\right)$

e. $P = \dfrac{Br(1 + r)^n}{(1 + r)^n - 1}$

On Your Own

7. a. \$1,355,121.84 **b.** \$803,195.64 **c.** \$493,537.82

8. a.

n	$f(n)$
0	P
1	$AP + B$
2	$A^2P + AB + B$
3	$A^3P + A^2B + AB + B$
4	$A^4P + A^3B + A^2B + AB + B$

b. $f(n) = A^nP + B\left(\dfrac{A^n - 1}{A - 1}\right)$

9. a. $f(36) = 1.005^{36} \cdot 12{,}000 - p\left(\dfrac{1.005^{36} - 1}{0.005}\right)$

b. \$365.06

Chapter 6
Lesson 6.1
On Your Own

8. $(\sqrt{13}, 2), (\sqrt{13}, -2), (-\sqrt{13}, 2), (-\sqrt{13}, -2)$

11. d. $AX = \sqrt{2}$, $BX = 4\sqrt{2}$, $CX = 4$, $DX = 2$, therefore $AX \cdot BX = CX \cdot DX = 8$

Lesson 6.2
Check Your Understanding
1. a. $|y - 2| = 3$

b.

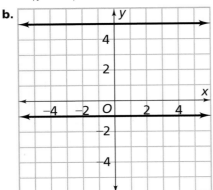

2. a. no **b.** yes **c.** If $a < 0$, this point must be closer to the y-axis than to $(4, 0)$ since $(4, 0)$ will be on the opposite side of the axis. Therefore, the distances could never be equal. **d.** $y^2 = 8x - 16$

3. a. No; the distance from $(5, 3)$ to $(15, 0)$ is $\sqrt{109}$, and the distance from $(5, 3)$ to $(6, 0)$ is $\sqrt{10}$.

b. $(9, 0)$ and $(-3, 0)$

c. $36 = (x - 3)^2 + y^2$

d. The graph is a circle with center at $(3, 0)$ and radius 6.

4. a. $y = 2x - 9$ **b.** $y = -\frac{3}{2}x + \frac{19}{2}$ **c.** $x = \frac{37}{7}$

5. a. Answers may vary. Sample: Any (x, y, z) fitting the equation $5 = \sqrt{(x - 2)^2 + (y - 3)^2 + (z - 4)^2}$ is in this set. Some examples include: $(7, 3, 4)$, $(2, 3, 9)$, $(2, 0, 0)$, $(-2, 0, 4)$, and $(2, -2, 4)$.

b. Answers may vary. Sample: Any (x, y, z) not fitting the equation in part (a) is not part of this set.

c. $(x - 2)^2 + (y - 3)^2 + (z - 4)^2 = 25$

6. a. a plane **b.** Yes, this point is part of the set.

c. $x + 2y + 3z = 14$ **d.** Yes, this point is part of the set.

e.

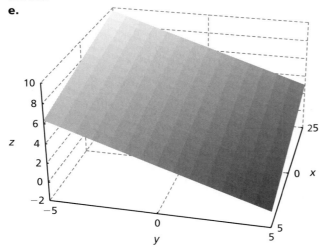

On Your Own
7. a. $y = -\frac{1}{3}x + \frac{10}{3}$ **11. b.** circle centered at $(0, 0)$ with radius 5

Lesson 6.3
Check Your Understanding
1. a. Answers will vary. One possible answer is $A(0, 0), B(a, 0), C(a, b), D(0, b)$

b. Using the coordinates from part (a), find the length of the diagonal using the distance formula.

$$AC = \sqrt{(a - 0)^2 + (b - 0)^2} = \sqrt{a^2 + b^2}$$
$$BD = \sqrt{(a - 0)^2 + (0 - b)^2} = \sqrt{a^2 + (-b)^2}$$
$$= \sqrt{a^2 + b^2}$$

2.

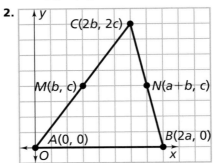

The midpoint of AC is $M(b, c)$ and the midpoint of BC is $N(a + b, c)$.

The length of segment MN, which joins the midpoints of sides AC and BC, is a.

The length of side AB is $2a$, which is twice that of MN.

Both segments are horizontal, therefore parallel, which completes the proof.

3. Assume a quadrilateral has vertices at $A(0, 0)$, $B(2a, 0), C(2b, 2c)$, and $D(2d, 2e)$.

Midpoints of the four sides are $M(a, 0), N(a + b, c)$, $P(b + d, c + e), Q(d, e)$.

The slopes of MN and PQ are both $\frac{c}{b}$ and the slopes of NP and MQ are both $\frac{e}{d - a}$. Therefore, since the slopes of both pairs of opposite sides are equal, this must be a parallelogram.

4. parallelogram

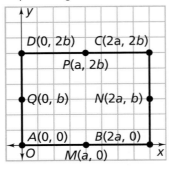

Selected Answers

Assume a quadrilateral has vertices at $A(0, 0)$, $B(2a, 0)$, $C(2a, 2b)$, $D(0, 2b)$.

Midpoints of the four sides are $M(a, 0)$, $N(2a, b)$, $P(a, 2b)$, $Q(0, b)$.

Similar to the previous problem, the slopes of MN and PQ are equal and the slopes of NP and MQ are equal. Therefore, since the slopes of both pairs of opposite sides are equal, this must be a parallelogram. Also, since $MN = NP$, $MNPQ$ is a rhombus.

5. Answers may vary. Sample: Joey assumes that the two lines of symmetry of the rhombus are perpendicular. He does this by placing them along the axes. It would be alright for Joey to place one line of symmetry on the axis, then prove the other must lie along the axis as well. But by building the rhombus in this way, Joey has assumed what he is trying to prove, which is invalid.

6.

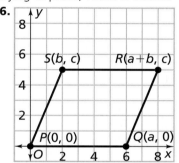

Assume a parallelogram has vertices at $P(0, 0)$, $Q(a, 0)$, $R(a + b, c)$, $S(b, c)$.

The slope of diagonal PR is $\dfrac{c}{a + b}$, and the slope of diagonal SQ is $\dfrac{c}{b - a}$.

If these diagonals are perpendicular, then
$$\frac{c}{a + b} \cdot \frac{c}{b - a} = -1$$
$$\frac{c^2}{b^2 - a^2} = -1$$
$$c^2 = a^2 - b^2$$
$$c^2 + b^2 = a^2$$

To prove $PQRS$ is a rhombus, you must show that two consecutive sides are congruent. The length of PQ is a and the length of QR is $\sqrt{b^2 + c^2}$. If the diagonals are perpendicular, then $a^2 = b^2 + c^2$, so $PQ = QR$ and the parallelogram must be a rhombus.

On Your Own

8. Answers may vary. Sample: One way is to use $B(2b, 0)$ and $C(0, 2c)$. Midpoint of BC is $D(b, c)$.

$$AD = \sqrt{b^2 + c^2}$$
$$BD = \sqrt{(2b - b)^2 + (0 - c)^2} = \sqrt{b^2 + c^2}$$
$$CD = \sqrt{(0 - b)^2 + (2c - c)^2} = \sqrt{b^2 + c^2}$$

All three lengths are the same.

11. Answers may vary. Sample: Assume coordinates $A(0, 0)$, $B(2a, 0)$, $C(2b, 2c)$, $D(2d, 2c)$.

The length of AB is $2a$ and the length of CD is $2b - 2d$. The average of these lengths is $a + b - d$.

The midline's endpoints are $M(d, c)$ and $N(a + b, c)$. The distance between M and N is $a + b - d$.

Lesson 6.4
Check Your Understanding
1.

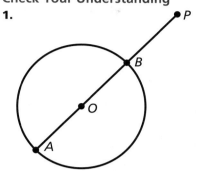

Consider point P outside the circle.

Pick $\overleftrightarrow{OP}$ where O is the center of the circle so that $OP = d$ and AB is a diameter.

$PA = d + r$ and $PB = d - r$, therefore the power of point P with respect to the circle is

$$PA \cdot PB = (d + r)(d - r) = d^2 - r^2$$

2. a. Center is $(-3, 4)$ and radius is 7.

b.

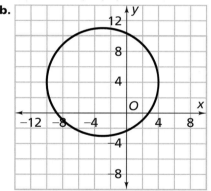

c. The two x-intercepts are $(-3 + \sqrt{33}, 0)$ and $(-3 - \sqrt{33}, 0)$.

The two y-intercepts are $(0, 4 + 2\sqrt{10})$ and $(0, 4 - 2\sqrt{10})$.

3. a. 24 **b.** 24 **c.** $(4, 4)$ and $(-3, -3)$; $P = 24$

4. As the intersection points get closer together, the line through P comes closer and closer to being a tangent of the circle. If PA is the tangent to the circle, then $(PA)^2$ equals the power of point P. This means that if point P is d units away from the center of the circle, and $d > r$, the length of the tangent from P to the circle is $\sqrt{d^2 - r^2}$.

5. Set $y = kx$ in the equation.

$$x^2 + y^2 + 6x - 8y - 24 = 0$$
$$x^2 + (kx)^2 + 6x - 8kx - 24 = 0$$
$$(k^2 + 1)x^2 + (6 - 8k)x - 24 = 0$$
$$x = \frac{8k - 6 \pm \sqrt{(6 - 8k)^2 - 4(k^2 + 1)(-24)}}{2(k^2 + 1)}$$
$$x = \frac{4k - 3 \pm \sqrt{40k^2 - 24k + 33}}{k^2 + 1}$$

Since the values of y are k times the values of x, the two intersections are at

$$\left(\frac{4k - 3 \pm \sqrt{40k^2 - 24k + 33}}{k^2 + 1}, \right.$$
$$\left. k \cdot \frac{4k - 3 \pm \sqrt{40k^2 - 24k + 33}}{k^2 + 1} \right)$$

To determine the power of P, find the distance between $(0, 0)$ and (x, kx).

$$\sqrt{x^2 + (kx)^2} = \sqrt{(k^2 + 1)x^2} = |x|\sqrt{k^2 + 1}$$

The product of the two distances will be $k^2 + 1$ multiplied by the two x-coordinates.

$$\frac{4k - 3 + \sqrt{40k^2 - 24k + 33}}{k^2 + 1} \cdot$$
$$\frac{4k - 3 - \sqrt{40k^2 - 24k + 33}}{k^2 + 1} \cdot (k^2 + 1)$$
$$= \frac{(4k - 3)^2 - (40k^2 - 24k + 33)}{k^2 + 1}$$
$$= \frac{16k^2 - 24k + 9 - (40k^2 - 24k + 33)}{k^2 + 1}$$
$$= \frac{-24k^2 - 24}{k^2 + 1}$$
$$= \frac{-24(k^2 + 1)}{k^2 + 1} = -24$$

(which is independent of k)

On Your Own

6. 20 **8. b.** 20

Lesson 6.5
On Your Own

6. $x = 16$

8. c.

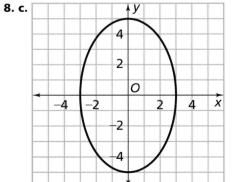

Lesson 6.6
Check Your Understanding

1. a. Answers may vary. Sample: The pins should be placed fairly close together. **b.** The pins should be placed far apart, a little shorter than the string length s but larger than $\frac{s}{2}$. **c.** If both pins are placed in the same spot, a circle will result. **2. a.** $b = 4, -4$ **b.** $a = 5, -5$ **c.** No; the sum of the distances between this point and the foci does not equal 10. **d.** $\sqrt{(x - 3)^2 + y^2} + \sqrt{(x + 3)^2 + y^2} = 10$ **3.** Your sketch should look like the one on page 471 but points D and E will coincide at the center of the circle. This will also be the point where the two spheres are tangent to the plane of the sliced circle. **4. a.** Answers may vary. Sample:

Any point that satisfies the equation
$$\left| \sqrt{(x - 3)^2 + y^2} - \sqrt{(x + 3)^2 + y^2} \right| = 4.$$

b.

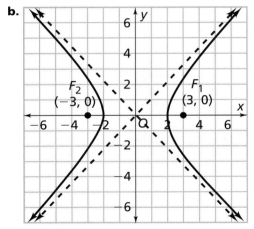

c. $\frac{x^2}{4} - \frac{y^2}{5} = 1$ **5.** If P is any point noncollinear with A and B, then the triangle inequality applies: if the shorter of PA or PB has length x, then the longer cannot be more than $x + 6$. So $|PA - PB| < 6$ is required. If P is collinear with A and B, then $|PA - PB| = 6$ is possible but no more. In the entire plane, no point P can satisfy $|PA - PB| = 10$.

On Your Own

6. a. no **b.** no **c.** yes **d.** no **9.** $x = \frac{1}{4}y^2$

10. a. Answers may vary. Sample: $3x + 25 = 5\sqrt{(x + 3)^2 + y^2}$

Lesson 6.7
Check Your Understanding

1. a. $25 \cdot (0)^2 + 169 \cdot (5)^2 = 4225$
$169 \cdot 25 = 4225$

b. Answers may vary. Sample: Any point satisfying the equation $\frac{x^2}{169} + \frac{y^2}{5} = 1$. **c.** The major axis is formed by the points (13, 0) and (−13, 0). The distance between these points is 26. **d.** $c = 12$

e.

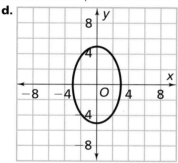

2. a. Answers may vary. Sample: Any points satisfying the equation $\frac{x^2}{9} + \frac{y^2}{25} = 1$. **b.** The major axis is formed by the points (0, 5) and (0, −5). The distance between these points is 10. **c.** $c = 4$

d.

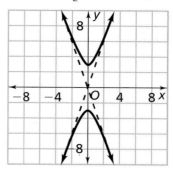

3. The graph will pass through the points $(a, 0)$, $(−a, 0)$, $(0, b)$, and $(0, −b)$.

If $a = b$, then this graph is a circle centered at the origin.

If $a > b$, the graph is an ellipse with major axis along the x-axis with foci points at $(\pm\sqrt{a^2 - b^2}, 0)$.

If $a < b$, the graph is an ellipse with major axis along the y-axis with foci points at $(0, \pm\sqrt{b^2 - a^2})$.

4. a. $y^2 - 9x^2 = 36$

$(\pm 6)^2 - 9 \cdot (0)^2 = 36$

b. $y = \pm 6.7082$ **c.** $y = \pm 16.1555$

d. $y = \pm 300.0600$

e. As x grows larger, the ratio of $\frac{y}{x}$ approaches 3 or −3 and the points on the parabola approach asymptotes defined by the lines $y = 3x$ and $y = -3x$.

5. a. This graph is a hyperbola that is a dilation with scale factor $\frac{1}{2}$ from the original in Exercise 5.

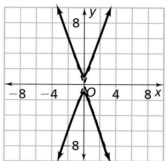

b. This graph is a hyperbola, even closer to the origin.

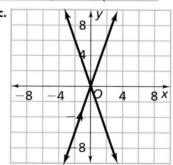

c.

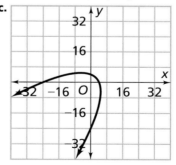

6. a. $x^2 - 2xy + y^2 + 20x + 20y - 100 = 0$

b. (−5, 5) and (−5, 35)

c.

On Your Own
7. $x = -\frac{1}{8}y^2$ **8. c.** The ratio $\frac{y}{x}$ approaches $\frac{3}{4}$.

Lesson 6.8
Check Your Understanding
1. a. (3, 2)

b.

x	y
6	undefined
7	2
8	4.25
9	5.3541
11	7.1962
13	8.8739
23	16.6969
43	31.8496
103	76.9400
1003	751.9940

c. The graph becomes asymptotic to the line $y - 2 = \frac{3}{4}(x - 3)$.

2. a.

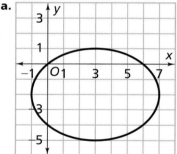

b. no

c.

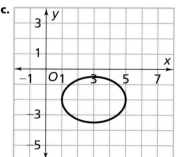

d.

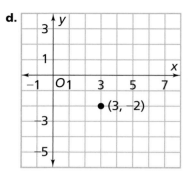

e. No graph, since the equation has no solution.
f. $N = 916$
3. a. Yes; hyperbola

b.

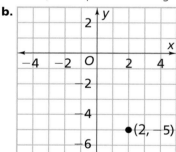

4. a. No; this equation is a single point

b.

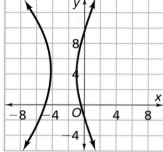

5. a. $(y - 2)^2 = 4(x + 3)^2 - 16$ **b.** The next step in solving this equation is to take a square root, which results in two answers (a positive and negative root).
c. $f_1(x) = 2 + \sqrt{4(x + 3)^2 - 16}$
$f_2(x) = 2 - \sqrt{4(x + 3)^2 - 16}$

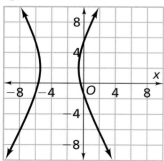

6.

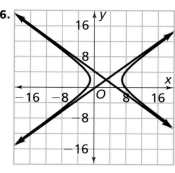

7. $y = \frac{1}{x}$

On Your Own

8. Answers may vary. Sample: The first equation is the sum of squares, and squares can never be negative. The second equation is the difference of squares, and that can be negative. **10. a.** $x \leq -16$ or $x \geq -2$ **11.** $(4, 10)$ and $(4, 0)$

Lesson 6.9

Check Your Understanding

1. a. $\frac{3}{5}$ **b.** $\frac{4}{5}$ **c.** $\frac{1}{5}$ **d.** $\frac{\sqrt{3}}{2}$ **2.** $\frac{(x - 8)^2}{16} + \frac{y^2}{12} = 1$

3. $\frac{(x - 8)^2}{16} + \frac{y^2}{12} = 1$; Center $= (8, 0)$

4. a. Center $= (-6, 5)$; vertices $= (-12, 5)$ and $(0, 5)$; foci $= (-15, 5)$ and $(3, 5)$ **b.** $e = 1.5$

c.

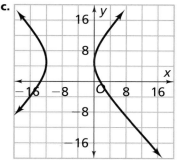

5. $e = 3$ **6. a.** If $e = 1$, the definition gives $PF = Pd$, which matches the locus definition of a parabola given in Lesson 6.6. **b.** Let $e < 1$ and use the distance formula to determine the equation of the ellipse.

$$\sqrt{x^2 + (y - 1)^2} = e|y + 1|$$

Solving this equation yields

$$\frac{x^2}{\frac{1 - e^2}{4e^2}} + \frac{\left(y - \frac{1 + e^2}{1 - e^2}\right)^2}{\frac{(1 - e^2)^2}{4e^2}} = 1$$

Based on this equation, $a = \frac{2e}{1 - e^2}$ and $b = \frac{2e}{\sqrt{1 - e^2}}$,

therefore $c = \frac{2e^2}{1 - e^2}$.

The eccentricity is given by $\frac{c}{a} = \frac{2e^2/(1 - e^2)}{2e/(1 - e^2)} = e$.

c. Using the same methods, find $a = \frac{2e}{e^2 - 1}$, $b = \frac{2e}{\sqrt{e^2 - 1}}$, $c = \frac{2e^2}{e^2 - 1}$ to show that $\frac{c}{a} = e$.

7.

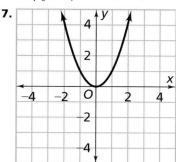

a. The graph looks very similar to $y = x^2$. **b.** Answers may vary. Sample: The ellipse must have a very high eccentricity and a vertex at $(0, 0)$.

On Your Own

10. a. $e = 6$ **12.** $(-5, 7)$

Lesson 6.10

On Your Own

6. c. $y = -\frac{1}{2}x + \frac{5}{2}$

8. a. The figure will be identical but all sides will be only half as long.

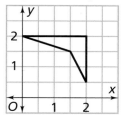

Lesson 6.11

Check Your Understanding

1. Assume point P has coordinates (x, y). Then point Q has coordinates $(x + c, y + d)$.

Assume point R has coordinates (m, n). Then point S has coordinates $(m + c, m + d)$.

a. The slope of $\overrightarrow{PQ}$ is $\frac{(y + d) - y}{(x + c) - x} = \frac{d}{c}$. Similarly, the slope of $\overrightarrow{RS}$ is $\frac{d}{c}$.

b. The length of $\overrightarrow{PQ}$ is

$$\sqrt{((x + c) - x)^2 + ((y + d) - y)^2} = \sqrt{c^2 + d^2}.$$

Similarly, the length of $\overrightarrow{RS}$ is $\sqrt{c^2 + d^2}$.

c. The displacement vector provides the direction. Since they have the same displacement, they must point in the same direction. **2.** If $\overrightarrow{PQ}$ has direction vector D, then $Q = P + kD$ for some positive scalar k. Similarly, $S = R + mD$ for some positive scalar m. The length of $\overrightarrow{PQ}$ is the length of kD, and the length of $\overrightarrow{RS}$ is the length of mD. But these are given to be equal; therefore $k = m$ as long as D is nonzero. Since $k = m$, then $Q - P = kD = mD = S - R$.
3. (6, 6) **4.** $A + U + V$
5.

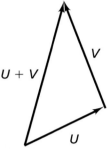

U + V

V

U

On Your Own
6. a. $(t_1 + a_1, t_2 + a_2)$ **e.** (1, 1, 1)

Lesson 6.12
Check Your Understanding
1. (4, 6): yes; (−5, −5): no; (13, 18): yes
2. $y = 2x - 2$ **3. a.** $\frac{4}{3}$ **b.** $\frac{3}{4}$ **c.** $\frac{4}{3}$ **d.** $\frac{4}{3}$
4. a–d. Answers may vary. Samples are given.
a. $X = (0, 1) + t(2, 3)$ **b.** $X = (5, 3) + t(1, 4)$
c. $X = (0, 3) + t(2, -3)$ **d.** $X = (-2, 3) + t(5, -2)$
or $X = (3, 1) + t(5, -2)$ are two equations.

5. $y = \frac{17}{3}$ **6.** no **7.** For the lines to be the same, it is necessary that D' be a scalar multiple of D (i.e., the lines are parallel). Once it is known that the lines are parallel, then check to see if P' is on the first line. If that turns out to be true, the lines are identical, since a line is uniquely determined by a point and a slope.
8. a.

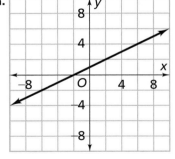

b.

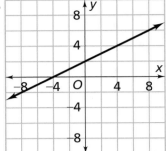

c. The direction vector is scaled, but the direction is not changed. Since the two lines have the same direction vector, they must be parallel.
On Your Own
9. Answers may vary. Sample: $X = (2, 3) + t(-3, 1)$
13. a. The paths intersect and these cars crash.
14. $z = 7$

Lesson 6.13
Check Your Understanding
1. a. $\overrightarrow{AB} = B - A = (3, 1) - (0, 0) = (3, 1)$.
Similarly, $\overrightarrow{DC} = C - D = (4, 5) - (1, 4) = (3, 1)$.
Therefore, sides AB and DC are parallel and equal in length, and $ABCD$ must be a parallelogram. **b.** (2, 2.5)
c. (2, 2.5)
2. Answers may vary. Sample: One way is to find the midpoints of two opposite sides, say AB and CD, draw the "midline" segment between them, and take the midpoint of that segment.

$$\frac{\frac{1}{2}(A + B) + \frac{1}{2}(C + D)}{2} = \frac{A + B + C + D}{4}$$

Another way is to draw both diagonals and mark the midpoints of each. Now take the midpoint of the segment between them.

$$\frac{\frac{1}{2}(A + C) + \frac{1}{2}(B + D)}{2} = \frac{A + B + C + D}{4}$$

3. a. They bisect each other. The midpoint of PR is

$$\frac{P + R}{2} = \frac{\frac{1}{2}(A + B) + \frac{1}{2}(C + D)}{2} = \frac{A + B + C + D}{4}$$

The midpoint of QS is also $\frac{A + B + C + D}{4}$. So the two lines intersect at their midpoints, bisecting each other.
b. They are parallel and equal in length. Prove that $Q - P = R - S$ to show that these are equivalent vectors.

$$Q - P = \frac{B + C}{2} - \frac{B + A}{2} = \frac{C - A}{2} \text{ and}$$
$$R - S = \frac{C + D}{2} - \frac{A + D}{2} = \frac{C - A}{2}$$

The vectors are equivalent, so PQ and RS are equal in length and parallel.

4. a.

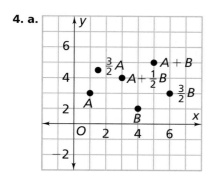

b. $\frac{1}{2}(A + (A + B)) = \frac{1}{2}((1, 3) + (5, 5)) =$
$(3, 4) = (1, 3) + \frac{1}{2}(4, 2)$ **c.** The midpoint of the
segment from A to $(A + B)$ is $\frac{A + (A + B)}{2} = A + \frac{1}{2}B$.
d. For any points C, D, the trisection point of CD
closer to C is $\frac{2}{3}C + \frac{1}{3}D$. Therefore, the trisection
point closer to $\frac{3}{2}A$ of the segment from $\frac{3}{2}A$ to $\frac{3}{2}B$
is $\frac{2}{3}\left(\frac{3}{2}A\right) + \frac{1}{3}\left(\frac{3}{2}B\right) = A + \frac{1}{2}B$. **5. a.** 1 to 3 **b.** 1 to 3
c. The quarter point of PC, the quarter point
of QB, and the midpoint of the median, are all
$\frac{1}{2}A + \frac{1}{4}B + \frac{1}{4}C$. Therefore, they are all the
same point. **d.** S bisects the median line.
6. The parallelogram can be fully labeled using the
given information.

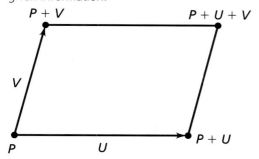

The midpoint of both diagonals is $P + \frac{1}{2}(U + V)$, so
the diagonals bisect each other.
7. Two sides are parallel if the direction vector for
one is a scalar multiple of the direction vector for the
other. So the figure includes the givens. To show that
opposite sides have equal length, you have to show
that $k = j = 1$. By the parallelogram law,

$U + V = jV + kU$

$(1 - k)U = (j - 1)V$

But since U and V are not parallel, the only way two
multiples of them could be equal is if the coefficients
are 0. That is $(1 - k) = (j - 1) = 0$.
Which implies $k = j = 1$ as desired.
On Your Own
8. $(1 - k)A + kB = A + d(B - A)$. If k varies
through all nonnegative numbers, you get all points

starting at A in the direction of B. You get beyond
B when $k > 1$. **9. a.** Given point D is inside the
triangle. Draw a line from vertex A through D to E
on side BC. Since E is between B and C, E is a convex
combination of B and C, and $E = (1 - k)B + kC$ for
some k with $0 < k < 1$. Because D is some convex
combination of A and E, then $D = (1 - j)A + jE$
for some j with $0 < j < 1$. By substitution,
$D = (1 - j)A + j(1 - k)B + jkC$. These
coefficients, $1 - j$, $j(1 - k)$, jk, are a, b, c. All of
these must be positive, and
$(1 - j) + j(1 - k) + jk = 1 - j + j - jk + jk = 1$

Chapter 7
Lesson 7.1
On Your Own
7. b. $\frac{19}{25}$ **d.** $\frac{35}{49}$ **8. a.** 120
Lesson 7.2
Check Your Understanding
1. a. $\frac{1}{2}$ **b.** $\frac{1}{4}$ **c.** $\frac{1}{2}$ **d.** $\frac{1}{2}$ **e.** 0 **f.** $\frac{1}{36}$ **g.** $\frac{35}{36}$
2. The results are not equally likely because there
are 5 ways to roll a sum of 8 on two dice out of
36 outcomes; $\frac{5}{36}$ **3.** 15; HHTTTT, HTHTTT, HTTHTT,
HTTTHT, HTTTTH, THHTTT, THTHTT, THTTHT, THTTTH,
TTHHTT, TTHTHT, TTHTTH, TTTHHT, TTTHTH, TTTTHH

4. $\binom{6}{2} = 15$; this represents 15 ways to pick two

items from a group of six. **5.** 20; this is the coefficient
of the t^3h^3 term; $(t + h)^6 = t^6 + 6t^5h +$
$15t^4h^2 + 20t^3h^3 + 15t^2h^4 + 6th^5 + t^6$ **6.** $\frac{21}{216}$
On Your Own
9. $\frac{84}{512}$ **10. a.** $\frac{1}{6}$ **11. a.** 36
Lesson 7.3
Check Your Understanding
1. a.

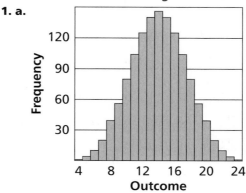

b. To roll a 5, the only possible roll is the four
variations of 1-1-1-2. To roll a 23, the only possible
roll is the four variations of 6-6-6-5. Also, the
frequencies appear symmetric on either side
of 14.

2. $\frac{1}{2}$ **3. a.** $x^2 + x^3 + x^4 + x^5 + x^6 + x^{10}$
b. 20; $\frac{95}{1296}$ **4. a.** Answers may vary. Sample: $2x^5$ represents the two faces with 5 on them, while the other exponents indicate single faces with 1 through 4 on them. **b.** 13; $\frac{164}{1296}$ **5. a.** $q(x) = 4x^{10} + 4x^9 + 5x^8 + 6x^7 + 7x^6 + 4x^5 + 3x^4 + 2x^3 + x^2$; this represents the frequencies of the sums when the 1-2-3-4-5-5 number cube is rolled twice. **b.** 36 **c.** 4

d. 4 **6. a.** $\frac{3}{50}$ or 0.06 **b.** $\frac{425}{1000}$ or 0.425
c. $\frac{7760}{10,000}$ or 0.776

On Your Own

7. a. $1 + x + 2x^2 + x^7$ **b.** $\frac{72}{625}$ **8. a.** 0.2; 0.2
b. $(0.2)^6 = 0.000064$

Lesson 7.4
Check Your Understanding

1. a. $\frac{1}{24}$ **b.** $\frac{3}{8}$ **2.** 1 **3.** $5719.53 **4.** There is nothing wrong with Daisuke's calculation. His mistake was in the interpretation of his results. Expected value is not a probability and can be greater than 1. $\frac{12}{8}$ represents the number of heads expected when you toss 3 coins.
5. a. $(0.2r + 0.8w)^6 = 0.000064r^6 + 0.001536r^5w + 0.01536r^4w^2 + 0.08192r^3w^3 + 0.24576r^2w^4 + 0.39322rw^5 + 0.26214w^6$; each term is the probability of getting a specific number of questions correct. **b.** 1.2
6. a. $(x^1 + x^2 + x^3 + x^{10})^3 = x^{30} + 3x^{23} + 3x^{22} + 3x^{21} + 3x^{16} + 6x^{15} + 9x^{14} + 6x^{13} + 3x^{12} + x^9 + 3x^8 + 6x^7 + 7x^6 + 6x^5 + 3x^4 + x^3$
b. $\frac{27}{64}$ **7.** 16
On Your Own
8. b. $14,925.80 **10. a.** 7 **b.** 10.5 **13.** 0

Lesson 7.5
Check Your Understanding

1.

Matches	Frequency
0 correct	2,118,760
1 correct	1,151,500
2 correct	196,000
3 correct	12,250
4 correct	250
5 correct	1

2. $\frac{5}{11}$ **3.** $\frac{44,800,030}{146,107,962} \approx 0.30662$
4. a. $\frac{1,000,000m + 28,800,030}{146,107,962} = 0.006844m + 0.197115$, where m is the number of millions
b. 0.88154 **c.** greater than $117,308,932
5.

Ticket Type	Frequency	Payout
5 balls + bonus	1	Jackpot
5 balls + no bonus	45	$250,000
4 balls + bonus	255	$10,000
4 balls + no bonus	11,475	$150
3 balls + bonus	12,750	$150
3 balls + no bonus	573,750	$7
2 balls + bonus	208,250	$10
1 ball + bonus	1,249,500	$3
Bonus only	2,349,060	$2
Losing ticket	171,306,450	$0
Total outcomes	175,711,536	

0.25029 **6.** $10.64.
On Your Own

7. $\frac{6}{7}$ **8. a.** $\frac{1,110,353,500}{65,530,000} \approx 16.9468$ **b.** $200,046,500
11. a. 720

Lesson 7.6
On Your Own
4. a. higher **d.** higher **e.** Bill should go higher for $n \leq 53$ and lower for $n \geq 54$.

Lesson 7.7
Check Your Understanding
1. a. 4.5 **b.** 1.5 **c.** 2.917 **d.** 1.708 **2. a.** 7 **b.** 3
c. 11.667 **d.** 3.4156 **3. a.** 3.3333 **b.** 1.3333 **c.** 2.2222
d. 1.4907 **4. a.** 3 **b.** 0 **c.** 0 **d.** 0 **5. a.** The mean increases by c, but the mean absolute deviation, variance, and standard deviation are unchanged. Answers may vary. Sample: Compare the data set 1, 2, 3, 4, 5, 6 with the data set from Exercise 1. The mean increased by 1, but the other values are the same.
b. The mean, mean absolute deviation, and standard deviation are multiplied by k, and the variance is multiplied by k^2. Answers may vary. Sample: Compare the data set 1, 2, 3, 4, 5, 6 with the data from Exercise 2. The mean, mean absolute deviation, and standard deviation were multiplied by 2. The variance was multiplied by 4. **6.** 3.96; 1.8018

7. Let the original data be $\{x_1, x_2, \ldots, x_n\}$ with mean $\bar{x}$. **a.** The new data is $\{(x_1 + c), (x_2 + c), \ldots, (x_n + c)\}$. The mean of the data $\frac{x_1 + c + x_2 + c + \ldots x_n + c}{n} = \frac{x_1 + x_2 + \ldots + x_n + n \cdot c}{n} = \frac{x_1 + x_2 + \ldots + x_n}{n} + c = \bar{x} + c$ Each deviation is $(x_i + c) - (\bar{x} + c)$; the value of c cancels. **b.** The new data is $\{kx_1, kx_2, \ldots, kx_n\}$. The mean of the data is $\frac{kx_1 + kx_2 + \ldots + kx_n}{n} = k \cdot \frac{x_1 + x_2 + \ldots + x_n}{n} = k\bar{x}$. Each deviation is $kx_i - k\bar{x} = k(x_i - \bar{x})$; each deviation is k times larger. The variance will be k^2 times larger since each deviation is the variance squared. **8.** 7; $\frac{35}{18}$; $\frac{35}{6}$; 2.415; the mean and variance are doubled and the standard deviation is $\sqrt{2}$ times as large. The mean absolute deviation is larger by factor of $\frac{35}{27}$ which doesn't seem to be part of the pattern.

On Your Own
9. a. $\frac{1}{2}$ **b.** $\frac{1}{2}$ and $-\frac{1}{2}$ **10. b.** 1, 0, 0, -1
12. b. $\frac{9}{2}$; 25

Lesson 7.8
Check Your Understanding
1. a.

Sum	Frequency
3	1
4	3
5	6
6	10
7	15
8	21
9	25
10	27
11	27
12	25
13	21
14	15
15	10
16	6
17	3
18	1

b. 10.5 **c.** $\frac{35}{4}$; $\frac{\sqrt{35}}{2}$ **d.** 3 times **e.** $\sqrt{3}$ times
2. a. 7; 25; 5 **b.** 16; 144; 12 **c.** 18; 256; 16

3. a.

+	1	7	13	25	34
2	3	9	15	27	36
12	13	19	25	37	46

b. 23; 169; 13
4. a.

Y	1	7	13	25	34
10	11	17	23	35	44
10	11	17	23	35	44
10	11	17	23	35	44
10	11	17	23	35	44
50	51	57	63	75	84

b. 34; 400; 20 **5.** 17 **6. a.** Spinner A: 5; Spinner B: 10.8; Spinner C: 12.8 **b.** 11.2 **c.** 16.32 **d.** Answers may vary. Sample: There is not an obvious pattern in the relationships of the mean absolute deviation of the combined spinners. **7.** Answers may vary. Sample: If the original standard deviations are a and b, and the new standard deviation is c. The numbers for the standard deviation are in the relationship, $a^2 + b^2 = c^2$.

On Your Own
8. a. $\frac{5}{2}$; $\frac{11}{12}$; $\frac{\sqrt{33}}{6}$ **12. b.** -6.25 cents; yes, the game will make money over time. **13. a.** 25; 5

Lesson 7.9
Check Your Understanding
1. $\frac{1}{5}$; 0.16; 0.4 **2. a.** $\frac{1}{25}$; $\frac{8}{25}$; $\frac{16}{25}$ **b.** 0.4; 0.32; $\sqrt{0.32} \approx 0.566$ **3.** 0.6; 0.48; $\sqrt{0.48} \approx 0.693$
4. 4; 3.2; $\sqrt{3.2} \approx 1.789$ **5. a.** $\frac{1}{4}$; $\frac{1}{2}$ **b.** $\frac{1}{2}$; $\sqrt{0.5} \approx 0.707$ **c.** 1; 1 **d.** $\frac{9}{4}$; $\frac{3}{2}$ **e.** 25; 5 **6. a.** 3 **b.** Answers may vary. Sample: Yes, it is unusual most results should be in the range 18 ± 3, between 15 and 21. Only 10 head is far outside this range. **c.** 0.003699 or 0.37% **7. a.** p; $p(1 - p)$; $\sqrt{p(1 - p)}$ **b.** np; $np(1 - p)$; $\sqrt{np(1 - p)}$
On Your Own
8. a. 781.25; 27.95 **c.** 3125; 55.90 **9. e.** $\frac{5n}{36}$; $\frac{\sqrt{5n}}{6}$

Lesson 7.10
Check Your Understanding
1. a. 0.0514 **2. a.** 0.0690 **3. a.** 40; 5.7735 **b.** Answers may vary. Sample: This is an unusual result. Most of the results should be from 40 ± 5.7735. This is roughly from 34 to 46. Getting only 20 sixes is far outside this range. **4. a.** Each question has $p = 0.2$ probability of getting a correct answer. They are independent of one another, so the probability of getting n consecutive questions right is 0.2^n.

b. 0.0115 or 1.15% **c.** 0.2054 or 20.54%

5. a. $f(n) = \binom{20}{n}(0.20)^n(0.8)^{(20-n)}$

b.

n	f(n)
0	0.0115
1	0.0576
2	0.1369
3	0.2054
4	0.2182
5	0.1746
6	0.1091
7	0.0545
8	0.0222
9	0.0074
10	0.0020

6. 0.2054; the coefficient is the probability of getting 3 correct and 17 wrong answers.

7. $p(1-p)^2 + p^2(1-p) = p(1-p)$
$$= p(1 - 2p + p^2) + p^2 - p^3$$
$$= p - 2p^2 + p^3 + p^2 - p^3$$
$$= p - p^2$$
$$= p(1-p)$$

8.

Number of Successes	Probability	Product
2	p^2	$2p^2$
1	$2p(1-p)$	$2p(1-p)$
0	$(1-p)^2$	0
Total		$2p$

Success	Deviation	Deviation²	Probability	Product
2	$2 - 2p$	$(2-2p)^2$	p^2	$(2-2p)^2 \cdot p^2$
1	$1 - 2p$	$(1-2p)^2$	$2p(1-p)$	$(1-2p)^2 \cdot 2p(1-p)$
0	$-2p$	$(-2p)^2$	$(1-p)^2$	$(-2p)^2 \cdot (1-p)^2$
Total				$2p(1-p)$

On Your Own

9. a. pq **b.** $(1-p)(1-q)$ **c.** $p + q - 2pq$

11. 14; $\frac{146}{1296} \approx 0.1127 \approx 11.27\%$

Lesson 7.11

On Your Own

5. a. $\frac{13}{162} \approx 0.0802$ **b.** 1 **9. a.** 0.2475 **c.** 0.0782

Lesson 7.12

Check Your Understanding

2. a. 0.2066; **b.** 0.2051 **c.** 0.73% **3. a.** 50; 5
b. 0.2995 **c.** 0.0301 **d.** 0.41% **4. a.** 1800; 900
b. mean doubles to 3600; standard deviation is multiplied by $\sqrt{2}$ to 42.43 **c.** 3558 to 3642

5. a.

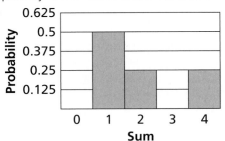

b.

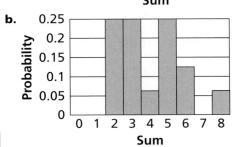

c.

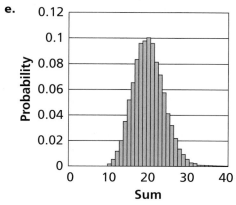

d.

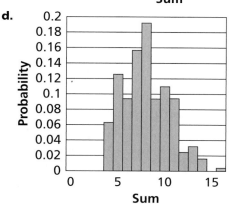

e.

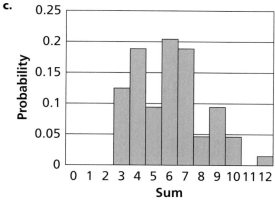

6. a. 100; 17.68 **b.** 82 to 118 **7. a.** 45 to 55 heads

b. $\sum_{k=45}^{55} \binom{100}{k} \cdot 0.5^k \cdot 0.5^{100-k} \approx 0.7287$

On Your Own
8. a. 1740 to 1860 heads **9. a.** 18; 3.55 **b.** 0.183 to 0.417 **12. c.** 0.040029 **d.** 0.040915

Lesson 7.13
Check Your Understanding
1. a. 68% **b.** 95% **c.** 2.5% **2. a.** 68% **b.** 60 to 78 inches **3. a.** 1250; 25 **b.** 16% **4. a.** 0.42074 **b.** 0.344578 **c.** 0.274253 **d.** 0.158655 **e.** 0.022750 **f.** 0.000032 **g.** 0 **5.** using the binomial theorem: 0.00013475, using the normal CDF: 0.00026605 **6. a.** .675 **b.** 1 **c.** 1.65 **d.** 2.58

On Your Own
7. a. 84% **b.** 10.6% **8.** 0.21% **12.** 52.2%

Chapter 8
Lesson 8.1
On Your Own
11. 3*ab* **13.** A regular polygon with *n* sides can be divided into *n* congruent triangles with base $\frac{p}{n}$ and height *a*. Each triangle has area $\frac{Pa}{2n}$, so the polygon has area $\frac{1}{2}Pa$.

Lesson 8.2
Check Your Understanding
1. The area should not change significantly, but tracing between the fingers will increase the perimeter. **2.** One idea: use string to carefully match the perimeter of the hand, then measure the length of string needed.
3. Answers will vary. **4.** Answers will vary.
5.

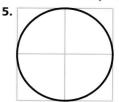

a. $A_{\text{lower}} = 0$; $A_{\text{upper}} = 4$ in.; $A_{\text{average}} = 2$ in.
b. $\approx 36\%$ **c.** $A_{\text{lower}} = 1$ in.; $A_{\text{upper}} = 4$ in.; $A_{\text{average}} = \frac{5}{2}$ in. **d.** $\approx 20\%$ **e.** A grid with squares of side 0.001 in. would be fine enough.
On Your Own
7. a. A dart is most likely to land in the "You win" region because this region takes up more than half of the board. **b.** The probability is equal to the "You win" area $\left(\frac{1}{4}\pi\right)$ divided by the area of the dartboard (1), which equals $\frac{1}{4}\pi \approx 79\%$.

Lesson 8.3
Check Your Understanding
1. Answers may vary. However, the following are essential to any algorithm.
• Divide the interval [0, 1] into the given number of equal pieces.
• For the lower sum: on each piece, build a rectangle with that base and height equal to the value of the function for the left-hand endpoint.
• For the upper sum: on each piece, build a rectangle with that base and height equal to the value of the function for the right-hand endpoint.
• To compute either sum, add up the areas of all respective rectangles.

2. Answers may vary. Sample:

program: sums(n, L, U, A, D)
   input   : n (number of subdivisions)
   output: L (lower sum), U (upper sum), A (their average), D (their difference)
$L \leftarrow 0$;
$U \leftarrow 0$;
$base = \frac{1}{n}$;
for $i = 1$ to n
   $L \leftarrow L + [(i - 1)/n]^2 \cdot base$;
   $U \leftarrow U + (i/n)^2 \cdot base$;
$A \leftarrow 0.5(L + U)$;
$D \leftarrow U - L$;

a.

n	$L_n[0, 1](x^2)$	$U_n[0, 1](x^2)$	Average	Difference
2	$\frac{1}{8}$	$\frac{5}{8}$	$\frac{3}{8}$	$\frac{1}{2}$
4	$\frac{7}{32}$	$\frac{15}{32}$	$\frac{11}{32}$	$\frac{1}{4}$
8	$\frac{35}{128}$	$\frac{51}{128}$	$\frac{43}{128}$	$\frac{1}{8}$

b.

n	$L_n[0, 1](x^2)$	$U_n[0, 1](x^2)$	Average	Difference
10	0.285	0.385	0.335	0.1
200	0.3308375	0.3358375	0.3333375	0.005
1000	0.3328335	0.3338335	0.3333335	0.001

c. $n > 100$; $n > 1000$

3. a.

$$\frac{1}{6} \cdot \frac{n(n + 1)(2n + 1)}{n^3} = \frac{1}{6} \cdot \frac{n}{n} \cdot \frac{n + 1}{n} \cdot \frac{2n + 1}{n}$$
$$= \frac{1}{6} \cdot 1 \cdot \left(\frac{n}{n} + \frac{1}{n}\right) \cdot \left(\frac{2n}{n} + \frac{1}{n}\right)$$
$$= \frac{1}{6}\left(1 + \frac{1}{n}\right)\left(2 + \frac{1}{n}\right)$$

b. $\frac{1}{3}$ **4. a.** $\frac{1}{3}$ **b.** yes **5. a.** The difference between the upper and lower sums is $\frac{1}{n}$; it approaches 0 as n gets larger and larger. **b.** The general claim is correct. If you know that the upper sum limit and the lower sum limit are the same, you need only find one of them.

On Your Own

6. a. $S[0, 2](x^2) = \frac{8}{3}$ **b.** $S[0, a](x^2) = \frac{a^3}{3}$ where $a > 0$. **c.** $\frac{b^3 - a^3}{3}$ (for $0 < a < b$) **8.** Answers may vary. Exact answers: **a.** $\frac{1}{4}$ **b.** $\frac{1}{5}$ **c.** $\frac{1}{6}$

Lesson 8.4
On Your Own

11. a. The graphs of $y = x^2$ and $y = \sqrt{x}$ are reflections of each other across the line $y = x$.
b. $A = A'$ **c.** $\frac{2}{3}$ **12.** $\frac{3}{4}$

Lesson 8.5
Check Your Understanding

1. $\frac{(n + 1)^2(2n^2 + 2n - 1)}{12n^4}$; $\frac{1}{6}$

2. a. $S[0, 1]\left(x^{\frac{1}{n}}\right) = \frac{1}{\frac{1}{n} + 1} = \frac{n}{n + 1}$;

$$S[0, 1]\left(\sqrt[m]{x}\right) = 1 - S[0, 1](x^n)$$
$$= 1 - \frac{1}{n + 1} = \frac{n}{n + 1}$$

The formulas are equivalent.
b. The formula makes sense for all n except $n = -1$.
3. $\frac{31}{5}$ **4.** $\frac{2^{m+1} - 1}{m + 1}$ **5.** $\frac{4}{3}$ **6.** $\frac{44}{15}$
7. Any integer k greater than 8

8. $\frac{b^4 - 1}{4}$ **9.** $\frac{b^5 - 1}{5}$

On Your Own

11. $\frac{15}{4}$ **12.** $\frac{1}{12}$

Lesson 8.6
Check Your Understanding

1. 0 can never be the leftmost point of the interval, since the second point of the subdivision must be r times the leftmost point and $0 \cdot r$ is always 0 no matter what r is.

2. a. $1, r = \sqrt[n]{2}, r^2, \ldots, r^{n-2}, r^{n-1}, r^n = 2$

b.

	Base	Height	Area
1st rectangle	$r - 1$	1	$1(r - 1)$
2nd rectangle	$r^2 - r = r(r - 1)$	r^m	$r^{m+1}(r - 1)$
3rd rectangle	$r^3 - r^2 = r^2(r - 1)$	$(r^2)^m = r^{2m}$	$r^{2(m+1)}(r - 1)$
4th rectangle	$r^4 - r^3 = r^3(r - 1)$	$(r^3)^m = r^{3m}$	$r^{3(m+1)}(r - 1)$
$\vdots$	$\vdots$	$\vdots$	$\vdots$
nth rectangle	$r^n - r^{n-1} = r^{n-1}(r - 1)$	$(r^{n-1})^m = r^{(n-1)m}$	$r^{(n-1)(m+1)}(r - 1)$

c. $LF_n[1, 2](x^m) = (1 + r^{m+1} + (r^{m+1})^2 + (r^{m+1})^3 + \cdots + (r^{m+1})^{(n-1)})(r - 1)$

d. $LF_n[1, 2](x^m) = \dfrac{2^{m+1} - 1}{\sum\limits_{i=0}^{m} r^i}$ **e.** It approaches $\dfrac{2^{m+1} - 1}{m + 1}$.

3.

	Base	Height	Area
1st rectangle	$r - 1$	r^m	$r^m(r - 1)$
2nd rectangle	$r^2 - r = r(r - 1)$	$(r^2)^m = r^{2m}$	$r^{2m+1}(r - 1)$
3rd rectangle	$r^3 - r^2 = r^2(r - 1)$	$(r^3)^m = r^{3m}$	$r^{3m+2}(r - 1)$
4th rectangle	$r^4 - r^3 = r^3(r - 1)$	$(r^4)^m = r^{4m}$	$r^{4m+3}(r - 1)$
$\vdots$	$\vdots$	$\vdots$	$\vdots$
nth rectangle	$r^n - r^{n-1} = r^{n-1}(r - 1)$	$(r^n)^m = r^{nm}$	$r^{nm+(n-1)}(r - 1)$

$UF_n[1, 2](x^m) = \dfrac{2^{m+1} - 1}{\sum\limits_{i=0}^{m} r^i} \cdot r^m$

4. Since the actual area, $S[1, 2](x^m)$, lies between $LF_n[1, 2](x^m)$ and $UF_n[1, 2](x^m)$ for each n and both the lower and upper sums approach $\dfrac{2^{m+1} - 1}{m + 1}$ as n gets larger, $S[1, 2](x^m) = \dfrac{2^{m+1} - 1}{m + 1}$.

5. a. $LF_n[3, 6](x^m) = \dfrac{6^{m+1} - 3^{m+1}}{1 + r + \cdots + r^m}$ **b.** It approaches $\dfrac{1}{m + 1} \cdot (6^{m+1} - 3^{m+1})$.

6. a. $LF_n[2, 3](x^m) = \dfrac{3^{m+1} - 2^{m+1}}{1 + r + r^2 + r^3 + \cdots + r^m}$
b. It approaches $\dfrac{1}{m + 1} \cdot (3^{m+1} - 2^{m+1})$.

7. a. $LF_n[2, 6](x^m) = \dfrac{6^{m+1} - 2^{m+1}}{1 + r + r^2 + r^3 + \cdots + r^m}$
b. It approaches $\dfrac{1}{m + 1} \cdot (6^{m+1} - 2^{m+1})$.

8. When $0 < a < b < hc$, this is true because of the additive property of area. Suppose A is the region under $y = x^m$ between a and b, B is the region under $y = x^m$ between b and c, and C is the region under $y = x^m$ between a and c. Then since the union of A and B is C and since A and B have no overlap, the area of C is the sum of the areas of A and B. That is, $S[a, c](x^m) = S[a, b](x^m) + S[b, c](x^m)$.

On Your Own

9. a. $LF_3[1, 2](x^5) = (r - 1)(1 + r^6 + (r^6)^2)$
b. $LF_5[1, 2](x^5) = (r - 1)(1 + r^6 + (r^6)^2 + (r^6)^3 + (r^6)^4)$
11. a. $LF_5[1, 2](x^2) = (r - 1)(1 + r^3 + (r^3)^2 +$
$(r^3)^3 + (r^3)^4)$ **b.** $LF_5[1, 2](x^2) = \dfrac{r^{15} - 1}{r^2 + r + 1}$
c. $r = \sqrt[5]{2} \approx 1.1487$; $LF_5[1, 2](x^2) = \dfrac{7}{(\sqrt[5]{2})^2 + \sqrt[5]{2} + 1}$
≈ 2.0183
12. $r = \sqrt[10]{2} \approx 1.0718$; $LF_{10}[1, 2](x^2) \approx 2.1736$
13. a. $LF_3[1, 2](x^4) = (r - 1)(1 + r^5 + (r^5)^2)$
b. $LF_4[1, 2](x^4) = (r - 1)(1 + r^5 + (r^5)^2 + (r^5)^3)$
14. $\dfrac{31}{5}$ **18. a.** $LF_n[5, 10](x^m) = \dfrac{10^{m+1} - 5^{m+1}}{\sum\limits_{i=0}^{m} r^i}$
b. It approaches $(10^{m+1} - 5^{m+1}) \cdot \dfrac{1}{m + 1}$

Lesson 8.7
On Your Own

3. a. $\dfrac{3}{8}$ **b.** yes **4. a.** 4 **b.** Computing $UF_n[0, 2](x^{-3})$ is impossible, since one of its rectangles has an undefined height ($y = x^{-3}$ is undefined for $x = 0$).

Lesson 8.8
Check Your Understanding

1. Answers will vary but should be close to the values in the table.

a	$\mathcal{L}(a)$
1	0
1.5	0.405465108108
2	0.69314718056
2.5	0.916290731874
3	1.09861228867
3.5	1.2527629685
4	1.38629436112
4.5	1.50407739678
5	1.60943791243
5.5	1.70474809224
6	1.79175946923
6.5	1.8718021769
7	1.94591014906
7.5	2.01490302054
8	2.07944154168
8.5	2.1400661635
9	2.19722457734
9.5	2.25129179861
10	2.30258509299

2.

3. From Exercises 1 and 2, $\mathcal{L}(2) < 1$ and $\mathcal{L}(3) > 1$. Therefore, $2 < a < 3$.

4. Using Theorem 8.1,

$$\mathcal{L}(2^3) = S[1, 2^3]\left(\tfrac{1}{x}\right)$$
$$= S[1, 2]\left(\tfrac{1}{x}\right) + S[2, 2^2]\left(\tfrac{1}{x}\right) + S[2^2, 2^3]\left(\tfrac{1}{x}\right)$$
$$= 3 \cdot S[1, 2]\left(\tfrac{1}{x}\right)$$
$$= 3\mathcal{L}(2)$$

5. $\mathcal{L}(r^m) = m \cdot \mathcal{L}(r)$, where $r > 1$ and $m \geq 0$.

6. The statement is true when $m = 0$, since $\mathcal{L}(r^0) = \mathcal{L}(1) = 0 = 0 \cdot \mathcal{L}(r)$.

Assume that $\mathcal{L}(r^{m-1}) = (m-1) \cdot \ln r$ where $r > 1$ and $m > 0$. Then

$$\mathcal{L}(r^m) = \mathcal{L}(r^{m-1} \cdot r)$$
$$= \mathcal{L}(r^{m-1}) + \mathcal{L}(r)$$
$$= (m-1) \cdot \mathcal{L}(r) + \mathcal{L}(r)$$
$$\text{(from the assumption)}$$
$$= m \cdot \mathcal{L}(r)$$

7. a. ≈ 2.71828 **b.** ≈ 7.38906 **c.** ≈ 20.085
d. ≈ 54.5982 **e.** ≈ 403.429

8. a. $\triangle_1 = \dfrac{b-a}{n}$

b. $\dfrac{1}{a}; \dfrac{n}{(n-1)a+b}; \dfrac{n}{(n-2)a+2b}; \dfrac{n}{(n-i)a+ib}$

c. $\dfrac{b-a}{na}; \dfrac{b-a}{(n-1)a+b};$
$\dfrac{b-a}{(n-2)a+2b}; \dfrac{b-a}{(n-i)a+ib}$

9. a. $\triangle_2 = \dfrac{tb-ta}{n}; \triangle_2 = t\triangle_1$

b. $\dfrac{1}{ta}; \dfrac{n}{(n-1)ta+tb};$
$\dfrac{n}{(n-2)ta+2tb}; \dfrac{n}{(n-i)ta+itb}$

c. $\dfrac{b-a}{na}; \dfrac{b-a}{(n-1)a+b};$
$\dfrac{b-a}{(n-2)a+2b}; \dfrac{b-a}{(n-i)a+ib}$

d. By comparing results we see that corresponding rectangles have equal areas. **e.** The two approximations consist of the same terms being added. Since the two sums contain exactly the same terms, they must be equal. **10.** Since the actual areas are the values the upper sums approach as n gets larger, and the sums are the same, the areas must be the same.

On Your Own

11. $U_3[1, 3]\left(\tfrac{1}{x}\right) = \tfrac{2}{3} \cdot 1 + \tfrac{2}{3}\left(\tfrac{5}{3}\right)^{-1} + \tfrac{2}{3}\left(\tfrac{7}{3}\right)^{-1}$
$$= \tfrac{2}{3} + \tfrac{2}{5} + \tfrac{2}{7}$$

$U_3[3, 9]\left(\tfrac{1}{x}\right) = 2\left(\tfrac{1}{3}\right) + 2\left(\tfrac{1}{5}\right) + 2\left(\tfrac{1}{7}\right)$
$$= \tfrac{2}{3} + \tfrac{2}{5} + \tfrac{2}{7}$$

15. Since there is no area under $y = \tfrac{1}{x}$ between 1 and 1, $S[1, 1]\left(\tfrac{1}{x}\right) = 0$, so $\mathcal{L}(1) = 0$.

Lesson 8.9
Check Your Understanding
1. a.

Fermat Lower Sum for $y = x^{-1}$ on $[1, 2]$			
	Base	**Height**	**Area**
1st rectangle	$r - 1$	$\frac{1}{r}$	$(r - 1)\frac{1}{r}$
2nd rectangle	$r^2 - r = r(r - 1)$	$\frac{1}{r^2}$	$(r - 1)\frac{1}{r}$
3rd rectangle	$r^3 - r^2 = r^2(r - 1)$	$\frac{1}{r^3}$	$(r - 1)\frac{1}{r}$
4th rectangle	$r^4 - r^3 = r^3(r - 1)$	$\frac{1}{r^4}$	$(r - 1)\frac{1}{r}$
$\vdots$	$\vdots$	$\vdots$	$\vdots$
nth rectangle	$r^n - r^{n-1} = r^{n-1}(r - 1)$	$\frac{1}{r^n}$	$(r - 1)\frac{1}{r}$

b. The sum of the rectangles is $n\left(\sqrt[n]{2} - 1\right) 2^{-\frac{1}{2}}$

2. a. 1 **b.** 2 **c.** 4 **d.** 100 **e.** 0 **3. a.** -1 **b.** -2 **c.** -3
d. -100 **4. a.** ≈ 1.39794 **b.** ≈ 0.30103
c. ≈ 1.69897 **d.** ≈ 6.09691 **5. a.** Note first that
$0 = g(1) = g(y \cdot y^{-1}) = g(y) + g(y^{-1})$, so
$g(y^{-1}) = -g(y)$. Then $g\left(\frac{x}{y}\right) = g(x \cdot y^{-1}) = g(x) + g(y^{-1}) = g(x) - g(y)$.
b. Since $g(5) = g((\sqrt{5})^2) = 2g(\sqrt{5})$, we know
$g(\sqrt{5}) = \frac{1}{2}g(5) = 0.349485$. **c.** The function g
satisfies all the properties of the common logarithm
(log base 10) function, denoted by log or $\log_{10}$.
d.

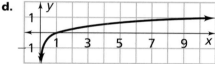

The graph of $y = g(x)$.
On Your Own
7. a. $\mathcal{L}(4) = \mathcal{L}(2 \cdot 2) = \mathcal{L}(2) + \mathcal{L}(2) = 2\mathcal{L}(2)$
9. From Exercise 8, $\mathcal{L}(1) = \mathcal{L}\left(\frac{r}{r}\right) = \mathcal{L}(r) - \mathcal{L}(r) = 0$.

Lesson 8.10
Check Your Understanding
1. a. $\dfrac{e^{1/n} \cdot (e - 1)}{n(e^{1/n} - 1)}$ **b.** $e - 1$ **2.** $e^{a+1} - e^a$

3. Answers may vary but should contain the following ideas:
- The constant a determines the direction and the rate at which the function increases or decreases: if a is positive, $f(x)$ grows when x grows, and the bigger a is the faster $f(x)$ grows; if a is changed to $-a$, the graph becomes reflected about the y-axis. So, if $a < 0$, $f(x)$ becomes smaller when x grows. If $a = 0$, the graph becomes a horizontal line, the graph of $y = 1 + b$.
- The value of b does not affect the shape of the graph, just how high or low on the coordinate plane it is located: $f(x) = e^{ax} + b$ is b higher than $g(x) = e^{ax}$ if $b > 0$, and lower than $g(x) = e^{ax}$ if $b < 0$. **4. a.** $e + 2$ **b.** $e - 1$ **c.** $e + 6$ **5.** e
6. a. The graphs of $\ln x$ and e^x are reflections of each other about the line with equation $y = x$. **b.** 1
7. $e^b - e^a$
On Your Own
8. a.

n	$\left(\dfrac{2n + 1}{2n - 1}\right)^n$
10	≈ 2.72055141
100	≈ 2.71830448
1000	≈ 2.71828205
10,000	≈ 2.71828183

b.

n	$1 + \dfrac{1}{1!} + \dfrac{1}{2!} + \cdots + \dfrac{1}{n!}$
4	≈ 2.70833333333
7	≈ 2.71825396825
10	≈ 2.71828180115
13	≈ 2.71828182845

9. a. $\dfrac{11}{4} = 2.75$ **b.** $\dfrac{106}{39} \approx 2.71794872$
c. $\dfrac{1457}{536} \approx 2.71828358$

Index

Index

Index

. . . . Acknowledgments . . . .

Staff Credits

The Pearson people on the CME Project team—representing design, editorial, editorial services, digital product development, publishing services, and technical operations—are listed below. Bold type denotes the core team members.

Ernest Albanese, Scott Andrews, Carolyn Artin, Michael Avidon, Margaret Banker, Suzanne Biron, Beth Blumberg, Stacie Cartwright, Carolyn Chappo, Casey Clark, Bob Craton, Sheila DeFazio, Patty Fagan, **Frederick Fellows**, **Patti Fromkin**, Paul J. Gagnon, Cynthia Harvey, Gillian Kahn, Jonathan Kier, Jennifer King, Elizabeth Krieble, Sara Levendusky, Lisa Lin, Clay Martin, **Carolyn McGuire**, Rich McMahon, Eve Melnechuk, Cynthia Metallides, **Hope Morley**, Christine Nevola, Jen Paley, Mairead Reddin, Marcy Rose, Rashid Ross, Carol Roy, Jewel Simmons, Ted Smykal, Kara Stokes, Richard Sullivan, Tiffany Taylor-Sullivan, Catherine Terwilliger, Mark Tricca, Lauren Van Wart, Paula Vergith, **Joe Will**, **Kristin Winters**, Allison Wyss

Additional Credits

Gina Choe, Lillian Pelaggi, Deborah Savona

Cover Design and Illustration
9 Surf Studios

Cover Photography
Peter Sterling/Getty Images, Inc.

Interior Design
Pronk&Associates

Illustration
Rich McMahon, Ted Smykal

Photography
Unless otherwise indicated, all photos are the property of Pearson Education, Inc.

Table of Contents: vi, Jim Richardson/CORBIS; **viii,** All Canada Photos/Alamy; **xi,** Roger Ressmeyer/CORBIS; **xiii,** Philip Gould/CORBIS

Chapter 1: Pages 2–3, Paul Chesley/Getty Images; **4,** Gilbert Iundt; Jean-Yves Ruszniewski/TempSport/Corbis; **13,** Arnulf Husmo/Getty Images; **23,** Jim Richardson/CORBIS; **28,** Patrik Giardino/CORBIS; **30,** 123luftbild/Peter Arnold, Inc.; **43,** Image Source Pink/Alamy; **49,** Lori Lee Miller/Alamy; **56,** Jeffrey Greenberg/Photo Researchers, Inc.; **59,** Siephoto/Masterfile; **73,** Bettmann/CORBIS; **77,** Ray Coleman/Photo Researchers, Inc.; **79,** Gerald Hoberman/drr.net

Chapter 2: Pages 82–83, CORBIS; **84,** Gregory Sams/Photo Researchers, Inc.; **92,** Image Farm Inc./Alamy; **105,** GIPhotostock/Photo Researchers, Inc.; **106,** Perry Mastrovito/Corbis; **118,** Grant Faint/Getty Images; **122,** Eddie Gerald/Alamy; **124,** Iain Masterson/Alamy; **131,** The Granger Collection, New York; **140,** The Granger Collection, New York; **144,** FoodCollection/SuperStock; **154,** travelstock44/Alamy

Chapter 3: Pages 164–165, Last Resort/Digital Vision/Getty Images; **166,** Peter Arnold, Inc./Alamy; **186,** Jim Craigmyle/CORBIS; **204,** Jim Sugar/CORBIS; **219,** All Canada Photos/Alamy; **227,** Funk Zone Studios/Getty Images; **230,** Funk Zone Studios/Getty Images; **238,** Michael Maslan Historic Photographs/CORBIS; **238,** Gérard Boutin/zefa/Corbis; **263,** Russell Illig/age footstock; **265,** The Granger Collection, New York

Chapter 4: Pages 274–275, Troy GB images/Alamy; **276,** FogStock/Alamy; **293,** Daikusan/Getty Images; **294,** Richard T. Nowitz/CORBIS; **300,** Photothèque R. Magritte-ADAGP/Art Resource, NY; **314,** Will Hart/Photo Edit, Inc.; **322,** Margot Granitsas/The Image Works; **335,** Alan Sirulnikoff/Getty Images

Chapter 5: Pages 340–341, Ben Welsh/age footstock; **342,** Scott Halleran/Getty Images; **370,** SSPL/The Image Works; **396,** Chris Potter/Alamy; **406,** Chris Howes/Wild Places Photography/Alamy; **408,** Joe Sohm/drr.net; **432,** Flint/Corbis

Chapter 6: Pages 438–439, Louie Psihoyos/Getty Images; **440,** Dennis Hallinan/Alamy; **454,** Roger Ressmeyer/CORBIS; **460,** Jack Hollingsworth/Getty Images; **464,** Jim West/Alamy; **466,** William Manning/Alamy; **488,** Martin Dohrn/Photo Researchers, Inc.; **500,** Roger Bamber/Alamy; **516,** Frank Krahmer/Getty Images; **520,** Bora/Alamy

Chapter 7: Pages 536–537, Paolo Curto/Getty Images; **538–539,** Gallo Images-Anthony/age footstock; **541,** John Gillmoure/CORBIS; **570,** Kevin Schafer/Getty Images; **572,** Court Mast/Getty Images; **579,** James W. Porter/CORBIS; **582,** UPI Photo/Brian Kersey/drr.net; **602,** Paul Katz/photolibrary.com; **612,** University Library, UGent

Chapter 8: Pages 630–631, John Pack/Stock Illustration Source/Getty Images; **632,** NASA/Corbis; **649,** The Bridgeman Art Library/Getty Images; **651,** SSPL/The Image Works; **652,** Philip Gould/CORBIS; **671,** 2008 photolibrary.com; **674,** Tim Wright/CORBIS; **695,** James King-Holmes/Photo Researchers, Inc.

Editorial Development
LaurelTech

Note: Every effort has been made to locate the copyright owner of material reprinted in this book. Omissions brought to our attention will be corrected in subsequent editions.